Claire Thacker and Cheryl Pelteret

with Herbert Puchta and Jeff Stranks

English in Mind

* Teacher's Book 1

CAMBRIDGE
UNIVERSITY PRESS

CAMBRIDGE UNIVERSITY PRESS
Cambridge, New York, Melbourne, Madrid, Cape Town, Singapore, São Paulo

Cambridge University Press
The Edinburgh Building, Cambridge CB2 8RU, UK

www.cambridge.org
Information on this title: www.cambridge.org/9780521750516

First published 2004
6th printing 2007

Printed in the United Kingdom at the University Press, Cambridge

A catalogue record for this publication is available from the British Library

ISBN 978-0-521-75051-6 Teacher's Book
ISBN 978-0-521-75046-2 Student's Book
ISBN 978-0-521-75050-9 Workbook with Audio / CD-ROM
ISBN 978-0-521-75052-3 Teacher's Resource Pack
ISBN 978-0-521-75053-0 Class Cassettes
ISBN 978-0-521-54504-4 Class Audio CDs

Contents

Map of Student's Book   4
Introduction   6

Teacher's notes and keys

Starter section   10

Module 1   Here and now   22
    1 Things we like doing   23
    2 School life   28
    3 A helping hand   34
    4 A healthy life   39
    Module 1 Check your progress   44

Module 2   Follow your dreams   45
    5 My hero!   46
    6 Good friends   52
    7 The secrets of success   57
    8 New ideas   63
    Module 2 Check your progress   68

Module 3   Far and wide   69
    9 The languages we speak   70
   10 We're going on holiday   75
   11 What will happen?   80
   12 Never give up!   85
    Module 3 Check your progress   90

Module 4   The things people do!   91
   13 Good intentions   92
   14 You shouldn't do that!   97
   15 How brave!   102
   16 It's a mad world   107
    Module 4 Check your progress   111

Projects   112

Workbook key   114

Acknowledgements   128

Starter section	A Nice to meet you	B Personal information	C Times and dates	D At home

Unit	Grammar	Vocabulary	Pronunciation

Module 1 — Here and now

Unit	Grammar	Vocabulary	Pronunciation
1 Things we like doing	Present simple (positive & negative). *like + -ing*	Hobbies & interests Everyday English	/n/ (ma*n*) & /ŋ/ (so*ng*)
2 School life	Present simple (questions & short answers) Object pronouns	School subjects Frequency expressions	Stress in frequency expressions
3 A helping hand	Present continuous for activities happening now Present simple vs. present continuous	Housework Everyday English	/ɜː/ (w*or*ld)
4 A healthy life	Countable & uncountable nouns. *a/an* & *some much* & *many*	Food & drink	The schwa /ə/ (water)

Module 1 Check your progress

Module 2 — Follow your dreams

Unit	Grammar	Vocabulary	Pronunciation
5 My hero!	Past simple: *be* & regular verbs *was/were born*	Phrasal verbs (1) Everyday English	*was* & *were* *-ed* endings
6 Good friends	Past simple: regular & irregular verbs Past simple questions	Sports Past time expressions	Word stress
7 The secrets of success	*have to / don't have to*	Jobs Everyday English	*have to*
8 New ideas	*some* & *any* Possessive pronouns	Sleeping & waking	Rhyming words

Module 2 Check your progress

Module 3 — Far and wide

Unit	Grammar	Vocabulary	Pronunciation
9 The languages we speak	Comparative adjectives Superlative adjectives	Language learning Everyday English	*than*
10 We're going on holiday	Present continuous for future arrangements	Future time expressions Holiday activities	/θ/ (think) & /ð/ (that)
11 What will happen?	*will/won't*	Expressions to talk about the future Everyday English	*'ll*
12 Never give up!	*too* + adjective Adverbs	The weather	/əʊ/ (go)

Module 3 Check your progress

Module 4 — The things people do!

Unit	Grammar	Vocabulary	Pronunciation
13 Good intentions	*be going to* (intentions & predictions) *must/mustn't*	Phrasal verbs (2) Everyday English	*must* & *mustn't*
14 You shouldn't do that!	*should/shouldn't* *What's it like?*	Personality adjectives Adjectives for expressing opinions	Silent consonants
15 How brave!	First conditional *when* & *if*	Adjectives of feeling Everyday English	Stress in conditional sentences
16 It's a mad world	Present perfect + *ever/never*	Animals Verb & noun pairs	*have* & *has* in the present perfect

Module 4 Check your progress

Projects ● Speaking exercises: extra material ● Irregular verbs and phonetics ● Wordlist

Speaking & Functions	Listening	Reading	Writing
Expressing likes & dislikes	Interviews about hobbies	An unusual hobby Story: Different – so what?	Letter about your hobbies
Talking about regular activities Talking about school subjects	Dialogue about a school timetable	At home – at school Culture: A school in Britain	Description of your usual school day
Talking about activities happening now Talking about housework	Radio interview with a volunteer in Belize	Hard work and no money Story: Where's Amy going?	Email about organising a party
Expressing quantity Ordering food Talking about food & fitness	Restaurant dialogue	Getting fat or keeping fit? Culture: What *is* British food?	Paragraph about food & fitness
Talking about the past Talking about when/where you were born	Presentation on 'My hero'	The woman who lived in a tree Story: Who's your hero?	Poster about your hero
Asking about the past Re-telling a story	Television comedy story	The start of a great friendship Culture: Using mobile phones	Email about an enjoyable day/weekend
Talking about obligations Describing job requirements	Presentation on success Descriptions of future jobs	Why are they so successful? The 1900 House Story: It's my dream	Description of a job
Talking about non-specific amounts Talking about possession Talking about sleep & dreams	Song: *What makes you think they're happy?*	4Tune's new music Dreaming up new ideas Culture: Pop idols	Imaginative story
Comparing things	Descriptions & interview about language learning	More than one language Amazing facts – or just lies? Story: I have to bounce!	Description or letter/email about language learning
Talking about arrangements Discussing holiday plans	Dialogues about holiday plans	Welcome to Ireland Culture: Adventure holiday in paradise	Magazine article about a class trip
Making predictions Talking about your future life	Science fiction story Future predictions Song: *Space Oddity*	Dialogue from a science fiction story Story: How embarrassing!	Competition entry about your life in the future
Describing the weather Giving advice Describing actions	Dialogue about the life of Wilma Rudolph	We can't give up! Culture: New Americans	Email giving advice to a friend
Talking about intentions	Dialogue about New Year's resolutions Dialogue about an unlucky day	New Year's resolutions Story: A birthday party	Email about New Year's Eve
Giving advice & recommendations Planning a friend's visit	Information about different customs	Quiz: Other cultures Culture: Tips for the tourist in Britain	Letter/email giving tips to a tourist
Expressing future possibilities Telling a story	Dialogues about bravery	Face-to-face with a gorilla Story: Dave's risk	Re-telling a story about facing danger
Talking about life experiences Talking about things you've done / never done	Interview about strange pets	Have you ever seen anything like it? John Evans, the Headbalancer Culture: Elvis lives	Letter/email about a visit to Los Angeles

Introduction

'If you can teach teenagers, you can teach anyone.' Michael Grinder

Teaching teenagers is an interesting and challenging task. A group of adolescents can be highly motivated, cooperative and fun to teach on one day, and the next day the whole group or individual students might turn out to be truly 'difficult' – the teacher might, for example, be faced with discipline problems, disruptive or provocative behaviour, a lack of motivation, or unwillingness on the students' part to do homework assigned to them.

The roots of these problems frequently lie in the fact that adolescents are going through a period of significant changes in their lives. The key challenge in the transition period between being a child and becoming an adult is the adolescent's struggle for identity – a process that requires the development of a distinct sense of who they are. A consequence of this process is that adolescents can feel threatened, and at the same time experience overwhelming emotions. They frequently try to compensate for the perceived threats with extremely rude behaviour, and try to 'hide' their emotions behind a wall of extreme outward conformity. The more individual students manage to look, talk, act and behave like the other members of their peer group, the less threatened and insecure they feel.

Insights into the causes underlying the problems might help us to understand better the complex situation our students are in. However, such insights do not automatically lead to more success in teaching. We need to react to the challenges in a professional way.[1] This includes the need to:

- select content and organise the students' learning according to their psychological needs;
- create a positive learning atmosphere;
- cater for differences in students' learning styles and intelligence(s), and facilitate the development of our students' study skills.

English in Mind has been written taking all these points into account. They have significantly influenced the choice of texts, artwork and design, the structure of the units, the typology of exercises, and the means by which students' study skills are facilitated and extended.

The importance of the content for success

There are a number of reasons why the choice of the right content has a crucial influence over success or failure in the teaching of adolescents. Teachers frequently observe that teenagers are reluctant to 'talk about themselves'. This has to do with the adolescent's need for psychological security. Consequently, the 'further away' from their own world the content of the teaching is, the more motivating and stimulating it will be for the students. The preference for psychologically remote content goes hand in hand with a fascination with extremes and realistic details. Furthermore, students love identifying with heroes and heroines, because these idols are perceived to embody the qualities needed in order to survive in a threatening world: qualities such as courage, genius, creativity and love. In the foreign language class, students can become fascinated with stories about heroes and heroines to which they can ascribe such qualities. *English in Mind* treats students as young adults, offering them a range of interesting topics and a balance between educational value and teenage interest and fun.

As Kieran Egan[1] stresses, learning in the adolescent classroom can be successfully organised by starting with something far from the students' experience, but also connected to it by some quality with which they can associate. This process of starting far from the students makes it easier for the students to become interested in the topic, and also enables the teacher finally to relate the content to the students' own world.

A positive learning atmosphere

The creation of a positive learning atmosphere largely depends on the rapport between teacher and students, and the one which students have among themselves. It requires the teacher to be a genuine, empathetic listener, and to have a number of other psychological skills. *English in Mind* supports the teacher's task of creating of positive learning experiences through: clear tasks; a large number of carefully designed exercises; regular opportunities for the students to check their own work; and a learning process designed to guarantee that the students will learn to express themselves both in speaking and in writing.

Learning styles and multiple intelligences

There is significant evidence that students will be better motivated, and learn more successfully, if differences in learning styles and intelligences are taken into account in the teaching-learning process.[2] The development of a

---

[1] An excellent analysis of teenage development and consequences for our teaching in general can be found in Kieran Egan: *Romantic Understanding*, Routledge and Kegan Paul, New York and London, 1990. This book has had a significant influence on the thinking behind *English in Mind*, and the development of the concept of the course.

[2] See for example Eric Jensen: *Brain-Based Learning and Teaching*, Turning Point Publishing, Del Mar, CA, USA, 1995, on learning styles. An overview of the theory of multiple intelligences can be found in Howard Gardner: *Multiple Intelligences: The Theory in Practice*, Basic Books, New York 1993.

number of activities in *English in Mind* have been influenced by such insights, and students find frequent study tips that show them how they can better utilise their own resources.[3]

The methodology used in *English in Mind*

Skills: *English in Mind* uses a communicative, multi-skills approach to develop the students' foreign language abilities in an interesting and motivational way. A wide range of interesting text types is used to present authentic use of language, including magazine and newspaper clippings, interviews, narratives, songs and engaging photo stories.

Grammar: *English in Mind* is based on a strong grammatical syllabus and takes into account students' mixed abilities by dealing with grammar in a carefully graded way, and offering additional teaching support (see below).

Vocabulary: *English in Mind* offers a systematic vocabulary syllabus, including important lexical chunks for conversation.

Culture: *English in Mind* gives students insights into a number of important cross-cultural and intercultural themes. Significant cultural features of English-speaking countries are presented, and students are involved in actively reflecting on the similarities and differences between other cultures and their own.

Consolidation: Four Check your progress revision units per level will give teachers a clear picture of their students' progress and make students aware of what they have learned. Each revision unit is also accompanied by a project which gives students the opportunity to use new language in a less controlled context and allows for learner independence.

Teacher support: *English in Mind* is clearly structured and easy to teach. The Teacher's Book offers step-by-step lesson notes, background information on content, culture and language, additional teaching ideas and the tapescripts. The accompanying Teacher's Resource Pack contains photocopiable materials for further practice and extra lessons, taking into consideration the needs of mixed-ability groups by providing extra material for fast finishers or students who need more support, as well as formal tests.

Student support: *English in Mind* offers systematic support to students through: Study help sections and Skills tips; classroom language; guidance in units to help with the development of classroom discourse and the students' writing; a wordlist including phonetic transcriptions and lists of irregular verbs and phonetics (at the back of the Student's Book); and a Grammar reference (at the back of the Workbook).

English in Mind: components

Each level of the *English in Mind* series contains the following components:

- Student's Book
- Class CDs or Class Cassettes
- Workbook with accompanying Audio CD / CD-ROM
- Teacher's Book
- Teacher's Resource Pack
- Website resources

The Student's Book

Student's Book 1 has a **Starter section** at the beginning. This is to allow teachers to revise, reasonably quickly, some of the key areas of language which students covered in the Starter level of *English in Mind* or in their previous learning. This section does not include the verb tenses covered in the Starter level, since Student's Book 1 itself revises these in the early units. An alternative use of the Starter section might be as diagnostic exercises, allowing teachers to gauge the strengths and weaknesses of their particular group of students before embarking on the level 1 material.

Modular structure: The *English in Mind* Student's Books are organised on a modular basis — each contains four modules of four units per module. The modules have broad themes and are organised as follows: a) a two-page module opener; b) four units of six pages each; c) a two-page Check your progress section.

Module openers are two pages which allow teachers to 'set the scene' for their students, concerning both the informational content and the language content of what is to come in the module itself. This helps both to motivate the students and to provide the important 'signposting' which allows them to see where their learning is going next. The pages contain: a) a visual task in which students match topics to a selection of photographs taken from the coming units; b) a list of skills learning objectives for the module; c) a short matching task which previews the main grammar content of the coming module; and d) a simple vocabulary task, again previewing the coming content.

The **units** have the basic following structure, although with occasional minor variations depending on the flow of an individual unit:

- an opening **reading** text
- a **grammar** page, often including pronunciation
- two pages of **vocabulary** and **skills** work
- either a **photo story** or a **Culture in mind** text, followed by **writing skills** work.

The **reading texts** aim to engage and motivate the students with interesting and relevant content, and to provide contextualised examples of target grammar and lexis. The texts have 'lead-in' tasks and are followed by comprehension tasks of various kinds. All the opening texts are also recorded on the Class CD/Cassette, which

---

[3] See Marion Williams and Robert L. Burden: *Psychology for Language Teachers*, Cambridge University Press, 1997 (pp. 143–162), on how the learner deals with the process of learning.

allows teachers to follow the initial reading with a 'read and listen' phase, giving the students the invaluable opportunity of connecting the written word with the spoken version, which is especially useful for auditory learners. Alternatively, with stronger classes, teachers may decide to do one of the exercises as a listening task, with books closed.

Grammar follows the initial reading. The emphasis is on active involvement in the learning process. Examples from the texts are isolated and used as a basis for tasks, which focus on both concept and form of the target grammar area. Students are encouraged to find other examples and work out rules for themselves. Occasionally there are also Look boxes which highlight an important connected issue concerning the grammar area, for example, in Unit 3, work on the present continuous has a Look box showing verbs which are hardly ever used in this tense. This is followed by a number of graded exercises, both receptive and productive, which allow students to begin to employ the target language in different contexts and to produce realistic language. Next, there is usually a speaking activity, aiming at further personalisation of the language.

Each unit has at least one **Vocabulary** section, with specific word fields. Again, examples from the initial text are focused on, and a lexical set is developed, with exercises for students to put the vocabulary into use. Vocabulary is frequently recycled in later texts in the unit (e.g. photo stories or Culture in mind texts), and also in later units.

Pronunciation is included in every unit. There are exercises on common phoneme problems such as /ɪ/ in *sit* vs. /iː/ in *seat*, as well as aspects of stress (within words, and across sentences) and elision. Vital areas such as the use of schwa /ə/ are dealt with on more than one occasion, and often in relation to a grammar area, for example, the pronunciation of 'than' when comparatives are taught.

Language skills are present in every unit. There is always at least one **listening skills** activity, with listening texts of various genres; at least one (but usually several) **speaking skills** activity for fluency development; **Reading skills** are taught through the opening texts and also later texts in some units, as well as the Culture in mind sections. There is always a **writing skills** task, at the end of each unit.

The final two pages of each unit have either a **photo story** (odd-numbered units) or a **Culture in mind** text (even-numbered units). The **photo stories** are conversations between teenagers in everyday situations, allowing students to read and listen for interest and also to experience the use of common everyday language expressions. These Everyday English expressions are worked on in exercises following the dialogue. The **Culture in mind** texts are reading texts which provide further reading practice, and an opportunity for students to develop their knowledge and understanding of the world at large and in particular the English-speaking world. They include a wide variety of stimulating topics,

for example, food in Britain, the use and language of mobile phones, manufactured TV pop stars, adventure holidays for American students in exotic locations and the influence of immigrant culture on the USA.

The final activity in each unit is a **writing skills** task. These are an opportunity for students to further their control of language and to experiment in the production of tasks in a variety of genres (e.g. letters, emails, reports, etc.). There are model texts for the students to aid their own writing, and exercises providing guidance in terms of content and organisation. Through the completion of the writing tasks, students, if they wish, can also build up a bank of materials, or 'portfolio', during their period of learning: this can be very useful to them as the source of a sense of clear progress and as a means of self-assessment. A 'portfolio' of work can also be shown to other people (exam bodies, parents, even future employers) as evidence of achievement in language learning. Many of the writing tasks also provide useful and relevant practice for examinations such as Cambridge ESOL PET or Trinity Integrated Skills Examinations.

When a module of four units closes, the module ends with a two-page **Check your progress** section. Here the teacher will find exercises in the Grammar, Vocabulary and Everyday English expressions that were presented in the module. The purpose of these (as opposed to the more formal tests offered in the Teacher's Resource Pack) is for teachers and students alike to check quickly the learning and progress made during the module just covered; they can be done in class or at home. Every exercise has a marking scheme, and students can use the marks they gain to do some simple self-assessment of their progress (a light 'task' is offered for this).

Beyond the modules and units themselves, *English in Mind* offers at the **end of the Student's Book** a further set of materials for teachers and students. These consist of:

- **Projects:** activities (one per module) which students can do in pairs or groups (or even individually if desired), for students to put the language they have so far learned into practical and enjoyable use. They are especially useful for mixed-ability classes, as they allow students to work at their own pace. The projects produced could also be part of the 'portfolio' of material mentioned earlier.
- An **irregular verb** list for students to refer to when they need.
- A listing of **phonetic symbols**, again for student reference.
- A **wordlist** with the core lexis of the Student's Book, with phonetic transcriptions. This is organised by unit, and within each unit heading there are the major word-fields, divided into parts of speech (verbs, nouns, adjectives, etc.). The wordlists are a feature that teachers can use in classrooms, for example, to develop students' reference skills, or to indicate ways in which they themselves might organise vocabulary notebooks, and by students at home, as a useful reference and also to prepare for tests or progress checks.

The Workbook

The Workbook is a resource for both teachers and students, providing further practice in the language and skills covered in the Student's Book. It is organised unit-by-unit, following the Student's Book. Each Workbook unit has six pages, and the following contents:

Remember and check: this initial exercise encourages students to remember the content of the initial reading text in the Student's Book unit.

Exercises: an extensive range of supporting exercises in the grammatical, lexical and phonological areas of the Student's Book unit, following the progression of the unit, so that teachers can use the exercises either during or at the end of the Student's Book unit.

Everyday English and **Culture in mind:** extra exercises on these sections in alternating units, as in the Student's Book.

Study help: these sections follow a syllabus of study skills areas, to develop the students' capacities as independent and successful learners. After a brief description of the skill, there are exercises for the students to begin to practise it.

Skills in mind page: these pages contain a separate skills development syllabus, which normally focuses on two main skill areas in each unit. There is also a skill tip relating to the main skill area, which the students can immediately put into action when doing the skills task(s).

Unit check page: this is a one-page check of knowledge of the key language of the unit, integrating both grammar and vocabulary in the three exercise types. The exercise types are: a) a cloze text to be completed using items given in a box; b) a sentence-level multiple choice exercise; c) a guided error correction exercise.

At the end of the Workbook, there is a **Grammar reference** section. Here, there are explanations of the main grammar topics of each unit, with examples. It can be used for reference by students at home, or the teacher might wish to refer to it in class if the students appreciate grammatical explanations.

The Workbook includes an **Audio CD / CD-ROM**, which contains both the listening material for the Workbook (listening texts and pronunciation exercises) and a CD ROM element, containing definitions for the wordlist items with a spoken model for each one. A range of carefully graded grammar and vocabulary exercises provide further practice of language presented in each module.

The Teacher's Book

The Teacher's Book contains:

- clear, simple, practical teaching **notes** on each unit and how to implement the exercises as effectively as possible

- complete **tapescripts** for all listening and pronunciation activities
- complete **answers** to all exercises (grammar, vocabulary, comprehension questions, etc.)
- **optional further activities**, for stronger or weaker classes, to facilitate the use of the material in mixed-ability classes
- **background notes** relating to the information content (where appropriate) of reading texts and Culture in mind pages
- **language notes** relating to grammatical areas, to assist less-experienced teachers who might have concerns about the target language and how it operates (these can also be used to refer to the Workbook Grammar reference section)
- a complete **answer key** and **tapescripts** for the **Workbook**.

The Teacher's Resource Pack

This extra component, spiral bound for easy photocopying, contains the following photocopiable resources:

- an **Entry** test which can be used for diagnostic testing or also used for remedial work for the Starter section
- **module tests** containing separate sections for: Grammar, Vocabulary, Everyday English, Reading, Listening (the recordings for which are on the Class Cassettes/CDs), Speaking and Writing. A key for the Tests is also provided
- **photocopiable communicative activities:** one page for each unit reflecting the core grammar and/or vocabulary of the unit
- **photocopiable extra grammar exercises:** one page of four exercises for each unit, reflecting the key grammar areas of the unit
- **teaching notes** for the above.

Web resources

In addition to information about the series, the *English in Mind* website contains downloadable pages of further activities and exercises for students as well as other resources. It can be found at this part of the Cambridge University Press website:

www.cambridge.org/elt/englishinmind

Starter section

This section is designed to serve as a review, giving students the opportunity to revise and practise language they already know, and it is also a tool for teachers to find out how much students know already and which areas students may need to do more work on before continuing with the course.

(A) Nice to meet you

1 Greetings and introductions

a 🔊 Students read through the words in the box and the gapped dialogue. Go through the example, if necessary. Students complete the exercise. Students can compare answers in pairs. Play the recording for students to listen and check, pausing the recording as necessary.

TAPESCRIPT

Liz   Hi! My name's Liz.

Monica   Hello, Liz. I'm Monica.

Liz   Oh, hi, Jack! How are you?

Jack   I'm fine, thanks. How about you?

Liz   OK, thanks. Monica, this is my friend, Jack.

Monica   Nice to meet you.

Jack   Hi, Monica.

Answers   2 I'm   3 fine   4 you   5 this   6 Nice

b In groups of three, students act out the dialogue in Exercise 1a. Students can change the names and invent new names for themselves, if they want. Monitor and help as necessary. Ask stronger groups to act out their dialogue in front of the class.

Remember

Go through the examples in the Remember box with students and remind them of subject pronoun and possessive adjective changes. If necessary, elicit the other subject pronouns and possessive adjectives from them and write them on the board:

I – my
you – your
he – his
she – her
it – its
we – our
you – your
they – their

2 Countries and nationalities

a 🔊 Read through the countries in the box as a class. Go through the example with students, making sure they locate Britain correctly on the map. Students complete the exercise. Play the recording for students to listen and check answers, pausing the recording as necessary for students to repeat.

TAPESCRIPT/ANSWERS
1 Britain   2 Belgium   3 Italy   4 Spain
5 Switzerland   6 France   7 Germany   8 Poland
9 Russia   10 Turkey   11 China   12 Japan
13 Canada   14 USA   15 Brazil   16 Argentina

b Go through the examples with students, pointing out the different endings for nationalities. In pairs, students complete the exercise. Check answers and clarify any spelling problems. Alternatively, you can put the table endings on the board and go through the examples with students. Then ask students to come out and write the other nationalities on the board under the correct ending.

Answers
-an/-ian: Brazilian, Canadian, German, Italian, Russian, American
-ish: Polish, Spanish, Turkish
others: Japanese, Swiss

To check understanding at this point, you can call out the countries from Exercise 2b and then call out a student's name. The student should supply you with the correct nationality.

OPTIONAL ACTIVITY

Call out a country and choose a student to name its capital. That student then chooses a country and calls out another student's name to give the capital and so on. For example:

T: Arturo, what's the capital of Japan?
S1: Tokyo. Sofia, what's the capital of Brazil?
S2: Brasilia. Anna, etc.

3 The verb *be*

Read through the grammar table with students. Check they remember all the forms of the verb *be*.

Remember

Remind them of all the personal pronouns in the Remember box (they should have seen these in Exercise 1).

(a) Go through the example with students and check they understand why *'re* is used (it's the contracted form of *are*). Students complete the exercise. Remind them to use short forms where possible. Check answers.

Answers 2 *'s/is* 3 *isn't / is not* 4 *'re/are*
5 *'s/is* 6 *'re/are*

(b) 🔊 Students read through the dialogue. Check any problems. Go through the example with them, if necessary. Remind them to use short forms where possible. Students complete the exercise and compare answers in pairs. Play the recording for students to check or change their answers. Play the recording again, pausing as necessary.

TAPESCRIPT

Jack Hi. My name's Jack, and this is Monica. She's from Italy.

Marek Nice to meet you. I'm Marek, and those two people are my friends, Barbara and Adam. Are you from Rome, Monica?

Monica No, I'm from Milan. Where are you from?

Marek We're from Poland. Adam and I are from Warsaw and Barbara is from Gdansk. Are you on holiday in Cambridge?

Monica No, I'm not. I'm a student at a language school here. Are you all students?

Marek Yes, we are. We're at a language school too.

Answers 2 *is* 3 *'s/is* 4 *'m/am* 5 *are* 6 *Are*
7 *'m/am* 8 *are* 9 *'re/are* 10 *are* 11 *'s/is*
12 *Are* 13 *'m/am* 14 *Are* 15 *are* 16 *'re/are*

(c) Read through the instructions with students. Choose a stronger student and read out the A part of the example dialogue and ask them to read out the B part. In pairs, students ask and answer questions. Monitor and check as necessary, making sure students are using the correct verb forms and the correct word order. If they are still having problems, refer them back to the grammar table at the start of the exercise.

B Personal information

1 Numbers

(a) 🔊 Elicit as many numbers as possible from 1–20 and write the numbers and words on the board. Go through the example if necessary. Students complete the exercise. Check answers. Play the recording for students to listen and repeat.

> **Language note:** Pay careful attention to students' pronunciation of the *-teen* numbers, making sure they are stressing these correctly on the second syllable (*four-teen*). Give them some extra practice with these, if necessary.

TAPESCRIPT

one	eleven
two	twelve
three	thirteen
four	fourteen
five	fifteen
six	sixteen
seven	seventeen
eight	eighteen
nine	nineteen
ten	twenty

Answers 3 *three* 5 *five* 7 *seven* 9 *nine*
12 *twelve* 14 *fourteen* 16 *sixteen* 18 *eighteen*

(b) 🔊 Students read through the numbers. Play the recording, for students to listen and repeat.

TAPESCRIPT

twenty-one	sixty
twenty-two	seventy
twenty-five	eighty
twenty-nine	ninety
thirty	a hundred
forty	a thousand
fifty	

(c) 🔊 Students look at the pairs of numbers. Explain that they will hear each pair of numbers and they must circle the number they hear. Play the recording, pausing it after the first pair to go through the example. Play the recording for students to complete the exercise. Check answers, playing the recording and pausing it again as necessary.

> **Language note:** Check students are pronouncing the numbers correctly especially *-teen* and *-ty* endings (e.g. *nineteen/ninety*). Give them a few more combinations like this for further practice, if necessary.

TAPESCRIPT/ANSWERS

1 17 (seventeen)
2 90 (ninety)
3 64 (sixty-four)
4 52 (fifty-two)
5 79 (seventy-nine)
6 28 (twenty-eight)

┌─ **OPTIONAL ACTIVITY** ─────────

Quick bingo
Students write down ten numbers between 1 and 100. You call out and put on the board (or note down) as you call them out, at random, a series of numbers. If you call out a number and a student has it, they can cross it off. Once students have crossed off all their numbers they can call out *Bingo!* The first one to cross off all their numbers correctly is the winner.

Remember

Read through the questions in the Remember box and ask a few students the questions to elicit the answers. Make sure students can form the questions and answers correctly. Remind them that the verb and subject pronoun swap places in questions. Point out the third person *is* in the verb *be*.

(d) Take the role of the A student in the dialogue and choose a student to take the role of B. Act out the dialogue with the student as an example. In pairs, students ask and answer questions. Monitor and help as necessary, making sure students are using the correct forms.

Stronger students who finish early can use the extension questions and ask about other family members.

Weaker classes: Elicit words for family members and write them on the board first (e.g. *brother, sister,* etc.).

2 Titles

Write the titles *Mr* /ˈmɪstər/, *Mrs* /ˈmɪsɪz/, *Miss* /mɪs/, *Ms* /məz/ on the board and practise the pronunciation with students. Explain your title to them. Explain that we usually use the title *Mr* for any man, *Mrs* refers to a married woman, *Miss* refers to a woman who is not married, *Ms* is used for a woman who may or may not be married. If necessary, go through the first item with students. Encourage them to look at the context of the picture before they choose the title. Students complete the exercise and compare answers in pairs. Check answers as a class.

Answers 1 Mrs   2 Mr   3 Ms/Miss   4 Miss/Ms

┌─ OPTIONAL ACTIVITY ───────────
Students can discuss in L1 if the same titles are used for people in their countries. Discuss any similarities or differences as a class.

3 The alphabet

(a) 🔊 Write the sounds of the alphabet on the board. Play the recording for students to repeat each letter. Go through the example sounds and letters with students, making sure they can hear the sound clearly.

Stronger classes: They can classify the remaining letters.

Weaker classes: It may be helpful to go through each letter individually with them, replaying the recording for them to hear the sound and then asking them to classify it.

Check answers. Play the recording again as necessary for students to practise the pronunciation.

TAPESCRIPT

A B C D E F G H I J K L M N O P Q R S T U V W X Y Z

Answers
/eɪ/: h, j, k
/iː/: c, d, e, g, p, t, v

/e/: l, m, n, s, x, z
/aɪ/: y
/uː/: u, w

(b) Read through the example with students. In pairs, students ask and answer questions about other numbers. Set a time limit, e.g. of three minutes, for students to ask and answer. Monitor and check as necessary. Revise any problem spellings once students have completed the exercise.

┌─ OPTIONAL ACTIVITY ───────────
Students each write down three countries and/or nationalities from Section A, Exercise 2. In pairs, students test their partner on the spellings.

4 Giving your personal information

(a) Look at the form with students and ask them if they have ever filled in a form like this before. If so, ask them what it was for. If not, explain the kind of information they will need to complete it. Read through the form with students and check any problems. Do the first item as an example with your own information. Give students a few minutes to complete the form. Then, in pairs, students compare information and check they have filled in the form correctly.

(b) 🔊 Students read through the completed form. Explain that there is one mistake in each line and they must listen and correct the mistakes. Go through the example with them, playing the recording and pausing it after she spells her name.

Weaker classes: Point out how it has been written down incorrectly. Then play the tape once for them to hear it through and then play it again for them to correct the mistakes.

Stronger classes: Elicit what the mistake is and ask them for the correct spelling. They can listen once only and correct the mistakes.

Check answers, playing and pausing the recording as necessary for students to check or change their answers.

TAPESCRIPT

Boy Good morning, Hartfield Sports Centre. Can I help you?

Girl Oh, hello. Yes, I want to become a member of the sports centre.

Boy OK, fine. Can you tell me your first name, please?

Girl Yes, it's Frances. F-R-A-N-C-E-S.

Boy Right. And your family name?

Girl Thompson. T-H-O-M-P-S-O-N.

Boy Thanks. And where do you live?

Girl I live in Hartfield.

Boy OK, and what's your address, please, Frances?

Girl It's 72 Grove Street, Hartfield.

Boy And your phone number?

Girl 01982 637410.

Boy And how old are you, Frances?

Girl I'm 16.

Boy Great. OK, it costs twelve pounds to be a member ...

Answers
Family name: Thompson not Tomson
Address: 72 not 27
Telephone number: 01982 637410 not 0982 637410
Age: 16 not 15

c Go through the example question with students, reminding them of word order in questions. Students complete the exercise. Check answers.

Answers
2 How do you spell it?
3 What's your address?
4 How old are you?
5 What's your phone number?

d In pairs, students ask and answer the questions from Exercise 4c. If necessary, ask a stronger pair to go through the example question and answer. Students ask and answer the questions, noting down their partner's answers. Monitor and check that each student is asking and answering. Students can change pairs and ask questions to a new partner. Ask for some students to report the information about their partner to the rest of the class.

C Times and dates

1 What's the time?

a 🔊 Students look at clocks 1–4. Play the recording, for students to listen and repeat.

TAPESCRIPT
1 two o'clock
2 five fifteen, quarter past five
3 eleven twenty, twenty past eleven
4 nine thirty, half past nine

Remember
Read through the examples in the Remember box with students, reminding them of the question forms. Ask them a few questions of your own (e.g. *What time is your English lesson? When is lunch time?*) to check understanding and to elicit the correct responses (*It's at ... / At ...*).

b Draw a clock face on the board and elicit *o'clock, half past, quarter past* and *quarter to*. Go through the example with students. Remind them of the different ways to say the times (e.g. *seven thirty* or *half past seven, eleven fifteen* or *quarter past eleven*, etc.).

Weaker classes: Call out a student's name and a picture number and the student says the time on that clock. Continue in this way until everyone has had a turn.

Stronger classes: They can do this in groups, taking turns to choose a group member and a clock for them to say what the time is.

Answers
2 seven thirty / half past seven
3 eight twenty / twenty past eight
4 four forty-five / quarter to five
5 one fifteen / quarter past one
6 four o'clock

┌ **OPTIONAL ACTIVITY**

If students need more practice, draw more clock faces with different times on the board and either ask students to come and write the times underneath or they can write the times in their notebooks.

2 Days of the week

a 🔊 Go through the example with students. Point out to them that column headings will give them a clue to the first letter of each day of the week. Students complete the exercise. Check answers. Play the recording, for students to repeat.

TAPESCRIPT/ANSWERS
Monday, Tuesday, Wednesday, Thursday, Friday, Saturday, Sunday

Language note: It may be interesting for students to think about the days of the week in their language and see if there are any similarities or differences in English.

b Go through the first item with students as an example, if necessary. In pairs, students ask and answer the questions.

3 Months and seasons

a 🔊 Write the months of the year on the board. Write *1* beside *January*, as in the example.

Stronger classes: They can simply order the months in their books.

Weaker classes: Ask students to come out and write the number *2* by the next month (*February*). Continue in this way until all the months have been ordered.

Play the recording for students to listen and check answers.

TAPESCRIPT/ANSWERS
January, February, March, April, May, June, July, August, September, October, November, December

Language note: It may be interesting for students to think about the months of the year in their language and see if there are any similarities or differences in English.

(b) 🔊 Underline the stress on *January* on the board and drill the pronunciation with students. Play the recording again for students to listen and underline the stress in the other months. Check answers by calling out *January* and then a student's name; the student must say the next month (*February*) with the correct stress. If it is pronounced correctly, move on to the next month, if not, ask a different student to try the problem month. Drill any problem pronunciation as a class.

Answers

January, February, March, April, May, June, July, August, September, October, November, December

(c) Students look at the pictures of the seasons and read through the names for each. Do the first season with them as an example. Students complete the exercise. Check answers.

Answers 1 b 2 d 3 c 4 a

Language notes

1 Check students' pronunciation of *autumn* /ˈɔːtəm/ and *spring* /sprɪŋ/. They may want to pronounce the *n* at the end of *autumn* and the *spr* cluster in *spring* may prove difficult for some students.

2 It may be useful for students to think about the words for the seasons in their language and see if there are any similarities or differences in English.

(d) In small groups, students discuss the questions. Ask for class feedback.

4 Dates

(a) 🔊 Students read through the list of dates. Point out the endings on the dates. Play the recording for students to listen and repeat. If there are any problems with pronunciation, drill the dates as a class.

TAPESCRIPT	
first	tenth
second	eleventh
third	twelfth
fourth	thirteenth
fifth	fifteenth
sixth	eighteenth
seventh	twentieth
eighth	twenty-first
ninth	twenty-second
	twenty-third

(b) 🔊 Go through the example with students, pausing the recording after the first number. Continue the recording for students to complete the exercise.

Check answers and play the recording again if necessary.

TAPESCRIPT/ANSWERS

1 third (3rd)   2 ninth (9th)   3 eleventh (11th)
4 sixteenth (16th)   5 twenty-second (22nd)
6 thirty-first (31st)

(c) Students read through the example dialogue. Refer students back to Exercise 3a on page 8 if they need to see a complete list of the months of the year. Students continue the dialogues taking turns to ask and answer about the months.

(d) Students look at the pictures and read through items 1–4. Go through the example with students, checking they understand the second number represents the month. Students complete the exercise. Check answers.

Answers

2 My birthday is on the fourth of March.
3 The football final is on the fourteenth of May.
4 Our national holiday is on the twenty-first of October.

(e) 🔊 Play the recording while students listen and tick the dates. Remind them that they will only hear one of the options in each dialogue. Play the recording, pausing it after the first dialogue and go through this as an example. Play the rest of the recording. Check answers. Play the recording again, if necessary.

TAPESCRIPT

1
Girl   Steve, when's your birthday?
Boy   It's on November the fourteenth.
2
Boy   When's the next holiday?
Girl   It's on the thirtieth of May.
3
Boy   When's your birthday, Julia?
Girl   My birthday? It's on the twenty-first of August.

Answers 1 14th November   2 30th May
3 21st August

(f) Go through the example with students, reminding them of how we say the years in English (see Language note).

Weaker classes: They may feel more confident practising saying these dates in pairs first.

Stronger classes: Choose a student, call out their name and a number from the exercise and the student has to say the date correctly.

Language note: In English, years before 2000 are said as 19 + 99 (*nineteen ninety-nine*) etc. Any year after 2000 is *two thousand and one, two*, etc.

(g) Write the date of your own birthday on the board. Elicit the question *When's your birthday?* and answer using that date. Then look at the example in the picture with students. In small groups, students practise asking and answering. Ask for class feedback. Are there any interesting findings, e.g. do any students have the same birthdays?

> **Language note:** Point out that when we reply to this question in English we use *on* + date (e.g. *On the twentieth of February*).

Remember
Go through the information in the Remember box with students. Remind them to use the written form when they next write a letter.

5 Question words

Students read the instructions. Look at the first item with them as a class and elicit the correct question word. Give students a few minutes to complete the exercise. Check answers.

Answers 1 What 2 How 3 Where 4 When 5 How 6 What 7 What 8 Where

D At home

1 Colours

Read through all the colours and check students know them all. Then read through the examples, explaining that students must find things in the classroom for each colour. In small groups, students complete the exercise. To make this more fun, you can set a time limit and the group who can match things to the most colours is the winner.

┌─ OPTIONAL ACTIVITY ─────────────
Call out a student's name and a classroom object; the student has to give you the colour of that object. Continue like this until you are sure students are confident with the colour adjectives.

2 Rooms and furniture

(a) Elicit as many rooms in a house as you can and write them on the board. Students then look at pictures A–F. Go through the example with them. Students complete the exercise.

If weaker students have problems labelling the rooms, give them further clues, e.g.:

You cook food in the … kitchen.
You eat in the … dining room.
You sleep in the … bedroom.
You watch TV in the … living room.
You have a bath in the … bathroom.

Students compare answers in pairs before a whole class check.

Answers B kitchen C dining room D bedroom E living room F bathroom

(b) Students read through the furniture vocabulary in the box. Check any problems. Go through the example with them, explaining that they must match the words in the box to the labelled items in each picture. Students complete the exercise. Check answers.

Answers 2 fridge 3 cooker 4 sink 5 window 6 table 7 chair 8 bed 9 cupboard 10 sofa 11 armchair 12 shower 13 toilet 14 bath

┌─ OPTIONAL ACTIVITY ─────────────
Mime an action in one of the rooms in Exercise 2, e.g. *cooking in the kitchen* and ask students: *Where am I? / Which room am I in?* Students guess using the phrases *In the kitchen/bathroom*, etc. until they get the correct answer. In small groups, students mime the other rooms and the other members of the group guess which room they're in.

3 Plural nouns

Books closed. Write the headings *Singular* and *Plural* on the board and put the word *chair* under the heading *Singular*. Elicit the plural form from students. Do the same with a few other classroom objects to make sure they have understood. Now follow the same procedure for the words *watch* and *dictionary*. Elicit the plurals from students and point out the spelling changes. Students open their books on page 10 and read through the table in Exercise 3. Check they understand the spelling rules and make sure they understand that some nouns have irregular plurals.

Students read through sentences 1–7. Go through the example with them, making sure they can explain why it is *policemen* and not *policemans*. Remind them to look at the singular noun ending to help them work out which plural ending will be needed. Students complete the exercise. Check answers.

Answers 2 families 3 friends 4 women 5 classes 6 children 7 boxes; matches

4 *There is / There are*

(a) Read the examples with students. Ask them if the nouns in each sentence are singular or plural, elicit the answers and then ask students to look at the expressions used with each. Make sure students understand that *There is …* is for singular and *There are …* is for plural.

Students read through sentences 1–5. Go through the first item with them as an example. Ask them to look at the noun and decide if it is singular or plural (singular) and elicit that *There's …* should be used. Students complete the exercise. Check answers.

Answers 1 There's a   2 There are   3 There's an
4 There are   5 There's an

> **Language note:** You could also quickly revise articles at this point. Use the *There is* example and point out the use of *a/an* and elicit from students why we sometimes use *a* and sometimes *an* (*a* is used before a singular noun starting with a consonant and *an* is used before a singular noun beginning with a vowel). Elicit a few more examples from students, if necessary.

(b) Students look at the picture in their books for 30 seconds. With books closed, in pairs, students make as many sentences as they can about the picture. They can do this orally or by writing their sentences down. Monitor and check they are using *There's / There are* and nouns correctly. To make this more fun, you can set a time limit and the pair with the most correct sentences is the winner!

(c) Read through the instructions and the prepositions in the box with students. Check students understand all the prepositions by giving them a few examples using things in the classroom, e.g. *My desk is between the board and the door. Your dictionary is in your bag.* etc. In pairs, students now make sentences about items in the picture. They can use *There is / There are* expressions with the prepositions or they can concentrate only on using the prepositions. Monitor and check they are using the prepositions correctly. Review any problems at the end of the exercise.

Example answers
There's a cat in the box. / The cat is in the box.
The box is next to the chair.
The door is behind the sofa.
The sofa is between the chairs.
The books are on the TV.
The TV is under the window.

(d) Students draw a plan of their own house/flat. Go through the examples in the book with the whole class. Students then talk about their house with a partner.

E In town

1 Shops and businesses

Read through the items in the box with students, making sure they understand them all. Go through the example, if necessary. Students complete the exercise. Check answers.

Answers a 4   b 2   c 3   d 5   e 6   f 7
h 9   i 8

2 *There is/are* negative and questions + *a/an* or *any*

Students read through the grammar table. Make sure they understand when to use *a/any* in negatives and questions. Elicit a few questions and answers from students about their town to demonstrate this point, e.g.:

T: Alex, is there a cinema in (name of students' town)?
S1: Yes, there is.
S1: Bertha, are there any supermarkets in (name of students' town)?
S2: Yes, there are.

(a) Students read through the instructions. Play the recording, pausing after the first item is mentioned to do this as an example. Continue playing the recording while students listen and mark their answers. In pairs, students compare answers. Play the recording again while students check or change their answers. Pause the recording as necessary to clarify any problems.

TAPESCRIPT

My town is small, but it's a nice place to live. There's a really great clothes shop in the centre of the town and the supermarket is OK. There are two music shops and they're quite good for CDs, but there aren't any bookshops. There are two or three cafés – my favourite is the Rainbow Café: I often go there after school. There isn't a cinema – we go to another town when we want to see a film.

There are four schools in the town, two for young children and two for teenagers. Sometimes we have school dances – that's good, because there aren't any discos in the town for young people. So it isn't a very exciting town really, but it's OK.

Answers ✓: clothes shop, schools, cafés, music shops, supermarket
✗: bookshops, discos, cinema

┌─ **OPTIONAL ACTIVITY** ─────────────
│ Play the recording in Exercise 2a again and ask students to note down the number of each thing the town has.
│
│ **Answers**
│ clothes shop: 1
│ schools: 4
│ cafés: 2 or 3
│ music shops: 2
│ supermarket: 1

(b) Students read through items 1–4 and a–d. Do the first item with them as an example, if necessary. Remind students they should look carefully at the verbs in items 1–4 and the nouns in a–d to see if they are singular or plural. Students complete the exercise. Check answers.

Answers 1 c   2 b   3 d   4 a

(c) Students read through questions 1–4. Go through the example with them, eliciting that *bookshops* is a plural noun. Students complete the exercise. Check answers.

Answers
1 aren't
2 Is there a; there is
3 Are there any; there are
4 Is there a; there isn't

(d) Students read through sentences 1–6. Do the first item with them as an example, if necessary. Remind them to look at the verb and the noun carefully before they choose *a* or *any*. Students complete the exercise. Check answers.

Answers 1 any   2 a   3 a   4 any   5 a   6 any

3 More places in town

(a) Books closed. Elicit as many words as possible for other places in the students' own town that have not been dealt with in Exercise 1. Put them on the board. Students open their books at page 13 and look at Exercise 3a. Read the instructions and check they understand the words in the box. They then match the words with the pictures. Do the first item as an example, if necessary. Students complete the exercise. Check answers.

Answers a 3   b 2   c 5   d 8   e 1   f 7
g 4   h 6

(b) Read through the instructions with students, making sure they understand what they have to do. Divide the class into Student A and Student B pairs. Tell all Student Bs to turn to page 136 and look at their information. Ask a stronger pair to demonstrate the example questions and answers. Do another example yourself with another student, if necessary. Students complete the exercise. Monitor and help as necessary, making sure students are using the question and answer forms correctly. Make a note of any repeated mistakes students make to look at after they finish the exercise.

Example answers
Langton:
Are there any sports stadiums in Langton? No, there aren't.
Are there any cafés? Yes, there are four cafés.
Are there any swimming pools? Yes, there are two swimming pools.
Is there a library? No, there isn't.
Are there any discos? Yes, there are three discos.
Is there an airport? Yes, there's one airport.
Is there a station? No, there isn't.

Wendford:
Are there any sports stadiums in Wendford? Yes, there's one sports stadium.
Are there any cafés? Yes, there are five cafés.
Are there any swimming pools? No, there aren't.
Is there a library? Yes, there's one library.
Are there any discos? Yes, there are two discos.
Is there an airport? No, there isn't.
Is there a station? Yes, there's one station.

(c) Put the same pairs into small groups and students discuss the questions. Ask for feedback. What is the class view and why?

(d) This can be done in class or set as homework. Using the information on Langton and Wendford as a model, students write about their own town. Remind them to use the expressions they have just been practising. Encourage students to present this to the class and illustrate it or use visuals if possible. Display some of the pieces of writing around the classroom.

F Family and friends

1 Members of the family

Students read through the words in the box then look at Stefano's family tree and the example. Make sure students understand the relationship between Stefano and the people in the picture. Students complete the exercise. Weaker students could work in pairs, to help each other. Check answers.

Answers 1 grandfather   2 grandmother   3 mother
5 aunt   6 uncle   7 brother   8 sister

┌─ OPTIONAL ACTIVITY ─────────────
This can be done for homework. Using Stefano's family tree as a model, students can draw their own family tree. If they want, they can include more information. Students can bring their completed family trees into class the next day and discuss them.

2 Possessive 's

Write the phrase *Stefano's family* on the board, pointing out the possessive *'s*. Explain to students that in English this is used to show possession – it is the family belonging to Stefano. Give them another example of your own to highlight the point, e.g. (pick up a student's pen) *This is Julia's pen*.

Students look at the pictures. Elicit why the apostrophe is in the position it is in each sentence (*John's book*: singular subject and noun; *my sister's bicycle*: singular subject and noun; *my sisters' dog*: plural subject but singular noun).

Students read through sentences 1–6. Go through the example with them, eliciting why it is *Antonio's* (because it is a singular subject and a singular noun). Students complete the exercise. Remind them to look carefully at the subjects and the nouns before writing their answers. Check answers, asking students to explain their choices.

Answers 2 Susanna's   3 My brothers'   4 My uncle's
5 My teacher's   6 My grandparents'

┌─────────────────────────────────
Language notes
1 Students may find it useful to note down the following rules for the possessive *'s*:
It is used with:
• person + thing: *John's book*
• person + person: *my mum's brother*

It is not used with:

- thing + thing: NOT ~~the TV programme's start~~. We say: *the start of the TV programme*.

2 Students may produce sentences like *The sister of Stefano*, so it may be useful for students to think about how they express the possessive in their language to make them more aware of the differences in English.

3 Possessive adjectives

Books closed. Write the subject pronouns (*I, you*, etc.) on the board and then the first possessive adjective (*my*). Elicit the others from students. Students open their books at page 14 and quickly read through the box in Exercise 3. They then read the instructions and the letter. Go through the example with them, asking them to explain why *your* is used (because it is referring to the writer of the letter). Students complete the exercise and compare answers in pairs. Check answers as a class.

Answers 2 your 3 Your 4 my 5 Their
6 her 7 his 8 our 9 His 10 your 11 your

> **Language note:** Although *it/it's* are used for animals, *he/his* and *she/her* can be used for animals if you know their gender (as in Exercise 3, question 9).

4 *have/has got*

Read through the grammar table with students. Remind them of the short and long forms and the inversion in questions. Ask a few questions of your own to make sure students understand this verb, e.g.:

T: Elisa, have you got any brothers or sisters?
S1: Yes, I've got ...

> **Language note:** Students may produce questions like *How many brothers have you?*, so they may find it helpful to think about how they say these things in their own language and compare them.

a ◁)) Read through the instructions and the questions with students. Elicit the words they are likely to be listening for to answer the questions (numbers). Play the recording. Check answers, playing and pausing the recording again as necessary.

TAPESCRIPT

Monica   Have you got a big family, Marek?

Marek   No, there's just me and my mother and my brother, Milos.

Monica   So you haven't got any sisters?

Marek   No, I haven't.

Monica   How old is your brother?

Marek   Milos? He's nineteen. He's at university

now. He's a really good-looking guy. He's tall and he's got fair hair and green eyes.

Monica   He sounds great.

Marek   What about you? Have you got any brothers and sisters?

Monica   Yeah, I've got two little sisters. There's Silvia – she's twelve. And then there's Lisa – she's nine.

Marek   Have they got black hair, like you?

Monica   Yes, we've all got black hair. Silvia's got brown eyes too, but Lisa's eyes are blue – they're amazing.

Answers
1 One brother, no sisters.
2 Two sisters, no brothers.

b ◁)) Look at the table with students and make sure they understand what they have to do. Elicit some different possible colours for hair and eyes. Play the recording for students to complete their tables. Check answers. Play the recording again, pausing as necessary for students to clarify any problems.

Answers
Milos: 19; fair; green
Silvia: 12; black; brown
Lisa: 9; black; blue

c Go through the example with students, showing them how each line must be followed to find out who has/hasn't got things. Students complete the exercise. Check answers.

Answers
2 Julie and Sam have got blue eyes.
3 My aunt and uncle haven't got a dog.
4 Jack's father has got a long nose.
5 Our new History teacher hasn't got a car.
6 Susan's sister has got brown hair.

d Students read through prompts 1–4. Go through the example with them and elicit the answer from a student. In pairs, students ask and answer the questions noting down their partner's answers. Monitor and make sure pairs are taking turns to ask and answer and are using the correct question and verb forms. Note down any repeated mistakes to go through as a class later.

Answers
2 Have you got a pet?
3 Have you got a bicycle?
4 Have your parents got a car?
5 Has your family got a flat or a house?
6 Has your flat/house got a garden?
7 (Students' own answers.)

e Read through the example with students, highlighting the use of *any* in negatives. Students use the information from Exercise d to write sentences about their partner. Ask a few students to read out their pieces to the class. Are there any interesting pieces of information for further discussion?

Activities

1 Verbs for activities

Read through the verbs in the box with students, checking pronunciation. You can mime some of these to help students understand, if necessary. Students then look at pictures 1–12. Go through the example with them. Students complete the exercise. They can compare answers in pairs before a whole class check.

Answers 2 read 3 close 4 jump 5 cry
6 open 7 smile 8 listen 9 shout 10 run
11 write 12 swim

2 Imperatives

Remember

Read through the information in the Remember box with students, making sure they understand it. Remind them of the negative auxiliary *don't*. Give them a few more examples, using the verbs in Exercise 1 if necessary. Give them the verb and then ask them to give you the positive or negative imperative of that verb, e.g.:

T: Giovanna, jump – negative.
S1: Don't jump!
T: Stella, smile – positive.
S2: Smile!

a Students read through items 1–6 and a–f. Go through the example with them, reminding them to look for connections in the verbs in the sentences they are matching. Students complete the exercise. Check answers.

Answers 2 d 3 f 4 b 5 a 6 c

b Read the instructions as a class and do the first item as an example, if necessary. Remind students to look at the pictures carefully and decide if they need a positive or negative imperative. Students complete the exercise. Check answers.

Answers 1 Close 2 Don't cry 3 Don't shout
4 Don't open 5 Jump

OPTIONAL ACTIVITY
Whole class. This gives further practice in positive imperatives. The aim of this activity is for students to follow your commands (using the verbs in Exercise 1) if you say *Teacher says ...* followed by an imperative. If you say an imperative only without *Teacher says ...* in front of it, students should NOT follow your instructions. Any student who follows an instruction which has been said without *Teacher says ...* is out of the game, e.g.:

T: Teacher says smile (students should all smile).
Teacher says jump (students should all jump). Cry (students should not cry).

After a few verbs, ask for student volunteers to come out and take the role of the teacher.

---

3 can/can't for ability

Read through the grammar table with students, making sure they recognise all the forms. Ask them some questions of your own to check understanding, e.g.:

T: Elisa, can you swim?
S1: Yes, I can. / No, I can't.
T: Milos, can you play the piano?
S2: Yes, I can. / No, I can't.

a 🔊 Read the instructions and ask students to look at the first two columns of the table (Marek and Liz) only. Remind them of the marking system. Play the recording, pausing after the first answer to check students understand what they have to do. Play the recording for students to complete the exercise. Check answers. Play the recording again, pausing as necessary for students to clarify any problem answers.

TAPESCRIPT

Liz Jack and Monica are at the swimming pool. Do you want to go there?

Marek No, not really. I can't swim.

Liz Really?

Marek Yeah. I'd like to learn to swim, though. Maybe you can teach me.

Liz No, I don't think so. I can swim, but not very well. You're good at music, aren't you?

Marek Well yeah, I can sing – I really like singing. And I can play the piano and the guitar.

Liz I can't play any musical instruments. We've got a piano at home, but I can't play it. And I can't sing either. When I sing at home, my brother shouts at me.

Marek Don't listen to him! Anyway, you're really good at art. You can paint and draw – I love your pictures.

Liz Can you paint?

Marek Oh, I can paint a bit, but not very well.

Answers
Marek: swim ✗; sing ✓✓; play the piano ✓✓; paint ✓
Liz: swim ✓; sing ✗; play the piano ✗; paint ✓✓

b Go through the example with students, reminding them to look carefully at how they have marked the table. Students complete the exercise. Check answers.

Answers
Marek can sing very well, but Liz can't.
Marek can play the piano very well, but Liz can't.
Marek can paint, but not very well. Liz can paint very well.

c Students now think about the activities in the table and complete the third column about themselves.

d In pairs, students ask and answer questions and complete the last column of the table about their partner. Ask one pair to demonstrate the example to the rest of the class. Students continue asking and answering until they have completed their table. Monitor and check students are using the correct forms and that they are taking it in turns to ask and answer. Ask some students to report back to the class what they found about their partner.

4 *can/can't* for permission

(a) Remind students how to use this structure by asking a few questions of your own, e.g. *Luca, can I borrow your pencil, please? Francesco, can you open the window, please?* etc.

Students look at pictures a–d. Play the recording, pausing after the first item, if necessary. Students complete the exercise. Check answers. Play the recording again, pausing as necessary for students to clarify any problems.

TAPESCRIPT

1

Man   It's very hot in here. Can I open the window, please?

Woman   Yes, of course.

2

Woman   Hi. Can I help you?

Girl   Oh, yes. Can I try on these trainers, please? Size 40.

3

Girl 1   Oh I love this dress! Can I borrow it for the party, please?

Girl 2   Yes, OK.

4

Boy   Dad, can I have an ice cream, please?

Man   No, sorry, I'm afraid you can't, Sam. We haven't got time.

Answers   a 3   b 1   c 4   d 2

(b) Students read through questions 1–4. Do the first item with them as an example, reminding them of what they heard in the dialogues in Exercise 4a. Students complete the exercise. Play the recording again for students to check answers, pausing as necessary.

Answers   1 Can I open   2 Can I try
3 Can I borrow   4 Can I have

(c) Students look at the four pictures. In pairs, they make dialogues about each one. If necessary, do the first one as an example. If you have weaker students, elicit the verbs for each picture first to help them. Stronger students can be encouraged to add as much information to the dialogues as they can.

Students complete the exercise. Ask some pairs to read out their dialogues to the rest of the class.

Example answers

Picture 1:   Can I borrow your bike?
            Yes, you can. / No, you can't.
Picture 2:   Can I have a chocolate?
            Yes, you can. / No, you can't.
Picture 3:   Can I switch the TV on?
            Yes, you can. / No, you can't.
Picture 4:   Can I try this jacket on?
            Yes, you can.

H Shopping for clothes

1 Clothes

(a) Books closed. Elicit as many clothes as students know and write them on the board.

Students open their books at page 18 and read the instructions for Exercise 1a. Go through the example with them. They then write in as many of the words as they can and then unjumble the other letters and match the words to the pictures to complete the exercise. Weaker students can work in pairs. Students complete the exercise. Check answers. Check any pronunciation problems at this point.

Answers   2 trainers   3 scarf   4 socks   5 jumper
6 jacket   7 jeans   8 shirt   9 dress   10 shoes
11 trousers   12 skirt

(b) Go through the examples with students, reminding them of the singular and plural forms of the verb *be*. Students can complete this exercise in pairs or you can call out the items from Exercise 1 and ask students to respond.

> **Language note:**   It may be useful to point out to students that colours come after the verb *be* in English. We say: *It's a blue shirt*. NOT ~~It's a shirt blue~~.

(c) Go through the example questions and answers with students. In pairs or small groups, students ask and answer about their favourite clothes.

2 Money and prices

Bring in some examples of US dollars, British pounds and euros, if you can, to show students before you begin this exercise.

(a) Students read through the list of prices. Remind them what the sign is for each currency. Play the recording, pausing it after the first item to do as an example, if necessary. Play the rest of the recording for students to complete the exercise. Check answers. Play the recording again, pausing as necessary for students to clarify any problems.

Answers 1 €17.50   2 €25.00   3 £15.99   4 $125
5 £2.50   6 $11.25

TAPESCRIPT

1   17 euros 50
2   25 euros
3   15 pounds 99
4   125 dollars
5   2 pounds 50
6   11 dollars 25

Remember
Go through the information in the box with students, making sure they understand how to say the written prices correctly.

(b) In pairs, students now go through the items in Exercise 1a and say the prices. With weaker students, you may want to call out an item and a student's name and the student has to say the price, so that you can check that everyone is saying the prices correctly.

Answers

1   Twelve pounds
2   Fifty euros
3   Nine pounds fifty
4   Five dollars twenty-five
5   Six euros fifty
6   A/One hundred and twenty-five pounds
7   Forty-two dollars seventy-five
8   Seven euros
9   Seventy-five pounds
10 Eighty-two dollars ninety-nine
11 Thirty-nine pounds ninety-nine
12 Three euros ninety

Remember
Read through the information in the box with students, making sure they can remember how to use the correct question form. Elicit the answer forms and remind them to use *It's* for singular and *They're* for plural. Ask a few questions of your own to check understanding, if necessary.

(c) In pairs, students ask and answer about the items in Exercise 1. Ask one pair to demonstrate the example dialogue. Monitor and check students are using the correct question forms and that they are taking turns to ask and answer.

3 *this/that/these/those*

Remind students of the demonstrative pronouns by pointing to things around the class and asking *What's this/that? What are these/those?*, etc.

(a) Students read through sentences 1–4 and look at the pictures. Do the first one with them as an example, if necessary. Students complete the exercise. Check answers.

Answers   a 4   b 1   c 2   d 3

Language note: Remind students that we usually use *that/those* when we refer to things that are further away from the speaker. *This/these* usually refer to things nearer the speaker.

(b) Students read and complete the table. Check answers.

Answers
Singular: that
Plural: these

(c) Students read through sentences 1–7 to check any problems. Go through the example with them and ask them to explain why this is the correct answer (because *film* is singular). Students complete the exercise. Check answers.

Answers 2 those   3 These   4 That   5 This
6 that   7 these

(d) Students look at pictures 1–8. Go through the example with them, making sure they understand why the answer is *Those* (because the girls are pointing at the T-shirts on the stall). Students complete the exercise. Check answers.

Answers 2 That   3 that   4 These   5 This
6 This   7 Those   8 these

Module 1
Here and now

YOU WILL LEARN ABOUT ...

Ask students to look at the photos on the page. Ask students to read through the topics in the box and check they understand each item. You can ask them the following questions, in L1 if appropriate:

1 *Where do you think the children in the photo are?*
2 *Does this look like your classroom?*
3 *Do you like this kind of food?*
4 *Where do you think she is?*
5 *What's your hobby?*
6 *Do you exercise?*

In small groups, students discuss which topic area they think each photo matches.

Check answers.

Answers
1 A typical school day in Britain
2 Learning at home
3 British food
4 A volunteer in Belize
5 An unusual hobby
6 Getting fat or keeping fit

YOU WILL LEARN HOW TO ...

Use grammar

Go through the first item with students. Stronger students should be able to continue with the other items on their own or in pairs.

Weaker classes: Put the grammar headings on the board and give an example of your own for each item, e.g. *I like teaching English. I teach you. I am teaching English now. Can I have a pencil, please? How many students are in this class?*

In pairs, students now match the grammar items in their book. Check answers.

Answers
like + -ing: She likes swimming.
Object pronouns: Sometimes our parents teach us.
Present continuous: Pauline is staying in Belize.
Countable and uncountable nouns: Can I have an apple and some juice, please?
much and *many*: How many eggs do you need?

Use vocabulary

Write the headings on the board. Go through the items in the Student's Book and check understanding. You can mime the *Hobbies and interests* and the *Housework* items if necessary. Now ask students if they can think of one more item for the *Hobbies and interests* heading. Elicit some responses and add them to the list on the board. Students now do the same for the other headings. Some possibilities are:

Hobbies and interests: *reading, playing computer games, going out with friends, playing football*

School subjects: *History, English, Physics, Chemistry, Biology, French, Art and Design, Physical Education (PE), Information Technology (IT)*

Housework: *do the washing-up, tidy your bedroom, clean the bathroom, wash the floor*

Food: *potatoes, carrots, pizza, chips, sausages, apples, bananas*

① Things we like doing

1 Read and listen

If you set the background information as a homework research task ask students to tell the class what they found out.

BACKGROUND INFORMATION

Australia: Is the world's largest island. Its capital city is Canberra. It has five states on the mainland (Queensland, New South Wales, Victoria, South Australia and Western Australia) and also the state of Tasmania, an island just off its south coast. As it is a vast country, the quickest and most effective way of travelling around it is by plane. The Aborigines (Australian native people) are thought to have come to Australia from Southeast Asia 50,000–60,000 years ago.

Brisbane: Is the capital of the state of Queensland and is also the main port in eastern Australia. It is the third largest city in Australia.

Sunshine Coast: This runs the length of the east coast of Australia and can be reached in 1–2 hours by car from Brisbane. It is a beautiful coast with unspoilt beaches where a whole variety of activities can be done, e.g. sea-kayaking, skydiving, canoeing, etc.

Helicopter Flying School: These can be found all over Australia and it is through schools like these that people learn to pilot helicopters and

other aircraft. Air travel is an important way of moving around Australia and there are a lot of jobs in the flying industry.

Warm up

Refer students to the photos. Ask them which country they think it is (Australia) and where the girl is (in a helicopter). Do not discuss what her hobby is at this point since this will be done in Exercise 1a.

a Pre-teach any vocabulary (*to hang out*, *driver's licence*, *take off*, *land*, *pilot*) or stronger students can use a dictionary to check the meanings. Ask students to read the two questions and predict the answers. Then students read the text quickly and find the answers to check their predictions. Remind students that they don't have to understand every word in the text to answer the questions. Check answers.

Answers
She's from Australia. Her hobby is flying helicopters.

> **Language note:** *Hang out:* This is a colloquial expression and describes what teenagers do when they spend time together.

b 🔊 Students read through the list of questions and check any vocabulary problems. Go through the first item as an example, if necessary. Play the recording for students to listen and read the text at the same time. Students complete the exercise and compare answers in pairs. Play the recording again, pausing as necessary for students to check or change their answers.

TAPESCRIPT

See the reading text on page 22 of the Student's Book.

Answers
1 She's 16.
2 She likes music, swimming, going to the cinema and hanging out with friends.
3 She learns how to fly a helicopter.
4 She doesn't like classroom work very much.
5 She wants to be a pilot.

┌─ OPTIONAL ACTIVITY ─────────────
Ask students if they have been in an aeroplane or a helicopter before. They can tell the class how they felt, what they saw and where they were going. This may be better done in L1 at this stage, since it requires the use of past tenses.

2 Grammar

Present simple (positive and negative)

a Books closed. Write an example sentence of your own on the board (e.g. *I come from Scotland. She doesn't come from Scotland.*). In pairs, students think of another similar sentence. Write a few of their sentences on the board.

Students now open their books at page 23 and read through the examples from the reading text. Ask them what they notice about the verbs in each sentence. (two end in -*s*). Ask them which verbs end in -*s* and elicit that they are the third person (*he/she/it*) forms.

Students complete the rules with the information they have. Check answers.

Answers you; they; -s

OPTIONAL ACTIVITY

If further practice with third person forms is needed, write the base forms from the examples on the board: *start, hate, get, like*. Call out students' names and ask them to use each base form in a sentence about a friend.

Look

There are certain third person singular spelling rules which it may be useful to explain to students once it is clear they understand the present simple. As follows:

• Verbs ending in -*sh*, -*ch*, -*x*, -*ss*, -*o*, add -*es* (e.g. *wash – washes*; *watch – watches*; *fix – fixes*; *kiss – kisses*; *go – goes*).
• Verbs ending in -*y*, change the -*y* to -*i* and add -*es* (e.g. *fly – flies*; *study – studies*).

Stronger classes: Ask them to give another example of each of these verbs in English.

Weaker classes: They can choose one of the sentences from the Look box and produce a sentence about themselves.

Grammar notebook

Students should use a grammar notebook and note down the spelling rules. Some students may find it useful to write down the base forms and the -*ing* forms.

b Go through the example with students. Ask them why it is *loves* and not *love* (Because Cristina is third person singular). Alternatively, you can write the first sentence on the board with two answer options, e.g. *Cristina love/loves parties.* Elicit the correct verb form and ask a student to come out and cross out the wrong form on the board. Students complete the exercise. Check answers.

Answers 2 hate 3 paint 4 writes 5 play 6 reads 7 get up

OPTIONAL ACTIVITY

If you feel students need further practice of the present simple positive form you can call out the first part of a verb (e.g. *I get up*) and ask a student to call out the next person. Continue like this with positive forms until you are sure students understand.

c Ask students to read through the words in the box first. Check they understand each item. Weaker students may find it more useful to match the words in the box with the pictures first. Explain to students what the verbs *like, love* and *hate* mean by giving examples of your own (e.g. *I like English. I love school. I hate Maths.*). Make faces to express each one as you say them. Go through the example with students, pointing out the third person verb and the boy in the picture.

Answers
2 I hate bananas.
3 She loves ice cream.
4 They like cats.
5 He hates winter.
6 We love football.

d Students read through the examples on the page. They can look back at the text on page 22 to see the sentences in context, if necessary. Ask them what they notice about the verb in these sentences compared to the verbs in the sentences in Exercise 2a. (These verbs use the negative auxiliaries *don't/doesn't* and the base form doesn't change.) Give students another example of your own if necessary (e.g. *I don't teach French.*). Ask some stronger students to give an example of their own.

Write *don't/doesn't* on the board and elicit the full forms (*do not/does not*). Students fill in the table. Check answers.

Answers Negative: don't; doesn't

Language notes
1 Explain to students that it is more common to use short forms when we speak and full forms when we write. Full forms tend to be more formal.
2 Students may produce statements like *She not like … / She not likes …* . Explain that English uses the auxiliary verb *do/does* in present simple negative statements. Ask students if the same or a similar thing occurs in their own language.

e Go through the first item as a class, reminding students that *likes* becomes *doesn't like* in the negative. Remind students to use short forms. Students complete the exercise. Check answers.

Answers
2 We don't write lots of emails.
3 My brother doesn't play the piano.
4 Helen doesn't learn Italian at school.
5 You don't listen to the teacher.

OPTIONAL ACTIVITY

If you feel students need more practice, call out base forms and ask students for the positive or negative form of it in a person of your choice (e.g. *I, he, you*).

(f) Check students understand all the verbs in the box. Go through the first item with students as an example, making sure students realise that they must look at the pictures to help them choose the verbs. Students complete the exercise. They can compare answers in pairs before a whole class check.

Answers
2 We don't swim in this river.
3 Jamie flies to Rome in the summer.
4 Bill's parents don't drive a big car.
5 Teresa doesn't know the answer.
6 Lesley runs in the park before school.

3 Vocabulary
Hobbies and interests

(a) 🔊 Students look at the pictures. Go through the first item with students as an example. In pairs, students complete the exercise. Play the recording, stopping to check their answers. Now play the recording again, pausing it for students to repeat the words.

TAPESCRIPT/ANSWERS
a 6 dancing
b 5 playing computer games
c 4 painting
d 7 listening to music
e 1 going to the cinema
f 2 reading
g 8 playing the guitar
h 3 swimming

(b) Ask students to look at the table. Do an example of your own from the table to check students understand what to do (e.g. *My brother plays computer games.*). Explain that you have chosen a person, a verb in the correct form and an activity and that this sentence is true about your brother. In pairs, students make sentences and tell their partner. Monitor, making sure students are using the correct verbs for each person.

Vocabulary notebook
In their vocabulary notebooks, students start a section called *Hobbies and interests*. They should note down any new vocabulary from this section and should add any new words as they come across them.

┌─ **OPTIONAL ACTIVITY** ─────────
See if they can think of one hobby for each letter of the alphabet.

4 Grammar
like + -ing

(a) Go through the examples from the reading text with students. Ask them what they notice about the verbs in bold (they all end in *-ing*.). Then ask them to look at the verbs which go before the *-ing* forms (*likes/enjoys/loves/hate*).

Students complete the rule with the information they have worked out.

Answers love; enjoy; hate (any order)
Check students have understood the rule by giving them an example of your own (e.g. *I like teaching English.*). Ask one or two students to give examples of their own using *like/love/enjoy/hate*.

Look
Read through the information in the box with students and explain that there are certain spelling rules when we add *-ing* to a verb in English:
1 If a verb ends in *-e*, we drop the *-e* before adding *-ing* (e.g. *dance – dancing; smile – smiling*).
2 If a verb ends in a vowel + a consonant, double the final consonant before adding *-ing* (e.g. *swim – swimming; run – running*).

┌─────────────────────────────────
Language notes
It may only be appropriate to give your students rules 1 and 2 (from the Look box) at the moment but note the further rules 3–5 below. Rule 4 applies to item 4, Exercise 4b.
3 Verbs ending in *-y*, *-x* and *-w*, add *-ing* (e.g. *play – playing; fix – fixing; show – showing*).
4 If a verb has two or more syllables and ends in a vowel + a consonant, if the stress is on the final syllable, double the final consonant and add *-ing* (e.g. *begin – beginning*).
5 If a verb has two or more syllables and ends in a vowel + a consonant but the stress is not on the last syllable, add *-ing* (e.g. *listen – listening*).
└─────────────────────────────────

(b) Check students understand the verbs in the box. Go through the example with students. Students complete the exercise. Check answers.

Answers 2 driving   3 talking   4 listening
5 running   6 going

┌─ **OPTIONAL ACTIVITIES** ──────────

Stronger classes
Ask students to decide which *-ing* spelling rule applies to each verb.

Weaker classes
Put the infinitives of the verbs in Exercise 4 on the board and ask students to see what patterns they can see when *-ing* is added to each.

5 Speak

Remind students of the hobbies mentioned in Exercise 3 (*going to the cinema, reading, swimming, painting, playing computer games, dancing, listening to music, playing the guitar*). Give students an example of your own with one of the verbs (e.g. *I love going to the cinema.*). In pairs, students make statements and note down what their partner says. Students should try and use each verb at least once.

Students report what their partner said to a different partner. Ask some stronger students to tell the class about their partner.

6 Listen

a 🔊 Copy the table onto the board. Explain that students are going to hear three teenagers talking about their hobbies. Students must decide if the teenagers like / don't like the hobbies by ticking or crossing them in the table.

Play the first part of the recording only (Kate's section). Pause the tape and go through the example with students. Ask them which verb she used with *tennis* (*like*). Play the rest of the recording for students to complete the exercise. Check answers. Play the recording again, pausing after each hobby for students to clarify any problems.

Weaker classes: This recording could be played through once and then paused after each section, allowing students time to note down their answers. Remind students they need to be listening for the key words they see in the table in their book and any like/love/hate words.

Stronger classes: After listening, students could identify the verb each teenager uses with their hobbies:

Kate: like tennis; love playing football; good at swimming; don't really enjoy it

Adrian: we like going to the cinema; I don't like sitting in front of the computer; love reading film books

Harry: hate dancing; love listening to music; enjoy playing the guitar; don't like playing the piano

TAPESCRIPT
Kate: My name's Kate. I do a lot of sport. I like tennis and I love playing football – I'm in the girls' football team at school. I'm good at swimming too, but I don't really enjoy it.

Adrian: Hi, I'm Adrian. I go out a lot with my friend, Jack. We're really into films, so we like going to the cinema. Jack also plays a lot of computer games, but I don't like sitting in front of the computer. I love reading film books, though.

Harry: My name's Harry. It's funny, I hate dancing, but I really love listening to music. I've got about 80 CDs at home. I also write music and I enjoy playing the guitar. I don't like playing the piano so much, because our piano isn't very good – in fact it sounds terrible!

Answers
Kate: tennis ✓ football ✓ swimming ✗
Adrian: cinema ✓ computer games ✗ reading ✓
Harry: dancing ✗ listening to music ✓ guitar ✓
piano ✗

b Ask a stronger student to take the role of Student B in the example while you take the role of Student A. Go through the example dialogue. Point out that the verbs used are in the third person and ask students if they can remember what happens in the negative (they need to use the auxiliary verb *don't/doesn't*). In pairs, students now discuss the teenagers from Exercise 6a. Remind them of the verbs in Exercise 5 and that they must be followed with an *-ing* form.

Monitor students and note down any mistakes with the third person verb forms and revise these some more if necessary. Check answers.

Answers
Kate's hobbies: She likes tennis and loves playing football – she's in the girls' football team at school. She's good at swimming too, but she doesn't really enjoy it.
Adrian's hobbies: He likes going to the cinema. He doesn't like sitting in front of the computer. He loves reading film books.
Harry's hobbies: He hates dancing, but he really loves listening to music. He enjoys playing the guitar. He doesn't like playing the piano.

7 Pronunciation
/n/ (man) and /ŋ/ (song)

a 🔊 Before listening, check students understand the difference between these two sounds. Do the first word for each sound as an example (*man/thing*). Ask students to repeat the word after you. Drill this several times. Now play the recording while students listen and repeat each word.

TAPESCRIPT
man, fun, town, Japan, Britain, Italian
thing, song, spring, morning, writing, reading

b Follow the same procedure for this exercise as for Exercise 7a.

TAPESCRIPT
Karen likes dancing and painting.
Dan enjoys running in the morning.
We sing songs at the station.

Different – so what?

If you set the background information as a homework research task ask students to tell the class what they found out.

BACKGROUND INFORMATION
Ballet: The popular form of ballet as we know it today was established at the end of the 18th century. Male ballet dancing was not as popular then as it is now, but the famous male dancers of the 20th century, Vaslav Nijinsky, Rudolf Nureyev and Mikhail Baryshnikov, have proved that it is a dance form as much for men

as it is for women. A recent popular film, *Billy Elliot*, dealt with this topic, showing how a young boy overcame prejudices within his family to make a success out of ballet dancing.

8 Read and listen

Warm up

Introduce the characters to students. They are Alex, Dave and Tony, three boys from the same school.

Ask students where the boys are (in the school playground) and what they might be talking about (Tony's hobby).

a Read the question with students. Play the recording for students to read and listen to find the answer.

TAPESCRIPT
See the photo story on page 26 of the Student's Book.

Answer
Tony Smith is different because he does ballet as a hobby.

b Go through the first item with students as an example. They can go back through the dialogue if they can't remember who said what.

Answers 1 Tony   2 Alex   3 Dave   4 Dave   5 Tony

c Students discuss this question in small groups. This could be done in L1. Encourage students to think about the following points: How would they feel if someone behaved like this towards them? How do they think Tony felt? Can they think of other sports/hobbies which are becoming more acceptable for both men and women to do? Which sports/hobbies do they traditionally associate with men/women?

OPTIONAL ACTIVITY
In groups, students can act out the dialogue from the photo story.

9 Everyday English

a Read through the expressions from the dialogue with students. Do the first item as an example. Ask students if they can remember (without looking back) who said this (Alex).
Students complete the exercise (looking back at the dialogue only if they need to). Check answers.

Answers 1 c Alex   2 e Dave   3 d Alex   4 a Dave   5 b Tony

b Ask students to read through the dialogues and check they understand them. Check any vocabulary problems. Go through the first item as an example. Students complete the exercise and compare answers in pairs before a whole class check.

Answers 2 guy   3 weird   4 So what?   5 What about

Vocabulary notebook
Student should start a section called *Everyday English* in their vocabulary notebooks and note down these expressions.

OPTIONAL ACTIVITIES
Stronger classes
Students can write their own short dialogues, using the expressions in Exercise 9a, and act them out in front of the class.

Weaker classes
They can act out the dialogues in Exercise 9b.

10 Write

a Explain to students that they are going to read a letter from a new penfriend. Before they answer the letter, they must read it quickly and answer the question.

Answers painting, playing tennis, riding her bike, watching TV, listening to music

b This can be set for homework. Ask students to read the letter again and match the four pieces of information with the different paragraphs in the letter.

Answers
para 1: your name, nationality and age
para 1: where you live
para 2: your hobbies and interests
para 3: some information about your friend(s)

Now remind students of the following information about informal letter writing (putting it on the board if you feel it will be useful):
- Address: We always put it at the top right-hand side.
- Date: This would usually go below the address
- Opening lines: Elicit various choices from students: (e.g. *Hi!/Hello!/Dear,*).

Remind students that after the opening line the writing continues on the next line.
- Paragraph 1: Elicit from students the kind of information this gives (introduction, including name, age, nationality).
- Paragraph 2: Elicit from students what information this gives (details of hobbies she likes).
- Paragraph 3: Elicit from students what information this gives (about her best friend and her favourite singer).
- Closing lines: Elicit from students various ways of ending an informal letter (e.g. *Write soon! / Love, / Keep in touch, / Hope to hear from you soon.*).

Students now plan and prepare their reply. They can bring their letters into class the next day for checking.

(2) School life

Unit overview

TOPIC: School and school subjects

TEXTS
Reading and listening: a text about learning at home
Listening: to a teenager talking about school timetables
Reading: a text about schools in Britain
Writing: a description of a school day

SPEAKING
Talking about how often you do things
Talking about your school timetable

LANGUAGE
Grammar: Present simple (questions and short answers);
Object pronouns
Vocabulary: School subjects; Frequency expressions
Pronunciation: Stress in frequency expressions

1 Read and listen

If you set the background information as a homework research task ask students to tell the class what they found out.

BACKGROUND INFORMATION

Chile: Is situated in the southwestern part of South America. It has borders with Peru, Bolivia, and Argentina and also has a coastline along the Pacific Ocean. It is a long, narrow country (4,630 km in length) but is only 430 km at its widest point. Its capital city is Santiago. The Andes mountains stretch the entire length of the east side and it is a country prone to earthquakes. The official language is Spanish. After many years of dictatorship under Augustin Pinochet, Chile elected its own president in 1990.

Arica: Is a port situated in the north of Chile on the west coast. It has a population of around 92,000 and is an important oil terminal. It is near the border with Peru.

Warm up

Look at the map on page 28 with students and ask them if they know which country this is (Chile). Ask if they can think of any other countries in South America and what languages they speak in those countries. Now focus on the boy in the photo and ask them what they think he is doing (learning at home). Do students know anyone who learns at home instead of coming to school?

Note: You may want to present Exercise 3 (school subjects) first before the reading text so that students have dealt with this vocabulary before tackling the text.

a Pre-teach any vocabulary before students read the text (*lonely*, school subjects [although these will be dealt with in Exercise 3]). Stronger students can look up any words they don't know in a dictionary. Remind students that they don't need to understand every word in the text. Read through the two questions with students and ask them to read the text and find the answers. Check answers.

Answers
He is in Arica, in Chile. He studies at home. He loves studying at home.

b 🔊 Read through questions 1–6 with students. Play the recording while students read, pausing it after question 1 to check students understand. Remind students to answer in full sentences. Play the recording again for students to complete the exercise. Check answers, playing and pausing the recording again as necessary.

TAPESCRIPT
See the reading text on page 28 of the Student's Book.

Answers
1 He is 15.
2 He studies at home because there aren't any English-speaking schools in Arica and he doesn't speak very good Spanish.
3 He studies Maths, English, History, Physics and Biology.
4 He likes studying at home because he can choose how to do things. He can study in his own way.
5 He doesn't get lonely because his brother and parents are with him and he has friends on the Internet and he has a few Chilean friends.
6 He sees his friends at the sports club every weekend and at a dance club twice a month.

c Put two columns on the board with the headings: *Advantages/Disadvantages*. Ask students to look at the text again and think about the advantages of studying at home that Matthew mentions (studying in his own way; can learn a lot; can choose how to do things). Ask students for one disadvantage of studying at home (can get lonely). In pairs, students think of two more advantages and disadvantages of studying at home.

Weaker classes: This can be done in L1. After students have discussed this for a few minutes, you could ask some stronger students to come out and add their suggestions to the columns on the board.

Example answers

Advantages: Can study what they like when they like; don't have to study at times you would do in a school; can listen to radio/music while studying; can watch TV
Disadvantages: Can get lonely; can't play and chat to friends in the playground; can't discuss difficult questions with friends; only see friends when you go to clubs

┌─ OPTIONAL ACTIVITY ─────────────

In small groups, students discuss if they agree on the advantages and disadvantages of studying at home. Would any of them prefer to study at home than come to school every day?

2 Grammar

Present simple
(questions and short answers)

a Read through the example questions and answers with students. If necessary, students can look back and locate these in the text on page 28. Remind them of the present simple positive forms they learned in Unit 1. Ask them what they notice about the verbs used in the questions (they use do/does and they are inverted). Then ask them to look at the questions and ask them what they notice about the verbs in the questions (the main verbs are not repeated; the auxiliaries do/does/doesn't are used). Students now complete the table. Check answers.

Answers
Questions: Do; Does
Short answers: don't; does; does

b Go through the example with students, reminding them that the third person singular uses the auxiliary verb does. Point out that the tick symbol means an affirmative (Yes) short answer is required and a cross symbol means that a negative (No) short answer is required. Students complete the questions and short answers. Check answers.

Answers
2 Do; don't
3 Do; they do
4 Does; Yes, she does
5 Do; No, I don't
6 Does; Yes, it does

Language notes
1 Remind students that a *you* question may need an *I* or a *we* answer.
2 Remind them that short answers do not repeat the main verb, e.g. *No, I don't*. NOT ~~No, I don't study~~.
---

c Go through the example with students. Remind students that they must choose the most appropriate verb from the box for each sentence and put it into the correct form. Students complete the questions

with verbs from the box. Check answers before students ask and answer the questions. Once you have checked answers, then, in pairs, students ask and answer the questions.

Answers
2 Do you like eating chocolate?
3 Does your family like living in a flat?
4 Do your friends like going to the cinema?
5 Does your mother like driving a car?
6 Do you like playing the piano?

┌─ OPTIONAL ACTIVITY ─────────────

Students look at the answers they gave to the questions in Exercise 2c and pairs can compare in groups and draw up a bar chart based on the group's preferences. With stronger classes this can be expanded from groups into a whole class survey.

3 Vocabulary

School subjects

Warm up

Weaker classes: Ask students to look back at the text on page 28 and find as many school subjects as they can. Give them one minute to do this.

Answers Maths, English, History, Physics, Biology

a 🔊 Read through the subjects in the box with students, explaining any new and difficult items. Go through the example with students. Students now match the subjects with the pictures. Play the recording for students to listen and check their answers.

TAPESCRIPT/ANSWERS
1 Geography
2 Information Technology (IT)
3 Science
4 Maths
5 English
6 Art
7 French
8 Drama
9 Physical Education (PE)
10 History

b In pairs, students discuss if they study any subjects which are not included in the list in Exercise 3a. This can be done in L1 if necessary. Ask students to give you their answers and put them on the board (to use in Exercise 3c).

Example answers Other languages, Design and technology, Business Studies, Food Technology, Music, Media Studies, Environmental Studies

c Students now choose five favourite subjects (from Exercise 3a and the list on the board) and discuss them with a partner. (e.g. *I like Maths. Ana doesn't like Maths, she likes English.*).

Ask some students to tell the class about themselves and their partner.

┌─ OPTIONAL ACTIVITY ─────────────────
Ask students if any of the words for school subjects are similar in their own language. This may help them remember the English words for the subjects.

Vocabulary notebook

Students start a section called *School subjects* and note down the vocabulary from this unit. Students may want to write the subject in their own language beside the items to help them remember them. They should add any more subjects to their list as they come across them.

4 Grammar
Object pronouns

(a) Ask students to look back at the text on page 28 and find the expressions. Once they have found them, go through the example with them. Point out that *it* refers to information that has appeared before and in this case refers back to *studying at home*.

Students now work through the other examples and decide what the object pronouns refer to. Check answers.

Answers
them: the usual subjects
us: Matthew and his brother Paul
him: Matthew's brother, Paul
me: Matthew

(b) Write the headings *Subject/Object pronouns* on the board. Then write the object pronouns from Exercise 4a under the relevant heading. Now ask students to think about what the subject pronouns are for each of the object pronouns they have found (e.g. *them – they*).

Now ask students to write the object pronouns in the spaces in the exercise. Check answers.

Answers you – you; he – him; she – her; it – it; we – us; they – them

┌─ OPTIONAL ACTIVITY ─────────────────
In order to check understanding at this point, ask students to supply the object pronouns in the following sentences:
1   *I like apples. I like* ....
2   *I like your jacket. I like* ....
3   *I like my brother. I like* ....
4   *I like English. I like* ....
5   *I like my mum. I like* ....

Answers 1 them   2 it   3 him   4 it   5 her

(c) Go through the example with students. Ask them what the subject of the first sentence is (*the CD*) and what object pronoun is used in the second sentence (*it*). Ask them why it is *it* and not *him* to check they understand why they are using *it* (because a CD is a thing not a person). Students complete the exercise and compare

answers in pairs. Ask a few students to read out their answers, explaining why they chose the object pronoun they did.

Answers
2   him (because subject is *that boy*)
3   me/us (because *I* am speaking)
4   them (because subject is *my shoes*)
5   us (because subject is *we*)
6   her (because subject is *Mariah*)
7   you (because *I* am speaking)

Grammar notebook

Students should make a table of subject and object pronouns in their grammar notebooks and learn the object pronouns for homework.

5 Vocabulary
Adverbs of frequency

(a) Draw the diagram on page 30 on the board. Give students the following example: *I … get up at 7.00.* Tell them that this is something you do every day. Show them 100% on the time line and the adverb *always*. Now put *always* into the example sentence you have written on the board: *I always get up at 7.00.* To check understanding, ask a student:

T: What time do you get up at every day?
S: I get up at … every day.
T: Do you always get up at … every day?
S: Yes, I do. / No, I don't.

Now ask students to think of one example of their own for each of the other adverbs of frequency in the diagram. Ask a few students to read out their sentences and put them on the board.

Now go through the example in the exercise with students, pointing out the adverb of frequency *never* is used because Matthew studies at home and never goes to school. Students now complete the exercise. Remind them to refer back to the text on page 28 if necessary. Check answers.

Answers
2   always
3   often
4   sometimes
5   hardly ever

(b) **Weaker classes:** Ask students to look at their completed item 5 from Exercise 5a. Ask them what they notice about the position of the adverbs of frequency with the verb *be* (the adverb of frequency comes after the verb). Then ask them to look at their completed item 4 and ask them if they notice anything different about the position of the adverb of frequency in this item (it goes before the verb). Students now complete the rule.

Stronger classes: They can look at their completed Exercise 5a items and work out and complete the rule themselves. Check answers.

Answers after; before

c Go through the example with students, pointing out that the verb *be* is used and elicit that the adverb of frequency is placed after the verb *be*. Students now complete the sentences putting the adverbs of frequency in the correct position. Check answers.

Answers

2 We sometimes go to the cinema.
3 Carlo hardly ever goes to bed early.
4 Those dogs are never quiet!
5 Elizabeth often listens to music.
6 You're usually good at Maths.

Language note

1 Adverbs of frequency can also go in initial or end position (e.g. *Usually you're good at Maths. We go to the cinema sometimes.*). However, students may not need to know this at this stage.

2 Students may produce statements like *Never I get up at 7.00.* Ask students to compare adverbs of frequency in English and their own language. Does the same thing happen with the verb *be* and the position of the adverb of frequency or does something different happen in their language?

Grammar notebook

Students should copy the diagram and the completed rules from Exercises 5a and b into their grammar notebooks and learn them.

┌─ OPTIONAL ACTIVITIES ─────────────

Weaker classes

Put the following prompts on the board: *get up, have breakfast, go to school, eat lunch, go home, do homework.* Explain to students that they must write sentences about their daily routines using the prompts on the board and adverbs of frequency.

Stronger classes

Students write some more sentences using adverbs of frequency about themselves, their friends or their families. Students compare sentences in pairs or small groups.

d Write the following prompts on the board: *sports club / every week*; *dance club / twice a month*; *study History / three times a week* and elicit the question and answer:

How often do you go to a sports club? Every week. Using the prompts on the board ask students to ask and answer across the class. Now ask students to look at the other expressions in the table on page 30. Explain that *once = one time* and *twice = two times*, above twice we always say the number + *times* (e.g. *three times*). In pairs, students now complete the exercise and report back to the class.

Language note

1 Check students are using the correct intonation and pronunciation in the *How often ...?* question (there should be a falling intonation at the end of each question and the pronunciation is /haʊ 'ɒfᵊn/).

2 Explain to students that the frequency expressions (e.g. *every day/once a week*) go at the end of sentences.

Grammar notebook

Students should copy down the time expressions into their grammar notebooks. They may find it useful to write an example of their own for each expression.

6 Pronunciation
Stress in frequency expressions

a 🔊 Before you begin the exercise, remind students of the pronunciation of some of the individual words in the time expressions. For example, drill the following words a few times: *once* /wʌns/, *twice* /twaɪs/, *every* /'evrɪ/.

Students read through the words and then listen and repeat each word after they hear it. Monitor and listen to students as they repeat the words, noting any pronunciation difficulties to deal with after the exercise.

b 🔊 Look at the first expression again with students. Point out the underlining and explain that this is where the word is stressed. Give an example sentence for students to hear the stress in context, for example: *I sometimes teach English on a Friday.*

Students now look at the expressions again and underline the main stress as in the example. Students compare answers in pairs, then listen and check.

TAPESCRIPT/ANSWERS

<u>some</u>times
<u>al</u>ways
<u>every</u> <u>week</u>end
<u>twice</u> a <u>day</u>
<u>usu</u>ally
<u>hard</u>ly <u>ev</u>er
<u>once</u> a <u>month</u>
<u>three</u> times a <u>week</u>
<u>twen</u>ty times a <u>year</u>

┌─ OPTIONAL ACTIVITY ─────────────

If you feel further practice is necessary, in pairs students write a sentence about themselves using the frequency expressions and then read it out to their partner who decides if they are pronouncing it correctly.

7 Speak

Ask students to read through the question prompts in their books and check any vocabulary problems. Remind students of the frequency expressions they practised in Exercise 6 and go through the example with them. Point out the *How often ...?* question and remind students of the use of the auxiliary *do*. In pairs, students ask and answer using the prompts.

Stronger students: Can use the prompts on the page and add some more of their own.

Weaker students: Use the prompts on the page only.

Ask several students to report back their answers to the class and discuss any interesting information about students.

8 Listen

a 🔊 With books closed, ask students: *How often do you study English?* and elicit the answer: *... times a week*. Explain to students that they are going to hear a girl talking about her school timetable and they must complete her timetable with the missing subjects listed in their books. Students read through the timetable on page 31 and look at the list of missing subjects. In pairs, students listen and complete the gaps.

Weaker classes: They can listen to this in sections with pauses between each section to allow them time to fill in the answers.

Play the recording again if necessary. Check answers. You can play the recording again, pausing at the relevant section to allow students to clarify any problems.

TAPESCRIPT

Boy   What's it like at your new school, Jane?

Girl   Oh, it's OK. You know, we finish at 3 o'clock every afternoon!

Boy   Great!

Girl   And after school they have games and clubs – it's cool!

Boy   Do you have PE?

Girl   Yeah, twice a week. We have PE on Mondays and Wednesdays at 12 o'clock.

Boy   Only twice a week?

Girl   Yes, I'm happy to say. I hate PE! But Information Technology's good, and we do it three times a week. Mondays, Wednesdays and Fridays at 9.45.

Boy   That's good. IT's fun.

Girl   Yeah. I love Drama too, but we only have Drama once a week – on Thursday, just before lunch, at 12 o'clock.

Boy   What about Art?

Girl   Only once a week. On Tuesday after lunch. But you know I don't like Art very much.

Boy   Hmmm. I'm sure you get a lot of English, though!

Girl   Yeah, four times a week! Mondays, Wednesdays and Fridays at 8.45, and Tuesdays at 12 o'clock.

Answers 1 English 2 IT 3 English 4 PE
5 Drama 6 Art

b 🔊 Remind students of the words for likes and dislikes they have learned up to now (*like, love, enjoy, don't like, hate*). Explain that they are going to listen to Jane again and they must decide if she likes or dislikes the subjects listed. Elicit the key words they should be listening out for (likes/dislikes words and school subjects).

Do the first item with them as an example, pausing the recording and asking them to listen carefully for the words they need. Elicit the answer and tell them to put a cross beside PE.

Weaker classes: This can be done in sections as for Exercise 8a.

Stronger classes: Ask them to listen and provide the like/dislike word with their answers.

Students listen and complete the exercise. Check answers by playing the recording and pausing as necessary.

Answers PE ✗   IT ✓   Drama ✓   Art ✗

c In pairs, students compare and contrast their school timetable with the one in their book. Go through the example with students, reminding them to use frequency expressions and the present simple tense.

Culture in mind

9 Read

If you set the background information as a homework research task ask students to tell the class what they found out.

BACKGROUND INFORMATION

English state school system: This is made up of primary and secondary schools (in most parts of England). Primary schools start at the age of 4/5 (Reception class) and end at the age of 11 (Year 6). Students are tested at various stages in their primary school, taking SATs (Standard Assessment Tasks) at the end of Years 2, 4 (optional), Year 5 (optional) and Year 6.

Secondary schools start in Year 7 (age 11/12) and end in Year 13 (age 17/18). During the course of a secondary school students must study certain subjects and take certain exams. In the first three years of secondary schools the following subjects are compulsory: Maths, English, Science, Design Technology, Information Technology, Religious Education,

PE and a foreign language. Students can also choose another three subjects.

In Year 10, students can choose between five and ten subjects to study for GCSE (General Certificate of Secondary Education) exams at the end of Year 11. After GCSEs students can leave school or stay on and study in the Sixth Form. They can then choose to study three or more subjects for A (Advanced) level exams. The A level studies are split over two years (Lower and Upper Sixth Form) and after the first year students take preliminary exams called AS levels. After students receive A level results they can decide whether they want to study at a higher level. It is these results which allow students to get into universities and colleges of further education.

The Scottish system has some differences from the education system in England, Wales and Northern Ireland.

Uniforms: These are not compulsory, although it is becoming more common for both primary and secondary school children to wear them.

Warm up

Ask students to look at the photos on the page and the title of the text and see if they can predict any facts about school in Britain that will come up in the text.

a Ask students to read the two questions and elicit the kind of words they might look for to help them with their answers (times/numbers, clubs). Students then read the text quickly to find the answers. Ask a few students to read out their answers and see if everyone agrees.

Answers
1 School starts at 8.50 and finishes at 4.00.
2 Alan stays on Mondays and Wednesdays to do a Photography and Athletics club.

b Students read through topics a–f. To help them with the matching and the text structure, remind them to think about the order of things in Alan's day and which things he is likely to do first, last etc. Students now read the text, matching each topic with a paragraph.

Students compare answers in pairs and then check answers with the whole class. Make sure all the students agree. If there are any disagreements, ask students to discuss them.

Answers a 5 b 4 c 1 d 3 e 6 f 2

> **Language note:** Explain to students that the expression *on Mondays and Wednesdays* uses the plural of the day of the week because it shows routine; it is something Alan does every Monday and Wednesday.

c Students now think about the information in the text and choose the correct word to make true sentences. Go through the example. Ask students why the answer is *doesn't wear* (because he only goes to school from Monday to Friday and he doesn't wear uniform at the weekend.). Students complete the exercise. Check answers.

Answers 2 mornings 3 likes 4 never 5 twice
6 does

d Ask students to read through sentences 1–6 and check they understand them all. Go through the first item as an example, eliciting the part of the text which tells them the answer (Para 1: *The girls wear ...*). Students answer the other questions. Remind them to think carefully about where they may find the information in the text. Check answers.

Answers
1 Yes, they do. (para 1)
2 No, they don't. (para 1)
3 No, he walks to school. (para 2)
4 He studies nine subjects. (para 3)
5 In the school dining room. (para 4)
6 Between 10 and 15. (para 5)

e Ask students about their school day and elicit the following information and put it on the board: *start time, finish time, subjects they study, what they do at lunch time, school clubs available, amount of homework they have, how often they have homework.* In pairs or small groups, students use their information and the information in the text about Alan's school day to discuss the similarities and differences.

Set a time limit for this and ask pairs/groups to give feedback to the class on what they think the main similarities/differences are.

┌─ OPTIONAL ACTIVITY ──────────────
  Students plan and draw up their ideal timetable.

10 Write

a Read through the questions. Students note down their answers to each question. Ask some students to tell the class when they do things.

b Remind students about the structure of the text about Alan and the content of each paragraph. Elicit the following information and put it on the board:

Para 1: Time he gets up
Para 2: How he gets to school; time school starts
Para 3: Number and name of subjects he studies
Para 4: Length of breaks and lunch time
Para 5: Time school finishes; what he does after school
Para 6: What he does at the end of the day; homework

Explain that they are now going to write about their school day with the notes they made in Exercise 10a. They must order the information. Students can complete the task in class or this can be set for homework and collected in the next day.

③ A helping hand

Unit overview

TOPIC: Working abroad on a gap year

TEXTS
Reading and listening: a magazine article about a student doing voluntary work in Belize in her gap year
Listening: to a radio interview with a student doing voluntary work
Writing: an email about organising a party
Reading and listening: photo story: *Where's Amy going?*

SPEAKING
Talking about housework
Talking about future arrangements and plans

LANGUAGE
Grammar: Present continuous for present activities; Present simple vs. present continuous
Vocabulary: Housework
Pronunciation: /ɜː/
Everyday English: *check it out*; *You're an angel.*; *She must be crazy.*; *Let's follow her.*

1 Read and listen

If you set the background information as a homework research task ask students to tell the rest of the class what they found out.

BACKGROUND INFORMATION

Gap year: In the UK it's become increasingly fashionable for school leavers to take a 'gap year', a year's working holiday before they start university. Many of these young people choose to work abroad in developing countries on various projects, for example helping with conservation, teaching (often English). Others choose to work in developed countries such as the UK or Australia. Their main aim is usually to gain experience of the outside world and other cultures, as well as to save money to help fund their future studies. The girl in the text, Pauline, has chosen to spend her gap year helping with conservation of the coral reefs in Belize.

Wales: Is one of the four countries which make up the United Kingdom. Its capital city is Cardiff. The Cambrian mountains include Mount Snowdon, the highest mountain in England and Wales. In parts of Wales people still speak Welsh as their first language, or are bilingual in Welsh and English.

Belize: Is often described as the 'jewel of the Caribbean'. It is in Central America and is the only country there where English is the official language. The capital is Belmopan and the chief port is Belize City. It is home to the world's second largest coral reef after the Great Barrier Reef in Australia. However, the coral reef is facing problems from overfishing and pollution.

Warm up

Encourage students to use non-linguistic clues such as pictures and headings to get information before reading. Ask them to look at the map of Belize and ask them what they know about Belize. Then ask them to look at the photo of the girl and predict how old they think the girl is (18).

(a) **Weaker classes:** You may want to pre-teach vocabulary in the text such as *volunteer*, *polluted*, and *research* before students read the text.

Stronger classes: Encourage students to guess the meaning of unknown vocabulary while reading.

As a lead in, you could give students background information about the gap year tradition in L1. Ask students to look quickly at the photos and the text. Let them guess the answers to the questions using the pictures and heading. Ask them to read the text very quickly and check their predictions. Check answers.

Answers
Pauline is 18. She is in Belize. She is working to protect the coral reefs / helping to do research on coral and fish.

(b) 🔊 Ask students to read the true/false questions and check they understand them. Play the recording while students listen and read. In pairs, students answer the true/false questions and note down the sentences from the text which gave them their answers. Check answers as a class, playing and pausing the recording again as necessary. Ask students to correct the false sentences.

TAPESCRIPT
See the reading text on page 34 of the Student's Book.

Answers 1 F (para 2: *She comes from Cardiff, Wales.*) 2 T 3 T 4 F (para 3: *I don't get any money, but that's OK.*) 5 F (para 3: *I want to travel around Belize and Central America.*)

(c) In pairs or small groups, students discuss the questions. Ask students to report back to the rest of the class.

Answers

1 She likes the work because she's learning a lot about the country, the people and herself.
2 (Students' own answers. Remind them to give reasons for their answers.)

┌─ OPTIONAL ACTIVITY ─────────────────

If students were positive about the idea of volunteer work abroad, ask which country they would like to work in. You could ask them if they know of any volunteer projects in their own country.

2 Grammar

Present continuous for activities happening now

a Books closed. Write on the board *I'm writing on the board*. Then underline the first person of the verb *be* positive form and elicit the other persons from students and put them on the board. Follow the same procedure for the negative and the question and short answers forms. Remind students that we do not repeat the *-ing* form in the short answers. Now write the following on the board: *We use the present continuous to talk about something that is happening now / every day*. Ask students to identify which alternative is correct and ask a student to come out and cross out the wrong one on the board.

Students open their books at page 35 and read through the three examples from the text. If necessary, students can refer back to the text on page 34 to see the sentences in context. Then they read through the grammar table and complete the gaps. Check answers.

Answers

Positive: are
Negative: isn't
Questions: Am; Are; Is
Short answers: are; aren't; is; isn't

Then they can read through the Rules box. Ask a few questions of your own to check understanding at this point: *Am I swimming now? Is it raining at the moment? Are you watching TV now?* etc.

Weaker students: At this point, you could ask them to go back through the text on page 34 and find more examples of the present continuous tense (*... but now she's living in Belize; I'm working with other people ...; I'm helping to do research; I'm learning a lot.*)

┌─ **Language notes** ─────────────────
1 Explain to students that normal long forms are seen to be quite formal and would usually be used in writing. Short forms are usually used in speaking.
2 Students may sometimes produce questions like this: *You're working?* Ask students if they have a tense like this in their language and have them

translate some of the examples in the grammar table so they can see any similarities and differences more clearly.
3 Remind students of the *-ing* spelling rules. They should be able to find these fairly quickly if they copied them down in their grammar/vocabulary notebooks.

b Go through the first item with students and ask them why it is *'s riding* (because it is third person singular subject) and ask them what the base form of the verb is (*ride*) and what spelling change has taken place (drop the *-e* and add *-ing*). Students now complete the exercise; remind them to use short forms where possible. Check answers.

Answers

2 're reading / are reading
3 's cooking / is cooking
4 aren't listening / are not listening
5 'm studying / am studying
6 aren't playing / are not playing
7 Are; watching
8 Is; doing

c Ask students to read through the verbs in the box and look at the pictures.

Do the first item with them as an example, if necessary. Students now complete the exercise. Remind them to look carefully at the context of each picture and decide if they need a positive or negative verb form. Check answers.

Answers

1 's writing / is writing
2 isn't watching / is not watching
3 are listening
4 'm not doing / am not doing
5 're playing / are playing
6 aren't working / are not working

┌─ OPTIONAL ACTIVITY ─────────────────

To check students have understood the form correctly, ask them questions about the pictures in Exercise 2c e.g.:
Picture 1: *What is grandfather doing? / Is grandfather reading a book?*
Picture 2: *Is Rosa playing a computer game? / What's Rosa doing?*

3 Pronunciation

/ɜ:/ (w<u>or</u>ld)

a 🔊 Play the recording for students to listen and repeat. You may want to focus on *birthday* and *university* and point out where the stress falls in them to make sure students pronounce them correctly. Drill any words students have problems with.

her world work learn birthday university

(b) 🔊))) Before listening, ask students to underline the /ɜː/ sound in the sentences. Go through the first one with them as an example. Play the recording for students to repeat the sentences. If there are any problems, drill the sentences a few more times.

TAPESCRIPT
1 All over the world.
2 He always works hard.
3 Learn these words!
4 They weren't at university.
5 I'm learning German.
6 This is her first birthday.

4 Grammar
Present simple vs. present continuous

(a) Ask students if they can remember when they use the present simple (for habits and routines) and when they use the present continuous (for activities happening now). Read through the examples of both tenses as a class, pointing out the time expressions used with each tense. Ask students to explain why each tense is used. Go through the first item in the exercise with students to check they understand. Ask students to think about their choice of verb each time and to look out for the time expressions used since this will help them choose the verb they need. Check answers, asking students to explain their choice of verb.

Answers 1 always wear   2 is wearing
3 It's raining   4 It rains   5 is cooking   6 cooks
7 He never listens   8 I'm listening

Look

Explain to students that there are some verbs in English which are hardly ever used in the present continuous tense. Read through the examples in the Look box with students. Ask them if the same thing happens with these verbs in their language.

Grammar notebook

Students can copy the notes from the Look box into their grammar notebooks and perhaps add some information about the verbs and how this works in their own language.

(b) Write the headings *Present simple* and *Present continuous* on the board. Read through the time expressions in the box with students.

Weaker classes: Ask them to look back at the example sentences in Exercise 4a and find as many of the expressions in the box as they can (*right now, at the moment, never, today*). Ask them which tenses they are used with and put the words under the correct heading on the board. Now go through the examples in Exercise 4b and students can then complete the exercise.

Stronger classes: Go through the examples in Exercise 4b and ask students to complete the exercise.

In pairs, students compare answers and give feedback. Write their answers on the board or ask one or two students to come out and write the answers under the correct heading.

Answers
Present simple: usually, every weekend, never, every evening, twice a year
Present continuous: at the moment, this afternoon, right now, today, this week

Grammar notebook

Students can copy these time expressions into their grammar notebooks and write an example of their own for each expression.

(c) Go through the first item with students as an example, focusing on the time expressions to help them work out which tense to use. Remind them to use short forms where possible and to check the spelling rules for the present continuous if they need to. Students complete the exercise. Check answers, asking students to explain their choice of verb.

Answers
1 walks; 's going / is going
2 have; 're reading / are reading
3 's studying / is studying; wants
4 know; don't remember
5 aren't dancing / are not dancing; don't like / do not like
6 does; mean

5 Listen

(a) 🔊)) Ask students if they can remember who Pauline is and what she is doing. (She is the character from the reading text on page 34 and she is working in Belize on a gap year project.) Discuss the three photos with students, asking them to explain what she is doing in each one. (Picture a: She is testing the sea water. Picture b: She is cooking something. Picture c: She is sitting on a beach / she is sunbathing.) Explain that students are going to hear Pauline talking about her work and that one of the pictures shows what she is doing during the interview.

Weaker classes: Ask them to predict some vocabulary items for each picture so they know what they might be listening out for.

Play the recording and ask students to listen and find the right picture. Check answers, asking students to justify their choices with words from the recording. Play the recording again, pausing it as necessary for students to hear the questions and Pauline's answers.

Interviewer   Good morning, and welcome to the *Morning Programme.* Our topic today is volunteer work. I'm in Belize, and I'm talking to a volunteer worker, Pauline Jones, about her life here. Hi, Pauline.

Pauline   Hello.

Interviewer   Now, you're living here in Belize for six months, is that right?

Pauline   Yes, that's right. I'm working on a project to protect the coral reefs.

Interviewer   And what are you doing right now?

Pauline   Well, I'm doing a test on the sea water here. I'm testing to find out if the water is polluted. It's part of my work.

Interviewer   And what do you do in your free time?

Pauline   I don't have much free time! I'm staying with a family here in Belize, and when I'm not working I help around the house.

Interviewer   Doing what, for example?

Pauline   Oh, sometimes I do the cooking and the washing, and of course I tidy my room. And I help with the shopping at the weekends, too.

Interviewer   Do you like the work here?

Pauline   Oh, yeah. The work we're doing on the reef is really important, I think. And I don't mind doing a bit of housework. Well, I don't like doing the washing – there isn't a washing machine, so we do the washing by hand. But that's not a problem, really.

Interviewer   So you're happy to be here?

Pauline   Yes, I love it here. I'm having a great time and I'm learning a lot too.

Interviewer   Well, that's great, Pauline. Thanks, and good luck with your work here.

Pauline   Thank you.

Interviewer   Now we go back to the studio …

Answer

Picture a is the correct picture. (Pauline says: *Well, I'm doing a test on the sea water here. I'm testing to find out if the water is polluted. It's part of my work.*)

b   🔊 Read through the questions with students and check they understand them all. Play the recording again for students to complete their answers. In pairs, students compare answers. Play the recording again, pausing as necessary for students to check or change their answers. Students can then correct the false answers.

Answers 1 T   2 T   3 F *(I help with the shopping at weekends.)* 4 F *(I don't like doing the washing …)* 5 T

6 Vocabulary
Housework

🔊 Read through the expressions in the box with students and check they understand them all. Go through an example with students. Students complete the exercise. They can compare answers in pairs before listening to the recording. Play the recording for students to check their answers. Play the recording again, so students can repeat the words.

TAPESCRIPT/ANSWERS

a   4   do the shopping
b   6   tidy up / tidy a room
c   1   do the cooking
d   3   do the washing
e   7   clean the windows
f   5   do the washing-up / wash up
g   2   do the ironing

Look

Look at the examples and explanations in the Look box with students and ask a stronger student to put each phrase into a sentence to check understanding.

Vocabulary notebook

Students should start a section in their vocabulary notes called *Housework*. They should copy down the expressions from Exercise 6 and the Look box. If necessary, they can translate them into their own language. Ask students if they know any more housework expressions they could add to the list.

OPTIONAL ACTIVITY

What am I doing?

In small groups, students each choose an activity and take turns to mime it to the rest of the group. The others have to guess what he/she is doing. Set a time limit of about 20 seconds for the students to guess. The person who guesses correctly has the next turn. This can also be done as a whole class activity.

7 Speak

a   Go through the example questions with students. Ask a few students the questions and check they use the correct tense when answering. Divide students into small groups to ask and answer questions about housework. Groups could appoint a secretary who notes down the results under each name. Ask for group feedback. Are there any general trends? Do boys do more / less / the same as girls? Put any interesting points on the board for further discussion.

OPTIONAL ACTIVITY

Groups can give feedback. Put the results on the board and students can draw up a class graph to show how work is distributed.

b Read through the instruction and the example with students. Point out the use of adverbs of frequency and the present simple tense. In pairs, students discuss the points. Ask for feedback and put any interesting points on the board for further discussion.

┌─ OPTIONAL ACTIVITY ──────────
Students can write up their discussions from Exercise 7b for homework.

Where's Amy going?

8 Read and listen

Warm up

Ask students to look at the photo story and tell you who the characters are (Amy, Alex and Dave). What can they remember about Alex and Dave, the characters from Unit 1? (Alex wasn't very nice to Tony – he teased him about doing ballet.) Students can now look at the title of the story and try and predict where Amy is going.

a 🔊 Read through the instruction and the question with students. Play the recording for students to read and listen. Check answers.

TAPESCRIPT
See the photo story on page 38 of the Student's Book.

Answer
She's too busy. (She can't go to the café because she is helping Mrs Craig. She is doing her shopping and she offers to do her ironing too.)

b Read through the two parts of each sentence with students and go through the example with them. Refer them back to the story if necessary. Check answers.

Answers 2 a 3 b 4 e 5 c

┌─ OPTIONAL ACTIVITY ──────────
In groups, students can act out the dialogue from the photo story.

9 Everyday English

a Students must decide who said these expressions from the photo story and to whom. Do the first one as an example if necessary.

Stronger classes: Can do this without looking back at the photo story.

Weaker classes: Can do this referring back to the photo story.

Answers 1 Alex (to Amy) 2 Mrs Craig (to Amy)
3 Dave (to Alex) 4 Dave (to Alex)

b Ask students to find the expression *Let's follow her* in the photo story. Can they guess the meaning from the context? Students now translate this into their own language.

c Ask students to find expressions 1–3 in the photo story. Ask students to match the expressions. Check answers.

Answers 1 b 2 a 3 c

d Read through the dialogues with students and check they understand. Remind students that they must use the expressions in Exercises 9b and c to complete the gaps. Students complete the exercise. In pairs, students compare answers before a whole class check.

Answers
1 She must be crazy.
2 check it out
3 let's
4 You're an angel.

Vocabulary notebook
Students should now note down the *Everyday English* expressions in that section of their vocabulary notebooks. Remind them to use translations or the other expressions from this unit to help them remember each one.

┌─ OPTIONAL ACTIVITIES ──────────
Stronger classes
Students can write their own short dialogues, using the expressions in Exercise 9, and act them out in front of the class.

Weaker students
They can act out the dialogues in Exercise 9d.

10 Write

Warm up

Ask students if they send or receive emails. How often? Who do they write to? What do they write about?

a Students read through the email quickly. Check any vocabulary problems. In pairs, students answer the questions. Remind them to use the present continuous tense in their answers.

Answers
1 The event is Peter's grandfather's sixtieth birthday. It is happening that evening.
2 There are about 40 people coming.
3 Peter's mother is cooking in the kitchen with his aunts. His dad is putting up lights in the garden. His uncle is organising the tables and chairs.

b Remind students of the differences between writing an email and a letter (Unit 1). Elicit/Give the following information about emails and write it on the board:

• Opening: include *To, From, Subject*.
• Greeting: Informal expressions like *Hi!* or *Hello!*
• Content: Does not have to be split into paragraphs as in a letter and can be very informal.
• Signing off: Does not need full sentences, can just have your name.

Students now choose one of the events and plan their emails. Students can prepare this in class and write the email for homework.

4 A healthy life

Unit overview

TOPIC: Food and a healthy lifestyle

TEXTS
Reading and listening: a text about healthy eating
Listening: to a dialogue in a restaurant
Reading: a text about British Food
Writing: a paragraph about food and fitness

SPEAKING
Talking about a health quiz
Ordering food in a restaurant

LANGUAGE
Grammar: Countable and uncountable nouns;
a/an and *some*; *much* and *many*
Vocabulary: Food and drink
Pronunciation: The schwa /ə/

1 Read and listen

If you set the background information as a homework research task ask students to tell the rest of the class what they found out.

BACKGROUND INFORMATION

Sumo wrestlers: The Japanese sport of Sumo or *Ozumo* (its traditional Japanese name) originated in ancient times as a religious performance to the Shinto gods. Today, Sumo is the Japanese national sport. Sumo wrestlers are usually aged between 20 and 35, follow special diets and live in special Sumo 'stables' which have very strict rules. A top Sumo wrestler is called a *yokozuna*. The principle of Sumo wrestling is simple: a wrestler who touches the floor of the Sumo ring with anything other than the sole of his foot or who leaves the ring before his opponent, loses. A Sumo match usually lasts for only a few seconds. Every year in Japan there are six Sumo tournaments, three of which take place in Tokyo.

Warm up

Ask students to look at page 40. Ask them if they know who the people are in the big photo (Sumo wrestlers). Now ask them what they can see in the photos in the article and what they think the connections are between them (keeping fit and eating a healthy diet keeps people in better health).

(a) Read through the questions with students and check they understand them. Pre-teach any vocabulary (*fat, meal, calories, heavy, wrestler, weight, worried, snacks, burn off, skinny*). Do the first item with them as an example. Students complete the exercise. Check answers. Remind students to copy new vocabulary into their notebooks once they have finished the exercise.

Answers
1 b (para 1, line 2: *Japanese Sumo wrestlers ...*)
2 c (advice box, point 2: *Eat five small meals ...*)
3 a (advice box, point 3: *It's a good idea to eat snacks ...*)
4 a (advice box, point 6: *Do some exercise every day ...*)

(b) Read through the questions with students to check they understand them all. Now play the recording while students listen and read and find the answers to questions 1–3. Students may need to answer question 2 in their mother tongue. Check answers. Then, in pairs students discuss question 4. Ask for class feedback.

TAPESCRIPT
See the reading text on page 40 of the Student's Book.

Answers
1 They usually eat *chankonabe*, a mixture of rice, meat and vegetables.
2 They go to bed straight after their dinner because they want to put on weight and get heavier, so they don't want to burn off the calories after eating.
3 They are overweight because they often eat unhealthy food and watch a lot of television or use the computer a lot.
4 (Students' own answers.)

2 Vocabulary
Food and drink

 With books closed, elicit as many food words from students as they know and write them on the board. Students now open their books and read through the food vocabulary in the box. Go through the first two examples with them as a class. Students then match the other items with the pictures. Students can compare answers in pairs. Play the recording for students to check or change their answers. Play it again, for students to repeat each word. Check answers.

TAPESCRIPT/ANSWERS
1 vegetables 2 fruit 3 meat 4 onions 5 eggs
6 water 7 rice 8 apples 9 tomatoes 10 sugar
11 pasta 12 grapes 13 carrots 14 bread

Language notes

1 Check students' pronunciation of these items, particularly: *vegetables* /ˈvedʒtəblz/, *onions* /ˈʌnjənz/, *tomatoes* /təˈmɑːtəʊz/, *sugar* /ˈʃʊgə/.
2 Ask students if there are any words which are similar in their language.

Vocabulary notebook

Students should start a section called *Food and drink* in their vocabulary notebooks. Students should copy these words down and add any more as they go along.

OPTIONAL ACTIVITY ════════════

I'm making a sandwich and …

This game can be played by the whole class or in groups. One student starts the sentence and adds a food item then the next student adds a new item and remembers the previous item, e.g.:

S1: *I'm making a sandwich and in it I'm putting onions.*
S2: *I'm making a sandwich and in it I'm putting onions and tomatoes.*
S3: *I'm making a sandwich and in it I'm putting onions and (adds another item).*

The game continues in this way until someone forgets an item or gets an item wrong. When a student makes a mistake they are out of the game and the person who remembers the most items is the winner. Set a time limit for this game.

---

3 **Grammar**

Countable and uncountable nouns

(a) Books closed. Write *onion* on the board. Elicit the plural from students and write it beside the singular. Elicit one more example of a singular and plural and put them on the board under *onion/onions*. Now write *sugar* on the other side of the board and ask students if they can count it. Elicit another example of an uncountable noun (e.g. *bread*) and write it below *sugar* on the board. Then write the headings *Countable* and *Uncountable* above each column on the board.

Students now open their books at page 41 and read through the five example sentences. Go through the first one with them as an example showing them which words to underline and which ones to circle. Students complete the exercise. Check answers.

Answers

1 Have some (bread.)
2 Eat five small meals.
3 Don't eat fried (food.)
4 Have some (bread,) an apple, some grapes or a carrot.
5 Eat some vegetables or some (fruit.)

Now read through the rules with students and check they understand them.

(b) Remind students of the information on the board from Exercise 3a and check they have understood the difference between countable and uncountable nouns. Go through the example with students. Students complete the exercise. Check answers. You can ask some students to come out and add their items to the list on the board.

Answers

Countable nouns: onions, eggs, apples, tomatoes, grapes, carrots
Uncountable nouns: meat, water, rice, sugar, pasta, bread

OPTIONAL ACTIVITY ════════════

To check students have understood properly, call out the nouns from Exercise 2 and ask them to answer *Countable* or *Uncountable* when you call out the noun, e.g.:

T: *Paolo, apples*
Paolo: *Countable.*
T: *Maria, bread.*
Maria: *Uncountable.*

---

a/an and some

(c) Using the lists on the board, ask students which word (*a/an* or *some*) we can put before *vegetable* (*a/an*) and *vegetables* (*some*). Ask students the same question with *bread* (only *some* can go before *bread*). Read through the rule with students, pointing out the example and then ask students to try and complete the rule. Check answers.

Answers countable; uncountable

(d) Go through the first item with students as an example if necessary. Focus on the noun after the gap and ask students to decide whether it is countable or uncountable. Remind them to do this in all the other items. Students complete the exercise. Check answers.

Answers 1 some 2 some; some 3 a 4 An; a 5 some; some 6 some; a

---

OPTIONAL ACTIVITY ════════════

Stronger classes

They can write their own gapped *a/an/some* sentences for a partner to complete.

Weaker classes

If you feel they need further practice in this area, give them the following sentences to complete:

1 *I want .... tomatoes.*
2 *Eat .... pasta. It's good for you.*
3 *There is .... carrot in the kitchen.*
4 *Drink .... water! It's hot.*
5 *Mark wants .... apple.*

Answers 1 some 2 some 3 a 4 some 5 an

---

40 Module 1

much and *many*

(e) Read through the examples with students. Ask them if the noun in each example is countable or uncountable (*meals*: countable; *water*: uncountable; *coffee*: uncountable; *vegetables*: countable). Now point out the words before each of these nouns (*much/many*) and ask them to read the rule and try and complete it. Check answers.

Answers
countable; uncountable

(f) Go through the example with students. Elicit that *milk* is an uncountable noun, therefore *much* is used before *it*.

Weaker classes: Go through items 2–6 in the same way and circle the correct word. Once they have completed this part of the exercise, check answers. Then match item 1 with the answers in the second column. Try various wrong possibilities first to show students how there is only one correct answer.

Stronger classes: They can do parts 1 and 2 together.

Students complete the exercise. Check answers.

Answers 1 much c   2 many d   3 much e
4 many a   5 many f   6 much b

Grammar notebook
Students should note down all the new grammar points from this unit in their grammar notebooks and try and learn one rule each day for homework.

4 Speak

(a) Pre-teach any new vocabulary from the Health Quiz on page 42 (e.g. *average*, *burn calories*) and read through the questions with the class. Ask students to work in pairs to discuss the questions and guess which answer is correct in each case. Check answers with the whole class.

Answers
1 c   2 a   3 c   4 b   5 c   6 a

(b) Ask the example questions to different students and elicit different answers. Ask students to suggest some more questions. Students then ask each other their own questions about things in the quiz, while the teacher monitors for errors. Get feedback with a few questions and answers from pairs at the end.

5 Pronunciation
The schwa /ə/ (wat*er*)

(a) Play the recording for students to listen and repeat. Make sure they do not try to stress the schwa sound, as it is always in a destressed syllable. Drill any words students have problems with.

TAPESCRIPT
water   tomato   exercise   sugar   banana   vegetable

(b) Ask students to listen to the recording and underline the syllables with the schwa sound. Play the example and check they understand that they must underline the schwa sound (and not the stressed syllable). Play the rest of the recording, pausing to allow them time to mark the correct syllable. Then play the recording again for them to check their answers. Play the recording one more time for them to listen and repeat.

TAPESCRIPT/ANSWERS
a carr*ot*   *an* orange
some bread   *some* apples   *some* oni*ons*
a lot   a lot *of* fruit   a lot *of* cal*or*ies
a lot *of* veget*a*bles

6 Listen
Warm up

Ask students if they ever eat in restaurants. Write the headings *Starters*, *Main meals*, *Desserts* and *Drinks* on the board. Elicit as many words as possible for these headings and write them on the board.

(a) Students read through the menu on page 43 and match each item with one of the pictures. Go through the first one as an example, if necessary. In pairs, students compare answers. Now play the recording, pausing as necessary for students to check or change their answers.

TAPESCRIPT/ANSWERS
a   9   tea
b   7   vegetable curry and rice
c   1   pasta
d   4   fish of the day
e   6   beefburgers
f   11 orange juice
g   8   coffee
h   3   seafood salad
i   10 mineral water
j   2   vegetable soup
k   5   chicken and mushrooms

(b) Ask students to read through the dialogue. Check any vocabulary problems.

Stronger classes: They can complete the dialogue first and then listen and check. Remind them to read the whole dialogue carefully and to look at other words around the gap to work out what is missing.

Weaker classes: They can listen to the dialogue and complete the gaps. Pause the recording as necessary, allowing students time to note down their answers.

Play the recording for students to check or change their answers.

TAPESCRIPT

Waiter   Are you ready to order?

Girl   Yes, I'd like to start with the soup, please, and then the grilled fish.

Waiter Certainly. Would you like vegetables or salad?

Girl Salad, please.

Waiter And to drink?

Girl I'd like an orange juice, I think.

Waiter Orange juice. Fine.

Boy And I'd like the seafood salad, please. And then the chicken with vegetables.

Waiter Chicken with vegetables. And to drink?

Boy Just some mineral water, please.

Waiter Right. Anything else?

Boy No, thank you.

Answers 1 fish   2 Salad   3 juice   4 seafood
5 chicken   6 water

OPTIONAL ACTIVITY

The food chain game

This can be played by the whole class or in small groups. Students think of an item of food and the next person must think of an item of food starting with the last letter of the previous one, e.g.:

S1: banana
S2: apple
S3: egg, etc.

If a student cannot think of an item of food, they are out of the game. The game continues until there is only one student left. Set a time limit.

---

7 Speak

In groups of three, students act out the dialogue in Exercise 6b. If space, then students can arrange their tables and chairs as if they were in a restaurant. Remind them to change the food items and choose different things from the menu. If time, students should swap roles.

Vocabulary notebook

Remind students to note down any new expressions from the menu and the dialogue in their vocabulary notebooks under their *Food* section.

OPTIONAL ACTIVITY

Stronger classes

They can make their own menus and should include their own favourite meals. They can decorate them.

Weaker classes

They can copy and decorate the menu on page 43. They could change the prices to their own currency.

All menus can be displayed on the classroom walls.

Culture in mind

8 Read

If you set the background information as a homework research task ask students to tell the rest of the class what they found out.

BACKGROUND INFORMATION

Fish and chips: This is a popular take-away meal from a fish and chip shop ('chippy').

Roast beef: Traditionally this is what British people are said to eat on a Sunday. Along with roast potatoes, Yorkshire pudding (a batter mixture of flour, water, milk and egg), vegetables and gravy, this is called 'a roast dinner'. A lot of pubs and restaurants specialise in roast dinners on Sundays.

Full English breakfast: This can include bacon, fried or scrambled eggs, tomatoes, mushrooms, fried bread, sausages and baked beans.

Take-away restaurants: Nowadays there is a variety of these, but the most popular are still fish and chip shops, Indian and Chinese take-aways. Many take-away restaurants now offer a door-to-door delivery service where a meal can be ordered by telephone and delivered to the person's house at a specific time.

Warm up

Ask students to look at the photos on page 44. Ask if they have eaten this type of food before or if they would like to eat the kind of food in the photos.

(a) Read through the items in the box as a class and check students understand them all. Do the first item with students as an example, if necessary. Students look again at photos 1–4 and match the words in the box with the photos. Check answers.

Answers
some cereal: photo 2
bacon and eggs: photo 2
restaurant food: photo 4
an omelette: photo 1
fish and chips: photo 1
some toast: photo 2
a sandwich: photo 1
a take-away: photo 3

(b) Students look at the headings from the article and decide which items from Exercise 8a match each heading. Students should read the text quickly, then check their answers.

Answers
1 cereal, bacon and eggs, toast
2 omelette, sandwich, fish and chips
3 restaurant food, take-away, fish and chips

Note: Fish and chips is included in the 'Lunch' picture here, but it is also often bought as a take-away from fish and chip shops.

(c) Pre-teach any vocabulary (e.g. *bowl, too much, it depends, holidays, enough*). Stronger students can look up any words they don't know in a dictionary. Read through questions 1–6 with students and check they understand them. Go through the first one with them as an example, if necessary. Students do the exercise and compare answers in pairs. Check answers with the whole class.

Answers
1 Roast beef.
2 No, she doesn't. She has tea and toast.
3 He has bacon and eggs at the weekends.
4 Sophie likes an omelette.
5 Because he lives in a small town where there aren't many restaurants.
6 He sometimes eats out in a Greek restaurant.

(d) Put the headings *Breakfast, Lunch, Eating out* on the board. Elicit as many examples of food for these meals as possible from students for each of the headings. You may also want to ask them about the times they have breakfast and lunch and when they tend to eat out. In pairs or small groups, students now discuss the differences between their eating habits and those of the teenagers in the article.

Weaker classes: Use the prompts on the board to encourage them to structure their discussion.

Stronger classes: They can go straight into their discussion without using the prompts on the board.

Ask for class feedback. Are there any similarities and differences between the students and the teenagers in the text? You may want to note down the main similarities/differences on the board in preparation for Exercise 9.

┌─ OPTIONAL ACTIVITY ──────────
Yorkshire pudding
If students are interested you could give them a British recipe to try out at home. Here is a recipe for Yorkshire pudding. Remind them this is a savoury accompaniment to a main meal.

You will need: One roasting tin with a shallow covering of olive oil; one whisk

Ingredients (for 4 people):
75 g plain flour
1 egg
75 ml milk
55 ml water
salt and pepper to season
some olive oil (for the roasting tin)

Method:
Put the roasting tin with the oil in it into the preheated oven (220°C).
1 Sieve the flour into a bowl.

2 Measure out the water and milk together in a jug and add to the flour.
3 Add the egg.
4 Mix everything together with the whisk.
5 Take the heated roasting tin out of the oven and pour the batter mixture into it.
6 Cook on the top shelf for 20–30 minutes or until golden brown.

Vocabulary notebook
Students should note down any new vocabulary from the reading text.

9 Write

This task can be set for homework with the preparation done in class.

(a) Read through questions 1–5 with students. Remind them to refer back to the notes on the board from Exercise 8d, if it will help them. Give students a few minutes to note down their answers.

(b) In pairs, students use their notes from Exercise 9a to exchange information and make notes about their partner.

(c) Read through the paragraph on page 45 with students. Focus on the structure of the paragraph with students and point out how it matches the order of the questions in Exercise 9a:

Question 1: sentence 1
Question 2: sentences 2 and 3
Question 3: sentence 4
Question 4: sentence 5
Question 5: sentences 7 and 8

Ask them to use the notes about their partner and write a similar paragraph. Remind them to use the present simple tense.

Students can read out their paragraphs to the class and some of the better ones can be displayed on the classroom walls.

┌─ OPTIONAL ACTIVITY ──────────
Stronger classes
In pairs, they can plan a healthy routine for a day. Remind them to use as much vocabulary from this unit and previous ones as possible: food, exercise, present simple for routines. Pairs can then compare with other pairs and give feedback to the class.

1 Grammar

a 2 her 3 us 4 them 5 him

b 2 lives 3 play 4 doesn't like 5 don't live
6 don't get up 7 gives 8 Do; like 9 Does;
work 10 Do; write

c 2 My friend is always late for school.
3 I don't usually watch football.
4 You are usually good at Geography.
5 My father hardly ever drinks coffee.
6 I go to a sports club twice a week.

d 2 works; 's working / is working
3 'm reading / am reading; don't usually read
4 's cooking / is cooking; cooks
5 don't watch; 're watching / are watching
6 A: Do; swim
  B: 're swimming / are swimming

e 2 an 3 much 4 many 5 Many 6 a
7 some; much

2 Vocabulary

a 2 Drama 3 Maths 4 English 5 Science
6 History 7 French 8 Geography
9 Information Technology 10 Physical Education

b Hobbies and interests: dancing, playing the guitar
Other possibilities: watching TV, reading, playing
computer games, going to the cinema, playing the
piano, seeing friends
Housework: doing the ironing, cleaning the windows,
tidying up
Other possibilities: doing the washing-up, tidying
your bedroom, laying the table, washing the floors

c 2 meat 3 onions 4 bread 5 water 6 juice
7 carrot 8 chips 9 apple 10 salad
The mystery word is: sandwiches

3 Everyday English

2 What about 3 Let's 4 must be crazy
5 So what 6 check out 7 an angel

How did you do?
Check that students are marking their scores. Collect
these in and check them as necessary and discuss any
further work needed with specific students.

Module 2
Follow your dreams

YOU WILL LEARN ABOUT ...

Ask students to look at the photos on the page. Ask students to read through the topics in the box and check they understand each item. You can ask them the following questions, in L1 if appropriate:

1 *Do you have/use a mobile phone?*
2 *Who is your favourite pop idol?*
3 *What is the woman doing?*
4 *What makes someone successful?*
5 *Do you know who the athletes are?*
6 *What do you think this teenager does?*
7 *What period of history is this?*

In small groups, students discuss which topic area they think each photo matches.

Check answers.

Answers

1 How British teenagers use mobile phones
2 Pop idols in Britain
3 A woman who lived in a tree
4 The secrets of success
5 A special friendship
6 Songwriting for a band
7 A family who went back in time

YOU WILL LEARN HOW TO ...

Use grammar

Go through the first item with students. Stronger students should be able to continue with the other items on their own or in pairs.

Weaker classes: Put the grammar headings on the board and give an example of your own for each item, e.g. *I worked in a different school last year. I taught English and French. You don't have to wear a school uniform. I've got some pencils. Is this pen his?*

In pairs, students now match the grammar items in their book. Check answers.

Answers

Past simple: *be*: The helicopter was very noisy.
Past simple regular verbs: Julia lived in a tree-house.
Past simple irregular verbs: They met in the 1936 Olympic Games.
have to / don't have to: Tom doesn't have to wear a uniform.
some and *any*: We haven't got any butter.
Possessive pronouns: Is this book yours?

Use vocabulary

Write the headings on the board. Go through the items in the Student's Book and check understanding. You can mime any of the items if necessary. Now ask students if they can think of one more item for the *Sports* heading. Elicit some responses and add them to the list on the board. Students now do the same for the other headings. Some possibilities are:

Phrasal verbs: *climb down, come up, turn up, turn down*
Sports: *football, golf, cricket, basketball, volleyball, tennis*
Jobs: *teacher, bus driver, doctor, cook/chef, waiter/waitress*
Sleeping and waking: *wake up, get up, dream, sleepwalk*

(5) My hero!

Unit overview

TOPIC: Heroes; The environment

TEXTS
Reading and listening: a magazine article about a protester
Listening: to a student's presentation about her hero
Reading and listening: photo story: *Who's your hero?*
Writing: a poster about your hero

SPEAKING
Talking about protesters and heroes
Talking about when and where you were born

LANGUAGE
Grammar: Past simple: the verb *be*; Past simple: regular verbs
Vocabulary: Phrasal verbs (1)
Pronunciation: *was* and *were*; *-ed* endings: /d/, /t/ and /ɪd/
Everyday English: *You can't be serious.; loads of people; That's amazing.; one day*

1 Read and listen

If you set the background information as a homework research task ask students to tell the rest of the class what they found out.

BACKGROUND INFORMATION

Julia Hill: On 10 December 1997, Julia 'Butterfly' Hill, then aged 23, climbed up a 1000-year-old redwood tree and made a house out of a platform she set up there. She wanted to prevent the destruction of the tree and nearby trees by the landowner, the Pacific Lumber Company. She relied on supplies brought to her by her supporters to survive in the tree. While she was up the tree she attracted a good deal of media attention and finally came down on 18 December 1999, after the Pacific Lumber Company agreed to save the area in exchange for her exit, and donated $50,000, which went towards university science research.

Warm up

You could give your students background information in L1 about the topic of forest destruction and ways people have tried to prevent it. Ask students to tell you the kinds of environmental problems we face (e.g. global warming and the 'Greenhouse effect') and what (if anything) is being done about them.

a Students look at the photo and title and read the instructions, silently. Collect ideas from the whole class (make sure they don't start reading the text yet) and write them on the board. Before students read the text, pre-teach *forest*.

Students read the text quickly to check their answer. Did anyone in the class get the answers right? (She wanted to stop the company from cutting down the tree and surrounding trees.)

b ◁)) This exercise is designed to help students guess vocabulary from context. Students read through items 1–4. Play the recording for students to read and listen. Pause the recording after the first item and go through it as an example. Do the first example with the whole class. Write the example on the board and refer students to the first word *company*. Ask the class for translations, giving clues when necessary. Do the same for *cut down*, pointing out if necessary that the adverb *down* gives them a clue to the meaning.

Students listen, read and complete the rest of the exercise. Check answers.

TAPESCRIPT
See the reading text on page 50 of the Student's Book.

c Look at the first question with the whole class. Ask students what kind of information the question is asking for and give prompts if necessary (*how tall the tree is, where it is, how old it is*). Students answer the questions individually, before checking with a partner. Check answers.

Answers
1 It was 70 m tall, and 1,000 years old. It was a redwood tree in California.
2 Two years and eight days.
3 Her friends cooked food for her.
4 She talked on a mobile phone.
5 The company which wanted to cut down the forest. They sent a big helicopter that flew near her tree-house and made a lot of noise/wind.

d Students work in small groups to discuss the questions. Alternatively, do this as a whole class discussion. Ask for class feedback and see which options were the most popular.

┌─ OPTIONAL ACTIVITY ──────────
In small groups, students discuss if they would do something like this. Do they know anyone who has made a strong protest about anything? If so, what and why? Do they believe strongly enough in something to do something similar? This can be discussed in L1 if necessary.

2 Grammar

Past simple: the verb *be*

(a) Write the following sentence on the board from the text: *Julia Hill was born in 1974.* Ask students if this is in the past or the present (past). Now ask students to look back at the text on page 50 and find more examples of the past simple of the verb *be*. Ask them if they can work out how to form the past tense. Elicit the positive forms and write them on the board under the heading *Positive*.

Answers
Paragraph 1:
… was born …
She was 23 years old …
… there were lots of …
… was 70 metres tall …
Paragraph 2:
… wasn't happy …
… were very helpful.
Paragraph 3:
… was very noisy …
… other people weren't …
… there was a lot of …
Paragraph 4:
… was successful.
… were very happy.

(b) Write the table headings on the board. Ask students to look at the examples they found in Exercise 2a and see if they can put them into the table. Check answers.

Answers
Negative: wasn't; weren't
Question: Was; Were
Short answer: was; wasn't; were; weren't

Check understanding by asking them when they use *was* (singular, except *you* form) and when they use *were* (all plural forms).

(c) Go through the example with students, asking them why the answer is *was* and not *were* (because Julia (*she*) = a third person singular subject). Students complete the exercise. Check answers.

Answers 2 were 3 was 4 wasn't 5 weren't

(d) Go through the example with students, reminding them of the word order for questions with the verb *be*. Students complete the exercise. Check answers.

Answers 2 Was 3 Were 4 Was 5 Were

(e) Go through the example dialogue with students, pointing out that if an answer is negative then they must provide the correct answer as well. If an answer is positive, they must try and provide more information to back up their answers. In pairs, students now ask and answer the questions in Exercise 2d. They can refer back to the text on page 50 if necessary.

Answers
2 Yes, it was. It was 1,000 years old.
3 Yes, they were. They cooked food for her every day.
4 Yes, it was. Julia didn't like it.
5 No, they weren't. They were very happy because the company agreed not to cut down the tree.

Grammar notebook
Make sure students copy the completed table from exercise 2b into their grammar notebooks.

3 Pronunciation

was and *were*

(a) 🔊 Put the following phonetic symbols on the board: /ɒ/, /ɜː/, /ə/. Read out the first sentence with the class and elicit which sound they heard in the word *was* (/ə/). Play the recording for students to listen and write which sound they think they heard in the underlined words. Ask students for their answers and write them under the relevant heading on the board. (Note that they hear the same /ə/ sound every time.) Play the recording again, pausing for students to repeat the words. Drill any words further, if necessary.

TAPESCRIPT
1 Julia was an American woman.
2 There were lots of trees in the forest.
3 Was the helicopter very noisy?
4 Were the trees very old?

Answer
The vowel sound in all the sentences is /ə/.

(b) 🔊 Go through the example with students (on the board) and tick the appropriate column. In order to make sure students have heard the correct pronunciation you could pronounce it in all three ways for them to see why /ə/ is the correct pronunciation. Play the recording for students to listen and decide which sound they hear. Check answers, playing and pausing the recording again as necessary.

TAPESCRIPT
1 I was unhappy.
2 He wasn't a good teacher.
3 My friends weren't at the park.
4 We were late yesterday.
5 Was it noisy?
6 Yes, it was.
7 Were you on the bus?
8 Yes, we were.

Answers 2 /ɒ/ 3 /ɜː/ 4 /ə/ 5 /ə/
6 /ɒ/ 7 /ə/ 8 /ɜː/

4 Grammar

was born / were born

Books closed. Write the following information on the board: *Name, Year of birth, Place of birth*. Now complete the information about yourself (the information can be real or invented). Point to *Year of birth* and repeat *In* + year. Now ask students: *When were you born? Where were you born?* Make sure they are answering using *In* + year and *In* + place.

Students open their books at page 51 and look at the two example sentences about Julia Hill. Ask them to fill in the gaps with the year and the place. Check answers.

Answers 1 1974   2 the USA

> **Language note:** Explain to students that in English, when we say a year before the year 2000, we split it into two parts (1999 = *nineteen ninety-nine*). For the years 2000–2009 we say the number (2001 = *two thousand and one*) and after 2010 we say it as two parts again (2012 = *twenty twelve*). It may be useful for students to compare how they say this in their own language.

5 Speak

a In pairs, students ask their partner when and where they were born. Remind students they need to use *in* + year and *in* + place to answer the questions. Ask a few students to give feedback to the class.

b In the same pairs, students now ask and answer about family members. Go through the example dialogue first, reminding students to use *was/were* as appropriate for the subject of their question.

Grammar notebook
Remind students to copy this information and some examples of their own into their grammar notebooks.

6 Grammar

Past simple: regular verbs

a Ask students to locate the example in the text on page 50 (para 2, line 2) and point out that the *-ed* ending means this is a past simple regular verb. Write the base forms of the verbs in this exercise on the board. Students now locate the other verbs in the text and write down the past simple. Check answers and write them on the board.

Answers cooked, lived, planned, stayed, travelled, tried, used, walked, wanted

b Ask students to read through the rule. Go through the first part with them as an example, referring back to the copy on the board from Exercise 6a. Students complete the rule. Check answers.

Answers -ed; -d; n/consonant; i; -ed

--- OPTIONAL ACTIVITIES ===

Weaker classes
To check students have understood this you can give them the following short exercise to choose the correct spelling:

stop: stopped/stoped
play: played/plaied
talk: talked/talkd
visit: visited/visitd

Once you are sure students have understood the rule, ask them to decide which part of the rule applies to the verbs in Exercise 6a.

Stronger classes
Ask them to decide which part of the rule applies to the verbs in Exercise 6a.

c Go through the first item as an example. Students then complete the exercise. Check answers.

Answers 1 wanted   2 lived   3 planned   4 tried; answered   5 travelled; visited   6 played; stopped; smiled

If you feel it would be helpful, ask students to decide which part of the rule in the Rule box applies to the verbs.

d Put the example on the board. Ask students to find a past simple positive form (*stayed*). Then draw their attention to the negative form (*didn't like*) and ask them what they notice about it (the auxiliary verb *did + not* is used). Ask them what they notice about the verb following the *not* + auxiliary part (it does not have *-ed*). Give them an example of your own (*I didn't cook yesterday*.). Now ask a few students to give you an example of something they didn't do yesterday to check they have understood the form. Students now complete the negative part of the box.

Answer
didn't

e Ask students to read through the verbs in the box and look at the pictures, then go through the example. Students complete the exercise. Check answers. Go through any problems at this point with the positive and negative forms.

Answers 2 stayed; didn't like   3 rained; didn't play   4 didn't watch; studied   5 tidied; didn't clean   6 talked; didn't say; stopped

Grammar notebook
Remind students to copy down the spelling rules for regular past simple verbs and to note down some examples for each rule. They can also note down the form of the past simple regular positive and negative forms.

--- OPTIONAL ACTIVITY ===

Students choose five verbs from Exercise 6e and write three true sentences about themselves and two false sentences. In pairs, students swap sentences and check their partner's items and guess which are the false sentences.

7 Pronunciation

-ed endings

🔊 Put the column headings /d/ or /t/ and /ɪd/ on the board. Do the two examples with students and check they can hear the difference. Then say *listened* with the three different endings and ask students which column it should go in (/d/). Tell them they are going to hear the verbs in the box and they must decide which ending they hear. Play the recording. Students note down the verbs according to the pronunciation of the endings. Check answers. Play the recording again, pausing as necessary to drill and repeat each verb.

TAPESCRIPT

walked, visited, listened, wanted, watched, climbed, started, tried, hated, decided

Answers

/d/ or /t/: walked, listened, watched, climbed, tried
/ɪd/: visited, wanted, started, hated, decided

Grammar notebook

Students should note down the different pronunciations and write examples for each one.

OPTIONAL ACTIVITIES

Stronger classes

They can add one or two more verbs for each ending to the lists.

Weaker classes

Ask students to look back at the past simple of the verbs in Exercise 6a. Students can classify these verbs according to their pronunciation.

8 Vocabulary

Phrasal verbs (1)

This is an introduction to phrasal verbs. All the example verbs in the Student's Book are literal – the meaning of the verb is reflected in the verbs themselves.

(a) Refer students to the examples from the text and check they understand the meaning of the verbs. Ask them if they can think of any other verbs that use *up* or *down*.

Stronger classes: Set a time limit and put students in pairs to think of verbs.

Weaker classes: Ask the whole class to think of verbs and write them on the board.

Check answers.

Example answers

Verbs with *up*: put up (e.g. a picture) sit up, get/stand up, move up, look up, turn up (volume)
Verbs with *down*: sit down, walk/drive/go down (e.g. the street/hill/road), put down, count down, look down, turn down (volume), stand down, set down (e.g. bus, train, etc.)

(b) 🔊 Go through the example with the whole class. Students now complete the exercise. Students can compare answers in pairs. Then play the recording for students to check their answers. Pause as necessary. Once students have checked their answers, play the recording again for students to repeat the verbs.

TAPESCRIPT/ANSWERS

a	2	Pick it up, please.
b	5	Polly! Come down!
c	8	Get out!
d	7	Take it off!
e	1	Climb up!
f	6	Put that knife down.
g	4	Get in.
h	3	Put them on.

(c) Go through the example with students. Explain to students that the verbs may not be exactly the same as in the example (*climb/come*). Students then match the opposites. Students can compare answers with a partner. Check answers.

Answers

pick up – put down
put on – take off
get in – get out

(d) Give an example of your own for the verb *climb up*, then ask for an example situation for *come down*. In pairs, students think of situations for the other verbs. Check answers.

OPTIONAL ACTIVITY

Weaker classes

Weaker students may enjoy the following simple TPR (total physical response) activity. It will help with recognition and comprehension of the verbs before students are required to actively produce them.

Pick several verbs from Exercise 8b and some examples students provided in Exercise 8a or 8c. Students listen and follow your commands.

T: Stand up!
Pick up your pen/book/pencil.
Put it down! etc.

If students are enjoying the activity, they can then take turns to be 'the teacher' and give the commands for the class to follow.

9 Listen

If you set the background information as a homework research task ask students to tell the rest of the class what they found out.

BACKGROUND INFORMATION

Chico Mendes: Was born on 15 December 1944 to a family of rubber tappers (*seringueiros*) in Brazil. The process of rubber tapping involves extracting sap from rubber trees which can then be used in the manufacture of car tyres, pencil erasers, etc. It is a process which causes no harm to the environment. However, the USA wanted to start destroying the rainforest in the Amazon and Mendes was opposed to their activities. He travelled to the USA to gain support for his opposition to the tree cutting and a huge organisation sprang up. However, opposition to his activities was also strong and he was murdered in 1988. His legacy is still strong today.

Warm up

Ask students to look at the poster and photos and elicit the meaning of *hero* (someone you admire greatly). Ask them why they think Chico Mendes is Amy's hero.

(a) Read the instructions aloud with the class. In pairs, students take a few minutes to discuss the questions and try to answer them. It is possible that they might only be able to answer numbers 1 and part of 4 and 5 at this point. (He was born in 1944, in Brazil. He wanted to stop people cutting down the trees. He died in 1988.)

(b) 🔊 Play the recording, pausing as necessary. Students note down the answers. Check answers.

TAPESCRIPT

Teacher OK, everyone. Quiet now, please, OK? Amy's going to give us her presentation now, about her project, all right? Now Amy, your project's about a Brazilian man, isn't it?

Amy That's right. His name was Chico Mendes.

Teacher Great. So, this is your poster. Can everyone see it? Yes? Good. So tell us about it, Amy.

Amy Right. Well, like I said, it's about Chico Mendes. Here's his picture, yeah? He was born in 1944, December 1944, in Brazil. And ... his father worked in the forests in North Brazil, in the Amazon. He was a rubber farmer – he took rubber from the trees there in the Amazon, like you can see here in this picture. They take rubber from the trees to make car tyres and things like that. And that's what Chico Mendes did too.

Teacher Do you know anything about his education, Amy? Did he go to school?

Amy Oh well, where Chico lived, a place called Xapuri, there wasn't a school at all. But Chico's father helped him learn to read and write.

Teacher Good. Thanks, that's fine. Go on.

Amy Anyway, when Chico was a rubber farmer, he saw people cutting down trees in the Amazon, because they wanted to get money for the wood. And Chico was very angry about that, so he started an organisation to try to stop it. And a lot of people helped him – after a few years, it was a big

organisation. And Chico was quite famous too. In 1987, he visited the United States – he travelled to Miami and Washington.

Boy Why?

Amy Well, he wanted to tell people about the problems in the Amazon. But some people in the Amazon – you know, the big farmers – they didn't like Chico and they wanted to stop him. And then one day, in 1988, two men arrived at Chico's house with guns and they killed him. It was terrible, you know?

Boy Who were the men who killed him?

Amy Two men, two brothers in fact – they worked for the wood companies. But, after that, I mean after Chico Mendes died, he was even more famous and now there are more organisations to stop cutting down trees in the Amazon. So – that's it. He's my hero, Chico Mendes. I think he was great because he worked hard for something very important, right, and because he died for that too.

Teacher Amy, that's great. Thanks a lot. OK, everyone – any questions?

Boy Yeah. Why did ...

Answers
1 1944; Brazil
2 Chico's father
3 (19)87
4 he wanted to tell people about the problems in the Amazon and to stop people cutting down the trees in the Amazon
5 (19)88
6 Two men
7 he became more famous and more organisations were set up to save trees

(c) Answer the question as a whole class and see if anyone predicted the answer in the warm up activity.

Answer
Chico Mendes is Amy's hero because he gave up his life and died for what he strongly believed in.

Who's your hero?

10 Read and listen

Warm up

Ask students to look at the title of the photo story and the photos and to predict what they think this episode will be about (who Lucy's hero is). You could also ask them who the girls are in this episode (Amy and Lucy) and where they are (in a classroom, at school).

(a) 🔊 Read through the instructions with students and see if students can guess the answers to the questions. Play the recording while students read. Check answers. Play the recording again, pausing as necessary for students to clarify any problems.

TAPESCRIPT
See the photo story on page 54 of the Student's Book.

Answers
Lucy's hero is her grandfather, because he saved lots of people. He was a firefighter.

(b) Read through items 1–4 with students and then do the first one as an example if necessary. Students answer the questions. Check answers. Students can also correct the false statements and provide the location in the text for their answers.

Answers 1 F (He was a firefighter, he doesn't work now.) 2 T 3 T 4 F (*I'd really like to meet him!*)

(c) Students discuss this question in pairs or as a class. Ask for feedback.

Answer
She thinks it unlikely that Lucy's grandfather could be someone's hero and wasn't expecting Lucy's answer.

┌─ OPTIONAL ACTIVITY ─────────
In groups, students can act out the dialogue from the photo story.

11 Everyday English

(a) Ask students to find the expressions in the photo story. If it helps, you can read them aloud or ask one or two stronger students to read them aloud with expression. Students can look back at the photo story if necessary. Students translate the expressions into their own language, checking in pairs, before a whole class check. Encourage them to guess the meanings from the context of the story.

Answers 1 Amy 2 Lucy 3 Amy 4 Lucy

(b) Students complete the dialogues in pairs or alone. If necessary, do the first one as an example with students. Check answers.

Answers 1 one day 2 loads of 3 You can't be serious 4 That's amazing

Vocabulary notebook
Students should note down these expressions in their *Everyday English* section.

┌─ OPTIONAL ACTIVITIES ─────────

Stronger students
Students can write their own short dialogues, using the expressions in Exercise 11, and act them out in front of the class.

Weaker students
They can act out the dialogues in Exercise 11b.

12 Write

The writing task can be set for homework or the preparation can be done in class and Exercise 12c can be set for homework.

If you set the background information as a homework research task ask students to tell the rest of the class what they found out.

BACKGROUND INFORMATION

Helen Thayer: She was the first woman to trek alone to either of the Poles. In April 1988 she trekked alone to the North Pole at the age of 50, with no teams of dogs to help her and no snowmobiles. Her only companion was her dog, Charlie. It took her 27 days to reach the Pole and she was constantly in danger from polar bears. She has also undertaken many other impressive expeditions. For example, she was the first woman to walk 1,400 miles (approx 2,250 km) across the Sahara Desert, and in November 1997 she spent her 60th birthday trekking 200 miles (approx 320 km) across the Antarctic.

(a) Students read the text silently and match the paragraphs and the questions. Check answers.

Answers a 2 b 3 c 1

(b) Ask students to think of people they admire and who they would like to find out more information about. These could be pop stars, sports heroes, adventurers, etc. You could elicit students' heroes as a whole class, or students could work in pairs to think of people.

Weaker students: They can work in pairs to choose a hero to write about, make a poster together and give a joint presentation for Exercise 12c.

It will help students organise their work if they use Dave's text as a model, and answer the three questions, in the same order.

(c) When students have finished their writing tasks, they use them to help them make the poster for their presentation. It may be useful to refer them to this section before they do their writing tasks, so that they can include photos, copies of extracts from newspaper articles, etc.

To help them make their posters, refer students back to Amy's presentation poster on page 53. They only need to include a few short pieces of information about their hero and if they have them, a photo or picture of their hero.

Students each give a two-minute presentation. Weaker students, who have worked in pairs, can give a joint presentation.

Unit 5 51

6 Good friends

Unit overview

TOPIC: Great friendships; Text messaging

TEXTS
Reading and listening: an article about a great friendship
Listening: to a television comedy incident
Reading: a text about mobile phones
Writing: an email to a penfriend

SPEAKING
Talking about what you did last night
Asking and answering about the past
Re-telling a story

LANGUAGE
Grammar: Past simple: regular and irregular verbs;
Past simple: questions
Vocabulary: Past time expressions; Sports
Pronunciation: Word stress

1 Read and listen

If you set the background information as a homework research task ask students to tell the rest of the class what they found out.

BACKGROUND INFORMATION

1936 Olympics: These were awarded to Berlin in 1931, two years before the Nazis came to power. The games presented Hitler with the perfect opportunity to demonstrate to the world how efficient Nazi Germany was.

Lutz Long: He was in the Nazi Germany team for the 1936 Olympics and had been training full time. He was their athletic superstar: a superb long jumper who matched the Nazi Aryan ideal of blond-haired blue-eyed racial superiority. However, he was beaten by Owens in the long jump, much to the German spectators' surprise.

Jesse Owens (1913–1980): He was born on 12 September 1913, the seventh of eleven children in Danville, Alabama. His real name was John Cleveland Owens and he was the most famous American athlete in the 1936 Olympic Games. He set records in the long jump and the 200 m race and he equalled the record for the 100 m race. He won a fourth gold medal in the 400 m relay race. He is still the only man to have won four track and field medals in a single Olympics.

He was an African American (and therefore racially inferior according to Nazi ideology).

Warm up

Find out how many students have ever done athletics. Ask them if they enjoy watching athletics.

(a) In small groups, students write down all the Olympic sports they know, then do a class feedback.

(b) Read through the questions with students and encourage them to read the text quickly to find the answers. Remind them they do not need to understand every word in the text. You could set a time limit of one minute to encourage students to 'skim read' the text (read quickly, looking only for the information required) and then check answers.

Answer
The event was the long jump and the winner was Jesse Owens.

(c) 🔊 Refer students to the pictures and check they understand what they have to do.

Stronger classes: Ask students to try to order the events before reading the text to check their answers. They can check their answers when the recording is played.

Weaker classes: Ask students to read the text slowly and carefully. Read it through with them, aloud, if you have a weaker class. Then they can read it again while the recording is playing. In pairs, students order the pictures. Check answers as a class. Play the recording again as necessary, pausing after each answer.

TAPESCRIPT
See the reading text on page 56 of the Student's Book.

Answers d 1   b 2   a 3   c 4

(d) Students can answer these in L1, if necessary. If time, put students into small groups or pairs to discuss their ideas and give feedback to the class.

2 Grammar
Past simple: regular and irregular verbs

(a) Write the following base forms on the board in jumbled order: *step, stay, die, have, go, beat*. Ask students to read through the sentences in 1 and 2. Ask them what they notice about the verbs in 1 and what they can remember from Unit 5 (these verbs are all regular past simple). Ask them to match the past simple forms with their base forms on the board. Now ask students to look at the sentences in 2 and see if they can match the verbs with their base forms. Ask them what they notice about these verbs (they are not regular: the verbs in 2 are irregular past simple).

(b) Students read through the list of verbs in the box. Go through the examples in the table with them. Students complete the exercise. Check answers.

Answers
Regular verbs: stepped, wanted, listened, happened, talked, died
Irregular verbs: told, left, said, became, beat, won, thought, went

To check students' understanding at this point, you can call out a few base forms of regular and irregular past simple verbs and ask students to call out the past simple form.

(c) Encourage students to read through the whole text first to try and get the general meaning. Go through the first example and elicit that the verb *be* is irregular. Students complete the exercise. Check answers.

Answers 2 had 3 thought 4 went 5 were
6 was 7 won 8 became 9 died

━━ OPTIONAL ACTIVITY ━━━━━━

Stronger classes
Write the infinitives of the verbs in the summary in Exercise 2c on the board, in jumbled order. Read the summary aloud, with students' books closed. When you come to a gap in the text make a sound, such as 'beep', to indicate where the gap is, and continue the sentence. Students supply you with the missing verbs from the list on the board, but in the past simple. With smaller classes, this could be done as a game in teams, with points awarded for the correct verb form and spelling.

Grammar notebook
Students should note down the regular and irregular verbs from this unit in their grammar notebooks.

Past simple: questions

(d) Put the following present simple question on the board:

Do | you | go | to the cinema | every week?

Quickly revise how to form present simple questions. Below the present simple question, add the following past simple question:

Did | you | go | to the cinema | last night?

Ask students what they notice about the two questions and elicit that the auxiliary verb is different and the time reference is different. Now ask one or two students the past simple question from the board and elicit the short answers. If necessary, ask a few more past simple questions with different time references (e.g. *Did you see the football match yesterday? Did you go to the park last weekend? Did you see Maria last night?* etc.). Students read through the examples in their books and complete the table. Check answers.

Answers
Question: Did
Short answer: did; didn't

(e) Students order the words to make past simple questions. Do the first item as an example, if necessary. Students complete the exercise. Check answers.

Answers
1 Did you go out last night?
2 Did you listen to music last weekend?
3 Did you drink coffee this morning?
4 Did you watch TV yesterday?
5 Did you go on holiday last year?

3 Speak

(a) In pairs, students now ask and answer the questions in Exercise 2e. Go through the example dialogue with a student. Students complete the exercise. Ask a few students to demonstrate their questions and answers to the class.

(b) Students now move to work with a new partner and report to the new partner what their other partner answered. Ask one pair to demonstrate to the class first, before pairs work together.

4 Vocabulary
Past time expressions

(a) Give students a few examples of your own using the time expressions (e.g. *I went to the bank yesterday morning. I saw a film last Saturday. I left home an hour ago.*) Now ask a few students to give you some examples. Read through all of the time expressions with students and ask them how they would say these things in their own language. Are there any similarities or differences?

Language notes
1 Students may notice that a different tense is used with these expressions in their language. Discuss this with them.
2 Some students may want to say *the last week / ago one hour* because of the way their own language works. Monitor students carefully when they are using these expressions and give them some extra practice if necessary.
3 Check the pronunciation of *ago* /əˈgəʊ/.
4 Explain that these time expressions can be used at the beginning or at the end of sentences.

(b) Do the first item as an example with information about yourself. Students complete the exercise. Students can compare answers in pairs. Ask for feedback and discuss any interesting facts.

Alternatively, students can write three pieces of false information and three pieces of true information about themselves. They can then work in pairs and their partner must guess the false information.

(c) Students read through the statements. Go through the example with students, reminding students that *ago* always goes at the end of the time expression. Students now complete the exercise. Check answers in pairs.

Answers 2 four days ago   3 an hour ago
4 two months ago   5 five hours ago

5 Speak

Remind students of the past simple questions from Exercise 2e. If necessary, write a past simple question on the board again and elicit where the *Wh-* word goes, e.g.:

… | did | you | go | last night?

Where | did | you | go | last night?

Remind them that the auxiliary goes before the person in questions. Now go through the example exchange with students, making sure they can see how to make the question from the prompt. Students ask and answer the questions.

Answers
When did you begin learning English?
When did you arrive at school this morning?
When did you meet your best friend?
(Students' own answers to the questions.)

> **Language note:** Point out to students that the expression *this morning* is a past time expression in this context.

6 Vocabulary

Sports

Warm up

Ask students if they practise any sports. If so, what? Do they play in a team or on their own? How often do they practise/play?

(a) 🔊 Elicit any sports which students already know and write the words on the board. Now ask students to look at the pictures in their books. Do the first item with them as an example and then students complete the exercise. Play the recording for students to listen and check their answers. Play the recording again, pausing for students to repeat each word.

TAPESCRIPT/ANSWERS
1 swimming
2 surfing
3 skiing
4 cycling
5 basketball
6 volleyball
7 ice hockey
8 skateboarding
9 snowboarding

(b) Do the first item as an example. Ask a student to give you the answer. (*Which sports always have teams? Basketball, volleyball, ice hockey.*) Students may wish to discuss other sports which are not always team sports but which can be, e.g. *cycling, swimming, skiing*. Students complete the exercise. In pairs or small groups, students answer the other questions.

Answers
2 cycling, skateboarding
3 swimming, surfing, skiing
4 skiing, snowboarding, ice hockey
5 (Students' own answers)
6 (Students' own answers)
7 (Students' own answers)

Vocabulary notebook
Students should start a section called *Sports* and note down the vocabulary from this unit. They can add translations or illustrations if it will help them.

┌─ OPTIONAL ACTIVITY ─────────────

Stronger classes
This is a vocabulary extension activity. In pairs or small groups, students write down the names of the places where the sports in Exercise 6a are done.

Answers
1 swimming: pool
2 surfing: sea
3 skiing: slopes; mountain; piste
4 cycling: track; cross-country
5 basketball: court
6 volleyball: court
7 ice hockey: rink/pitch
8 skateboarding: ramp
9 snowboarding: slope

7 Listen

Warm up

Ask students if they can remember what kind of programme a comedy is (*funny*).

Ask them if they like comedies and what their favourite comedy programmes are on TV. How often do they watch them? This can be done in L1 if necessary.

(a) Refer students to the names of the characters. Read them aloud so they can recognise the names on the recording (Jane /dʒeɪn/, Louise /luːˈiːz/, Danny /ˈdæniː/, Sylvia /ˈsɪlvɪə/).

(b) In pairs, students try to put the pictures into the correct order to make the story. Explain they will listen and check their answers and it doesn't matter if they don't get the right order, the aim is that they understand the general idea before listening.

(c) **Stronger classes:** Ask pairs or groups of three students to look at the words and phrases to try to work out their meaning. Encourage them to use a dictionary if they can't work them out on their own. Ask them to match the phrases to the correct picture.

Weaker classes: Go through the words as a class and translate when necessary. You could also provide these words in sentences of your own or mime them for students to try and guess their meanings.

Answers
go out with someone: to spend a lot of time with someone (e.g. with close friends or a boyfriend/girlfriend)
push: to use force to move someone/something away from you
pour: to make a liquid flow from its container
have an argument: to have a disagreement / angry discussion with someone
cream cake: a sweet food made from flour, sugar, eggs, butter and milk and cooked in the oven then filled with cream

d 🔊 Play the recording. Students listen and check their answers. Play the recording again if necessary, pausing it after each 'picture' to help weaker students.

TAPESCRIPT

Girl 1   I saw a funny programme on TV last night. It was called *The Cream on the Cake*. Did you see it?

Girl 2   No, I didn't. What was it about?

Girl 1   Well, there were these two girls called Jane and Louise. They were really good friends. So one day they had lunch together and they met a boy called Danny – he came and sat down at their table. The problem was, both Jane and Louise liked him.

Girl 2   Oh, yeah ...

Girl 1   Well, Jane went out with this boy Danny – they went to the cinema together – and Jane thought he was wonderful, you know? So she was really happy. But then the next day she was in the bus, and she looked through the window and she saw Danny and her friend Louise together!

Girl 2   Oh no! So what happened?

Girl 1   Well, the two girls had a big argument later that day. They stood there in the street and shouted at each other.

Girl 2   So that was the end of their friendship, right?

Girl 1   No, wait! The next minute, the girls looked across the street and who did they see? Danny! He was at the café, and he had a big cream cake in front of him and a drink, and he was with a different girl, called Sylvia.

Girl 2   So what did they do?

Girl 1   Well, they walked over to the café together. And Jane pushed Danny's face into the cream cake and Louise poured the drink down the back of his shirt. Yeah, he looked really funny and he was incredibly angry – he had cream all over him. And then Jane and Louise left together and they just laughed and laughed.

Girl 2   So they stayed friends, right?

Girl 1   Yeah, of course.

Girl 2   I wonder what happened to Danny.

Girl 1   I don't know. But he didn't enjoy that cream cake.

Answers
a 3   b 5   d 4   e 8   f 2   g 7   h 6

8 Speak

a **Stronger classes:** Choose one or two stronger students to start off the first part of the story. Remind them to use the pictures and verbs in Exercises 7b and c to help them. In pairs, one student starts telling the story, the other continues. They take turns to add a line to the story until it is finished. Choose a few pairs to demonstrate to the class.

Weaker classes: They can think of one sentence for each picture and work in pairs to put their sentences together.

b Students discuss their ideas in pairs. Alternatively, you could do this as a class discussion point.

┌ OPTIONAL ACTIVITY ────────
Students write a paragraph about their friends for homework. They can include information about how long they have known their friend, what they like doing together and why they like them.

9 Pronunciation

Word stress

a 🔊 Write the words on the board and ask students to read through the list on page 59. Repeat the first word in isolation and ask them how many syllables it has. Write the number of syllables on the board. If necessary, remind students what a syllable is. In pairs, students now work out how many syllables the other words have. Play the recording for students to listen and check answers. Play the recording again, pausing for students to repeat.

TAPESCRIPT/ANSWERS
1   surfing (2)
2   basketball (3)
3   sport (1)
4   cycling (2)
5   skateboarding (3)
6   Olympics (3)

b 🔊 Write the stress patterns on the board. Go through the first example with students, writing *surfing* under the two-syllable pattern. Students now use their answers from Exercise 9a and match the words with the stress patterns. Play the recording again for students to check answers. Play the recording once more, pausing as necessary for students to repeat each word.

Answers
1 surfing ●●
2 basketball ●●●
3 sport ●
4 cycling ●●
5 skateboarding ●●●
6 Olympics ●●●

Culture in mind

10 Read

Warm up

Ask students if they have a mobile phone of their own. If so, when do they use it? How often do they use it? What do they use it for? Do they send text messages?

(a) Ask students to look at the mobile phone text message on page 60. In pairs or small groups, ask them if they can work it out without looking at the text. Give them a few minutes to do this. Ask them to read the text quickly to check their answers.

Answer
See text, para 2.

(b) Students read the text again, this time more slowly, in order to answer questions 1–4. If necessary, do the first question with them as an example.

Answers
1 She is shopping / in a (clothes) shop.
2 Because it's quick, easy and cheap.
3 They often ring during classes and students often send text messages during classes.
4 They can use them at break, lunch time or after school.

(c) **Stronger students:** They can work this out without referring back to the text.

Weaker students: They can use the glossary within the reading text and try and work out the message.

Check answers.

Answer
Hi Matt,
How are you? I'm in town today. Are you going to Steve's party tomorrow? Do you want to buy a present for him? Please call me before tonight. Bye for now! Have a nice day! Mike

┌─ OPTIONAL ACTIVITY ─────────
│ Students can write their own text message and send it
│ to a partner for them to work out.

(d) In small groups, students decide if they agree with Clare's opinion from the text. Ask for feedback. Is there a general consensus within the class?

11 Write

BACKGROUND INFORMATION

Oxford Street: This is the main shopping area in central London. Selfridges, one of the biggest department stores in London, is in Oxford Street.

Students choose one of the tasks. They can do the preparation in class, and complete the writing at home, or if time allows, do everything in class. This can be done in pairs.

(a) Encourage stronger students to choose option a, which is more demanding as there's less guidance. Encourage them to look back at the pictures and verbs in the unit to make sentences. Remind students about the following points when writing a diary entry:

• The tone is honest and personal: nobody else is meant to read your diary, except you, the writer!
• Abbreviations, as in the text messages, can be used.

When they have finished, ask students to read their diary entry to a partner.

(b) Read questions 1–3 aloud as a class. Tell students to read the email only to find answers to the questions. Students can then read the email. Check the meaning of any difficult vocabulary.

Answers
1 She went to her cousin's house in London.
2 She went bowling on Friday, went shopping (in Oxford Street) on Saturday and went for a meal in the evening.
3 She asks Julia to send her some photos of Julia's holiday.

Remind students about the following points when they are writing emails:

• The tone is informal and the language can be informal, e.g. use contractions.
• Opening greetings are usually things like *Hi!*, *Hello!*
• Opening paragraph: usually includes questions.
• Main paragraph: this includes all the information from the sender.
• Closing paragraph: Asks the receiver for information and signs off.

Students write their email at home. They can bring them into class the next day and 'send' their email to a classmate to read.

7 The secrets of success

1 Read and listen

BACKGROUND INFORMATION

Bill Gates: The founder of Microsoft computer programs was born on 28 October 1955 in Seattle, Washington State, USA. He was a very talented mathematician as a child and wrote his first computer program at the age of 13. He studied law at Harvard but still maintained an interest in computers. With his old school friend, Paul Allen, Gates designed a software program for a computer which was soon recognised by the Massachusetts Institute of Technology. He set up a company and called it Microsoft and by 1986, at the age of 31, Gates was a billionaire.

Penelope Cruz: Was born Penelope Sánchez Cruz on 28 April 1974 in Madrid, Spain. She first became known for her roles in the films of the famous Spanish director, Pedro Almodóvar. She made her breakthrough in America as the co-star with Tom Cruise in the film *Vanilla Sky* in 2001. She has been linked romantically over the years with various actors including Matt Damon, Johnny Depp, Nicholas Cage and Tom Cruise.

David Beckham: Was born David Robert Joseph Beckham in Leytonstone, London on 2 May 1975. He signed as a trainee for

Manchester United in 1991 and in 1992 played for them for the first time. He was a very influential player in Manchester United until 2003, when he transferred to the Spanish club, Real Madrid. He has also played many times in the England team, having captained it in the 2002 World Cup. He is married to the former Spice Girl singer, Victoria Adams, with whom he has two sons, Brooklyn and Romeo.

J. K. Rowling: The author of the famous Harry Potter series, was born Joanne Kathleen Rowling on 31 July 1965, near Bristol, England. She lived in Portugal in the early 1990s until she moved to Edinburgh with her daughter and began work on a book. The idea for Harry Potter is said to have come to her as she was travelling on a train from Manchester to London in 1990. By the summer of 2000 the first three Harry Potter books had earned almost $480 million in three years. J. K. Rowling is now said to be one of the richest women in Britain.

Naomi Campbell: Is the well-known British-born supermodel who made her debut on the catwalk but has become a singer and a writer too. She has also starred in a film with Madonna.

Robbie Williams: Was born Robert Peter Williams in February 1975, in Stoke-on-Trent, England. His early show business experiences were with local theatre companies and in local musicals. At the age of 16, in 1991, he saw an advert for a band who were looking for a fifth member, and he joined Take That. After five years with the band he was dismissed. His solo career had a slow start but the hit single *Angels* saw him at the top of the charts again and he continues to be a very successful solo artist.

Warm up

Ask students to look at the pictures and say what they know about the people and what they think the people have in common. (They are all famous/talented/successful/wealthy.)

a Ask students to read through jobs 1–6. Go through the first one with students as an example, if necessary. Students match the people and the jobs. Check answers.

Answers a 2 b 5 c 3 d 6 e 1 f 4

Elicit the meaning of *successful* (achieving highly). Ask students to read the text quickly once and tell you what the topic is.

Ask students to suggest other famous people who have these jobs. In small groups, students can discuss who they think is the most successful person. Find out if there are any class favourites and where they come from, e.g. USA, students' own country, UK.

b 🔊 Discuss questions 1, 2 and 3 as a whole class. Students then read the text again and see if they can answer the questions. Play the recording while students read the text again to check or change their answers or find their answers. Ask for class feedback.

TAPESCRIPT

See the reading text on page 62 of the Student's Book.

Answers

1 Some are men, some are women. They come from different countries, have different interests and professions.
2 They are all successful.
3 A lot of people think it is because they are talented.

c Ask students to read through the list. Check understanding. Explain any problem items in L1 if necessary or ask stronger students to look up anything they don't know in a dictionary. Students work on their own to answer the question, then compare answers with a partner. Ask for class feedback and find out what most of the class ticked as requirements for success.

OPTIONAL ACTIVITIES

Stronger classes

In small groups, students discuss each of these things and then rank them in order of importance for success.

Weaker classes

They could classify these in order in L1 and discuss them in L1.

Ask for feedback and discuss any interesting points.

d 🔊 Read the instructions with the class. Elicit the kind of words and phrases they think they may hear; refer students back to the list in Exercise 1c.

Weaker classes: Ask them to copy down the items from Exercise 1c and then they can tick the ones Alex mentions.

Stronger classes: Can make notes without using Exercise 1c.

Play the recording. Students note down Alex's ideas about what makes a successful person.

Find out if his ideas are the same or different to most of the class's ideas. Ask students to report their ideas to the rest of the class.

TAPESCRIPT

OK. I also wanted to find out *why* these people are successful, right? So I found some books about them, and I looked on the Internet. And I found some interesting things, some things that all these people have in common. OK – so, to be successful, this is what you have to do.

First, you have to have a dream. I mean, you have to know what you want. And it's not good enough to say, for example, 'I'd like to be a writer'. You have to have some practical ideas about what you want to write, and when and how.

Then the next thing: you have to be determined. You know, never give up. Sometimes things are difficult, things go wrong. But you can't give up – you have to keep going, keep working, keep trying.

Next, you have to have a few good friends. All the successful people say that help from friends was important. Because good friends say 'Well done!' and 'That's great!' and 'You can do it!' – things like that. So, good friends are important.

Er … what's next? Oh, yes. This is *really* important. You have to work hard! Yeah, sorry, guys! All the really successful people work very hard. But you *don't* have to work 24 hours a day! You have to relax sometimes – that's important too.

So – those are the big things if you want to be a big success! You don't have to have lots of money or rich parents, and you don't have to get good school results. Some really successful people weren't good at school, but they were good at other things and they worked hard.

OK, that's it. Oh, one last thing. You need a little luck sometimes – that always helps! But you have to *use* your luck too.

So … that's my presentation. Any questions?

Answers
have a dream (know what you want)
be determined
have good friends
be hard-working
be lucky

e Students work in pairs and discuss the question. They should agree on someone they want to talk about and discuss why that person is successful.

OPTIONAL ACTIVITY

Who am I?

In small groups (or as a whole class), students take turns to choose a character from Exercise 1. The others have to guess who they are by asking present simple questions, e.g.:

S2: Do you play football?
S1: No.

The person who has chosen the character can only answer using *Yes* or *No*. The person who guesses correctly can choose next. If the person answers using words other than *Yes* or *No*, they must tell the rest of the group who they chose. Then the next person can choose.

2 Grammar

have to / don't have to

a Read the examples with the class. Give an example of your own if necessary (e.g. *I have to be in school at 8.00 every day.*). Students complete the rule, comparing in pairs before a whole class check. After completing the rule, students complete the table. Check answers. To check understanding, ask a few students some questions about themselves, e.g. *Do you have to wear a school uniform? Do you have to do homework every day?* etc.

Answers
Rule: have to / has to; don't have to / doesn't have to
Table:
Positive: has to
Negative: don't; doesn't
Question: Do; Does
Short answer: do; don't; does; doesn't

b Students read through the sentences. Go through the first item with them as an example if necessary. You can ask them why the answer is *have to* and not *has to* to check they are using the correct form. Students complete the sentences. Check answers.

Answers 1 have to 2 has to 3 doesn't have to
4 don't have to 5 have to 6 don't have to

3 Pronunciation

have to

🔊 Read the instructions with the class. Play the recording and ask them to listen for the /f/ sound in *have* and the weak form of *to*. Students listen and repeat. Play the recording again, if necessary.

TAPESCRIPT
1 I have to go.
2 You don't have to shout.
3 He doesn't have to come.
4 We have to learn English.
5 You have to have money.
6 Does she have to work hard?

4 Speak

a Students look at the pictures. Check they understand all the words (they should remember some of these from Unit 3). Do the first item as an example if necessary. Students tick the types of housework that they have to do at home and cross the ones they don't have to do.

b In pairs, students ask and answer about the housework they have to do. Go through the example dialogue with them, reminding them of the questions and short answer form. Find out how many have to do each type of housework listed. Ask *Who has to do the washing-up? How many people in the class have to do their own ironing?* If there are any interesting results these can be discussed further with students.

5 Vocabulary

Jobs

a 🔊 Ask students to read through the list of jobs, making sure they know the meanings of the words. If necessary ask them the following questions to check understanding: *Which person flies a plane? Serves drinks on a plane? Looks after sick people in a hospital? Treats sick people? Builds bridges and machinery? Types letters? Treats sick animals? Teaches students? Helps people with legal problems? Looks after people's teeth?* In pairs, students match the jobs to the pictures. Check answers. Play the recording for students to check or change their answers. Play it again for students to repeat each word.

TAPESCRIPT/ANSWERS
a 8 pilot
b 3 nurse
c 5 doctor
d 1 engineer
e 10 secretary
f 4 vet
g 6 flight attendant
h 2 teacher
i 7 lawyer
j 9 dentist

> **Language notes**
> 1 Students may need some extra practice in the pronunciation of *secretary* /'sekrət°ri/ and *engineer* /endʒɪ'nɪəʳ/.
> 2 You may want to remind students that we always use articles when we talk about jobs in English.
> We say *She is a lawyer*. NOT ~~She is lawyer~~.

b Students write the names of four other jobs they are interested in. They can look them up in a dictionary or check with you.

Set a time limit for this and once students have finished, ask for feedback and write any interesting/ unusual jobs on the board.

In small groups, students can discuss why they are interested in the jobs they chose.

Vocabulary notebook
Remind students to go to their vocabulary notebooks and make a mind map or list of the words for jobs in Exercise 5a, and to add the words they have just looked up in Exercise 5b.

c 🔊 Explain that they are going to hear four teenagers talking about jobs. Go through the list of jobs with them and elicit some of the words/ phrases they think they may hear when they listen. Write them on the board. Play the recording while students listen and match the people with the jobs. Check answers. Play the recording again if necessary, pausing for students to check answers.

TAPESCRIPT

Mike My uncle's a vet and in the holidays I often help him. It's great for me because I really love animals. Of course I know you have to study hard and for a long time, but that's my dream and I'm sure I can do it.

Tina I want to work in IT – Information Technology. You have to be really good to get the best jobs, and then you can earn a lot of money. But money isn't the only thing. I just love computer programming and I really want to do something in this field.

Tony I love this game and my dream is to play professionally. I know you have to practise a lot, so I joined a club and I practise almost every day. I hope I can win some big matches some day …

Judith Well, talent isn't enough – you also have to have a lot of luck to get to the top. But I'm a good singer, I think, and I play the guitar quite well, and I just love music. So maybe I'll be lucky and get into a band. That's what I'd really love to do.

Answers 1 Mike: vet 2 Tina: computer programmer 3 Tony: tennis player 4 Judith: singer

┌─ OPTIONAL ACTIVITY ────────────

Ask students to look back at the list of jobs in Vocabulary, Exercise 5a. Ask them to complete these sentences with *has to / doesn't have to*.
1 A vet .... like animals.
2 A dentist .... test people's eyes.
3 An engineer .... be good at music.
4 A nurse .... like helping people.
5 A secretary .... study medicine.
6 A pilot .... like travelling.
7 A teacher in your country .... speak Japanese.
8 A doctor .... study Biology.
9 A flight attendant .... be polite.
10 A lawyer .... be a man.

Answers 1 has to 2 doesn't have to 3 doesn't have to 4 has to 5 doesn't have to 6 has to 7 doesn't have to 8 has to 9 has to 10 doesn't have to

6 **Speak**

a 🔊 Ask students to read through the list of words and the gapped dialogue. Check they understand everything.

Stronger classes: They can look at the words and phrases and predict some of the content of the conversation they are going to hear.

Weaker classes: Go through the first item with students as an example, if necessary. Remind students to look at the context round a space to help them work out which words go in. Students complete the exercise and compare answers in pairs.

Play the recording, pausing as necessary, for students to check or change answers.

TAPESCRIPT

Jenny What do you want to be when you leave school?

Mark I want to be a pilot.

Jenny Really? What do you have to do for that?

Mark Well, you have to get good school results and you have to be good at Maths and Physics. And you have to speak English really well too. What about you? What do you want to do?

Jenny I'm not sure, but I think I'd like to be a vet.

Answers 1 leave school 2 be a pilot 3 have to do 4 get good school results 5 Maths and Physics 6 speak English 7 not sure 8 I'd like

b Remind students what Jenny said she wanted to be in the dialogue in Exercise 6a (a vet). Refer students back to the dialogue and focus on the questions Jenny asked Mark. In pairs, students now read the phrases in the box and continue the dialogue. Remind them that Mark will be asking the questions and Jenny will be answering them. Ask some pairs to act out their dialogues in front of the class.

Example answers
Mark: Really? What do you have to do for that?
Jenny: Well, you have to get good school results and you have to be good at Medicine. And you have to study for five years.
Mark: That sounds like hard work! Do you have to do anything else?
Jenny: Well, of course, you have to like animals!

┌─ OPTIONAL ACTIVITY ────────────

Students can memorise the whole dialogue from Exercise 6a and act it out with a partner.

c In pairs, students ask and answer about jobs they want to do. Remind them of the sort of questions Jenny and Mark asked in Exercises 6a and b. Monitor and check that students change roles so that each person has a turn to talk about his/her job. Ask for feedback from several students about themselves and their partners (e.g.: *I want to be a photographer. I have to go to college and study for three years. Gerhard wants to work in media. He has to go to university and study for three years. He has to be good at talking to people.*).

┌─ OPTIONAL ACTIVITY ────────────

What's my line?
Divide students into teams. Each team chooses a job or profession for one of its members. That student has to answer the other team's questions about this job, as they try to guess what it is. The student can discuss answers with his/her own team, but can only answer *Yes* or *No*. The questions have to be about duties,

qualifications, talents etc., using *have to*, wherever possible. The opposing team should try to guess the job in less than 20 questions. Then it's their turn to answer questions.

Example:
Do you have to work with animals? (Yes.)
Do you have to study Biology at school? (Yes.)
Are you a zoo keeper? (No.)
Are you a vet? (Yes.)

7 Read

BACKGROUND INFORMATION

The 1900 House: In 1999 a television programme was made where a modern family volunteered to live in a house from the 1900s in exactly the same conditions as that period in history. The programme recorded how the family coped with the changes to their lifestyle and how they felt about it.

Warm up

Ask students to look quickly at the pictures and title and tell you what the text will be about (a house in 1900, in England). Ask students what they know about Victorian England (around 1900). Ask if they think people then had to do more housework than we do these days, and why. (Yes, they did, because there wasn't electricity, and there weren't modern appliances.)

a Ask students to read through the questions and elicit and put on the board any ideas they may have about what the text will say. Remind them they do not have to understand every word in the text. Students read the text quickly and check their predictions. Were any of them correct?

b Pre-teach any vocabulary before students read the text in detail (*electricity, gas, furniture, shampoo, share*). Stronger students can look these words up in a dictionary. Read through questions 1–3 with students and check they understand them. Students read the text and find the answers to the questions.

Answers
1 Six (Paul, Joyce, Kathryn, Ruth, Hilary and Joe Bowler)
2 For three months.
3 To film the family's everyday life.

Look

Draw students' attention to the Look box. Elicit that in the past tense there is only one form for all persons in the affirmative case (*had to*) and in the negative case (*didn't have to*). Students may find it useful to think about how they say these things in their own language. Do they have a special verb for *have to*?

c Draw a table on the board, with the headings *had to* and *didn't have to*. Go through the words in the box and check understanding. Go through the example with students. Students work in pairs and make a list under each heading, referring to the text and the words listed. When checking answers, ask them to give a reason why they had to do certain things, and didn't have to do other things.

Answers
1 They had to use an outside toilet (because there wasn't a toilet inside).
2 The sisters had to share a bed (because there weren't enough beds for everyone to have their own bed).
3 They didn't have to go to school (because most girls didn't go to school in Victorian times).
4 They had to wear Victorian clothes (because they had to live like Victorians).
5 They didn't have to do their own shopping (because the TV company did it for them).

d Students work in pairs and talk about things they have to / don't have to do using the items from the box in Exercise 7c. Find out who has to do the same things.

e Students work in pairs or small groups to discuss the questions, before a class feedback session.

It's my dream

8 Read and listen

BACKGROUND INFORMATION

Paper round: This is a common way for many British teenagers to earn some extra money. Teenagers are employed by a local newsagent's to deliver newspapers either early in the morning or in the late afternoon. The teenagers arrive at the newsagent's, collect a large bag full of papers and then deliver them to the houses on a list they have. A lot of teenagers do this by bike but others do this on foot.

Warm up

Ask students to name the two characters in this episode (Amy and Dave). Then ask them to look at the title and the photos and to predict what they think it will be about.

a 🔊 Read the question through with students. Play the recording while students listen and find the answer. Play the recording again, pausing as necessary for students to check their predictions.

TAPESCRIPT
See the photo story on page 66 of the Student's Book.

Answer
Amy's dream is to be a singer.

(**b**) Ask students to read through the questions and check they understand them all. Students read the text again and answer them. Students can compare answers in pairs.

Answers
1 A newspaper round.
2 Dave thinks it's a lot of work for hardly any money.
3 Yes, she does. (... *in the cold and the rain*.)
4 She wants to buy a good guitar.
5 No, he hasn't. (*I'm not really sure ...*)

(**c**) Read through the questions with students. In small groups, students discuss questions 1–4. Ask for feedback from each group and compare group results. Are there any interesting points for further discussion?

Weaker classes: They may need more help with this. Provide them with some prompts to help them, e.g.:

Question 2: *Do they work in shops? If so, what kind of shops? Where else do they work? Libraries? Fast-food restaurants? Bars?*

Question 4: Write *Good jobs* and *Bad jobs* on the board and elicit some examples of each from students. Ask them for reasons why they think some are good and some are bad.

┌─ OPTIONAL ACTIVITY ────────────
In groups, students can act out the dialogue from the photo story.

9 Everyday English

(**a**) Read the expressions aloud with the class. Tell them to find them in the photo story and to try to match them with their meaning. Check answers.

Answers 1 c   2 b   3 d   4 a

(**b**) Students read the dialogues and then complete them with the expressions from Exercise 9a. Go through the first item as an example, if necessary. Check answers.

Answers
1 doing a paper round; saving up
2 pocket money
3 hardly any money

Vocabulary notebook
This would be a good time to refer students to their vocabulary notebooks. They should note down these expressions under their *Everyday English* category.

┌─ OPTIONAL ACTIVITIES ────────────

Stronger classes
Students can write their own short dialogues, using the expressions in Exercise 9, and act them out in front of the class.

Weaker classes
They can act out the dialogues in Exercise 9b.

10 Write

Students can do the preparation for this task in class, and complete the writing at home.

(**a**) Students read through the questions. Then ask them to read through Hakan's paragraphs, checking any vocabulary problems. Students match the questions with the order of the paragraphs. Check answers.

Answers a 3   b 1   c 2

(**b**) Students interview a friend in class or someone at home and write their paragraph for homework.

Weaker classes: They may need some more help with the structure of this. Remind them first to make notes on what the person says and then to expand their notes into full sentences within each paragraph. Remind them about what should be included in each paragraph:

Paragraph 1: What the person's job is, when they decided to do it and what they had to do to do it.

Paragraph 2: What the job involves and how long the person has to work each day/week.

Paragraph 3: What the person likes / doesn't like about their job.

8 New ideas

Unit overview

TOPIC: Daydreams and ideas

TEXTS

Reading and listening: a school magazine interview with Nick from the band 4Tune

Listening: to a song and an interview

Reading: a magazine article about Walt Disney

Reading: a text about *Pop Idol*

Writing: a visualisation exercise

SPEAKING

Talking about the differences between two pictures

Talking about sleep and dreams

Talking about non-specific amounts

LANGUAGE

Grammar: *some* and *any*; Possessive pronouns

Vocabulary: Sleeping and waking

Pronunciation: rhyming words

1 Read and listen

Warm up

Ask students to look at the photo and the title of the text and predict what it will be about.

a Ask students to read the questions and discuss them in pairs, before a whole class discussion. Find out why students like/dislike a particular singer or group.

b Read the instructions with the class. Explain that this text is only the first part of the interview with Nick (they will hear the rest of it later in the unit). Ask students to read the text in pairs. They can do this aloud, with each member of the pair taking one of the roles to read. Ask them to tell you the answers to the questions and to give you the point in the text where they found their answers.

Answers
1 Nick (*well, I write a lot of them ...*)
2 Karen (*Karen writes too ...*)

c 🔊 Ask students to read through items 1–7 and check they understand them all.

Stronger classes: They can answer these by reading the text alone and then listening to check.

Weaker classes: Play the recording while they read, pausing as necessary to give them time to find their answers. Check answers. Students then correct the false statements.

TAPESCRIPT
See the reading text on page 68 of the Student's Book.

Answers 1 F (They aren't all finished. There's still some work to do.) 2 T 3 F (There's a party at the end of next month.) 4 T 5 T 6 (Not always.) 7 F (He wrote it when he was away from his desk.)

2 Grammar

some and *any*

a Write the headings *Countable* and *Uncountable* on the board and elicit an example for each category and write it on the board. Now go through the examples with students. Ask them the following questions:

Sentence 1: *Is* information *countable or uncountable?* (uncountable) *Is the verb positive or negative?* (positive)

Sentence 2: *Is* ideas *countable or uncountable, singular or plural?* (plural countable) *Is the verb positive or negative?* (positive)

Which words are used before these words? (*some*)

Sentence 3: *What do you notice about the verb in this sentence?* (It's negative.)

What is the word before ideas? (*any*)

Now ask students to complete the rule. Check answers.

Answers
some; any

b Ask students to read through items 1–5 and check they understand them. Go through the example, eliciting the second answer from students. Ask them if the verb in the second part is positive or negative and which word they think they should use before they answer. Students complete the exercise. Check answers.

Answers 1 any 2 any; some 3 some; any
4 some; any 5 some; some; any

3 Speak

Divide the class into Student A and Student B pairs. Explain that all Student Bs should turn to page 136 and look at the picture there. Student As should look at the picture on page 69. Students must ask and answer questions to find out what the differences are between the pictures. Go through the example exchange with students. Remind them to make questions using *Is there / Are there* ... and to use *some/any* in their answers.

Weaker classes: They may need some help with vocabulary. If necessary, pre-teach the following words: *paper, pens, a bottle of orange juice, paper, a jug of coffee*. You can also tell them that there are four differences they must find.

Set a time limit for this exercise. Check answers.

Answers
The differences are:
Picture A: 5 pens; bottle of orange juice; 2 oranges; pot of coffee and cup of coffee
Picture B: 4 pens; bottle of water; 2 bananas; no coffee and cup

4 Grammar
Possessive pronouns

a Bring in a few objects of your own for this (e.g. passport, keys, marker pen) and collect up a few things from students (e.g. pens, pencils, rubbers, books, etc.). Put all the objects in a bag. Pick one object out (preferably one of your own) and ask *Whose (passport) is this? It's mine.* Continue taking things out of the bag and asking questions with *Whose ...* . If students answer using the possessive *'s*, e.g. *It's Julia's.* Say *Yes, it's hers.* etc. to make sure they know they should be answering using a possessive pronoun. Now ask them to complete the table with the possessive pronouns. Check answers.

Answers mine; yours; ours; hers

> **Language note**
> Students may answer *It's my (passport).* If this happens, show them on the board how *my* is an adjective in this statement and it changes to a possessive pronoun when we talk about the owner: *It's (mine).*

b Students read through items 1–6. Go through the example. Students complete the exercise. Check answers.

Answers 2 his   3 hers   4 theirs   5 mine   6 ours

OPTIONAL ACTIVITY
If you feel students need further practice of singular possessive pronouns put students in small groups. They collect some of their belongings together and put them into a bag (as in the presentation in Exercise 4a). The first student picks something out of the bag and asks the question *Whose ... is this?* The other students must answer by pointing at the student it belongs to and using the correct possessive pronoun *It's his/hers/mine.* The bag is then passed on to the next student and it continues like this until everyone has had a chance to ask the question.

Grammar notebook
Remind students to note down the possessive pronouns from this unit. They may find it helpful to copy the whole table from page 69 with the subject pronouns and possessive adjectives.

5 Listen

a 🔊 Students read through questions 1–3. Pre-teach *What makes you think they're happy?, fly off, scared, late, guys.* Ask students to think about the context in which Nick wrote the song. Make notes about their ideas on the board. Play the recording. Do not give students the correct answers at this point.

TAPESCRIPT
See the song text on page 70 of the Student's Book.

b 🔊 Now play the rest of the interview and let students check their answers to Exercise 5a.

TAPESCRIPT

Reporter So, Nick, you were saying that you wrote this song after you heard a conversation. Where was that?

Nick Well, I was going on a holiday with my parents, and we were sitting in the airport. The plane was a little late, so we had some time, and we decided to get some coffee. So we went to the airport café, and while we were sitting there, I heard these two people talking. One of them was a waiter, and the other one was, I think she was one of the people who clean the tables, you know. And I heard her say, 'I hate this place. I want to get out of here!' And she talked about all the people there in the airport, and you know, that they all had a lot of money, and they were all flying to these really interesting places, but she had this boring job. And she just talked and talked about how lucky they were and that they had all this money to go to all these beautiful places, and they get holidays and time in the sun ... and the waiter was listening to this, and he didn't say anything, but when the woman finally stopped, he just said, 'What makes you think they're happy?' And I thought, yeah, good question! And I liked the sound of the question too, you know. 'What makes you think they're happy?' And it stayed in my head, and a little later, when I was on the plane, I looked at some of the other people on the plane and they *didn't* look very happy. And I remembered the waiter in the café and I got out some paper and I wrote the song.

Reporter So you just got the idea in an airport café listening to these two people ...

Answers
1 He was sitting at the airport, waiting for his plane.
2 A waiter and a cleaner.
3 The holidaymakers who fly to foreign places.

6 Pronunciation
Rhyming words

a 🔊 Explain that rhyming words are important in most songs and ask students for some examples from songs they like to listen to. Read out the words.

Do the first pair as an example, if necessary. Students match the other rhyming pairs. Play the recording for students to check answers. Play it again, pausing for students to repeat each word.

TAPESCRIPT

1 plane, Spain
2 fun, sun
3 floor, more
4 late, great
5 night, right

Answers 1 d   2 e   3 b   4 c   5 a

(b) 🔊 Students now do the same with the new words. Read the words aloud for students before they start. You could set a time limit for this exercise to make it more fun! Play the recording once for students to check answer, then play it a second time for students to repeat the words.

TAPESCRIPT

1 keys, please
2 red, said
3 thought, short
4 shirt, hurt
5 won, run
6 talk, fork

Answers 1 b   2 e   3 d   4 a   5 c   6 f

— **OPTIONAL ACTIVITY** —

Students add more words to each pair they have already found in Exercises 6a and b. Students work in small groups, using dictionaries if necessary. Set a time limit of, e.g. three minutes, and the group with the most words for each pair in the time is the winner!

Example answers

plane, Spain, main, train, drain
fun, sun, done, won, run
floor, more, door, wore, four, tore
late, great, gate, mate, eight, wait
night, right, sight, light, white
keys, please, cheese, sneeze
red, said, bed, dead, led
thought, short, bought, taught
shirt, hurt, dirt, skirt
won, run, sun, fun, done
talk, fork, walk, pork

7 Read

If students researched the background information for homework ask them to tell the class what they have found out.

BACKGROUND INFORMATION

Walt Disney: Walter Elias Disney was born on 5 December 1901 in Chicago, Illinois, USA. Walt Disney was not an academic child and left school at the age of 17, when he served as an ambulance driver in the First World War for a short time. He then did an apprenticeship as a commercial illustrator and made some advertising cartoons. By 1922 he had set up his own shop with a friend, Ub Iwerks. In 1923, Disney went to Hollywood with his older brother and this was where he invented Mickey Mouse, in a cartoon called *Steamboat Willie*. He made a series of shorts in the 1930s and characters such as Mickey Mouse, Donald Duck, Minnie Mouse and Goofy were invented. The first feature-length Disney cartoon was *Snow White* in 1937 and other classics followed, such as *Pinocchio* and *Bambi*. By the time of his death in 1966, Disney had produced 21 full-length animated films, as well as a great many short subjects, live action films, 'true-life' adventure features and TV programmes. The popularity of Disney continues today with the various theme parks in California, Florida, Tokyo and Paris and the continuation of Disney as a film producer.

Isaac Newton: The famous mathematician and physicist was born on 4 January 1643 in Woolsthorpe, Lincolnshire, England. At the age of 19 he went to study at Trinity College, Cambridge. He developed the law of universal gravitation between 1664 and 1666; he developed calculus and also discovered that white light is made up of every colour in the spectrum. In 1668 he built the first reflective telescope. He died in March 1727, leaving behind him a wealth of information to help prepare people for the age of technology.

Warm up

Ask students to look at the text and the photos and see if they can predict what the text will be about (Walt Disney and how he got his ideas). Ask them if they know who Walt Disney was and see if they can name any cartoons he made.

(a) Read through the questions, explaining them in L1 if necessary. Students discuss them in small groups. Ask for feedback. If there are any interesting results, put them on the board to discuss after reading the text.

(b) Pre-teach the following vocabulary if necessary: *imagination, universal gravity, creative, dreaming, daydream, cartoon.* Read the instructions and ask them to find the answer after reading the text. Let them read it silently first, before reading it aloud with them, if necessary. Elicit the correct answer.

Answer
Picture 2

8 Vocabulary
Sleeping and waking

a 🔊 Read the examples and instructions with the class. Go through the example, making sure students remember that it is the opposite they are looking for. Students match the opposites. Play the recording for students to listen and check their answers. Play the recording again for students to repeat the words.

TAPESCRIPT/ANSWERS

1	to go to bed	c	to get up
2	to go to sleep	a	to wake up
3	to be asleep	b	to be awake

b Students work in pairs to discuss the phrases, before giving their answers.

Answers
To dream: to be in the state of experiencing mental images while you sleep
To daydream: to fantasise while you are awake

c Students read through sentences 1–7. Go through the example with students, reminding them to look at the context of the sentence to help them work out which verb is needed and which form it is needed in. Students complete the sentences. Check answers.

Answers 2 go to sleep 3 dreamed/dreamt
4 is asleep 5 was awake 6 woke up; got up
7 daydreams

9 Speak

Students work in pairs and take turns to ask and answer the questions. Ask several pairs to report their answers to the rest of the class. Find out if anyone has the same answers.

Vocabulary notebook
This would be a good time to refer students to their vocabulary notebooks. Students can start a section called *Sleeping and waking* and note down any new expressions. They may find it useful to illustrate some of them or translate them into their own language.

Culture in mind

10 Read

If students researched the background information for homework ask them to tell the class what they have found out.

BACKGROUND INFORMATION

The Beatles: The English rock music group of the 1960s who are said to influence music to this day. The group were from Liverpool and were John Lennon (1940–1980), Paul McCartney (1942–), George Harrison (1943–2002) and Ringo Starr (Richard Starkey) (1940–). Lennon and McCartney did most of the song writing and music. The group had their first number one hit single in 1963 with the song *Please Please Me* and they went on to have many more hits. The Beatles split up in 1971.

The Rolling Stones: Another popular rock group from the 1960s. They were Mick Jagger (1943–), Brian Jones (1944–69), Keith Richards (1943–), Ron Wood (1941–), Bill Wyman (1941–) and Charlie Watts (1941–). Mick Jagger and Keith Richards wrote most of the music and songs for them and their many hits include songs like *Satisfaction, Jumpin' Jack Flash* and *19th Nervous Breakdown.*

Take That: Were a famous five-member boy band formed in 1991. The band were Robbie Williams, Gary Barlow, Howard Donald, Jason Orange and Mark Owen. They had a lot of hits in the early 1990s but dismissed one of their band members, Robbie Williams (see Unit 7, Exercise 1), in 1996 and then split up. Both Gary Barlow and Robbie Williams went on to have successful solo careers.

The Spice Girls: They were a pop sensation of the late 1990s and were Victoria Adams, Melanie Chisholm, Geri Halliwell, Melanie Brown and Emma Bunton. The girls had replied to an advert in a magazine for females who could sing and dance and they were put together to form the group. In 1996 they had their first hit with *Wannabe* which went straight to number 1 in the charts. Geri Halliwell left the group in 1998 and the group later split up.

Popstars: A television programme where thousands of young hopefuls auditioned to become members of a pop band. In the end five people were chosen and they became the pop group Hear'Say. Their first hit single *Pure and Simple* made them famous but shortly after that one of the members left. The band split up in October 2001.

Pop Idol: A similar television programme (October 2001) to *Popstars,* but this time the aim was to find a solo artist. By February 2002, out of the 10,000 people who auditioned originally there were two left: Will Young and Gareth Gates. Will Young won the public vote and became Pop Idol. Both singers have since gone on to have successful solo careers.

Warm up

Ask students to look at the title of the text and the photos and predict what they think the text will be about (the television programme *Pop Idol*).

(**a**) In small groups, ask students to look at the photos and see if they recognise anyone on them. What can they tell you about the ones they recognise?

(**b**) Read the question with students and then ask them to read the text quickly and find the answer. Remind them they don't have to understand every word.

Answer
Hear'Say won the TV programme *Popstars* and Will Young won the *Pop Idol* programme.

(**c**) Students now read the text again in detail and decide if the statements are true, false or if there isn't enough information in the text. Remind them that they may not find information in the text to answer all of them. Do the first item as an example, if necessary. Students complete the exercise. Students can compare answers in pairs. Check answers.

Students can then correct the false statements and provide the sentences from the text where they found the information for their true answers.

Answers
1   N (para 2: *started in the 1990s ...*)
2   T (para 2: *was extremely popular with TV audiences ...*)
3   F (para 3: *after some time there were 50 contestants ...*)
4   F (para 3: *to find a new solo singer.*)
5   N
6   T (para 4: *he argued with the judges.*)
7   T (para 5: *Will is now a big star.*)

(**d**) Read through the questions with students. In small groups, students discuss and give feedback.

(**e**) Refer students back to the text on page 72 and ask them to read the question again at the end of the text. In pairs or small groups, students discuss the question, then report back their opinions to the whole class.

11 Write

(**a**) ◁» Explain to students that this activity is a creative visualisation. They will listen to a recording and be asked to do various things. Some students may feel slightly embarrassed about this but explain that everyone will have their eyes closed and no one will see others.

Read the instructions with the students. Tell them to relax, close their eyes, and when they are ready to listen, play the recording.

TAPESCRIPT

Sit there with your eyes closed, and relax ... While you're listening to these words ... and the music ... imagine it's a beautiful sunny day ... and you're standing somewhere on a beautiful beach ... And while you're standing there, you can hear the water ... and the sound of the sea on the beach ... and you can feel the warm sun on your face, on your arms and your legs ... and the warm sand under your feet.

Take your time ... and look around ... What can you see?

Then somewhere on that beach, in front of you ... you can see a tree. Think about the tree. What does it look like?

Now you can see that tree ... you start walking ... along the beach ... and you're getting close to the tree ... You can see something under the tree ... It's a box ... there's a box under the tree. Think about the box. What does it look like?

Now you can see your name on the box ... and you open the box ... There's something inside the box, something for you ... a present. You can look at it, and pick it up, and hold it in your hands. What is it?

And now it's time to close the box again ... walk back to the place on the beach where you started from ... but you can take the present with you ... What do you do with the present?

And now it's time to open your eyes again and come back to your classroom.

(**b**) Students open their eyes again and look at the second part of the exercise in their books. Ask two students to read aloud Stefano's story.

(**c**) Now students write their own paragraphs based on their visualisation while listening. Read the instructions and the list of questions with them. Remind them to answer all the questions in their paragraphs. Students write this privately, in class.

(**d**) When they have finished, they exchange work with a partner, looking for differences and similarities. Ask them what they deduce from the differences between their visualisations.

Module 2 Check your progress

1 Grammar

(a) 2 were   3 was   4 was   5 Was   6 wasn't
7 were

(b) 1 saw   2 became; won; was   3 won   4 jumped;
stopped; said

(c) 1 didn't enjoy   2 did; say   3 Did; see; didn't see;
saw   4 went; didn't go

(d) 1 any   2 any; some   3 any; some   4 some; some;
any

(e) 2 yours   3 ours   4 Mine   5 theirs   6 hers

2 Vocabulary

(a) 2 up   3 down   4 on   5 out   6 in   7 out
8 up; down

(b) 1 snowboarding   2 basketball   3 cycling
4 swimming   5 skiing   6 hockey   7 surfing
Mystery word: Olympics

(c) 2 dentist   3 doctor   4 nurse   5 pilot
6 lawyer   7 secretary   8 engineer

3 Everyday English

2 pocket money   3 hardly any   4 saving up
5 one day   6 loads

How did you do?
Check with students on their progress and if necessary
spend time with students helping them in the areas
they need more work on.

Module 3
Far and wide

YOU WILL LEARN ABOUT ...

Ask students to look at the pictures on the page. Ask students to read through the topics in the box and check they understand each item. You can ask them the following questions, in L1 if appropriate:

1 *Do you like science fiction stories? Can you give any examples?*
2 *Have you ever visited Ireland?*
3 *What do you do on an adventure holiday?*
4 *Who do you think are the world's best language learners?*
5 *When did Europeans go to live in America?*
6 *Where do you think the mountain climbers are?*

In small groups, students discuss which topic area they think each picture matches.

Check answers.

Answers
1 A science fiction story
2 Holidays in Ireland
3 An adventure holiday
4 The world's best language learners
5 Europeans who went to live in America
6 Four young mountain climbers

YOU WILL LEARN HOW TO ...

Use grammar

Go through the first item with students. Stronger students should be able to continue with the other items on their own or in pairs.

Weaker classes: Put the grammar headings on the board and give an example of your own for each item (e.g. *English is more difficult than (L1). English is the easiest language in the world. I'm going to Spain in the summer. I won't study English next year. This exercise is too difficult, can you help us? I am speaking slowly.*).

In pairs, students now match the grammar items in their book. Check answers.

Answers
Comparative adjectives: Pronunciation is more difficult than grammar.
Superlative adjectives: It's the longest river in the world.
Present continuous for future arrangements: We're visiting Ireland next summer.
will/won't: It won't hurt!
too + adjective: We can't do it – it's too difficult.
Adverbs: They stood up slowly.

Use vocabulary

Write the headings on the board. Go through the items in the Student's Book and check understanding. Now ask students if they can think of one more item for the *Language learning* heading. Elicit some responses and add them to the list on the board. Students now do the same for the other headings. Accept suggestions in L1 and translate them into English as necessary. Some possibilities are:

Language learning: (*good/bad*) *pronunciation, fluent, make mistakes*

Future time expressions: *next week/month/year, in a week's time, in two years' time*

Holiday activities: *hillwalking, swimming, canoeing*

The weather: *windy, snowy, rainy, hot, cold*

The languages we speak

Unit overview

TOPIC: Languages and language learning

TEXTS

Reading and listening: a text about people who speak more than one language

Listening: to teenagers talking about language learning

Listening: to advice about language learning.

Reading and listening: photo story: *I have to bounce!*

Writing: write about your language; write a letter or an email

SPEAKING

Comparing things

Talking about language learning

LANGUAGE

Grammar: Comparative adjectives; Superlative adjectives

Vocabulary: Language learning

Pronunciation: *than* /ðən/

Everyday English: words for *good* through the ages

1 Read and listen

If you set the background information as a homework research task ask students to tell the class what they have found out.

BACKGROUND INFORMATION

Florida: Is one of the states of the USA. It forms the peninsula between the Atlantic Ocean on the east and the Gulf of Mexico on the west. A large percentage of the population speak Spanish.

Vaupés River: Is the largest tributary of the Rio Negro in northern Brazil.

Tukano language: Is one of the languages of the Tukano community who live in the Amazon. In 1995 there were said to be 3,500 Tukano people living in Brazil. Their communities range from 20 to 100 people, all living together in a *maloca* (a multi-family dwelling).

Warm up

Ask students how many languages they speak, or are learning at the moment. Find out if anyone in the class speaks more than two languages. Ask them which one they think is easier / more difficult to learn, and why.

OPTIONAL ACTIVITY

If the class is interested in the topic, you may like to give them a quick quiz about languages. Write, in random order, the following languages on the board: *Mandarin Chinese, English, Hindustani, Spanish, Russian, Arabic, Bengali, Portuguese, Malay-Indonesian, French.* They are in the correct order here. Ask students to guess which three are the most widely spoken languages in the world (Chinese, English, Hindustani).

a Read the questions with students. In pairs, students read the text quickly and answer the questions. Remind them they don't need to understand every word in the text and that they should only be looking for the answers to the questions. Check answers.

Answers

They are the Vaupés River Indians from the Amazon. They are special because all of them speak three languages or more.

b 🔊 Read through items 1–4 with students and check they understand them. Remind students to look for some of the key words from the statements in the text to help them with the answers. Play the recording while students listen. Check answers, asking students to justify their answers with evidence from the text. Students can correct the false statements.

TAPESCRIPT

See the reading text on page 78 of the Student's Book.

Answers

1 T (para 1: … *a lot of people speak Spanish as their mother tongue.*)

2 F (para 2: *All of the Vaupés River Indians speak three languages …*)

3 T (para 2: … *he or she has to marry someone who speaks a different language.*)

4 F (para 2: … *Tukano, the language that all Vaupés Indians have in common.*)

c Students discuss the questions in small groups. Ask them to think of the people they know who speak more than one language. Do their parents speak more than one language? Ask: *What other languages, apart from English, do people speak or try to learn, in your country?* Ask for feedback and discuss any interesting points further as a class.

d If you chose to do the optional activity (above) then students should be able to answer the question. If you have not done it already, do it now. Ask students to choose an option and see how many get it right.

Answer

Chinese

2 Listen

a 🔊 Ask students to look at the photos of the teenagers and the notes below each photo about which languages they speak. Play the recording while students read and listen.

TAPESCRIPT

Roberto My Spanish is good – it's better than my German. Of course, for me Spanish is easier than German. That's because it's got a lot of words that are almost the same as Italian. The grammar is very similar, too.

Gabriela Portuguese pronunciation is difficult for me. But of course, English pronunciation is more difficult! I never know how to pronounce a new word, because the writing and the pronunciation are often very different.

b 🔊 Students read through the texts, ignoring the spaces. Go through the first item as an example, pausing the tape at the relevant point. Play the recording again while students complete the spaces.

Answers
Roberto: Spanish; German; Spanish; German; Italian
Gabriela: Portuguese; English

3 Grammar
Comparative adjectives

a Focus on the adjective *easy* in the grammar table and ask students to find a word similar to it in Roberto's text in Exercise 2b (*easier*) and read the full sentence. Explain that he uses this word to compare Spanish and German and it is followed by *than*. Now ask students to find examples in the texts of other adjectives of comparison.

Students complete the chart. They can compare their answers in pairs, before a whole class check.

Answers
shorter, easier, more important, better

Now ask students if they notice anything about the spellings in the comparative column of the table. Elicit the spelling rules.
Short adjectives: Add *-er.*
Adjectives ending in *-y*: Change the *-y* to *-i* and add *-er.*
Longer adjectives: Use the word *more* before them
Irregular adjectives: Learn them!

> **Language notes**
> 1 The above is a simplified version of the rule: in actual fact, we only double the last consonant in short adjectives ending *t, d, g, m, n* where the last syllable ends consonant-vowel-consonant. Examples: *big – bigger, red – redder, hot – hotter,* BUT *long – longer, quiet – quieter, loud – louder.*

2 Students may produce comparatives like *more bigger than* ... or *It's hotter that* ... . Remind them that in English we compare two things using *more ... than.*

> **OPTIONAL ACTIVITY**
> If you feel students need further practice in forming comparative adjectives, ask them to write the comparative form of the following: *fat, tall, noisy, intelligent, old, pretty, young, careful.*

b Read through sentences 1–5 with students. Go through the example, if necessary. Students complete the sentences. Check answers.

Answers 2 shorter than 3 bigger than 4 more difficult than 5 farther from; than

> **OPTIONAL ACTIVITY**
> Ask students to change the adjectives in the sentences in Exercise 3b, and rewrite them so that the meaning is the same. Do the first one as an example.
> **Answers**
> 1 Latin is older than Italian.
> 2 The Nile is longer than the Amazon River.
> 3 India is smaller than the Amazon rainforest.
> 4 For most Europeans, learning Italian is easier than learning Chinese.
> 5 My country is closer to Paris than Sydney.

Grammar notebook
Students should copy the comparative table into their grammar notebooks.

4 Pronunciation
than

a 🔊 Write the first sentence on the board and read it out as an example. Ask students to tell you where the stressed syllables are and underline them on the board. Students read the other sentences while listening to the recording and mark the stressed syllables. Check answers, playing the recording again.

TAPESCRIPT/ANSWERS
1 Pronunciation is more difficult than grammar.
2 Spanish is easier than German.
3 My speaking is better than my writing.
4 Is French more interesting than English?

b 🔊 Write *than* on the board and ask students to pronounce it: /ðən/. Explain that *than* is pronounced in its weak form when it is unstressed. Students repeat, paying particular attention to the schwa sound /ə/. Play the recording again, for students to repeat.

5 Speak

Read through the adjectives in the box with students, making sure they know them all. Do the first item as an example, giving your own opinion, e.g. *I think books are more interesting than CD-ROMs.* Students work in pairs or small groups and make comparisons. Find out how many have the same opinions. Ask: *How many of you think that dogs are more intelligent than cats?* etc.

> **Language note**
> We do not normally use *beautiful* (or *pretty*) to describe a man; rather, *good-looking*, *handsome* or *attractive*.

OPTIONAL ACTIVITY

Ask students to give you the names of two popular actors/actresses, bands, football teams, etc. Write them on the board, along with the adjectives:

good, attractive, young, talented, successful, famous, popular, funny

Students now work in pairs to make interesting comparative sentences. Ask some pairs to read out their answers. Does everyone agree?

---

6 Listen

a 🔊 Read the instructions with the students and explain that they are going to listen to Matthew talking about the five languages he speaks, and where/how he learned them. Students should only focus on the first column of the table at this point.

Play the recording and pause as necessary. Give students time to note down their answers. Check answers with the class.

TAPESCRIPT

Interviewer They say that British people aren't very good language learners. Well, perhaps that's true. But there's one British person who is very, very good at learning languages. Matthew Dawson is 16 and speaks five languages fluently. He's here with us in the studio. Hello, Matthew.

Matthew Hello.

Interviewer Five languages! That's amazing. Can you tell us which languages they are?

Matthew Sure. English, of course, and French. Er, Spanish and German, and Italian.

Interviewer Hold on! English, French, Spanish, German, Italian. Is that right?

Matthew That's right!

Interviewer And you're only 16, Matthew. Tell me, did you learn these languages at home, at school ...?

Matthew Well, the first thing to say is that my father's English but my mother's French. And my

father always speaks English to me – of course! – and my mother always speaks French. I've got two first languages, really, English and French. So they were really easy.

Interviewer OK. What about the others?

Matthew Well, the second thing is ... about ten years ago we went to live in Madrid. And I went to school there for four years, a real school for Spanish children, so of course I had to speak Spanish. So I learned Spanish actually there in Spain, in the country.

Interviewer OK. So what about the other two – what were they?

Matthew German and Italian. Well, I learned German at school here in England, I started when I was 13. And I don't know, I just found German really easy to learn. And I love languages, I think they're great, so I decided to learn more. I learned Italian at home. I bought a special book and some cassettes to listen to, and that was it.

Interviewer Incredible. But Matthew, let me ask you ...

Answers 1 English 2 French 3 Spanish
4 German 5 Italian

b 🔊 Read through the other column headings in the table with students. Play the recording again, pausing it at the example to show students what Matthew said. Now play the rest of the recording while students complete the other columns.

Weaker classes: You can pause the tape after each answer, if necessary.

Check answers, playing the recording again and pausing as necessary.

Answers
1 English: from his parents
2 French: from his parents
3 Spanish: in the country
4 German: at school in England
5 Italian: taught himself

c 🔊 Ask students to read through sentences 1–6 and check understanding. They can predict what they think Matthew will say and listen and check their predictions.

Play the recording while students complete the exercise. Check answers.

TAPESCRIPT

Interviewer Incredible. But Matthew, let me ask you: are there special things that people need to do to learn a new language? For example, if I want to learn French, what should I do?

Matthew Um, well ... I think you have to read and listen as much as you can, you know, in the foreign language, the language you're learning.

Interviewer OK, so read and listen a lot. Anything else?

Matthew Yeah. You have to remember lots of new words, of course, so I have some ways of testing myself, so that I can remember the new words. Um, for example, I write new words on cards and test myself on the bus when I'm going to school.

Interviewer Mmm …

Matthew Another thing is about pronunciation. For me that's the most difficult thing – it's quite hard. So, I practise a lot. I listen to my cassettes and I try to use the same pronunciation as the people on the recording. I usually do that in my bedroom – I don't want people to hear me! Er, but it helps a lot, you know. Imitating the accent. Listening and trying to say it the same way.

Interviewer Yeah, that makes sense.

Matthew Oh, one more thing. It's about making mistakes. Er, I try not to make mistakes if I'm speaking or writing. But I think it's really important not to worry too much about mistakes. It's more important to communicate, you know. Just open your mouth and speak!

Interviewer Matthew Dawson, thank you, and good luck with the next language you learn.

Answers
Matthew talks about 1, 3, 4 and 6.

(**d**) In small groups, students discuss which of the ideas in Exercise 6c they do when speaking English and which they think they would like to try. Ask some stronger students to explain why they find the ideas helpful. Do the class agree on the general ideas?

OPTIONAL ACTIVITY
Students choose one of Matthew's ideas or one of their own to help them improve their English. They should write it down and try it out over the next week.

7 **Vocabulary**
Language learning

(**a**) 🔊 Go through the words in the box with the class. Students work in pairs and try to work out the meanings of each word or phrase. As a way of checking, use each word or phrase in a sentence or context, and ask students to give you their definition. Play the recording for students to check and repeat each word or phrase.

TAPESCRIPT
make mistakes, imitate, corrects, translate, look up, have an accent, means, guess, communicate

(**b**) Ask students to read through the whole text, ignoring the spaces. Check any vocabulary problems. Go through the first item with them as an example.

Students work individually to complete the spaces, then compare their answers in pairs. Check answers.

Answers 2 imitate 3 means 4 guess 5 look up
6 translate 7 make mistakes 8 corrects
9 communicate

Vocabulary notebook
Students may find it useful to copy down any new words or expressions from this section. If necessary, they could write translations beside each one.

OPTIONAL ACTIVITY
Ask students to work in small groups and discuss the advice in the text. Which of it do they agree with? Which of it, if any, do they find difficult to follow or accept? Why?

Ask students to write down any other advice their group has about language learning and to share it with the class.

8 **Grammar**
Superlative adjectives

(**a**) Read the amazing facts through with the class. Check that they understand any new words. Students guess which statements are not true, and why.

Answers
Statements 1 and 3 are untrue. (The longest town name in Britain is the famous 58-letter Llanfairpwllgwyngyllgogerychwyrndrobwllllantysiliogo-gogoch, also in Wales. The station name in 7 was invented to beat this record!)

(**b**) Read through the three questions with students, then with books closed (or the text covered) students try to remember the answers. In pairs, students compare answers. Books open, students read the texts again quickly to check their answers.

Answers 1 Africa 2 Y and U 3 the

(**c**) Students read through the adjectives in the box and the spelling rules in the table. Go through the examples in the table with students eliciting the rules for superlatives (short adjectives: add -est; longer adjectives: add *most* before the adjective). If further work is necessary before students begin the exercise, ask students to give you the comparative and superlative form of another adjective from the table to check understanding.

Students now add the adjectives from the box to the table and complete the comparative and superlative forms. You may wish to do this on the board as a whole class activity, inviting students to come and fill in the chart for their classmates to check.

Answers
(short) – (shorter) – shortest
(small) – smaller – smallest
big – bigger – biggest

(easy) – (easier) – easiest
happy – happier –happiest
difficult – more difficult – most difficult
fantastic – more fantastic – most fantastic
important – more important – most important
(bad) – (worse) – worst
(good) – (better) – best
(many) – (more) – most

> **Language note**
> It is important for students to know when to use the comparative or superlative form of the adjective. Ask if anyone can guess the rule. (We use the comparative when we compare two things, and the superlative when we compare more than two things.)

(d) Read through sentences 1–6 with students and check any problems. Go through the example with students. Students complete the exercise. Check answers.

Answers 2 happiest 3 most important
4 smallest 5 worst 6 longest

Grammar notebook
Students should note down the comparatives and superlatives and the spelling rules from this unit and learn them.

┌─ OPTIONAL ACTIVITY ──────────────
This activity can also be given as homework to complete, for students who finish early in class. Students work in pairs or groups and write a questionnaire for other pairs or groups, using superlatives. Encourage students to start with the opposites of the adjectives in Exercise 8, e.g. *What's the saddest film you can think of? What's the most useless invention in the world?*

Students exchange their quizzes and discuss the new questions in their groups or pairs.

I have to bounce!

Warm up
Ask students to look at the photos and say who appears in this episode (Amy, Lucy and Dave).

9 Read and listen

(a) 🔊 Read through the questions with students and ask them to predict the answers by looking at the photos and the title. Play the recording while students read. Check answers.

TAPESCRIPT
See the photo story on page 82 of the Student's Book.

Answers
I have to bounce means *I have to go.* Lucy doesn't understand it because she's not American.

(b) Read through sentences 1–5 with students and check any problems. Students do the exercise in pairs. Remind students to justify the true answers with evidence from the text and they can also correct the false answers. Check answers.

Answers
1 T
2 F (She says it's *cool*, which means she likes it.)
3 F (It means 'someone not very nice'.)
4 F (*Beats me!* means she doesn't understand.)
5 T

┌─ OPTIONAL ACTIVITY ──────────────
In groups, students can act out the dialogue from the photo story.

10 Everyday English

Read through the instructions with students and look at the words in the picture. Ask how many words for *good* they have in their language. In small groups, students discuss which words are popular with teenagers in their country. Ask for feedback.

Vocabulary notebook
They should note down the different words for *good* and any words they have come up with in Exercise 10 and their translations.

11 Write

This section ends with a writing task on the theme of language learning. Students can do the preparation in class, and complete the writing assignment as homework. Read through the tasks with the class and make sure students realise they only have to choose ONE of the topics.

(a) Students who choose topic a should refer to the texts on page 79. Tell them to underline all the comparative adjectives, and to try to use them, or similar adjectives, as a starting point when writing about their own language learning experiences.

(b) Students who choose topic b should look carefully at the questions first, and think about possible answers. Tell students to think about any vocabulary they will need for ideas to build on in their evaluation of their imaginary English course. Students may also need reminding of the format of emails and informal letters (see Units 3 and 6).

10 We're going on holiday

Unit overview

TOPIC: Future plans and holiday arrangements

TEXTS
Reading and listening: web page holiday adverts; teenagers discussing holiday plans
Reading: a magazine article about Ireland
Reading: a text about adventure holidays
Writing: an article for a school magazine

SPEAKING
Talking about future plans
Talking about holidays

LANGUAGE
Grammar: Present continuous for future arrangements
Vocabulary: Future time expressions; Holiday activities
Pronunciation: /θ/ _think_ and /ð/ _that_

1 Read and listen

If you set the background information as a homework research task ask students to tell the class what they have found out.

BACKGROUND INFORMATION

Ireland (Eire): Is the second largest island of the British Isles. It is divided politically into Northern Ireland (part of the United Kingdom) and the Republic of Ireland. The capital city of the Republic of Ireland is Dublin and the country is popular as a holiday destination because of its beauty and the friendliness of the Irish people. The country is also famous for its pubs, its Guinness (a special type of black Irish beer) and its rugby.

Dublin: The capital of the Republic of Ireland, situated on the east coast of the island in the province of Leinster. It has two universities and is the birthplace of many famous people, including the writers James Joyce, George Bernard Shaw and Jonathan Swift.

Aran islands: A small group of islands in Galway Bay in the west of Ireland. The largest island is Inishmore. They are popular holiday destinations.

River Shannon: This is the longest river in Ireland.

Warm up

Ask students if anyone has ever been to Ireland. If so, ask for some more details about where they went, what they did, etc. Then ask students to look at the photos and name as many of the holidays as they can (staying on a farm, staying in a hotel, horse-riding, canal boat holiday, hiking/walking holiday).

(a) Following the Warm up, ask students which type of holidays they think are good and bad ideas. It may be useful to elicit different types of people who go on holiday at this point and write them on the board. Students can then discuss in small groups which type of holiday would suit which type of person, e.g. young people, retired people, young families, single people, students. Ask for feedback. Does the class agree?

(b) Students now listen to two teenagers discussing the holidays in the photos. They must number the photos in the order they are mentioned. If necessary, play the first part of the recording as an example and pause it when it mentions the first holiday. Remind students to listen for key words describing each holiday.

Weaker classes: The recording can be played in sections, pausing after each holiday is mentioned.

Stronger classes: They can listen to the recording without pauses.

Play the recording. Then play the recording again, pausing it as necessary for students to check their answers.

TAPESCRIPT

Kate   Greg! Come here and help me.

Greg   What are you doing?

Kate   Mum and Dad asked us to plan the summer holiday in Ireland, so I'm looking at this web page.

Greg   Oh, right. Looks good. What's this? Horse-riding? Hmm – I don't think that's a good idea!

Kate   No, nor me. But what about this? Canal boats. 'Travel around Ireland in a boat – enjoy total freedom.' What do you think?

Greg   Wonderful! Let's do that. I like boats.

Kate   Yes, maybe a week on a boat. Nice and relaxing! And this one – hiking around Ireland. Let's do that!

Greg   What? Are you crazy? Hiking! No way – too much work!

Kate   OK, maybe you're right. But how about an elegant hotel in Dublin?

Greg   Much better! Yes, that's a good idea.

Kate   OK. So ... canal boats, and then some time in Dublin. But look, we've got two weeks, so let's do something else.

Greg What about these farms on the Aran Islands? You like farms and animals and things, don't you?

Kate Yes, I do. OK, so in the second week we can stay on a farm there.

Greg Right. That's it. Now, let's tell Mum and Dad about it ...

Answers
1 Horse-riding
2 Canal boat holidays
3 Hiking
4 Dublin
5 Aran islands

OPTIONAL ACTIVITIES

Ask students what kind of holiday Kate and Greg decided on in the end (canal boat holiday for a week and then two days in Dublin in a hotel and then a farm on the Aran islands).

Then, in small groups, students must agree on and choose a holiday in Ireland. Each group appoints a spokesperson who can give feedback to the class.

c Students read through the dialogue first, ignoring the spaces. Check any problems. Explain to students that it is verb forms that are missing and go through the first item with them as an example.

Stronger classes: They could complete the dialogue without the recording and then listen and check only.

Weaker classes: They can listen to the recording and complete the dialogue while listening. Pause the tape as necessary for them. Alternatively, put the base forms of the verbs on the board for them to choose from as they listen.

Play the recording while students complete the exercise. Students compare answers in pairs. Play the recording again, pausing as necessary for students to check or change answers.

TAPESCRIPT

Maggie Hey, Kate! How was your weekend?

Kate Good! My brother and I planned the family summer holiday.

Maggie Excellent! Where are you going?

Kate We're going to Ireland in August.

Maggie Oh! How are you getting there?

Kate We're travelling by ferry. And we're spending a week on a canal boat on the River Shannon.

Maggie Great! Are you only staying a week in Ireland?

Kate No, two weeks. After the canal boat, we're going by train to Dublin and we're staying in a really nice hotel there for two nights. And then we're flying to the Aran Islands. We're staying on a farm there.

Maggie I think you'll have a great holiday! Are all your family going?

Kate Yeah. My Dad says it's a bit expensive, but he's seeing the bank manager tomorrow!

Answers 1 going 2 getting 3 travelling
4 spending 5 staying 6 going 7 staying
8 flying 9 staying 10 going 11 seeing

OPTIONAL ACTIVITY

In pairs, students can act out the dialogue between Maggie and Kate.

2 Grammar
Present continuous for future arrangements

a Students should already be familiar with the form of the present continuous, which they saw in Unit 3. Ask students *Where are Kate and Greg going on holiday?* (Ireland). *What tense is this?* (present continuous). To check understanding ask them, in L1 if necessary: *Is this happening now or in the future?* (future). *Is this a plan or an arrangement?* (plan). Now read through the examples from the dialogue and remind students of the negative and question forms, giving a few examples of these if necessary. Students go through Exercise 1c and underline any more examples of the present continuous. Check answers.

Answers
We're going to Ireland in August.
How are you getting there?
We're travelling by ferry.
We're spending ...
Are you only staying ...?
... we're going ...
... we're staying ...
... we're flying ...
We're staying ...
Are all your family going?
... but he's seeing ...

Now read through the Rule box with students. You may want to remind them of the spelling rules for the *-ing*.

b Students read through the plans in the sentences 1–6. Check any problems. Go through the first item with them as an example, if necessary. Remind them to use short forms where possible. Students complete the exercise. Check answers.

Answers
1 'm visiting / am visiting
2 're having / are having
3 's taking / is taking; 're leaving / are leaving
4 A: Are you going; B: 'm staying / am staying
5 isn't coming / is not coming; 's working / is working
6 'm seeing / am seeing

Grammar notebook
Remind students to note down the rules and some examples of the present continuous for future use.

3 Vocabulary
Future time expressions

(a) Students read through the time expressions and in pairs decide how they say them in their own language. Discuss any similarities and differences in these expressions. Ask students a few questions using the future time expressions and the present continuous (e.g. *Nicolo, what are you doing tomorrow after school? Anna, what are you doing on Saturday?*)

> **Language note**
> It may be useful to point out to students that there is no article before *next week/month* etc. in English. We don't say ~~The next week~~ ...

(b) 🔊 Students read through questions 1–4. Check any problems and do the first one as an example, if necessary. Students complete the exercise. Students can compare answers in pairs. Then ask a few students to read out their answers to the class. Play the recording, for students to repeat the questions.

TAPESCRIPT
1 What day is the day after tomorrow?
2 What day is it in three days' time?
3 How many days is it until next Sunday?
4 What is the month after next?

4 Speak

Read through the bullet points with students and check they understand them all. Go through the example dialogue with a student highlighting the use of the present continuous. In pairs, students ask and answer questions to find out what they are doing and when. Make sure students swap roles to allow both to ask and answer.

Weaker classes: They may find it useful to have some ideas about leisure activities on the board. Elicit a few before they start (e.g. staying at home, watching TV, going to a restaurant, going to the cinema, doing my homework, playing computer games, seeing my friend, etc.).

Ask a few students to give feedback on what their partner's plans and arrangements were.

Grammar notebook
Students can note down the future time expressions and their translations from Exercise 3a.

5 Read

If you set the background information as a homework research task ask students to tell the class what they have found out.

BACKGROUND INFORMATION
U2: They are a popular Irish band from the 1980s who are still producing hit singles today. Other famous Irish singers and bands are The Corrs, Van Morrison, Westlife and Ronan Keating.

Warm up
Ask students to look at the photos and say which type of holiday they would choose.

(a) Students read through the questions and choose answers. Go through the example with them before they start and remind them that if they don't know the answer, they should guess.

(b) Students read the text to check their predictions from Exercise 5a. Check answers.

Answers 2 about 2,000,000   3 3,000,000   4 U2

(c) **Weaker classes:** They can go through the text and underline any adjectives they find. Once they have done this look at the example with them, explaining that *warm* can describe people as well as, for example, the weather. Students now continue the exercise using the adjectives they have underlined and the categories in the exercise.

Stronger classes: They can read the example and find the other adjectives in the text, checking their answers in a dictionary.

Check answers as a class.

Answers
The people: friendly
The country: charming, beautiful
The music: exciting
The hotels: comfortable
The museums: fascinating

Vocabulary notebook
Students can note down any new adjectives and their meanings from this exercise.

--- OPTIONAL ACTIVITY ---

Tourist brochure
This task can be set for homework. Students can write a tourist advert for their own city using the Ireland text as a model. They can use the adjectives from this unit and find some more. They should think about the following areas:
- number of tourists who visit each year
- what the city's attractions are: sights, museums, hotels, restaurants, people
- types of holidays you can have there
- culture and music.

Students can add photos or pictures of their own city.

6 Vocabulary
Holiday activities

a 🔊 Books closed. Elicit as many holiday activities as you can. Remind students of the activities Kate and Greg talked about in Exercises 1b and c. Put students' suggestions on the board. Students now open their books at page 87 and read through the activities in Exercise 6a. Go through the first one as an example or choose one of the responses students gave you with books closed and match it to one of the pictures. Students complete the exercise. Play the recording for students to listen and check answers. Play the recording again, for students to repeat.

TAPESCRIPT/ANSWERS
1 windsurfing
2 camping
3 horse-riding
4 sightseeing
5 snorkelling
6 canoeing
7 sunbathing
8 sailing

b In pairs, students discuss which of the activities in Exercise 6a they like doing on holiday. Remind them if necessary of the expressions they learned in Unit 1, *like/don't like/love/hate + -ing*. Go through the example with students, if necessary. Set a time limit for this and ask for some students to give feedback to the class about themselves and their partner.

c **Stronger classes:** With books closed, write the following verbs on the board: *hire, travel, stay, buy, spend*. Ask them to check the meaning of the verbs in a dictionary. Remind them that there may be several uses of one verb.

Weaker classes: Read through the verbs in the box with them and sentences 1–5. Check they know the meaning of each verb and the words in the sentences 1–5. Give them some examples with the verbs in context to help them understand the meaning (e.g. *I always hire a car when I go on holiday./I like to travel by plane when I go to Spain.*). Students complete the exercise. Check answers.

Answers 1 buy 2 stay 3 travel 4 spend
5 hire

> **Language notes**
> 1 Point out to students that we use *by* with means of transport: *by ferry/car/plane/train/coach* but we say *on foot*.
> 2 The verb *spend* can also be used in the expression *to spend money*.

Vocabulary notebook
Students could start a section called *Holiday activities* in their notebooks and note down any new words from this unit.

7 Speak

Read through the instructions and the question prompts with students. Go through the example dialogue, reminding students to use the present continuous tense for future plans and arrangements. In pairs, students discuss their plans. Ask for feedback from some pairs.

┌─ OPTIONAL ACTIVITY ─────────
Students use the activities from this unit and plan an ideal holiday. They choose a place they want to go to. They then decide when they are going to go on their holiday, what they are going to do and in what order.

8 Pronunciation
/θ/ (think) and /ð/ (that)

a 🔊 Write the words *think* and *that* on the board and drill the pronunciation of each a few times. Explain that one is voiced (*that*) and the other unvoiced (*think*), elicit which is which. Divide the class into two and ask half the class to say *think* and the other *that*. Can they hear the difference? Students doing the voiced sound may find it useful to put their hand to their throat and feel the vibration. Swap sounds after a few minutes.

Students read through the words. Play the recording for students to listen and repeat.

TAPESCRIPT
1 think, three, month, something, toothache
2 that, those, with, brother, sunbathing

b 🔊 Go through the first item as an example without the recording. Make sure students are clear about which sound to underline and which to circle.

Weaker classes: This can be done in two parts: first they listen for the /θ/ sound and underline it then they listen for the /ð/ sound and circle it.

Play the recording for students to listen and underline/circle. Play the recording again, pausing for students to repeat.

TAPESCRIPT/ANSWERS
1 Give me (th)ose <u>th</u>ings.
2 (Th)ere's no<u>th</u>ing in my mou<u>th</u>.
3 I <u>th</u>ink it's <u>Th</u>ursday.
4 Your clo(th)es are in the ba<u>th</u>room.
5 My mo(th)er <u>th</u>inks I'm crazy.
6 (Th)is mon<u>th</u> we're staying at a you<u>th</u> hostel.

┌─ OPTIONAL ACTIVITIES ─────────
1 **Stronger students:** They can think of more words themselves. Put them on the board and drill them.
2 **Weaker students:** If you feel students need more practice with these sounds, give them a few more words to work out which sound it is and practise them. For example:

/ð/: *brother, this, those, these, sunbathing*
/θ/: *through, something*

Culture in mind

9 Read

If you set the background information as a homework research task ask students to tell the class what they have found out.

> ### BACKGROUND INFORMATION
>
> **New York:** Is the name of one of the US states on the east coast and also of the largest city in the USA.
>
> **Hawaii:** Is the 50th state of the USA. It is a group of eight major islands and some smaller ones in the Pacific Ocean, southwest of San Francisco. Its capital is Honolulu. The islands are volcanic and have beautiful coral reefs around them.

Warm up

Ask students to look at the title of the text and the pictures and to predict what they think it will be about (a teenager going on holiday to Hawaii).

(a) Students now read through the questions and read the text quickly to find their answers and the answers to their warm up predictions. Check answers.

Answers
He is going on a camping holiday in Hawaii. He is staying there for three weeks.

(b) Pre-teach any vocabulary (*summer camp, teenagers, kids, backpacks, jungle, trail, waterfalls, spectacular, valley, surf, instructor, coast, sea turtle, caves, couch potatoes, fit, experience*). Look at the pictures a–h and elicit the activities; write the activities on the board. Students now read the text and tick what Paul is doing. Do the first item as an example, if necessary.

> **Language note:** The expression *couch potato* is usually used to describe someone who spends a lot of time on a sofa/couch (or a chair) watching television.

Answers snorkelling, kayaking, hiking, surfing, planting trees

(c) Students read through sentences 1–8; check any problems. Go through the first item with them as an example, if necessary. Students complete the exercise. Remind them to provide information from the text to back up their true answers and they can correct the false answers. Check answers.

Answers
1 F (para 1: *... he usually goes away to a summer camp ...*)
2 T (para 2: *... leaving on 23 July ...*)
3 F (para 2: *... for kids from 14 to 18.*)
4 T (para 3: *... hiking through the jungle... /* para 4: *After this five-day walk ...*)
5 F (para 4: *... I don't know how to surf ...*)
6 T (para 6: *... we're sailing for three days ...*)
7 T (para 7: *Every night for the three weeks, we're camping in tents ...*)
8 F (para 7: *I think it's going to be a fantastic experience.*)

(d) In small groups, students decide if they would like to go on a summer camp like this and give their reasons. They can then decide which activities from Exercise 9b they would choose to do.

Weaker classes: It may be helpful to elicit some reasons why they may / may not want to go on such a trip and put them on the board, e.g.:

Against: too long; would miss their friends and families; too far from home

For: good experience; living outdoors is very healthy; learning about lots of new things; would get to know new people and make new friends

Vocabulary notebook
Students should note down any new vocabulary from the text.

10 Write

This activity can be prepared in class and completed for homework. Read through the instructions and prompt questions with students. Go through Paul's text in Exercise 9 with them again and focus on the sequencers (para 3: *First*; para 4: *After this*; para 5: *Then*; para 6: *After that*; para 6: *Finally*) explaining how and why each one is used. Remind students that they are writing this for a school magazine so the style can be fairly informal. Students make notes on the question prompts and then plan their articles. They can prepare a draft version which they can swap with a partner to check and then write up final versions.

11 What will happen?

Unit overview

TOPIC: The future; Science fiction

TEXTS
Reading and listening: to a dialogue inside a spaceship
Listening: to two teenagers talking about the future
Listening: to a song: *Space Oddity*
Reading and listening: photo story: *How embarrassing!*
Reading and writing: about your life in the future

SPEAKING
Asking and answering about future personal predictions

LANGUAGE
Grammar: *will/won't*
Vocabulary: Expressions to talk about the future
Pronunciation: *'ll*
Everyday English: *Anything else?*; *the best bit.*; *nonsense*; *How embarrassing!*

1 Read and listen

a Ask students to look at the picture. Read the instructions. Students answer the question. Elicit that the scene is set in the future. A spaceship is travelling through space. A planet (not Earth) is visible through the window of the spaceship. (Students might think the planet is Mars – known as the 'red' planet – but this will become clearer when they listen to the dialogue on the recording in Exercise 1b.)

Answer
They are in a spaceship.

b 🔊 Play the recording. Students say why Samantha and Jake are frightened.

TAPESCRIPT

Samantha Jake, we went into space nearly two years ago and we're still looking for planet Vulcan. What do you think? Will we find it?

Jake Oh, yeah. I'm sure we will. Relax, Sam. The universe is a big place, but we've got the computer to help us. We're in a new galaxy now. Perhaps we'll find it here.

Samantha OK, but I'm not sure about the computer. I know it's the most powerful computer in the world, but it tells terrible jokes.

Computer Good morning, you lucky space travellers! This is your friendly computer speaking. Did you sleep well?

Samantha Oh, hi, Bob. Yeah, fine, thanks. How about you?

Computer Excellent! My last night of sleep was excellent.

Jake Last night of sleep? What do you mean?

Computer Oh, sorry, guys. Didn't I tell you? That red and blue planet out there – can you see it? Our spaceship will crash into it in exactly … um … one minute from now.

Jake What? We can't! You have to do something!

Computer Sorry! I'd like to help, but the spaceship is out of control and there's nothing – I repeat, nothing – I can do. So in 45 seconds, we'll all be dead.

Samantha Help! Do something!

Computer I can't. But don't worry. When we die, in exactly … um … 30 seconds from now, it'll be very quick and it won't hurt! So I just want to say that I really enjoyed being with you on this spaceship. Thank you for being such good friends! 'We'll meet again, don't know where, don't know when …'

Answer
They are going to die. Their spaceship is going to crash into the red and blue planet.

c 🔊 Before you play the recording again, read through the words in the box with students. Check they understand them.

Weaker classes: They can work in pairs and try to fill in the spaces with the words in the box. They might remember some of them from the first listening.

Stronger classes: They can complete the dialogue with the words. Then play the recording and let them check or change their original. Check answers by asking three students to read the dialogue, taking the roles of Samantha, Jake and the computer.

Answers 1 space   2 universe   3 galaxy   4 jokes
5 planet   6 crash   7 spaceship

> **Language note:** The gap filling exercise should help clear up any problems with vocabulary. If not, ask students to help each other by explaining words, or ask them to look up the words in their dictionaries first, to see whether they still have problems.

OPTIONAL ACTIVITY

Stronger classes
Ask students to match these related words and their definitions:
1 galaxy
2 planet
3 space
4 universe

a the large group of stars which includes the Sun and all the planets

b all of space, including the stars and planets

c the area outside Earth's air, where the stars and planets are found

d a very large round object which moves around the Sun or another star

Answers 1 a   2 d   3 c   4 b

(d) Read through the ideas in the box with students first. Then, in pairs, students discuss the question. They can choose the most likely idea and say why they think this will happen or they can make a different prediction. Ask for feedback at the end of the exercise and discuss any interesting ideas further.

(e) 🔊 Play the recording. Find out how many students were right about their predictions.

TAPESCRIPT

Computer   ... I really enjoyed being with you on this spaceship. Thank you for being such good friends! 'We'll meet again, don't know where, don't know when, But I know we'll meet again some sunny day ...'

Samantha   Look! The planet's getting closer! Jake, we have to do something!

Jake   I know Sam, I know. Don't worry – I'll think of something. Um .... um ...

Computer   15 seconds, guys! It was nice knowing you!

Samantha   Well? Jake? I don't want to die, Jake!

Jake   Oh, my darling. Remember what the computer said? 'It won't hurt.' Let's just ... close our eyes ...

Computer   Five seconds!

Jake   I'll never forget you, Sam.

Samantha   Jake! I love ...

Computer   Whooaarmmmmm!!

Samantha   What was that?

Jake   Wow! We missed it. Our spaceship suddenly turned right at the last minute! What happened?

Computer   Ha, ha, ha, ha, ha! Fooled you! Remember what day it is today?

Jake   Let me see. Um ... April the first 3003.

Computer   April Fool!

Samantha   Oh! When we get back to Earth, I'm going to tell them about you, and they'll break you into little pieces.

Computer   Oh, come on, Samantha!! Just my little joke! Ha, ha ...

Language note: 1 April is the day people usually play tricks or jokes on each other. If someone falls for the joke (i.e. believes it is true) they are called *April Fool*. The joke has to be played in the morning, no later than midday.

2 Grammar

will/won't

(a) Read the example sentences with the class. Ask them to find the word (positive or negative) that is next to each verb in each sentence (*will* ('*ll*) / *won't*). Students look for and underline other examples of *will* ('*ll*) or *won't* in the text. Check answers.

Answers
Jake: *I'm sure we will.*
Jake: *Perhaps we'll find it here.*
Computer: *Our spaceship will crash into it ...*
Computer: *... we'll all be dead.*
Computer: *... it'll be very quick and it won't hurt.*
Computer: *We'll meet again.*

(b) Read the instructions aloud with the students. Do the first item with students as an example, if necessary. Students complete the table and the rule. Check answers.

Answers
Positive: 'll
Negative: won't
Question: Will
Short answers: will; won't
Rule: 'll; won't

Language notes
1 *'ll* is the contracted form of *will*.
The negative form of *will* is *will not*, which is contracted to *won't*.
Both *will* and *won't* remain unchanged for all persons, singular and plural.

2 When we use a third person noun (not pronoun), we don't usually contract *will*, because this can sometimes be clumsy to pronounce, e.g.:
My mother will be cross. NOT ~~My mother'll be cross.~~ / *The doctor will know you're not ill.* NOT ~~The doctor'll know you're not ill.~~

(c) Ask students to read through the verbs in the box and the dialogue. Go through the example with students. Students then complete the exercise. Check answers.

Answers 1 won't get   2 'll be   3 won't go   4 'll stay   5 won't help   6 will give   7 'll find

(d) Students practise the dialogue in pairs. Ask a few stronger students to act the dialogue out for the class.

Grammar notebook
Students may find it useful to note down the grammar table and the rules in their notebooks for future reference.

3 Pronunciation

'll

a 🔊 Ask students to read through sentences 1–4. Tell students that they are going to listen to the sentence pairs. Explain that in each sentence a there is a verb without 'll and in sentence b, the contraction of will ('ll) is heard. Read the first two sentences aloud yourself, if necessary, for students to hear the difference. Play the recording. Students say whether they hear sentence a or b in each pair. Check answers.

TAPESCRIPT
1 I'll ask the teacher.
2 They go to school early.
3 We'll have a lot of work to do.
4 I'll go to London by train.

Answers 1 b   2 a   3 b   4 b

b Students read out the b sentences, paying attention to the contraction 'll.

c Students work in pairs. Monitor them as they work, making sure students swap roles. If necessary, drill any items which are still causing students problems.

Stronger classes: They can think of their own sentences in the style of Exercise 3a and work with a partner to guess which ones they are saying.

4 Listen

🔊 Read the instructions aloud with the class and make sure they understand what they have to do while listening. (Tell them to ignore the last two columns for the time being.)

Play the recording. If necessary, pause the tape after the example item and go through it with students to check they understand what to do. Continue with the recording for students to mark their charts, before comparing in pairs. Check answers.

TAPESCRIPT

Interviewer Cristina, what do you think will happen in your future?

Cristina Oh well, I think I'll get married and I'll probably have two or three children. I love children.

Interviewer Do you think you'll go to university?

Cristina Yes, I think so. I'll probably go to university.

Interviewer And do you think you'll get a good job?

Cristina Well, I don't know. But I hope to get a good job, yes.

Interviewer How about living abroad? Do you think you'll do that?

Cristina No, I doubt it. I'll probably go on holiday to other countries, but I don't think I'll live abroad.

Interviewer Will you learn to drive when you're older?

Cristina Yes, I will – when I'm 18 or 19.

Interviewer One last question. Lots of young people dream of being famous. Do you think you'll be famous one day?

Cristina Oh, no – I doubt I'll be famous!

Interviewer OK. Now here's Paolo. Hi, Paolo, how are you?

Paolo Hi. I'm fine, thanks.

Interviewer What about your future? What do you think will happen?

Paolo Well, maybe I'll get married one day, but I'm sure I won't have children.

Interviewer Really? Why's that?

Paolo I just don't want to be a father, really.

Interviewer Oh, OK. What about your job?

Paolo Well, it's difficult to know, but I hope to find a good job. I don't think I'll go to university but I'll go and live in another country for a few years. I want to learn one or two foreign languages. I think that will help me to find an interesting job.

Interviewer What about driving a car?

Paolo Oh yes, I'm sure I'll learn to drive when I'm 18.

Interviewer How about becoming famous? Do you think you'll be famous one day?

Paolo No, I don't think so!

Interviewer Right. Thanks very much, Paolo ...

Answers
Cristina: get married ✓; have children ✓; go to university ✓; get a good job ✓; live abroad ✗; learn to drive ✓; become famous ✗
Paolo: get married ✓; have children ✗; go to university ✗; get a good job ✓; live abroad ✓; learn to drive ✓; become famous ✗

5 Vocabulary

Expressions to talk about the future

a Read the instructions with students. Students answer the question and then think about how they say I hope to in their own language.

Answer
She wants to get a good job but she's not sure if she will.

b Read through sentences 1–8 with students and write the column headings on the board. Give an example of your own for each column before students start (e.g. I think I'll teach in this school next year. I don't think I will go to England this summer. I'll probably go to England for Christmas.) Ask them which of these things you believe will happen (sentence A), which won't happen (sentence B), and which is possible that it will happen (sentence C). Students now classify the sentences under each heading. Check answers.

Answers 1 A   2 C   3 B   4 B   5 C   6 B   7 C   8 A

Vocabulary notebook
Students should note down these expressions and some translations or example sentences in their notebooks.

6 Speak

(a) Students go back to the chart at the top of page 92. This time, they complete the *Me* column.

(b) Read the example dialogue with students before they begin. Students then work in pairs to ask the questions and note down their partner's answers in the column marked *My Partner*. Ask several pairs to demonstrate their dialogues to the class. Ask other students to say whether their partners think they will be married / live abroad, etc. Are there any interesting answers? If so, discuss these in more detail as a class.

OPTIONAL ACTIVITY
Students use the information in the table in Exercise 4 and go around the class asking other students their opinions. Students pool the information and draw up a chart showing the general opinions in the class.

7 Listen

If you set the background information as a homework research task ask students to tell the class what they have found out.

BACKGROUND INFORMATION
David Bowie: Was born David Robert Jones in London in 1947. He changed his name in 1966 since there was another singer called David Jones. His first hit was with *Space Oddity* in 1969 and the song was based on the Stanley Kubrick film *2001: A Space Odyssey*. Throughout the 1970s David Bowie had many more musical successes and was also well known for his extreme costumes and outfits on stage. He has also acted in films, e.g. *The Man Who Fell to Earth* (1976), *Merry Christmas, Mr Lawrence* (1983) and *Basquiat* (1996).

Space Oddity: See above.

NASA: The National Aeronautics and Space Administration was created on 1 October 1958 by the USA. Its purpose is to conduct research and develop space programmes for people to travel into space, amongst other things.

(a) Read the instructions aloud with the class. Elicit the meaning of *astronaut* (A) (traveller in a spaceship) and *Ground Control* (GC) (person on Earth who is in contact with a spaceship as it travels through space).

As there is some potentially tricky vocabulary in the song, you may wish to pre-teach some of the vocabulary (try to elicit the meanings first by asking questions):

1 *pills*: What kind of food do astronauts eat? Do they get fresh food? Or do they take tablets/pills? (Answer: *pills*)
2 *helmet*: What do we call the 'hat' astronauts wear on their heads? (Answer: *helmet*)
3 *commencing countdown*: Before the space ship takes off (= moves up into space), there is a countdown, ending with ... 3, 2, 1, Blast off!
4 *check ignition*: When you start a car or motorbike, where do you put the key? In the door? In the ignition? (Answer: *the ignition*)
5 *You've really made the grade*: When you do a test, and the teacher says, 'Well done, you've really made the grade!' What does this mean? Have you done well or badly? (Answer: *well*)
6 *the papers want to know whose shirts you wear*: Explain that when someone becomes famous, the newspapers want to know all sorts of details about them, e.g. which shops they shop at, which designer clothes they buy, etc.
7 *capsule*: Explain that this is the part of the spaceship where the astronaut sits, which breaks away from the rest of the space ship and returns to Earth with the astronaut.
8 *floating in a most peculiar way*: Explain that there is no gravity in space, so you can't walk on the ground like we do on Earth. Your feet don't touch the ground, you float (almost like flying) in a strange (peculiar) way.
9 *tin can*: What does the space capsule looks like from far below, on Earth? Does it look a bit like a can of fizzy drink?
10 *circuit's dead*: Ask how the radio connection between space and Earth works. Explain there is an electrical current connecting them. *What happens when this electrical circuit 'goes dead'? Does it still work, or not?* (Answer: *not*)

Play the recording. In pairs, students mark each verse A or GC. Check answers, playing and pausing the song again as necessary.

TAPESCRIPT
See the song on page 93 of the Student's Book.

Answers
Verse: 1 GC   2 GC   3 GC   4 A   5 A   6 A   7 GC

(b) Students read through questions 1–6. Check any problems. In pairs or small groups, students answer the questions.

Answers
1 Because he is a famous person/astronaut.
2 It's the space capsule.
3 Out of the space capsule.
4 He is floating because there is no gravity in space.
5 Very calm (*I'm feeling very still*).
6 Probably he will die in space, as something has gone wrong.

If students still have problems with some of the vocabulary in the song, ask them to help each other work out the meaning, or look up the words in a dictionary.

(c) 🔊 If students have enjoyed listening to the song, play the recording again and students can sing along.

Vocabulary notebooks
Students may find it useful to note down some of the vocabulary from the song in their notebooks.

How embarrassing!

8 Read and listen

If you set the background information as a homework research task ask students to tell the class what they have found out.

BACKGROUND INFORMATION
Fortune cookies: These are small Chinese cakes which contain a slip of paper, on which a prediction is made. They are often given at the end of a meal in a Chinese restaurant.

Warm up

Ask students to look at the pictures and the people. Ask them who the people are (Lucy, her parents and her brother, Rick). Then ask them to look at the title and predict what they think is embarrassing.

(a) 🔊 Read through the questions with students. Students answer the questions quickly and find the answers to their predictions in the Warm up. Play the recording while students listen and check answers.

TAPESCRIPT
See the photo story on page 94 of the Student's Book.

Answers
1 A Chinese restaurant.
2 The end (because the bill has arrived).

(b) Go through the example, if necessary. Students then work in pairs and complete the exercise. Check answers by asking different students to read out different sentences in the correct order.

Answers a 3   b 6   c 1   d 7   e 5   f 4   g 2

┌ **OPTIONAL ACTIVITY** ─────────────
In groups, students can act out the dialogue from the photo story.

9 Everyday English

(a) Read the expressions aloud with the class. In pairs, students find them in the photo story and decide who said them (and to whom). Check answers. Students then translate them into their own language.

Answers
1 The waiter to Dad
2 Lucy to Dad
3 Lucy to Dad
4 Mum to everyone
5 Mum to Dad

(b) Students complete the sentences with the vocabulary from Exercise 9a. Do the first item as an example, if necessary. Remind students to read through the whole dialogue before deciding which expressions to use. Check answers.

Answers
1 the best bit
2 Anything else?
3 I don't believe it!
4 nonsense
5 How embarrassing!

Vocabulary notebook
Students should note down the expressions from the dialogue on page 95 under the *Everyday English* section.

┌ **OPTIONAL ACTIVITIES** ─────────────
Stronger classes
Students can write their own short dialogues, using the expressions in Exercise 9a, and then act them out in front of the class.

Weaker classes
They can act out the dialogues in Exercise 9b.

10 Write

Students can do the preparation in class, and complete the writing at home.

Ask students to read the model provided and point out the use of *will, won't, probably, hope to,* etc.

Students then work in pairs and discuss their ideas about their future job, family life, friends, house, money, car, etc. They make notes under each heading. Remind students that they must expand their notes when they do their final piece of writing.

Students can read each other's finished competition entries and vote for the winner.

12 Never give up!

Unit overview

TOPIC: Doing difficult things, not giving up

TEXTS
Reading and listening: a magazine article about a mountain climbing trip
Listening: to biographical information about Wilma Rudolph
Reading: a text about New Americans
Writing: an email to a friend, giving advice

SPEAKING
Describing actions
Re-telling a story

LANGUAGE
Grammar: *too* + adjective; Adverbs
Vocabulary: The weather
Pronunciation: /əʊ/ *go*

1 Read and listen

BACKGROUND INFORMATION

Nepal: Or The Kingdom of Nepal is in Asia. It is bordered by China to the north and India to the west, south and east. The capital is Katmandu.

Himalayas: The Himalayan mountains are in the north of Nepal and include Mount Everest, the world's highest mountain.

Warm up

Ask students if they have ever been mountain climbing. If so, where? If not, would they like to? Who did they go with and how high was the mountain they climbed?

(a) Students look at the picture and answer the questions. They can discuss these in pairs, or you can ask the whole class for their ideas.

Answers
They are climbing a mountain. They could fall, there could be an avalanche, they could get caught in a snow storm, etc.

(b) Read through questions 1–3 with students and tell students to read the text through very quickly to find the answers to the questions. Now read the text slowly with the class for them to check their answers.

Answers
1　Mountain climbers: Glen Stephens and his friends Gaby, Craig and Tom.
2　In Nepal, in the Himalayas.
3　There was an avalanche.

(c) Students look at the title of the text again and in pairs decide what it means. Ask for ideas from the class.

Answer
It means to continue doing something (with determination) despite having problems.

(d) 🔊 Read through the definitions with students. Play the recording for students to find the words to match them. Check answers.

Stronger classes: Could do this without listening and listen only to check.

Weaker classes: Pause the recording at the relevant points for each answer and play it again as necessary.

Answers 1　bitterly　2　suddenly

TAPESCRIPT
See the reading text on page 96 of the Student's Book.

(e) In small groups, students discuss the questions. Ask for class feedback.

OPTIONAL ACTIVITIES
You may want to ask some more general comprehension questions on the text:
1　*Why was it too dangerous to continue climbing?*
2　*Why did they decide to continue?*
3　*Why did they start falling?*
4　*How far did they fall?*
5　*How were they hurt?*
6　*How many days later did they reach the top of the mountain?*

Answers
1　Because the weather was very bad, there was snow and it was bitterly cold.
2　Because the weather got better.
3　An avalanche started.
4　50 metres.
5　Tom's leg was hurt and Gaby's arms were cut.
6　Two days later.

Stronger classes:
Ask students to find the opposites of these words in the text:
1 *safe*　2 *light*　3 *late*　4 *bad*　5 *quiet*　6 *easy*
7 *energetic*

Students can use dictionaries, if necessary.

Answers 1　dangerous　2　dark　3　early　4　good
5　loud　6　difficult　7　exhausted

2 Grammar

too + adjective

(a) Read the sentences aloud and match the first one as an example with students. Students match the other items. Check answers. Then ask students to translate the underlined expressions into their own language. Do they notice any similarities or differences?

Now ask students to look at the adjectives in the second part of each sentence and ask them what they think the word *too* does to the adjective (it intensifies it). Elicit a few more adjectives and put them on the board, then elicit a few sentences from students using *too* + one of the adjectives on the board.

Answers 1 b   2 c   3 a

> **Language note:** It may be useful to tell students that when we put *too* in front of an adjective it usually implies a negative meaning. Compare: *It was very dark to continue the climb. / It was too dark to continue the climb. Too* + adjective is often used in the construction *too* + adjective + infinitive, e.g. ... *too dark to climb.*

(b) Go through the adjectives in the box with students and then the example. Students work in pairs or individually to complete the sentences. Check answers.

Answers 1 too difficult   2 too short
3 too expensive   4 too cold   5 too young

(c) Read through the expressions in the box with students and go through the example. Remind students of the differences between using *very* and *too* with adjectives (see Language note above). In pairs, students complete the exercise. Check answers.

Answers 1 very big   2 too big   3 too heavy
4 very heavy   5 very old   6 too old

OPTIONAL ACTIVITIES

Ask students to find the opposites of the words in Exercise 2b. Check the answers by calling out one of the words in Exercise 2b and asking students to give you the opposite.

Answers
difficult – easy; tall – short; expensive – cheap; cold – hot; young – old

Stronger classes
Give students some more adjectives, such as in the list 1–8 below. Ask them to find the opposites. Students can use a dictionary if necessary.

1 *wide*   2 *new*   3 *beautiful*   4 *early*
5 *dark*   6 *dry*   7 *full*   8 *quiet*

Answers
1 narrow   2 old   3 ugly   4 late
5 light   6 wet   7 empty   8 noisy

Grammar notebook
Students may find it useful at this point to note down the key points from this grammar section and any useful translations.

3 Vocabulary

The weather

(a) 🔊 Give students an example using the weather today, for example:

T: What's the weather like today, Alberto?
Alberto: It's hot/cold etc.

Then read through the weather expressions with students and tell them to match them with the pictures. Students can compare answers in pairs. Then play the recording for students to listen and check. Play the recording again, for students to repeat each expression.

TAPESCRIPT/ANSWERS
a 1 It's hot today.
b 4 It's cold today.
c 3 It's cool today.
d 2 It's warm today.

> **Language note:** It may be useful to point out to students that English uses the verb *be* for weather expressions, e.g. *It's hot.* NOT ~~It makes/does hot~~. Ask them to translate the expressions into their own language and compare them with English.

(b) Students read through the weather expressions in the box. Check any problems. Go through the example with students. Students complete the exercise. Check answers.

Answers 1 foggy   2 snowing   3 cloudy   4 windy
5 sunny   6 raining

4 Grammar

Adverbs

(a) Read through the examples from the text with students. If necessary, refer them back to the text where they can see each sentence in context. Write the headings *Adjectives* and *Adverbs* on the board. Look at the example sentences again and ask students the following questions: *How cold was it?* Elicit *bitterly.* Do the same for the other sentences: *How did his leg hurt?* (*badly*), *How did the snow fall?* (*heavily*), *How do they work?* (*hard*).

Explain to students that adverbs describe adjectives. Ask them to look at each adverb and try and work out which adjective they come from (*bitter, bad, heavy, hard*). Read through the rule with students and then students complete it. While they are doing this put the adverbs and the elicited adjectives they come from on the board. Check answers. To check understanding at this point, call out a few adjectives and ask students for the adverb (e.g. *quick – quickly, soft – softly*).

Answers
verbs; -ly; i; -ly

b Refer students back to the text on page 96 and tell them to go through it and find examples of adverbs. Students can compare answers in pairs. Ask some pairs to read out their answers to the class.

Answers
Para 1: ... *they like to play hard too* ...
Para 2: ... *but suddenly it changed* ...
Para 2: ... *so they started early* ...
Para 3: *Luckily, their ropes* ...
Para 3: *They stood up slowly.*

At this point you can ask students to work out which adjectives these adverbs come from.

Answers
hard – hard, sudden – suddenly, early – early, lucky – luckily, slow – slowly

c Read through the tables with students and go through the regular and irregular examples with them. Using the information from Exercises 4a and b, students now complete the tables. Check answers.

Answers
Regular adverbs: badly, loudly, quietly, luckily, easily
Irregular adverbs: early, hard

d Students read through sentences 1–5. Check any problems. Go through the example with them, eliciting the second adverb (*well*). Remind students to read the whole sentence and to look carefully at the second sentence since they will find the information there to help them choose their adverb. Check answers.

Answers 1 well 2 quietly 3 late 4 slowly
5 hard

─── OPTIONAL ACTIVITY ───

In small groups or in front of the class, students can act out some mini-scenes with adverbs. The other students have to guess the whole sentence or the adverb. Set a time limit of one minute for students to guess the answers. Students get one point for guessing the correct adverb and two points for guessing the whole situation correctly. The group/student with most points is the winner.

Example sentences/situations (or students can provide their own):
- *eating a banana slowly*
- *arriving late for your class*
- *speaking English quickly*
- *singing loudly in the shower/bath*
- *walking quietly out of the house*

5 Speak

a Read through the three questions with students. If necessary, do the first question and answer as an example. For example:

T: Silvia, do you get up early or late?
Silvia: I get up early. I get up at 6.30.

Then, in pairs, students ask and answer. Do not ask for feedback at this stage.

b Read through the adverbs in the box and go through the example dialogue first. Students then continue from Exercise 5a asking and answering about other things they can do. Remind them to use present simple tenses when asking and answering. Set a time limit for this. After a few minutes, swap pairs and students can give information about their partner to a new partner, e.g. *Silvia gets up early and she can speak English well. She can't play the piano well but she can sing.*

Grammar notebook
Students should copy down the Adjective and Adverb tables from this unit and learn the adverbs. They can ask a partner to test them on the adverbs.

6 Pronunciation
/əʊ/ (go)

a Drill the word *go* a few times and check students are clear how it is pronounced. If students are having problems with this sound, show them how to make their lips very round as in the English exclamation *Oh!* and practise a few more times. Play the recording, for students to repeat each word.

TAPESCRIPT
show, no, clothes, rope, homework, houseboat, snowing

b Students read through sentences 1–6. Explain that they will listen to the recording and they must underline the /əʊ/ sound in each sentence where it occurs. Do the first item as an example aloud if necessary.

TAPESCRIPT/ANSWERS
1 Only a few more metres!
2 They stood up slowly.
3 They decided to go on.
4 The snow was bitterly cold.
5 Sorry! I broke the window.
6 A: Who's on the phone?
   B: I don't know.

7 Listen

If you set the background information as a homework research task ask students to tell the class what they have found out.

BACKGROUND INFORMATION

Wilma Rudolph: She was born on 23 June, 1940. Her father had eleven children from a first marriage and she was the fifth of eight children in his second marriage. She contracted polio at the age of four and lost the use of her left leg. She was the first American woman runner to win three gold medals in the Olympic Games. In the 1960 Olympics she made history in Rome when she was the first American woman to win three gold medals in track and field events. There is more information about her in the tapescript.

Bill Clinton: Born William Jefferson Blythe on 19 August, 1946, he became the 42nd president of the USA in 1992. A Democrat, he studied at Georgetown University and also at Oxford University, UK.

(a) Read the instructions with the class and ask students to look at the photos. Ask them who they think Wilma Rudolph was. (She was a black American athlete in the 1960s.)

They work in pairs to predict the correct order of the pictures. Do not check answers at this stage.

(b) ◁))) Now play the recording. Students check or change their order, if necessary.

Weaker students: It may help to pause the recording after each answer.

TAPESCRIPT

Amy ... so I have to find out about a sportsperson, and ... well, I don't know who to write about.

Mother I know someone you can choose.

Amy Who?

Mother Wilma Rudolph.

Amy Who?

Mother Wilma Rudolph. She was a great runner and a really interesting woman.

Amy Tell me about her.

Mother Well, she was born in Tennessee in the USA in 1940 and her family were very poor. When Wilma was a baby, she got a very dangerous illness called polio. She didn't die, but she couldn't walk very well and when she was five, she started to wear a metal thing – a brace – on her leg, to help her to walk.

Amy Hang on – you mean she couldn't walk when she was young, but she became a great runner?

Mother That's right. Every day her parents helped her to walk. And when she was 11 ... well, one day, when she was in church, she just took off her leg brace, and started walking.

Amy Wow!

Mother Then she got interested in sport, especially running. And when she was 14, she got a sports teacher to help her, and she worked very hard and she became a really good runner. So in 1956 she went to Australia, to the Olympic Games, and she won a bronze medal in the relay race. And she was only 16, remember.

Amy Brilliant!

Mother Hang on, that's not all. She kept running – her dream was to win a gold medal – and four years later, in 1960, she went to Rome and she won three gold medals for running.

Amy What an amazing woman. Huh! Is she still alive?

Mother No, she died in 1994. But before that, after she stopped running, she became a school teacher when she was about 25. And in 1993 – I think it was 1993 – she got a special prize from the president, Bill Clinton, remember him?

Amy Yes, Mum, I *do* know who President Clinton was!

Mother OK, fine. Well, there's someone you can write about for your project.

Amy Yeah, maybe I will. So, tell me again ... she was born in 1940 ...

Answers a 3   b 5   c 6   d 8   e 7   f 2   g 1   h 4

(c) ◁))) Play the recording again, pausing it at the point where the first age/date is mentioned. Students write the date or age, as in the example. Continue playing the recording. Check answers, replaying the recording as necessary.

Answers
a 11 years old
b 1956 and 16 years old
c 1960
d 1993
e 25 years old
f 5 years old
g 1940
h 14 years old

8 Speak

Using the pictures in Exercise 7 and the information in Exercises 7b and c, students talk about Wilma Rudolph. They can work in pairs, and try to remember as much about her life as possible. Ask several pairs to tell their stories to the class, and see if anyone can add any details.

Culture in mind

9 Read

If you set the background information as a homework research task ask students to tell the class what they have found out.

BACKGROUND INFORMATION

John F. Kennedy: Born 29 May, 1917 in Brookline, Massachusetts. He was the 35th president of the USA from 1960 until his assassination in 1963.

Irish migrants: It is estimated that 1,600,000 Irish people emigrated to the USA between 1847 and 1854 as a result of the Great Potato Famine of 1845–49.

Warm up

Ask students if they know anyone who has emigrated. If so, where did they go and why? This can be done in L1 if necessary.

(**a**) Students read the questions and look at the photos and the people in them. They then read the text quickly to check their predictions. Remind them that they don't need to understand every word of the text.

(**b**) Pre-teach the following vocabulary if necessary or ask stronger students to look up the words in a dictionary (some of these items will be dealt with in Exercise 9c): *jobs, opportunities, migrant, country, farm, strange, determined, succeed, look down on, newcomers, share, apartment, crowded, building, manual, skyscraper, gradually, successful, business, enrich, strengthen, fabric.*

Read through sentences 1–6 with students. Check any problems. Go through the first item with them as an example. Remind students in a multiple-choice activity they should find the correct place in the text for the answer and check all the possibilities first with the information in the text. Students can check answers in pairs and then give feedback to the class.

Answers 1 b 2 a 3 a 4 b 5 c 6 a

(**c**) Read through items 1–6 with students. Do the first item with them as an example. Students complete the exercise. Check answers.

> **Language note:** *Apartment* is the American English word for a flat and *skyscraper* is also an American English word.

Answers 1 century 2 returned 3 newcomers
4 apartments 5 manual 6 skyscrapers

Vocabulary notebook
At this point students should note down any new vocabulary from the text in their notebooks.

10 Write

(**a**) Students read the question and then Spiros's email. Check any vocabulary problems.

Answer
Because he's finding English very difficult and he's getting terrible test results.

(**b**) This can be set for homework. Read through the expressions in the box and check students understand how and when to use them. Then look at the start of the email reply with students and explain that they must continue the reply using the expressions from the box. Students plan their reply and complete the exercise in class or at home.

Module 3 Check your progress

1 Grammar

(a) 2 more difficult   3 easiest   4 worst   5 bigger
6 better   7 worse   8 most important

(b) 2 's meeting / is meeting Gerard in a café.
3 are going to the cinema.
4 are having lunch.
5 she's doing / is doing her homework.
6 her cousins are arriving from Canada.

(c) 2 'll stay / will stay   3 'll become / will become
4 won't rain   5 Will; go   6 won't be

(d) 2 badly   3 easy   4 well   5 slowly   6 loud
7 slow; late

2 Vocabulary

(a) 1 communicate   2 mean   3 imitate   4 translate
5 accent   6 guess; look up

(b) in/on water: windsurfing, snorkelling, canoeing,
sailing
not in/on water: camping, horse-riding, sightseeing,
cycling, sunbathing

(c) Across: Down:
5 raining   1 sunny
7 cloudy   2 warm
8 cold   3 foggy
                    4 windy
                    6 hot
                    7 cool

3 Everyday English

2 nonsense   3 the best bit   4 believe it
5 embarrassing   6 anything else

How did you do?
Check students' results with them and if necessary
give students extra practice in weaker areas.

Module 4
The things people do!

YOU WILL LEARN ABOUT ...

Ask students to look at the pictures on the page. Ask students to read through the topics in the box and check they understand each item. You can ask them the following questions, in L1 if appropriate:

1 *Have you ever seen a gorilla?*
2 *Do you think customs in China are very different from your country?*
3 *Do you know any world records?*
4 *What do you do at New Year?*
5 *Who was Elvis Presley?*
6 *What does a tourist need to know about British customs before they visit the country?*

In small groups, students discuss which topic area they think each picture matches.

Check answers.

Answers
1 A meeting with a gorilla
2 Different cultures
3 Amazing records
4 New Year celebrations and resolutions
5 The fans of Elvis Presley
6 Tips for tourists in Britain

YOU WILL LEARN HOW TO ...

Use grammar

Go through the example with students. Stronger students should be able to continue with the other items on their own or in pairs.

Weaker classes: Put the grammar headings on the board and give an example of your own for each item, e.g. *You must do your English homework every weekend. You shouldn't watch TV when you're doing your homework. What's your new teacher like? If I don't do my homework, I won't pass my exam. Have you ever been to London?*

In pairs, students now match the grammar items in their book. Check answers.

Answers
be going to: I'm going to get fit.
must/mustn't: You must remember to feed the dog.
should/shouldn't: You shouldn't arrive late.
What's it like?: What's the new girl like?
First conditional: If I don't move, he'll go away.
Present perfect + *ever/never*: I've never been to Paris.

Use vocabulary

Write the headings on the board. Go through the items in the Student's Book and check understanding. Now ask students if they can think of one more item for the *Phrasal verbs* heading. Elicit some responses and add them to the list on the board. Students now do the same for the other headings. Accept suggestions in L1 and translate them into English as necessary. Some possibilities are:

Phrasal verbs: (Unit 5) *climb up, pick up, put on, get in, come down, put down, take off, get out, work out, take away, keep (something) up*

Personality adjectives: *sensible, nice, happy, sad, funny*

Opinion adjectives: *brilliant, wonderful, terrible, great*

Animals: *cat, dog, zebra, rhino, gorilla, monkey, giraffe*

13 Good intentions

Unit overview

TOPIC: Intentions and resolutions

TEXTS
Reading and listening: about New Year's resolutions
Reading and listening: about an unlucky day
Writing: a reply to an email about New Year
Reading and listening: photo story: *A birthday party*

SPEAKING
Talking about future intentions
Making offers

LANGUAGE
Grammar: *be going to*: intentions and predictions; *must/mustn't*
Vocabulary: Phrasal verbs (2)
Pronunciation: *must/mustn't*
Everyday English: Making offers using *'ll*

1 Read and listen

If you set the background information as a homework research task ask students to tell the class what they have found out.

BACKGROUND INFORMATION

New Year's Eve: In Scotland this is called *Hogmanay*. It is traditional to sing the Scottish song *Auld Lang Syne* at midnight. The song was written by Robert Burns (1759–1796), a famous Scottish poet. Another new year tradition associated with Scotland is that of 'first footing' – people visit the houses of friends and relations to continue the celebrations after midnight and sometimes take small gifts! It is supposed to be good luck to be the first person in someone's house after midnight.

Auld Lang Syne: This was a song written by Robert Burns (1759–1796), a famous Scottish writer and poet. The chorus is the most famous part of the song and the song itself describes how people come together and remember the past and look forward to the future. *Auld Lang Syne* means 'times gone by'. The words of the chorus are as follows:

For Auld Lang Syne, my dear,
For Auld Lang Syne,
We'll tak a cup of kindness yet
For the sake of Auld Lang Syne.

Warm up

Ask students what they did last year / usually do at New Year. Do they have certain traditions they always carry out at New Year?

a Read the question with students and then ask them to read the text quickly to check their ideas. Remind them that they don't need to know every word in the text in order to answer the question. Check answers.

Answer
They have parties in their homes or in the streets and sing songs.

b Students read through the words/phrases. Do the first one with them as an example, locating the relevant point in the text. Students complete the exercise. Check answers.

Answers 1 New Year's Eve   2 midnight   3 dawn

c (🔊) Pre-teach *New Year's resolutions*, giving an example of your own. Check students understand they are going to listen to the teenagers in the photo talking about New Year's resolutions. Students read through resolutions 1–6. Check understanding. Play the recording, pausing it after the first item and asking students who said it. Elicit *Mark* and explain that they must write *M* in the box. Continue with the recording while students complete the exercise. Check answers, playing and pausing the recording as necessary for students to check or change their answers.

TAPESCRIPT

Annie Well, here we are – the first of January, a new year. Have you got any New Year's resolutions, Mark?

Mark Yes! I'm going to be more healthy this year.

Annie Yeah? How? What are you going to do?

Mark No more chocolate, for a start. I'm going to give up chocolate completely. From now on, it's going to be healthy food for me. I'm going to eat fruit every day. Also I'm going to take up scuba diving. I'm really determined to do that.

Annie Well, I've got two resolutions. First, I'm going to organise my life better. I'm going to clean out my room and throw away all my old papers and rubbish. It's going to be a totally new working environment!

Mark Oh, yeah, Annie. Can I believe this? What's your other resolution?

Annie Well, it's to do with my sister. We have arguments all the time, and we both get really angry and upset. But this year we're going to talk more and work out our problems.

Mark Do you think you can keep it up?

Annie   Well, we're going to try, anyway.

Mark   Good. I think it's going to be an interesting year.

Answers 1 M   2 M   3 A   4 M   5 A   6 M

── OPTIONAL ACTIVITY ──────────────

Students in small groups discuss New Year's resolutions they have made. If so, what were/are they? Have they been able to keep them? If not, why not?

2 Vocabulary
Phrasal verbs (2)

a 🔊 Ask students if they can remember what phrasal verbs are. Elicit a few examples from the ones they saw on the Module opener page or in Unit 5. Students read through verbs 1–5 and the definitions. Do the first item with them as an example, if necessary. Students complete the exercise. Check answers. Then play the recording for students to listen and repeat the phrasal verbs. To check understanding at this point, give an example of your own and ask a few students to give you examples for the other verbs.

Ask students which verb is usually associated with New Year's resolutions (*give up*). Remind them of Mark and Annie's conversation in Exercise 1c.

TAPESCRIPT
1 take up
2 give up
3 throw away
4 work out
5 keep up

Answers 1 b   2 d   3 a   4 e   5 c

b Students read through sentences 1–5. Go through the example with them, substituting all the other verbs and showing them why *give up* is the only possibility. Students complete the exercise. Remind them to use the correct form of the verb. They compare answers in pairs and then give feedback to the class.

Answers 2 worked out   3 took up   4 keep; up   5 threw; away

> **Language note:** Explain to students that some phrasal verbs can be split and a pronoun can be inserted between the first and second part. Highlight this using items 4 and 5 from Exercise 2b. This is not possible with all phrasal verbs and has to be learned.

── OPTIONAL ACTIVITIES ──────────────

Stronger students
Call out a list of verbs and ask students to give you the relevant particle to go with them to make them into phrasal verbs.

Weaker students
They can work in pairs. Write these verbs down and look them up in a dictionary to find the various particles.
Climb (up/down)
Turn (up/down/around)
Work (out)
Take (up/down/in/out)
Keep (up/in/out)

Vocabulary notebook
Students should note down the phrasal verbs from this unit in their *Phrasal verbs* section.

3 Grammar
be going to: intentions

a Books closed. Ask students if they can remember the dialogue between Mark and Annie in Exercise 1c. Ask them: *Who is going to be more healthy?* (Mark). *Who is going to be more organised?* (Annie). Then ask: *Were Mark and Annie talking about the past or the future?* (future). Explain that they were talking about future intentions and elicit the form of *be going to* which was used. It may be useful to write this on the board at this stage. Students now open their books at page 107. Read through the Rule box in Exercise 3a with them and check they understand. You can do this by asking them a few questions, e.g. *Alicia, are you going to do your homework tonight?* and elicit the short answer, *Yes, I am. / No, I'm not.* Students now complete the grammar table. Check answers.

Answers
Negative: aren't; isn't
Questions: Are; Is
Short answers: am; are; isn't

b Read through the words in the box with students and check understanding. They should remember most of these from the dialogue in Exercise 1c.

Students read through items 1–6. Go through the example with students, asking why *are going to* is used (because it is a plural subject) to check students have remembered all the forms of *be*. Students complete the exercise. Remind them to change any pronouns as necessary to match the subject. Check answers.

Weaker classes: They may find it useful to listen to Exercise 1c dialogue again before starting this exercise.

Answers
2 isn't going to be untidy
3 are going to work out their problems
4 is going to stop arguing with her sister
5 isn't going to eat unhealthy food
6 Mark: Are; going to throw away your rubbish
   Annie: am

── OPTIONAL ACTIVITY ──────────────

If it is appropriate, you could ask the groups to think of class resolutions which could be set for this year / the rest of the year. In small groups, students discuss the areas where they could be better as a class and write down at least two intentions using *going to*. Groups then give feedback and the class can vote on the best intentions. These could then be decorated and displayed on the walls.

be going to: predictions

(c) Read through the rule with students and give them another example of your own (e.g. *Look at those black clouds. It's going to rain soon.*). Check students understand that this is prediction because there is present evidence. Students read through items 1–6, then go through the example with them. Students complete the exercise. Remind them to use short forms where possible. Check answers.

Answers
2 isn't going to be / is not going to be
3 're going to love / are going to love
4 're going to be / are going to be
5 isn't going to get / is not going to get
6 Are; going to win

(d) Students look at the pictures and read through sentences 1–6. Explain that they must match one sentence with each picture. Do the first one as an example, if necessary. In pairs, students complete the exercise. Check answers.

Answers a 2 b 6 c 5 d 1 e 3 f 4

(e) This can be done for homework. Read through the instructions with students. Do the first item with them as an example. In pairs, students complete the exercise. Check answers.

Answers 1 P 2 I 3 P 4 I 5 P 6 I

4 Speak

(a) In pairs, students discuss their intentions.

Weaker classes: If necessary, elicit a few ideas about possible intentions and put them on the board, e.g.:

This evening / Next weekend: watch TV, do homework, go to the cinema, listen to music, go to a café

Next holiday: Spain / Greece / parents' village / grandparents' village / Britain / America

(b) Pairs now work with a new partner and tell them what their first partner's intentions are. Ask for some pairs to give feedback to the rest of the class. If there are any interesting intentions, discuss them further with the class.

5 Read and listen

(a) 🔊 Students look at the top picture and decide what they think Simon's parents want him to do. Elicit a few predictions. Students now read through the dialogue quickly; check any problems. Play the recording while students listen and check their answers. Were any of their predictions correct?

TAPESCRIPT
See the dialogue on page 108 of the Student's Book.

Answer
Post a letter and feed the dog.

(b) 🔊 Read through the questions with students. They look at the second picture to find the answers. Play the recording for students to check answers.

TAPESCRIPT

Mother I can't believe it. I'm never going to leave you alone in this house again!

Simon Oh, Mum, listen ...

Mother Well, just look at the dog. She's really hungry! Come on, Blackie.

Simon I know. I'm sorry, but ...

Mother You didn't even post the letter! And it was important, you know that.

Simon Look, Mum, you don't know what happened.

Mother Happened? Tell me, then.

Simon Well, when I left the house to post the letter, I heard someone shouting for help. It was Mr Smith next door.

Mother Oh, really? What was the problem?

Simon Well, he fell over and he really hurt himself. He couldn't stand up, and he was in a lot of pain.

Mother Oh, I'm sorry, Simon. Oh, the poor man. What did you do?

Simon Well, I called the ambulance, but that was only the beginning. When the ambulance arrived, I was going to post the letter – but then I realised I didn't have any money. So I went back to the house to get some money, and guess what? The door was closed, and the key was inside. So I couldn't get in!

Mother Oh dear!

Simon So I had to cycle to Grandma's place to get a key. And then ...

Father I can't believe it!

Mother It's OK, Richard. Just listen to his story first.

Father Sorry, no time for stories.

Mother What's going on?

Father It's awful. The car's locked, and the key's inside the car!

Mother Oh, no!

Answers
1 She's going to be angry with Simon. He hasn't posted the letter or fed the dog.
2 He didn't do what she asked because he was helping Mr Smith.

(c) 🔊 Write the letters a–g on the board. Remind students of the dialogue in Exercise 7b when Simon's parents return. Ask them: *What did Simon do first?* (He left the house to post the letter.) Write the number 1 beside e on the board. Explain that students must now order the other sentences. Play the recording again.

Students compare answers in pairs. Ask for volunteers to come out and order the sentences/items on the board. Play the recording once more, pausing after each answer if necessary.

Answers a 4   b 6   c 7   d 2   e 1   f 5   g 3

d In small groups, students discuss an unlucky day they have had. Remind them to use the past simple when re-telling their stories to the rest of the class.

Weaker groups: It may help them to elicit some prompts and put them on the board, e.g. *When was it? Who were you with? Where were you? What were you doing? What happened?*

┌─ OPTIONAL ACTIVITY ──────────────
│ Students can write out their unlucky day stories
│ for homework.

6 Grammar
must/mustn't

a Read through the example sentences with students. Ask students why Simon's mum asked him to do these things (because they were important). Now students read through the Rule box and the grammar table and complete the table. Check answers. To check understanding at this point give an example of your own and elicit a few more from students, e.g. *I must remember to go to the supermarket after school today. Maria, is there anything you must remember to do today?* etc.

Answers
Positive: must
Negative: mustn't

b Students read through the verbs in the box and look at the pictures. Go through the example with them. Students complete the exercise. Check answers.

Answers 2 must practise   3 mustn't miss
4 mustn't say   5 mustn't touch   6 must listen

7 Pronunciation
must & mustn't

a 🔊 Read out the first sentence, making sure that the stress on *must* is clear. Ask students which word was stressed in the sentence (*must*). Read through the instructions and the other sentences with students. Play the recording. Play the recording again, for students to repeat.

TAPESCRIPT
I must go to the post office later.
You <u>must</u> work harder.
You <u>must</u> come to my party!
We must go home now.

Answers
Sentences 2 and 3. Because it is important that these things are done.

b 🔊 Drill the pronunciation of *mustn't* /ˈmʌsənt/ a few times. Play the recording for students to listen and repeat.

TAPESCRIPT
You mustn't eat that!
We mustn't forget.
You mustn't drive too fast.
I mustn't be late.

c 🔊 Refer students back to the sentences they completed in Exercise 6b. In pairs, students take turns to read the sentences to each other and check their pronunciation. Monitor and drill *must/mustn't* if more practice is necessary. Play the recording for students to listen and check their pronunciation.

TAPESCRIPT
1   I mustn't be late for school.
2   You must practise more often.
3   We mustn't miss the beginning of the film.
4   I mustn't say anything stupid!
5   You mustn't touch it.
6   You must listen to this CD – it's great!

A birthday party
8 Read and listen
Warm up

Ask students if they have birthday parties. If so, what do they do? Students then look at the photo story. Ask them who features in this story (Lucy and her mum) and ask them to predict what they might be discussing.

a 🔊 Students read the photo story and answer the questions. Play the recording for students to check their answers and their predictions from the Warm up. Were any of their predictions correct?

TAPESCRIPT
See the photo story on page 110 of the Student's Book.

Answers
She's not happy about her parents being there or about the time they'll be back / the time the party will finish.

b Students read through the sentence parts. Do the first one with them as an example. Students complete the exercise. Students compare answers in pairs. Check answers. Play the recording again, if necessary.

Answers
a   at 10.30 in the evening. 5
b   she doesn't want her parents to be at the party. 3
c   16 next week. 1
d   to go out for the evening. 4
e   to have a barbecue at home. 2
f   too early for the end of the party. 6

9 Everyday English

a Students read the instructions and sentences 1–3.
Do the first one with them as an example, if necessary.
Check answers.

Answers
1 Simon to his mum (Exercise 5a).
2 Lucy's mum to Lucy.
3 Lucy's mum to Lucy.

b Read through the sentences with students and check
any problems. Go through the example with them.
Students complete the exercise. Remind them to read
each item carefully and look for any clues in the other
part that will help them match the offers. In pairs, they
compare answers. Check answers.

Answers 2 e 3 b 4 a 5 f 6 d

c Students read through the verbs in the box and look at
the pictures. Students use the verbs in the box to write
an offer for each picture. Do the first item with
students as an example, if necessary.

Answers 1 I'll answer 2 I'll fix 3 I'll help
4 I'll pay

10 Write

This exercise can be set for homework. The planning
can be done in class and the email written up at home.
Remind students how Scottish people celebrate New
Year (see Background information at the start of this
unit). Explain that Jessie is from Scotland and has
written this email. Students read through Jessie's email;
check any problems. To remind students how to
structure their reply ask them to match each item to
a paragraph in Jessie's email. Students then complete
the exercise. Collect these in to mark or students can
swap with a partner and the partner can correct
their email.

Answers
Jessie's New Year's Eve: para 2
Jessie's New Year's resolution: para 3
A resolution made by someone in Jessie's family:
para 3
What Jessie's doing this week: para 4

(14) You shouldn't do that!

Unit overview

TOPIC: Customs around the world; Advice

SKILLS

Reading and listening: about a magazine quiz and people discussing different cultures

Reading: a text with travel tips for people visiting Britain

Writing: a letter or email to a penfriend about to visit your country

SPEAKING

Giving advice and recommendations

Talking about what people/things/places are like

LANGUAGE

Grammar: *should/shouldn't*; *What's it like?*

Vocabulary: Personality adjectives; Adjectives for expressing opinions

Pronunciation: Silent consonants

1 Read and listen

If you set the background information as a homework research task ask students to tell you what they found out.

BACKGROUND INFORMATION

Photos show:

Brandenburg Gate, Berlin, Germany: Built 1788–91. From 1961–89 it was located in no-man's land between East and West Berlin and became a symbol of a divided city. In 1989 the borders between the two German countries were opened and the gate became the centre of German reunification.

The Great Wall, China: Over 2,000 years old, it is about 6,000 km long and up to 7.8 m high.

Big Ben, London: Big Ben is the name of the bell inside the tower, not the tower itself. Part of the Houses of Parliament, the clock dates back to 1858.

Mecca, Saudi Arabia: Birthplace of the prophet Mohammed and the religion he founded, Mecca is the centre of the Islamic world. It is estimated that each year, 2–2.5 million Muslims from around the world make a pilgrimage to Mecca.

Temple of the Emerald Buddha, Bangkok, Thailand: The temple was constructed to house what Thais consider to be the most sacred of all Buddhist images, the Emerald Buddha.

Mount Fuji, Japan: One of the most famous volcanoes in the world, Mount Fuji is 3,500 m above its surrounding plain. Its most recent eruption was in 1707–08.

Blue Mosque, Istanbul, Turkey: It was built by Sultan Ahmet in 1609 and took seven years to complete. It is called the Blue Mosque because of the beautiful blue Iznik tiles which decorate the inside.

The Taj Mahal, India: The building is in fact a tomb, as well as a 'symbol of eternal love'. It was built by the 5th Mughal emperor, Shah Jahan, in 1631 in memory of his second wife, Mumtaz Mahal, a Muslim Persian princess who died while giving birth to their 14th child.

Warm up

Ask students to look at the pictures and the title of the unit and the text. Ask them what they think the unit will be about (customs around the world). Check they understand the word *culture* in this context (the customs and attitudes that have developed in a particular country, influenced by the religion, history, etc. of that country).

(a) This activity will help them to understand the meanings of any difficult words. Go through the first one as an example with students. If necessary, students can check the words in their dictionaries, or ask you. Students work in pairs and match the pictures and the words. To check students understand you could mime *bow* and *cow*, touch the top of your head, indicate your pocket, point to an item made of leather and elicit the correct answers.

Answers 1 c   2 e   3 d   4 a   5 f   6 b

> ┌─ **OPTIONAL ACTIVITY** ─────────
> Before you do Exercise 1b, ask students the following questions to increase interest in the topic:
>
> *Where are the following countries?* (If possible, students should point them out on a map or explain exactly where they are): *Thailand, Japan, Saudi Arabia, Turkey, India, China, Germany, England.*
>
> Refer students to the photos a–h. Can they name the famous places? What do they know about them? They can do this in L1 if necessary.

(b) In pairs, students read through the sentences and try to match them with the countries. Explain that it doesn't matter if they don't know the answers as they'll find out when they listen to the recording; the aim is to get them to read the text and try to predict. Encourage students to guess the meaning from context and check any words or phrases they don't know in their dictionaries. Do the first item with them as an example, if necessary.

c 🔊 Play the recording for them to listen and check answers.

TAPESCRIPT

Boy Did you know that in Japan, children usually bow to their teacher when he or she enters the classroom?

Girl Yes, I know. It's polite to bow.

Woman My Chinese friend says you shouldn't give someone a clock in China.

Man Why not?

Woman It's bad luck, I think.

Man Apparently in Saudi Arabia you shouldn't give a toy dog as a present. In fact, you shouldn't give someone a card with a dog on it.

Woman Really?

Man Yes, it's in this book I'm reading about Saudi Arabia.

Boy Here in Turkey you shouldn't cross your arms when you're talking to someone.

Girl Oh?

Boy Yes, for Turkish people crossing your arms looks rude and unfriendly.

Girl I'm going to Germany next month. Is there anything I should remember?

Boy Well, one thing: if someone invites you for dinner, you should try not to be late. It isn't polite to come late.

Girl Oh, OK. In England it's usual to arrive a bit late. But only about five or ten minutes.

Man It says here that in Thailand you shouldn't touch the top of someone's head.

Woman That's interesting.

Man Apparently it's not polite.

Girl I want to buy a present for my Indian friend. What should I get?

Man Well, you shouldn't get anything made of leather. For the Hindus in India, cows are sacred.

Answers

1 e
2 b (the sound for *clock* is the same as the sound for *death* in Chinese characters)
3 d
4 g
5 c (although it's not rude to arrive on time, many people think it's more polite to be 5–10 minutes late to give the host/hostess time to make final preparations)

6 a (most Germans are good time-keepers and would consider it rude if you arrived late)
7 f (the top of the head is considered the most sacred part of the body in Thailand)
8 h (the cow is considered a sacred animal in India and is therefore not usually killed for meat or hide)

— OPTIONAL ACTIVITY ————

Ask the class which of the customs they found most interesting or surprising. Ask what customs there are in their own country that might be 'new' to foreigners, e.g. How do they normally greet friends or strangers? Do people shake hands when they meet, or do they embrace (put their arms around each other)? Are there any 'rules' foreigners should know about when they have a meal in the students' country?

2 Grammar
should/shouldn't

a Read through the example sentences with the class.

Books closed. Write the example sentences on the board, but with the target language gapped (*should/shouldn't*). Can they remember which words go in the spaces and what they mean? Ask students to quickly find more examples of *should* and *shouldn't* in the quiz on page 112 and underline them.

Read the rule with the class. Make sure students are clear that we usually use *should/shouldn't* when we are giving advice to someone.

b Students complete the grammar table. Point out that *should* is a modal verb and explain that we don't need to add *do* or *does* to make questions or negatives. Ask them what other modal verbs they can think of (*can, will, must, might,* etc.).

Answers
Negative: shouldn't
Short answers: should; shouldn't

c Students read through the verbs in the box and items 1–6. Go through the example. In pairs, students complete the exercise. Check answers by asking pairs to read one of their dialogues to the class.

Answers 2 should watch 3 Should; go; shouldn't watch 4 should go 5 Should; wear; should wear 6 shouldn't go

3 Speak

Divide students into pairs.

Weaker classes: It might be an idea to let all the Student As read Student A's role card together in pairs, so that they can discuss 'their problem' and possible solutions. Student Bs can work together and do the same with 'their' problem (see Student's Book pages 113 and 137).

Stronger classes: If your class is strong enough, you can write examples of some other ways of giving advice on the board, and encourage students to use these structures as well, e.g. *If I were you, I'd … . Why don't you (talk to your parents)? What about (talking to your parents)?*

Student A works with Student B and, taking turns, they tell each other about the problem on their role card and give each other advice, using *should/shouldn't*.

Ask several pairs to demonstrate their roleplays to the class. Find out what everyone thinks of the advice they were given.

4 Vocabulary
Personality adjectives

a 🔊 Students read through the adjectives in the box. Play the recording, for students to listen and repeat each adjective. Make sure students are stressing them in the correct place.

TAPESCRIPT
kind, hard-working, polite, honest, organised, cheerful, relaxed, friendly

┌─ OPTIONAL ACTIVITY ──────────────────

Stronger classes
Before going on to the next exercise, ask students if they can give definitions of the words.
A kind person … (helps other people and thinks about their feelings).
A polite person … (always says *please* and *thank you*).

b In pairs, students read the sentences and use the adjectives in the box in Exercise 4a to complete them.

Weaker classes: Do the first two or three examples with the whole class first. This exercise should help them work out the meaning of the adjectives, so don't worry if they are new to the students.

Encourage students to use their dictionaries, if they have them, and to help each other.

Answers 1 cheerful   2 honest   3 relaxed
4 hard-working   5 organised   6 kind   7 friendly
8 polite

c 🔊 Write the adjectives from Exercise 4a on the board. Students read through the adjectives in the box. Ask them if they can see any words which are similar to the adjectives in Exercise 4a (*dishonest, unfriendly, unkind, disorganised*).

Elicit from students that by adding the prefixes *dis-* and *un-* these adjectives are the opposites of the ones in Exercise 4a. Go through the first item with students and then students match the other adjectives to the pictures. Students check answers in pairs. Then play the recording for students to check or change their answers. Play the recording again, for students to repeat.

TAPESCRIPT/ANSWERS

1	disorganised	5	lazy
2	rude	6	miserable
3	unkind	7	unfriendly
4	dishonest	8	nervous

d Remind students of the opposite adjectives they matched in Exercise 4c. Ask them to put them into the table. Students now go through the other adjectives in Exercise 4c and try and match them to their opposites.

Answers 1 unkind   2 miserable   3 rude
4 dishonest   5 disorganised   6 nervous   7 lazy
8 unfriendly

┌──┐
│ **Language note:** Check students put the correct │
│ stress on the adjectives when a negative prefix is │
│ added: *happy – unhappy*. │
└──┘

┌─ OPTIONAL ACTIVITY ──────────────────

Stronger classes
Ask students to underline the prefixes in the adjectives in Exercise 4d. Give them the adjectives suggested below, without the prefixes, and ask students to make their opposites, using one of the prefixes they have underlined (*un-* or *dis-*):

(un)attractive, (dis)contented, (un)important, (un)exciting, (dis)pleased

Vocabulary notebook
Students should note down the table of adjectives from Exercise 4d and add any new adjectives when they come across them.

5 Pronunciation
Silent consonants

a 🔊 Students read through words 1–7. Do the example with them. Play the recording for students to listen and repeat. Students then underline the silent consonants in each word. Check answers.

TAPESCRIPT/ANSWERS

1 <u>h</u>onest   2 shoul<u>d</u>   3 sc<u>h</u>ool
4 <u>w</u>rite   5 clim<u>b</u>   6 <u>k</u>now   7 t<u>w</u>o

b 🔊 **Stronger classes:** They can underline the silent consonant in words 1–6 without listening first.

Weaker classes: Play the recording, pausing after each word for them to underline the silent consonant.

Play the recording again for students to check their answers, then play it again for students to repeat.

TAPESCRIPT/ANSWERS

1 shoul<u>d</u>n't   2 <u>Th</u>ailand   3 foreign   4 lis<u>t</u>en
5 i<u>s</u>land   6 fas<u>c</u>inating

c (◁))) Students read through the sentences then listen and repeat them. Play the recording again.

TAPESCRIPT
1 They should go to school.
2 I speak two foreign languages.
3 I know he's an honest person.
4 It's a fascinating island.
5 You shouldn't climb on the wall.

─── OPTIONAL ACTIVITY ────────────
Ask students to think of as many more words as they can with silent letters.

Example answers
knife, autumn, often, climb, hour, should, wrong, science

6 Grammar
What's it like?

a Ask students: *What's the weather like today?* (*It's sunny, cloudy*, etc.) Then ask them: *What was the weather like yesterday?* (*It was sunny, cloudy*, etc.) Elicit the difference between the two questions (*one is present, one is past*). If students are still not sure about this difference, ask a few students questions, e.g.:

T: Pietro, what was your last holiday like?
Pietro: It was good/bad, etc.

Students now read through questions 1–5 and answers a–e. Go through the first item with them as an example. Students complete the exercise. Check answers.

Answers 1 d 2 e 3 a 4 c 5 b

b Read the instructions with students and students complete the table. Make sure students understand when we use *is/are* and when we use *was/were*. Ask them why they chose the verb forms and tenses in Exercise 6a to check this, if necessary.

Answers
What is/*was* he/*she/it like?*
What *are/were* they *like?*

┌─────────────────────────────────────┐
│ **Language note:** Explain that when we use this │
│ question in the present tense singular we normally │
│ use the short form *What's it like?* (not *What is ...*). │
└─────────────────────────────────────┘

c Students read through the dialogues. Go through the example with them. Ask them why the verb is *was* to check they have understood. Students complete the exercise and compare answers in pairs. Ask pairs to read out their completed dialogues to the class.

Answers
2 's/is it like
3 's/is she like
4 was the weather like
5 are they like
6 were they like

Grammar notebook
Students should copy the completed table into their grammar notebooks. If necessary, they can add some example sentences or translate some.

7 Vocabulary
Adjectives for expressing opinions

a (◁))) Put the column headings + and − on the board. Give students an example of your own to show the meaning of *brilliant* and *boring*. Elicit that *brilliant* is a positive adjective and *boring* is a negative adjective and write them under the relevant heading on the board.

Stronger classes: They can now classify the other adjectives in the box under the relevant headings.

Weaker classes: They may need more help with the meaning of each adjective so elicit some example sentences or, if no one knows a word, provide example sentences for them, to show the meaning.

They can then classify the adjectives under the headings.

Students can compare answers in pairs. Ask students to come out and write the adjectives under the headings on the board. Then play the recording for students to listen and check. Play the recording again, for students to repeat.

TAPESCRIPT
boring, brilliant, interesting, attractive, fantastic, awful, cool, dull, ugly, dreadful

Answers
+: interesting, attractive, fantastic, cool
−: awful, dull, ugly, dreadful,

┌─────────────────────────────────────┐
│ **Language note:** *Cool* is used to express │
│ a positive opinion, colloquially, especially by │
│ young people (to mean 'very good', e.g. *Her new* │
│ *trainers are really cool.*). *Cool* can also be used │
│ about the weather (e.g. *It's rather cool for July.*). │
└─────────────────────────────────────┘

b Do the first item as an example with students. Either give students an example of your own or ask a stronger student the question: *Have you seen [title of a recent film]? What was it like?* and elicit one of the positive adjectives from Exercise 7a. In pairs, students discuss which adjectives apply to the other items. Check answers.

Answers
1 interesting, boring, brilliant, fantastic, awful, dull, dreadful
2 boring, interesting, attractive, awful, dull, ugly, cool
3 boring, brilliant, interesting, fantastic, awful, dull, ugly, dreadful
4 boring, brilliant, fantastic, awful, cool, dull, dreadful
5 brilliant, fantastic, awful, cool, dull, dreadful

8 Speak

Students read through the items in the box. Go through the example dialogue with them, eliciting another adjective to complete the second sentence. In pairs, students now ask and answer questions about the things in the box. Remind students to use the adjectives from Exercise 7a and they can also revise and practise adjectives of personality from Exercise 4a here. Ask some pairs to report back to the class on their conversations.

Culture in mind

9 Read

Warm up

Ask students if they have ever been to Britain. If so, ask them what they noticed about British customs, rules of the road, etc. that were different from those in their own country and/or which surprised them. If no one in your class has been there, ask them if they know of any British customs, e.g. queueing. The text is meant to be a light-hearted look at British customs, although the 'rules' given are true.

a Read the instructions with students and then ask them to predict the answer to the question. Students now read the first two paragraphs quickly to check their predictions. Encourage students to guess the meaning of the words from the context.

Answer
Tips are useful pieces of information/advice.

b Refer students to the pictures.

Weaker classes: Ask students what the people are doing in picture c (queueing), and write *queue* on the board. Read the text aloud with the class, and ask them to do the matching exercise as you read. They can work on this after reading too, for a few minutes.

Stronger classes: Students read silently and match the pictures to the paragraphs. They can then check their answers in pairs before the class check.

Check answers.

Answers a 5 b 3 c 1 d 2 e 4

c Go through the example with students before they begin. Students work in pairs to write the sentences. Remind them to use *should/shouldn't* in their sentences. Check answers.

Example answers
b She should say 'Pardon?' or 'Sorry?' / She shouldn't say 'What?'
c He should wait in a queue at the bus stop. / He shouldn't push past people in a queue.
d She should say 'Please' when she asks for something. / She shouldn't just say 'I want …'.
e He shouldn't kiss people he doesn't know. / He should only kiss family or friends.

d In pairs, students discuss the similarities and differences between their own country and the things in the text about Britain. Ask groups to give feedback to the class.

e Students use the information they have found out in Exercise 9 and make a list of useful tips about their own country which tourists will find helpful. Remind them to use *should/shouldn't* where possible.

OPTIONAL ACTIVITIES

Stronger classes
They can expand their notes and write a text for a tourist brochure. They can collect pictures and make this into a mini-project.

Weaker classes
Students can write out their tips into a fuller text (using the Exercise 9 reading text as a model) and decorate them. These can be displayed on the classroom walls.

10 Write

Students can do the preparation in class and complete the writing at home.

a Read the paragraph headings aloud with the class, then either read the letter aloud or ask students to read the text silently and quickly. Students match the paragraphs and headings.

Answers a 3 b 2 c 1

b Students write an email or letter to an imaginary penfriend who is visiting their country. Tell students to use the model text to help them organise their work. Remind students of language used to start and end informal emails/letters:

Greetings: *Hi, Dear*

Endings: *Love, Bye, Love from, Best wishes* (slightly more formal)

Before students start writing, ask them, in groups, to make a list of ideas for things to take and things the penfriend should or shouldn't do.

When they have finished, ask them to 'send' their letter or email to a classmate to read.

15 How brave!

Unit overview

TOPIC: Acts of bravery; Taking risks

TEXTS

Reading and listening: a magazine article about a brave incident with animals

Listening and speaking: a conversation between people about bravery

Reading and listening: photo story: *Dave's risk*

Writing: about a film, book or TV programme where someone was in a dangerous situation

SPEAKING

Talking about what will happen if/when something else happens

Talking about brave people

LANGUAGE

Grammar: First conditional; *when* and *if*
Pronunciation: Stress in conditional sentences
Vocabulary: Adjectives of feeling
Everyday English: *No way!*; *How should I know?*; *Hang on.*; *No big deal.*

1 Read and listen

If you set the background information as a homework research task ask students to tell the class what they found out.

BACKGROUND INFORMATION

Gorillas: They are the largest ape and are native to the forests of West Africa. The male gorilla can be anything from 150 to 190 cm tall and can weigh up to 450 kg in the wild. Females tend to be about half the size of males. They have brown or black coats. Gorillas are actually quiet and retiring animals and are mainly vegetarian.

Warm up

In pairs or small groups, students look at the text title and the photo and predict what they think will happen in the text. Ask for predictions and put them on the board.

a Read the questions with students. They discuss the options in pairs before choosing the ones they think are true. Find out how many answer *True* for number 1, 2 or 3.

b Read the instructions aloud. Students read the text; remind them to do this quickly and not to worry if they don't understand every word. If you have a weaker class, read it aloud with them. Then ask them to look at their answers to Exercise 1a, and change them if necessary. Check answers.

Answers

1 T
2 F (They only attack when you show you're afraid.)
3 T

c Students answer the question or refer back to their Warm up predictions. They can rely on their memory first, but encourage them to read the text again to check their answer.

Answer

2: A woman who takes a baby gorilla back to its family

d 🔊 Play the recording while students read and listen to the text. In pairs, students answer the questions. Remind them to find evidence in the text for their answers. Check answers.

TAPESCRIPT

See the reading text on page 118 of the Student's Book.

Answers

1 Because she wanted to take it back to its family. (para 1: ... *I had to take it back to its family.*)
2 Because she knew the gorilla would attack her if she ran away. (Para 3, lines 6/7: *If I turn and run away, this gorilla will attack me.*)
3 Because he wanted to frighten the woman. (para 4: *But he wanted to frighten me ...*)
4 Yes, he did. (para 4: *He went over to the baby, picked it up ...*)

e Read through the meanings with students. Then in pairs, students find the words in the text. Check answers. If it helps students, these words can be translated into their own language. Students can see if there are any similarities or differences in the translations. Students may want to note these words down in their vocabulary notebooks.

Answers 1 well 2 recognise 3 lifted

┌─ OPTIONAL ACTIVITY ────────────

Stronger classes

Students work in pairs and set more 'definition' games for another pair. They write the definitions of five other words from the text, along with the paragraph where they can be found, and ask another pair to try and find the words.

f Students work in pairs to discuss the questions. Alternatively, you can do this as a whole class activity.

Ask some pairs to give feedback and see what the general class opinion is.

2 Grammar
First conditional

a Read the instructions with the class and ask them to try and match the sentence halves without referring to the text. Students then check the text on page 118 and change their answers if necessary. Check answers as a class.

Answers
1 b If I turn and run away, the gorilla will attack me.
2 c If the mother doesn't recognise the baby, she won't take it back.
3 a If I don't move, he'll go away.

Ask students to look at the first half of each sentence and find one word which is in the present tense in each sentence (*If I turn*) and one word (positive or negative form) which refers to the future in the second half of each sentence (*will/won't*). Read the Rule box with the class. To check understanding at this point, give a few examples of your own, gapping one word in each half to elicit the tenses from students (e.g. *If you … hard, you'll pass your English exam.*)

b Students complete the grammar table. This will remind them of the full and short forms of *will / will not* which they should remember from Unit 11. Check answers.

Answers
'll; won't

c Students read through the sentences. Go through the first item with them as an example and show them how the *If* clause doesn't always have to come at the start of a sentence (see Language note below). Students complete the exercise. Check answers.

Language note: Draw students' attention to the fact that the *If* clause doesn't always come first in the sentence. It can also come at the beginning of the second clause. When this happens the comma is omitted from the sentence.

Answers
1 If I see Jane, I'll tell her. / I'll tell Jane if I see her.
2 If I'm late, my parents will be angry. / My parents will be angry if I'm late.
3 If I remember I'll bring it to school tomorrow. / I'll bring it to school tomorrow if I remember.
4 If you come to my party, you'll meet my new friend Jake. / You'll meet my new friend Jake if you come to my party.
5 If it doesn't rain tomorrow, we'll go to the beach. / We'll go to the beach tomorrow if it doesn't rain.
6 If I don't feel better tonight, I won't go to the concert. / I won't go to the concert if I don't feel better tonight.

OR: If I don't feel better, I won't go to the concert tonight. / I won't go to the concert tonight if I don't feel better.

d Students read through sentences 1–6. Go through the example with them and elicit the verb for the second half of the sentence (*'ll finish*) to make sure they have understood how the first conditional works. Students complete the exercise. Students compare answers in pairs. Then check answers as a class.

Answers
1 'll finish
2 won't meet; don't go out
3 'll come; says
4 doesn't want; 'll eat
5 will be; hears
6 buy; won't have

Language notes
1 Remind students we don't use *will/won't* in the *If* clause. We say *If I work hard, …* NOT ~~*If I will work hard …*~~
2 Students may find it useful to think about how this structure works in their own language. They may want to translate some of the sentences in Exercises 2c and d to show this.

Grammar notebook
Students should copy the completed table into their notebooks and any translations of sentences for Exercises 2c or d or examples of their own which may help them remember this structure.

3 Speak

With books closed, divide the class into Student As and Bs and put As and Bs together into pairs. Student As turn to page 119 and Student Bs turn to page 137. Students read through the questions on their cards and check any problems with you. Student A should ask their questions first and then Student B answers. Students then swap roles with Student Bs asking their questions and As answering. Students should note down their partner's answers and then some can report them back to the class. If there are any interesting answers, ask the student(s) to give the class more details.

4 Pronunciation
Stress in conditional sentences

a 🔊 Students read through sentences 1–6. Read the first sentence aloud as an example, putting extra stress on the underlined words. Check students can hear the stressed words and understand which parts of conditional sentences are stressed. Play the recording. Students mark the stressed words in the sentences. Check answers.

TAPESCRIPT

1 If it <u>rains</u>, I <u>won't go</u> to the <u>beach</u>.
2 We <u>won't pass</u> the <u>test</u> if we <u>don't work hard</u>.
3 I'll <u>give</u> him the <u>card</u> if I <u>see</u> him.
4 If you <u>decide</u> to <u>come</u>, I'll <u>meet</u> you at the <u>cinema</u>.
5 She <u>won't arrive</u> on <u>time</u> if she <u>misses</u> the <u>train</u>.
6 If he <u>doesn't</u> <u>phone</u> his <u>parents</u>, they'll <u>worry</u> about him.

b 🔊 Play the recording again, for students to listen and repeat.

┌─ OPTIONAL ACTIVITY ───────────────
│ Working in small groups (of three or four), students
│ make a chain of first conditional sentences. Each group
│ is given the start of a sentence and the first student
│ completes it. Student 2 must then take the second part
│ of Student 1's sentence and make a new first
│ conditional sentence, e.g.:
│
│ *S1: If it rains this weekend, I'll go to my friend's house.*
│ *S2: If I go to my friend's house, I'll listen to some CDs.*
│ *S3: If I listen to some CDs, I'll dance.*
│ *S4: If I dance, I'll get tired.*
│ *S1: If I get tired, I'll go home and go to bed!*
│
│ Example sentences (or stronger students can think of
│ their own):
│
│ *If it rains this weekend, …*
│ *If the weather's nice, …*
│ *If I go out this evening, …*
│ *If I play football tomorrow, …*
│ *If I cook the dinner tonight, …*

5 # Grammar
when and *if*

a Read through the questions and sentences 1 and 2
with students. Elicit that sentence 1 uses *when* in the
first conditional and sentence 2 uses *if*. Ask students
if they see any difference in meaning, and ask them
the second question in their book. (Sentence 1 means
the speaker is sure he/she will see John.) Put another
example of your own on the board at this point to
check they have understood the difference clearly.

b Students read through sentences 1–4. Go through
the first item with them as an example, making sure
they are clear about the speaker's certainty. Students
complete the exercise. Check answers.

Answers 1 when   2 If   3 if   4 when

6 # Vocabulary
Adjectives of feeling

a With books closed, write the adjectives *frightening*
and *frightened* on the board. Ask students: *How do you
think the woman in the text about gorillas on page 118
felt when she saw the gorilla?* Elicit *frightened*. Then
say: *She was frightened because the situation was … .*

Elicit *frightening*. Ask students: *Have you ever felt
frightened or been in a frightening situation?* Elicit
some examples from the class. Students now open
their books on page 120 and read Exercises 6a and b
instructions.

b In pairs, students go through the text and find
examples of *-ed* adjectives. Check answers. You could
ask some students to put the adjectives into sentences
of their own.

Answers
Para 1: worried
Para 3: frightened
Para 3: scared
Para 4: terrified

┌───┐
│ **Language note:** It may be useful to remind   │
│ students the spelling rules for *-ed* adjectives   │
│ at this point.   │
│   │
│ Noun/Verb + *-y* : Change the *-y* to *-i* and add *-ed*. │
│ Noun/Verb + other consonant: Add *-ed*.   │
│ Students may also find it useful to know that the   │
│ pronunciation of *-ed* adjectives is the same as past │
│ simple regular endings.   │
└───┘

c 🔊 Read through the adjectives in the box with
students. Check they understand them all. Do the
first item with students as an example. Remind them
to look carefully at each picture and think about how
the person is feeling. Once students have completed
the exercise, play the recording. Students check their
answers. Play the recording again, for students to
repeat each word.

TAPESCRIPT / ANSWERS
1 bored   2 frightened   3 interested   4 tired
5 excited   6 annoyed

d Students read through sentences 1–8. Go through
the example with students, reminding them again
of when *-ed* and *-ing* adjectives are used. Students
complete the exercise. Check answers.

Answers 2 interested   3 frightened   4 exciting
5 interesting   6 frightening   7 annoyed   8 tiring

┌─ OPTIONAL ACTIVITY ───────────────
│ Students copy and complete the following table.
│
│ | Verb | *-ed* adjective | *-ing* adjective |
│ |------|------------------|-------------------|
│ | *worry* | *worried* | |
│ | *frighten* | | *frightening* |
│ | *interest* | | |
│ | *excite* | | |
│ | | *annoyed* | |
│ | *tire* | | |
│ | *exhaust* | | *exhausting* |

Vocabulary notebooks
Students note down the new adjectives from this unit
and add any more of their own as they come across them.

7 Listen and speak

a Read through the words in the boxes with students
and check understanding. Explain that students must
make up a noun for each picture with a word from
each box. Go through the example with them, showing
them how the words have come from each box.
Students complete the exercise. In pairs, students
compare answers. Stronger students could check
answers in a dictionary. Check answers as a class.

Answers 2 firefighter   3 underwater photographer
4 parachute jumper   5 racing driver

b Read through the list of nouns and verbs with students
and check they understand them all. Stronger students
can check any words they don't know in a dictionary.
Go through the example with students, explaining that
there is one noun and two verbs for each picture.
Students complete the exercise. In pairs, students
compare answers. Check answers as a class.

Answers
Picture 2: burn, building, collapse
Picture 3: shark, attack, swim
Picture 4: parachute, land, open
Picture 5: race, crash, overturn

┌─ OPTIONAL ACTIVITY ─────────────────
Students can write first conditional sentences about
each picture using the nouns and verbs from Exercise 7b
(e.g. Picture 1: *If the rope breaks, he'll fall.*).

c Students read the instructions. Discuss their views
on picture 1 and elicit a score for this from the class.
In pairs or small groups, students discuss the other
pictures and give them a score. Groups can give
feedback to the class. Are there similar results?

d 🔊 Explain to students that they will hear two people
talking about the pictures in Exercise 7a. They should
listen carefully and write in the first column of their
table the number of the picture being talked about.
Go through the example with students, playing the
recording and pausing it after the first answer. Play
the recording again for students to complete column 1.
Check answers.

TAPESCRIPT

Jenny OK, Franco – what about this person? What
score did you give him?

Franco I gave him two. These drivers have a big team
of people to look after the cars, and they just drive
round and round. I don't think they're all that brave.

Jenny But the races are dangerous! I think you have
to be very brave to drive that fast. If you make one
little mistake, the car might crash. I gave him four.

Franco Four. OK, then.

Jenny What did you give the next person?

Franco Oh, that! Look at that man! He's so brave.
What will he do if the shark attacks him? I gave
him five. What about you?

Jenny I only gave him three.

Franco Really? Why?

Jenny Well, most sharks are harmless – they don't
attack people. They're more interested in small fish.

Franco Mmm, well I wouldn't like to do what he's
doing.

Jenny The last one here ... I gave her a score of four.

Franco Yes, me too. I think people have to be very
brave to jump out of a plane. I know lots of people
do it, but if your parachute doesn't open, you'll die.

Jenny Yes, and you might land in a tree or in the
water.

Franco Scary. I'll keep my feet on the ground.

Jenny So, we both agree on four for her.

Answers
Column 1: Pictures 3 and 4

e 🔊 Play the recording again for students to note
down the scores Franco and Jenny give to each picture.
Pause after the first score is given and go through the
example in column 2 of the table. Continue playing
the recording for students to complete the scores.
Check answers.

Answers
Franco: Picture 3 – 5 points; Picture 4 – 4 points
Jenny: Picture 3 – 3 points; Picture 4 – 4 points;
Picture 5 – 4 points

┌─ OPTIONAL ACTIVITY ─────────────────
Ask students to get into small groups and discuss
their own reactions to Franco and Jenny's scores.
Do they agree or not? Why? / Why not?

f Ask students to look at the example dialogue,
and then to work in new pairs and discuss their
own choices for Exercise 7c. Ask several pairs to give
feedback to the class.

Dave's risk

8 Read and listen

Warm up

Ask students to say who the boys are in the photo
story (Alex and Dave) see if they can remember what
the two were up to the last time they appeared in
a photo story episode.

(a) 🔊 Students look at the title and the story and answer the question quickly. Play the recording. Students listen and read to check their predictions.

Answer
If he asks Amy out, she might say no.

(b) Students read through sentences 1–6. Go through the first item with them as an example, if necessary. In pairs, students complete the exercise. Remind them to provide evidence from the text to back up true answers and ask them to correct the false ones. Check answers.

TAPESCRIPT
See the photo story on page 122 of the Student's Book.

Answers
1 T (*She's lovely.*)
2 T (*How should I know?*)
3 F (Alex talks to Dave about it.)
4 T (*... she won't want to be my friend any more.*)
5 F (*I'd love to go tomorrow.*)
6 F (*It's her dad's birthday today, that's why she can't go.*)

┌─ OPTIONAL ACTIVITY ─────────────
In groups, students can act out the dialogue from the photo story.

9 Everyday English

(a) Read the expressions aloud with the class. Tell them to find them in the photo story. Who says each one and to whom? Check answers. Students then match phrases 1–4 with the expressions a–d. Check answers.

Answers
1 d Dave to Alex
2 b Dave to Alex
3 a Amy to Dave
4 c Dave to Amy

(b) Students translate the expressions into their own language, checking in pairs, before a whole class check.

(c) Students read through the dialogues. Check any problems. Go through the first item as an example, if necessary. Students complete the dialogues. Students compare answers in pairs. Check answers as a class.

Answers
1 Hang on
2 How should I know?
3 No way!
4 No big deal.

┌─────────────────────────────────
Language note: *No big deal* is very colloquial and informal and is only appropriate when speaking to friends or people you are very familiar with.
└─────────────────────────────────

┌─ OPTIONAL ACTIVITIES ───────────
Stronger classes
Students can write their own short dialogues, using the expressions in Exercise 9, and act them out in front of the class.

Weaker classes
They can act out the dialogues in Exercise 9c.

10 Write

Students choose one of the tasks in Exercise 10b for their writing assignment. They can do the preparation in class, and complete the writing at home.

(a) Students read through questions 1–6; check any problems. Students then read the book review and answer the questions. Do the first item with them as an example, if necessary.

Answers
1 The book was called *A Picture to Remember*.
2 A girl called Christina.
3 She was in the gym and later in the street.
4 Because she had seen the robbers' faces and they planned to kill her.
5 She drove away from the hospital, followed by the robbers. She was frightened but she kept calm.
6 The robbers' car crashed. One of the robbers died and the police caught the other one.

(b) Using the text in Exercise 10a as a model, students choose one of the topics to write a review on. Go through the text again in more detail with them, looking at its structure. Remind them of or elicit from stronger students the following:

- Para 1: Introduction: title of story, name of main character, summary sentence
- Para 2: What happened next
- Para 3: Conclusion, giving details of what happened in the end.

Remind them of the brave events they have read about in this unit and see if they can think of a book or film which has a brave character or someone who escapes from a dangerous situation. Students should also use the questions in Exercise 10a to help them structure their reviews. Students can swap reviews with a partner and give a score to it.

Ask students if they would like to see the film or read the book their partner has mentioned. Discuss some of the more popular titles with the class.

┌─ OPTIONAL ACTIVITY ─────────────
Students can illustrate their reviews and some of the better ones can be displayed around the class.

16 It's a mad world

Unit overview

TOPIC: Record holders; Animals

TEXTS

Reading and listening: extracts from the Guinness Book of Records

Listening: to an interview with someone who wants to break a record

Reading: a text about a record breaker

Reading: a text about Elvis Presley

Writing: a letter or email from Los Angeles

SPEAKING

Asking and answering about past experiences

LANGUAGE

Grammar: Present perfect + *ever/never*

Vocabulary: Animals; Verb and noun pairs

Pronunciation: *have* and *has* in the present perfect

1 Read and listen

If you set the background information as a homework research task ask students to tell the class what they have found out.

If you have a copy or can get hold of a copy of the *Guinness Book of Records* it may be useful to bring it in for this lesson.

BACKGROUND INFORMATION

Guinness Book of Records: This was first published in 1955 and the idea came from the director of the Irish Brewing company, Guinness. It has been published annually ever since and today it holds the all-time sales record for a copyrighted book. There is a museum featuring a lot of the records from the books in Tennessee, USA.

Warm up

Ask students if they have ever seen the *Guinness Book of Records*. Perhaps they can tell you about an interesting record they know about, e.g. the tallest person in the world, etc.

(a) Students read through the texts quickly. Check any problems. If necessary, go through the first one with them as an example. Students then match each paragraph with a picture. Students can compare answers in pairs. Check answers.

Answers a 4 b 2 c 3 d 1 e 5

(b) 🔊 Explain that one of the records 1–5 in the text is NOT true. Play the recording for students to read and listen. In pairs or small groups, students give their ideas about which record is not true and give their reasons. Find out why they think certain records are not true. Find out by a show of hands who votes for which one, and then ask students to check the answers on page 129. How many were correct?

TAPESCRIPT

See the reading text on page 124 of the Student's Book.

2 Vocabulary

Animals

🔊 Books closed. Elicit as many animals as possible from students and write them on the board. Students open their books at page 125 and read the instructions for Exercise 2. Go through the first item with students as an example, if necessary. Students complete the exercise. Students compare answers in pairs. Play the recording for students to check or change their answers. Play the recording again, pausing for students to repeat each word.

TAPESCRIPT/ANSWERS

1 cow 2 alligator 3 snake 4 rabbit 5 tiger
6 dog 7 mouse 8 tarantula 9 frog 10 horse
11 cat 12 parrot

3 Listen

(a) 🔊 Read the instructions with the class. Let students guess what record Mr Brown wants to break. Play the recording for students to listen to and find out whether anyone was correct.

TAPESCRIPT

Interviewer Mr Brown, you're trying to become a world record-holder, is that right?

Mr Brown Yes, that's right.

Interviewer By having more pets in your house than anyone else, I believe.

Mr Brown That's right. Up to now I've got over 25 pets.

Interviewer Really? And I suppose you have many different kinds of animals?

Mr Brown Oh, yes. Um, I've got two tarantulas ... um, some lovely frogs, um ... a dog ... several rabbits ... a snake, a very large snake ... a white mouse ... um ... a parrot, and er ... oh, all kinds of things. I haven't made a list of them all.

Interviewer Quite a lot of animals, then?

Mr Brown Yes indeed! Oh, I almost forgot. The alligator! How could I forget!

Answer
He wants to have more pets in his house than anyone else.

(b) 🔊 Play the recording again. Students tick the animals Mr Brown has. Check answers.

Answers
tarantula, frog, dog, rabbit, snake, mouse, parrot, alligator

(c) 🔊 In pairs or small groups, students work together to make sure they understand the words. (They can share the task of looking one of the words up and explaining it to the other member(s) of the pair or group.) Students read through the whole dialogue, ignoring the spaces. Play the first part of the recording, pausing after the first space for students to decide which word goes in it. Check answers. Remind students to look at the whole sentence to help them find the word which fits in each space. Continue playing the recording for students to complete the exercise. Students compare answers in pairs then play the recording again for students to check or change their answers.

TAPESCRIPT

Interviewer Is it difficult to have so many animals all in the same house?

Mr Brown Sometimes. You see, I can't have the alligator in the same room as the other animals. It's eaten some of the smaller ones. It loves frogs.

Interviewer Yes, I see. So have you ever had any problems yourself? Some of these animals are dangerous, aren't they?

Mr Brown Well, the tarantulas have bitten me once or twice.

Interviewer What do your neighbours think about all these animals?

Mr Brown Well, they've never complained.

Interviewer Have any of your pets ever escaped?

Mr Brown Yes. The parrot escaped in 1998. But the alligator and the tarantulas have never escaped.

Interviewer Oh, good! And tell me, Mr Brown: how many animals do you need to break the record?

Mr Brown Well, unfortunately, there's a woman in America with more than 60 pets in her house, so I have a long way to go.

Answers 1 room 2 frogs 3 dangerous 4 never 5 parrot 6 record 7 woman

(d) Students read through sentences 1–5 and a–e. Go through the first item as an example, if necessary. Students match the sentence halves, referring back to their completed dialogue in Exercise 3c if necessary. Ask several students to read out complete sentences for the rest of the class to check.

Answers
1 c 2 e 3 d 4 a 5 b

(e) In pairs or small groups, students discuss what they think about Mr Brown. Find out how many agree or disagree with each other.

┌─ OPTIONAL ACTIVITIES ─────────

Stronger classes
Students choose one of the animals on this page or choose one of their own and say why they would like to have it as a pet.

Weaker classes
Ask students to say which of the pets they think are most dangerous, most unusual, most scary, etc.

Vocabulary notebook
Remind students to start a section called *Animals* in their vocabulary notebooks. They should note down the animals from this unit and any others as they come across them. Students may find it useful to classify the animals under the categories *Pets* and *Wild animals*.

4 **Grammar**
Present perfect + *ever/never*

(a) Read the sentences with students. Ask them what they notice about this tense (it uses *has/have*). Read through the Rule box with students and then ask them to complete it. Point out that the use of *ever* here means 'at any time in your life' and that *never* means 'at no time in your life'.

Answers
Rule: have

Students then look at the grammar table and complete it. Check answers. To check understanding at this point, ask a student a question of your own and elicit their response. The student can then choose another student and ask the question, continue like this until you are sure students are confident using this structure, e.g.:

T: *Alberto, have you ever been to London? / worked in a restaurant? / seen a tiger? etc.*
S1: *Yes, I have. / No, I haven't.*
S1: *Silvia, have you ever been to France?*
S2: *Yes, I have. / No, I haven't.*

Answers
Positive: have; has
Negative: has not
Questions: Have; Has

┌─────────────────────────────
Language notes
1 Explain that *ever* is used in questions and *never* is used in negative statements. Students should note their positions: *ever* is positioned between the subject pronoun and the past participle in questions and *never* is positioned after the *have/has* and before the past participle.
2 Remind students that *it's* can mean *it is* or *it has*. They should read the whole sentence and work out from the context which *it's* is being used.
└─────────────────────────────

b) Put the headings *Base form* and *Past participle* on the board. Read through the list of verb forms with students and go through the example with them. Elicit and write on the board any other irregular past participles students know. Using the Irregular verbs list on page 138, students complete the exercise. They can compare answers in pairs before a whole class check. To check students have understood the past participles, call out a few base forms (with irregular past participles) and ask students to give you the irregular past participles.

Answers 2 done 3 gone 4 seen 5 written
6 bitten 7 spoken 8 eaten 9 driven
10 flown 11 swum 12 won

c) Students read through sentences 1–6. Go through the example with them, reminding them of the position of *never*. Students complete the exercise. Remind them to use short forms where possible. Students can compare answers in pairs. Students can compare answers in pairs, then check answers with the whole class.

Answers 2 Has; ever studied 3 've never seen
4 Have; ever driven 5 Have; ever flown
6 's stayed; 's never eaten

Grammar notebook
Remind students to make a note of these irregular past participles and to note down any more as they come across them.

5 Pronunciation

have and *has* in the present perfect

a) 🔊 Read through the example dialogues with students. Play the recording and ask students to listen carefully and note down what they think the difference is between the pronunciation of *have* and *has* in each exchange. Play the recording again for students to listen and repeat.

TAPESCRIPT

A: Have you <u>ev</u>er <u>dri</u>ven a <u>car</u>?

B: <u>Yes</u>, I <u>have</u>.

A: Has she <u>ev</u>er <u>stud</u>ied a <u>for</u>eign <u>lan</u>guage?

B: <u>Yes</u>, she <u>has</u>.

Answer
In each dialogue, the first one is unstressed, the second one is stressed.

b) 🔊 Go through the first item with them as an example if necessary. Play the recording. Students underline the stress. Students listen and check. Then they listen again and repeat, with the correct stress.

TAPESCRIPT/ANSWERS
1 I've <u>never</u> <u>lived</u> in A<u>mer</u>ica.
2 A: Have you <u>ev</u>er <u>seen</u> an <u>all</u>igator?
   B: <u>No</u>, I <u>haven't</u>.
3 A: Has he <u>ev</u>er <u>swum</u> in a <u>riv</u>er?
   B: <u>Yes</u>, he <u>has</u>.

6 Speak

a) Read the part of A in the dialogues, with a student reading the part of B and demonstrate the dialogues in front of the class. Read through the prompts with students and explain that they have to make similar dialogues, using the prompts.

Divide students into pairs and ask them to take turns to ask and answer questions. Monitor them as they work. At the end of the activity, ask several pairs to demonstrate their dialogues to the class.

b) In pairs or small groups, students make up more questions for each other with the verbs given. Ask them to demonstrate their questions to the class.

7 Read

a) Students read the instructions and make their predictions. Students can refer to the objects by their numbers, but you may want to give them the words *bricks* for 1, *cans* for 2 and *milk crates* for 3, and perhaps explain that in Britain milk is traditionally stored in bottles in milk crates and delivered to houses by a milkman. Then ask them to read the text silently and check their answer. If you have a weak class, you may prefer to read the text aloud with the class following in their books.

Answer
He balances all the objects in the pictures.

b) Read through questions 1–7 with students and check understanding. Students read and answer the questions. Check answers.

Answers
1 29 times.
2 He was a builder.
3 When he was a builder he balanced bricks on his head.
4 In 1992.
5 He balanced 96 milk crates on his head and broke the record.
6 When he started breaking records and appearing in TV shows.
7 Yes. He has raised £56,000 so far.

c) In small groups, students discuss the questions. Ask for class feedback. Are there any interesting answers? If so, discuss them further with the class.

8 Vocabulary

Verb and noun pairs

(a) Read through the examples with students, referring them back to the text in Exercise 7 if necessary. Ask students to find and match each of these expressions in the list below. Students complete the exercise and compare answers in pairs. Check answers.

Answers 2 b   3 d   4 f   5 c   6 a

(b) Students read through sentences 1–5. Do the first item with them as an example, if necessary. Remind students to look at the context of each sentence and to check the verb form they need. Students complete the exercise. Check answers.

Answers   1 won; broke   2 building   3 raises
4 took   5 tells

Vocabulary notebook

Remind students to copy down these expressions in their vocabulary notebooks. They can translate them into their own language if necessary or note down some examples to help them remember them.

--- OPTIONAL ACTIVITY ---

Stronger classes
They can think of their own gapped sentences using these verb and noun pairs and give them to a partner to fill in the gaps.

Culture in mind

9 Read

If you set the background information as a homework research task ask students to tell the class what they found out.

BACKGROUND INFORMATION

Elvis Presley: Was born Elvis Aaron Presley on 8 January, 1935 in Tupelo, Mississippi. At the age of ten he won a school singing competition and taught himself the basics of guitar playing, although he never could read music properly. After graduating from high school in 1953 he began work as a truck driver and also began training as an electrician in the evenings. In July 1954 he recorded his first single *That's All Right Mama.* He continued recording songs and then in 1956 released the million-selling single *Heartbreak Hotel.* He then served in the army from 1958 to 1960 and returned not only to singing but to acting. His last chart hit while he was alive was in 1969. He died at the age of 42 in 1977 but is still regarded by many as the King of Rock and Roll.

Warm up

Ask students to look at the photos and the text title and to predict when this singer was popular (in the 1950s).

(a) Students read through the questions and predict their answers. Then they read the text and check their predictions. How many of them were correct?

(b) Students read through the information in this part of the exercise. Go through the first item with them as an example if necessary. Remind them that they should be looking for the specific information in this exercise. Then they read the text again and complete the exercise. Check answers as a class.

Answers 1 d   2 e   3 a   4 f   5 b   6 c

(c) Students read through meanings 1–6. Go through the first one with them as an example. Students complete the exercise. Check answers.

Answers 1 hit   2 fans   3 huge   4 middle-aged
5 wheelchairs   6 anniversary

(d) In small groups students discuss the questions. Groups give feedback to the rest of the class. If there are any interesting experiences ask students to share more details about them with the rest of the class.

10 Write

(a) Students can do the preparation in class, and complete the writing at home.

Students read the letter and answer the question.

Answers
She asks about:
- the family her friend is staying with
- things her friend has done in Los Angeles
- people her friend has met
- if her friend has visited Hollywood
- if her friend has seen any film stars

(b) Remind students about the form for a personal letter or email. If students need help, ask them to look back through the book and find models of emails (e.g. see pages 39, 61, 101 and 111). Ask students to suggest ideas to answer the questions, and write them on the board.

Read through the suggested beginning for the letter or email. Students write their letters or emails at home. When they have finished, ask them to 'send' their work to a classmate to read.

1 Grammar

a) 2 's/is going to help me
3 'm not / am not watching
4 Are; going to wear
5 are going to visit
6 isn't / is not going to ride
7 're/are going to dance

b) 2 must   3 must   4 mustn't   5 mustn't
6 must   7 mustn't

c) 2 should   3 should   4 should; shouldn't
5 shouldn't   6 Should

d) 1 'll/will buy
2 comes; will be
3 will complain; make
4 have; 'll/will get
5 don't / do not get up; you won't / will not have
6 won't / will not pass; doesn't / does not study

e) 2 My brother has never studied a foreign language.
3 My parents have never flown in a plane.
4 I've never got 100% in a test.
5 Richard has never eaten frogs' legs.
6 Has your teacher ever shouted at you?
7 Have you ever spoken to a British person?
8 Have your parents ever won a competition?

2 Vocabulary

a) 2 unkind   3 disorganised   4 miserable
5 unfriendly   6 impolite/rude   7 lazy

b) 1 tiring   2 excited; boring   3 frightening;
frightened   4 fascinating; interested

c)

R	A	B	A	I	P	A	R	G	O
T	R	V	L	T	A	R	A	N	T
A	G	U	L	S	R	A	X	T	I
R	I	Q	I	L	R	O	D	O	G
F	R	O	G	M	O	U	S	R	E
T	A	R	A	N	T	U	L	A	R
H	A	M	T	E	R	T	I	B	R
O	W	M	O	U	S	E	J	B	A
R	H	O	R	S	E	B	F	I	B
S	N	A	K	E	F	R	O	T	T

d) 2 won   3 take   4 tells   5 raise   6 broke

3 Everyday English

2 Hang on
3 It's no big deal
4 How should I know
5 No way

How did you do?
Ask students to complete this. Check their results and if necessary provide extra practice in their weaker areas.

Project 1

1 Prepare the survey

You may find it useful to take in some magazine questionnaires with you for this lesson and to make copies of the questionnaires before students do Exercise 1d.

(a) Read through the instructions with the class. In groups of three or four students discuss the topics and choose one.

(b) Read through the instructions and the example with students, reminding them of different question forms.

Weaker classes: Elicit more examples from students, if necessary. Students complete the exercise.

(c) Look at the model questionnaire extract with students and show them some examples from magazines if you have brought them in. Go through the example answers with students and explain that they must think of three answer options for each question they have written in Exercise 1b or make it a 'yes/no' question.

Students complete the exercise; make sure each student makes a copy of the questionnaire.

(d) Students ask the other students in their group the questions and note down their answers. Then students circulate round the class asking as many students as they can, noting down their answers.

2 Write up the results

(a) Students regroup in their original questionnaire group (from Exercise 1) and discuss their answers. Look at the model charts with students, explaining that they should draw up their results in this way. They can work out how many people they interviewed and what percentage answered in the same way.

(b) Read through the example with the class and show how it relates to the results in the model charts in Exercise 2a. Using their own information from Exercise 2, students now write sentences to describe their results. Make sure each student in the groups completes this task. Monitor and help as necessary.

(c) This can be set for homework. Students now transfer all their information (chart and sentences) onto a poster and add illustrations and more details if they want.

Present your information

Groups present their posters and their findings to the rest of the class. Each groups appoints a spokesperson to lead the presentation. If there are any interesting results, these can be discussed with the class.

Project 2

Divide the class into groups of about four to six. Read through the instructions with the class.

1 Brainstorm

(a) Students follow the instructions and read the texts in Module 2 again.

(b) This part of the project can start off as a class project. Write the headings from Exercise 1b on the board. Elicit some more categories from the class which they may be interested in. Then ask students to suggest people for each category.

(c) Read the instructions with students. Groups appoint a notetaker and then give them a few minutes to come up with ideas and agree on who they are going to research. Monitor and help as necessary, making sure each student in the group is getting a chance to speak.

2 Research

Read the instructions. Students decide which part of the project they will find out about. They should brainstorm ideas for resources: names of magazines, newspapers, books they have heard of, website addresses, etc. They should try to answer all the questions, with as much additional interesting information as they can find. Give students a week or so to collect their information and bring it to class.

Read through the instructions for Presentation too at this point, so that students know they have to collect visuals, and discuss, if they want to, ideas for music.

3 Presentation

Students work on this in class. They will need to go through all the information they have collected, and decide which of it they are going to use, and how. It is important to tell them how long the presentation should be. If you have a large class and you want all the presentations to be done in one lesson, for example, it would be advisable to keep the length of each presentation to a maximum of ten minutes.

If students want to (and if you have time) a presentation can take the form of a large poster, with handwritten or printed text, pictures, photos, drawings, etc. Students can then use the poster as a background for the oral presentation. Alternatively, members of the group can talk about the person, using visuals, music, etc.

Read through the examples for making presentations with the class and let groups decide on a way to present their information. They will need to practise the presentation. They can do this in their groups in class.

Students should do their presentations in the next lesson.

Project 3

Divide class into groups of about four or five.

1 Brainstorm

a Read through the instructions as a class and look at the example topics. Each group decides which topic they are going to write about. Give them a few minutes to do this and monitor the discussions making sure each student has a chance to voice their opinion.

b Students now take a few minutes to decide how far into the future they are going to look. Give them a few minutes to make their decisions, making sure each member of the group is happy with the decision.

c Read through the instructions and example questions with students. Remind them of different question forms and also remind them to think about how the questions will be answered. It is a good idea here to encourage students to include open questions which will require more than a 'yes/no' answer. If necessary, answer a few of the example questions to highlight this point. Students complete this part of the activity in class.

2 Make the poster

a This part of the project can be set for homework. As a class, brainstorm ideas for finding visuals, website addresses, magazines, comics, etc. Students should bring in their visuals to the next class.

b Students look at the pictures the groups have collected and select a few to illustrate their poster. The groups must agree on the visuals. Students work in their groups and write predictions about each picture they are going to include on their poster. This should be done in their notebooks or on rough paper. When students are satisfied that their predictions are written correctly and grammatically, they can transfer them to the poster.

c Supply each group with a large sheet of paper, sticky tape or glue, for them to start making their posters. They should write the title at the top.

d Students now write their personal opinions of the predictions made on their posters. If they have written, e.g. *Robots will do the housework in most people's homes*, ask them to write their opinions of this. Will they miss doing the housework themselves? etc. Students can check their texts in their groups before deciding on final versions and sticking them onto their poster.

3 Presentation

Each group should prepare a short presentation to explain their poster to the rest of the class. Encourage other groups to ask questions about posters. Posters can then be displayed on the classroom walls.

Project 4

1 Listen

Read the instructions and ask students to predict from the picture what one of the stories is about (a sports team and fans). Play the recording. Check answers

TAPESCRIPT

1 One really sad thing that happened this year was that my dog died. She was called Mitzi, and I really miss her. She was 14 years old – that's old for a dog – and we got her when I was very young, so we sort of grew up together. She died in April this year. We knew she wasn't very well, and then ...

2 I want to talk about the fire that broke out in our town earlier this year. It happened two months ago. The fire started in the shoe shop in Miller Street, early in the evening. We first realised something was wrong when my mother noticed a lot of smoke outside, and then we heard the fire engines ...

3 Football is the most important thing in my life, and the best thing that happened this year was when Chievo won the European Cup. The Flying Donkeys! It was brilliant. The final was on the twenty-sixth of May and they played against Manchester United at the Bernabeu stadium in Madrid. My friends and I watched the match on television and ...

Answers
1 Someone's dog died.
2 A fire in a town.
3 The football team, Chievo, won the European Cup.

2 Choose a topic

Read through the instructions with the class. Give them some time to think about a topic.

3 Plan

a Read through the questions with the class.

b Students work on their own to make a list of important words for their topic. Students make notes (on small pieces of card they can look at as they speak).

c For homework, they should collect visuals, or music etc. to make their presentation really interesting.

d Using their cards and visuals, students quietly practise their talk in class. Monitor and help.

4 Give the talk

Divide the class into small groups and students give their talk to the others in their group.

Workbook key

1 Things we like doing

1 2 pilot   3 car   4 start   5 doesn't enjoy   6 loves
   7 lands   8 don't want

2 **(a)** 2 studies   3 get up   4 writes   5 sleeps
       6 drive   7 like   8 gets

   (b) 2 watches   3 write   4 flies   5 go
       6 knows   7 finishes   8 talk

   (c) 2 doesn't like cats
       3 don't read books
       4 don't watch TV
       5 doesn't fly a helicopter

   (d) 1 runs   2 reads   3 listens   4 teaches
       5 start   6 finish   7 sings   8 don't get
       9 goes   10 doesn't get up

3 **(b)** 2 reading
       3 swimming
       4 playing computer games
       5 dancing
       6 painting
       7 listening to music
       8 going to the cinema

   (c) 2 swim e
       3 plays computer games b
       4 dance f
       5 listens to music a
       6 play tennis d

4 **(a)** 2 going   3 driving   4 swimming   5 dancing
       6 smiling   7 studying   8 getting

   (b) 2 loves/likes/enjoys painting
       3 hates/doesn't like/enjoy playing football
       4 loves/likes/enjoys running
       5 hate/don't like/enjoy flying
       6 hates/doesn't like/enjoy dancing
       7 love/like/enjoy playing computer games
       8 hates/doesn't like/enjoy watching TV

5 **(a)** 🔊 TAPESCRIPT/ANSWERS
       1 listen   2 opening   3 wrong   4 wins
       5 spring   6 go in   7 coming   8 driving

   (b) 🔊 TAPESCRIPT
       1 Ann enjoys talking in Italian.
       2 Martin is good at swimming and singing.
       3 Learning Russian is interesting.
       4 Kevin doesn't like going to his dancing
         lesson.

6 1 What about   2 weird   3 Shut up   4 So what
   5 guy

7 Music activities: playing the piano
   Places: cinema, beach
   Other activities: reading, dancing, painting
   Sports activities: playing football, swimming

8 🔊

Sally: learn ballet, go dancing
James: talk to friends, write emails
Richard: go to the swimming pool, go to the cinema
Nadia: ride a bicycle, listen to pop music

TAPESCRIPT
1 **Sally**
  My favourite hobby is dancing. I learn ballet –
  I go to ballet lessons on Wednesday after school,
  and I really enjoy that. And I often go dancing
  with my friends on Saturday nights.
2 **James**
  I spend a lot of time talking to my friends
  on the phone. Writing emails is fun too, but
  I haven't got a very good computer.
3 **Richard**
  I like swimming, but I don't live near the coast,
  so I go to the local swimming pool. My other
  hobby is going to the cinema – I love watching
  films.
4 **Nadia**
  My friend and I go for long bicycle rides –
  we both like riding bikes. And at home I listen
  to the radio a lot. I really enjoy listening to
  pop music, obviously.

9 Matthew

Unit check

1 1 cinema   2 like   3 watches   4 talking
   5 teaches   6 doesn't   7 games   8 weird   9 guy

2 2 b   3 a   4 a   5 b   6 b   7 c   8 b   9 c

3 2 Ben's mother ~~drive~~ *drives* us home from school.
   3 I ~~not like~~ *don't* like flying.
   4 We enjoy ~~to run~~ *running* in the park.
   5 Tony and his brother love ~~swiming~~ *swimming*.
   6 Sue and Catherine ~~doesn't~~ *don't* ride bikes.
   7 Elise ~~studys~~ *studies* in the library after school.
   8 My sister ~~not~~ *doesn't* get up before 7 o'clock.
   9 In the summer, Dad ~~watchs~~ *watches* the tennis
     on television.

2 School life

1 1 e 2 d 3 b 4 a 5 f 6 c

2 **(a)** 2 Do; listen 3 Does she like 4 Do they study 5 Does he speak 6 do; live
7 do; go 8 does she wear

(b) 1 Do your parents help with your homework?
2 Do you study in front of the television?
3 Does your English teacher give you a lot of tests?
4 Do all your friends learn English?
5 Where do you have lunch?
6 When does the school day finish?
(Students' own answers)

(c) 1 meet 2 go 3 do; go 4 drink 5 don't go 6 get up 7 play 8 doesn't get up
9 Does; work 10 works 11 doesn't like
12 come 13 don't go 14 do

3 **(a)** S O I T Y R H: History

(b) 2 Geography 3 French 4 Science 5 Art
6 History 7 IT/Information Technology
8 Drama 9 PE/Physical Education

4 **(a)** 🔊 TAPESCRIPT/ANSWERS
1 Drama 2 Italian 3 Science 4 History
5 Geography 6 Biology 7 Physical Education 8 Information Technology

(b) 🔊 TAPESCRIPT
1 I like Maths and Art.
2 In Science we study Physics.
3 History is my favourite subject.
4 Geography, Biology and Technology.

5 2 him 3 it 4 me 5 you 6 her 7 us

6 **(a)** 2 Cathy usually walks to school
3 never wear a uniform
4 sometimes walks to school
5 always wears a uniform
6 hardly ever get up early

(b) 2 four times a week
3 twice a year
4 three times a day
5 once a year
6 twice a day

7 1 walks 2 students 3 uniform 4 always
5 dining 6 studies 7 Twice 8 clubs 9 do
10 exams

8 **(a)** Verbs: 1 use 2 plays 3 bring; eat
4 walk; catch
Nouns: 1 computer 2 orchestra
3 students; sandwiches; school 4 bus

(b) Nouns
Subjects: Art, Geography
Other nouns: exam, uniform
Verbs
teach, write

9 **(a)** Lunch time and after-school activities

(b) 1 Music 2 Sport 3 Art and photography
4 Study

Unit check

1 1 subjects 2 Science 3 live 4 train 5 every
6 twice 7 stays 8 time 9 usually

2 2 c 3 a 4 c 5 c 6 c 7 b 8 b 9 c

3 2 *Do* you bring your lunch to school?
3 What time *does* the film ~~starts~~ *start*?
4 I use my computer every ~~days~~ *day*.
5 Our cat ~~sleeps always~~ *always sleeps* in my room.
6 They go swimming three ~~time~~ *times* a week.
7 Sarah ~~doesn't~~ never ~~drink~~ *drinks* coffee.
8 What *do* your parents do on Sunday evenings?
9 Our Art classes ~~usually are~~ *are usually* very interesting.

3 A helping hand

1 1 b 2 a 3 b 4 c 5 c

2 **(a)** 1 're/are 2 's/is 3 aren't / are not 4 isn't
/ is not 5 'm/am 6 're/are 7 are

(b) 2 ~~driveing~~; driving
3 ~~are~~; is
4 ~~swiming~~; swimming
5 ~~they are~~; are they
6 ~~is~~; are
7 ~~geting~~; getting
8 ~~listenning~~; listening

(c) 2 Irene is sitting in the garden. The birds are singing.
3 Danny is sitting on his bed. He's reading.
4 Olga and Joanne are watching TV. Sandro is cooking.
5 Sam is playing the guitar. Tony is painting.
6 Franca is cycling in the park. The dogs are running in the park / beside her.

(d) 1 d 2 e 3 f 4 a 5 c 6 b

(e) 2 'm/am doing 3 don't; stay 4 goes
5 isn't using 6 're/are watching 7 's/is
doing 8 do; do 9 Are; playing
10 don't understand

3 **a** 🔊

2 Tidy up 3 Do the cooking 4 Wash the car
5 Do the washing-up 6 Do the washing

b 2 's/is cleaning the windows
3 are tidying up
4 are doing the washing-up
5 's/is cooking
6 are doing the shopping

4 **a** 🔊 TAPESCRIPT
1 bored, bird
2 born, burn
3 walk, work
4 short, shirt

b 🔊

/ɜː/ girl: learning, working, birthday
/ɔː/ more: door, always, talking

TAPESCRIPT

girl, more, door, always, learning, working,
talking, birthday

c 🔊 TAPESCRIPT/ANSWERS
1 All over the world.
2 I was born in Turkey.
3 Bert is working in Portugal.
4 The girls are organising their research.
5 Laura was early for work this morning.

5 1 Let's 2 must 3 crazy 4 check 5 out
6 You're 7 angel

7 **b** 🔊 1 living 2 right 3 what 4 water
5 is 6 do 7 don't 8 family 9 cooking
10 help

TAPESCRIPT

Interviewer I'm in Belize, and I'm talking
to a volunteer worker, Pauline Jones, about her
life here. Hi, Pauline.

Pauline Hello.

Interviewer Now, you're living here in Belize
for six months, is that right?

Pauline Yes, that's right. I'm working on
a project to protect the coral reefs.

Interviewer And what are you doing right
now?

Pauline Well, I'm doing a test on the sea water
here. I'm testing to find out if the water is
polluted. It's part of my work.

Interviewer And what do you do in your
free time?

Pauline I don't have much free time! I'm
staying with a family here in Belize, and when
I'm not working I help around the house.

Interviewer Doing what, for example?

Pauline Oh, sometimes I do the cooking and
the washing, and of course I tidy my room.
And I help with the shopping at the
weekends, too.

Unit check

1 1 morning 2 up 3 moment 4 the 5 is
6 hate 7 right 8 works 9 shopping

2 2 c 3 c 4 b 5 c 6 b 7 a 8 b 9 b

3 2 I'm ~~listen~~ *listening* to the radio at the moment.
3 They aren't here – they*'re/are* studying at the
library.
4 Sally ~~wears~~ *'s/is wearing* white trainers today.
5 Is Giorgio ~~use~~ *using* the computer at the moment?
6 Irena often ~~do~~ *does* the housework.
7 ~~Are~~ *Do* you often write letters?
8 Where ~~you are~~ *are you* going?
9 ~~I'm not wanting~~ *don't want* to read this book.

4 A healthy life

1 1 heavy 2 healthy 3 worried 4 unhealthy
5 sweet

2 **a** Across: Down:
        1 cheese   1 carrots
        4 oranges   2 eggs
        6 tea   3 butter
        9 potatoes   5 sugar
                      7 apples
                      8 water

b 1 Apples/Oranges; oranges/apples
2 Potatoes/Carrots; carrots/potatoes
3 Cheese/Butter; butter/cheese
4 tea/water; water/tea 5 eggs 6 Sugar

c 1 bread 2 coffee 3 milk 4 onions
5 tomatoes 6 grapes

3 **a** Countable: oranges, potatoes, carrots, eggs,
apples
Uncountable: cheese, tea, butter, sugar, water

b 1 is 2 is 3 are 4 is 5 is 6 are 7 is
8 are

c 1 some; some; some 2 an; some 3 a; an
4 an; some 5 some; some 6 some; some
7 some; an 8 a; some

e 1 many calories 2 much sugar 3 much
weight 4 much exercise 5 many hours
6 many emails

f 1 many 2 much 3 many 4 much
5 many 6 much 7 much

4 **(a)** 🔊 TAPESCRIPT/ANSWERS
sal(a)d brea(k)fa(s)t ham(b)urger exerci(se)
take-away ov(er)weight

(b) 🔊 TAPESCRIPT/ANSWERS
1 s(o)me min(era)l wat(er)
2 s(o)me bac(on)(and) eggs
3 (a) lot (of) (p)otatoes
4 (a) hun(dred) kil(o)grams
5 (a) terrib(le) super(m)arket

5 **(a)** 1 T (She only has one piece.)
2 F (*I love bacon and eggs at the weekend.*)
3 T (*... fish and chips*)
4 F (*... omelettes for lunch.*)
5 T (*... often get a Chinese take-away.*)
6 F (*... I often go there with my friends.*)
7 F (*... I sometimes go to a Greek restaurant.*)

7 **(a)** 1 Maria 2 Max 3 Maria 4 Dianne

(b) Meat and fish: beef, seafood, chicken
Fruit and vegetables: tomato, salad, onions,
garlic, carrots, potatoes, orange
Other food: pasta, milk, cheese, spices, yoghurt,
rice, bread, toast

Unit check

1 1 some 2 breakfast 3 beef 4 fish 5 doesn't
6 vegetables 7 eats 8 apple 9 grapes

2 2 c 3 b 4 a 5 b 6 c 7 a 8 c 9 b

3 2 How ~~much~~ *many* carrots do you want?
3 I'd like ~~a~~ *some* rice and some vegetables, please.
4 Andrew eats lots *of* bread.
5 I've got some grapes and ~~a~~ *an* apple for lunch.
6 How ~~many~~ *much* food does your dog eat?
7 There isn't ~~many~~ *much* butter in the fridge.
8 I think Joanne has got ~~a~~ *some* money.
9 How ~~much~~ *many* people can you see?

(5) My hero!

1 1 c 2 e 3 b 4 a 5 d

2 **(a)** 1 were 2 was 3 weren't 4 Were you
5 was 6 was 7 Were 8 was

(b) 🔊 1 was 2 Was 3 was 4 wasn't
5 was 6 was 7 were 8 was 9 were
10 weren't 11 was

TAPESCRIPT

Gran Oh, look at this old record!

Sally Who is it, Gran?

Gran It's Buddy Holly. He was my favourite singer
when I was young!

Sally Was he British?

Gran No, he was American.

Sally I don't know him at all.

Gran No, of course you don't. He died in 1959. And
he wasn't very old – he was only 22.

Sally What happened?

Gran Well, he was in a small aeroplane, in winter.
Two other singers were in the plane with him. The
plane crashed, and they all died.

Sally Oh, that's terrible.

Gran Yes, I was very sad. I cried all day!

Sally Tell me more about him.

Gran Well, *Peggy Sue* and *That'll be the day* were
his famous songs in the 1950s. But they weren't
my favourites – my favourite Buddy Holly song
was *Everyday*. Do you want to hear it?

Sally OK, Gran – play it for me!

(c) 2 hated 3 climbed 4 stayed 5 listened
6 cried 7 planned 8 decided 9 talked
10 stopped 11 studied 12 cleaned

(d) 2 cleaned 3 listened 4 cried 5 stopped
6 talked

(e) 2 didn't answer 3 didn't cook 4 didn't
speak 5 didn't study 6 didn't do

(f) 1 didn't stay 2 stayed 3 didn't like
4 visited 5 talked 6 didn't want
7 walked 8 didn't have 9 didn't play
10 started

3 **(a)** a 3 b 1 c 4 d 2

(b) 2 Take it off! 3 Put them down!
4 Put them on!

(c) 2 grows up 3 Turn off 4 sit down
5 go out

4 **(a)** 🔊 closed 1 decided 3 watched 1
walked 1 needed 2 studied 2 started 2
shopped 1 protected 3 worked 1

TAPESCRIPT
closed, decided, watched, walked, needed,
studied, started, shopped, protected, worked

(b) 🔊 TAPESCRIPT
1 She wanted a drink.
2 They watched a good film.
3 He walked a long way.
4 We visited our friends.
5 I hated that book!
6 She climbed the hill.
7 We decided to go home.

5 1 serious 2 Loads 3 one day 4 amazing

6 **(b)** wakes up, goes off, turns on, gets up, puts on,
sets off, goes on, slow down, gives up

7 **(a)** 1 b 2 e 3 a 4 c 5 d

(b) 1 F 2 T 3 T 4 F 5 F 6 T

(c) 1 favourite 2 hero 3 thief 4 rich
5 beautiful

Unit check

1 1 travelled 2 born 3 was 4 planned 5 didn't
6 trees 7 discovered 8 were 9 wasn't

2 2 b 3 a 4 b 5 a 6 b 7 c 8 b 9 c

3 2 ~~Is~~ *Was* your friend at school yesterday?
3 There ~~isn't~~ *weren't* many people at the party last night.
4 Where ~~are~~ *were* you born?
5 We ~~cook~~ *cooked* lunch for the family last Sunday.
6 Petra ~~studyed~~ *studied* History when she was at university.
7 They ~~wasn't~~ *didn't* live here in 2003.
8 We ~~stoped~~ *stopped* painting when it started to rain.
9 I watched the film but I ~~not liked~~ *didn't like* it.

6 Good friends

1 2 c 3 b 4 d 5 f 6 g 7 a

2 **(a)** 2 wanted 3 said 4 enjoyed 5 wasn't
6 met 7 became 8 left

(b) 2 left 3 won 4 went 5 began 6 met

(c) Names (from left to right)
Angela: did not finish/sixth
Judy: fifth
Maria: fourth
Sandra: third
Pat: second
Liz: first

(d) 1 Did you meet a famous athlete?
2 Did she speak to you?
3 Did the volunteers stay in the Olympic village?
4 Did you work hard?
5 Did (the) people enjoy the Olympic Games?

(e) 🔊 1 Did; see 2 didn't 3 were 4 had
5 met 6 liked 7 went 8 thought
9 was 10 looked 11 shouted 12 did; see

TAPESCRIPT

Esra I saw a funny programme on TV last night. It was called *The Cream on the Cake*. Did you see it?

Wendy No, I didn't. What was it about?

Esra Well, there were these two girls called Jane and Louise. They were really good friends. So one day they had lunch together and they met a boy called Danny – he came

and sat down at their table. The problem was, both Jane and Louise liked him.

Wendy Oh, yeah …

Esra Well, Jane went out with this boy Danny – they went to the cinema together – and Jane thought he was wonderful, you know? So she was really happy. But then the next day she was in the bus, and she looked through the window and she saw Danny and her friend Louise together!

Wendy Oh no! So what happened?

Esra Well, the two girls had a big argument later that day. They stood there in the street and shouted at each other.

Wendy So that was the end of their friendship, right?

Esra No, wait! The next minute, the girls looked across the street and who did they see? Danny! He was at the café, and he had a big cream cake in front of him …

3 **(a)**
Across:
1 May
3 Friday
5 hour
6 months
8 April
10 years
11 day

Down:
1 March
2 weeks
3 February
4 Yesterday
7 ten
9 Last

(c) b 8 c 11 d 7 e 12 f 9 g 1 h 3 i 2
j 10 k 6 l 5

4 **(a)** 🔊 TAPESCRIPT/ANSWERS
1 <u>happened</u> 2 <u>listened</u> 3 be<u>gan</u> 4 ar<u>rived</u>
5 <u>studied</u> 6 be<u>came</u>

(b) 🔊
●•: medal, athlete, friendship
•●: July, tonight, today
●••: stadium, teenager, exercise
•●•: important, fantastic, beginning

TAPESCRIPT
morning, November, yesterday, because, July, stadium, medal, athlete, important, tonight, teenager, fantastic, friendship, beginning, today, exercise

5 1 d 2 c 3 f 4 e 5 a 6 b

6 **(a)** 1 made 2 got 3 came 4 saw 5 took

(b) 1 swim 2 forget 3 speak 4 drink 5 give

7 🔊 a 3 b 2 d 2 e 1 f 3

1

I met my friend Greg when we were five years old. We started school together on the same day, and we quickly became friends after that. Now we're at different schools, but I often see him at the weekend. We've both got bikes and we do a lot of cycling together.

2

Peter is another good friend of mine. I met him three years ago when his family came to live in the flat next to us. I see him almost every day. We usually walk to school together, and we sometimes help each other with our homework.

3

Michael's 18 and he's my boyfriend. I met him a year ago – we met at my cousin's 16th birthday party. He asked me to dance and then we started talking, and I really liked him. We're still going out together. I see him about three times a week and we go to the cinema together every Saturday, because we really love watching films.

Unit check

1 1 surfing   2 didn't   3 was   4 looked   5 began
6 said   7 became   8 ago   9 friendship

2 2 c   3 b   4 a   5 a   6 c   7 a   8 b   9 a

3 2 Antonio ~~go~~ *went* to the stadium yesterday.
3 ~~Had they~~ *Did they have* a good time at the concert on Saturday?
4 They ~~was~~ *were* in the best team.
5 I ~~not ate~~ *didn't eat* much for lunch yesterday.
6 What ~~he watches~~ *did he watch* on TV last night?
7 The film began at 8 o'clock and ~~finish~~ *finished* at 9.30.
8 Where *did* you ~~met~~ *meet* Elizabeth?
9 Anna ~~leave~~ *left* the swimming pool an hour ago.

(7) The secrets of success

1 (a) 2 e   3 f   4 b   5 a   6 c

(b) 1 I have to do my homework after school.
2 Doctors don't have to be good at painting.
3 A teacher doesn't have to know everything.
4 We have to do the washing-up after lunch.
5 You don't have to get up early tomorrow.
6 Roberto doesn't have to work in the holidays.

(c) 1 doesn't have to   2 have to   3 has to
4 have to   5 doesn't have to   6 don't have to

(d) 2 Julie Baker doesn't have to go to the helicopter school by bus.
3 Matthew and his brother don't have to go to school.
4 Alan Martin has to wear a white shirt at school.

5 Pauline Jones doesn't have to work in Belize.
6 Successful Sumo wrestlers have to be heavy.
7 Text messages have to be short.

(e) 2 Yes, they do.   3 No, he doesn't.   4 No, she doesn't.   5 Yes, she does.   6 No, they don't.

(f) 2 Do Giovanna and Stefano have to do the washing-up? Yes, they do.
3 Does Giovanna have to do the ironing? No, she doesn't.
4 Do Helena and Stefano have to clean the windows? No, they don't.
6 Do you have to do the ironing? Yes, I do. / No, I don't.

2 (a)

(b) 1 teacher   2 pilot, flight attendant   3 doctor, nurse   4 secretary   5 vet   6 engineer
7 tennis player   8 dentist

3 1 had to   2 have to   3 have to   4 have to
5 have to   6 had to

4 (a) 🔊 TAPESCRIPT
1 We have to leave now.
2 They don't have to go out.
3 She has to do the washing.
4 He doesn't have to study tonight.
5 He had to cook this evening.
6 Does he have to drive to the shop?

(b) 🔊 1 has to   2 had to   3 has to
4 have to   5 had to   6 have to

TAPESCRIPT
1 Sam has to help his parents at the weekend.
2 I had to go to the dentist yesterday.
3 Teresa has to work on Saturday mornings.
4 We have to buy a present for Dad's birthday.
5 My sister had to get a new computer.
6 You have to go to bed early tonight.

5 1 Dave   2 Dave   3 Amy   4 Amy   5 Amy

6 🔊 1 c   2 g   3 a   4 h   5 d   6 f   7 b   8 e

TAPESCRIPT/ANSWERS
1 <u>do</u>ctor   2 <u>pi</u>lot   3 engi<u>neer</u>   4 <u>ath</u>lete
5 <u>secretary</u>   6 <u>flight</u> attendant   7 <u>foot</u>ball player
8 pho<u>to</u>grapher

7 1 e Picture e (Claudia Schiffer)   2 c Picture a
(Edmund Hilary)   3 a Picture b (Charles Dickens)
4 b Picture d (Ludwig Van Beethoven)
5 d Picture c (Harrison Ford)

8 (a) singer; rich; job; round; guitar

Unit check

1 1 dentist   2 doctors   3 job   4 player   5 dream
6 have   7 hours   8 has   9 successful

2 2 a   3 b   4 c   5 c   6 a   7 c   8 a   9 b

3 2 A nurse usually ~~have~~ *has* to wear a uniform.
3 Engineers have to ~~being~~ *be* good at Maths.
4 My parents ~~not~~ *don't* have to work at the weekend.
5 Maria ~~has~~ *had* to go to the dentist last week.
6 ~~Is~~ *Does* Giorgio have to learn English at school?
7 I ~~has~~ *had* to get up early yesterday morning.
8 ~~Have you~~ *Do you have* to do a lot of homework?
9 My little sister ~~not has~~ *doesn't have* to do much
homework.

8 New ideas

1 1 a songwriter   2 writing songs   3 always easy
4 an idea   5 some paper   6 writes songs
7 the band   8 school party

2 (a) 1 e   2 c   3 b   4 a   5 f   6 d

(b) 1 Was; wasn't   2 Is; there's   3 are   4 wasn't
5 Are   6 are

(c) 1 some   2 some   3 any   4 some   5 any
6 any   7 some   8 any   9 any

(d) 1 a; any   2 any; some; a   3 an; a   4 some;
any   5 any; some; some; an

(e) 2 mine   3 yours   4 Ours   5 theirs   6 hers

(f) 1 theirs   2 his; hers   3 our; ours   4 yours;
you   5 mine; mine

3 (a) 🔊 TAPESCRIPT/ANSWERS
/eɪ/ say: Spain, plane, late
/ʌ/ up: sun, fun, won
/ɔː/ more: fork, floor, talk
/aɪ/ my: night, right, nine
/iː/ see: keys, please
/e/ bed: said, red
/ɜː/ her: hurt, shirt

(b) 🔊 TAPESCRIPT/ANSWERS
I thought my holiday in Spain
Was going to be great.

But when I got into the *plane*,
They told me I was *late*.

I ate some food, I wanted more:
They asked me not to talk.
I dropped my knife onto the *floor*,
I only had a *fork*.
The plane was flying in the night,
But the sky was blue and *red*.
'It's strange,' I thought, 'this isn't *right*.'
'You're in a dream,' they *said*.

4 (a) 2 Joe went to sleep at work and his boss wasn't
very happy.
3 The baby is asleep so please be quiet –
I don't want her to wake up.
4 Maria had a dream about flying.
5 I went to bed at midnight but I read until
two in the morning.
6 The baby is awake so you don't have to
be quiet.

5 1 popular   2 contest   3 groups   4 audience
5 judges   6 sold   7 cruel   8 chose

6 Positive: excellent, healthy, fantastic, successful,
delicious, creative, beautiful
Negative: lonely, polluted, stupid, crazy, unhappy,
difficult, weird

7 (a) a 2   b 4   c 6   d 5   e 7   f 1   g 3

(b) 2 a butterfly with open wings
3 a singing bird
4 a spider
5 buzzing bees
6 a sleeping cat
7 a running horse

Unit check

1 1 at   2 some   3 his   4 ideas   5 asleep
6 to bed   7 wake up   8 to   9 dream

2 2 b   3 c   4 a   5 c   6 c   7 a   8 c   9 b

3 2 We can't find ~~some~~ *any* information in this book.
3 That scarf doesn't belong to her, but the jacket
is ~~her~~ *hers*.
4 Have you got ~~a~~ *any* milk in the fridge?
5 Leo and Karen haven't got a pet, so the dog
isn't ~~ours~~ *theirs*.
6 My parents give me ~~a~~ *some* pocket money
on Saturdays.
7 There aren't ~~some~~ *any* music shops in our town.
8 Is this CD ~~your~~ *yours*?
9 No, it isn't ~~my~~ *mine*. I think it's Barbara's.

9 The languages we speak

1 (a) free, small, local, old, excellent, Russian,
different, strange, good, determined, big, exciting

(b) -er: quiet – quieter, big – bigger, lonely – lonelier, cheap – cheaper, noisy – noisier, old – older

more ...: difficult – more difficult, expensive – more expensive, successful – more successful, relaxing – more relaxing

irregular: bad – worse, far – further/farther

(c) 2 Café Paradiso is newer than Efes Café.
3 The coffee in Café Paradiso is cheaper than the coffee in Efes Café.
4 The coffee in Efes Café is more expensive than in Café Paradiso.
5 The sandwiches in Efes Café are more expensive than the sandwiches in Café Paradiso.
6 The sandwiches in Café Paradiso are cheaper than in Efes Café.

2 **(a)** 1 e 2 c 3 d 4 a 5 b 6 h 7 f 8 g

(b) 1 means 2 guess 3 look up 4 have
5 imitate 6 make 7 translate

3 **(a)** -est: big – biggest, easy – easiest, thin – thinnest, heavy – heaviest, short – shortest, rich – richest

most ...: beautiful – most beautiful, important – most important, delicious – most delicious, creative – most creative, intelligent – most intelligent

irregular: bad – worst, good – best

(b) 1 most delicious / best 2 biggest
3 most boring / worst 4 most beautiful
5 easiest/best 6 richest / most important
7 heaviest

(c) 1 most interesting 2 most expensive
3 bigger 4 older 5 best 6 friendlier
7 more difficult 8 most delicious 9 better
10 most successful 11 more exciting
12 worst

4 **(a)** and **(b)**

🔊 TAPESCRIPT/ANSWERS
1 Cars are faster than bicycles.
2 Chocolate is sweeter than butter.
3 Paula is more creative than her brother.
4 The Maths exam was more difficult than the Science one.
5 Robert is the youngest student in our class.
6 Vegetables are the healthiest things you can eat.
7 It was the most expensive jacket in the shop.
8 They were some of the most talented writers in the country.

5 1 cool 2 can't 3 pocket; save up 4 What about you?; check out

7 **(a)** 🔊
1 Juliette e
3 Alice d
4 Carla a
5 Mary b

(b) 🔊 1 T 2 F 3 T 4 T 5 F 6 F

TAPESCRIPT

My name's Adrian. I'm 16 and I'm interested in Art. I want to be a painter when I leave school.

I've got four sisters. Mary is the oldest, but she isn't the tallest – she's smaller than Carla and Alice. Mary's got very short hair – our parents don't like it, but I think it looks cool. She's got a boyfriend called Terry and she talks about him all the time. It gets a bit boring, really.

Juliette is my favourite sister. She's the youngest – she's only ten, but I think she's very intelligent and she's also the funniest person in our family – she can really make you laugh. She loves animals and she keeps a pet rabbit in the garden.

Carla and Alice are twins – they were born on the same day, and now they're both 12. They look similar, but Carla's got longer hair and bigger eyes than Alice. They have arguments about music all the time. Carla loves all the young girl bands but Alice hates them. Alice is a sporty kid – she's a good swimmer and she's in the girls' football team at school.

Unit check

1 1 speak 2 than 3 difficult 4 easier 5 worst
6 guess 7 look 8 accent 9 imitate

2 2 b 3 b 4 a 5 b 6 a 7 b 8 b 9 c

3 2 I think History is more interesting ~~then~~ *than* Geography.
3 Mont Blanc is the ~~higher~~ *highest* mountain in Europe.
4 The book was ~~more good~~ *better* than the film.
5 Your hamburger is ~~biger~~ *bigger* than mine!
6 Football is the ~~popularest~~ *most popular* sport in the world.
7 The Science exam was ~~worst~~ *worse* than the Maths exam.
8 My cat is ~~most~~ *more* intelligent than my dog.
9 The day I met Laura was the ~~more lucky~~ *luckiest* day of my life.

10 We're going on holiday

1 a 4 b 2 c 1 d 5 e 3

2 **(a)** 1 isn't / is not staying
2 's/is having
3 are paying
4 's/is going
5 aren't flying

6 're/are travelling
7 'm not / am not hiking
8 're /are spending
9 're /are staying

(b) 2 Sorry, I'm having lunch with Grandma on Saturday.
3 Sorry, I'm meeting Uncle Jack at the airport (at 4.30) on Friday.
4 Sorry, my cousins are arriving from Germany on Sunday.
5 Sorry, Helen's coming to my place on Monday.
6 Sorry, I'm studying for a Maths test on Wednesday.
7 Sorry, I'm going shopping with Dad on Tuesday.

(c) 1 Is Peter coming?
2 he isn't
3 Are Ann and Paul coming?
4 they are
5 Are you and your family going
6 we are
7 Are you travelling
8 we aren't
9 Is your sister going
10 she is

(d) 1 F 2 N 3 N 4 F 5 F 6 F 7 F 8 F 9 N

3 (a) 2 in two days' time
3 in three hours' time
4 next year
5 in two months' time
6 in three weeks' time

(b) 1 horse-riding 2 canoeing 3 windsurfing 4 camping 5 snorkelling 6 sailing 7 sunbathing 8 sightseeing

(c) stay: on a farm, in a hotel
travel: by plane, to London, by car
hire: a boat, a car, canoes
spend: a week, some time, three days
buy: souvenirs, a postcard, presents

(d) 1 buy; souvenirs 2 spent three days 3 hired a car 4 travelled by plane 5 stayed in a hotel

4 (a) 🔊
/θ/ think: maths, thousand, thirteen, athlete, throw
/ð/ that: clothes, those, father, brother

TAPESCRIPT
clothes, those, Maths, father, thousand, thirteen, athlete, throw, brother

(b) 🔊
1 It's my sixteenth birthday next month.
2 They're sunbathing together on the beach.

3 Her grandfather is healthy but he's very thin.
4 My brother can throw this ball further than me.

5 1 backpack c 2 waterfall f 3 volcano b 4 airport d 5 turtle a 6 jungle e

6 (a) 2 verb 3 adjective 4 preposition 5 singular 6 plural

(b) 1 e 2 c 3 d 4 a 5 b

(c) 2

7 2 On Saturday night in a hotel in town.
3 Her aunt and uncle.
4 On Friday.
5 Because their flat is very small.
6 Her grandfather, because he's still in hospital.
7 They're going to buy some new clothes to wear.

8 🔊 1 ✓ 2 ✓ 3 ✗ 4 ✗ 5 ✓

TAPESCRIPT
Emma   Hello.
Adam   Hi, Emma. It's Adam.
Emma   Oh, Adam! Hi.
Adam   How are you? How was the party on Saturday?
Emma   Oh, it was really good. Well, most things were good, anyway. The room looked fantastic – the decorations were lovely and the flowers looked really beautiful.
Adam   And the food?
Emma   Great – delicious. Everyone really enjoyed the food. The only thing was, the birthday cake was a bit of a disaster. Mum cooked it too long, so it was black on the bottom and it was very dry. Mum wasn't very happy about that.
Adam   No, that's a shame.
Emma   The other problem was the jazz band. Two of the musicians didn't come! They went to the wrong address.
Adam   Oh, no!
Emma   Yeah, can you believe that? My brother had to run home and get a CD player and some CDs. But it didn't seem to matter, really. Everyone danced and had a good time. And there were loads of presents for Dad and he loved them. I think he had a very good night.

Unit check

1 1 coach 2 breakfast 3 sailing 4 sunbathing 5 hiring 6 aren't 7 campsites 8 youth 9 is

2 2 c 3 b 4 a 5 b 6 b 7 c 8 a 9 b

3 2 My friend is arriving the day after ~~the~~ next.
3 Are you ~~cook~~ *cooking* the dinner this evening?
4 My brother ~~not~~ *isn't / is not* going out this weekend.
5 Helen and Tony ~~bring~~ *are bringing* some CDs to the party on Friday.

6 I'm starting a new job the day ~~next~~ *after* tomorrow.
7 Rebecca ~~doesn't sing~~ *isn't singing* at the concert next week.
8 Stefano is seeing the doctor ~~for~~ *in* three days' time.
9 When ~~Alex is~~ *is Alex* coming home from school this afternoon?

11 What will happen?

 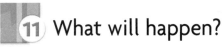

1 a

1 Will we find
2 we'll all be
3 it'll be
4 it won't hurt
5 I'll never forget you
6 they'll break you

TAPESCRIPT

Samantha Jake, we went into space nearly two years ago and we're still looking for planet Vulcan. What do you think? Will we find it?

Jake Oh, yeah. I'm sure we will.

Jake You have to do something!

Computer Sorry! I'd like to help, but the spaceship is out of control and there's nothing – I repeat, nothing – I can do. So in 45 seconds, we'll all be dead.

Samantha Help! Do something!

Computer I can't. But don't worry. When we die, in exactly ... 30 seconds from now, it'll be very quick and it won't hurt!

Computer Five seconds!

Jake I'll never forget you, Sam.

Computer April Fool!

Samantha Oh! When we get back to Earth, I'm going to tell them about you, and they'll break you into little pieces.

b a 5   b 8   c 6   d 2   e 1   f 7   g 4   h 3

c 1 'll be / will be   2 won't be   3 won't win
4 'll help / will help   5 'll find / will find
6 won't wear   7 won't hurt   8 will see

d 1 Will; get   2 Will; come   3 Will; go
4 Will; be   5 will; finish   8 will; see

e **Example answers**
2 You'll win lots of money but you won't be famous.
3 You won't have a big house but you'll have a fast car.
4 You'll get married when you're 30 but you won't have children.

2 a **TAPESCRIPT**
I'll go now.
She'll help you.
They'll be here on Monday.
You'll see him later.
That information will be on the Internet.
The universe will continue to get bigger.

b 1 'll   2 'll   3 will   4 will   5 0   6 0
7 'll   8 will

TAPESCRIPT

1 Don't worry. I'll do this for you.
2 We'll do our homework after lunch.
3 The spaceship will land in 20 minutes.
4 The countdown will start soon.
5 During a flight, astronauts eat lots of vitamins.
6 Go to university. I'm sure you see how important it is for your future.
7 I doubt they'll be here in half an hour.
8 They say this capsule will take people to the planet Jupiter.

3 a 1 I think I'll enjoy it.
2 I think the baby will wake up.
3 I don't think he'll give it back.
4 I think he'll know how to do it.
5 I don't think they'll be late.
6 I think I'll finish before 9 o'clock.

b 1 probably   2 doubt   3 not sure   4 maybe
5 hope   6 sure

c 1 stars   2 planet   3 spaceship   4 countdown
5 helmet

4 1 Anything else   2 the best bit   3 nonsense
4 don't believe   5 embarrassing

5 a Sentences 1 and 3 are nouns. Sentence 2 is a verb.

b 1 b   2 d   3 c   4 a

6 2 lines 2–6   3 lines 26–29   4 lines 24–26   5 lines 22–33   6 lines 2–9   7 lines 15–17   8 lines 7–9

Unit check

1 1 think   2 abroad   3 probably   4 to find   5 don't
6 sure   7 nonsense   8 maybe   9 she'll

2 2 c   3 a   4 c   5 b   6 b   7 a   8 a   9 c

3 2 This town ~~is~~ *will be* bigger in ten years' time.
3 Maybe they *'ll / will* have guitar lessons next year.
4 ~~I'll be~~ *'m / am* sure Emma will get a good job.
5 ~~You will~~ *Will you* watch a video this evening?
6 Lisa ~~won't probably~~ *probably won't* arrive before 10 o'clock.
7 Will your parents ~~to~~ drive us to the airport?
8 They ~~doesn't~~ *won't* go there next year.
9 I ~~won't~~ *don't* think our team will win the competition.

12 Never give up!

1 a a 6 b 2 c 5 d 4 e 1 f 3

2 a 2 a 3 e 4 f 5 b 6 c

b 2 too 3 very 4 too 5 very 6 too

c 2 too difficult 3 too cold 4 too small
5 too far 6 too young 7 too easy
8 too expensive

3 a 2 warm; rainy 3 cold; foggy 4 hot; windy
5 cold; snowy 6 hot; sunny

4 a 1 quickly 2 safely 3 noisy 4 early
5 hard 6 brilliantly 7 good 8 fast
9 easily 10 late

b 1 quietly 2 stupid 3 slowly
4 dangerously 5 usual 6 healthy

c 2 's/is working hard
3 's/is playing badly
4 're/are running quickly
5 's/is smiling happily
6 're/are shouting loudly
7 's/is winning easily
8 's/is getting up late

5 1 newcomers d 2 skyscrapers e 3 manual c
4 railway f 5 century h 6 migrants g
7 apartments a 8 succeed b

6 a 🔊 TAPESCRIPT
job, what, want, foggy, belong, probably
rope, won't, joke, kilo, going, tomorrow

b 🔊 TAPESCRIPT/ANSWERS
1 Our dog has got a cold nose.
2 Bob and Tom don't go to the coast.
3 The foreign politician told a good joke.
4 John wants to own a mobile phone.
5 Those tomatoes are old.
So what? Throw them in the pot!

7 *o*: potato, hello
ow: tomorrow, window, follow
oa: boat, soap
o + consonant + *e*: nose, joke, hope

Unit check

1 1 too 2 heavily 3 windy 4 bitterly 5 snowed
6 weather 7 happily 8 sunny 9 angry

2 2 c 3 b 4 a 5 a 6 b 7 c 8 a 9 a

3 2 That music is very ~~loudly~~ loud.
3 The shop was busy and we had to work ~~hardly~~ hard.
4 It's ~~to~~ too hot to wear a jumper.
5 If you walk ~~quick~~ quickly, you can get to the station in five minutes.

6 My grandfather is ~~too~~ very old, but he's fit and healthy.
7 Alison talks ~~slow~~ slowly, so it's easy to understand her.
8 I can't lift the piano – it's too ~~heavily~~ heavy.
9 Our team didn't win, but they played ~~good~~ well.

13 Good intentions

1 1 circle 2 December 3 countdown 4 seconds
5 fireworks 6 kiss 7 Eve 8 midnight 9 dawn
10 resolutions 11 Happy

2 a 1 e 2 d 3 b 4 a 5 c

b 1 keep; up 2 throw away 3 take up
4 work out 5 give up

3 a 1 F 2 F 3 T 4 T 5 F 6 F

b 1 'm/am 2 's/is 3 Are 4 aren't 5 isn't
6 're/are 7 'm not 8 Is

c 2 A: Is; going to learn B: she is
3 A: Is; going to move B: he isn't
4 A: Are; going to wear B: I'm not
5 A: Are; going to do B: they are
6 A: Are; going to hire B: we are

d 2 'm not going to enjoy
3 're/are going to have
4 aren't going to see
5 're/are going to miss

f 1 mustn't eat 2 must do 3 mustn't use
4 must wear 5 mustn't bring 6 must be

4 🔊 1 mustn't 2 must 3 must 4 mustn't
5 must 6 mustn't

TAPESCRIPT
1 You mustn't do that.
2 You must sit here.
3 She must speak to him.
4 We mustn't give her the letter.
5 I must stay here.
6 You mustn't forget me.

5 1 I'll drive you home.
2 I'll fix it for you.
3 I'll pay for your meal.
4 I'll open the window.
5 I'll make an omelette for you.
6 I'll ask my parents.

7 a 🔊 1 b 2 b 3 a 4 b 5 c

TAPESCRIPT
Denise Hi, Robbie, Happy New Year! It's Denise here.

Robbie Denise! Happy New Year! Good to hear from you. How are you? What's happening in your life?

Denise Oh, big news. My father's got a new job and that's going to mean a huge change for my family. It means we're going to move from London to Newcastle.

Robbie Newcastle – is that close to London?

Denise No, it's miles away, in the north of England. We're moving out in five weeks' time.

Robbie Gosh! Have you got a new place to live?

Denise Yes, we're going to move into a house in Newcastle. My parents say it's a nice house, and it's bigger than our London flat – it's got four bedrooms and a garden. But I haven't seen it yet. I'm going to have a look at it next weekend.

Robbie So what's happening with the flat in London?

Denise We're going to sell it. That's OK with me, it isn't a very nice flat and it's too small. But still, it's going to be hard to leave London. I'm really going to miss my friends here and it's going to be difficult starting in a new school. I'm not looking forward to it, really.

Robbie What about your mother?

Denise Mum? She can't wait. She's going to give up her job and she's really happy about that. And she wants to take up painting again – she was a good artist, you know, before she got married.

Robbie Well, it sure will be a big change. I hope it all goes well …

Unit check

1 1 resolutions 2 must 3 going 4 isn't 5 keep 6 to 7 stick 8 give 9 take

2 2 a 3 a 4 c 5 a 6 b 7 b 8 c 9 b

3 2 We're/are going to study hard before the exams.
3 Anna ~~doesn't go~~ isn't going to watch TV this evening.
4 They must ~~being~~ be home before 12 o'clock.
5 I'm/am not going to take my guitar with me.
6 Are you going to take up windsurfing next year?
7 We mustn't ~~to~~ forget Mum's birthday.
8 ~~Does~~ Is it going to rain soon?
9 They ~~don't~~ aren't going to travel by bus.

14 You shouldn't do that!

1 **(a)** 1 b should 2 c should 3 a shouldn't 4 d should

(b) 2 should be nice to people
3 shouldn't buy expensive clothes

4 should have music lessons
5 shouldn't go to bed late
6 should talk to his teacher about it

(c) 2 Should students bow
3 Should you bring a present
4 When should you use
5 Should people take off
(Students' own answers.)

(d) **Example answers**
2 She should go to the doctor.
3 You should go to England for a year.
4 You should study tonight.
5 He should save up his money.
6 You should study hard and pass your exams.
7 He shouldn't buy so many CDs.
8 They should have a party.

2 **(a)** 2 cheerful 3 lazy 4 polite 5 miserable 6 hard-working 7 organised 8 rude 9 nervous

(b)
James: b
Sally: a
Cathy: a
Joanne: c
Max: b

TAPESCRIPT

James is usually very happy. He smiles a lot and you often hear him laughing.

I like Sally because she always tells you what she thinks. Sometimes you don't like what you hear but you know she's being truthful.

Cathy's great. She doesn't worry a lot about problems. And she hardly ever gets angry, even when people are unfriendly or unhelpful.

Joanne hardly ever does her homework and she never makes her bed or tidies her room. She sleeps until 11 o'clock at the weekend and she watches TV all the time.

Max is a strange guy. He doesn't like to talk to anyone and he doesn't speak when he sees you. He always works alone and he never invites people to come to his place.

3 **(a)** TAPESCRIPT/ANSWERS
1 answer, twenty
2 kind, knife
3 often, faster
4 autumn, station
5 climber, robber
6 horse, hour
7 went, wrong
8 hold, should
9 Science, disco

(b) 1 b 2 l 3 k 4 n 5 w

1 lamb 2 could 3 kneel 4 column
5 wrap

4 2 What are your new sunglasses like
3 What's the weather like
4 What were Helen's friends like
5 What was the party like
6 What's your neighbour like

5 (**a**) 1 c 2 d 3 a 4 b

6 (**b**) 1 dull 2 brilliant 3 ugly 4 interesting

1 Can I have 2 Pardon 3 You're welcome
4 please 5 Thank you

7 (**b**) dis-: orderly – disorderly,
obedient – disobedient
un-: healthy – unhealthy, usual – unusual,
lucky – unlucky
Different adjective: beautiful – ugly,
quiet – loud, stupid – clever

8 (**c**) im-: possible – impossible, perfect – imperfect
-less: useful – useless, careful – careless

3 F (*I made friends with other French people.*)
4 F (*The children were … great teachers.*)
5 F (*You should leave your dictionary at home …*)
6 T
7 T
8 F (*… don't study too hard.*)

Unit check

1 1 cheerful 2 miserable 3 lazy 4 shouldn't
5 dishonest 6 like 7 disorganised 8 kind
9 should

2 2 c 3 c 4 b 5 a 6 c 7 a 8 b 9 b

3 2 They shouldn't ~~to~~ talk loudly in the library.
3 I don't think you ~~shouldn't~~ *should* go out without
a coat. / I ~~don't~~ think you shouldn't go out without
a coat.
4 What *are* your new teachers ~~are~~ like?
5 We should ~~to~~ get up early tomorrow.
6 He ~~doesn't~~ *shouldn't* smoke when people are eating.
7 ~~Do I should~~ *Should I* send an email to Martin?
8 You shouldn't be lazy, ~~do~~ *should* you?
9 What'~~s~~ *was* the concert like last night?

15 How brave!

1 1 d take it back 2 a will kill 3 e didn't hit
4 c picked it up 5 b are scared

2 (**a**) 1 you finish 2 don't 3 he'll have to
4 you'll be 5 she'll send

(**b**) 1 If Judith misses her bus, she'll be miserable.
2 If the train doesn't come soon, we'll walk
home.
3 You won't get wet if you wear a raincoat.
4 I won't sing well at the concert if I'm too
nervous.
5 If my friends see me, they won't recognise me.

(**c**) 1 will go for a bike ride / go cycling.
2 rains, she'll read a book.
3 gets up early, he'll go shopping.
4 doesn't get up early, he'll listen to some music.

(**e**) 1 the rope will break
2 the dog will attack her
3 they won't find us
4 they'll/will have a crash
5 you'll/will feel better
6 the plane won't take off

(**f**) 1 when 2 when 3 if 4 If 5 if 6 when

3 (**a**) ◁)) TAPESCRIPT/ANSWERS
1 If the <u>mo</u>ther doesn't <u>rec</u>ognise the <u>ba</u>by,
she <u>won't</u> take it <u>back</u>.
2 They <u>on</u>ly at<u>tack</u> when you <u>show</u> you're
<u>scared</u>.
3 If I <u>turn</u> and run a<u>way</u>, this gorilla will
at<u>tack</u> me.
4 But if I don't <u>move</u>, he'll go a<u>way</u>.

(**b**) ◁)) TAPESCRIPT/ANSWERS
1 <u>Neil</u> will <u>look</u> for a <u>job</u> when the summer
<u>hol</u>idays be<u>gin</u>.
2 I'll do my <u>home</u>work when I <u>get home</u>.
3 We'll <u>take</u> a <u>taxi</u> if <u>Dad can't</u> meet us at
the <u>sta</u>tion.
4 If you <u>waste time</u>, you <u>won't fin</u>ish your
<u>work</u>.
5 It'll be <u>great</u> if I <u>win</u> this <u>com</u>peti<u>tion</u>!
6 We'll have a <u>big</u> cele<u>bra</u>tion when you <u>turn</u>
twenty-<u>one</u>.

4 (**a**) 1 c 2 e 3 d 4 f 5 a 6 b

(**b**) 1 interesting 2 worried 3 exciting
4 terrified 5 annoyed 6 frightening

(**c**) 1 crash 2 land 3 attack 4 overturn
5 fall 6 collapse 7 burn

5 1 Hang on 2 No way 3 No big deal

7 (**a**) a 2 b 1 c 4 d 5 e 3

(**b**) 1 An old lady.
2 She threw some stones.
3 It barked at Sharon.
4 Because its owner arrived.

Unit check

1 1 bored 2 exciting 3 annoying 4 tired
5 when 6 interested 7 I'll 8 arrives 9 I'm

2 2 b 3 c 4 b 5 a 6 a 7 b 8 c 9 b

3 2 If ~~you'll~~ *you* go to bed now, you'll wake up early tomorrow.
3 Sam ~~is~~ *will be* healthier if he eats more fruit.
4 Paula will sing well if she ~~not gets~~ *doesn't get* nervous.
5 If it's rainy tomorrow, we ~~don't~~ *won't* go horse-riding.
6 You'll miss the bus ~~when~~ *if* you don't run.
7 I'*ll/will* stop writing to Jane if she doesn't answer my letters.
8 If Tim goes to university, he will ~~becomes~~ *become* a lawyer.
9 ~~If~~ *When* the winter comes, we will get some snow.

16 It's a mad world

1 **(a)** 1 John Evans balances things on his head.
2 The man from Scotland grows onions.
3 The man from Thailand never cuts his hair.
4 Len Vale Onslow has never had an accident.
5 Susan Smith never gets out of bed.

(b) 1 grow 2 getting out 3 cut 4 balance

2 **(a)**

```
R I S N A K E D P E
F R I T P C J A D R
T A R A N T U L A M
A B Y T I D U L E O
L B S I O T P I K U
N I V G F R O G E S
O T C E T O S A N E
R C O R W N A T L D
E M W P A R R O T H
H A E L G H O R S E
```

(b) 1 tiger 2 snake 3 cow 4 tarantula
5 alligator 6 parrot 7 frog 8 rabbit

3 **(a)** 1 played 2 worked 3 driven
4 learned/learnt 5 eaten 6 written
7 listened 8 done

(b) 1 ~~I'm~~ *I've* read this book three times.
2 This actress has ~~be~~ *been* in about 30 films.
3 Annette and Luke ~~has~~ *have* never played ice hockey.
4 Martin hasn't ~~spoke~~ *spoken* to my parents.
5 We'*ve/have* never been in a helicopter.
6 You've ~~travel~~ *travelled* to a lot of countries.

(c) 2 A: Has a snake ever bitten you?
B: No, I've never seen a snake.
3 A: Have you ever flown to America?
B: No, I've never been in a plane.
4 A: Have your friends swum in this pool?
B: No, they've never learned to swim.

(d) 2 Have you ever met a pop star?
3 Have you ever eaten Mexican food?
4 Have you ever tried windsurfing?
5 Have you ever been in hospital?
(Students' own answers.)

(e) 1 've/have never seen
2 've/have never had
3 Have; had
4 've/have never been there
5 have driven
6 've/have never cycled
7 has never killed
8 Have; eaten

(f) 🔊
1 have bitten me
2 they've never complained
3 pets ever escaped
4 have never escaped

TAPESCRIPT

Interviewer So have you ever had any problems yourself? Some of these animals are dangerous, aren't they?

Mr Brown Well, the tarantulas have bitten me once or twice.

Interviewer What do your neighbours think about all these animals?

Mr Brown Well, they've never complained.

Interviewer Have any of your pets ever escaped?

Mr Brown Yes. The parrot escaped in 1998. But the alligator and the tarantulas have never escaped.

4 🔊 **TAPESCRIPT/ANSWERS**
1 I cut my finger.
2 Have you seen the parrot?
3 He's spoken to my mother.
4 They've won lots of prizes.
5 He's seeing the doctor.
6 She's eaten the chocolate.

5 1 win a prize 2 took a risk 3 raise money
4 break the record 5 told a joke

6 **(a)** 1 parachute 2 wheelchair 3 anniversary
4 skydiver 5 ghost

(b) 1 F 2 F 3 T 4 F 5 T 6 T

7 No change: cut – cut – cut
Same past simple and past participle: make – made – made, meet – met – met
Different past participle: write – wrote – written, fly – flew – flown, break – broke – broken, drive – drove – driven, go – went – gone

8 🔊 1 mushrooms   2 do you want   3 please
4 cut   5 four   6 six   7 can eat six pieces
8 mine   9 decide   10 red   11 blue
12 rains   13 black horse   14 bigger than
15 brown one

TAPESCRIPT

Boy   This is one of my favourite jokes. Listen.
A man goes into a pizza place and asks for
a pizza. The girl asks him what he wants on it.
'Oh, ham and mushrooms and olives, please.'
'Fine,' says the girl. 'And what size pizza do
you want?'
'What sizes have you got?' asks the man.
'Well, you can have small, medium or large.'
'Oh,' says the man. 'Um ... medium, please.'
The girl says: 'OK. And do you want me to
cut it into four pieces or six pieces?
The man thinks about it and says, 'Just four
pieces, please. I'm not really very hungry.
I don't think I can eat six pieces!'

Girl   Yeah, that's a good joke. But I think this
one's good too.
Two farmers go out one day and they buy
two horses, one each. They put the two horses
in a field.
'Wait a minute,' says one farmer. 'How will
we know which horse is yours and which horse
is mine?'

So the two farmers sit down and think about
it. They decide to paint the horses' tails – one
tail will be red and the other tail will be blue.
But that night, it rains, and the paint comes
off. So the two farmers think about it again.
Then one of them says, 'Oh, what stupid
farmers we are! Look, it's easy. Your black horse
is bigger than my brown one!'

Unit check

1 1 pets   2 mouse   3 cow   4 snake   5 never
6 parrots   7 spoken   8 ever   9 been

2 2 a   3 c   4 b   5 b   6 b   7 a   8 c   9 b

3 2 Alan ~~have~~ *has* painted some excellent pictures.
3 I've ~~work~~ *worked* in five different jobs.
4 Tom and Claudio ~~haven't never~~ *have never /
haven't ever* played football.
5 ~~You ever have~~ *Have you ever* stayed in Paris?
6 I've ~~wrote~~ *written* to Lily a few times, but she
hasn't answered.
7 Sally ~~not has~~ *hasn't / has not* had a meal at this
restaurant.
8 *Has* the dog ever bitten you?
9 He's never stayed at your house, ~~hasn't~~ *has* he?

Acknowledgements

The publishers are grateful to the following contributors:

Fran Banks: editorial work
Cheryl Pelteret: initial script writing
Pentacor Book Design: text design and layouts
Claire Thacker: final script writing

Co-Creation Spirituality:
A Breath of Fresh Air

Are you ready for an exciting spiritual challenge? Finally, there is a well-thought-out way to bridge the gap between Pagan/Wiccan practice and the esoteric Christian Mysteries.

Founded upon the universal truths of all positive religions, Co-Creation Spirituality is a non-judgmental approach to Divinity. *Cauldron of Transformation* is a refreshing alternative to all forms of mainstream religion.

Cauldron of Transformation contains everything you need to create your own spiritual tradition. This material is based upon the experience of over 20,000 people who have benefited from the teachings offered by Our Lady of Enchantment—one of the first Pagan/Wiccan metaphysical centers in the United States open to the general public.

Cauldron of Transformation skillfully examines the wisdom of Buddhism, the lore of Celtic Druidism, and the grace of Christianity while exploring the ecstatic vitality of Santería and Shamanism.

Cauldron of Transformation shows you how to reclaim the power of the Old Religion without needlessly throwing away the compassion and wisdom of early Christianity. Decide for yourself what is spiritually satisfying and begin the rewarding work of creating a personally meaningful religious tradition with the guidance of *Cauldron of Transformation*.

About the Author

For the past eighteen years, Lady Sabrina has been actively involved in the study of comparative religion, the metaphysical sciences, and the Wiccan/Pagan movement. Sabrina is well versed in comparative religion, Wicca, and the Pre-Christian mystery traditions. She is an initiated High Priestess and a legally ordained minister of Wicca.

In 1978, Sabrina founded Our Lady of Enchantment, a church and school of the Old Religion. Since those early beginnings, Our Lady of Enchantment has blossomed into the first Wiccan Metaphysical Center open to the public in the United States.

Sabrina has personally written and prepared all six of the school's home study courses, along with her first book, *Reclaiming the Power,* a Llewellyn publication. She actively works with students in comparative religious studies and in the magical arts through public presentations and workshops.

To Write to the Author

If you wish to contact the author or would like more information about this book, please write to the author in care of Llewellyn Worldwide and we will forward your request. Both the author and publisher appreciate hearing from you and learning of your enjoyment of this book and how it has helped you. Llewellyn Worldwide cannot guarantee that every letter written to the author can be answered, but all will be forwarded. Please write to:

Lady Sabrina
c/o Llewellyn Worldwide
P.O. Box 64383, Dept. K600-9, St. Paul, MN 55164-0383, U.S.A.

Please enclose a self-addressed, stamped envelope or $1.00 to cover costs.
If outside the U.S.A., enclose an international postal reply coupon.

Free Catalog from Llewellyn

For more than 90 years Llewellyn has brought its readers knowledge in the fields of metaphysics and human potential. Learn about the newest books in spiritual guidance, natural healing, astrology, occult philosophy, and more. Enjoy book reviews, New Age articles, a calendar of events, plus current advertised products and services. To get your free copy of *Llewellyn's New Worlds of Mind and Spirit,* send your name and address to:

Llewellyn's New Worlds of Mind and Spirit
P.O. Box 64383, Dept. K600-9, St. Paul, MN 55164-0383, U.S.A.

Cauldron of Transformation

A New Vision of Wicca for Modern Pagan Practice

LADY SABRINA

1996
Llewellyn Publications
St. Paul, Minnesota 55164-0383, U.S.A.

Cover design: Maria Mazzara
Cover photography: Russell Lane
Interior illustrations: Tom Grewe and Maria Mazzara
Photographs: Lady Sabrina
Book design and layout: Ronna Hammer
Editor: Rosemary Wallner
Project Coordinator: Jessica Thoreson

Library of Congress Cataloging-in-Publication Data

Sabrina, Lady.
    Cauldron of transformation: a new vision of Wicca for modern pagan practice /
Lady Sabrina. — 1st ed.
          p.   cm.
    Includes bibliographical references and index.
    ISBN 1-56718-600-9 (pbk.)
    1. Witchcraft. I. Title.
BF1571.S22 1996
133.4'3—dc20

                                             95-51457

Llewellyn Publications
A Division of Llewellyn Worldwide, Ltd.
P.O. Box 64383, St. Paul, MN 55164-0383

Other Books by the Author

Reclaiming the Power: The How and Why of Practical Ritual Magic, 1992

To all the members of Our Lady of Enchantment, especially Aristaeus, Autumn, Balaam, Brie, Cassius, Damaclease, Galadriel, Lisa, Leonard, and Lucy. Also, thank you Nancy, Jessica, and all the Llewellyn staff who made this book a reality.

Contents

Preface: A New Vision of Wicca   ix

Introduction: Co-Creation Spirituality   xiii

PART I: The Cauldron of Reflection   1

Where History and Tradition Meet

1. Religion: The Dream of the Human Mind   3
   Preface to Tradition (Chapters 2 through 6)   13
2. The Druids and Celtic Paganism   15
3. Christianity: A Covenant with Christ   23
4. Santería: An Old Religion in a New World   31
5. Buddhism: The Ascetic Way of Life   41
6. Shamanism: The Natural Way of Spirituality   47

PART II: The Cauldron of Light   53

The Birthplace of Divinity

7. Discovering Divinity   55
   Preface to Deity (Chapters 8 through 12)   61
8. Africa: Home of the Orisha   63
9. Asia: The Land of Many Gods   75
10. Egypt: Valley of Temple and Tomb   83
11. Europe: Alive with Myth and Mystery   95
12. Those Who Ever Shine Brightly   107

PART III: The Cauldron of Inspiration   119

Where Symbol and Spirit Unite

13. Tools and Symbols of the Sacred   121
14. The Oracle as a Voice of Truth and Wisdom   135
15. Harmony and the Elements of Nature   147
16. A Place for Prayer and Worship   159

PART IV: The Cauldron of Transformation   171

A New Vision of Expression

17. The Office and Obligation of the Priesthood   173
18. The Observance of Essential Requirements   181
19. Sacraments, Sacred Rites, and Prayers   195
20. The Creative Spirit   265

Bibliography   271
Index   275

A New Vision
of Wicca

Over the last eighteen years, almost 20,000 people—mostly mail-order students—have passed through Our Lady of Enchantment. The majority of these people were well-educated, over thirty years of age, and from a Christian background. For the most part, they were tired of the politics and dogma of the Christian Church but still had a healthy regard for deity and spirituality. They were looking for something new and different—something that would support their future but not invalidate their past. Most found what they were seeking through our study programs.

Our Lady of Enchantment teaches a form of alternative spirituality that is based on the principles of metaphysics,[1] magic,[2] and mysticism[3] in combination with ceremonial worship of the God and Goddess. This formulation of doctrine and ritual, what we call *Co-Creation Spirituality,* essentially sprouted from Wiccan/Pagan roots.

Like all offspring that have been cherished and nurtured, our system has grown and matured far beyond our original expectations. Because we have refined and perfected our theology and practices, the commonly accepted term "Wicca" no longer accurately describes our religious practices. For the most part, Wicca has become a social movement based on politically correct agendas to which a sprinkling of New Age spirituality has been added. Wicca's religious aspect seems to have been lost somewhere between the Eco-feminism and the Poly-amorous lifestyles.

Wicca, in its principal form, traces its origins back to the early 1940s and to Gerald Gardner, a British occultist. Gardner's frustration with both Christianity and the complexity of ceremonial magic prompted him to create something different. The result was a system combining the worship of deity with the practice of ritual magic.

Gardner's spiritual child has grown, developed, and amassed a great many followers over the years. Just like all children, it has created many of its own problems. Some of these problems, such as the absence of specific rules and regulations concerning beliefs and practices, were ones we could not tolerate. The disregard for structure within the Wiccan movement has created confusion and chaos, leading to constant jousting between Wiccans for validation of doctrine and positions of superficial power.

This lack of comprehensive spiritual direction, coupled with the fact that Wicca does not allow the expansion of its "keep it free, easy, and simple"[4] doctrine into any of the Christian mysteries, prompted us to renovate our system. There was also the problem with the word *Christian*. For some reason, that word seems to cause a flurry of criticism and ridicule from those practicing the Wiccan faith. We felt this was unreasonable because esoteric Christianity, like all mystery traditions, had something of value to offer.

Because of Wicca's lack of spiritual regulations and the basic Christian phobia, Our Lady of Enchantment formulated a new system of study that allowed us to combine many different esoteric practices into one working religious unit. We wanted something that would bridge the gap between Wiccan-Pagan ideology and the original intent of the Christian mysteries. We wanted something that everyone could relate to and feel comfortable with. Our efforts produced a progressive arrangement based on both Pagan and Christian principles—Co-Creation Spirituality.

Co-Creation Spirituality is a more extensive and inclusive religious system than the singular, tradition-bound Wiccan method. Because it is more extensive, we were able to create a comprehensive doctrine and incorporate a variety of spiritual disciplines into our practices. Also, by encouraging Co-Creationism, we open the doors of our religious system to all sincere seekers—be they from a Christian or Pagan background.

A principal characteristic of our system (to which some object) is this inclusion of Christian thought and symbolism into our practices. This inclusion, coupled with the fact that we acknowledge the Cosmic Christ—as in Jesus Christ, sun[5] of god—seems to send chills down the spines of most Wiccans. And when we express our understanding and appreciation for the symbolism of Christ's passion—as a divine victim or sacrificial king—their Pagan feet start running.

The combination of Christian symbolism and our structured doctrine has created a major wedge between us and some more vocal members of the Neo-Pagan/Wiccan movement (not to mention the distress we seemed to have caused by having an image of Jesus Christ in our chapel, even though there are far more Pagan deities represented therein). Personally, I think this aversion to Jesus is pure foolishness that stems mainly from ignorance. Wiccans, like Christians, seem to confuse deity with the political faction of the presumed offending religion.

To my way of thinking, all gods and goddesses are divine and, therefore, should not be subject to simple human prejudice. Jesus, in his spiritual aspect, was a composite of previous solar-savior divinities.[6] He was the Mithras, the Sol Invictus, and the Unconquered Sun of the Piscean Age. In the corporeal sense, he was a rebellious Jewish rabbi on a collision course with the religious establishment of his day.

Jesus was a mystic, healer, and a man of enlightenment. The followers of Jesus and those who came later distorted the teachings and esoteric symbolism of the Christ. They are the ones who should be censured, not Jesus the man or Christ the god.

As a religiously inclined individual, I have a problem with this vehement prejudice toward any and everything Christian, when in fact Christianity, especially Catholic Christianity, is nothing more than Pagan-plagiarism with some exasperating patriarchal overtones.

The whole Christian concept began with a group of insurgent Jews and Pagan Gentiles who wanted to start a religious movement of their own—something new, different, and separate from the established religions of their time. What they envisioned way back when is totally different from what we have today.

For those who have taken the time to do any research at all, it is no secret that the early Church absorbed most of the rites and symbology of the ancient Greek, Roman, and Persian mystery religions. Most importantly, these early merchants of theological wisdom could read and write when most everyone else didn't know the difference between a book and stepping stone. Because of their knowledge, many of their records and writings are invaluable when delving into the history of religious beliefs and practices. It is a shame that today's Wiccans and Pagans cannot see past the Church's politics and appreciate some of its initial beauty and mystery. This reminds me of a story I want to share with you.

I once had a Great Dane named Ralph who weighed in at 150 pounds. One afternoon, I was invited to a barbecue party at a friend's house. She had a good deal of property, so I took the dog with me. Dogs being dogs, Ralph was a pest and had his nose into everything. One exceptionally astute guest chained the 150-pound dog to an aluminum yard chair (chairs weigh approximately three pounds). Ralph moved, the chair collapsed, and pandemonium ensued.

The dog took off like a bat out of hell with the devil in hot pursuit. We took off after the dog. No matter how fast poor Ralph ran, he could not get away from the chair, which, of course, was chasing him.

After the hysteria was over, the flower beds were ruined, the lawn was torn to pieces, and the vegetable garden was uprooted. When we stopped running, the dog calmed down and someone was able to free poor Ralph from his object of terror.

My point is that no matter how fast we run, we cannot outrun the shadow of our Christian heritage. However, if we stop running and calm down, maybe, just maybe, the hand of reason can free us from our imagined bondage.

The purpose of this book is to help you decide for yourself what is spiritually satisfying. Every person on the face of this earth is unique. Because of this, physical, emotional, and spiritual needs vary from person to person. Many students have expressed their discomfort with Pagan deities, which presents a problem. People are not happy with the dogma of the Church but are still devoted to Christian deities. What do they do? They create their own spiritual paths.

For the most part, this book embodies and advocates the use of Co-Creation Spirituality as the alternative to most modern religious systems. Symbolically, Co-Creation Spirituality is a cauldron that can simultaneously brew many different combinations of ingredients. Like the cauldron, our system allows for the mixing and merging of many concepts and beliefs to create a potpourri of spiritual refreshment.

The cauldron's principal purpose is change. Through time, we see the symbolic cauldron transform itself from the magical brewing pot of our ancestors into the mythical Grail of modern spiritual quests. Likewise, our Wiccan ideal grew and evolved into Co-Creation Spirituality, becoming a more sophisticated and comprehensive form of Paganism.

In conclusion, there is no one right and only brew when it comes to personal spirituality and religion. The only stew or brew in your spiritual cauldron should be the one of your creation or choosing. What makes you feel good, enhances your life, and allows you to progress spiritually is what you should be cooking!

ENDNOTES

1. *Metaphysics* is an accepted doctrine that all things are a part of one source and that each thing—animate or inanimate—should be respected for its particular form, independent function, and contribution to the main source.

2. *Magic* is an art that comprises a system of concepts and methods using the more subtle forces of nature to help individuals balance their emotions. Magic develops control of human will; magic uses incantations, ceremonies, symbols, and objects to manipulate the subtle forces to achieve a desired result.

3. *Mysticism* seeks hidden wisdom and a relationship between visible and invisible beings and powers. Mysticism attempts to enjoy a communion with the highest energies and eventually God; it seeks union with God and understanding of the laws that make this union possible.

4. *Simple* does not mean to imply, in any way, that Wicca does not have value or substance. It is a valid spiritual path and certainly has its own merits for those who feel comfortable with it.

5. *Sun of god* refers to Jesus the Christ as the spiritual sun or light at the center of the soul and spiritual universe. In the ancient mystery traditions, the spiritual sun was Mithras, the "Sol Invictus" or Unconquered Sun.

6. Solar-Savior divinities would include Mithra, Osiris, Tammuz, Dionysus, Adonis, and others from earlier Pagan pantheons.

Co-Creation Spirituality

What I am sure of is that any future forms of religious experience will be quite different from those we are familiar with in Christianity, Judaism, or Islam, all of which are fossilized, outmoded, drained of meaning. I am sure that new forms, new expressions, will come. What will they be? The great surprise is always the freedom of the human spirit, its creativity.

Mircea Eliade in *Ordeal by Labyrinth*

The following is a description of Co-Creation Spirituality and what Our Lady of Enchantment promotes as an extensive working religion and personal spiritual system. We find these principles highly practicable because we view spirituality as an ongoing process of learning, growing, experiencing, and progressing. Realizing this, we constantly strive to improve our theology, rites, and personal spiritual discipline.

Throughout this book, Co-Creation Spirituality is used to illustrate the method by which a religion is created and takes form. If one wishes to practice this form of the Wiccan religion, it is necessary to follow the basic format of the system. Of course, you will need to supplement the structure with your own individual symbols, prayers, and practices. No hard and fast rules exist when it comes to spirituality. However, there are universal truths, intelligent decisions, and certain formulas that are known to produce a working system.

A Definition of Co-Creation Spirituality

Co is a prefix meaning "complement of." *Creation* is "the continuous cyclically recurring process that emanates through our universe." As Co-Creationists, we see ourselves as a complement to the Unmanifested[1] and all physical nature. We have the ability to imagine, devise, and conceive of new ways to progress spiritually. We align ourselves with natural forces, cycles, and seasonal changes to bring harmony back into our lives.

We see our place in the universe as a counterpart to both the creative force and manifestation process. We do not seek to dominate our universe nor do we subjugate ourselves to it. We try to *co-exist,* in a peaceful yet meaningful way, with the world around us.

We view the nature of the Unmanifested, or God Force, as the ultimate source of all power and energy. The God Force is without gender, physical attributes, or emotion—it always was and always will be. Because the God Force rules such a vast universe, it has no time to involve itself directly with human affairs. Therefore, it is considered that the God Force rules in absentia by the projection of its energy as an expression of itself through the universe's primary natural principles.

The co-creation system teaches us that the God Force or Unmanifested is too extensive to be understood in its totality. So as individuals we pick a portion of the God Force and try, through comprehension of the part, to gain some knowledge of the whole. These portions of the God Force are lines of energy that are channeled through a deliberately conceived multicultural pantheon of masculine and feminine deities. These heavenly gods and goddesses, as well as many other spectral beings, form a communication link between our spiritual consciousness and that of the Unmanifested. By attuning ourselves to these intermediary deities, we learn to appreciate and use our own god-like qualities to achieve spiritual satisfaction.

Through sacred myth, a reverence for nature, and an acceptance of reincarnation, we co-create continuity and balance and learn the truth of life. We have found that the most effective way to reach spiritual inner harmony is through religious ritual and ceremony. Ritual provides a physical expression of spirituality, bringing it out and making it real. Because we are all unique and have different views of divinity, we stress the importance of individual participation and connection with deity.

We believe that each person is both co-creator and experiencer of his or her reality. As such we have the right and responsibility to reaffirm our god-like abilities through acts of magic, ritual, and worship. Ritual not only strengthens and encourages our spiritual being, but also makes us feel good about ourselves.

We recognize the power, potential, and universal truth in all genuine belief systems. Although we are not of the Christian persuasion, we are not by any means anti-Christian. We find merit in righteousness no matter what its origin. As Co-Creationist and sincere seekers of enlightenment, we respect and use all universal truths to aid us in our practices.

Our ceremonies become plays for the benefit of the higher consciousness, with the participants as the actors. By physically acting out what we want to happen, we become one in sympathy with our desires. These desires, once acted upon, become thought forms that in turn are projected into the universal consciousness. With the right amount of force and energy, proper thought forms will become reality.

The Co-Creation Principal Belief System

As Co-Creationist, we believe in the existence of the original source of creation known as the Unmanifested. We believe in and realize the importance of the communicative secondary creative powers revealed through various forms of gods and goddesses, as well as in the subtle forces of nature.

As Co-Creationist, we are neither matriarchal nor patriarchal in our religious focus. We seek the middle path of balance. We realize the truth, wisdom, and creative power that comes from the union of the masculine and feminine forces of nature.

As Co-Creationist, we believe in the value and need for organizational structure within our religious system. Structure and organization begin with good leadership. We value the opinions of all our devotees, and so our administration of spiritual knowledge is expressed through an equal-partnership priesthood comprised of both men and women. We also respect the authority given to those who are spiritually mature and advanced in the theology of other valid religious systems.

As Co-Creationist, we believe in magic, defined as "the ability to create change at will." We use physical symbols and tools, as well as metaphysical concepts, to help focus and direct our energies toward the manifestation of desire. We respect the abilities and rights of all our members to work toward their own goals and spiritual progress within and without the group.

As Co-Creationist, we believe there is a need to respect and harmonize with the social structure of our time, while maintaining our individual rights and personal freedoms. Simply, this means we maintain a level of moral ethics acceptable to our present-day society.

As Co-Creationist, we believe that our religion as well as our lives are part of an ever-changing process that is integral to our personal and spiritual growth and progress. Because everything we see or know is in a constant state of change, our practices, beliefs, and expressions of spirituality must also change to fit the system[2] in which they are personified.

As Co-Creationist, we gladly accept and encourage suggestions, additions, or modifications to our beliefs, practices, and magical systems from our student membership, congregation, and priesthood.

The Co-Creation Symbol and What It Means

Crescent (waning) Moon: Signifies the wisdom, authority, and good judgment that comes with experience and age.

Equal-Armed Cross: Embodies the masculine and feminine powers of heaven and earth; represents the four cardinal directions and the crossroads of choice.

Eight-Pointed Star: The light coming from the East, the vision of tomorrow, the spirit of enlightenment, and the ability to see beyond the physical.

Together, these create and reaffirm balance, vision, and the ability to co-create a new reality.

ENDNOTES

1. The Unmanifested is the source of all creation, the divine spirit, the Universal Force, the God in sense of neutral—both male and female, good and evil, all that ever was or will be.

2. System here refers to the twentieth century in which we live. Regression into the Paleolithic or romantic Renaissance ages can be fun, but has little to do with progress of any kind.

PART I

The Cauldron of Reflection

Where History and Tradition Meet

CHAPTER 1

Religion: The Dream of the Human Mind

Religion. A daughter of Hope and Fear explaining to Ignorance the nature of the Unknowable.

Ambrose Bierce (1842–1914)

Man is born to believe. And if no Church comes forward with its ti-tle-deeds of truth…to guide him, he will find altars and idols in his own heart and his own imagination.

Benjamin Disraeli (1804–1881)

Religion and Reality

Creating a religion or spiritual path is similar to building your own home. The first requirement of home building is the drawing of a set of plans. If you don't have experience with architecture, you take a course or have someone teach you how to lay out and draft your design. Next you purchase land and pour the foundation. Then you start on the framework, exterior walls, and roofing.

Sound like a big project? Well, it is. This is why most people buy a house already built or stick with what they have—those solutions are easier and more convenient. Nowadays, almost everything—including religion—is based on the "buy it ready made or make it yourself" concept. If you want something truly unique and different, you must make it yourself. However, before you attempt to create anything, you need a basic understanding of the essential elements required to produce the end product.

Like the home builder who needs a background in architecture, the spiritual craftsman needs a background in religious studies and concepts. Once you have the necessary knowledge, you will be able to draft your own set of plans and create something original.

As we begin to study religion as a whole, we find humanity's greatest accomplishments and most conspicuous failures. Respectively, the religions of the world should bring peace, love, and harmony. Instead, they seem to be the cause of war, hatred, and destruction. In human history, more people have died in the name of religion than for any other cause. Something is wrong with the system when the religions of the world do exactly the opposite of what they should.

The problems most religious organizations incur stem from their ecclesiastic severity and unmanageable size. Humans by nature are independent and territorial first. Subordinate and tribal needs place second, and then only when hearth and home are threatened. In other words, individuality and personal space are prerequisites over communal supervision and support.

When in their own backyard, by all rights, individuals are the ever-reigning king of the mountain. However, when they gather with others, certain social regulations prevail, and they are not necessarily lord and master of all they perceive. Individuality is relinquished for the common good of the group and for the sanction it creates through sheer mass power. Crowd domination is necessary for political conquest and military purposes, but it leaves much to be desired in conjunction with spirituality.

This condition of "quest for validation through majority approval" is not limited to the Christian religions. Every religious body seems to suffer from it—including those within Neo-Paganism. Head count and notoriety seem to be the priority, with theological significance coming somewhere after the social hour. This need for sanction by vast numbers of people induces power struggles in leadership and creates a political rather than spiritual agenda. Left unchecked, the politics soon infects the system and eventually causes its decline and spiritual death.

The contradictions within our species are numerous. We enjoy our privacy, but are social by nature and seek a certain amount of interaction with others who have similar ideas. This is especially true for the spiritually inclined who seem to seek out others of like mind. These champions of religious zeal also manage to gather frequently in order to show their spiritual prowess.

Religious and spiritual gatherings should be times of celebration and worship, not partisan assemblies where people meet to compete with each other. The sad part of this is that most of the New Age earth religions have mimicked, as closely as possible, the Christian gathering neurosis of "the more people you have, the more valid you are." It's not the substance of what they offer anymore that counts, but rather the ability to lure many people onto their turf or into their campgrounds.

Nothing is inherently wrong with proselytizing if the religious body has strong, unified binding principles and beliefs that its followers can all agree upon and work toward. However, from what I have seen, most large Pagan gatherings are more like

Easter Sunday at the Catholic Church. Everyone shows up to see who has the most flamboyant hat—only to go home and ridicule them while devising equally outrageous concoctions of their own.

The primary goal of religion is to transform the individual soul through a progression of spiritual initiations and incarnations, not to engage in spiritual buffoonery. Sadly, this concept has been lost and the essential spiritual initiation process has been replaced with secular objectives. The entire point of becoming involved in religion and spirituality is to learn how to receive and assimilate divine energy through identification with deity. Once the identification process has been completed, a bond or communication link between the individual and his or her god is established. This bond of communication then empowers the individual with those eminent qualities of the deity itself. In time, the individual is able to raise his or her level of spiritual consciousness.

Unfortunately, in their quest for copious amounts of followers, most religious systems have strayed from this original goal. In the face of their unresponsive and indifferent demeanor, tolerance and consideration for individual spiritual needs has been lost. For years now mainstream religious movements have herded people into their churches only to bore them to death with fund drives, moral rebukes, and impersonal theology. Is it any wonder that the once faithful are looking elsewhere for their spiritual comfort?

What is really amusing is the lack of insight from the seemingly astute theologians, both Pagan and Christian. These individuals should at least be able to see, if not get a grip on, what is happening. History repeats itself. The same conditions of religious populace appeasement that prevail today existed in the Roman Empire over 1600 years ago. Only then, a state type of Paganism and the Mystery cults were the dominant means of spiritual expression.

Then, like now, humanity was growing[1] into a New Age. Change was in the air and what used to be was in the midst of passing away. Over the decades, Paganism and the Mystery traditions had become vapid, sterile, and lifeless. They were losing their adherents to Christianity, the new, more enigmatic, system. Christianity was fresh, modern, and different. It presented itself to the majority rather than the minority. Rich or poor, illiterate or scholarly—there was a place for everyone and everyone was able to receive the sacraments of the god.

Christianity began like all religions do, in secret, for fear of condemnation and persecution. The teachings that would bestow on it world importance were a compilation of Mosaic Law, cultural Paganism, and a synthesis of Mystery cult symbolism. People were familiar with and could relate to these teachings. The only difference was that Christianity presented these teachings in a new, more organized format and with zealous enthusiasm.

Christianity captured the attention and admiration of the majority not only because it was new, but also because it offered something for everyone. Judaism had become entirely too rigid and punitive; Paganism seemed pointless and was boring; the Mystery cults were closed, exclusionary, and sexist, allowing only military, state elite, or the well-educated to become distinguished members.

With the entrance of the Piscean Age, Judaism retreated into itself; Paganism saw its final sunset; and the Mystery traditions lost their appeal. Now with the coming of the Aquarian Age, the Christian Church and all its factions are floundering and are about to beach themselves like dying whales. Each of these religious traditions, in their own time, had something special to offer. Like everything, they sprouted, blossomed, and brought joy; faded; and passed away. Birth, life, and death are part of the cycle that affects all things, whether they are animate or inanimate, conjecture or fact.

With the coming of the New Age, it is once again time for religiously progressive individuals to show initiative and be creative. The archaic morality and political commercialism of today's mainstream religions need to be discarded so the true essence of spiritual idealism can once again flourish. The morals, doctrines, and rites that represent known truths need to be revised and presented in a new and compelling way. When this happens, religion and spirituality will once again rekindle the divine spark within and reunite humanity with deity and its destiny.

Religion by Definition

From the earliest times of prehistory down to the present day, religion has provided humanity with a means of explaining our deepest thoughts and convictions. It is through a complex mixture of conjecture, doctrine, and intuition that religious traditions are formed and become repositories of spiritual energy. When devotees tap into these repositories, they provide a revelation or mystical experience. The joy that follows the revelation or mystical experience is what keeps the individual's divine spark alive and creates a living religion.

Because of its illusive nature, religion and the mystical experience are difficult to define in precise terms. For this reason, most religions tend to express their esoteric nature through ritual or some form of art, such as sculpture, music, or dance. These symbolic methods of interpretation bridge the language barrier, allowing the individual to experience within (rather than verbalize, which tends to inhibit) the true ecstasy of spiritual enlightenment.

Religion is universal ideation that is necessary for balanced existence—which is why it can be found in every society and culture at all stages of human history. The word itself comes from the Latin *religio*, meaning re-linking or reunion and is the restoration of the bond between humans, nature, and god. The entire concept of religion, at least in theory, is to bring humanity into alignment with deity for spiritual enlightenment, progress, and eventual reconciliation with the creator.

One of the most outstanding features of religion—and why it has always been important—is that it gives value and meaning to life. Religion helps to develop an awareness, or feeling, that life is not accidental and meaningless but has direction and purpose.

Religion and most forms of genuine spirituality create a sense of security and stability within the believer. This sense of stability, of knowing there is something more to life than just the physical, brings promise for the future. When this sense of security is combined with true love and affection for deity, the void of the soul is filled and the need for constant distraction[2] ceases.

All religions have something in common and can be seen to have five separate, though related, divisions. No aspect by itself constitutes a religion, but when they are combined they create a working spiritual arrangement. As you read through the following divisions, speculate on how they relate to your own personal beliefs and spiritual realizations. By reflecting, you begin the creation process that in time will give form to your own system.

1. **Beliefs and Faith**

   Beliefs and faith are the essential part of any religion and show how those involved deal with the universe, life and death, ancestors, spirits, magic, and divinity. The beliefs can be written down as in scripture, passed on through myth, or acted out in ritual.

2. **Practices and Ceremonies**

   Group activities are an important part of any religion. Through religious practices, members express their beliefs and faith in practical terms. These practices include praying, performing rituals and ceremonies, making sacrifices and offerings, and observing special customs. Because each religion has its own method of practices, I can only generalize about common observances. The most common group activities are seasonal celebrations; harvest remembrances; rites of passage for birth, puberty, marriage, and death; festivals for deities and ancestors; and appreciation or recognition of natural phenomenon.

3. **Religious Objects and Places**

   These are the items and places that have been set aside as sacred or holy. They are not commonly used except for a specified religious purpose. Many religious objects and places are considered to be sacred. Humans created some; nature herself created others. Once something has been designated as sacred and holy, both the community and the individual practitioner hold it in high regard.

   All religions have special tools, symbols, and objects that designate their intention and purpose to both priest and practitioner. These objects and the places where worship occurs help to formulate the religion's physical aspect.

4. **Values and Morals**

   Values and morals include truth, justice, right and wrong, good and evil, respect for people and property, rights, and responsibilities. Values and morals also exhibit the character and integrity of those involved in the belief system. The values and morals help individuals to live with one another, settle their differences, maintain peace and harmony, and allow them to have a relationship with their environment.

5. **Leaders and Priesthood**

   These are religion's trained, initiated, or designated leaders. They conduct the ceremonies, lead the people in prayer, perform divination, and provide counseling for their believers. They can be found in all religions and may hold office as the medicine man, local king, parish priest, diviner, rain maker, or church elder. The position and title of the leader or priest will depend on the tradition, philosophy, and social and cultural designation of the religion itself.

   Whatever their title, the leaders are trained specialists and experts in religious matters. They are the human keepers of the religious tradition, its laws, rituals, and heritage. They are the arbitrators in matters of disputes and the dispensers of divine wisdom.

Religion and the Spiritual Process

As you can see, religion is a complex mixture of social, cultural, and philosophical impressions. The five aspects mentioned above are essential to its makeup and together create a whole orderly process. In reality, these divisions constitute the formula used to generate new religions based on eternal truths, established procedure, and contemporary thinking.

Working with Co-Creation Spirituality as the example, I will show how the five divisions help to compose and structure a religious system. In addition to the required elements, Co-Creation Spirituality as a new religion sanctions the individual interpretation of deity and its related expression in ritual. This inclusion of personal perception into a structured religious system creates an active rather than passive process. When this happens, the devotees become participants rather than just spectators—and their religion manifests as a progressive means of spiritual growth.

Co-Creation Beliefs

From the Introduction, it is evident that Co-Creation Spirituality believes in a Supreme Being. This Force is referred to as the All or Unmanifested and is a form of pure energy beyond the comprehension of human understanding. This ultimate

Force exudes and radiates primal energy that transforms itself through a set of secondary principles, which in turn manifest as the gods and goddesses comprising the various pantheons of different world religions.

The Co-Creation system teaches that it is ultimately up to the individual to choose the god and/or goddess he or she wishes to work with. As we commonly appreciate and hold in high esteem all genuine forms of deity, we are in essence omnithestic[3] and therefore nonjudgmental in our approach to deity.

For the church and Sabbat Masses at Our Lady of Enchantment, we use Cerridwen and Cernunnos as the projections of the masculine and feminine energies of deity that form the link between us and the Unmanifested. We use both a god and goddess because all life is shared between the negative and positive, masculine and feminine forces of the universe. For our established ceremonies, we have found it best to support the same god and goddess each time. This allows the group, as a whole, to build a relationship with a centralized spiritual force that in turn helps to spiritually unite the members.

In addition, we encourage our members to seek out their own special gods and goddesses. This creates a balance between group worship and solitary work, allowing for the expansion of spiritual knowledge and growth through shared experience.

Co-Creation Ceremonies and Practices

Co-Creation Spirituality stresses the value of energy that resides within the universe, nature, and the human form. Therefore, as a group as well as individually, we stress the importance of personal alignment with the rhythms and vibrations of our environment. We work with the seasonal changes[4] for planning, planting, nurturing, and accepting in accordance with desire and the life cycle. These times of reverence include Yule, Imbolc, Vernal Equinox, Beltane, Summer Solstice, Lughnasadh, Autumn Equinox, and Samhain.

In addition to celebrating the eight divisions within the calendar year, we also acknowledge the god in his aspect of the Divine Victim and resurrected Lord. This special Eucharist Mass takes place at sunset on Good Friday. On September 7, we celebrate the Feast of the Blessed Virgin in honor of the goddess in all her sacred forms. The Eight Seasonal Sabbats, along with Good Friday and the Feast of the Blessed Virgin, constitute our Ten Days of Holy Obligation.

In practice, Co-Creation Spirituality also stresses the concept of initiation as a palingenesis of individual consciousness. Because of this, Our Lady of Enchantment makes ordination into the priesthood available for those who wish to progress. Even though we have three levels of achievement when one has been initiated and ordained as a priest or priestess, the individual becomes a fully functioning member of the organization with all rights and privileges.

Co-Creation Religious Objects and Places

Co-Creation Spirituality as practiced at Our Lady of Enchantment designates sacred space as a permanent area set aside for worship of deity. We believe that energy can be confined and maintained over a period of time in a properly constructed space. All our members set aside a room or area for personal prayer and worship in their home. For our common meetings, we gather in the chapel at Our Lady of Enchantment, which has been consecrated, blessed, and dedicated specifically for the worship of the god and goddess.

As Co-Creationists, we value and appreciate all religious symbolism and works of art. We understand that some items are passive, such as icons, paintings, and statues. We see these as having the ability to contain the eminent force or energy of the god or goddess. However, we realize these objects are not in reality the god or goddess they represent, but a receptacle for the deity's specific force field.

We also recognize the value of religious objects, which in symbolic form constitute an active part of our worship. Some of these come from traditional Wiccan roots, while others are borrowed from the Pagan Mystery traditions and early Christian teaching. We also have added several other objects that have a traditional significance but are in a new form and therefore are unique to Co-Creation Spirituality.

The sacred tools and symbolic objects we use to represent deity and the elemental forces of life are the Chalice, Vessel of Creation, Dagger, Rod of Authority, and cauldron. In addition, we use the censer, aspergillum, bells, and Paten—all of which will be thoroughly discussed later in this book.

Each of these objects takes on a special significance when used in the context of ritual. The most important contribution tools make is in their ability to help the individual focus his or her attention at the proper time. Eventually, if properly cared for, all sacred objects retain and become reservoirs of divine energy that, when needed, can be tapped by the sincere devotee.

Co-Creation Values and Morals

Our values and morals reflect the substance of the culture and society in which we live. State and federal laws take precedence over individual impulse, which we consider to be common sense. In addition, we have personal reflections that we feel are realistic and beneficial to our membership.

Moderation: A criterion whereby we judge our works and our actions. Excess of any kind leads to imbalance in both the physical or spiritual sense.

Function: Realism as to the attitude and actions of members in regards to their place and purpose within a group or social structure. Everyone is unique, has his or her own talents, and is respected according to his or her works, not words.

Respect: For leaders, as in the Priesthood, in regards to their earned ability to direct and produce spiritual realization within the congregation and working structure of ritual.

Observation: Of the lack of perfection within the scope of individual participation. We see these imperfections as an obvious flaw in all humanity, which does not create or cause disruption but is a reason for understanding, tolerance, and love.

Knowledge: We expect those in positions of authority to express what they know and be willing to learn about what they are not in possession of. Knowledge is a privilege and should be treated with respect, and so should those who give of it freely.

Wisdom: We regard all positive religions with an open mind and do not fear accepting or using those beliefs that are in alignment with our philosophy and teachings, be they Christian or Pagan. We know our position and walk the middle path with awareness and understanding of those around us.

Co-Creation Leadership

As Co-Creationists, we firmly believe in a strong, trained, and disciplined priesthood. The quality of leadership is a direct reflection on the fundamental endowment of philosophy, belief, and practice of our—or any, for that matter—religious organization.

We consider a central authority to be mandatory. Just as a building has one foundation, so our religious association has one common ground of management. This central authority is evidenced through our board of qualified priests and priestesses who have been fully trained and educated in the comparative religious studies of Wicca and Co-Creation Spirituality. By having this point of reference, there is continuity and perpetuation of our specific religious and spiritual ideals.

This structure in no way hinders the individual from freedom of expression but instead provides guidelines for personal growth and development. Simply, without direction and established rules of conduct, chaos exists. Everyone needs to know their boundaries. When boundaries are fully recognized, the growth process is productive, not random and dysfunctional. For this reason, Our Lady of Enchantment has a two-step program designed to help educate those who wish to become members of the priesthood.

The program we offer is simple and straightforward and provides extensive training in religious theory and the Metaphysical arts. Upon completion of our training program, the student may apply for ministerial credentials and eventual initiation and ordination into the Wiccan priesthood.

The path of the priesthood is not a vocation for everyone or for every member of our organization. Many of our members feel the need for spirituality in their lives but have not been called to the priesthood. These people share and participate in all our public Masses and enjoy all the privileges of a formal religious tradition. It is the interaction of the priesthood with the laity that generates the constant flow of new energy and spiritual revelation that benefits all of us.

In closing, we feel that Co-Creation Spirituality complies with the five necessary requirements that constitute a working religion. Because we see the need for personal interpretation in spirituality, we stress knowledge as a fundamental requirement for both the congregation member and the ordained priesthood. The more someone knows and understands about his or her religion, the more likely he or she is to get involved and progress spiritually.

ENDNOTES

1. At this time, we were at the very beginning of the Piscean Age. Pisces is represented by two fish swimming in opposite directions, coincidentally the symbol for Christianity. Pisces was an age of duality, internal struggle, and world conflict. Pisces can never seem to make up its mind one way or the other.

2. Distraction is usually concealed in the form of excessive habits: the constant need for buying or acquiring new and better toys; the longing for physical affection or attention; in some cases, illness and substance addiction.

3. Omnitheistic/Omnitheism is the belief in all forms of theism, as in all deities, gods and goddesses, as both separate from but connected to all other life and spiritual forms.

4. A complete explanation of the eight seasonal Sabbats and their accompanying rituals is found in Chapter 19.

Preface to Tradition
Chapters 2 through 6

It would be difficult, if not impossible, to thoroughly describe all the world's major and minor religions in a single book. First, too many of them exist; second, religion is a complex subject. Even though all religions have something in common, social and cultural differences lead to major variations in beliefs and practices.

Not being able to cover all religions presents a problem. In order to understand religion as a whole, one needs to examine and compare a variety of traditions. By learning and comparing, the student can then separate a tradition's politics and social customs from the mysteries and spiritual truths upon which the tradition is based. Once this has been accomplished, a real sense of religion's rationale becomes apparent and it is then possible to choose or create wisely.

The following chapters discuss five different systems in reference to their origins, customs, and beliefs. These discussions will help you become familiar with the various traditions available, as well as introduce you to some of their practices and sacred symbology. Through comparison, obvious similarities and truths will surface and distinct differences and political factions will become apparent. Knowing the difference between spiritual fact and social custom will be useful if you decide to compose your own belief system.

Chapters 2 through 6 cover Celtic Druidism, Christianity, Santería, Buddhism, and Shamanism. These religious traditions were selected because I feel they are good examples of popular belief, spiritual discernment, and metaphysical discipline. In one way or another, all these traditions have contributed to Our Lady of Enchantment's system of Co-Creation Spirituality. Another reason for my selections was the fact that all these traditions are still being practiced today and therefore allow for further examination.

Besides the reasons already mentioned, I felt the traditions' separate and distinct regional positions, living conditions, and societies presented an extensive view of cultural religion. Personally, I think that by using dissimilar systems it is easier to pinpoint spiritual truths in contrast to the political and social precedents, which tend to color all religious traditions. As truth is the one concept all religions value, once it has been uncovered, it is only a matter of applying the truth in order to produce a workable system.

To introduce as much information as possible, each religious tradition is presented in an extended outline style. Though these outlines are complete in their primary form, they are in no way conclusive in their entirety. To fully explain any religion in detail, one would need more space than I am allotted here. However, plenty of references are listed for the curious student to follow up on.

CHAPTER 2

The Druids and Celtic Paganism

To the peoples of antiquity, the isle of Britain was the very home and environment of mystery, a sacred territory, to enter was to encroach upon a region of enchantment, the dwelling of gods.

Lewis Spence, *The Mysteries of Britain*

The History of the Celts

To understand the Pre-Christian Celtic religion—of which the Druids were the Magi, philosophers, and priesthood—it is necessary to appreciate the early Celtic lifestyle. Religion is, and always has been, a community affair, reflecting the cultural and social structure of its time.

The Celts were a branch of the Indo-European people who migrated from their homeland, west of the Black Sea, into Europe around 3000 B.C. From around 400 B.C., they became recognizable as a culture. They were by tradition a cattle-herding, horse-breeding, and a head-hunting people.[1] Short swords, lances, and chariots were some of their sophisticated war-making implements. Among their sports were fishing, hunting, and, of course, fighting—which they loved above all. They were not a docile, peaceful race, but aggressive, barbaric, and war-loving.

As a whole, the Celts were tall and robust in comparison to the shorter and slighter Greeks and Romans whose territory they invaded. Because of their size, tattoos, and bleached hair, the Celts must have seemed like weird giants to the civilized Romans. Even their clothing was strange as both sexes generally dressed alike in breeches, knee-length tunics, and brightly colored cloaks. They adorned themselves with rings, bracelets, armlets, and ornate buckles along with intricate gold and silver brooches, which held their cloaks in place.

The Celts were known for their fairness in law, which among other things guaranteed the place of women. In Celtic society, a woman could own property, choose her own husband, and divorce her spouse. Women also took their place in the line of battle next to their husbands. If a woman's husband died, she ascended to his role as chief in their family line.

Within the Celtic tribe or clans, three divisions of recognition existed. First was the king, a descendent of a hero or warrior leader who was recognized for his prowess in battle. Next were the warriors, chosen for their ability to protect and defend the tribe or clan during times of attack. The last designation was the common people, who were the herders, farmers, and other producers of products needed for sustaining daily life.

Separate from the tribe or clan, yet intrinsically part of it, were the Druids or Celtic priesthood. This special clergy, like the clan or tribe, was divided into three classes or grades, each with its own functions and responsibilities. First in order was the Druid/Derwydd, who was advisor to the chief or king and acted as judge and lawyer to the people. He also held authority in worship and ritual. Next were the Ovates/Ovydd, who were the priests and priestesses in charge of prophecy and divination. The last grade was the Bards/Bardd, who were poets, musicians, and keepers of tradition. They were trained in music, history, and song-spell. An Arch-Druid ruled all these groups. The senior brethren (ones considered to be the most learned) elected the Arch-Druid by lot.

The Celtic cosmology and Drudic system were based on the fundamental belief in the law of three or the logical order of the triad, which was the association of humans with nature combined with divinity. This produced a religious system that was monotheistic (belief in one creator) in its underlying creed, but polytheistic (belief in many gods and goddesses) in its ritualistic practices. Prior to Christianity, this dualistic approach toward religion was common, especially among the agricultural and livestock breeding peoples. By virtue of their association with the land and animals, these people were more aware of the subtle energies and power potential of natural phenomenon.

The one problem with accurate Drudic and Celtic religious history is that some zealous Christian priests destroyed most of the written records. According to historian Dr. Kennedy in *Dissertation about the Family of the Stuarts*, more than 300 volumes of the Celts' fables, superstitions, and worship were burned. These, along with other lost books written by Roman historians who had contact with the Druids, leave us with little viable information. What is left comes to us from the records of liberal Irish monks who wanted to preserve their heritage, and what can be gleaned from archeology and ancient art. As with anything, the astute individual—with time and patience—will be able to piece together a fairly accurate picture of the Celtic spiritual system.

Beliefs and Practices of Celtic Druidism

The Druids were the priests of the Celts, which therefore puts them in the position of religious dissemination. The term *Celtic* refers to the culture of the people. *Drudic* indicates their religious system.

The Drudic faith centered on One Supreme Creative Force that manifested through:

a. *Divinity:* the gods, goddesses, angels, and nature spirits.

b. *Nature:* the elements of earth, air, fire, and water—places where energy was present, such as caves, rivers, wells, mountains, tree groves, and the ocean.

c. *Animated Existence:* humanity, animals, birds, fish, and all living creatures great and small.

Druid beliefs extended to reincarnation as expressed in the Spiral of Abred, the circle of creation. This was the great circle on which the cycle of life moved like a wheel from birth to death and then back again. Each turn allowed for more experience to be gained in order to elevate the individual's spirit closer to its original source.

Belief in reincarnation or an afterlife was paramount with tribal people. Living conditions and life in general were less than comfortable; with effort and work, one could almost guarantee a position of reason in the afterlife and progress in those lifetimes to come.

The Druids' systematic view of God was expressed in a triad known as "The Transcendent Three."[2]

The Transcendant Three

1. The principal employment of God is to:

- enlighten the darkness
- invest nonentity with a body
- animate the dead

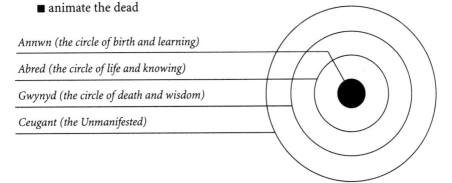

Annwn (the circle of birth and learning)

Abred (the circle of life and knowing)

Gwynyd (the circle of death and wisdom)

Ceugant (the Unmanifested)

The Spiral of Abred
(the circle of creation)

2. The three agents of God are:
- will
- wisdom
- love

3. The three things beyond the human realm are:
- extreme limits of space
- beginning and end of time
- the work of God

Along with their philosophical viewpoints and ideas about God, some physical areas of significance carried great amounts of power and deserved people's respect. It must be remembered that these were people of the land—farmers, herders, and craftsman—who honored and revered anything of natural importance. Nowhere is this more clearly communicated than in their "Five Forces of Influence."

The Five Forces of Influence
1. Influence of place
2. Richness of time
3. Treasures of tribe
4. Glory of ancestors
5. Joy of journey

The Celtic culture was based on livestock breeding and agriculture, which no doubt influenced their religious customs and the practices of the Druids. Because of their dependence on the land and the herd, they recognized the four elements and the seasonal changes as being of great consequence. As with most early peoples, everything that affected the tribe—including the weather—had some sort of mystical significance.

The Four Elements and Their Corresponding Symbols of the Land

Air	Slea Blue (spear)
Fire	Climah Solis (sword)
Water	Cauldron of Dagada
Earth	Lia Fail (stone of destiny)

The Eight-Fold Plan of the Year

As a pastoral people, the Celts had great respect for the land and all that rose from the soil. From their appreciation for the bounty of Mother Earth came their observance of seasonal rites. In the eyes of the Celts, planning, planting, and harvesting were an integral part of life that could be governed through ritual observance. Their legacy of celebration is still with us today in the form of the eight Sabbats.

The Eight Sabbat Celebrations

1. *Imbolc/Candlemas:* February 1; the time of natural beginnings and preparation for the growing season.

2. *Alban Eiler/Spring Equinox:* March 21; the time of fertile ground when planting begins; also the time of equal day and night.

3. *Beltane/May Day:* May 1; the time of fertility when both animals and land are ready for impregnation by seed.

4. *Alban Heruin/Summer Solstice:* June 21; the highest point of the sun; the time to nurture the young and appreciate the eternally moving circle.

5. *Lughnasadh/Lammas:* August 1; the marriage of light and fire; the baking of the first loaf; the beginning of the harvest.

6. *Alban Elued/Autumnal Equinox:* September 21; the time of ripened achievement; equal day and night; also known as the harvest home.

7. *Samhain/Hallowmas:* October 31; the union of the two worlds of spirit and man; slaughter of the animals for winter food; the beginning of rest.

8. *Alban Arthuan/Winter Solstice:* December 21; the death and rebirth of the sun; the lowest point of the sun; the prayers for the return of the sun.

Commentary: Co-Creation spirituality recognizes the subtle changes of the seasons. As human beings, we are connected to each other and the earth; therefore, what influences one will have direct bearing on the actions of the other. When it is time to plant, it is time to plant; and when it is time to accept reward, it is time for celebration. We do not attempt to plant the seeds of our desires in the dead of winter just as we do not expect compensation with the first bud of spring. Cooperation with and participation in the seasons is enjoyable and rewarding and the reason why some customs never die out. Because of their impact and specific energy force, Our Lady of Enchantment incorporated the Eight Seasonal Festivals into our system as part of our Holy Days of Obligation.

The Druids, like many religions and spiritual traditions, had a symbol that expressed their philosophy in a simple form. This sacred symbol was the three columns that translated into the letters *O, I,* and *U.* These mystic letters and corresponding lines represented the three attributes of God:

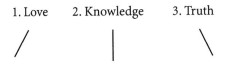

1. Love   2. Knowledge   3. Truth

The Celtic Druids were deeply appreciative of nature and her marvelous wonders. Because of their relationship with the land, they did not believe that God should be housed in a building. Thus they practiced their faith in what was called a Nemeton, sacred ground that had been consecrated for spiritual use. For added power and energy, the Nemeton was set in a grove of trees, upon a hill, or near a sacred well.

The Nemeton was usually made in the form of a large rectangle, marked on the ground and surrounded by a ditch in which water was placed. The fire pit, sacrificial altar, votive depositories, the sacred stone, and those items used for ritual working were placed within the boundaries of the Nemeton.

The Nemeton

Celtic and Drudic Symbols

Celtic and Drudic Symbols

Cauldron, sword, spear, oak, harp, flute, drum, horse, apple, silver, gold, shell, chalice, golden-sickle, holy-stone, earth, air, fire, water, pearl, emerald, ruby, sun, moon, dragon, snakes, mistletoe (All Heal), well, Ogham Tree Alphabet, rainbow, egg, glass boat, lots of three, bread, wine, white robes.

Synopsis

The influence of both the Druids and the Celtic culture cannot be ignored. Because of their association with the land and natural phenomenon, they left a rich heritage of symbol, celebration, and worship. Probably the most recognized of their customs are the seasonal celebrations. The Druid festival of Samhain became All Hallows Eve, which we celebrate as Halloween. The fertility festival of Beltane became May Day. Carving pumpkins, kissing under the mistletoe, Easter egg hunting, and May pole dancing were all passed down to us from our Celtic ancestors.

As the priesthood of the Celtic people, the Druids taught a belief in the soul's eternal nature and that all forms of creation contained a living spirit. An ancient Druid saying portraying this outlook was, "Spirit sleeps in the mineral, breathes in the vegetable, dreams in the animal, and wakes in man." The Druids also believed that souls could be contacted after death and that eventually the soul would reincarnate.

The Drudic teachings as a whole are consistent with the beliefs of most pantheistic nature religions, including those of Neo-Paganism, Wicca, and Shamanism. The major differences between the modern nature religions and Druidism is that the Druids were highly structured, systematic in their training, authoritative in their disposition of hierarchy, and persistent in proper procedure. They realized early on that, without structure and suitable leadership, chaos and corruption were unavoidable. Unfortunately, these conceptions of structure and leadership are missing in today's Neo-Pagan and Wicca movement. When someone is foolish enough to broach the subject, that person is usually met with contempt or shunned altogether. Goddess have mercy if anyone should infringe on the free spirit of anarchy!

For the most part, Druidism is a practical approach to living in harmony with the world around us. It teaches respect for nature, god, and the creative force within. The major problem with Druidism is within its structure of practice. Today's urban community is not prepared to accommodate practitioners of nature religions. The availability of private woods, isolated mountain tops, and secluded oceanfront property do not exist—and where they do, they are usually posted as private property. Therefore, in order for Druidism to work, it needs to be modernized. Rituals need to be rewritten for the urban practitioner in a manner that preserves their original essence and at the same time supports a twentieth-century lifestyle.

ENDNOTES

1. The Celts, like a lot of barbarian tribes of this time period, took heads as war trophies. The Celts placed the heads on poles as warning signs; triumphant warriors hung the heads from their belt.

2. The reason for the belief in threes was due to the fact that it takes two to create a third, which is in essence part of both original components and at the same time separate and individual. This is one concept that Co-Creation embraces, as we firmly believe that the continuance of life involves the union of the masculine and feminine aspects of nature.

CHAPTER 3

Christianity: A Covenant with Christ

Even those who have renounced Christianity and attack it, in their inmost being still follow the Christian ideal, for hitherto neither their subtlety nor ardor of their hearts has been able to create a higher ideal of man and virtue than the ideal given by Christ of old.

The Brothers Karamasov, 1880, Part II, Book IV

The History of Christianity

Christianity is a vast and overwhelming subject—you would need volumes of text and a lifetime to explore it. Even then, I am not sure you would be able to do justice to the phenomenon of its jurisdiction. In addition to its formidable history and extensive size, hundreds of divergent sects deserve consideration. One small chapter can do nothing more than present a fleeting, but concise, glimpse into the events that led up to this wonder child of the Piscean Age.

Looking back, we find that Christianity actually started several hundred years before Jesus stumbled into it—which makes one wonder about the nature of Jesus himself. Was he the Messiah foretold in Jewish scripture or did he identify with their myth for reasons of his own? Did Jesus die on the cross or did Mary Magdalene revive him and orchestrate his escape? Will we ever know, and does it really matter? We know Jesus was there, Christianity was born, and its effects are with us today.

From the conventional viewpoint, Christianity seems to have blossomed forth from profoundly Jewish soil with a focus on the teachings of Jesus as their long-awaited Messiah. But this view lacks foundation for several reasons—one of which was that

Jesus was critical of the practices of Judaism. He preached love instead of Mosaic law and was quick to condemn the religious leaders for hiding spiritual truths from the people. It also seems reasonable to assume that Jesus had no intention of being part of the old Judaic tradition or of starting a new religion of his own. He was too opposed to the organized and political piety of what he saw in the temple.

Then there is the problem with Jesus himself, who was a thorn in the side of the Jews from his birth. The Jews were looking for a liberating monarch to ride in on his proud steed and rescue them. What they got was an insurgent Jewish Rabbi who came from a simple background, consorted with fishermen and prostitutes, and had the audacity to dispute religious rulership. It is suspect that Judaism may not have played a role in Christianity that some would like to think it did.

In reality, Christianity is basically a Greek religion, and one that was in development long before Jesus was a twinkle in his mother's eye. At the time of Christian inception, Orphism was a popular movement.[1] Its doctrine taught, through a resurrection myth, that humans contained a divine spark that came directly from deity, although humans were prone to evil as well. It was the responsibility of the individual, through purification by initiation, to free the divine part from the evil part in order to attain everlasting life. This concept was Hellenistic in principle, but decidedly foreign to Jewish doctrine.

It is true that Judaism provided Christianity with the notion of a Messiah as well as some eccentric social rules and laws. But the most important aspect of Christianity is in the Greek concept of resurrection, which came from the reincarnation myth of Dionysus.[2] This was the primary appeal of Christianity to the average believer. Through Christ it was possible to have a personal relationship with a resurrected divinity, thereby being granted everlasting life. The idea of such a thing would have rankled the most permissive Jew, as this type of thinking was alien to them.

Orphism rather than Judaism helped pave the way for Christianity because Orphism already taught the concepts of original sin, punishment of the wicked in an afterlife, the metaphorical interpretation of myth, and the belief in eternal life. Similarities existed between Orpheus and Jesus as well. Orpheus possessed the power to move stones and tame wild beasts. He was also known as the "Good Shepherd."

Parallels between Christianity and the Pagan Mystery traditions existed as well. One glowing example was the similarity between the solar divinity Mithras and Jesus.[3] Both deities celebrate their birthdays on December 25, which marks the return of Sol Invictus, the Unconquered Sun. It is also believed that Mithras, like Jesus, was born in a cave or grotto.

The Mithraic mysteries have other things in common with Christianity, such as a meal of bread and wine and the shedding of blood for the salvation of humankind. Though these similarities are not exact in their presentation, they are similar in consequence—as is the way Mithraism promoted initiation as a death and rebirth process whereby the individual was "born again" into the light.

There is no doubt that Christianity was an amalgamation of a variety of traditional beliefs and practices. The most obvious contributions come from the Pagan practices of Mithraism, the Orphic beliefs, and Mosaic Law. When these are combined, the final result was the new religion called Christianity. In its pristine state, Christianity was intended to synthesize the best elements of Greek, Jewish, Egyptian, and Persian spirituality for a world religion. Unfortunately, somewhere it slipped off track and became infected with political greed and corruption.

What was and could have been is past. Christianity captured Rome and the Roman Catholic Church became the wonder child of the civilized world. It also absorbed every bit of Paganism it could. What it did not absorb, it eliminated. The church, and the Roman Catholic Church in particular, confiscated all written records, accounts, and information on philosophy and the Mysteries. For this reason, it is crucial for the seeker to investigate some of the Catholic Christian mysteries and read between the lines as he or she searches for the truth.

Beliefs and Practices of the Catholic Church

The Roman Catholic Church bases its beliefs on the life and teachings of Jesus Christ, the Messiah, who came to redeem humanity from sin. He gave his life and shed his blood on the land so the faithful would be granted everlasting life through his resurrection.

Jesus (Yeshua ben Joseph) was born around 4 B.C., toward the commencement of the Common Era, just before the death of Herod the Great. He was born in Bethlehem to Mary and Joseph and raised in Galilee. Little is known about his early life except that he received a full education in the Old Testament, may have spent time with the Essenes, and worked as a carpenter, like his father.

Jesus' meeting with John the Baptist set in motion the future of his public ministry. John had called Israel to return to God. In the river Jordan, he baptized those who responded to his message. Jesus joined John's ministry and stayed with him until John was imprisoned. Jesus returned to Galilee to continue with the ministerial work he had begun with John.

Jesus was a charismatic and authoritative speaker and drew large crowds whenever he preached. To those he attracted, as well as his disciples, he brought a message of love, purity, deliverance, and repentance. He also warned against becoming preoccupied with material possessions. Jesus was popular with the common people, but he soon aroused opposition with the Jewish leaders and authorities. His habit of mixing with ostracized people, his contempt for affluence, his free attitude toward Sabbath observance, and his high regard for women made him a threat to the Jewish religious establishment.

It no doubt was this last sacrilege, his attitude toward women, that finally brought about the animosity of the Pharisees. In Jewish society, women had no rights. One saying was, "Be it better to burn the Torah than teach it to a woman, as she is considered inferior in all things." Jesus found this attitude intolerable and did not help things when he said to the priests and elders, "Verily I say unto you, that the publicans and the harlots go into the kingdom of God before you" (Matthew 21:31).

Jesus' ministry lasted only three years. His teachings and influence on his followers, as well as the general populace, was perceived as threatening to the Jewish priests. The opposition came to a climax at the Passover festival when Jesus rode into the city of Jerusalem in a deliberately messianic gesture, then carried out a demonstration against the temple. He proceeded to get into a serious and bitter argument with the Jewish religious authorities who charged him with blasphemy.

Temple guards subsequently arrested Jesus with the help of Judas, a disgruntled apostle. He was tried for blasphemy under Jewish law, and the Sanhedrin no doubt gave him a death sentence. But this sentence was not good enough for the Jewish leaders who were incensed by Jesus' claim of his messianic character. They wanted as much public fanfare as possible, so they pushed for a Roman conviction as well.

Early on Friday morning, Jesus was taken to Pilate, who made a futile effort to transfer him to another jurisdiction. The Jews cornered Pilate and threatened him with denunciation. They said that if he acquitted Jesus he would be "no friend of Caesar." Jesus was found guilty of sedition. Pontius Pilate carried out the execution that very day by having Jesus crucified.

It was not so much the passion or death of Jesus that launched the Christianity we have today, but rather Jesus' resurrection three days later. His followers and apostles saw his resurrection as both vindication and validation of his claims to be god's agent. The resurrection, coupled with his appearance to Mary Magdalene and his disciples, is what crystallized and set the foundation for the Christian ministry.

Practices of Roman Catholicism

Christianity is a social religious system, and the Church represents the spiritual and moral pattern of the community. This pattern is expressed through the organized teachings, rituals, and celebrations conducted by the priesthood for the benefit of the community or congregation.

The word *Catholic* means "universal" and *Roman Catholic* refers to the Latin western church. Roman Catholics recognize the Pope, through apostolic succession, as the head of the Church and final authority on doctrine. The emperor Constantine granted religious freedom to Christians in A.D. 313 and subsequently converted the entire Roman Empire to Christianity, which dignified the Roman Catholic Church.

The basic format of the Catholic Church is the belief in:

- The existence of one God, the Creator and Lord of the universe.
- The idea that humans are made in the image of God, but rebelled and now stand in judgment.
- Jesus Christ as the Son of God, who was revealed to and rejected by the nation of Israel.
- The idea that someday God will establish his rule with Jesus Christ as his appointed agent.
- The Holy Bible as the word of God, especially the New Testament.
- Redemption of sin, at death, which means humans are assured a place in heaven with God and Christ.

The Seven Sacraments

The above beliefs in combination with the following Seven Sacraments, or seven obligations, are what give foundation to the Catholic creed.

1. *Baptism:* The ritual washing by which a person is made clean of sin and thereby ready for admission into the fellowship of the church.

2. *Confirmation:* A public confession of faith in the church and a ratification of vows from baptism. A bishop or priest administers this sacrament by the laying on of hands and anointing of the candidate.

3. *Holy Communion or Eucharist:* Eucharist[4] comes from the Greek word *eucharistein*, meaning to give thanks. The Eucharist is the central act of worship or sacrament of the church. The giving of thanks was a direct request of Jesus at the Last Supper before his death. At the Last Supper, he requested his followers to do this in remembrance of him.

4. *Confession:* Penance or repentance for sins or wrongdoing in accordance with the individual's religious beliefs. Here the person, by going through the priest, is granted absolution for his or her errors in judgment.

5. *Holy Orders:* The act of ordination in which a person is admitted to the ministry of the church. A cup or chalice and a Host resting on a Bible is this sacrament's symbol.

6. *Matrimony:* The sacrament whereby a man and woman enter into an agreement to give and receive rights over one another for the act of generation and the fostering of mutual love.

7. *Extreme Unction:* The act of anointing with sacred holy oil an individual who is in a state of grace and in danger of death. A bishop or priest administers the sacrament and completes the act of penance.

Commentary: Co-Creation Spirituality has similar ideals of sacraments. We use Dedication as our Baptism; Initiation in place of Confirmation; The Great Rite of Union as the Eucharist celebration; Ordination is our method of bestowing Holy Orders; Marriage is basically the same no matter who you are; and for Extreme Unction we use the Ceremony of Release. Although our names are different, the basic principles remain the same. It is for everyone's benefit to have the regular ceremonial observances defined in an organized manner.

Holy Days of Obligation

Holy days commemorate important events in the history of the Catholic Church. These special times are celebrated by attending mass and partaking of the Eucharist. The mass is usually followed by a social gathering of family and friends. These gatherings are reminiscent of a time when people gathered to give thanks and praise to their gods and celebrated with a feast afterward.

Advent is the beginning of the Christian calendar. It is the four weeks of preparation before Christmas in celebration of the birth of Jesus Christ. Advent begins on the Sunday following St. Andrew's day, which is on November 30. Advent is marked by the making of wreaths and the lighting of candles.

Christmas, the English name for the Feast of the Nativity, is celebrated on December 25 and coincides with the Pagan festival of Yule as the rebirth of the sun. Because Jesus Christ was considered the Sol Verus, or true sun, his birthday was commemorated on this date.

Lent is a forty-day period of preparation for Easter. It corresponds to the forty days that Jesus spent fasting in the wilderness before beginning his public ministry.

Palm Sunday, the Sunday before Easter, recalls Jesus' triumphal entry into Jerusalem and is marked by the blessing of palm branches.[5]

Good Friday commemorates the passion of Jesus, beginning with the agony in the garden, scourging at the pillar, crowning with the thorns, carrying the cross, and the crucifixion.[6]

Easter Sunday is the greatest of the Christian festivals and celebrates Jesus' resurrection. The date of Easter changes each year and is calculated from the first Sunday after the full moon following the Spring or Vernal Equinox.

Ascension Day is when Jesus ascended to heaven. It is celebrated forty days after Easter.

Pentecost/Whitsun is the celebration of when God sent his Holy Spirit to the apostles ten days after Jesus' ascension. This festival marks the birth of the church.

Christian Symbols

Almond, altar, angels, apple, ark, arrow, bell, Bible, bramble (acacia), candle, censer, chalice, circle, Chi-Rho, cope, cross, dagger, dove, eye, font, four elements, gold, goose, grapes, heart, incense, key, lamb, ladder, lamp, lance, lily, mirror, owl, palm, paten, rainbow, ring, rock, rosary, salt, scales, shell, sparrow, tabernacle, throne, triangle, veil, vine, wafer, wand, water, whip, yew.

Synopsis

How does one sum up Christianity? It is a difficult topic to begin with, and one that seems to bring out animosity in the most docile of people. What makes a summarization so hard is that no matter which side an individual takes, the other side comes raging forth all teeth and claws. This subject can not be broached without arousing someone's anger and subsequent resentment.

To its early followers, Christianity was a social and spiritual ideal of collective religious teachings. These visionaries saw it as the New Song, the New Hope, the Promise of Universal Harmony. In their wildest dreams and worst nightmares they could never have imagined what it would become.

The creative scholars, mystics, and philosophers of the early Piscean Age perceived their new religion as a synthesis of the great spiritual wisdoms of the known world. By drawing on the Greek, Hebrew, and Egyptian mysteries, they hoped to assemble a collage of the most celebrated teachings of their time. By bringing these concepts together, they would create a worldwide living spiritual temple—one that would invite a diversity of thought and practice to all who participated in it.

Early Christianity was far more eclectic than most of our religious systems today. The developers were zealous, energetic, and devoted. They picked, chose, and appended where necessary in order to create a cohesive working process. There was room for everyone and their opinions, and every aspect was a subject for discussion. These individuals were truly inspired and sought to set a new spiritual precedent.

The Golden Age of Christianity came and went, and with it died the hope of a universal religion. Once Christianity became a formal organization, the retention of funds for jobs, operating expenses, and the building of churches was necessary. It was not long before the Church's secular side became more important than its original spiritual ideals. As the growth and power of the Roman Catholic Church continued, it became increasingly more rigid, dogmatic, and orthodox.

The Church soon began to emphasize the bishops' historical claim to being the true emissaries of Jesus and God through apostolic succession, and as such were the sole dispensers of spiritual truth. This was purely a political move to justify their ecclesiastical existence and to maintain their temporal authority. It was not long before these same pompous merchants of theological wisdom proclaimed that the

Catholic Church was indeed "The one truth and only way to salvation." No other religion except Judaism had ever been so bold.

In closing, I want to say that I am not promoting the Catholic Church nor am I condemning Christianity. The purpose of this chapter is to help the individual distinguish between politics and spirituality. As far as I am concerned, all religious philosophies—and I stress *philosophy* rather than political agenda—are open for investigation. This is why Co-Creation Spirituality is so important; it does not pigeonhole any one specific tradition. Judgment is left to a higher authority and participation is invited by the sincere seeker of truth and spiritual wisdom.

Endnotes

1. Orphism is a religious movement supposedly founded by Orpheus. It was the first Greek religion to embody its doctrines in literature.

2. Greek myth relates how the young god Dionysus was slain and dismembered. He was then put back together, restored to life, and sent up to heaven.

3. Co-Creation Spirituality recognizes Jesus as the Sol Invictus and/or the composite form of all past solar-savior deities who do not necessarily belong conclusively to any specific tradition. We feel his energy is as available to us as to anyone and without judgment.

4. The celebration of the Eucharist is a concept that was easily worked into Co-Creation Spirituality. From the basic meaning of giving thanks, it only makes sense to include this age-old practice in our rituals and make it as elaborate and ceremonial as possible in a show of true respect and appreciation.

5. Palm branches are a Pagan symbol of victory, adopted by the early Christians to signify the triumph over death of their saints and martyrs. Palms were spread before Jesus when he rode into Jerusalem as the Messiah.

6. For Our Lady of Enchantment, Good Friday and the concept of deep appreciation for Jesus the Christ and all solar-savior divinities who have shed their blood and given their lives for the good of humanity—whether in actuality or symbolically—is in arrangement with our Co-Creation belief system.

CHAPTER 4

Santería: An Old Religion in a New World

Santería is a miracle of spirit brought out of crushing human suffering. Its history shows that a people placed under the most difficult conditions imaginable can fashion a spiritual world of beauty and hope.

Joseph M. Murphy, *Santería: An African Religion in America*

The History of Santería

To millions of practitioners, Santería is more than just a religion; it is a way of life, involving a complex mixture of social morals, spirit contact, and deity worship. To fully appreciate this intricate system, you must understand its Cuban beginnings. Through a meshing of African myth and Spanish Catholicism, in combination with cross-cultural integration, the path for this new religion was paved.

From A.D. 1500 on, Spain enticed people to relocate to Cuba by offering land grants and monetary rewards. As the Spanish settled in their new land, they established their own form of government, which included Roman Catholicism as the state religion. All other forms of worship, including Judaism and Islamic practices, were forbidden. This created problems because of the diverse ethnic background of the local as well as emigrant populations.

During this time period, the Catholic Church prevailed and enveloped all phases of life with its antagonistic oppression and domination of spirit. Cuba, however, was different from other Catholic countries because Spanish Catholicism was not like its rigid Roman ancestor. This difference may have been due to a counter reformation or a negative reaction to the Protestant movement, or it could have been the response to living in a new country with other races. Whatever the reason, differences existed between the two.

In Cuba, the Spanish Catholic religion was divided into two systems. The first was a basic cult dedicated to the Seven Sacraments that seemed to be the province of Church officials and affluent land owners. The second division, embraced by the lower Creole classes, was a cult predisposed to the personages of Jesus, the Virgin Mary, and every conceivable Saint known to humans. This second division was the most widely practiced form of Catholicism. Followers actively celebrated the legends and miracles of the Saints through yearly festivals and pilgrimages to their shrines.

From this second cult, dedicated to the Saints, a third faction emerged and was considered to be a form of Catholic folk magic. The practices of this third division involved lighting candles, saying prayers, and providing offerings to the Saints in exchange for their blessings. These folk incorporated herbal remedies, love potions, and all manner of natural substances in their craft. Had they not been devoted Catholics working under the watchful eye of their Saints, they could have been accused of Witchcraft.

During the 1700s, Cuba was growing by leaps and bounds, and it was impossible for the Church to govern everyone's actions. As a result, this third cult, with its veneration of the Saints, transformed into a form of domestic worship that the Church seemed to ignore. Home altars, local shrines, and personal spiritual practices soon took precedence over Church doctrine, especially among the Creole and country population.

The Church being the Church, it tried to get its hands in everybody's pocket, including those of the large sugar plantations. The Church made every effort to teach the slaves Christianity. However, this venture was soon considered a lost cause because the plantation owners resented the Church's interference, and the slaves, who worked eighteen-hour days seven days a week, did not have time for religion.

By the late 1870s, Cuba's black population began to grow due to an influx of Africans the British had set free on Cuban shores. These people migrated into the cities and smaller farming communities. This influx of Africans, coupled with the local growth from the black Creoles, created a discrimination problem. Everyone wanted to be white, and mulattos, along with other races, were buying white citizenship. Segregation of the races, which up to now had been a class issue, was becoming a color issue. Few spheres of life existed where people of African descent and European descent met on any level of equality.

One area of integration was religion, because there was no segregation in the Catholic Church; blacks had equal rights with whites. The Afro-Cubans could also take refuge from racism in their own clubs and fraternal organizations. The number of African clubs and bars increased and soon became meeting places for the preservation of the Yoruba (traditional African) religion and Creole culture.

These clubs, or Cabildos,[1] served as centers for recreation, spiritual devotions, and general social interaction. The Church saw these centers as the perfect place to convert the Afro-Cubans to Christianity. Under the direction of a diocesan priest, each Cabildo was assigned a Saint to watch over it and the activities of its members.

As long as Christian doctrine, prayers, and practices were taught, the African customs were allowed to prevail. It was hoped that in time the Africans would give up their Pagan rites and follow Christianity.

In the Cabildos, the syncretism of the Yoruba religion and Catholicism began. This religion was not a forced consolidation of beliefs and practices, but a gradual combination that took place over generations. With the Catholic authority always present, and in view of the Church's social position, it is only natural that it would influence some of the Yoruba customs. With the help of the Church, not only was the Yoruba faith allowed to continue, but also, through assimilation and adaptation, it evolved into the new religion of Santería.

By looking at the religion of the Yoruba, which is called Ifa, we get a basic idea of the formal principles that helped fashion the Santería religion. Ifa is an intricate combination of theology and ritual, revolving around the teaching of nature as God or the Supreme Being. The significance of this presents itself in a belief that nature is a divine being composed of many different controlling forces. These forces manifest in natural phenomena such as thunder, rain, fire, and lightning. The controlling forces also appear as human interest and endeavor in love, war, marriage, and fertility.

In Ifa, Olodumare is the supreme God who is thought to be a sort of cosmic energy from which the universe was made. Because Olodumare has to care for such a vast universe, he rules in absentia through Olofi, a personal god set to care for humanity.

Olodumare transmits a pure vital energy force which is called *ashe*. This *ashe* is transmitted from Olodumare to Olofi, who in turn channels it through a pantheon of other deities, called Orisha. The intention of the religion is to determine which Orisha need to be appeased or praised through *ebbo* (sacrifice) in order to receive some of their *ashe*. This in turn will help the individual maintain a balanced and happy life.

Belief and Practices of Santería

The five distinct aspects of Santería include the following: the worship of the Orisha and Saints; the use of divination to ascertain the wishes of the Orisha or Saints; initiation in order to receive the mysteries of the Orisha; *ebbo* or sacrifice in order to appease or give thanks to the Orisha; and ancestor worship.

Santería also functions on the basic principle that the spiritual and physical aspects of an individual should work together. Their philosophy is that each individual should live up to his or her potential. If you wish to be rich and famous, you should strive for that. On the other hand, if you wish to serve and help the needy, this should be your goal. It does not matter what you choose to do as long as you do it to the best of your ability.

The religion also stresses the concept of good sense and for the most part loathes the idea of "thou shalt not." God gave us brains and we are expected to use them; through right effort, work, and communion with deity, humans will learn to live in harmony with each other and nature.

The Orisha

Each Orisha represents a different[2] aspect of the creative force and has the ability to manipulate his or her *ashe* according to the sphere of influence each exemplifies. In Santería, each of the Orisha, besides being independently powerful, is identified with a corresponding Catholic Saint. The Saint which represents the Orisha is also believed to be endowed with the Orisha's *ashe* or power.

In Santería, the Orisha's *ashe* or power is contained in the *otanes* (sacred stones) that are kept in a *sopera* (tureen). Also inside the *sopera* are a set of tools that symbolize the expression of the owner Orisha. During Asiento, the initiate is presented with four *sopera,* corresponding to Oshun, Yemoja, Obatala, and Shango.[3]

At this point it is necessary to introduce the Orisha because it is impossible to explain Santería without understanding their significance. The Orisha are the religion's main purpose and point. But because several hundred Orisha exist, it would take an entire book to relate them all. For this reason, following is a list of the most popular, including the "Seven African Powers" conveyed in the initiation of Asiento or El Santo.

Orisha	Saint	Attributes
Olofi	Christ (God)	One of the three aspects of Oldumare
Obatala	Virgin of Mercy	Father of Orisha; guardian of morality, order, and tradition
Shango	Saint Barbara	God of thunder, lightning, and fire; the wrath of Oldumare; rules passion
Oya	Virgin of La Candelaria	Guardian of the cemetery and justice; concerned with death and the business world
Oshun	Virgin of Caridad del Cobra	Patroness of love, money, sex and marriage, and yellow metals
Yemoja	Virgin of Regla	Mother of the saints/Orisha, Goddess of the sea; mother of the world; rules maternity

Eleggua	Holy child of Atoche	Messenger of all Orisha; keeper of doors and crossroads; rules chance, communication, and hazards
Babaluaiye	Saint Lazarus	Patron of the sick; father of the world because of his power over sickness
Ogun	Saint Peter	God of iron, warfare, and sacrifice; rules employment
Orunmila	Saint Francis	Owner of Ifa divination; guardian of Assisi; knowledge of past and future

Divination

Santería's major object is to find out, through different methods of divination, what the Orisha want. What is needed in order to appease them, through *ebbo* (sacrifice), so they will grant you some of their *ashe?* The four methods of divination used in Santería follow:

1. *The Obi* are four coconut rinds and is the most common method used to determine what the Orisha want and if they are pleased with an offering. Although anyone can use this system, only people who have undergone the initiation of the warriors should do so.

2. *The Diloggun* is a set of twenty-one cowrie shells, of which sixteen are used for the reading. This system is complicated and proficiency requires many years of practice; only initiated priests and priestesses use this system.

3. *The Okuele* is a chain set with eight medallions made of coconut shell. Only high priests of Santería, known as Babalawos, use this method of divination.

4. *The Table of Ifa* is the Oracle of Santería and is the highest form of divination. Only Babalawos use this form during rituals and ceremonies where the ruling Orisha of a person is to be decided.

Santería Divination Tools

Commentary: This concept of being able to talk with, and get an answer from, deity inspired the creation of Our Lady of Enchantment's Vessel of Creation. As will be explained in Chapter 13, the Vessel contains symbols and tools along with a set of Speaking Stones, which are attuned to the practitioner's principal goddess. By working with this specific tool, the individual is allowed to speak directly to his or her goddess and, most importantly, receive an answer. Because all of the symbols and objects in the vessel are receptive to the goddess, they act like a magnet, attracting her essence and energy into the Vessel.

Initiation: El Santo

Essential to the practice of Santería are four secrets that make up the formal initiation ceremony of "El Santo"—the use of herbs, water, cowrie shells, and stones. Without these, the practice of the religion is next to impossible.

The initiation ceremonies in Santería make it possible to practice the religion. One can be an adherent of the philosophy without being initiated, but in order to really practice Santería, initiation is mandatory. The secrecy involved in the religion and the fact that the information needed to work with the Orisha is only given to initiates are two reasons why initiation is mandatory. The four initiations are the *Collares*, or *Elekes*; *Los Guerreros*; *Asiento*; and the *Consecration of Ifa*.

The *Collares* or *Elekes* (necklaces). This is a one-day ceremony in which the recipient receives a set of beaded necklaces representing Eleggua, Obatala, Chango, Yemoja, and Oshun. The necklaces protect the initiate from danger.

Los Guerreros (Eleggua and the warriors). In this special ceremony, the initiate receives a cement head representing the Orisha Eleggua; a cauldron of working implements belonging to Ogun and Oshosi; and a small cup surmounted by a rooster and bells, which represent Osanyin. Los Guerreros and the Collares initiations are considered to be the foundation of Santería.

Asiento, also known as *Kariocha*. This is the major initiation in which the person's guardian Orisha is placed in his or her head. This initiation takes seven days to complete and a year of training, during which the initiate is referred to as the *iyawo*. After this initiation, the person is now a priest (Santero) or priestess (Santera) of Santería.

Santería is an initiatory religion that involves a traditional hierarchy. When one enters training under a Santero or Santera, he or she becomes that teacher's godchild. From this point on, the godchild refers to his or her Santero or Santera as Padrino or Madrina. Each Santero or Santera has his or her own working group, which is designated as his or her "house." Each group or house is independent in their worship and magical workings. On special occasions, such as the initiation of Asiento and designated holidays of importance to the Orishas and Saints, houses will gather in celebration.

Consecration of Ifa is also known as Olofi or receiving of "God's mysteries." These are the highest initiates known as the Babalawos and are always men. In Santería, they are considered the high priests and diviners serving in a judicial capacity, largely as consultants for the Santeros and Santeras.

Sacrifice, the Ebbo

The term *ebbo* means sacrifice[4] or offering and is probably the most misunderstood aspect of the entire religion. Santería is not the first religion to incorporate sacrifice into its practices. Almost every religion in the world—both Christian and Pagan—at one time or another has done the same. Most of the Pagan religions, however, died out long ago and are only now reviving; they are choosing not to use sacrifice. The religion of the Yoruba did not die out; it only changed its name and appearance for a new world.

Sacrifice is believed to be essential to human well-being. Thousands of items are used for sacrifice, including money, fruit, liquor, kola nuts, palm oil, special foods, and virtually anything else that may appeal to the Orisha. On occasion, when the problem is severe, the life of an individual is at stake, or during an initiation, the sacrifice may include the offering of blood. When an animal is offered, all of the animal is put to use. The meat is properly butchered, cooked, and eaten by those in attendance. The hooves, hides, and horns are used for drums and magical implements.

Ancestor Worship and Reincarnation

Ancestor worship is very much a part of Santería but separate in its placement and rituals. The idea of ancestor worship is more in the form of respect for those who have passed on, realizing they may have beneficial knowledge to share with the living.

This concept of the ancestors also involves reincarnation. In Santería, as in Ifa, it is believed that when one dies he or she spends time on the other side being refreshed before returning. During this transition time, loved ones may communicate with relatives on the earth. Once the transition of reincarnation takes place, the person is believed to be reborn in the same blood line in which he or she once lived.

Symbols and Celebrations

The symbols used in Santería are all associated with the Orisha and Saints; they will sometimes vary from house to house. The celebrations are geared to coincide with Saint Holy Days and days associated with certain Orisha. The following are some of the more popular days celebrated:

Feast of Yemoja: September 7; celebrated by acknowledging the power of the Mother aspect of the Goddess.

Feast of Oshun: September 8; celebrated to give thanks to Oshun for the love and prosperity in one's life.

Feast of Chango: December 4; recognizes the power of the fire and passion of the god.

Feast of Babaluaiye: December 17; a time to ask for protection and give thanks for personal blessings.

Feast of Eleggua: June 13; a time for those who have received Eleggua to celebrate his function within the pantheon.

Synopsis

Because I have received several initiations in Santería, I feel qualified to speak about this system. Santería is a beautiful and powerful religion. The power comes from a pantheon of deities that have survived for thousands of years in their original form. The beauty comes from the ability to communicate directly with these gods on a personal level and incorporate their desires with a modern lifestyle.

Santería is not an easy religion to get into. First, it is held in the greatest of secrecy and, second, most Santeros, who are of Hispanic descent, do not trust the average white American. Only after several initiations and a dedication to learning will the Madrina or Padrino open up, and even then with much reserve and resistance. In some ways, this resistance is good because it protects the religion from the insincere.

Santería—unlike many of the New Age, earth-oriented religions—cannot be gleaned from reading books and then dubbing oneself high priest or priestess. The religion requires both study and training, which can only be gained by learning from a trained Santero or Santera. The discipline, training, and initiation through proper channels has allowed this system to remain alive, pure, and powerful.

Santería allows for the expression of the individual both physically and spiritually. Even though there are set procedures and etiquette that must be followed, plenty of room exists for each person to be creative, interact with deity, and contribute original material to their practices. In fact, creativity and personal input are encouraged and seen as the way to keep the religion in a continual state of progress and growth.

My last comment on Santería is on the concept of sacrifice and to those who object to it. I have been to many Neo-Pagan gatherings and seen people dressed in elaborate animal skin costumes complete with horned head gear and feathers. I wonder, did these people ever consider for one moment how or why the animal—which now adorns their body for the sole purpose of admiration from their peers—died? "Let he who is without sin cast the first stone."

Endnotes

1. A Cabildo was any assembly, meeting, council or cathedral chapter, or temple of the Afro-Cuban peoples where African religions and culture were taught.

2. *Different* is a concept that Co-Creation spirituality recognizes as well. We believe that all gods and goddesses are different. Each god and goddess is a separate and distinct energy force or emanation extending from the All. As such, each has a specific quality and distinct energy force.

3. This concept of the power of the deity being attracted to and residing within symbolic objects kept in a special vessel is applicable to any system; and one we readily accepted and worked through in our Co-Creation tradition.

4. Sacrifice is the giving of something valuable and loved in thanksgiving or for the petitioning of a request. Valuable depends upon the situation. To a poor farmer, a basket of vegetables or a chicken would be considered valuable, but to a bank president these would have little meaning.

CHAPTER 5

Buddhism: The Ascetic Way of Life

Does the eagle know what is in the hole?
Or wilt thou go ask the mole?
Can wisdom be put in a silver rod?
Or love in a golden bowl?

William Blake, *The Book of Thel*, 1789

The History of Buddhism and Buddha

Asia is a land of 70,000 temples, exotic incense, and the mysterious chanting of saffron-cloaked monks. This land is where we find Buddhism, the great missionary religion of India. Here, Siddharta Gautama, who was dissatisfied with the conventional sacrificial religion of Brahmanism and the excessive austerity of Jainisim, discovered the fundamental truth of the Middle Way.

Siddharta Gautama, later to become known as the Buddha or Enlightened One, founded the Buddhist religion. He was born about 560 B.C. and died at the age of eighty. His father was the rajah of Kapilavastu and raised Siddharta as a prince in resplendent luxury. Siddharta married at an early age and had a son. When he reached the age of twenty-nine, however, he decided to leave his world of splendor and become a homeless holy man.

Several events contributed to Siddharta's choice. The first was his shock and horror at seeing suffering in the streets, which he had been unaware of due to his sheltered life. The second was his knowledge of the Upanishads[1] and their orientation toward a more inward approach to religion. These two motivations, coupled with the idea of homelessness as the true and proper method of seeking spiritual truth, led Siddharta to embark on his remarkable journey.

Siddharta studied with many religious teachers, learning the disciplines of an ascetic way of life. After an extended fast, when all his body hair fell out, he found his enlightenment. This event marked the turning point in his life, as he realized the futility of denying the physical in search of the ultimate spiritual truth. He found that without food and the necessities of daily life, the body becomes weak, the mind distracted, and spiritual concentration decreases.

Shortly after his experience of enlightenment, or return of common sense, Siddharta began to teach and won many disciples who followed him in his vagabond way of life. The mission of the Buddha and his disciples was to imbue on their followers, and the general public, a more meditative lifestyle, which they believed led to nirvana.[2]

Eventually, Buddhism evolved and developed into many different traditions. Though their practices may vary, they all hold to the core of the Buddha's teachings of the Four Noble Truths. The most widely practiced forms are Theravada Buddhism and Mahayana Buddhism, with Tibetan Buddhism and some of the others being offshoots of the two larger denominations. The selection here discusses the Middle Path of Mahayana Buddhism.

Beliefs and Practices of Mahayana Buddhism

Buddhism is a solitary system that grew out of the basic tradition of Indian religious thought. It is not a religion that leads to ecclesiastical approval; rather it stresses the importance of following the Four Noble Truths and Eight-Fold Path taught by the Buddha. In essence, it emphasizes the principles of gentleness, reverence for life, and profound self-reflection.

The Four Noble Truths

1. The universal human experience of suffering—mental and emotional as well as physical—is the direct effect of karma.

2. The perception of such suffering is due to craving or grasping for the wrong things, or for the right things in the wrong way. The basic human problem is a misplaced sense of value, assigning to things or persons in the world a value they cannot sustain. Nothing in the material world is worthy of reverence or can be depended upon in any ultimate sense.

3. It is possible for human suffering to cease and for the ultimate human dilemma to be solved.

4. The Noble Eight-Fold Path is the solution, which forms the basic teaching of the Buddhist lifestyle.

The Noble Eight-Fold Path

The first two truths of the Noble Eight-Fold Path come under the classification of wisdom or understanding, the next three under ethical conduct, and the last three under mental discipline.

1. Right knowledge

2. Right attitude

3. Right speech

4. Right action

5. Right living (occupation)

6. Right effort

7. Right mindfulness

8. Right composure

Reincarnation: Through reincarnation, all human beings reap good or evil, depending on the quality of their actions, thoughts, and deeds in previous lives. What one did in his or her last life will determine the circumstance and quality of a future life.

Karma: The law of karma is the law of cause and effect. It operates on both physical and moral levels of human behavior. To gain liberation from karma, one must understand the human situation and observe the Noble Eight-Fold Path.

Nirvana: Nirvana is the goal of life. This is not the annihilation of the self, but the transformation of the human consciousness. It is the true refuge, a state of blissful inactivity or spiritual enlightenment.

Dharma: Dharma is an unknown principle that pervades the whole universe and regulates its harmonious action. It is the way to the goal of nirvana. Dharma is a personal dynamic that gives inner power and quality to life.

The Buddhist Calendar

A visit to the Buddhist temple to pray might take place at any time as there are no fixed weekly meetings. However, like all religions, certain times of the year are set aside for celebration and ritual.

The New Year: On this night, the ritual known as *Joya No Kane* is celebrated with the toning of the temple bells 108 times (symbolizing the 108 forms of defilement) as midnight approaches to mark the end of the old year.

Annual Ceremonies for the Dead: These ceremonies are held on March 21 and on September 23 or the Spring and Autumn Equinoxes in remembrance of the family members.

Obon: The traditional Japanese "All Souls Day" is usually celebrated sometime between July and August.

Birthday of the Buddha: Known as Hanamatsuri, this holiday is also known as the annual Flower Festival and celebrated on April 8.

Death of the Buddha: Celebrated on February 15, this marks Buddha's entrance into nirvana.

Buddhist Symbols

Buddhist Symbols

Conch, umbrella, canopy, mystic knot, fish, lotus, vase, scroll, Wheel of the Law, rope, begging bowl, incense burner, sacrificial cup, fan, cock and sun, hare and moon, fly whisk, rosary, goad, spear, ax. The footprint of the Buddha, which contains the swastika, wheel, conch, fish, varja, crown, and vase.

Synopsis

Buddhism has contributed a great deal to both religion and the New Age movement. One of the most important aspects of Buddhism is its ability to transcend the mundane physical world and look within. This introspection allows the individual to realize his or her true place within the universe and at the same time creates a feeling of oneness of self and nature. This feeling, coupled with the ability to discipline both the mind and body, provides the training necessary for working with other realms of awareness.

For people born and raised in the Western culture, some drawbacks to Buddhism exist. The major obstacle comes from the West's conditioned thinking, motives, and actions that extend from an outward point of view. In the East, the mind is reflective and meditative, creating an inward nature or outlook. Because all religions reflect the culture and frame of mind in which they are developed, it is difficult for the Western mentality to adapt easily to the Eastern intellectual process of looking within.

This opposition of outlook creates the biggest problem for the Westerner. First is the lack of adventure in discovering spiritual truths for oneself. To the Buddhist, everything has already been done, written down, and preformulated by former teachers. All the seeker needs to do is learn the appropriate discipline in order to achieve results. In Western traditions, on the other hand, are spontaneous encounters, adventures into other realities, and discoveries of new approaches to age-old mysteries.

Another problem is that the Buddha preached a religion devoid of any metaphysical speculation. Questions—such as: *Is the soul the same as the body or is it something different?, Is the world infinite or not?, Is there life after death?*—were considered unimportant. Buddha considered this type of discussion to be superfluous and nothing more than a greed for views. Unfortunately, asking these types of questions is why most people become interested in religion—they want and need answers.

The biggest obstacle with Buddhism, at least from my point of view, is that anything even faintly resembling the supernatural is condemned. This includes any type of divination or forecasting. I find this irrational, as the whole purpose of religion is to reunite the individual with deity. To me, this means there has to be communication between humanity and God. How can people ever hope to evolve spiritually if we are denied the ability to emit and receive divine inspiration?

What it amounts to is East is East and West is West and cross-cultural coupling is difficult, if not, in some ways, impossible. Our natural instincts, reasoning attitudes, and spiritual perspectives are different. Many Westerners are impulsive, aggressive, and presumptuous; many Easterners are reticent and speculative. One is not superior or inferior to the other, far from it; it is two different ways of approaching the same concept.

Even though I find it difficult to relate to much of Buddhism, this in no way hinders my affection for and admiration of the Buddha himself. The vast majority of his teachings were oral and what was in actuality his, or what has been reworked through time, is only speculation. The Buddha's most important contribution was his realistic attitude. So many people get involved in spirituality and feel that to be truly spiritual they must drift off into the fog of austerity or relinquish all their worldly goods and live on bread and water. These ideas are not what the Buddha taught; he taught moderation as the key to enlightenment and believed that deprivation or excess would cause imbalance.

ENDNOTES

1. The Upanishads are ancient teachings of the Hindu religion, containing the records of spiritual experiences of the sages of ancient India.

2. Nirvana is an awareness utterly devoid of content; a state of blissful inactivity; a state of spiritual enlightenment or illumination that releases the individual from suffering, death, and birth.

CHAPTER 6

Shamanism: The Natural Way of Spirituality

Shamanism is a great mental and emotional adventure. In Shamanism, the maintenance of one's personal power is fundamental to well-being.

Michael Harner, *The Way of the Shaman*

Shamanism, Nature, and Spirituality

Shamanism is more a personal approach to life, the universe, and god than an organized religion. However, with the coming of the New Age and the awareness of how we treat Mother Earth, Shamanism should be considered as an option. For the most part, North American Neo-Shamanism will be examined, as it is most readily available to those who feel this path to be their calling.

Shamanism is probably the oldest spiritual system in the world and traditionally comes from Siberia and Central Asia. Its practices include the use of visions, altered states of consciousness, and contact with nature gods and spirits. Evidence of Shamanism can be seen almost everywhere; the most often cited examples are found in the cave paintings in southern France. These paintings date back to 35,000 B.C. and depict early humans dressed in animal skins, performing a hunting ritual. Through imitation and participation with the animals and the natural world, the shaman obtained his or her empowerment.

When our Paleolithic ancestors came to North America from Siberia by way of a land bridge across the Bering Strait, they brought their spiritual practices with them. As these groups spread across the continent, different cultures, folkways, and belief systems developed among the tribes. Many forces dictated the behavior and characteristics of each tribe. Climate and terrain also influenced their way of life, prompting some to become hunters, some farmers, and some fisherman.

The beliefs of the Shaman ancestors was expressed according to their region, social structure, and cultural viewpoint. Individually, however, they held certain theories and truths in common. Respectively, most Shamans believed in a God that was presented as the "Great Mystery" and was responsible for the movement of all things. There seemed to be a common mindset as to the earth representing creation and all living things, including humans, and being interconnected. It was also accepted that the earth did not belong to humans exclusively, but rather humans belonged to the earth. This belonging was seen as a form of a stewardship in which humans served and rendered assistance where needed.

The Shaman had respect for the earth and all that resided on it. He or she also observed the spirits inherent within all living things, communing with them through daily activities and ceremonies. It was believed that as the Shaman worked with the spirits, the spirits worked with the Shaman in return. Most often, the Shaman communicated with these spirits while in an ecstatic state of consciousness that allowed him or her access to the upper, lower, and middle worlds.

The practices and rites of the Shamans were geared to the tribe's cultural orientation. The Shaman of a hunting tribe would usually work with the spirits of animals; the Shaman of a tribe involved with agriculture would work with the elements that supported a good harvest. Special times such as births, deaths, marriages, and puberty were also considered to be of importance, as were the changing of the seasons.

When the French, Spanish, and English began to conquer North America, they imposed their Christian religion on the native peoples. Like many other earth-oriented religions, Shamanism secreted itself away, allowing only the most dedicated and sincere to partake of its mysteries. For hundreds of years, it seemed to lay dormant except to those who were of its privileged priesthood. In the 1960s and early 1970s, a new, more-spirited version of Shamanism appeared as a practice of hippies, Witches, and Neo-Pagans. Today, Shamanism is once again reclaiming its place in the spiritual world.

Beliefs and Practices of Neo-Shamanism

Originally, the Shaman was a member of the tribe who, through trance, journeyed to other worlds. While the Shaman was in this altered reality, he would commune with spirits, gain wisdom, and acquire new methods of healing. The prime purpose of the Shaman was to bring back information from his journey. Other activities, such as physical healing and ritual work, were presided over by the medicine men and women.

In today's world, Shamanism implies a wider range of activity that basically combines the journey or pathworking of the Shaman with the physical healing and ritual work of the medicine man or woman. The techniques and procedures to follow are generally considered to be those practiced by most Neo-Shamans. However, as with most New Age spirituality, methods and standards will vary from group to group and Shaman to Shaman.

The Journey and Vision Quest

The Shaman is a trained individual who enters and leaves states of consciousness at will. When in these states of altered consciousness, he or she journeys to various domains of the inner world. This journey usually puts him or her in contact with spirits of ancestors, totem animals, and higher plane teachers. The purpose of the journey is to obtain power, knowledge, and wisdom from the inner world contacts, and bring it back to the realm of reality.

Also included in the process is the custom of going on a *vision quest*. In the traditional vision quest, the individual is sent off into seclusion, without food and only a blanket for warmth, to "catch a spirit." During this time of separation from the world of reality, the person acquires his or her guardian spirit and a portion of his or her medicine power.

Medicine Power

The term *medicine* refers to an individual's own unique talent or skill and the ability to blend these skills or talents with the forces of nature. When it is combined with the knowledge and wisdom gained from an inner world journey or vision quest, it becomes the *medicine power* used to heal and help others.

Places, personal objects, fetishes, and animals are also considered to have medicine power. When the Shaman goes into a trance, it is for this special power of the place, object, or spirit that he or she searches. Once the answer to the question, problem, or situation has been acquired, the Shaman returns to the world of reality, bringing the healing answer with him.

Cleansing and Smudging

Prior to every ceremony or healing, the individuals participating are cleansed of bad feelings and negative vibrations that may be attached to them. This cleansing is accomplished by passing smoke from the burning of certain herbs over the body. The most commonly used herbs are sage (to drive out unwanted spirits), cedar (to carry prayers to the creator), and sweetgrass (to bring in good spirits and influences).

Another form of purification (considered to be the best) is that of the sweat lodge. During the rite of the sweat lodge, all the powers of the universe—earth, water, fire, air, breath, and sky—are called upon. The lodge is built from red willows covered with hides. In the center of the lodge is a pit into which heated rocks, called the *Stone People*, are placed. As each stone is placed in the pit, it is named and receives a force or power of nature. During the sweat lodge, the sacred pipe along with smudge and prayers are used to cleanse and purify those taking part in the ceremony.

Commentary: Every religion or spiritual path should include some sort of cleansing procedure to release negative energies from the physical and mental body. Before coming to any ritual at Our Lady of Enchantment, all members ritually bathe to clean and refresh themselves. Fasting for at least four to six hours prior to a ritual helps eliminate lethargy caused by the digestive system. Meditation and breathing exercises also help prepare the body for assimilating divine energy.

Drumming and Dancing

The drum is one of the Shaman's most used possessions as it is literally the vehicle that carries him or her to the other world. Often, the drum is associated with a horse or other animal whose skin is used in its manufacture. There is also the association between horse and drum because the drum is used as a mode of transport from one reality to another. The monotonous rhythm of the drum allows the Shaman to "ride" into the upper and lower worlds.

Dancing in combination with drumming aids in entering an ecstatic state of consciousness. Once the individual has entered another state of reality, he or she is able to acquire new knowledge. For the Shaman, there are many ways of dancing. One method is referred to as "dancing your totem animal," which brings one closer and more in tune with an animal. In ceremonial medicine wheel dances, members strengthen their individual contact with the earth and nature. Dancing is almost always used in rituals that celebrate and mark changes in seasons and personal lives.

The Sacred Pipe

The sacred prayer pipe is the "tool of tools," the most powerful and cherished gift of all the Native American tribes. The prayers and desires of humans are carried to the Great Spirit and Sky Father on the smoke of the pipe. The pipe is used in all Native American ceremonies and is considered to be the "axis mundi"[1] that forms the bridge between earth and sky. The pipe acts as a traveling altar, which becomes the center of focus for all rituals or ceremonies.

The pipe's bowl represents the feminine, goddess, and Earth Mother aspect of the Great Spirit. The pipe's stem is seen to be the masculine, god, and Sky Father part of the Great Spirit. When these two elements are united for the purpose of sharing breath, they create peace, harmony, and unity among those participating in the ceremony.

The Medicine Wheel

The medicine wheel is a symbol of the universe and represents completion. It is a place where men and women learn to sing the song of the world, become whole again, and unite with the Earth Mother and Sky Father. When properly constructed, the medicine wheel becomes a powerful tool for transition, self-realization, and communication with the spirits of nature.

The wheel is constructed by clearing an area large enough to accommodate the people using in it. A stone or stake driven into the ground to symbolize the Great Spirit marks the center of the wheel. Stakes or rocks painted in corresponding elemental colors mark the four cardinal points. Other rocks, sticks, sacred objects, flowers, and feathers may be used to mark certain areas. Simple or elaborate, the medicine wheel serves as a place for meditation, a symbol of the universe, or a circle of protection for sacred ceremonies.

The Guardian and Totem Spirit

The Shaman believes that everyone is born with a guardian spirit. This belief is common among many peoples, especially those practicing nature-oriented religions. During initiations, vision quests, and trance, the individual is able to communicate with his or her guardian spirit. Some societies believe that this guardian spirit is related to the spirit of the individual, a sort of eternal cosmic twin energy.

The totem spirit can be a badge or emblem of a tribe or clan, representing their principal purpose or focus. The totem can also serve as a sacred personal talisman, chosen for its special relationship and symbolism pertinent to the individual's personality. In either case, it usually provides protection, gives counsel during times of trouble, and, when properly appeased, brings prosperity.

Traditional Symbols

Sun, Moon, Medicine Wheel, Great Spirit, Sacred Pipe, Rainbow, Four Directions, Life Tree

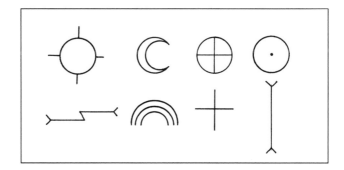

Synopsis

Shamanism is a outgrowth of humanity's desire to work and live in harmony with nature. Everything the Shaman does revolves around a special awareness of and connection to the earth and all the living spirits that inhabit it. The respect and appreciation with which all creatures, both great and small, are treated speaks of the Shaman's sincerity.

The beauty of Shamanism is that anyone, anywhere, can practice it. All you need is imagination, quiet time, and a desire to reconnect with the living forces of nature. There are no complicated rituals that require years of training—only the truth and beauty that comes from honest prayer and worship. Because of the simplicity of Shamanism and its reunion of humans with nature, it has become a popular alternative for many New Age enthusiasts. When the majority of one's time is spent engulfed in a crowded city—surrounded by all manner of high-tech equipment—Shamanism and its alignment with nature is a breath of fresh air.

Today's Shamanism is a personal path of rediscovery and alignment with the earth. You can find your medicine power through personal symbols, meditation, and simple prayers to the gods and spirits of nature. The only problem with Shamanism is the nonrestrictive value it places on human behavior. By this I mean trust in personal integrity. There are those who claim to be pipe carriers or initiated Shaman healers who are not. This abuse can lead to a corruption of the system, which in turn affects those who sincerely practice it. If you choose Shamanism as your path, and wish to teach and help others, find a reputable teacher who can properly train and initiate you.

I feel the one major contribution from Shamanism, especially where Co-Creation is concerned, is in the idea of personal involvement and experience. It is important to get actively involved with your religion, if you expect to receive any benefit from it. Sitting in a pew or standing at the rim of a circle once a month is all well and good, but the only ones benefiting from the performance are the acting priests. For sensory stroking, this type of religious encounter is fine, but for the awakening of the spark within it leaves much to be desired.

ENDNOTES

1. Axis mundi is the cosmic axis, the central point of time and space; the supreme support of all things; that which connects heaven and earth. It is sometimes seen as a rod, staff, tree, pillar, spindle, or umbilical cord.

PART II

The Cauldron of Light

The Birthplace of Divinity

CHAPTER 7

Discovering Divinity

Divinity is in its omniscience and omnipotence like a wheel, a circle, a whole, that can neither be understood, nor divided, nor begun, nor ended.

Illustrations of Hildegard of Bingen

History and the Divine

The existence of God has been heavily debated for millenia. When it comes to this issue, humans are the same today as they were thousands of years ago. Although our lifestyles may have changed, our curiosity about the creative forces of the universe has not changed. We still poke our noses into every conceivable hypothesis available, as we desperately search for information that will shed light on the nature of divinity.

Throughout history, the wonders of the universe have been a constant inspiration to the indomitable questing soul of humanity. And while men and women studied and observed the world around them, time and nature moved on. Were our lives not so short, we might be able to determine the reasons for this constant need to know the answers to the questions *Why are we here? Who put us here? What should we be doing?* But our time is limited and so we feel compelled to find answers about our origins, purpose, and destiny. Amazingly, these questions always seem to culminate with thoughts of deity.

In all probability, our ancestors had a better chance than we do of answering these questions and understanding the world. They were not constantly bombarded by media propaganda, distracted by television, or caught up in this high-tech world. Because they led simpler lives, they were closer to the awesome powers of creation. Granted, some of their familiarity with the world around them was necessary for their survival. Even so, they still had an aptitude for blending with, and becoming part of, nature that we just do not have today.

Looking back, we find it was humanity's relationship with the environment that led early humans to discover the real essence of their divine potential. Through observation and instinct, early humans realized there was more to nature than what they could see and feel. Something greater than themselves had control of the world, and they needed to develop a relationship with that greater power if they were going to survive.

Just when humans began to designate and separate the forces of nature is not known. But they did step back, identify, and classify all they could see, hear, feel, and touch. Along with the identification of the physical, the unseen forces and powers of creation were included as well. Eventually, through the projection of a greater awareness, these forces manifested into a multitude of intangible, invincible beings and sympathetic spirits.

From the beginning, our ancestors sensed the wonder in a storm, recognized the power of a raging flood, and marveled at the miracle of birth. It did not take a genius to distinguish between the times of abundance and plenty and the times of scarcity and destitution. Somewhere along the line, humanity figured out there had to be something that would compensate for both their successes and misfortunes. Whatever that something was, it was all-encompassing and responsible for life's obstacles and pleasures.

Through a combination of anxiety and awe, the worship of deity came into being. Out of instinctive emotion, humans created living repositories for the designated forces of nature. These reservoirs of dynamic energy were classified according to their power, function, and use. They were the living potentials of nature; though they were independent from humanity, they were dependent upon humans for their survival. Humans believed that if they ignored these forces, destruction would result. However, when humans showed deference and made offerings, peace prevailed.

From the start, these energies were considered to be higher octaves of humans. They were endowed with individual characteristics and assigned personal qualities, symbols, and areas of emphasis. They were the gods of nature; everything possessed, in some form, a portion of their energy potential. The larger and more impressive the object, the more powerful the god or spirit who occupied it. This principle was applied to the unrestrained forces of nature as well.

The most powerful of these gods inhabited the sky, shone forth as the sun, and ruled the mountain tops. When heated by passion, they brought the thunder, lightning, and fire from the heavens. The great goddesses were in charge of the earth, the night sky, and the nourishing river waters. When provoked, they manifested as the tempest storms and raging winds; they brought barrenness to the land and all that lived on it. Our ancestors were uncomplicated. When the gods were happy, all was well. When they were not, all hell broke loose. In most cases, whether the result was feast or famine, the actions of the gods were thought to be in direct relation to human activity.

As humanity evolved, developed, and matured, the gods did likewise. They moved with their people and left the natural habitats of their origin. From sacred groves to sanctuaries, from mounds to monuments, the gods progressed as their worshippers demanded. From simple cave paintings and primitive clay sculptures came noble statues and majestic temples proclaiming the glory of the gods.

Creating a Relationship with Divinity

One of the essential elements of all religions is the interpretation of deity, which must be both specific and conceivable in its intrinsic and functional nature. For a complete understanding to be attained, an explicit analysis of the appearance, temperament, position, and archetypal expression exhibited by deity is required. In other words, one needs to have a reasonable explanation of the deities and know what they represent and how they function before they can have a relationship with them. It is impossible to become comfortable with an unknown entity, let alone an abstract concept. Identification of the god form is necessary before developing a relationship with it or beginning worship..

This introduction to deity is not a difficult process and should remain simple. All that is needed is an acceptance of an originating concept in and of itself, and the energies that radiate from it. Monotheism, polytheism, and pantheism are three methods of identifying a deity.

Monotheism recognizes an ultimate cause of all creation. This omnipotent, omnipresent, and omniscient source is referred to as the *All* and is the infinite causation of the universe.

Polytheism states that many gods and goddesses exist, each with separate and distinct functions and various aspects of nature to supervise.

Pantheism is the doctrine that God is All; the sum total of everything that exists. God is part of creation but not separate and distinct from it.

These three definitions are correct and usable for people creating their own system. But which one do you choose if you happen to relate to more than one explanation of theism?[1] Co-Creation spirituality uses the term *omnitheism*,[2] which considers all forms of theism to be equally valid.

Omnitheism's definition eradicates the right-wrong duality that is so prevalent in world religions and allows for everyone to be right. From the standpoint of Co-Creation spirituality, omnitheism proclaims a belief in a single source, the All, which exudes energy in order to form a divine dualism, the total feminine or Goddess concept and the total masculine or God concept. These two dynamics create a secondary[3] pantheon of deities that help humanity develop, progress, and spiritually advance through the various stages of personal experience and initiation.

Who are these magnanimous beings we call gods and goddesses? How do we get to know them? In reality, these beings are the energy forces that emanate throughout the universe. These beings have been restrained and are compelled to make known their potential through the manifestation of spiritual revelation. In the ancient world, these beings were considered to be etheric world intelligences that could communicate with humans. In today's world, those people who are devoted to this idea relate to the gods in much the same way. The gods are seen as higher forms of natural intelligence with the potential for providing guidance, protection, and hope for the future.

The God

Like all deities, the God has many faces. He appears as the radiant, brilliant, and illuminating Sun of Righteousness; the divine victim who spills his blood for the love of the land; the warrior king whose fight for truth and justice is revealed in the battle between good and evil. To the followers of Neo-Pagan religions, the God is the symbol of virility, the fertilizing and regenerating energy force of nature. He is the personification of all that is masculine, potent, and powerful.

The God's most obvious and dominant characteristic is his ability to regenerate. Although his countenance may change with time and culture, he continually returns to live and die for the land he loves. We have known him as Osiris, Tammuz, and Adonis. We have seen him manifest as the Unconquered Sun or compassionate savior Mithra, Helios, and Christ. Whatever his incarnation, he is always the potentate of power, strength, and authority—and the final judge before the gate of the Goddess.

The Goddess

After centuries of exile, the Goddess has made her way back to her land, people, and position as the personification of feminine dominion and perception. She is the Earth Mother and Mistress of Magic; she is all that is beauty and bounty. What the God inaugurates, the Goddess materializes. The God impregnates her with the seed of desire and she gives birth to reality. The Goddess is the creative process through which all physical levels are made manifest.

From the spiritual aspect, the Goddess is the intuitive and instinctive side of nature. Her inconceivable powers of transition and transformation radiate like the translucent beams of celestial light, for she is the mystery and magic. Beneath her full moon she is invoked as Arianrhod, Diana, and Hecate by those seeking her favors. Everything psychic and mysterious belongs to her alone.

Together, the God and Goddess permeate all levels of existence. Their presence promulgates life in its purest state. Once an intimate relationship has been developed with them, it is impossible to imagine living without their divine inspiration. For the most part, they become the principal considerations in daily life and primary factors in all religious ritual and worship. Whether individually or collectively approached, they are the fundamental reasons behind all spiritual enlightenment.

Synopsis

"All gods are one god, and all goddesses are one goddess." This is a popular euphemism that is both erroneous and misleading. While all deities share the same nature in that they are omniscient, omnipotent, and divine, the similarity ends there.

Deities, like human beings, are channels of consciousness that receive outside information or input and then transmit to an original source. Each channel or strain of consciousness—be it human or god—is unique, and so is its feedback. The ultimate logic of the universe testifies to its intention by having created millions of separate life-forms. There would be no reason for this multitude of energy forces if all life-forms were transmitting the same message. We must realize that it is the incredible amount of diverse information—processed and fed back to the Ultimate Force—that maintains the momentum of universal existence.

Simply put, early humans learned how to relate to the energy patterns of the universe; they learned to recognize their differences and identify with them. One does not mistake a raindrop for an earthquake, and so one should not confuse a goddess of fertility with one of war. It is understood that each goddess is feminine and therefore capable of feminine actions, just as all gods are masculine and capable of masculine actions. However, gender capacities do not suppress or diminish individual ability. It is therefore best to learn what type of energy a deity will manifest before one proceeds to invoke their wrath, rather than their blessing.

ENDNOTES

1. Theism is the belief in the existence of gods and goddesses.

2. *Omni* is the Latin prefix meaning all. Omnitheism is the belief in all theism, or gods and goddesses, including the original causation.

3. Secondary refers to the thousands of deities that confirm natural energies, emotions, and concepts important to the structure of the universe.

Preface to Deity
Chapters 8 through 12

Images of gods and goddesses grace our museums, great cathedrals, and personal altars. Tales of fearless encounters, passionate love affairs, and enchanting rites of magic are passed from generation to generation. Through myths and legends, their power, folly, and wisdom quietly enrich our lives and the lives of our children. Paying tribute to each god and goddess we revere would take great amounts of time and volumes of printed material. Even though my space is small, it is still possible to present an extensive list of deities by limiting the selection.

As the enthusiastic student of mythology is well aware, innumerable texts listing god after god exist. These texts pay little if any attention to detail, other than giving the deity's name and his or her placement within a pantheon. Helpful as this may be with identification, it does little to inspire or encourage the connection to deity within the life of the seeker.

Personally, I feel it is better to have comprehensive information about a few deities rather than a multitude of names with only basic facts. For this reason, chapters 8 through 12 focus on the principal deities from the most popular pantheons. By limiting the selection, you will find a more extensive arrangement of details concerning the qualities and correspondences related to each god and goddess.

The deities were chosen with respect to their authority, classical image, geographical location, and function within the pantheon. As much information as possible has been given for each deity. Though the information is by no means complete, it will help you get started.

Remember that the gods and goddesses are representations of natural energies that have been culturally humanized. The deities authorized, if not encouraged, this classification in order to make their dominion felt by those seeking their knowledge and wisdom. Acceptance of their virtue is primary to understanding their sovereignty and their ultimate relationship with humanity.

Personification of deity is the heart and essence of all religions. Whether you worship at a local church or create your own system, the delegation of deity should be your primary consideration. Through personal experience and use of these forces, the ultimate realization of divinity manifests. The only way to get to know the God and Goddess is to actually learn about them, and then, through prayer and supplication, approach them with an open mind and heart.

CHAPTER 8

Africa: Home of the Orisha

Aye! There's places in Africa where you get visions of primeval force....In Africa the past has hardly stopped beating.

Trader Horn

The Land of Great Mystery

Africa is the mysterious land of vast jungles and dark secrets. It is a place where witch doctors summon spirits of the dead and the steady drumming of the Bata[1] fills the air. It is a land abounding with superstition, strange magic, and exotic gods—a land where ancient customs and rites still live on.

To some, Africa is the birthplace of humanity and the location of the Garden of Eden. Whether this is true or not, Africa remains the home of some of the oldest deities known to humans. These charismatic gods and goddesses have controlled the elements of African culture and life for thousands of years. To the people of the jungle, these gods are the original intention, power, and purpose behind reality.

The Orisha are viewed as being very much alive and anthropomorphic in their appearance, attitudes, and desires. Because they are so human-like, African religious practices are festive occasions, with music and much food and drink—because humans like and enjoy these things, the gods must delight in them as well. For the most part, Africans see their Orisha as friends and allies rather than as remote or indifferent gods who take no interest in human affairs.

These wonderful beings are believed to reside in certain objects and places. By coming in contact with them in their homes, a measure of their *ashe* can be absorbed. By procuring the Orisha's *ashe,* humans gain the power to protect themselves and their families as well as manifest their desires. To receive a portion of *ashe,* favorite foods and drink are given to refresh and cool[2] the Orisha. This concept of exchange—giving in return for receiving—helps maintain the balance between humanity and the gods.

Africans keep a close working relationship with the Orisha. One of the primary reasons for this closeness is that the Yoruba believe that as a person grows, the world hardens him or her and tends to throw the person off balance. The individual must contact his or her guardian Orisha and learn what to do to get back into alignment with his or her fate. Once the person finds out what is required to live correctly, he or she will offer *ebbo* (sacrifice) as a means of thanksgiving. Because of this giving and receiving custom, a constant flow of energy exists between the individual and his or her Orisha. As a result, great friendships develop between the Africans and their gods.

The Orisha described below are considered to be the most powerful and popular of the pantheon. Because of their widespread acceptance, practitioners of both Ifa and Santería usually contact and work with these Orisha during ritual. Because of their popularity and the growing interest in African traditions, Orisha's statues and sacred objects are easily obtainable.

The Orisha, Gods of Africa

Yemoja (Mother of the World, Origin of Life)

Yemoja is the ultimate symbol and personification of motherhood. She represents the place of origin and the maternal source of divine, human, animal, and plant life. She is considered the top level of the ocean where plant life grows, which is the largest environment for life on earth.

Yemoja embodies the principle of everlastingness; she gives humans the ability to exist. Yemoja is the matriarch who presides over the bloodstreams of the world. All rivers by their natural motion dump their cargoes at Yemoja's door. She is in a state of constant motion; never at peace, never resting. Even when she is calm on the surface, things are brewing below. Yemoja is the ultimate manifestation of female power and therefore the greatest Witch of all.

In myth, Yemoja had a son named Orungan. He became so inflamed by his sexual passions that he pursued his own mother. His approaches repelled Yemoja and she made every attempt to avoid him. She became so tired of fleeing his presence that she fell to the floor. When she fell, Yemoja's chest and stomach opened up and vast amounts of water flowed from her, creating a lagoon. From this lagoon the Orisha were born.

Yemoja's connection with water is shown in her association with docks, boats, and all other maritime activities. Her altar is round and usually placed on a mound covered in blue material. During her festivals, people dance around her in a circle to emphasize the idea of roundness and the cycle of life with which she is associated.

Correspondences

Archetype	Divine Mother
Expression	Mistress of magic
Element	Water
Nature	Emotional, nurturing
Association	Our Lady of Regla
Symbols	Fish, ocean, river, docks, boats, ship's wheel and anchor, mermaid, ducks, birds, seagulls, the peacock feather, shells, rattle, fan
Colors	Blue, white, crystal-clear
Number	7
Plants/Foods	Sheep, goat, turtle, rooster, duck, pork, bacon, watermelon, green grapes, plantain, coconut candy, popcorn, cane syrup, white yam, lettuce, black-eyed peas, lettuce, spearmint, purslane, watercress, river fern
Places	Ocean, shore, river
Misc.	Feast day: September 7

Oshun (Love, Beauty, Civilization)

Oshun is the Goddess of love and beauty. She is considered to be the enchantress, expressing the quality of beauty that comes from within. She is refinement, taste, and delicacy. Oshun represents all human sentiments and deep feelings. She is the virgin because of her purity of spirit, but she is also the temptress of deep and unexplained feelings.

Oshun is the river and sweet water that sustains life and makes everything worthwhile. She is the energy force that focuses on the present as well as on life's comfortable sensual pleasures. Oshun is the desire that raises human passions. Through her sexuality she is able to fulfill her goal of conceiving and bearing children, whom she leaves in the competent care of Yemoja.

From myth we learn that Oshun met the great god Chango at a Bembe[3] and fell madly in love with him. Chango, however, was busy eating and dancing and did not notice her. Oshun dipped her finger in the honey pot she carried at her side and spread the sticky liquid on Chango's lips. Chango reacted to the sweet honey and began to dance with Oshun. It wasn't long before Chango and Oshun became lovers.

As a result of his admiration and love for Oshun, Chango allowed her to wear his red beads in her yellow necklace.

Oshun is also important when it comes to money and possessions, as she provides the tenacity to maintain achievement. She is a master of strategy and understands the use of charms and magic, especially when it comes to the manipulation of the sexes. However, she can also be overindulgent in the pleasures of life and sometimes needs to be reminded of her true place and goal in the scheme of things.

Correspondences

Archetype	Creator of Civilization
Expression	Love, beauty
Element	Water
Nature	Loving, soothing, unpredictable
Associations	La Caridad del Cobre, Venus, Erzulie
Symbols	Peacock feather, pumpkin, fan, mirror, comb, gold, cowrie shell, brass bells, needle, anything brass or copper, fish, honey, butterfly, mermaid
Colors	Yellow, amber, red
Number	5
Plants/Foods	Castrated goat, hens, red snapper, egg custard, raw fish, cornmeal mush, white yam, cooked pumpkin, pineapple, yellow rice, honeydew/muskmelon, watercress, pumpkin, aniseed, corchorus, cinnamon
Places	River, shore of river, lakes, streams
Misc.	Feast day: September 8

Obatala (Judgment, Purity, and Wisdom)

Obatala is the "King of the white cloth" and is considered the king of the Orisha because of his great age. In the Yoruba culture, age is a key factor in the ability to wield power, and Obatala holds this position because of his honored maturity. He is the force of nature that represents the morals and obligation to do the right thing.

Obatala is humility, calmness, ethics, clearness of thought, and purity. God selected him to be the leader; he owns all the heads, even those of the other Orisha. Owning these heads gives Obatala prominence because it is believed that the human soul exists in the head, making it the seat of the soul. Because the head holds the soul, everything in Santería is done to the person's head.

Obatala is considered a creator deity because he shapes the fetus within the womb. Folklore states that Obatala got drunk from palm wine while he was sculpting humanity from clay. Due to his intoxication, he misformed some of the human beings, thus creating people who are dwarfs, hunchbacks, disabled, and with limited hearing and sight. It is believed that these people are Obatala's special children.

Obatala lives on top of a mountain where he maintains a clear view of humanity. He is represented by both sexes, because good judgment and reason are not considered to belong to one particular sex. He has a sense of humor and tries to see the element of laughter in all situations. His totem animals are the snail, boa, chameleon, and elephant—due to the enormous strength these creatures possess in comparison to their size. The exception is the elephant, which is not only strong but also wise.

Obatala represents the wisdom attained through age and is the one who appreciates the nuances and calamities of life. Wisdom and experience enable him to see the humor behind human's follies.

Correspondences

Archetype	Father, creator
Expression	Judgment, propriety, moderation
Element	Earth
Nature	Cool headed, amicable, confident
Associations	Our Lady of Mercy, Mercedes
Symbols	White cloth, clay, white shells, sun, gorilla, snail, elephant, boa, chameleon, judge's gavel, cotton, cascarilla, white doves, fly whisk
Color	White
Numbers	8, 16, 24 (any combination of 8)
Plants/Foods	Female goat, doves, milk, pears, white grapes, rice pudding, meringue, custard, breads of all kinds, rice and rice bread, white cornmeal, white yam, farina, sage, black-eyed peas with skin removed, green grapes, tobacco, basil, cotton (Obatala's offerings must never contain salt)
Places	Mountaintops, hills, close to the sky
Misc.	Feast day: September 24

Eleggua (Choice, Options, and Balance)

Eleggua is the Orisha who offers choices. He sits at the threshold of every decision and offers the options that decide the future. He was present at the creation of the world and will be there when it ends. Eleggua represents our ability to choose and bring about new circumstances. He teaches that the present is a reflection of the past and an indication of the future.

Eleggua likes to bring out the fool in humans. He is the provocateur and instigator who tricks humans into making wrong decisions for no other reason than to see how they will rectify the situation. As Eleggua is always right, he looks for right action

Eleggua

and proper conduct in those he chooses as his children.

Legend tells that Olodumare became ill and none of the other Orisha could make him well. The elder deities did not consider the young Eleggua to be someone who could help the situation. However, when Eleggua learned that Olodumare was ill, Eleggua rushed to his side and asked for the chance to heal him. The elder Orishas laughed at Eleggua, but Olodumare silenced them and gave Eleggua a chance. Eleggua reached into his knapsack, which always hung by his side, and pulled out some herbs. He prepared an herbal brew and gave it to Olodumare to drink. As soon as Olodumare drank the liquid, he was healed of his illness.

Olodumare called all of the Orisha together and proclaimed that from that day forward Eleggua would be honored first in their ceremonies. He gave Eleggua the keys to every door. Olodumare also gave him the power of life and death and the ability to solve problems. Because Olodumare knew that Eleggua possessed a great sense of justice, Olodumare also made him the arbitrator of human affairs and the master of fate.

Eleggua is the perfect balance in nature; the Equinox is his symbol because everything is in perfect balance at this time. Eleggua is the guardian of the crossroads and potentiality. He is the communicator between the worlds, between humans and the Orisha. He changes human's language into nature's language and nature's language back into human's language, creating a link between them.

Correspondences

Archetype	Divine balance
Expression	Trickster
Elements	Earth, Air, Fire, Water
Nature	Unpredictable, mischievous
Associations	Anthony of Padua, Saint Martin
Symbols	Comb, whistle, spoon, cross, checkerboard, erect penis, toys, red car, red parrot feather
Colors	Red, black, white
Number	3
Plants/Foods	Coconut, goat, rooster, baby chick, bush rat, smoked herring, dry fish, cigars/tobacco, dry wine, all fruit, cakes, yellow bananas, popcorn, boiled yams, cornmeal, okra, toasted corn, rum, guava, corn, bastard lime, dub grass

| Places | Crossroad, house threshold, marketplace, curve in the road |
| Misc. | Feast days: June 13, August 16; he is also honored at all Santería ceremonies and rituals |

Chango (Instant Illumination and Retribution)

Chango

Chango can be considered to be the wrath of God. He is instant illumination and retribution. He is the lightning that illuminates the night sky—allowing you to see in a flash things that otherwise would remain in the dark. When Chango spits fire at someone, he is showing who he is angry with as well as letting others know they could be next.

Chango is suave and debonair; he is a Casanova who loves to dance. It is said he also possesses the gift of gab. He is quick-witted, able to think on his feet, and can excite the masses with his wit and words. He is and can be everything to everyone; the consummate politician.

Chango was not only a great warrior and dancer, but he was also a skillful diviner and owner of the table of divination. However, Chango's real love was dancing. One day, upon meeting with Orumila, the Orisha's gifted dancer, Chango offered to trade his table and gift of divination for Orumila's ability to dance—Chango knew his proficiency at dancing would greatly increase his popularity with the ladies. Orumila and Chango traded and have lived happily ever after.

Chango is a fireball and lives for adversity. He enjoys being able to get out of tricky situations that he has created, mainly to test himself. He is the idea of surviving against the odds and represents two things: force and wisdom. He is the ultimate adventurer, connoisseur, visionary, and artist. Chango is the "King of Divination," the owner of drums; a revolutionary, herbalist, magician, bum, and dancer.

Correspondences

Archetype	Illumination
Expression	Force and power
Element	Fire
Nature	Vitality, dominant, charismatic, passionate
Association	Saint Barbara
Symbols	Double-headed ax, horse, cats, inverted mortar, Bata drum, gourd rattle, wand, sword, palm or cedar tree, tortoise shell

Colors	Red, white
Numbers	4 or 6
Plants/Foods	Ram, tortoise, turtle, rooster, dry white wine, green bananas, red apples, pomegranate, cornmeal, okra, rice bread, fufu, black-eyed peas, obe ayaba, cinnamon, cedar, teak, camwood, plantain, bonset
Places	Foot of the palm or cedar tree, woods
Misc.	Feast day: December 4 or 6

Cauldron of Ogun

Ogun (Energy, Strength, and Firmness)

Ogun is energy, war, inheritance, medicine, and perspiration. He is the force of nature that keeps matter in motion—and is in constant motion himself. Once God gives a being life, Ogun sustains it. Ogun is one of the oldest gods in the Yoruba pantheon. He is force, locomotion, contraction, expansion, and give and take. He is the magnetic stone.

Ogun is an earth deity who lives inside an iron cauldron, which represents the womb of the earth, the mine, and the primordial abyss. Symbolically, the womb or cauldron is the individual's ability, and Ogun's tools are a gift that will help to bring out or extract their potential and wealth to enhance life.

The main tools of Ogun are the anvil, the ability to transform; shovel, the ability to dig for one's potential; machete, used to clear the path and protect; rake, used to gather and smooth rough areas of the self; hoe, human's ability to cultivate one's potential; hammer, used to bend and shape one's faculties; and pick, used to pierce or penetrate the hardened areas of the self.

Ogun is the force that animates life—he is the only one allowed to take a life. During a blood sacrifice, he is always fed first. Ogun is the owner of the knife, which is the first thing to taste the blood in any sacrifice; only a person who has received the initiation can perform a sacrifice using a knife.

When working with Ogun, it is necessary to understand that he deals with things that are in reach, within the reality of the person. He must be able to keep an eye on what he is doing.

Correspondences

Archetypes	Force and motion
Expression	Strength and will
Element	Fire
Nature	Strong, self-determination, initiative
Association	Saint Peter
Symbols	Cauldron, anvil, shovel, machete, rake, hoe, hammer, pick, magnets, railroad spikes, iron train, knife, dog
Colors	Red, green, black, white
Number	3
Plants/Foods	Pigeon, white rum, red wine, black-eyed peas, roasted hen, same foods as Eleggua
Day	Tuesday
Places	Deep forest, woods, door with Eleggua
Misc.	Feast day: June 29

Osanyin (The Balance of Nature)

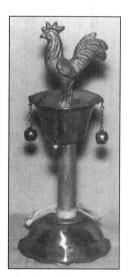

The Osun (Symbol of Osanyin)

Osanyin is the Yoruba god of herbalism who lives in the forest and controls the power contained therein. In this sense, he controls the curative and poisonous herbs and plants that grow in the forest. The leaf is his knife and his wand. He is the chemist of the Orisha; he represents the two sides of herbal power: the side that cures you and the side that kills you.

Osanyin represents the balance of nature. Just as the tree stands on one leg, Osanyin helps humanity retain balance by preventing and curing diseases of the mind and body. He symbolizes the scientist who ventures into the unknown. Nature is his sanctuary, where one escapes the hazards of civilization. Osanyin is also the permanent sentinel of sacred groves where the individual can go for refuge of the mind and cool, logical thinking. Osanyin is the owner of all herbal ingredients and, therefore, protects one against the evils of witchcraft.

Osanyin is considered a weapon of war because of his knowledge of witchcraft, potions, and charms. He is the greatest of witch doctors. He is the king of the trees and is compared to the Araba tree (the tallest tree in Africa). Many believe that his symbol of the staff surmounted by a bird represents his tree. The bird is symbolic of swiftness and has the ability to carry prayers to God.

Correspondences

Archetypes	Nature and movement
Expression	Swift hunter
Element	Air
Nature	Quiet, strong, fast, wise
Association	Saint Joseph
Symbols	Osun (staff surmounted by a cup with bells and a rooster), leaves and all herbs, birds, bow and arrow, all trees, beads
Colors	Green, red
Number	3
Plants/Foods	Guinea hen, venison, fish, almonds, liquor, beans, toasted corn, all fruit, cigars, yams, same foods as Eleggua and Ogun
Places	Forest, trees, outland, inside of house door
Misc.	The Osun is placed in a high place for protection; if it falls over, it is a bad omen and a warning of trouble
	Feast day: December 31

Synopsis

An entire book, if not several, would be needed to fully explain and elucidate the qualities, properties, and functional capabilities of the Orisha, not to mention their contemporary Saint versions. The most I could hope to convey in this short chapter is their essential characteristics and corresponding symbolic purpose.

One needs to realize and understand that the Orisha are *not* the Catholic Saints with whom they are associated. The Orisha are natural forms of energy that have been designated to correspond with human emotions and needs. These energies are brought to reside in Otanes (stones), tools, and symbols that are kept in specially prepared vessels called *soperas*—these, not the Catholic Saints, are the living, physical representations of the Orisha.

The Saints, on the other hand, are not African gods but Christian deities who have evolved from righteous humans into divine beings. They are represented by their statues, colors, symbols, and attributes. Because of the syncretism or spontaneous combination of Orisha with Saint, the Saint has become an intermediary through which the Orisha energy is channeled. It was this syncretism that made it possible for the early Orisha worshipers to commune with their deities under adverse conditions.

Becoming involved with the Orisha is a big responsibility. These are not deities who have been neglected and forgotten for hundreds of years—they are very much alive. The Orisha are raw, primitive power, and should be treated with respect. As repositories of great energy, they are more than willing to lend a helping had to humanity, but they do expect *ebbo* (sacrifice and offering) in return for their efforts.

Probably the most attractive concept of Orisha worship is the physical response the deity transmits to the devotee. When something is demanded of the Orisha, they respond and, more often than not, manifest a physical phenomenon as proof of their presence. I have seen them dehydrate fruit, wither perfectly healthy plants, and create temperature changes in short periods of time. When they are happy, everyone is happy; when they are not, it is better to hide.

If you are interested in Santería, Ifa, and the Orisha, take the time to find a reputable teacher, as this is not a religion that can be gleaned from books. You can gain a background from reading, but to understand and work with it, initiation is necessary. This secrecy is a safeguard to protect both the seeker and the Orisha's power from abuse.

It is possible, however, to set up altars to the Saints and through them get to know the Orisha. You can do this safely through personal study and organized observation of results. In time, if it is meant to be, the Orisha will provide the devotee with the proper teacher and guide.

ENDNOTES

1. The Bata is a double-headed drum sacred to the Orisha—especially to the god Chango—and often played in their honor.

2. *Cool* is a term meaning to make calm, to have a gentleness of character; it is the correct way for humans to behave.

3. Bembe (Bem-BAY) is a drum and dance festival celebrated for and in honor of the Orisha.

CHAPTER 9

Asia: The Land of Many Gods

If the radiance of a thousand suns were to burst into the sky, that would perhaps be like the splendor of the Mighty One.

Amaury de Riencourt, *The Eye of Shiva*

Hindu and Buddhist Worship

Aromatic incense, the resonating sound of a gong, and the melodic chanting of saffron-robed monks fill the air, creating an atmosphere of meditative tranquillity.

Asia, like Africa, still harbors pre-Christian religious philosophies, most of which are steeped in thousand-year-old myths and traditions. These captivating beliefs are based on mythical deities, local folklore, and inspired scripture. Although Buddhists and Hindus remain separate in some regions, an interweaving of doctrine has occurred in other regions, leading to a merging of deities and practices.

The teachings and beliefs that originated in the East are different from those of Western cultures. For one, the Eastern perspective does not fit the conservative, analytical boundaries of Western thought. The Western Judaic, Christian, and Islamic patterns focus on one (male) god whose laws must be obeyed unquestionably. In the Eastern point of view, universal truths and personal enlightenment are presented without judgment; salvation is considered to be an individual responsibility.

Many different traditions, representing a variety of spiritual disciplines and beliefs, comprise the culture and teachings of the Indian subcontinent. The beliefs are an established set of eternal truths gleaned by the Rishis, or great seers. The Rishis incorporated their knowledge into massive religious texts, one of which was the

Vedas. These volumes of spiritual knowledge contain a cosmology of polytheistic and pantheistic mythologies in poetic form, which describe humans' various relationships with God.

The most obvious aspect of the Asian deities is that they all express their nature. They are perfect examples of the transmutation of elemental energy into physical form. Each deity represents an aspect of life or nature that is fundamental to humans' pleasure or survival. Because the gods and goddesses of this area are so lifelike, they have captured and held the hearts of people for thousands of years. Even though their culture is far removed from ours, the power and passion of these divine beings still project the magic and mystery of forgotten times.

The Gods of Asia

Ganesha

Ganesh, Ganesha (Lord of the Ganas, Dwarf-demon)

Ganesh, one of the most popular Indian gods, has the head of an elephant and the body of a potbellied man. As a god of good enterprise, his statues can be found everywhere—from the sacred temple to the common marketplace. He is practical wisdom, the remover of obstacles; he represents the union of humans with the universe.

Ganesh is the son of Parvati and Shiva and guards the gate of his mother's house. He is usually pictured with four arms and riding on a rat or mouse. In his hands he carries an elephant goad, a rosary, and an alms bowl.

This extraordinary-looking deity is also the god of the sciences and skills. He was the first scribe; in this aspect, he is likened to the Egyptian god Thoth. Ganesh is called upon when traveling and opening a business, before writing a book, and during wedding negations. Being part elephant and part man, he has a ravenous appetite and is pleased when offered abundant offerings.

Legend tells that Parvati created Ganesh. She wanted a guardian to prevent Shiva from spying on her while she was bathing. She took her bath oil and other secret substances and formed the body of a man with a fat belly. Then she sprinkled him with her bath water (Ganges water) and he came to life. When Shiva arrived, Ganesh would not let him near Parvati. In his wrath, Shiva cut off Ganesh's head. Fearing Parvati's displeasure, Shiva replaced the head of the man with that of an elephant.

In another myth, the gods thought that it was too easy for humans to enter heaven. They went to Parvati for help because the heavens were becoming over-crowded with meritorious people. Parvati rubbed her body with a special oil and in time gave birth to a fat man with four arms and the head of an elephant. She pronounced that this monster would present an obstacle to people's enterprises unless he was properly propitiated.

Ganesh is a popular deity. He is calm, generous, and loves humanity. His good sense of judgment and friendliness are only part of the reason for his popularity. Ganesh has been known to bestow riches and success on those he favors. Nothing should begin—whether it is worship or enterprise—until Ganesh has been honored.

Correspondences

Archetype	God of Knowledge
Expression	Benefactor of humanity
Elements	Water, earth
Nature	Kind, calm, generous, protective, philosophical
Associations	Thoth, Hermes
Symbols	Alms bowl, rat, snake, elephant goad, rosary, pen, elephant, books, ivory, tusks
Colors	Yellow, brown
Number	4
Plants/Foods	Apples, carrots, straw, all fruits and vegetables, sweet pudding, rice and coconut balls, candy, flour, sugar
Places	River, riverbank, jungle
Misc.	The feast of Ganesh is celebrated toward the end of August; at the end of the ten-day celebration, people create statues of the god from clay and throw them into the river for blessings

Kali Ma (Black or Dark Mother)

Kali is the Hindu triple goddess and venerated life force. She is the mother or vir-gin, great goddess, and ultimate reality. She has been identified as Parvati in her cre-ative countenance and as Uma in her destructive aspect. Kali is the ideal image of birth and death, as she both gives life (as the womb) and reclaims it (as the tomb).

Kali's image is usually represented in black, wearing a garland of fifty human heads, symbolizing her knowledge and wisdom. Her girdle of human hands signifies the action of karma and accumulated deeds. Her three eyes indicate the past, pre-sent, and future; her disheveled hair forms the curtain of illusion. Kali has four arms and holds in one left hand a severed head, symbolizing freedom from the ego. In one of her right hands, she carries a sword that frees humanity from bondage. Her emp-ty right hand gestures to dispel fear; her empty left hand proposes spiritual strength.

Kali Ma

Kali is the active power and the creative force, reminding us that to be born means to accept death. She calls people's attention to the process of liberation; she emphasizes that the concept of remaining in a confined space only creates stagnation. Kali is all that is benign and all that is terrible; she is against all evil in the eternal struggle of the cosmos. After all has come and passed, Kali alone remains—she was the inspiration behind the genius who created her, allowing for the birth of the gods.

In myth, Kali can be seen dancing on the dead body of her husband, Shiva, swinging his severed head in one hand and a sword in the other. During this seemingly terrible occurrence, Kali is also having intercourse with the body (reminding us of Isis copulating with the dead Osiris). As the goddess of death, Kali must destroy everything, including her husband, since no visible or physical thing is eternal.

Correspondences

Archetype	Destroyer
Expression	Ultimate feminine force
Elements	Water, fire
Nature	Creative, consuming, powerful, transcending
Associations	Parvati, Uma, Sekhmet
Symbols	Skull, sword, yoni, snake, lotus, bells, gold armlets, cowrie shell, trident, Ur-text, pot, triangle, Kali Yantra
Colors	Red, black, white
Number	9
Plants/Foods	Lily, lotus, cypress, crab, rose, beet, blood root, cucumber, yogurt
Places	River, cave, mountain, cemetery
Misc.	During the festival of Durga, special hymns to Kali are sung; many believe that Kali favors Wednesdays

Shiva (Benevolent, Moon God of the Mountains)

Often, Shiva is called the lord of the dance or the dancing god; he is the supreme example of cosmic rhythm and the cycle of birth, death, and rebirth. It is said that he has the moon in his hair through which flows the River Ganges.

In the beginning, the gods agreed to the descent of Ganga, the heavenly river, whose sheer mass of water would have engulfed the earth. Shiva offered to lessen the shock of the river by allowing her to flow through his tangled hair. Ganga wandered about his head for several years. Finally, Shiva divided the river into seven streams and she descended without causing harm.

As the lord of the mountains, Shiva sits facing the south, toward India. He is the master of the mountain; the one with whom the sages meditate, learning his exalted wisdom. Shiva sits on a tigerskin rug to demonstrate his control over greed and aggression; his snow-white hair signifies his asceticism. His faithful companion, Nandi, a white bull, and his son Ganesha accompany him.

In myth, Parvati, one of Shiva's consorts, playfully held her hands over his eyes, which were always open. At once darkness spread

Shiva

over the entire universe; there were no sun, stars, or moon—all was dark. Shiva created a third eye in the center of his forehead so that light would return to the world, and with the light came order and justice.

Besides being a god of the rivers, Shiva is also lord of the forest, indicating his ability as both fisherman and hunter. He holds a trident, expressing his capacity as a fisherman, and a bow, depicting his hunting abilities. In ancient times when humans wandered the forest in search of game, the hunters prayed to the god of the hunt, in this case Shiva, to send the animals their way. Hunters and fishermen often made offerings to Shiva before entering his forest so as not to offend him. Today, in some remote areas, bundles of fruit and vegetables are left as offerings in hopes of obtaining Shiva's favor.

Correspondences

Archetype	God of Light
Expression	Master of magic
Elements	Fire, water
Nature	Creative, wise, justice, order, truth, wisdom
Association	Vishnu
Symbols	Trident, serpent, elephant, bow, moon, javelin, noose, deer, lion, spear
Color	White
Number	3
Plants/Foods	Rice, milk, dosa (Indian pancakes), yogurt, almond milk and pudding, pine, lily
Places	Mountain, river, forest
Misc.	Shiva's annual festival is Mahashivatri (The Great Night of Shiva), celebrated on February 19

Kuan Yin

Kuan Yin (She Who Harkens to the Cries of the World)

Kuan Yin is a celestial Bodhisattva[1] whose origin is speculative at best. In some areas, she is the feminine aspect of Avalokita, a direct manifestation of Amitabha Buddha. Others feel that she is the unification of Tara and Mio Shan, brought together by Avalokita, in order to create the concept of compassion. How or why Kuan Yin came into being is of little consequence as she is probably one of the most venerated of all the Eastern goddesses. For thousands of years, all kinds of people have worshiped her. Today, her image can be found in almost every traditional Eastern temple and household.

As the goddess of fecundity and healing, Kuan Yin hears the cries of the world. She has sacrificed her Buddhahood for the sake of all who suffer and remains in the world to help others achieve salvation. She has been described as a teacher of magic, an oracular goddess, and a protector of those who travel the seas.

One of Kuan Yin's most dramatic qualities is her ability to rescue those who call upon her. She has saved sailors, fisherman, and those caught in storms at sea. She is also a divine savior, guiding people to the Pure Land and helping them make the transition from life to death.

In myth, Kuan Yin descends into the land of the dead in order to alleviate the torments of those residing there. Her radiant and virtuous presence puts out the fires of torment and changes the instruments of torture into beautiful flowers. When she recites the Buddhist scriptures, the land of the dead becomes a paradise; everyone there exists in unbounded happiness.

Depictions of Kuan Yin can be found everywhere in China and Japan. Generally, she is idealized in human female form, wearing a long robe and hoodlike head dress. The ornaments that adorn her head, throat, wrists, and ankles symbolize her status as Bodhisattva.

Kuan Yin appears in two distinct positions. The first is standing on a giant lotus petal with one hand raised and the other pointing down in benediction. In this particular pose, she usually holds a dew pot (vase) in her pointing hand and a willow spray in the other. These emblems symbolize her compassion and wisdom. When seated, her right leg usually rests on her left thigh with the left leg extended. In this depiction, Shan Ts'ai, a young child, and Lung Nu, the dragon maiden holding a pearl, attend her.

Archetype	Divine Savior
Expression	Supreme love
Element	Water
Nature	Compassion, kindness, understanding
Associations	Tara, Mio Shan, Virgin Mary
Symbols	Lotus, dew pot or vase, rope, jeweled bowl, sword, vajra-dagger, bird, rabbit, bow and arrow, jade bracelet, mirror, rosary, conch shell, bell, golden wheel
Colors	White, blue, violet
Number	3
Plants/Foods	Lotus, willow, lily, rice, milk, honey, eggs, fish, fowl, grapes, jasmine, cherry, white rose, lilac, orchid, peach, pear, violet, yarrow
Places	Ocean, river, lake, docks, seashore
Misc.	Feast day: July 19 (the rites may last several days)

Synopsis

It is amazing how we incorporate, in most cases unconsciously, the forces and powers of deities into our lives. I was in an antique shop in an arty-tourist area of New England. Sitting on a shelf behind the counter—and looking very regal—was a statue of Ganesh. He was about two feet tall, made of brass, and wore a devilish grin. Being a greedy statue collector, I asked the Irish-looking gentleman behind the counter how much he wanted for the Ganesh. Well, you would have thought I had asked for a piece of the Great Isle Herself. In no uncertain terms, the man said that the statue was not for sale—it was his Ganesh and the protector of the store's profit. Since then, I have noticed many Ganesh and other deity statues gracing the marketplaces of this country.

Ganesh is not the only one I see watching from behind the counter, positioned over the cash register, or peeking around the corner. All manner of shops, businesses, and New Age stores possess favorite deities who protect and provide for them. Near my home, Kuan Yin graces the window of the health food store and Hoti proudly occupies center stage of the display window at a local New Age bookstore. At the Asian restaurant downtown is an altar to Shiva, bedecked with flowers and floating candles.

For the most part, I doubt that these people are religiously inclined but they still use the god's or goddess' power to benefit their life. Subconsciously, the energy of these deities attracts people.

Centuries ago, these Eastern gods and goddesses began crossing the oceans to grace us with their presence for mutual favor and support. They are helping us to understand that the mystery and magic of myth still lives and can enhance our lives if we only give it a chance.

Even if you are not of an Eastern mind, it is still possible to have a rapport with these gods and goddesses. A four-foot-high statue of Kuan Yin adorns the entrance to the chapel of Our Lady of Enchantment. In an alcove inside, a life-sized Buddha, from a temple in Taiwan, watches as we conduct ritual. Though the Buddha is not the center of focus, he lends much to the atmosphere and energy levels of our ceremonies. Hoti and Ganesh both keep an eye on our gift shop; Shiva and other deities greet visitors as they tour our metaphysical center.

The calm, quiet, meditative quality of Eastern deities can enhance everyone's life. You do not need a great deal of space or time to give one of these lovely gods or goddesses a home. Fresh flowers, incense, and an occasional token of appreciation will yield three times their worth in the peace and harmony that will prevail.

ENDNOTES
1. Bodhisattva is one intent on enlightenment and works to overcome imperfections and serve civilization as a whole.

CHAPTER 10

Egypt: Valley of Temple and Tomb

Concerning Egypt I will now speak at length, because nowhere are there so many marvelous things, nor in the whole world beside are there to be seen so many things of unspeakable greatness.

Herodotus, fifth century B.C.

The Valley of Kings and Priests

The beauty of Co-Creation spirituality, Wicca, and Neo-Paganism lies in their diversity and freedom of choice. This is particularly true when it comes to worship of deity. Unlike most monotheistic Christian sects, nature-oriented religions delight in a variety of gods and goddesses to work with and worship.

For the most part, regional folklore, myth, and legend have kept many of the ancient gods and their traditions alive. Because of this, it is a fairly simple process to match a legendary god or goddess with his or her respective beliefs and practices. However, this is not the case with the gods and goddesses of Egypt. The actual beliefs and practices of the ancient Egyptians died with the last of the ruling pharaohs. We have only tombs and artifacts to speak for this once-great culture.

Rameses II was the last of the great pharaohs. In the ninety years following his death, eight more kings would take the throne. During this time they competed with the priesthood for power and managed to remove religion and its hierarchy from the control of the pharaoh. During this time of separation (about 1070 B.C.), Egypt went into its third and final decline.

When the religion of Egypt became less important than governmental concerns, the priests lost their power and position within society. No one was left to protect or preserve the spiritual traditions which had made Egypt the marvel of the ancient world. Over the centuries, invaders chipped away at Egypt's empire; then Christianity arrived. What had not been obliterated by foreign warring factions was eventually eradicated by the cross. Around A.D. 500, the Islam Sunites made their move and consumed the last of Egyptian spiritual history, and the glory of Egypt was buried beneath the sands of time.

To this day it can only be hypothesized exactly what the religious practices and beliefs of these ancient people were. This is why there is no specific religious tradition chapter preceding this discussion of Egyptian gods and goddesses.

However, the lack of detailed theology should not discourage the student of Egyptian myth and legend. The gods and goddesses of Egypt are just as vital and relevant to us today as they were to the builders of the pyramids. In fact, many Wiccan and Pagan groups honor and worship these glorious forces of the desert sun. Because of this power, potential, and popularity, these deities are included in the text. If you feel a special kinship with, or calling from, the gods of Egypt, study their culture and create your own system.

The ancient Egyptians assigned an immeasurable amount of commitment to their architectural, religious, and scientific communities. The impact of the pyramids and their precision of measure are unequaled, as are the distinctive temples, sacred hieroglyphs, and tombs of gold. In almost every way, Egypt was and still is a focus of myth, mystery, and magic.

To some degree, people of classical Egypt were monotheistic because they thought of the universe as the conscious creation of one supreme force. This force, however, was expressed through a pantheon of secondary deities called the Neterw.[1] These secondary deities were Egypt's gods and goddesses who were a reflection of a particular aspect of the original potential. Also important was the belief that certain animals—such as the hawk, jackal, cat, and hippopotamus—were embodiments of specific divine principles. The acceptance of these forms as divinity led to the practice of polytheism, the worship of many gods and goddesses.

The Egyptians also believed that humans carried within themselves the spark or seed of the supreme god. However, this force or potential could only be realized through the king, who was the embodiment of the personal and spiritual destiny of humanity.

The king was a direct reflection of the supreme god force and as such duplicated the creator's heavenly actions on earth. The king generated order out of disorder and conquered the forces of anarchy and chaos. He represented the forces of light in their eternal conflict with the forces of dark; he was both ruler and spiritual leader of his people.

The Egyptian religion was elitist; participation was reserved for the privileged priesthood and the pharaoh. The temples were not open to the public and only certain priests and the king had access to the inner sanctuaries. Rituals performed in the secrecy of these sanctuaries imbued sacred objects and the statue of the god or goddess who resided there with supreme power. During special religious festivals, the image of the god or goddess would be carried out of the temple, procession-style, among the common people.

The gods and goddesses of Egypt were served by both priests and priestesses. In most cases, the priests and priestesses were of equal rank and each serviced their own particular deity. Even though priests presided over most of the temples, some temples were dedicated specifically to a goddess and priestesses were entrusted with her care. Only at certain pageants or during designated festivals, where a god and goddess were brought together, would the priests and priestess perform conjointly. Otherwise, they kept to themselves, involved in their own religious activities.

The temples in Egypt were like miniature cities, and their function was to see to the comfort of the god or goddess who dwelled within. These self-contained monuments to deity must have been a beehive of activity. From dawn to dusk the kitchens, bakeries, and laboratories were busy creating special foods, baking breads, and making unguents for the pleasure of the gods. There were morning purification rites, afternoon ablutions, and sacrifices, followed by evening prayers and devotions.

A typical day included the morning purification bath of the high priest or priestess, after which he or she dressed in white linen robes. The priest or priestess entered the temple and performed cleansing ceremonies in the outer corridors. When these ceremonies were completed, a procession of offering-bearers entered with their litters of foods, breads, libations, and incense. Singers and chanters praising the glory of the gods accompanied these lesser priests and priestess.

For the most part, daily rituals were timed to coincide with the movement of the sun. The morning purification ceremony paved the way for the celebration of high noon and the formal dressing of the god/goddess and his or her feast. What was left over from the god's feast was shared among the priesthood and constituted their main meal of the day. As the sun crossed the sky and dusk approached, all activities were geared to the closing ceremony, which consisted of prayers, invocations, and songs to the god or goddess and the ritual sealing of the temple for the day.

As mentioned earlier, the Egyptians' actual religious practices have been lost for centuries; no way to present an accurate tradition[2] for them exists. Because there is a great deal of interest in their folklore and customs, I feel it is appropriate to present their deities here. The gods and goddesses described below are some of the more popular members of the pantheon. Because they are more popular, much information is available about them, including fine paintings, statues, and artifacts.

The Gods of the Egyptians

Isis

Isis (The Great Goddess)

Isis (from the Greek for *aset*, meaning throne) is the personification of the Great Goddess in her aspect of maternal devotion. Isis is the daughter of Seb and Nut, wife and sister of Osiris, and mother to Horus. She is always represented as a woman and wears on her head a symbol of the throne, which is also the hieroglyph for her name. However, at times her headdress changes to that of the solar disk with horns or to the vulture's cap.

Isis was probably the greatest goddess in Egypt and was worshipped for more than 3,000 years. Her influence was not confined to Egypt and spread to Greece and the Roman Empire. Isis appeared in various images. She was the goddess of serpents of the primeval waters; milk-giving cow goddess; Sirius, the star goddess, who brought about the inundation of the Nile; fertility pig goddess; bird goddess; and goddess of immortality.

Isis was the female principle of nature and therefore a goddess of a thousand names. She was worshipped as "the great magic" who protected her son Horus from predators and other dangers. Because she protected her son, many believed she would protect mortal children from the perils of daily life as well.

Myth and legend confirm Isis as a true wife and mother. When her husband Osiris was killed by his jealous brother, Set, Isis spared no pains in finding his hidden body. Once she found the body, however, Set recaptured it, cut it into fourteen pieces, and scattered the pieces throughout the land. Isis hunted down all the pieces. She magically reconstituted the body and made love to it. Through this union with Osiris, Isis conceived Horus, who eventually revenged his father's death.

Correspondences

Archetypes	Mother, protector
Expression	Mistress of magic
Elements	Water, earth
Nature	Cultivated, authoritative, resolute
Associations	Ishtar, Demeter, Virgin Mary
Symbols	Thet (knot or buckle), scepter, cup, horns, mirror, snake, owl, hawk, ram, white cow, girdle
Colors	Sky blue, green, gold, white

Numbers	2, 8
Plants/Foods	Fig, willow, lotus, lily, narcissus, myrtle, myrrh, iris, date, sycamore tree, cooked goose, bread, beer, wine, honey, celery, papyrus
Places	Marshes, river's edge
Misc.	Feast days: May 14, August 21, October 31 (most festivals lasted for about three to four days each)

Osiris (He Who Occupies the Throne)

Osiris

Osiris (from the Greek *asar*, meaning power of the eye) symbolizes the divine in mortal form. He is the personification of physical creation and the cycles of life. His death and resurrection symbolized the succession of the seasons and gave humanity hope for another life. He is the highest of all powers, the king who brought civilization to Egypt. He is husband and brother to Isis, father of Horus, and son of Seb and Nut.

It is believed that Osiris once lived as king upon this earth. Before his reign, the tribes of Egypt were nomadic hunters, constantly at war with each other. However, Osiris changed all this. He took his sister Isis for his queen and ruled the land. Osiris taught people the arts of agriculture and making tools to tend the crops. He showed them how to grow wheat, grind it, and make it into bread. He taught his followers how to grow grapes, make wine, and brew beer from barley, which was considered to be cultured behavior.

Osiris also founded temples and elaborately decorated them with fine carvings and statues. He organized the rituals of worship and designated religious practices. By his actions and works, he encouraged people to live noble and just lives, and he provided them with civil laws as well.

Set, Osiris' brother and the power of evil and darkness, treacherously murdered Osiris. After Osiris' death and resurrection, he became lord of the underworld and judge of the dead. He presides in the scenes of judgment, when the heart of the deceased is weighed against the feather of Ma-at and Thoth records the verdict.

Osiris is usually portrayed as a mummified, bearded man wearing the white crown of the North. At times, his mummy wrappings were colored green to reflect his nature as a god of growth and regeneration. Around his neck is an elaborate pectoral necklace and the menat counterpoise. He carries the shepherd's crook, the symbol of sovereignty and responsibility, and the flail that separates the wheat from the chaff.

Correspondences

Archetypes	King, priest
Expression	Father of stability and growth
Elements	Earth, water
Nature	Mature, refined, controlling, organized
Associations	Tammuz, Jesus Christ
Symbols	Djed, crook, flail, menat, was (scepter), agricultural tools, hawk, jackal, ape, bull
Colors	Gold, yellow, green, white
Numbers	1, 7, 14
Plants/Foods	Corn, barley, willow, ivy, mallow, bread, beer, wine, all harvest grain, fish, sycamore tree, cypress, thorn, acacia, ivy, papyrus, orris, lily, storax, bay, frankincense, dittany
Places	Desert, field, riverbank
Misc.	The Isis festival celebrated in November commemorates the death and resurrection of Osiris

Hathor

Hathor (from the Greek *athyr*, meaning the dwelling of Horus) was a sky deity originally described as the wife of Horus and daughter of Ra. Because her name meant "the dwelling of Horus," she was often seen as the mother of Horus as well. This complex condition is explained by her enclosing the sun god each night within her breast so he was protected and could be born again the following day.

Hathor is also described as the great celestial cow who gave birth to the universe, including the sun. In this aspect, she is represented as a cow or cow-headed goddess. Her most popular depictions are those of a woman wearing a lunar crown with cow's horns or heavy tresses and cow's ears.

Like the Greek goddess Aphrodite, Hathor was a patroness of women, mistress of merriment, and sovereign of music and dance. Her temples were homes of intoxication and places of enjoyment. Because of her association with music, the sistrum became one of her symbols and was used to drive away evil spirits and confer blessings during her rituals.

Despite the fact that Hathor was a goddess of joy and love, she was equally respected and cherished as a patron of the dead. In fact, she was the protector of the Theban necropolis under her title of "Queen of the West." It was said that Hathor would wait in the foliage of the sycamore tree at the edge of the desert and welcome the dead with bread and water.

Hathor was worshiped at Dendera, the location of her principal sanctuary. In this temple, people celebrated great festivals, especially the anniversary of her birth on New Year's Day. On that day, the priestess prepared her toilet and, just before dawn, brought Hathor's image out into the temple garden so that it was exposed to the sun's first rays. Great celebration and rejoicing—including much singing and drinking—followed this first ritual of the day.

Hathor was the passionate, consummate lover and nurturing mother; she was the intoxication of life. However, as with all goddesses, she had an opposing aspect that was noticeably expressed through her association with Sekhmet, the lion-headed goddess of war, death, and destruction. Certain ancient texts maintain that Sekhmet is the destructive side of Hathor; other texts placed them as separate entities. In either case, the two are related because they appear to have been granted the power of the "eye of Ra." It is possible the Egyptians were trying to imply that the goddess had both a loving and destructive side to her nature. When loving, she was Hathor; when destructive, she was Sekhmet.

Correspondences

Archetype	Mother, sustainer
Expression	Queen of the West
Elements	Water, fire
Nature	Passionate, loving, fertile, destructive
Associations	Aphrodite, Sekhmet
Symbols	Sistrum, cow, horns, lunar disc, lioness, sycamore tree, papyrus stalks, menat, lynx, sparrow
Colors	Sky blue, turquoise, copper, gold
Number	7
Plants/Foods	Beer, barley, mandrake, rose, sycamore, myrtle, milk, bread, benzoin, clover, papyrus, sandalwood, palm, pomegranate
Places	Sky, heavens, desert
Misc.	The fifteenth day of every month was sacred to Hathor; her major festivals were on November 21 and New Year's Day

Horus

From the beginning of the dynastic civilization, there is mention of Horus (from the Greek *heru*, meaning "He Who is Above"), the falcon-god and "lord of the sky." He was represented as a falcon or as a falcon-headed man. His most distinguishing characteristics were his eyes; his right eye symbolized the sun and his left eye symbolized the moon. In a fight with Set, Horus lost his left eye—which was eventually recovered and aided in the resurrection of Osiris. In time, this eye became known as the "Wadjet Eye." It symbolized the power of light and was used as a talisman against evil.

Originally, about twenty-five different gods were named Horus. The most distinguished of these were "Horus the Elder," son of Ra, brother of Set, and husband of Hathor; and "Horus the Child," son of Isis and Osiris. Over a period of time, the Egyptians became either unwilling or unable to distinguish between the two. Horus

Horus

the Elder and Horus the Child merged into one being. Horus the Child (son of Isis and Osiris) eventually claimed the heart of the people.

In the myth, which resembles the Old Testament story of Moses, Horus is born in secret and hidden in the marshes or bulrushes. Because Isis had conceived Horus after the death of Osiris, she feared Set would kill him as well. With time, Horus grew to maturity and sought out Set in order to revenge his father's death. The many battles between Set and Horus were considered symbolic of the continual struggle between the powers of light and darkness and the powers of the king and the enemy.

Horus had four sons (Imset, Qebehsenuf, Duamuttef, and Hapi) who were guides for the dead. Their pictures and names were painted on each side of a coffin and their likeness was sculpted on the lids of canopic jars.[3] They protected the dead from hunger and thirst as they watched over the internal organs. As with the "Wadjet Eye," we find Horus, this time through his offspring, as an agent of protection.

Along with his protective attributes, Horus was also the representation of resurrection and regeneration because he was the posthumous son of Osiris. As the matured seed carried by Isis, he represented the ability to transform. Also contributing to his imagery of regeneration was his personification as the rising sun, a symbol of kingship, which represented the rebirth of the god each day.

Correspondences

Archetypes	Sun god, savior god
Expressions	Kingship, protector
Elements	Fire, air
Nature	Protective, fearless, avenging, authoritative
Association	Apollo
Symbols	Wadjet (Eye of Horus), winged disk, falcon, canopic jars, sun, moon, double crown, feather, lion, snake, crocodile, club, bow and arrow, papyrus, pillar
Colors	Gold, yellow, amber, silver, blue
Numbers	5, 10
Plants/Foods	Bread, grain, nettle, absinthe, laurel, lotus, papyrus reed, onions, frankincense, myrrh, milk, pepper, pine
Places	Sky, horizon, tops of trees, tops of temple gates, desert
Misc.	He is honored at the Spring and Fall Equinoxes

Sekhmet

Sekhmet (from the Greek *sakmis*, meaning the powerful) represents the feminine aspect of creative fire and is usually depicted as a bare-breasted woman with the head of a lioness. She is the daughter of Ra and the consort of Ptah of Memphis. Her son is Neferten, the lotus god. Sekhmet was as loved as she was feared because she could be both benevolent and malevolent, depending on the circumstance.

Sekhmet was one of the goddesses adopted by the pharaohs as a symbol of superiority and bravery in battle. She would ride next to the king in his chariot and breathe fire on the enemy, burning them to death. As a goddess of war, one of Sekhmet's titles was "lady of bright red linen," which described her blood-soaked garments and may have also referred to the color of her homeland.

One legend describes Sekhmet's negative nature very well. The sun god Ra was afraid that humans were plotting against him. The other gods urged Ra to call down retribution on humans by sending forth his avenging eye. Ra had two avenging eyes—Hathor and Sekhmet—and he sent Sekhmet to teach humanity a lesson. Sekhmet, however, became blood-thirsty and would not stop killing. Ra ordered seven thousand drums of beer to be colored red and taken to the desert. Sekhmet drank the beer (thinking it was blood), became intoxicated, and forgot what she was doing. As a result, humanity was spared complete destruction.

Sekhmet was also a goddess of plagues; people assumed that what she could bring, she could also take away. In this aspect, she was the "Lady of life." Her priests recited prayers to Sekmet over their patients, asking her to heal them. She became Sekhmet the healer; petitioning her became an integral part of medicine.

One of the fascinating things about Sekhmet is her dual nature. She can be destructive—tearing, rending, and consuming that which is profane. However, she can also be beneficial in her ability to counteract illness and death. In these aspects, she has been equated with both Hathor and Bastet—the positive sides of the feminine force—with Sekhmet being nature's pernicious face.

Correspondences

Archetype	Destroyer
Expression	Warrior goddess
Element	Fire
Nature	Rending, power, transformation
Associations	Hathor, Bastet, Kali
Symbols	Lion, rosette, scepter, linen, vulture, solar disk, uraeus, arrows, claw, knife, red ochre, ankh
Color	Red
Number	7
Plants/Foods	Pomegranate, beer, rose, myrtle, cake, red meat, papyrus reed, tobacco, red wine, pepper, dragon's blood, orange, thistle, wormwood, olive

Places	Desert, sky
Misc.	Feast day: January 7

Ptah

Ptah (The Sculptor and Cosmic Architect)

Ptah was known as the "Ancient One" and considered to be the creator of the gods. He existed before Nun[4] and conceived the idea of creation in his heart. Through prolonged meditation and abundant love, he manifested existence. This was accomplished by splitting his original thought into Nun, the masculine, and Nunet, the feminine counterpart of genius.

Nun and Nunet gave birth to Atum,[5] who was bestowed with the title of "The Thought of Ptah." With this title, Atum represented the heart of Ptah, which, to the Egyptians, was thought to be the seat of the mind.

Thoth and other primary deities followed, but the belief in Ptah as the first word or original source placed him, his wife Sekhmet, and their son Neferten, at the head of the Memphis triad.[6]

Besides being a source of origination, Ptah was thought to have created the skills of design and sculpture. In the Old Kingdom, his priests were known as *werkherep hemut*, which translated as "supreme leader of craftsmanship." It is interesting to note that limestone quarries were located near Ptah's temples, conveniently producing the materials for artisan priests to carve into statues and sacred objects.

Ptah was unique in his appearance as well as in his province. He was depicted as a bearded man with his head enveloped in a tightly fitting skull cap, leaving only his ears and face in view. He was wrapped totally in linen with only his forearms emerging. He wore a large necklace and held the "was," scepter of dominion. At the uppermost part, this scepter combined the ankh and the djed topped by the crooked head of a dog. The staff's lower portion was forked.

In Memphis at Ptah's great temple, a bull named Hap (or Apis, the more commonly held Greek name) was kept. This animal was considered to be the physical incarnation of the god himself and was chosen for his color and markings.

Because of his identification with the god, the bull was treated with great care and respect. It was indulged with every comfort possible, even to the point of providing it with a harem of cows. When at an old age the bull finally died, he was mummified, as befitted royalty, and placed in a special sacred crypt.

For the most part, Ptah did not have much to do with the funerary cults nor did he play a large part in the underworld. Ptah-Sokar, a composite deity, was involved with the afterlife. However, Ptah did have influence and played a major role in the "opening of the mouth" ceremony, which was performed on mummified corpses and statues of the deceased.

Correspondences

Archetype	Architect of the universe
Expression	Divine craftsman
Elements	Earth, air
Nature	Creative, constructive, artistic, inventive
Associations	Hephaestus, Vulcan
Symbols	Mummy, heart, potter's wheel, cosmic egg, bull manet, tongue, crafts, ankh, djed, clay, wood, limestone
Colors	Gold, yellow, violet
Number	8
Plants/Foods	Juniper, cinnamon, lotus, wisteria, storax, frankincense, myrrh, lilac, fish, bread, wine, milk, honey
Places	Temples, blacksmith forge, museums

Synopsis

Since the beginning of time, people's egos have led to fashioning their deities in their own likenesses. The ancient Egyptians were similarly inclined, and for this reason they created a pantheon of gods and goddesses who closely resembled humanity in every aspect. They lived, loved, and died as the mighty warrior, tempestuous virgin, and triumphant hero. Their myths and tales present exultant victories, passionate love affairs, and invincible powers. They are what humans could be if they were smarter, stronger, and immortal.

Through the centuries, the ancient Egyptians evolved into a civilized and sophisticated society. As the people developed, so did their culture, gods, and rituals. The Egyptians were an urban people with vast resources, incredible architectural knowledge, and the discipline to create a civilization that lasted more than 3,000 years. Because of their refinement, their deities are more conservative and reserved than those of other pantheons.

When approaching the gods and goddesses of Egypt, keep in mind their history and culture, as this will be where communication begins. Records from tablets, tombs, and scrolls tell us that primary purification and extensive toilet rituals were performed first. Prayers, chants, and songs followed. A great amount of time and energy also went into the presentation of libations and food offerings. The dressing of the deity and its adornment were a priority, as was the proper preparation of all unguents, oils, and perfumes.

Make an effort to duplicate the customs of a culture as closely as possible to recreate an atmosphere conducive to receiving the deity's energy force. Because the Egyptian gods and goddesses were refined, you need to invoke them in the same fashion as they were originally invoked. That is, reserve a special place for the deity's altar and set aside specific times to perform ceremonies for their benefit.

The Egyptians respected and deferred to their gods and goddesses. If you plan to work with these deities, do the same. Keeping things clean, neat, and orderly will go a long way toward setting the mood and proper conditions for inviting the presence of these deities. As with any deity, learn about them, in as much detail as possible, before you attempt to call them forth. Once encouraged, the gods become allies; once offended, they usually withdraw from our awareness.

Commentary: In our system of Co-Creation spirituality, we use methods similar to the Egyptians' methods for temple maintenance and deity intensification. We firmly believe that everything associated with the god or goddess form should be kept clean, including the images or statues themselves. Bathing and purification rituals should be done to enhance the representation of the god or goddess as well as clear the area of any unwanted energies.

Negative thoughts and vibrations float through the air like particles of dust and gather on anything and everything possible. Regular cleansing rituals remove unwanted energies and create a tranquil atmosphere conducive to communication with a deity. We have also noticed that deity statues enjoy being washed, perfumed, and adorned with scarves, drapes, and jewelry.

Remember that once the image or statue has been ritually charged, it becomes a physical receptacle for the divine energy force and will respond accordingly to the attention being paid it.

ENDNOTES

1. Neterw (pronounced net-er-oo) singular, neuter: the Egyptian word for god or divinity.

2. Even though no accurate tradition is available, you can still create one. Knowing what constitutes a religion and spiritual system allows you to create your own traditions using whatever gods and goddesses you choose.

3. Canopic jars were four large jars used to store the wrapped internal organs of the deceased. The jars' lids were carved with one of the faces of the four sons of Horus. The faces were those of the ape, jackal, man, and falcon.

4. Nun is the primal chaos out of which all life began. Ptah personified the primal waters, which contained the potential for all things.

5. Atum is the sun god and creator of the universe.

6. Note that the Egyptian triads (a group of three closely related parts) were composed of a mother, father, and son arrangement; Christianity later imitated this idea in their concept of Mary, Joseph, and Jesus as well as in their symbolic trinity.

Chapter 11

Europe: Alive with Myth and Mystery

All Europe by conflicting Faiths was rent,
And e'en the Orthodox on carnage bent;
The blind avengers of Religion's cause
Forgot each precept of her peaceful laws.

Nicholas Boileau-Despreaux (1636–1711)

Where Lance and Grail Meet

The journey from Stonehenge to the Parthenon is filled with the magic of dragon caves, fairy mounds, and mist-shrouded moors, speaking of ancient times. The journey includes meetings with courageous gladiators, knights in shining armor, and secret gatherings in the Druid grove.

As Europe contained a variety of cultures and belief systems, it was and still is a land of myth and mystery. The openness to cultures and beliefs was especially true of the pre-Christian Celtic, Germanic, Greek, and Roman peoples. Though separated to some degree by social structure and natural boundaries, their beliefs eventually blurred into each other. Because the Celtic and Germanic systems belonged to the Indo-European language group (which also included the Greeks and Romans), exchange of religious myths became a popular method of cultural interaction.

Early Northern European people shared information by way of the spoken word, especially regarding their spiritual practices. For the most part, the Greeks and Romans—with their dedication to the written word—composed most of the documents concerning the Celtic people. Polubius, Tacitus, and other writers in contact with the Celts provided most of the information we have today regarding Celtic religious systems. If not for these scholars, the majority of pre-Christian Celtic practices would have been lost forever.

Both mythology and folklore were methods of preserving many religious and secular traditions of Northern Europe and the Mediterranean. One popular custom that helped to ensure the keeping of established myths was the transmutation of deity, which usually happened when one tribe or legion captured or seized another. In transmutation, the local gods and goddesses were brought into the new and imposing culture's systemin an effort to control the local inhabitants.

By looking back just prior to Christianity, we find that religion was an intrinsic part of life rather than a politically mandated crusade. Deities were localized and affiliated with the agricultural and cyclic processes. Each god and goddess commanded respect and held power over those who lived within their jurisdiction. Frequently, customs, rites, and practices varied extensively among tribes and villages; these differences in no way inhibited a deity's influence or power.

The contrast in lifestyles between the Celts and Greeks must be considered when considering European deities. Most Northern people (Celts) were herdsmen and transient farmers. Their occupations created a different emphasis in beliefs and practices in comparison to the more urban, trade-oriented Greeks and Romans.

Because of their nomadic and farming lifestyle, the Celts were more appreciative of natural settings for their religious celebrations. Outdoor ceremonies may have seemed primitive to the more sophisticated Greeks, who practiced their devotions in stately constructed temples.

For the most part, the Celts were concerned with war and agriculture whereas the Greeks were more interested in philosophy and art. Their gods and goddesses, for the most part, reflected their primary interests. Even though many differences in lifestyle and spiritual persuasions existed, many deities from dissimilar cultures had similar qualities, characteristics, and attributes. These common traits probably made it easier for the Celts, as well as the Greeks and Romans, to adopt each other's deities.

The Gods of Europe

Brighid (Bright or Exalted One)

Brighid, the daughter of the Daghdha, has been linked with Danu and Anu (or Ana). She is the embodiment of poetry, inspiration, and divination and was considered the personification of the Celtic triple goddess.

Brighid was originally a sun and fire goddess known as Brighid of the Golden Hair. Because of her connection with fire, Brighid was associated with inspiration and the art of smithcraft. To the early Celts, little, if any, difference existed between the inner psychological and outer scientific worlds. They saw the fires of inspiration, hearth and home, and the forge as aspects of this essential element.

Along with her fire aspect, Brighid was also an important fertility goddess. A Celtic custom of requesting successful childbirth included praying and using votive offerings at Brighid's sacred springs and wells. During the pregnancy and the birthing process, Brighid was called upon to protect both mother and child.

With the coming of Christianity, Brighid became one of the most popular Saints in the Celtic Catholic Church. A special order of nineteen sisters (or nuns) worshipped and cared for her in a monastery at Kildare, Ireland. The nuns kept a perpetual fire burning for the goddess. Each of the nineteen nuns tended the fire for one day; on the twentieth day, Brighid herself would appear and attend to the fire personally. Brighid's

Brighid

fire or eternal flame was kept in a courtyard surrounded by a hedge. No man was permitted to enter the sanctuary lest he burst into flames and die on the spot.

When Brighid was Christianized, she kept much of her original Pagan mystique and power. Some stories said she was raised in a Druid household and fed the milk of magical Otherworld cows while being taught the enchantments of healing and prophecy. Other legends declare her to be Jesus' foster mother, wearing a crown of lighted candles on her head to distract Herod's soldiers away from the Divine Child. She may also have been midwife at the birth of Jesus, anointing him on the forehead with spring water, thus bestowing the virtues of purity and wisdom.

Whatever the myth or legend, Brighid still plays an important role in the lives of many Britons. Her festival is celebrated on February 1, the Pagan commemoration of Imbolc, and the welcoming back of the Virgin aspect of the Goddess. In honor of this auspicious occasion, young maidens gather, dressed in white and carrying corn-dollies made in her image. There are candlelight processions, purifications, and blessings, as well as fertility games and much feasting and merrymaking.

Correspondences

Archetypes	Virgin, Divine Bride
Expressions	Inspiration, healing, fertility
Element	Fire
Nature	Sustainer, creator, artist, healer
Associations	Minerva, Danu, Ana
Symbols	Bell, spindle, flame, well, rainbow, bag of healing herbs, candle, swan, snake, cow, ewe/lamb, cockerel, eternal flame
Colors	Blue, white, yellow, gold
Number	19

Plants/Foods	Milk, bread, jasmine, wheat, honey, eggs, rosebud, blackberry, rosemary, hyssop, orange, apple blossom
Places	Wells, mounds of earth, Isle of Avalon
Misc.	Feast day: February 1 (Imbolc)

The Daghdha (The Good God, Mighty One of Knowledge)

The Daghdha (Dagda), the greatest of the Irish gods, was associated with wisdom and considered to be omnipotent—the true father figure. He is usually pictured as potbellied, ugly, and coarse, wearing a short tunic, exposing his buttocks. His imprudent appearance may have been created to mask his real inner powers and abilities.

In his position of primal father deity, the Daghdha brings to life two of the Celts' most valuable magical tools: the cauldron and staff. The Daghdha's cauldron dispensed endless satisfaction through a perpetual supply of food. The club or staff he carried brought life with one end and death with the other, suggesting the polarity of power. Both symbolic tools appear again in medieval texts about the Holy Grail and the legends of King Arthur.

Along with his other attributes, the Daghdha had an enormous appetite for life's physical pleasures. One myth reveals that just before the second battle of Magh Tuiredh, the Daghdha's Fomhoire adversaries encouraged him to eat a great amount of porridge. This was no average bowl of cereal—it consisted of eighty cauldrons full of oats, milk, and fat topped with whole sheep, pigs, and goats. Once finished with this tasty repast, the Daghdha made love to a Fomhoirean woman. She was so impressed with his sexual prowess that she agreed to help him and turned her magical powers against her own people. In another myth, on the eve of Samhain, just before battle, the Daghdha made love to the fierce Morrigan as she stood astride the river Unius.

The Daghdha was both the defender and nourisher of his people. His club could strike a man dead with one end and bring him back to life with another. His cauldron brought physical refreshment as well as spiritual satisfaction. He was the unquestionable king: strong, sexually potent, fierce in battle, and passionate toward his people.

Correspondences

Archetypes	All Father, King
Expressions	Strength, wisdom
Element	Earth
Nature	Passionate, potent, all-knowing, skilled
Association	Sucellos
Symbols	Cauldron, club or staff, torc, pig, goat, harp, cup, tunic, rope or cord, triple spiral

Colors	Brown, yellow, gold, green, russet
Numbers	1, 8
Plants/Foods	Oats, wheat, barley, milk, pig, goat, oak, nuts, patchouly, rye, vetivert, quince, primrose, potato, rhubarb
Places	Sidhe-mounds, hollow hills, mountains
Misc.	The eve of November 1, or Samhain, is associated with the Daghdha due to its death and rebirth aspect

Lugh (Shining One)

Lugh

Lugh is the shining god of light; he is a warrior, sorcerer, and master of all crafts. He belongs to the Ulster Cycle and is related by birth to both the Tuatha De Danann and their enemies, the Fomorians. He was a sun god; the summer festival of Lughnasadh on August 1 is celebrated in his honor.

In myth, Lugh appears at Tara (the royal court of Nauda, king of the Tuatha De Danann). When the guard at the royal gate asked Lugh the name of his craft, Lugh replied that he was a carpenter. The guard told Lugh that the court already had a carpenter. Lugh then said he was a smith. On learning that there was already a smith, Lugh said he was a warrior. Lugh kept naming crafts, including harpist, poet, historian, and sorcerer, and the guard kept saying that the posts were already filled. Finally, Lugh announced that indeed he was master of all these crafts. He demanded to meet with Nauda. When Lugh approached the king, he asked Nauda if he had any one person who, as he, was master of all these skills. The king admitted there was no one with such talent and admitted Lugh to the court.

Once Lugh became a member of the court, he encouraged Nauda to stand up to the Fomorians. In turn, Nauda relinquished his kingship to Lugh who orchestrated the military campaign against the Fomhoireans. In preparation for battle, Lugh hired three craftsman-gods to forge a magic spear, slingshot, boat, and sword. During the ensuing fight, Lugh killed Balor, the king of the Fomhoireans, with his slingshot.

In his aspect of "the Shining One," Lugh represented the power of good or light overcoming the power of evil or darkness. The constant battle between good and evil is a popular theme in Celtic legends, as it helps to illustrate morals, ethics, and proper conduct. Because tribal life was difficult, correct action and just behavior were important.

Correspondences

Archetype	Warrior God
Expression	Craftsman

Element	Fire
Nature	Able, artistic, defender of light, honorable
Associations	Mercury, Daghdha
Symbols	Spear, slingshot, raven, boat, sword, caduceus, ram, cock, tortoise, forge, all musical instruments
Colors	Gold, yellow, silver, red, orange
Numbers	1, 4
Plants/Foods	Corn, bean, bittersweet, blackberry, bergamot, sunflower, oranges, apples, ale, marigold, cornbread and barley soup, benzoin, cinnamon
Places	Fields, sidhe, hills, river
Misc.	Feast day: August 1, Lughnasadh; established in the memory of Lugh's foster mother

Cerridwen

Cerridwen (The Initiator)

Cerridwen, associated with Astarte or Demeter, is the Celtic mother goddess of the moon and grain. She is especially known for her fearsome death totem, a white corpse-eating sow. Cerridwen's harvest celebrations express her ability to both give life and take it away.

Cerridwen is also known as the goddess of inspiration and knowledge because of her inexhaustible cauldron[1] in which she brewed a magic draught called greal. This draught would give inspiration and knowledge to any who drank it.

Cerridwen's concepts are expressed clearly in the myth about Gwion Bach. In the myth, some liquid from Cerridwen's cauldron spilled onto the young boy's finger and gave him the gift of knowledge. Because the liquid was meant for someone else, Cerridwen became angry and relentlessly pursued Gwion. In his attempt to hide, Gwion changed into different creatures, but so did Cerridwen. Finally, Gwion turned himself into a grain of wheat and hid in a pile of grain. Cerridwen turned herself into a hen and swallowed the grain. Nine months later, she gave birth to a male child. Immediately, Cerridwen set the baby adrift upon the river. He was later discovered and in time became the great bard, Taliesin.

Even though all goddesses manifest three phases of ability, they usually have one phase that is predominately expressed over the other two. In the case of Cerridwen, her mother phase is the one most often invoked. For this reason, Cerridwen's mother phase provides the most effective form of her energy for ritual use.

Archetypes	Crone, Initiator
Expression	Mother of inspiration
Elements	Earth, water
Nature	Inspiration, cunning, protectiveness, wisdom
Associations	Astarte, Demeter, Medusa
Symbols	Cauldron, cup, sow, hound
Colors	Silver, white, green
Numbers	3 and any combinations of 3
Plants/Foods	Corn, barley, helbore, patchouly, belladonna
Places	Woods, water's edge
Misc.	Samhain, winter and harvest festivals, are celebrated in her honor

Cernunnos (The Horned One)

Cernunnos

Cernunnos means horned one and this god appears to be the Celtic god of vegetation, fertility, and the underworld. Cernunnos was the pre-Christian stag god, Lord of the Beasts, and master of woodland animals. On the famous Gundestrup Cauldron, he is depicted with ram's horns, holding a serpent and surrounded by animals. To early hunters and warriors, horns were a symbol of strength, power, and virility. Serpents were important because they symbolically represented the concept of regeneration.

Cernunnos is often pictured as a half-man, half-beast with horns. This image alludes to his fecundity as well as presents him as the virile guardian of the portals to the underworld. Cernunnos ushered those seeking transformation into the mysteries.

Little if any mention of Cernunnos exists in myths and legends because he was not a warrior god, but a god of the country and common people. Few peasant gods, including Cernunnos, would have fond their way into the songs, ballads, and myths the nobility preserved.

Cernunnos, like most horned gods, was concerned with the earth and human life's parallels to the earth's rhythms and cycles. Of prime importance to his role in the community was the idea of growing and becoming strong to ensure the survival of life and the land. Though these concepts may seem unimportant today, their implications can still be applied and used symbolically.

Correspondences

Archetypes	Guardian, Regenerator
Expression	Father of life

Element	Earth
Nature	Fertility, observant, generous, sensible
Associations	Herne, Silvanus
Symbols	Torc necklace, horns, cornucopia, stang, stag, ram, serpent, dog
Colors	Red, orange, forest green, brown
Number	6
Plants/Foods	Wild boar, deer, benzoin, bay, stew, mistletoe, wild honey, oak, beer and ale
Places	All woods, forests, groves
Misc.	Feast days: September 9 and the beginning of the New Year

Hecate

Hecate (Queen of Night)

To the Greeks, Hecate was one of the oldest embodiments of the triple moon goddess. She held power over the heavens, earth, and the underworld, where she was in control of birth, life, and death. Representing her triple qualities, she possessed the key, rope, and double-edged dagger. The key unlocked the door to the underworld, opening the way to the mysteries and secrets of knowledge and the afterlife. The rope represented the umbilical cord of rebirth and renewal, the connection between humanity and the Goddess. The double-edged dagger symbolized her power and ability to cut through delusion.

Hecate was the giver of visions, magic, and regeneration. She could grant the ability of second sight and teach those seeking the deepest secrets of magic. Hecate and her lover Hermes were the guardians at the gates of the underworld, easing the transition from this life to the next.

Because of her role as guardian at the gateway between the worlds, Hecate was associated with crossroads. When one reaches a crossroad, as in death, it is possible to see what lies ahead as well as what has gone before. Crossroads have long been considered a place where the physical world and the otherworld intersect. They were symbols of the transition between this life and the afterlife, and therefore a good place to contact deity. Altars and obelisks were placed at crossroads in honor of Hecate and offerings were left there in order to win her favor.

In Greece, Hecate was one of the feminine trinities. Although she was characterized as having all three aspects, her Crone, or underworld, aspect was most emphasized. Because of her association with the underworld, Hecate was called on in rites of divination, magic, and consultation with the dead.

While Hecate walked outdoors, her worshipers gathered inside to eat "Hecate suppers" in her honor. At these gatherings, people shared magical knowledge and the secrets of sorcery. When the supper was over, the leftovers were placed at the crossroads as an offering to Hecate and her hounds of death.

Because Hecate was also the goddess of the moon, she was also a goddess of the earth. She ruled the spirits of the dead and possessed the powers of regeneration. As queen of the underworld, she could hold back the spectral hordes from the living if she chose. Consequently, Greek women would call on her for protection before they left their homes. They would also place images of Hecate at their doors to let unwanted spirits know that all who lived in the house were under her protection.

Correspondences

Archetype	Queen of the Underworld
Expression	Death Crone
Elements	Water, earth
Nature	Regenerator, protector, sorceress, psychic
Association	Artemis
Symbols	Moon, besom, crossroads, triangle, bow and arrow, key, cross, sword or dagger, rope, torch, hound, bear, lion, snake, horse
Colors	Black, dark blue, silver, white
Number	3
Plants/Foods	Cypress, alder, poplar, yew, poppy, almond, moonwort, mugwort, myrrh, civet, hazel, jasmine, lily, patchouly, garlic, belladonna, hemlock, mint, palm date, monkshood or wolf's bane, corn
Places	Crossroads
Misc.	Feast day: August 13

Hermes, Mercury (Messenger)

Hermes was the god of communication, commerce, twilight, and the wind. His Greek name suggests movement so people viewed him as a guardian of travelers. They placed his image where country roads branched and at the crossroads in towns. People also believed that he escorted the souls of the dead to the underworld.

Hermes was the son of Zeus and the nymph Maia and was born in a cave while the gods and humans slept. Soon after his birth, he displayed his mischievous sense of humor by stealing his brother Apollo's celestial cattle. Hermes slipped away in the night and found the divine herd. To confuse his brother, Hermes placed enormous sandals on his feet and made the cows walk backward to a secret hiding place. Through divination, however, Apollo discovered the truth and seized Hermes, bringing him before Zeus. Hermes' defense was so skillful and spirited that Zeus ruled there should be a friendly settlement between the brothers.

Apollo reclaimed his cattle but remained annoyed with Hermes and continued to reproach him bitterly. As a peace offering, Hermes made Apollo a lyre out of a turtle shell, ox hide, and sheep gut. When Apollo heard the music that came from this magical instrument, his anger died. He was so delighted with his gift that he gave Hermes a golden wand in return—a prototype of the caduceus—and entrusted him with his heavenly herd. Thus, Apollo became the god of music and Hermes the protector of flocks.

Because of his expressiveness and eloquence, Zeus also made Hermes the god of the spoken word. Hermes was honored by this highly valued position because it is through speech that exchanges are made, gallantries expressed, and knowledge conveyed. As with everything, however, this position had its negative side: lying, disguised truth, and confusion. For this reason, Hermes also became seen as a divine trickster.

Correspondences

Archetype	Divine Messenger, Divine Trickster
Expression	Benefactor of humanity
Element	Air
Nature	Articulate, quick-witted, brilliant, imaginative
Associations	Mercury, Thoth
Symbols	Caduceus, cow, flute, goat, lyre, crossroads, staff, tortoise, wings, feathers, cup, lamb, purse, sandal
Colors	Yellow, orange, silver
Number	4
Plants/Foods	Cake, honey, lamb, olive, palm, almond, May apple, orange, clover, lavender, lily of the valley, lemon verbena, pecan, mace
Places	Caves, crossroads, mountains
Misc.	Festival days: February 4 and April 24

Demeter (Mother Earth)

Demeter was the daughter of Kronos and Rhea and belonged to the family of eminent Olympians. She was associated with corn, vegetation, fertility, and the fruitful earth. As the goddess of vegetation, she was the founder of agriculture and the civic rite of marriage. Her mysteries, called the "Thesmophoria," were held each April and her cult center was at Eleusis, south of Athens.

Demeter had several consorts, including Zeus and Poseidon. In the form of a bull, Zeus tricked her and laid with her, making her the mother of Persephone.

Demeter loved her daughter above all else. One day when Persephone was picking flowers with her friends, she noticed a narcissus of striking beauty. As she went to pick it, the earth opened and Hades seized Persephone, dragging her into the depths of the underworld.

Demeter, hearing her daughter's cries for help, rushed to her aid but could not find her. In her dismay, Demeter renounced her divine duties and left the Earth until such time as her daughter was returned. The goddess' exile made the Earth barren. Because Zeus was responsible for order in the world, he demanded that Hades return Persephone. However, because Persephone had already eaten some pomegranate seeds, binding her to the underworld, a compromise had to be reached. It was decided that Persephone would return to the Earth with the first flower of spring and return to the underworld with the first seed of fall.

Demeter

At Eleusis in Crete, Demeter's temple was raised and the Eleusian Mysteries began. In September and October, the candidates for initiation would purify themselves in the sea. They would form a procession and walk the path from Athens to Eleusis, arriving at the temple by nightfall. Once within the sacred grounds, the secret initiations took place. These initiations were called mysteries because the system was a closely guarded secret.

Correspondences

Archetype	Earth Mother
Expression	Patroness of the mysteries
Element	Earth
Nature	Loving, productive, beautiful, fertile
Association	Ceres
Symbols	Basket, bull, scepter, torch, cow, box, well, corn, water jug
Colors	Yellow, orange, gold, green
Numbers	3, 9
Plants/Foods	Corn, barley, honey, wheat, pennyroyal, poppy, all harvest fruit and grain, cornbread, beans, rose, wax plant, beef
Places	Fields, farms
Misc.	September 23 begins the first day of the "Greater Eleusian Mysteries" in honor of Demeter and her daughter

Synopsis

When looking to the gods and goddesses of early Europe, it is important to understand their historical development—even though this may seem irrelevant in today's world. These extraordinary beings were created for a reason and therefore have a purpose. Their myths and legends helped our ancestors understand the phenomena of celestial movement and seasonal change and provided guidance in the transitions from life to death. Whatever the situation, a god or goddess could be petitioned for help and advice. The security of knowing a superior being was in charge made life much less frightening.

As stated earlier, the Celts were an agricultural people and, because of this, the seasonal changes were an important part of their life. Because of their affiliation with the land, most of their gods and goddesses align with the solar festivals such as Imbolc, Beltane, Lughnasadh, and Samhain. It is easy to integrate Celtic deities into modern earth religions because of the deties' like to natural cycles.

The Greeks and Romans, however, were more cultured and led an urban lifestyle. Where the Celts were pragmatic and concerned with fighting and survival, the Greeks and Romans were romantic and interested in philosophy and statecraft. These differences led to disparate viewpoints about deity and the practice of ritual. Thus, dissimilarities in the contrasting characteristics and energy levels exist between the Celtic and Greco-Roman gods and goddesses. These differences do not imply that one pantheon is better than the other, but presents a variety of options.

One of the most important aspects to consider when choosing a deity to work with is their fundamental energy level. This is especially important with the gods and goddesses of Europe as they represent such divergent lifestyles. A person who is refined and artistic and wishes to enhance his or her talents should consider a deity with a similar type of energy. A Greek or Roman deity would be a good choice for this person. However, a Celtic deity would probably be a better choice for a person who is inclined to the robust, earthy, outdoors lifestyle.

When looking for a god form with which to work, consider your feelings about the god's culture. If you are unable to relate to his or her society's fundamental customs, then you will probably be uncomfortable with that society's deities as well.

ENDNOTE

1. This cauldron, called Amen, is considered to be the symbol of life, death and regeneration. The cauldron is symbolic of the womb and its creation process.

CHAPTER 12

Those Who Ever
Shine Brightly

God who creates and is nature, is very difficult to understand,
but his is not arbitrary or malicious.

Albert Einstein, words carved above the fireplace
in Fine Hall, Princeton, New Jersey

Supplementary Gods and Goddesses

The deities in this chapter display a unique richness of character and, within their specific cultural environment, are commonly recognized as being a dominant force. These deities have been given the same attention to detail as was afforded the gods and goddess previously discussed. However, the introductory section has been shortened because it does not correspond to previously considered areas of tradition.

A deity does not need to come from a traditional pantheon in order to be used effectively in spiritual practice. The affinity you feel for a particular god or goddess should be the criterion for your choice. Many lesser known gods and goddesses work as well, if not better, than the more popular ones promoted by the general Neo-Pagan voice. Choose a deity according to its ability to function within your life rather than relying on the standards set by others.

Additional Choices of Deity

Two Statues of Ishtar

Ishtar and Enki

The gods and goddesses from Mesopotamia are some of the oldest known. Their mysteries and spiritual significance have inspired countless myths, poems, and invocations. Because the Babylonians were an urban people and kept written records, it is possible to access the power and potential of these deities who reigned thousands of years ago. Many of the customs and beliefs of the Babylonians have survived, including the idea that the temple is the house or home of the god; the enactment of the sacred marriage; and the ritual celebration at the time of harvest. It is only a matter of retracing the steps of our ancestors to find ways of approaching and using their gods or goddesses.

Ishtar (Morning Star)

In Babylonian scripture, Ishtar was called the Light of the World, Hierodule of Heaven, Leader of Hosts, and Opener of the Womb. The Sumerians also knew her as the Lady of Battles and considered her valiant among the goddesses. She was the goddess of the morn and goddess of the evening, the divine personification of the planet Venus, and the dispenser of the never failing waters of life.

Ishtar's image and role as the Hierodule of Heaven comes from the Neolithic idea of the Great Mother as procreation itself. This idea of procreation augments the concept of virginity and the true power of the goddess. To our ancestors, virginity was not a physical condition but rather the ability to maintain a constant state of creativity. Creativity and the ability to transform empower the essence of the feminine principle and our concept of goddess.

Fertility and all aspects of creation were Ishtar's domain. Sacred prostitution was an integral part of her cult and was looked upon with respect. Prostitution, like many things over the span of time, has been misinterpreted. The original meaning of the word *prostitute* was "to stand on behalf of" and was sacred work for a woman. Through sexual intercourse with the priestesses of Ishtar's temple, men experienced the state of bliss associated with the divine union. Prior to Christianity, sex and giving birth were considered channels through which the gods' divine energy poured. To be a temple prostitute was to validate and strengthen, or stand on behalf of, the highest potentials of the goddess herself, those of sacred union and creation.

With her attributes of love and beauty, Ishtar was also a goddess of life and death. In Babylonia as well as in old European cultures, no separate image of a "terrifying" goddess of death and destruction existed. These images were connected because life and death were intertwined and considered to be two aspects of the whole. Ishtar was identified with both the destructive and the nurturing powers of life. She could bring forth a bountiful harvest or destroy it through the power of the storm. Because of her awesome powers over the forces of nature, in time Ishtar became a war goddess favored by victorious kings.

Even today Ishtar's image can be seen in many works of art, including Assyrian cylinder seals, vases, and friezes. She is easy to recognize because of her symbols, which always appear with her: the eight-pointed star, the crescent moon, and the vessel containing the waters of life. At times, she is also shown holding a staff upon which two serpents intertwine, again reminiscent of her duality. Many times, she is depicted with the lunar horns of a crescent moon on her head, showing her to be a descendent of the ancient goddess who originally was the sky, earth, and underworld.

Correspondences

Archetype	Virgin Queen
Expressions	Divine harlot, principle of justice
Elements	Water, air
Nature	Loving, astuteness, propensity
Associations	Venus, Isis, Virgin Mary
Symbols	Eight-pointed star, crescent moon, caduceus, rainbow, rosette, water jug, double-headed ax, torch, tablets of law (called the Me), cow, lion, sparrow, snake, dove
Colors	Blue, green, sapphire blue
Numbers	8, 14
Plants/Foods	Apple, olive, sycamore, cedar, date palm, violet, corn, barley, orchid, rose, foxglove, dates, grapes, eggs, figs, raisins, beer
Places	Sacred wells, fountains, springs, lakes, rivers
Misc.	March 28 was the beginning of an eight-day festival and celebration in honor of Ishtar

Enki (Lord of the Earth)

In Sumeria, Enki was the organizer of life on earth and ruled destiny. He came from Dilmun, the land of copper, where he slept beside his virgin wife. When she asked for life to be brought into the world, Enki mated with her. Their daughter became the source of all life. His wife suggested that Enki copulate with his granddaughter in order to bring forth all plant life.

Enki was the God of great understanding, a magician and master of all practical knowledge who spent his time making up for the mistakes of the other gods.

At his height of popularity, Enki was the possessor of the "Me," the tablets containing the elements of social life and civilization. The goddess Inanna wanted the Me for her own city of Uruk because they reflected justice and made the city of the holder superior. She journeyed to Eridu, Enki's city, and ate a banquet with him. He offered her the Me and she took them back with her. Enki regretted his decision in giving her the tablets, and tried to get them back. Six times, Enki sent fearsome monsters to bring back the Me; each time they failed. In the end, Enki conceded defeat and forgave Inanna because he was an intelligent god, always thoughtful and sensible.

In spite of the story above, Enki succeeded in all of his undertakings. Enki taught early humans to fish and make garments. He was the patron of carpenters, stonecutters, and goldsmiths. He instructed humanity in the arts and taught people about farming, architecture, magic, and the law.

Correspondences

Archetype	Creator God
Expression	Divine Craftsman
Elements	Earth, water
Nature	Thoughtful, sensible, creative, understanding
Associations	Ea, Ptah, Lugh
Symbols	Me, copper, brush, wand, chisel, hammer, knife, melting pot, carving tools, crown, lahama, clay, staff
Colors	Gold, green, russet
Number	1
Plants/Foods	Apples, oranges, barley, wheat, fish, flour, tamarisk branches, cedar, juniper, aromatic resins, eggs, figs, raisins, beer
Places	Wells, underground springs, ocean, all waterways
Misc.	The greatest festival honoring Enki was that of the New Year, which took place during the first eleven days of Nisan, the month of the Spring Equinox

Erzulie and Damballah Wedo

The Voudoun religion comes from an African heritage transported to the New World with the slave trade. Voudoun is a living religion and a system of magic that has evolved, progressed, and matured through the centuries. Voudoun, much like Santería, has incorporated Catholic ideology into its system as well as aligned its deities, known as the Loa, with many Catholic saints. The Voudoun religion's prime objective is to contact and communicate with the Loa to gain information and wisdom that will help the individual lead a better life. Contact and communication are accomplished through elaborate rites that usually culminate in possession of the celebrant by one of the Loa. Although most people find possession an unusual practice, to Voudoun believers it is common and considered the principal reason for ritual.

Erzulie (Maitresse Erzulie—Haitian Virgin)

Erzulie is the goddess of the independent, fulfilled woman. She is the mistress of love, marriage, beauty, abundance, music, and art. All acts of romantic love and pleasure are her delights. She is seen as being fabulously rich and moves in an atmosphere of luxury and refinement. She likes jewelry and perfume and wants everything meticulously clean, as she is vain about her appearance and surroundings.

In Voudoun, Erzulie is the divinity of dreams, the Goddess of Love, and the muse of beauty. She is the mother of myth and gives meaning to what life holds in secret. She is all that is seductive. Because she can be both vengeful and loving with those who grace her presence, she is also mysterious.

Erzulie is the Haitian/Voudoun Goddess of Love, much like Oshun is in the Yoruba/Santería pantheon. Both goddesses are sacred harlots, like Ishtar, and are similar to Aphrodite or Venus.

Erzulie, like Oshun, is a goddess of fresh water, lakes, rivers, and streams. Water is necessary to life and pleasure and is both refreshing and dangerous. Because of her association with water, Erzulie can control human's movements. Water provides commerce, lush vegetation, and food from its dark depths—all of which are essential to Haitian life.

The goddess also governs those things that make life worth living. Erzulie's petitioners call on her to bring love into their lives, help acquire money, and find husbands for their daughters.

In Haiti, Erzulie is associated with the Catholic Saints the Virgin Mary and Our Lady of Charity. In every Voudoun sanctuary, a room or corner of a room is dedicated to Erzulie. In her area, her special items and objects are kept ready for use during ritual.

Correspondences

Archetype	Virgin Mistress
Expression	Eloquence
Elements	Earth, water
Nature	Loving, passionate, lusty, vain, wealthy
Associations	Virgin Mary, Oshun, Venus, Aphrodite
Symbols	Fan, rattle, mirror, comb, shells, peacock feathers, bells, jewelry, boat, scarf, three wedding bands, gold, peacock, vulture, parrot
Colors	Yellow, coral, pink, red
Number	5
Plants/Foods	Pumpkin, orange, honey, cinnamon, allspice, clove, nutmeg, basil, white wine, creme de menthe, champagne, French pastry, rum, sweet fruit, candy, yellow or pink rose, lily, honeysuckle, white hen and quail

| Places | River, riverbank, lake, stream, all waterways |
| Misc. | Feast Day: September 8; Tuesdays and Thursdays are her days |

Damballah Wedo (The Good Serpent of the Sky)

Damballah Wedo is the personification of the DA, the universal current of psychic power. He is the dynamic of pure action, of which his own movement is a graphic representation. He is the great father: benevolent, paternal, and compassionate; his followers come to him for blessings as well as for protection.

Damballah is the positive force that encircles the universe; he has no malevolent sense. He stands for the powerful dead who lived too long ago to be remembered. He existed before the mythic time and before the world fell into trouble. Damballah is at the top of the spiritual hierarchy and is the oldest and most respected of the Voudoun Loa.

All trees are resting places for Damballah. Being both a snake and aquatic deity, he rests among the branches in the marshes, springs, and rivers. He moves between the land and the water, as snakes do, generating life with his coiling movements. Like the snake which can survive in the hottest and most arid terrain, Damballah represents the will to live and remain vital in an inhospitable environment.

Damballah is pictured as a snake arched in the path of the sun. Sometimes, half the arch is composed of his female counterpart Ayida Wedo, the rainbow. Together, Damballah and Ayida represent the ultimate totality of sexual unison. They encompass the cosmos and are pictured as intertwined serpents coiled around the world egg.

As the coiling, sinuous snake, Damballah is seen as the life force that unites the past, present, and future. He is the serpent that gives up his skin in order to recreate himself. Voudoun practitioners see this recreation as an example of how they should be flexible and adapt to whatever the future brings.

Correspondences

Archetype	Cosmic Force
Expression	Power of regeneration
Elements	Water, earth
Nature	Expression, power, superiority, sovereignty
Association	St. Patrick
Symbols	Asson, bell, staff, snake, wand, cosmic egg, rooster, rams, calabash, sun, rattle
Colors	Red, white
Number	4
Plants/Foods	Apples, bananas, eggs, cornmeal, palm, cola, cola nuts, white flour, white cake, milk, powdered sugar, bone marrow, coconut, yams

| Places | Trees, marshes, creeks, rocks |
| Misc. | March 17 and Thursdays are devoted to Damballah |

The Virgin Mary and Jesus Christ

Without a doubt, these two deities are the most widely recognized of all. Because Christianity is one of the world's largest and most regularly practiced religions, the spiritual prominence of Mary and Jesus is obvious, as is their value and worth. Unfortunately, for the most part Christianity has turned these engaging deities into paragons of perfection far beyond the reach of mortals. For centuries, the church has maintained that the only ways to reach Jesus and Mary were by way of pulpit and priest. This is unfortunate because many people have benefited from their energy and presence. Whether an individual is Christian or Pagan, these deities offer power and potential when their intention is fully realized.

Virgin Mary (Queen of Heaven, Mother of God)

The Virgin Mary is unique. She has been bestowed with extraordinary powers and set apart from all other human beings because she is the mother of god. However, the Christian church does not consider her to be divine. Mary has been denied the status of goddess because the Church refuses to acknowledge the feminine aspect of deity. This denial is a shame because the Virgin Mary fulfills all the qualifications of a goddess. She is omnipotent, immortal, savior, protector, and promoter of fertility. She serves in the same capacity as goddesses have for thousands of years, and she provides miracles, presentations, and hope for those devoted to her.

The Mary myth relates how Gabriel, an angel, visited Mary in Nazareth, telling her she would conceive and bear a male child whom she would call Jesus. The child, Gabriel told her, would be called the Son of God, given the throne of David, and reign over the House of Jacob; his kingdom would endure forever. Mary was doubtful. She was betrothed to Joseph but not married to him and did not see how she could possibly be with child. The angel explained that the Holy Spirit was upon her and that God would overshadow her doubt. Mary consented. Joseph, though uncertain, placed his faith in God as well. The angel's visitation becomes the foundation of the immaculate conception and Mary's role as coredeemer in some Christian theology.

Mary's high standing within Christianity seems to stem from her vow to abstain from sexual intercourse. By abstaining, she had, in the eyes of the Church, refused to fall into sexual indulgence. Therefore, she remained pristine and whole physically; she was spiritually moral and superior to others of her station. Because of her purity, she became a channel through which the grace of God would flow to the earth.

Mary, as the Mother, has been associated with the concept of fertility. Because she conceived a child in such a miraculous manner, many believe she has the power to

Virgin Mary

bestow this gift on others. In Italy and Spain, newlywed couples travel to Mary shrines in hope of having a fruitful marriage. In gratitude for her blessings, they leave toys, baby clothes, and dolls.

Mary's connection with fertility extended past conception to growth, prosperity, and abundance. Around the eighteenth century, Mary became associated with spring and the month of May. Celebrations and festivals were held to honor her as the May Queen. In some areas, her devotees decorated her statue and carried it through flower-lined streets.

One tradition tells how a Mary shrine was built on the exact location of the Roman temple dedicated to the goddess Ceres. Here, the image of Mary, Santa Maria, is showered with corn, wheat, and other offerings on feast days that coincide with planting and harvesting. Even today in some areas, the first fruits, loaves of bread, and grain are brought into shrines to be blessed by the Virgin.

Whether orthodox theology wants to admit it or not, by all definitions Mary is a goddess. As with all goddesses, her roles have included those of virgin, bride, mother, and redeemer. Before Mary, this magnificent feminine force appeared in other guises, such as Kuan Yin, Isis, and Ishtar. Once accepted as a goddess, Mary's compassion can help bridge the gap between Christian and non-Christian faiths. As a Mother, she truly loves her children no matter what their race, color, or creed.

Correspondences

Archetype	Mother of God
Expression	Divine Virgin
Element	Air
Nature	Purity, spiritual, compassionate, loving
Associations	Isis, Ishtar, Kuan Yin
Symbols	Cross, heart, cup or grail, veil, rosary, dove, crown, cord, girdle, sword, staff, lamp, crescent moon
Colors	Blue, white
Number	3
Plants/Foods	Lily, myrrh, frankincense, myrtle, corn, barley, wheat, milk, honey, bread, fish, jasmine, palm, rice, marigold
Places	Cave, well, temple
Misc.	Lupercalia in February, the month of May, September 8, and July 2 are a few of the feast days celebrated for the Virgin Mary

Jesus Christ (The Son of God)

Jesus Christ is a model for Christian theology and an archetype of the greatest mystical ideal. The groundwork and foundation of the Christian faith were already in motion before the birth of Jesus. It was only a matter of time before the Jewish prophecy of a Messiah was fulfilled. However, ancient Jewish prophecy is not important or of interest here. What is important is the association and unification of concepts and deities into a central figure of worship.

Jesus Christ

From the mystical point of view, Jesus was born to Mary and Joseph in a stable or barn. When he was thirty years old, Jesus was baptized. During the ceremony, he allowed his mind and body to become a vehicle for the service of the highest god. This higher force worked through the body of Jesus for three years. At Jesus' crucifixion, the force departed. Jesus' life gave humans an example to follow whereby they offer their mind and body so that the Christ or divine spark within can manifest.

The figure of Christ aligns with and becomes a compilation of all previous solar savior deities. He assimilated the properties of Mithras, who was born on December 25 in a grotto and was seen to bestow everlasting life upon his followers. An inscription from one Mithraic sanctuary reads, "Us too you have saved by shedding of blood which grants eternity." It is interesting that initiation into the Mithraic mysteries was seen as a rebirth into the light.

Christ, as Apollo, was the personification of harmony. The urging to avoid extremes and excess was inscribed on the temple at Delphi, as was the commandment to "know thyself." Apollo was also known as a great healer and the god of light. The early Christians saw Jesus as the Logos, so the Greeks portrayed Apollo and Hermes as their Logos. It is essential to realize that Christianity was basically a Greek creation and, therefore, would naturally adopt some of the latter mythos into its teachings.

Even though Jesus appeared in a physical existence, his essential nature as Christ[1] was developed to exemplify the spiritual rather than the temporal. Because Christianity was a child of Pagan practice and Jewish law, naturally their savior god would incorporate those qualities so long revered. Jesus thus became the dying god, who descended to the realm of the dead to be resurrected and ascended into the light.

Jesus, as a man, rejected the material possessions of a corporeal world for the ultimate spiritual experience. He did this for the emancipation of his own divine spark and to serve as an example to his followers and all humanity. The fact that this man may be all myth and legend matters not; it is the intention, meaning, and purpose behind the story that becomes the standard for spiritual evolution. To find the

Christ within is to discover that invisible seed or divine spark that is a part of the totality of God and perfect it for reunion with its original source. The process is personal and has nothing to do with Christian dogma, political convention, or popular Pagan opinion.

Correspondences

Archetypes	Divine Savior, King of Kings, Light of the World
Expressions	Messiah, Good Shepherd, Messenger
Elements	Air, fire
Nature	Brilliant, charismatic, constant, honorable, radical
Associations	Sol Invictus, Mithra, Helios, Apollo, Dionysus
Symbols	Cross, Chi-Rho, sun, crown of thorns, lamb, cup or chalice, crooked staff, ciborium, monstrance, fish, star, cock, sacred heart
Colors	Red, purple, yellow, gold
Number	3
Plants/Foods	Balsam, olive tree and oil, palm, frankincense, bread, fish, wine, lily, all grains, grape, chrysanthemum, orange, chicory
Places	Caves, grottos, desert, flower gardens, church
Misc.	Festivals: Christmas, December 25; Palm Sunday; Good Friday; Easter, held on the first Sunday after the full moon following the Vernal Equinox; Ascension Day, forty days after Easter

Synopsis

Religion is about the worship of and communion with deity. It is the process of veneration and appreciation for the continuous multi-leveled arrangement of energies that flow through our universe. These energies transcend and eclipse human emotions, perception, and reasoning as they manifest through an endless continuation of vigilant gods and goddesses.

There are as many forms of deity as there are human beings on this earth. Each responds differently when called upon by the mere mortals they oversee. The gods and goddesses do not sit in judgment or condemn human vulnerability, nor do they love, hate, or get angry. These are human emotions, not divine attributes. However, the gods do respond to human supplication and need when properly approached.

The first step for those seeking true spiritual revelation is a firm faith and belief in the power and potential of deity. This can only be accomplished through a personal relationship with the gods themselves, so choice of deity becomes an important factor.

In selecting a god or goddess, you can approach the process in various ways. Take a good look at your racial and ancestral heritage. Looking into your heritage provides insight into your cultural conditioning. Use your personal interests or previous religious training to help you decide. Some people find it helpful to study ancient myths and legends, as these can inspire and encourage the searching soul.

Always remember the main purpose behind choosing a god or goddess: the desire to relate to divinity on an individual basis. Whether you choose to work with Isis, Chango, Kuan Yin, or Jesus, the choice is yours, and yours alone. Bringing the power and potential of a god and goddess into your life is an awesome experience; one that will provide joy and contentment for a long time. Some people's gods may be dead, but ours are not; they are only waiting for us to bid them welcome once again.

ENDNOTE

1. The Greek word for Christ, *Kristos*, means anointed; in Hebrew the word means messiah. The word *Christ* does not refer to any specific person; it is a title; the Logos of Infinities.

PART III

The Cauldron of Inspiration

Where Symbol and Spirit Unite

CHAPTER 13

Tools and Symbols
of the Sacred

The symbol expresses or crystallizes some aspect or direct experience of life and truth, and thus leads beyond itself.

J. C. Cooper, *Traditional Symbols*

Whoever has the symbol has thereby the beginning of the spiritual idea; symbol and reality together furnish the whole.

Odo Casel, *Mysterium,* 1926

The Value of Symbols and Sacred Objects

Symbols are the fabric from which we form a fundamental understanding of life and our relationship to the universe. They are an intrinsic part of communication and experience, essential to all religious traditions. Whether symbols are created through associative or aesthetic reasoning, they convey in a nonverbal manner the presence of deity, higher wisdom, and spiritual awareness.

Religious art is the most dramatic and influential method of expressing a symbol's essence. Paintings, wood carvings, sculptures, and etchings illustrate divine beliefs and concepts. These artistically presented symbols address issues, intentions, and considerations through a silent presentation of ideology. Without effort, an individual's consciousness is automatically elevated to a realm of higher perception and understanding.

Religiously, as well as mundanely, symbols create a connection between the conscious and unconscious mind. They reveal and veil certain realities and truths, according to each individual's level of understanding. Because of their ability to both unite and separate higher levels of consciousness, symbols have become the language of all sacred mystery and religious traditions.

Symbols have a life and energy of their own, and the medium in which they are expressed reveals their nature. A good example is feeling the passion of Christ that a vivid painting portrays; becoming quiet and meditative when in the presence of an elegant image of Kuan Yin; or feeling a sense of family and warm reflection when viewing a colorful holiday display. An individual's reaction to the energies and inherent meaning of the symbolic objects or articles displayed causes these emotions.

When common objects are converted into religious tools, they become sacred and represent spiritual thoughts and actions that imply higher spiritual values and sentiments. By coming in contact with a sacred object, attention is automatically directed from mundane thoughts to spiritual ones. This change in focus allows the individual to feel and explore other realms of awareness.

Objects become sacred tools when they portray spiritual intentions, ideas, and, in some cases, deity itself. Most importantly, sacred tools serve as channels of communication between the devotee and his or her personal deity. Once communication between an individual and a deity has begun, higher levels of consciousness are reached and personal potential increases.

The primary function of any religion is to connect, in an intimate sense, the individual with deity. This connection usually begins with the process of association between the external material world and the symbolic spiritual world. Once contact has been accomplished, even the vaguest sacred symbolism will unite the devotee with his or her god form. This unity establishes the line of communication that will, in time, reveal the higher spiritual concepts sought by the believer.

All religions and spiritual paths have symbology as their primary language. The mysterious and elusive quality of pure thought and the ultimate creative essence cannot be expressed verbally; these must be felt and recognized within. Once some stimuli has activated inner awareness, the individual's emotions are transformed into spiritual energy. This energy forms the translucent beam of light that both sends and receives messages from the ethereal planes. Symbols and tools become like the telephone—objects that make communication at a distance accessible and possible.

The Symbols of the Sacred

Co-Creation Spirituality advocates the use of traditional Wiccan/Pagan and some Christian symbolism within the context of ritual. However, to enhance the personal aspects of our system, we have added two new tools, the *Vessel of Creation* and the *Rod of Authority*, to our individual altars. These additions are personalized and designed to bring the individual into direct contact with the god and or goddess with whom he or she is working.

As Co-Creationists, we believe that daily personal meditation and worship is essential to spiritual development. We therefore, as individuals, keep and maintain our own sacred space, tools, and altars. By regularly affirming our personal communication with deity, we progress beyond the limits of structured communal worship. As a result, our members are religiously mature and radiate spiritual composure—which adds momentum to our group celebrations.

For both communal and personal worship, the following objects and tools represent, in some way, higher, spiritual ideals, concepts, and divinity. The tools described in this chapter are indispensable in our religion. As with all aspects of spirituality, including sacred objects and tools, no specific requirements exist. The significance, strength, and value of any object comes from personal interpretation. Decide for yourself what is appropriate to use. No two people will place the same value on the same object; and what may seem foolish to you, will become an important part of someone else's spiritual journey.

The Chalice or Grail

Chalice and Paten

The Chalice is receptive and feminine in nature. It is restrictive and controlling because it contains the hidden mystery of life. By design it is emblematic of the womb, the Mother Goddess, and the ability to regenerate. These symbols probably account for its presence in so many ancient Egyptian and Babylonian temples and even Christian churches, as it was through the process of spiritual rebirth that an individual gained wisdom, inspiration, and enlightenment.

In most religions, the Chalice represents mystery, hope, and promise. It is open to observation, while only the surface of what it contains can be seen. One must delve deeply within to discover its secrets. The emotional factor of the unknown will create a powerful energy flow.

Because the Chalice will be used for the Rite of Union and to hold sacred wine for blessing, spare no expense in acquiring one. The only restrictions include the following: the Chalice must be opaque, as it contains the mystery of life, and it must be feminine in shape and design. The color, style, and texture should reflect your image of the Goddess.

The Chalice we use for our Sabbat celebrations (see photo) was purchased from a church supply store. It is eight inches high and gold-plated; it also has a matching paten for the Eucharist blessing. For our less formal rituals, such as Friday night church, we use a plain pewter chalice. The choice is up to the individual or group and depends on what you can afford. I feel that money should not be a factor when obtaining major working tools. Many ways to save money exist, if necessary, but altar tools are not the place to cut costs.

Paten

The Paten is a small, flat, circular silver or gold-plated dish, symbolic of the dish used during Jesus' Last Supper, on which he placed the bread of the Eucharist. You can use this small plate for spiritual offerings as well, but we use it strictly to hold the host or bread prior to blessing in the Rite of Redemption. The Paten is usually placed on top of the Chalice, covering the mystery within. When purchased in most church supply stores, the Chalice and the Paten usually come as a set, although the pieces can often be purchased separately. No matter what your tradition, these tools make a wonderful addition to the altar.

Athame

The Athame and Sword

The Athame and Sword are symbols of masculine strength, power, and potential. Countless myths have been developed about the young hero, wielding a magical weapon, coming to the rescue of lady, land, and ideal. Probably the best-known sword is Excalibur, the mighty sword of King Arthur given to him by the Lady of the Lake. As long as Arthur was in possession of the sword, he was invincible.

In most Wiccan/Pagan circles, the Athame and Sword represent the male and the God (whereas the Chalice represents the female and the Goddess). When the Athame or Sword, and Chalice are conjoined, their energy and force unite for the blessing of all those in attendance. In Co-Creation Spirituality, this unity is called the "Rite of Union" and is the most sacred point within the mass or ritual.

Because the Athame or Sword is masculine in nature, this symbolic weapon best serves those aspects of ritual involving power and protection. And a weapon it is when in the hands of the trained priest or priestess wielding it. Through the Athame or Sword, the priest or priestess focuses his or her personal power in order to banish all negative energies and create a sacred space for deity.

Traditionally, the Athame is a double-edged, black-handled knife about nine inches in length. Not everyone agrees upon this appearance, however. As previously mentioned, tools are symbols and their design and use will vary from one person to another. Remember that the tool that uplifts you is what you should be using.

My Athame has a natural wood handle and is about seven inches in length. The Athame used in our public church services (see photo) is about ten inches in length and solid brass. With the Athame, the shape and size are not important, but rather the feelings and ability of the person using it. In time, all ritual tools take on an energy and force of their own, which complement and enhance the practitioner's potential.

The significance of the Athame and Sword is in their function as symbolic weapons capable of directing personal power. They have the inherent ability to help focus energy in a desired direction for a specific purpose. They help regulate as well as conduct the flow of internal expression toward a desired destination.

The Vessel of Creation

The ability to create or give birth belongs to the realm of the Goddess and the feminine aspect of nature. Through her power of restriction, the capacity to contain, the formation of thought becomes reality. From conception to delivery, the confines of the womb embrace, nurture, and protect the spark of life. Within this feminine vessel of creation, the mystery of life begins and develops.

The Vessel of Creation

In today's society—with its technology and scientific resolutions—the power of giving life is a mystery still. Even though it can be reproduced through laboratory processes, the components of its primary arrangement, those of the masculine and feminine elements, are needed. Once these elements have come together, they are still in need of containment in order to reproduce themselves. Whether in the physical womb or the mystical vessel, the system of rendering remains the same. Something must confine the energy until it is ready to manifest.

The idea of a vessel to contain the life-giving properties of the feminine aspect is not a new one. The Grail legends relate how the power of life can come by restricting feminine power in sacred cauldrons and holy wells. The ability to contain, energize, and bring forth a new presence, be it tangible or intangible, is the quest of humanity. We all want to manifest our desires in some fashion or another. This need is a requirement of survival.

The Vessel of Creation is a symbolic tool which helps an individual to transform thoughts into physical reality. Through the essential elements placed within the vessel, the Goddess' natural energy is attracted and drawn into the vessel itself. Once properly consecrated and charged, the vessel becomes a living representation of the Goddess and the feminine forces of nature. Learning how to work with this special tool will bring its power and potential to you.

The Vessel of Creation (see photo), besides being a representation of the Goddess force, also serves as an oracle of communication. Stones and tokens, which are symbolically etched and numbered, are kept in the Vessel. These special items relate to the goddess you are working with and attract her energy to them. Through constant work and effort with these special objects, a link is formed between you and the goddess. In time, this link becomes a line of communications.

Throughout history, many religious systems have used special methods and tokens as a means of communicating with their gods. It only makes sense that if you are honoring, praying, and working with a specific god force you should be able to communicate with it. This force should be able to answer as well. It is difficult to build a rapport with another individual, let alone a god force, if there is only one way of communication.

How to Make the Vessel of Creation

First, choose a goddess with whom you will be working and learn everything you can about her. What major symbols, colors, herbs, flowers, plants, trees, and stones does your goddess prefer? Next, choose a container to serve as the vessel. Import stores are the best places to look for a vessel. These stores have a wide variety of jars, vases, bottles, and other suitable objects, which are reasonably priced and new. This is not the time to use a relic from an old aunt's attic, no matter how quaint it is. The container you choose must be new and free of vibrational buildup.

Carefully choose your container and the items that will be placed inside. Remember, this vessel is a representation and reflection of the goddess herself; each and every detail is of vital importance. To attract and maintain the energy level of the goddess within the vessel, everything associated with it must be in agreement.

Essential Requirements

The Vessel. Vases with large openings, ginger jars, and ceramic canisters work well. The vessel will need a lid, so choose something that comes with a covering or can easily be fitted with one. The container must be opaque and large enough to hold all the necessary items.

The Vessel Oracle Items

Along with the necessary empowering items, the Vessel also contains an oracle. This oracle consists of stones, symbols, and a reading cloth that allows you to speak directly with the goddess.

The Speaking Stones. To make the speaking stones, you will need nine fairly flat stones in the primary color of the goddess you are working with. (An example would be green for Ishtar or black for Hecate.) These stones will make up the major part of the oracle that will allow you to communicate directly with your goddess. Choose stones that are similar in shape and size and will fit into the vessel.

The Key Stones. These are four round, flat stones of a different color also associated with your goddess. If you are not using black or white as the color for your speaking stones, use one or the other for the key stones. Whatever the color, these stones should be round, smooth, and flat so that one side can be painted.

The Totem. This is the last item needed to complete the oracle and should be the animal, bird, fish, or reptile that is connected to your goddess. It may be a miniature representation or it can be painted on a small disk of wood or stone. (For example, you could use a small hand-carved lion for Ishtar because that animal is her totem animal.)

The Oracle Reading Cloth. This is a circular piece of plain material with the four elements (Air, Fire, Water, Earth) marked on one side. Use the Reading Cloth to read the oracle and wrap the speaking stones.

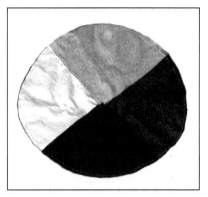

To make the cloth, cut a thirteen-inch diameter circle from a piece of cloth. On one side, mark off four equal sections and color these accordingly. You will have a section for air (blue), fire (red), water (green), and earth (yellow). Use paint or sew colored cloth to the sections. Your finished product should look like the photo.

Oracle Reading Cloth

Wrap your speaking stones, key symbols, and totem in the oracle cloth and place them inside the Vessel. (Chapter 14 provides more information on the speaking stones.)

Vessel of Creation Fundamentals
Other symbolic objects are placed in the vessel along with the oracle. They are used to attract and maintain the energy of the goddess' potential inside the Vessel.

The Natural Powers. These are herbs and plants that correspond to your goddess and naturally attract her energy and power. Select several plants to represent her different aspects; for example, flowers for the maiden; herbs for the mother; and woods to align with the crone. Make three separate bundles, tie with appropriate colored cord, and place inside the Vessel.

Sacred Fluid. The sacred fluid is symbolic of the feminine life force and is essential to attracting and maintaining the goddess' essence within the Vessel. The Sacred Fluid is made from pure spring water and your goddess' favorite herb.

You will need to buy a small (new) bottle, with a tight fitting cap, that will fit inside the Vessel. Thoroughly clean the bottle and fill it with spring water. Add a sprig of your goddess' favorite herb. Keep the bottle outdoors for three nights so it can absorb the energy from the moon.

Once your Vessel has been properly consecrated, the energized water will become activated. You can use it for anointing, mixing in other beverages, or for creating sacred space.

The Rod of Authority

The Rod of Authority

Manifestation of desire is the intent of the masculine force of nature. Through the Rod of Authority, this basic fundamental concept is realized. With its phallic shape and hollow shaft, it provides the passageway for the seeds of potential to flow. All that is needed is a passive receptacle, such as the Vessel of Creation, to nourish and support it to maturity.

Looking at the rod in its most basic form, we can realize its importance. The rod is the basis of all measurement. It is essential to movement, as in transportation, because it forms the spokes and axle of the wheel. Rodlike antenna for radio and television communication allow global interaction. Rod-shaped pens, pencils, arrows, spears, and pipes make life easier and more accommodating now or in the past. These rod functions are of a masculine nature and indispensable to our daily activities.

One of the first things that comes to mind when looking at the Rod is its resemblance to the male reproductive organ, which can generate new life. Even though the Rod is a symbolic representation of this, it is still effective, proficient, and capable of creation. Whether the creation process is propagation of the race, bringing forth a desire, or heightening spirituality, it is no less an accomplishment. The Rod, with its hollow shaft, serves to deliver the seeds of creation from origination to manifestation.

The Rod has a twofold purpose. The first is to represent the masculine force of deity. The second is to provide a suitable receptacle to house this force. Once this force has been contained, it can be used for personal direction. Containing this force becomes obvious when the Rod is used in conjunction with the Vessel of Creation to manifest desire. In most cases, the phenomenon of divine union provides inner awareness, physical euphoria, and spiritual promise.

Additional attributes of the Rod include concepts of discipline and authority. Through discipline we learn to maintain and control the magnetism of ethereal potential. Authority is the result of discipline and establishes the individual's right to call on and work with the higher spiritual forces of the universe.

How to Make the Rod of Authority

Choose a god to work with and learn as much about the god as possible, including the plants, colors, objects, and symbols that best represent his nature.

Once you are in sympathy with your god, it will be easy to choose a suitable rod. The rod will need to be strong and hollow. Brass, copper, and silver tubing work well, as does heavy cane bamboo. If you choose a solid wood, drill through it or have someone do it for you. The rod must be completely hollow.

For my Rod (see photo), I chose a heavy cane bamboo, the kind found in most garden and import shops. Because I am working with Tammuz, a dying and resurrecting vegetation god, bamboo was a perfect choice. It is masculine in nature, phallic in shape, and dies every winter to return the following summer. The fact that it is naturally hollow was an added bonus.

Think carefully about what your god represents. If he is a solar deity, a brass or gold tube would be ideal. If he is of lunar energy, silver would work well. If he suggests death and rebirth, use bamboo or an appropriate corresponding wood.

Essential Requirements

The Rod. The hollow rod should be at least ten inches long and one inch in diameter with a shaft opening of three-fourths of an inch.

Once you have drilled and finished the rod portion, affix a suitable point to create the head of the rod. This point may be a crystal, stone, or wooden knob. The choice is yours, but it should reflect your god's personality and nature.

For my Rod, I chose a rutilated smoky quartz crystal. It is projective because of its rutilations and receptive because of its color. Because it is a crystal, it is masculine-, fire-, and solar-oriented.

The last item you will need is an end piece, which may be in the form of a cap or plug. You must be able to remove the end piece when needed, and it must cover the end opening.

Rod of Authority Fundamentals

The following symbolic objects also are placed in the Rod's hollow shaft. Align these items with your deity so as to attract and maintain his energy and force. These items represent, symbolically, the principles of creation.

The Natural Powers. These are herbs and plants that correspond to your god. Choose two and tie them with a small piece of appropriately colored string. I used wheat and bay tied with a thin, yellow thread.

The Sacred Fluid. The sacred fluid is symbolic of the masculine life force and is represented by scented oil. It is kept in a small vial placed inside the Rod. Make the Sacred Fluid from essential oils that are associated with your god; color it appropriately and place a sprig of his favorite herb or resin in the bottle. Once the oil is activated through the consecration of the Rod, it will be used for anointing the body and sacred objects during specific rituals.

The Active Force. For this you will need a pinch of salt, a small bit of earth, a stone or crystal sacred to your god, and a glass vial (small enough to fit inside the Rod). Pulverize the stone or crystal, mix it with the earth and salt, and put the mixture into the glass vial. Place the vial in a protected spot where it will receive direct sunlight for six days. When the Rod is consecrated, this mixture will be activated and used for purification, as an ingredient in incense, or for creating sacred space.

The Active Symbol. This is a small item special to your god's nature. It is put into the Rod and represents your god's unique abilities, qualities, and powers. My active symbol is a small handcrafted ear of corn, which represents fertility, abundance, rebirth, and vegetation.

Place the active symbol, oil, salt mixture, and herbs inside the rod and place the cap over the end. Be sure the cap is secure but can be removed as you will be working with the contents of the rod periodically.

The Cauldron

The Cauldron

The Cauldron is one of the oldest symbols of the Goddess. It represents her power of transformation and symbolizes the Great Mother Goddess and her womb of the earth. It comes to us from our prehistoric relatives and has managed to survive intact.

Nourishment, sustenance, and transformation are some of the Cauldron's inherent qualities. Much like the Grail, the cauldron is a symbol of life and death, birth and renewal. Cauldrons have also served as containers for magical potions and mystical spells, such as the Cauldron of Cerridwen with its powers of inexhaustibility, regeneration, and inspiration.

The Cauldron has many uses, both as a physical tool and as a symbol or representation of the Goddess. When the Staff (see below) accompanies it, the Cauldron represents the totality of life through the divine union of the god and goddess. Together, the Staff and Cauldron create their own altar where offerings to deity may be placed.

With a lit candle inside it, the Cauldron represents the animating force of life and serves as the focal point in seasonal rituals or rites of renewal. In the chapel at Our Lady of Enchantment, we have a large, black, cast-iron Cauldron (see photo). We keep a seven-day candle burning inside for the Goddess. For city dwellers who do not have fireplaces or backyard firepits, the Cauldron can be used as a place to burn petitions and herbal offerings.

The Staff

The Staff, like the Rod, represents masculine authority, dominion, and dignity. The Staff also symbolizes a disciple's journey toward his or her spiritual goal. This concept is openly displayed in Christian art. Most commonly, Christ, seen as the Good Shepherd, holds a staff and herds his flock of devotees toward God's intention.

The Staff is associated with magic power and knowledge, along with the quality of transformation. This transformation quality was exemplified in the Old Testament when Moses threw his staff at the Pharaoh's feet, and it turned into a serpent. Joseph of Arimathaea plunged his staff into the ground, and it grew into a tree. In Greece, Hermes' staff, in the form of a caduceus, heralded divine messages from the gods. The Egyptian Osiris used a staff in his position as judge of the dead.

The Staff is unique because it is symbolic and suggestive of performance by its stature and design alone. To convey its message, the staff does not have to be used, it only has to be present. It remains a symbol of skill in many traditional religions and mystical orders. Depending on its shape, size, and design, it distinguishes the neophyte from the adept.

The Staff should be made from a wood that is sacred to or held in high regard by your god. Its length should be the same as your height. The ground end should contain a piece of metal or stone that is associated with your god; the top should be phallic in shape. Color, markings, and decoration should be in keeping with your tradition and deity preference.

The Aspergillum and Censer

The aspergillum is used for purification, blessing, and dispelling of negativity. It is a small perforated globe that contains consecrated (holy) water. The aspergillum may also be made from sprigs of hyssop (which is traditional) or from your deity's favorite herb, plant, or tree. If made from a herb or tree branch, be sure there is enough greenery to retain water so the water may be sprinkled in a ritual manner. In our rituals, we use the aspergillum for blessing at the beginning of the benediction to all our rituals.

The Censer and Aspergillum

The censer is the vessel in which incense is burned in offering, prayer, and sacrifice to deity. It is usually made of brass, silver, or gold and has a chain or handle for carrying. The censer is used in traditions where incense carries the devotees' petitions to the gods or where it blesses and protects.

You will find a censer in church supply centers, New Age shops, and import stores. If possible, especially if you are starting out, purchase new tools and ritual items. It is much easier to cleanse a new object than something that has had years of negative vibrational buildup. Take the time, spend the money, and buy good tools the first time.

God and Goddess Statues

To emphasize your religious intentions, an image of your deity commands respect and consideration. A statue of the god and goddess on the altar emphasizes their presence and sovereignty—reasons why, throughout history, humanity has repeatedly fashioned images of gods. Humans want to physically behold their gods' glory.

A statue of your deity helps intensify invocations, personal petitions, and ritual. When you regularly perform acts of devotion before the statue, the raised energy is absorbed and compounded. Over time, the statue literally illuminates the area or room where it is kept. This illumination or energy accentuates the presence of the god or goddess and heightens the ritual experience.

When statues of gods and goddesses are displayed, they fascinate, enchant, and compel attention. These feelings are especially true when the image has been expertly sculptured with attention to detail. I have seen statues in museums that actually looked as if they were breathing.

Statues are wonderful symbols of deity as they physically represent archetypal energies. They come to us from the past and bring new meaning and purpose to the present. When images of the divine, along with their sacred tools, are incorporated into ritual, they elicit a change in consciousness. This transition from the secular to the spiritual is the objective of all religious philosophies. Visual aids and tools make the process easier.

There are many ways to work with statues of deity to develop their ability to absorb energy. By placing stones, herbs, and totems inside the statue itself, you increase the attraction of a specific energy. Draping the image with corresponding colored scarves and jewelry enhances its physical presence. The ritual washing and perfuming, along with the offering of candles, incense, and foods, seem to bring the image to life. These physical actions show love and respect to the god or goddess the statue represents.

We realize that the statue is not the god or goddess, but a representation of their being. However, like the Vessel of Creation, the image of the deity can become a container for their energy. Once this happens, devotion during worship or invocation will bring forth their presence.

The Rite of Consecration

The following simple ceremony allows you to remove negative thoughts and vibrations that might be attached to your tools. In the process, you will energize your tools with your positive feelings.

You will need your altar covered with a white cloth, two white candles, sandalwood incense and censer with a lighted charcoal in it, a small bowl of salt, a small bowl of water, and your tools.

1. Light the altar candles (right first, then left) as you say the following:

   Let now the Lord and Lady of Life and Light be with me, guide me, and bless me this night.

2. Sprinkle some incense on the lighted coals. Pick up a tool, hold it in offering, and sprinkle salt and water over it in blessing as you say:

   Let all negative thoughts and vibrations be driven from this tool. Let all impurities and unholy thoughts be cast forth. Let only my desires remain within from this moment on. So shall it be done in the name of the Lord and Lady.

   Repeat this step for each tool.

3. Begin with your Athame (followed by each of the tools), hold it high in salute, then consecrate it with each of the four elements: pass it through the flame of the candle; the smoke of the incense; sprinkle some salt on it; sprinkle some water on it. For each tool, say the following (inserting the name of your god and goddess):

   By the power of the Lady _____
   And by the power of the Lord _____
   Do I bless and consecrate thee
   Unto the path of righteousness
   For all that brings life and light
   Now and forever, so mote it be!

4. Once you have blessed all the tools, take a few moments and, in your own words, thank the god and goddess. Ask them for their blessings on all you do.

Synopsis

Symbols, statues, and tools are visual aids that enhance and accentuate the different aspects of your spiritual work. Whether you are meditating, praying, or performing a special ritual, these objects create atmosphere, aid in concentration, and focus energy. Religious statues and symbols make contact with deity and changes of consciousness easy to accomplish; this is why they have been used throughout the centuries.

For personal reflection, the most significant expressions of deity are the Vessel of Creation and the Rod of Authority. With proper use, these tools become more than just symbols; they empower you with the ability to communicate directly with your god or goddess. They are the repositories of the dynamic energy you channel from divinity and, therefore, provide the substance of your spiritual intention. With them, you can travel to the heavenly spheres and retrieve the knowledge, wisdom, and understanding available only to those of vision.

For those who have an aversion to idols, the Vessel of Creation and Rod of Authority will provide the necessary god and goddess symbolism needed for any ritual. Candles are another way to represent these two forces, using a black one for the goddess and a white one for the god. I have also seen people use a shell for the goddess and a stone for the god.

The only real requirement is that whatever you choose to represent the deity should be consistent. If you constantly change the object, divine energy has no substantial place to reside. The idea is to establish a permanent home for the god and goddess so they are always with you.

ENDNOTE

1. The oracles of the ancients were used for different purposes. The oracles were a tool for divination, personal counseling, and a contact point between humans and divinity. Prior to Christianity, the oracles were the providence of women and the priestesses who guarded them.

CHAPTER 14

The Oracle as a Voice of Truth and Wisdom

To see clearly is poetry, prophecy, and religion, all in one.
John Ruskin (1819–1900)

A Conversation with Deity

The lure of the unknown and the lore of hidden things have long intrigued humanity. Along with skills such as fashioning flint spearheads and making clay vessels, primitive humans developed more subtle crafts, such as forecasting weather by the way the wind blew or predicting death from the patterns of birds. Many of the techniques, such as meteorology, used by scientists today evolved from these simple beginnings.

At some point, everyone has wondered what the future holds for them. Speculating about the future seems to be a characteristic of human nature, as we are the only creatures who modify our behavior on the basis of potential outcome. Because of our need to speculate, divination has become a principal means of arriving at choice without the uncertainty of chance.

The meaning of the word explains much about why we are fascinated with divination. *Divination* literally means gift from the divine. Divination is information received from god; the ability to receive such information is acquired by one's own initiative and link with deity.

Psychoanalyst Carl Jung believed that divination was an effective tool for the maintenance of mental health. He developed this theory by showing that apparently unrelated events could trigger unconscious experiences and images leading to expanded awareness. He also recognized that symbols could be used to form a type of visual language for understanding and communicating with other levels of consciousness. This ability to increase comprehension, realize advanced concepts, and acquire information from higher sources is reason enough to learn some form of divination.

One of the most important aspects of divination or religious prophecy is that it helps eliminate the fears that motivate people. Most people act and react to things that are of little consequence because they fear what others will think. They also harbor phobias about death, illness, and all sorts of trivia. Most of these anxieties stem from trying to live according to society's standards, rather than in harmony with divine wisdom.

When oracles[1] are properly consulted regarding spiritual needs, they provide the guidelines for living a balanced and productive life. Oracles divine which influences are favorable and which are apt to cause trouble. In a short time, they can help eliminate all sorts of personal fears through their positive predictive qualities. Individuals gain confidence because they know they have access to resources that will aid them in problem solving.

The idea of having an oracle directly linked to deity was one of the things I found attractive about the Ifa and Santeria religions. Their religious tradition included a system of communication between humans and gods for the retrieval of divine information. At some point during every Santerian ritual, divination is performed to question the gods in relation to the ceremony as well as to ask for spiritual guidance. Because divination was, and still is, essential to their religion, direct contact with deity has always been a part of their belief system. In my opinion, the ability to communicate with the gods or goddesses one worships is an essential part of any religion.

When developing Co-Creation Spirituality, it seemed reasonable to incorporate a system of divination into the religion's basic framework. In this way, contact with a deity would become an intrinsic part of the system, creating a continual line of communication between the worshipers and their gods. As worshipers used these lines of communication, the connection with a deity would become strong and secure, providing the practitioners with sources of spiritual information.

Just as Co-Creation Spirituality is a fresh approach to traditional religious theory, so is the oracle within the Vessel of Creation a modern approach to established prophecy. All that was needed to create this new procedure was a logical order of symbolism that could be built into the system from the start—a system that would harmonize directly with a deity and include a set of definitions to allow for interpretation. The oracle evolved as a set number of Speaking Stones that are read in relation to the four elements.

The concept of incorporating a system of divination into the Co-Creation process worked, as did the oracle itself. Once the oracle was activated, it functioned like a magnet, attracting the forces it represented into itself. The reason for its success was attributed to the numerical precision of the stones, the elemental disposition of their placement, and the symbolic alignment of the oracle with a deity.

Since divination, by nature, is a feminine and intuitive function, the oracle was predetermined to align with the sovereignty of a goddess. To protect and preserve the magnetism of the oracle, it was designed to fit inside the goddess' sacred Vessel of Creation. By making the oracle part of this feminine religious object, it assimilates the goddess' potential and energy. The oracle becomes a connection between the believer and his or her goddess.

The following instructions explain how to make your own oracle and set of Speaking Stones. The necessary items are easily obtained and the process of making the oracle is simple. Once you have decided upon your goddess and obtained her Vessel, the rest will fall into place.

The Oracle

To make your own set of Speaking Stones you will need nine reasonably flat stones of equal size. These stones should be in the primary color attributed to the goddess with whom you are working. For example, I am working with Ishtar and green is her principal color. I chose the stone adventurine. Other examples are black onyx for Hecate and blue lace agate for Isis.

The Oracle

Take the time to hold the nine stones and feel their energy. Make sure no imperfections such as cracks or chips exist. When you are comfortable with your choice of stones, number them from one to nine. Etch or paint a number on one side of each stone; leave the other side plain.

Next, mark your Key Stones (see Chapter 13) in the same manner as you did the Speaking Stones. Paint or engrave a circle on one side of the round flat stones to designate its face or key side.

When your set of stones is completed, wrap them in the Oracle Reading Cloth (again, see Chapter 13) and place it in the Vessel of Creation. The Vessel of Creation is now complete and your oracle is ready to use. Because the Vessel is a spiritual tool, bless and consecrate it as you would any other sacred object. The Benediction (Blessing) in Chapter 18 was intended for this purpose; however, you may use any blessing or consecration ritual you feel is appropriate.

Using the Oracle

In ancient Greece, before the priestess of Apollo attempted to receive wisdom from the Oracle of Delphi, she fasted, bathed in cleansing waters, and performed special prayers and rites. The fasting and cleaning with water were done to purify the body, and the prayers opened the way for the priestess to receive divine inspiration and wisdom.

Today, with all our technology, social pressures, and general rushing around, proper preparation for spiritual working is especially necessary. If one truly wishes to commune with the higher forces of the universe, the mind and body must be calm. When individuals are relaxed, they become sympathetic to the subtle vibrations that emanate from the deity during divination. A simple bath and meditation[2] will enhance personal sensitivity and susceptibility to divine revelation.

The Interpretation of the Oracle

The following definitions apply to the nine numbered stones. Toss the Speaking Stones onto the Reading Cloth. Add those numbers facing up until a single digit number is attained. This single digit number is considered the primary statement the oracle is rendering.

For example, if a 6, 2, and 4 are face up, add these numbers together and you get the number 12. Add the digits 1 and 2 together to form the single digit 3. The number 3 would be the definition you would consult.

The Meaning of the Numbers on the Stones

1. The qualities of the number one vibration are creativity, new beginnings, freedom, self-motivation, and faith in oneself. Now is the time to become more self-motivated, set your sights on your goal, and begin to work toward it.

2. The qualities of the number two vibration are contrast, balance, duality, diversity, and the quiet side of judgment. Look for contrast; see what is needed and what can be eliminated from your actions. Look at both sides of issues and make judgments accordingly.

3. The qualities of the number three vibration are harmony, arbitration, self-expression, and favorable conditions. Three is also the number of resolve, as it takes two to create an argument and one to arbitrate the situation. Through truly seeing and listening, you will come to a place of peace within. Try to maintain this level of inner harmony.

4. The qualities of the number four vibration are unity, endurance, steadiness, effort, and reward for work well done. Four is the first building block of stability. As you progress toward your goal, set a firm foundation. Take your time and do the job well; what is earned is valued.

5. The qualities of the number five vibration are independence, self-indulgence, excess, and the inability to make correct decisions. Five represents the selfish, I-deserve-more side of the personality. Independence is good if kept in perspective.

6. The qualities of the number six vibration are strength, wisdom, courage, accomplishment, and the ability to face challenge. Here is the vibration of the ability to meet life at face value. You have been through a lot and because of this earned personal power that is an accomplishment in itself. Achievement and success are on the horizon.

7. The qualities of the number seven vibration are knowledge, study, talent, imagination, and mystery. Seven is the mystery number and represents the hidden side

of nature. However, through study comes the knowledge that will help you seek out and unlock hidden doors.

8. The qualities of the number eight vibration are success, prosperity through expansion, materialism, and determination. The number eight is another form of stability, but in completion rather than origin. A foundation well laid will always produce success and prosperity.

9. The qualities of the number nine vibration are completion, fulfillment, spirituality, and deep understanding of the nature of things. With the material world in control, the time has come to seek spiritual fulfillment. Learn to work with and understand the real you and the nature of the world you live in. Money and material goods only buy distractions, not true happiness and self-respect.

Interpretation of the Stones in Conjunction with the Elements

After the primary statement has been determined, observe where the stones landed on the Reading Cloth. Their placement will constitute the second part of the reading, which provides insight into possible problem areas within your nature or present situation. As the stones fall, they will land within the scope of one or more of the elements on your Reading Cloth. By combining the meaning of the stone or stones with that of the element, you will be able to pinpoint trouble areas.

For example, you may be exerting too much fire and not enough water, or there may be a need for more air and less earth at this time. By finding out what is needed and what is not, you can balance your energies with those of the natural world around you.

To determine the meaning of the stones in combination with the elements in which they landed, add up the number stones, as you did before, and reduce them into a one digit number. The difference here is you only add them according to the element in which they are positioned.

For example: If you have a 3, 9, and 1 in the element of Air, add these together and you get number 13. Add the 1 and 3 together to form the single digit 4. The number 4 in Air would be the definition you would consult.

If only one stone is in the element, use that number. Element sections with no stones or stones with their blank side up are not read as they are silent and do not affect your life at this time.

The definitions of the Speaking Stones and the four elements follow.

The Element of Air is intellect, the ability to think and be creative; it deals with the realm of the spirit. Stones that land in this element express the fact that there is a need for more thinking and less physical activity. It could also mean there is too much "spacing out" and there is a need to ground at this time. The following meanings apply.

1 in Air: Time to be more creative and have faith in yourself. With effort and thought, you can do it. Clear thinking is crucial at this time of new beginnings.

2 in Air: Balance is needed; there should be equal time spent on spiritual as well as mundane activities. Action should follow thought or there will be no manifestation of desire.

3 in Air: Harmony prevails. Whatever you are doing at this time is in accordance with your ability and should be accepted as such.

4 in Air: Endurance is needed at this time. Also, a joyful attitude will bring reward. Remain steadfast and positive. Do not try so hard that you stagnate, but continue with calm reserve.

5 in Air: Excessive thinking and rationalization of the issues will bring failure. At this time, too much confusion to make a sound judgment exists. Stand back and give yourself room to think.

6 in Air: The challenge before you will take strength and courage. Use wisdom rather than emotion. Carefully weigh your options.

7 in Air: More knowledge of the subject is needed at this time. Use your imagination—it is the key to unlocking the mystery before you.

8 in Air: Through determination, you will be successful. Do not allow others to talk you out of what you know is right and what you know will work. Listen with discernment.

9 in Air: Completion and fulfillment of spiritual desires flow through you at this time. Look within and realize how your intentions affect your objective.

The Element of Fire is what motivates us on the material plane. It is energy, personal power, and aggression. It deals with survival in a primitive sense. Stones that land in this element are telling us to look at how we are reacting to the situation at hand. Are we using too much force? Being too aggressive? Are we allowing others to dominate us? The following meanings apply.

1 in Fire: Now is the time to put creative ideas into action. Take a firm stand and do not allow others to manipulate your opinions. Stand firm in your convictions.

2 in Fire: Balance is needed. This is not the time to start an argument or attempt to push others into action. Think before you act and temper your actions with wisdom.

3 in Fire: Conditions are favorable at this time. You are in control of your emotions and in harmony with the elements. Share your warmth, energy, and feelings of security with others.

4 in Fire: Endurance has paid off and you are in a position of power. However, do not allow this to go to your head. Maintain your self-control and acknowledge a higher authority; reward will be yours.

5 in Fire: Self-indulgence and too much independence are negative and destructive. It is not wise to make important decisions when you are confused. Stop and think before you react.

6 in Fire: Whatever the task, you have the strength and power to overcome the obstacles put before you. If you control your temper, courage and determination will be your allies at this time.

7 in Fire: Temper the fires within by learning more about your objective. There are powers greater than yours and you must acknowledge this fact. Knowledge brings peace and freedom.

8 in Fire: Determination is an asset if it is tempered with wisdom at this time. Achievement of a goal is a wonderful thing as long as you do not have to compromise your values or spiritual development.

9 in Fire: Completion is close at hand. Keep your emotions and actions in control and never forget what it took to achieve your objective. Use your fire to spark other projects and ignite the spirit within.

The Element of Water expresses emotion and what you feel deep within. Emotions determine how you react to your environment and those around you. Temper your emotions with wisdom and thought rather than allowing the fire of survival to control them. Emotions are energy and can be your best friend or your worst nightmare. The following meanings apply.

1 in Water: Give birth to the seeds of your imagination. Allow others to share in your experience and, through this sharing, develop new and greater relationships.

2 in Water: Balance between your emotions and what you know is right is needed now. Caution should be used in relationships that are shaky at this time.

3 in Water: There is harmony between your mind and your emotions at this time. Avoid emotional behavior, and relationships built during this period of stability will flourish.

4 in Water: The effort you put toward controlling your emotions will pay off. There is a need to show more respect for friends, family, and coworkers at this time. Respect is a quality that is earned.

5 in Water: Your independence is showing to excess. Emotions are running high; decisions made during crisis and based on emotions never prove fruitful.

6 in Water: Strength and wisdom surround you; do not be afraid to allow others to help at this time. As you share your need, they will share their energy. Learn to ask when you need help.

7 in Water: The time has come to explore the hidden side of your personality. Go deep within and find out what is making you react this way. Make an effort to harmonize your thoughts, emotions, and actions.

8 in Water: Expansion always produces a reaction. As you progress, be sure to do so honorably. Temper your determination with wisdom and regard for others.

9 in Water: Completion and fulfillment are at hand. As long as you maintain control of your emotions, any partnerships or relationships entered into at this time will flourish.

The Element of Earth protects, provides for us, and nourishes us in times of need. The earth also represents responsibility and the capacity for personal achievement. The earth can bring you abundance if you are willing to heed her messages and learn her ways. Stones that land in Earth express the need for more physical effort. Simply put, if you want to be successful and accomplish your goals, now is the time to stop talking and start doing.

1 in Earth: The time has come to concentrate on the material world. Get your ideas out of your head and into physical form. Create something tangible at this time; do not rely on others to do it for you.

2 in Earth: Things are not always as they appear. Be careful, plan, and double-check everything you do. Lack of proper judgment at this time could result in failure. Do not rush into something that has not been properly established.

3 in Earth: Now is a good time to express yourself and give form to ideas. This is also a good time to form partnerships in business or purchase things needed for the manifestation of desire.

4 in Earth: Build and create on the physical plane. Unite with others of like mind to help make your dreams come true. Now is the time to work hard, in a physical sense, toward your goal.

5 in Earth: Excess at this time will result in failure in your projects. If you indulge and give in to your impulses, there will be loss both in a monetary as well as physical sense. Curb your independence and seek guidance from others with more experience.

6 in Earth: Meet the challenge head on; you have the strength and the courage to make things happen at this time. However, only you, through your own effort, can produce the results you want. If you want it done right, do it yourself.

7 in Earth: Put down the hammer and pick up the book. Be sure you know how to do what it is you are trying to do before you begin. There is no substitute for knowledge; study and use your imagination and the project will flourish.

8 in Earth: Now that you have succeeded in your goal, assume responsibility for it. See things through to the end and hold on to what you have gained. Success and prosperity are yours.

9 in Earth: Completion. Feel the exhilaration and celebrate a job well done. Thank those who have helped and give recognition where it is deserved. Enjoy what you have accomplished but do not feel this is the end. Now is the time for reward and beginning again.

Definitions for the Four Key Stones

The four flat stones with a painted circle on one side are used for yes and no answers only. These are used apart from the Speaking Stones but in conjunction with your oracle reading as a whole. If you have asked a question about a situation and want a simple yes or no answer after your interpretation of the oracle itself, then cast your Key Stones.

To cast the Key Stones, put aside the other stones and turn your Reading Cloth over. Hold the four key stones in your hand and formulate your question so it could be answered yes or no. Toss the stones onto the cloth and interpret them as follows:

Four Circles Up
The situation is fixed. The answer is positively yes.

Three Circles Up
Things look good, but may change; the answer is favorable and will tend to stay so.

Two Circles Up
Maybe yes, Maybe no; ask again.

One Circle Up
Things do not look good at this time. This is not a good time to make any move. Conditions are not favorable at this time.

Four Blank Sides Up
The answer is definitely no; all conditions are unfavorable at this time.

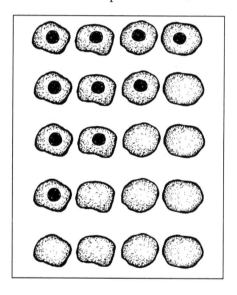

Use of the Totem in the Oracle

The totem you choose should personify the archetypal force of the goddess whom the vessel represents. In this way, it can be used to delineate or target related energy patterns that may hinder or enhance the reading.

For my totem, I chose a small replica of a full-grown lion, which is sacred to Ishtar. In antiquity, the lion was associated with fertility and wisdom because of its intractable power. Symbolically, the lion represents light, strength, and courage—qualities displayed by the goddess herself.

It is easy to use the totem in conjunction with the oracle. Just before you do a reading, spread out the Reading Cloth and ask, "What vibrations surround me at this time?" Toss the totem onto the Reading Cloth and note which element it lands on. The placement will reveal which element is dominant and should be given extra consideration.

For example, if my totem, which represents courage and power, were to land on fire, the goddess might be trying to tell me to use less force or have more courage, depending on what the oracle itself had to say.

Synopsis

To some people, the world is a complex and disconcerting place. One of the reasons for this confusion is due to being out of touch with the rhythms of life and the higher spiritual self. Another reason for the trepidation is our technology, which propagates the illusion of being in control when we are truly at the mercy of the unexpected.

However, for those who are willing to extend themselves beyond the bounds of mediocrity, divination provides the tools that will help them navigate through the storms of uncertainty.

A perfect example was a reading I did prior to making some dramatic changes in our ritual format. I wanted to know if it was the right time and a good idea to make the changes. My concern was justifiable because, to the inexperienced or ignorant, the similarity between the ritual additions and various parts of the Christian Mass might be construed as identical. In reality, however, they were only modernizations and modifications of ancient Mithraic and Orphic Rites. The answer I received came from a point of authority and was not predisposed to personal interpretation.[3] This lack of predisposition is a principal reason why the oracle is such a useful tool; deviation is difficult when only specific commentary is rendered. I will share my query and response as an example of how the oracle works.

First, I asked my question: Is it wise to make changes in the rituals at this time? I held the Speaking Stones and concentrated on the question. After a moment, I tossed them onto the Reading Cloth; 7, 2, and 1 were face up. After adding them together, I reduced them to a single digit of 1 ($7 + 2 + 1 = 10; 1 + 0 = 1$).

The number 1 relates to creativity and new beginnings. It also stresses setting goals and working toward them. The answer to my question was both positive and motivating; it seemed that now was a good time to add new material to the rituals.

The next step was to read those stones in conjunction with the elements for more insight into the situation. The 7 was in Air (this suggested I should be sure I had all my facts straight and that with right imagination these new rituals would unlock new mysteries); 2 was in Fire (it warned me not to be pushy about the new material but rather to temper my enthusiasm with wisdom); and 1 was in Water (it reaffirmed my decision by telling me that I should give birth to the seeds of my imagination and share the results with others).

Finally, I turned the Reading Cloth over. I asked, "Will the new material work?" and tossed the Key Stones. All four marked stones were facing up, meaning yes.

We all suffer moments of doubt and wonder if others will accept what we are about to do. Many times, this self-doubt keeps us from doing what we should and what will enhance our lives. By having a tool such as the oracle, we can eliminate many of the fears we face and begin doing instead of just wishing.

I am glad I did the reading and added the new ritual material. The final results were positive and generated better rituals for our church services. Everyone loves the additions and cannot imagine ritual without them.

ENDNOTES

1. Oracle (Greek) is any person or thing that serves as an agent of divine communication.

2. Meditation is any soothing and relaxing exercise. One type of meditation is mentioned in Chapter 15.

3. Personal interpretation is common with other less rigid definitions. For example, when reading Tarot cards, each card has many different sets of symbols and can be interpreted in several different ways. With short set definitions, as in the oracle, the ability to read in personal desire is limited.

CHAPTER 15

Harmony and the Elements of Nature

Nature, as a whole and in all its elements, enunciates something that may be regarded as an indirect self-communication of God to all those ready to receive it.

Martin Buber, *At the Turning*

Elemental Theory

The world we live in is a combination of many forces, working together to maintain life. These forces are comprised of both physical (chemical) and metaphysical (spiritual) elements, which are fundamental to the creation process and essential for supporting life as we know it. We need to understand these principal forces if we are to understand ourselves, the universe, and the dynamic energy that controls it.

The principal forces are the four elements of Air, Fire, Water, and Earth. These elements are responsible for the structure of this world and other basic phenomena. In general, most Wiccan, Pagan, and metaphysical philosophies consider these elements to be symbolic representations of potential energy that radiates from a deity as well as from various archetypal sources.

Our ancestors, who were responsible for creating and developing the early magical-religion systems, considered these natural constituents to be a power unto themselves as well as an emanation from deity. Early people sensed that alignment with these natural forces would render most gods and goddesses vulnerable to human's needs and desires. As a result, humanity devised different ways to use the surroundings in the honor and worship of deity.

Humanity first enlisted nature's powers through hunting rituals. These rituals employed a horned god (whose nature was in harmony with the animals) for assistance during the hunt. By acting out the hunt in front of a drawing or image of the god, early people thought the god would take notice and protect the men from danger as well as provide them with a successful hunt.

Another way of awakening the gods to humans' needs was through the powers of early fertility rites. Through the sexual act performed during ritual, the atmosphere was stimulated with human energy. This energy would in turn motivate the gods to quicken the propagation of the herd or increase the harvest yield.

Generally, most people will agree on the existence of the four primordial elements, even though today we know many more make up the world of matter. Philosophically and symbolically, the four elements—Air, Fire, Water, and Earth—remain the primary focus of power and energy in most New Age and magical religious systems. These elements are believed to be universal principles, which when understood, controlled, and arranged in a certain way, help the individual devise a more perfect reality.

Co-Creation Spirituality, like many traditions, endorses the importance and employment of the basic primary energies of life; we also know it is necessary to learn about them. These energies or elements affect the way we think, feel, and behave; they are indispensable to the creative processes. The understanding of nature, environment, and self is a prerequisite to the understanding of spirit and deity.

The elements are essential building blocks of nature and create a framework in which to define energy, emotion, and expression. The use of these forces is paramount in creating a spiritual system in which you can function and work to your greatest potential.

Learning about the elements and the areas of your life they control are important steps in your spiritual development. Once you begin to harmonize with these magical forces of nature, you become aware of their knowledge and wisdom. The insight you gain from interacting with the elements will help balance your thinking and emotions. This balancing is important because spiritual focus is difficult if you are overwhelmed with passion, inflamed with anger, or given to flights of fancy.

Almost everything we come in contact with is associated with the elements. The elements correspond to the seasons; different times of the day and night; and even plants, stones, and places. Astrologically, the elements provide the data to understand personality types and modes of expression. Without a doubt, the elements are one of nature's greatest contributions. They are a wondrous storehouse of knowledge waiting to be explored.

Understanding the Principles of Nature

The Element of Air

Air is a subtle material realm between the physical and spiritual plane. Air speaks to the intellect and brings forth the true essence of the individual through the creative imagination. The element of Air represents new beginnings, the thought process, and creativity.

Air has always been associated with breath, which is synonymous with the spirit or soul of all living creatures. The idea of Air or breath giving life to the soul or spirit dates back to the time of matriarchal rule. After giving birth, the mother would gently breathe[1] into her child's mouth, initiating the breathing process. In Greece, the female Air soul was Pneuma (meaning breath), or the Muse who always brought inspiration, giving poets and seers the power of understanding.

Breathing is paramount to life itself. Breath enters our bodies at birth and withdraws at death. Many have believed that the soul or spirit leaves the body at death on the person's breath. For this reason, in the past, mirrors were held close to the mouth of a dying person in hopes of capturing his or her soul in the mirror. This belief was echoed in folklore that spoke of mirrors as soul traps and the realm of the dead as the Hall of Mirrors.

Air is the bridge between spiritual inspiration and the conscious projection of ideas. Fresh, clean Air is exhilarating; it is movement; it inspires creativity. Air is feminine and innovation; it is the ability to conceive of new ways of doing things. Air is the tie that binds us together through conversation, intellectual sharing, and the endless seeking of knowledge.

Air and Personality Qualities

Aquarius, Gemini, and Libra are the three astrological Air signs.

The principal concern of Air people is communication. People with a predominance of Air think, communicate, analyze, and theorize. They love freedom and truth and have a strong sense of justice and fair play. Air people can change circumstances with amazing speed; like cats, they usually land on their feet.

Air people's devotion to abstract ideas and the hard time they have making commitments can make them seem elusive as well as exasperating at times.

Air people are thinkers. They rely on rationality rather than intuition or emotion to explore a situation. Their philosophical approach to matters allows them to endure hardships that others could not. They can tolerate almost any circumstance as long as there is a rational explanation for it.

Those of the Air element have great leadership capabilities and make good judges and crusaders for social issues. They have a reputation for being fair; they expect everyone to follow the same standards as they do. They cannot understand why everyone does not think and act as they do.

Air becomes a negative influence when it tries to rationalize mistakes that should be seen as learning experiences. Air people who cannot cope with reality have a tendency to live in a fairy tale world of their own creation.

Spiritual Considerations for Air

Spiritually, Air comes from the East on the wings of the Archangel Raphael, whose name means Healer of God. One of this magnificent creature's abilities is to heal both the physical body and the spirit. Raphael is usually depicted with a bow and arrow and a crystal vial of healing balm.

Air Correspondences

Colors	Blue, silver, white, gray
Symbols	Circle, bird, bell, sylph, flute, chimes, clouds
Tools	Wand, rod, staff
Plants	Almond, broom, clover, eyebright, lavender, pine
Stones	Amethyst, sapphire, citrine, azurite
Places	Sky, mountain tops, treetops, bluffs, airplanes
Zodiac	Aquarius, Gemini, Libra
Archangel	Raphael
Times	Spring, dawn
Direction	East
Process	Thinking, reading, speaking, praying, singing

Air Meditation

Air is an important element and one that needs to be experienced. Working with Air can lift your spirits and bring forth creative ideas. The best way to align with Air is by working with it in meditation. The meditation I have used for years, and which I have found to work exceedingly well, is outlined below. Work with this meditation on a regular basis; it will help you connect with the element on a personal level.

Choose a symbol or object from the list of Air correspondences and make yourself comfortable and relaxed. Hold the object and focus your attention on it. Use your breath to control your thoughts. Breathe in to a count of five; then exhale to a count of five. Do this breathing several times until your concentration is fixed upon the object.

Feel the object become light, so light it could float. Because you are holding it, you too are so light you can float.

Feel yourself floating upward toward the blue sky; you drift like a feather in the wind. Feel the sun and fresh Air upon your face as you float higher and higher; upward into the clear blue sky. As you soar above the ground, feel yourself being totally free and able to do anything you wish.

While you are in this state, look around. What do you see? How do you feel? What thoughts present themselves? Keep floating, feeling free and able to do as you wish.

During this time, original ideas will come to you. Remember these ideas, as they represent your higher consciousness and its creative ability. These are the thoughts and ideas you should work on. These thoughts and ideas are the things that you, the real you, want to do, create, and complete.

Take your new thoughts and ideas with you as you begin to descend. Slowly float downward until your feet touch the earth, and you begin to feel the weight of your body. You are now totally in touch with reality and have the knowledge of your Air journey to help guide you toward your desired goal.

The Element of Fire

Fire is transformation; it is the life-giving generative powers of the sun. Fire is emblematic of the masculine deity in many cultures and is the element of fervent intensity, aspiration, and personal power. Fire is the force that motivates and drives all living organisms. Fire, along with Air, creates energy, gets us going, and provides stamina. It has been said that what the mind can imagine (Air), the will (Fire) can create. Fire is bright, brilliant, and flamboyant. Unfortunately, it is neither stable nor logical. Fire leaps intuitively to grasp the moment with little regard for what is around it. Fire is reckless, seeking, and passionate; it knows only itself. Fire is unique because in order for it to create, it must first consume or destroy. For example, in a forest fire, the Fire burns, consumes, and destroys the trees and underbrush. In time, however, new plants will grow. Fire is the active element within us. Fire pushes toward the new by getting rid of the old.

To use Fire constructively, you must first contain it. When you contain Fire, you can direct its energy toward a desired purpose, such as heat or light. You can also direct it with the personal forces it dominates, such as passion, anger, and aggression. When you control these emotions and channel their energy in a positive way, they bring about beneficial reconstruction. When these feelings go unchecked, they bring destruction and create chaos—just like Fire.

Fire and Personality Qualities
The astrological signs for Fire are Aries, Leo, and Sagittarius.

The best way to describe a Fire person is to say that he or she is the essence of passion. *Passion* here does not mean sexual desire, but rather all-powerful emotions. Most Fire people have intense appetites for living life to the fullest. They experience love, hate, anger, enthusiasm, desire, pain, and death with extreme intensity.

To Fire people, everything is intense; when nothing is happening, they will create something—even if what they create causes trouble for them. They seek passion and are willing to suffer for it in order to avoid boredom.

The mind of the Fire person is quick and active; most people find them attractive if not a little dangerous at times. They seem to attract people just as the Fire in the hearth attracts people on a cold day. With an emphasis on adventure and a vivid experience, the Fire person often hurts others in the process. They are so blinded by their own desires they respond without consideration for those around them.

Fire people are quick to fly into a rage when angry and just as quick to forget about it. These emotions cause problems because Fire people cannot understand why others are still hurt and brooding once the anger has passed. Those with much Fire tend to get involved quickly but may lack the staying power of the other elements. Fire lives for the moment with passion and brilliance.

Spiritual Considerations for Fire

Michael, the supreme commander of the armies of Light, spiritually brings us Fire. This illuminating agent of Divine Light, whose name means Perfect of God, is the guardian of the southern quarter. He is visualized as a Roman soldier, dressed in red and gold and ready to battle evil.

Fire Correspondences

Colors	Red, red-orange (as in flames), amber
Symbols	Triangle, lightning, flame, salamander
Tools	Sword, dagger, fire pot, double-headed ax
Plants	Basil, blood root, dragon's blood, ginger, orange, tobacco
Stones	Ruby, garnet, diamond, bloodstone, flint, topaz, sunstone
Places	Volcanoes, ovens, fireplaces, deserts
Zodiac	Aries, Leo, Sagittarius
Archangel	Michael
Times	Summer, noon
Direction	South
Process	Passion, anger, quick, active, energy, power

Fire Meditation

Fire is one of the elements everyone needs to learn to control in his or her life. Fire can be a blessing or a curse, depending on how you project the Fire aspect of your personality. If you have too much Fire, you can tone it down and get control of it. On the other hand, if you have too little Fire, work toward rekindling the spark within.

The following meditation will help to get you acquainted with your Fire element so you can learn to work with it in a productive manner.

Choose a symbol or object from the list of Fire correspondences and make yourself comfortable and relaxed. Hold the object and focus your attention on it. Use your breath to control your thoughts. Breathe in to a count of five; then exhale to a count of five. Do this breathing several times until your concentration is fixed upon the object.

As you hold onto the object, feel yourself growing hot; feel the heat and energy of the Fire element flowing through your body. Feel yourself totally engulfed in flames, yet not harmed in any way. You are all-powerful; you have the energy and ability to accomplish anything you wish. You are strong, forceful, and filled with energy. Point your fingers and see flames shoot from their tips. See these flames turn into energy and power; power that allows you to move things without touching them. See the pure energy of life being projected from the tips of your fingers.

See yourself doing things. Make things happen through your personal power and energy. You are as the flame—hot and powerful—and you can do what you set out to do. You burn with passion and power and will accomplish your goals. Allow this impression of your ability to achieve to be burned into your consciousness.

Slowly feel the warmth begin to cool. Slowly come back to reality while retaining that sense of personal power; that knowledge of your ability to manifest your desires.

The Element of Water

Water is passive and receptive. It has long been seen as the source of all potentialities in existence, and has long been associated with the Great Mother, the universal womb, birth, and fertility. Water is emblematic of the universe's life-giving and life-destroying abilities. Water is used to cleanse or purify physically as well as psychically.

Where Air is the intellect and Fire the energy or drive, Water is the emotional response to situations. Fluid, responsive, and giving, Water is sensitivity and emotion. Water is like the Great Mother and, when heated by the Fire god's passion, life is brought forth. When cooled by the midnight air, silence and death are eminent. Many religions use immersion in Water to symbolize the return to a primordial state of purity. In essence, the baptism or dunking of an individual in Water signifies death and rebirth of both body and spirit.

The element of Water is both detached and willful as it flows freely. However, there are times when Water will allow itself to be contained. Water is a gentle element, and it inspires intuition and the desire to worship. The element of Water is truly linked to and part of the goddess within all of us. Water is remembering the past and foreseeing the future. As Water brings life, it can also bring destruction; the key is in governing its energy.

Water and Personality Qualities

The astrological signs for Water are Cancer, Scorpio, and Pisces.

Water people are sensitive—they sense the feelings of others; they are in tune with and aware of their surroundings on an emotional level. The Water person seems to sense the vibration of the universe and the mythic meaning behind reality.

Water people seem to live in a spiritual world where everything can become sacred if so desired. They become involved with other people and are prone to nurture, tend, help, and heal with little effort. They can be tremendously protective and loving of the world around them; sometimes they find it hard to draw a line between those things they should care about and those they should leave alone.

The major problem of the Water person is their sensitivity. As with anything, if the Water person's sensitivity is not balanced by other energies, he or she becomes hypersensitive to the world. Some Water people break under the stress of feeling too much. Sometimes, if they cannot control their sensitivity, they seek escape through drugs, alcohol, or other addictions. This lack of control also leads to holding grudges. Water can flow with love, bringing green pastures in its wake; or it can gouge and erode the landscape through flooding until nothing is left.

A strong spiritual system can make the difference in the Water person's outlook and in his or her dealings with others on firm ground. A good system provides support and allows for creativity; it also acts as a channel for his or her emotions.

Spiritual Considerations for Water

Gabriel is the Archangel of the West and the spiritual aspect of Water. He is destined to sound the last trumpet. Gabriel, like Water, is fertility in all its forms. His role is that of initiator of physical life, and he is pictured holding the Grail as he emerges from the sea of immortality.

Water Correspondences

Colors	Green, turquoise
Symbols	Crescent, shells, boats, ship wheel, anchor, cup
Tools	Vessel, grail, chalice, cauldron
Plants	Aloe, cucumber, dulse, gardenia, lily, lotus, willow
Stones	Aquamarine, chrysocolla, moonstone, mother-of-pearl
Places	Ocean, rivers, lakes, ponds, waterfalls, beaches
Zodiac	Cancer, Scorpio, Pisces
Archangel	Gabriel
Times	Autumn, sunset
Direction	West
Process	Love, nurture, sensitivity, psychic ability, healing

Water Meditation

Water is an important element and should not be overlooked because of its passivity. We all have feelings and emotions, and we need to keep them in perspective. Our emotions are of no use if they create hypersensitivity. On the other hand, they are of no use if we keep them in check to the point that they manifest in some sort of addiction. The key, as with all elements, is to create a balance within. The following meditation will help to balance your Water element.

Choose a symbol or object from the list of Water correspondences and make yourself comfortable and relaxed. Hold the object and focus your attention on it. Use your breath to control your thoughts. Breathe in to a count of five; then exhale to a count of five. Do this breathing several times until your concentration is fixed upon the object.

As you hold or look at your Water symbol, begin to feel cool, clear, fresh Water surrounding you. You are floating on top of the waves. It is restful and quiet; you can see the clear blue sky overhead. Slowly allow the Water to cover you; sink beneath the surface of the Water until you are completely immersed. Do not be afraid; like a fish, you are completely at home. Swim around under the surface of the Water. See the other fish, plants, and underwater growth. Feel the calmness and quiet. You are aware of everything around you, yet nothing can harm you or disturb your sense of peace. The Water absorbs your problems and negative thoughts; you feel a deep emotional security. You know that no matter what happens to you, the Water restores your vitality. It provides you with the rest you need to regenerate and reorganize your thoughts.

This is a time of total quiet, when you can reach deep inside and feel your total being. It is a time to learn how your emotions react; a time to get in touch with the real you. When in the Water, you are safe from the outside world; you can take the time to just be.

Slowly float to the surface. See the sky above as you emerge from the Water; feel the warmth of the sun and the cool breeze as it refreshes you. Remember how you felt while you were underwater. Take with you this feeling of total psychic and emotional cleanness and freshness. Know that when you begin to get emotional about something, you can wash this feeling away with the Water element. This knowledge will allow you to see things as they really are because they will not be clouded by negative emotions.

The Element of Earth

Earth has the vibrational frequency that forms a solid quality; Earth is passive in nature and negative in polarity. The Earth symbolically represents both the womb and the grave; that which brings life forth and that which takes it away or reclaims it. However, unlike Water, the Earth is stationary and does not actively create. The Earth is seen mystically as the final outcome. It provides the other three elements with a place to physically manifest a desire. Earth is our base of operation where we exhibit the final product of our imagination.

Earth is related to the flesh and all physical matter. It holds, nourishes, and affirms. Earth sees, touches, smells, senses, and feels; it is both sensual and practical. It can be stubborn as well as generous and has instinct rather than feelings for the cycles and seasons of time. Earth is slow, steady, and ever-changing while remaining the same.

Earth and Personality Qualities

Taurus, Virgo, and Capricorn are the three Earth signs; their essential quality is that of strength.

Most Earth people are practical and like organization. They are slow, steady, and solid in their efforts. Earth people have a strong sense of responsibility and see themselves as builders and defenders.

The Earth signs are concerned with reality and the constants of home, family, and work. Earth people are sensual and like things they can touch, feel, smell, and see and things they can buy or sell. They rarely get into fads or trends and tend to be conservative in their approach to life. Earth people are kind but also cautious. It can take years to win their trust and friendship, but once you have it, they are loyal forever. They seem to hold on to what they have with fierce determination.

Because Earth people are concerned with strength, they also are attracted to power. Those of the Earth need to be aware of their desires and not become entangled in power for power's sake. Power games, possessiveness, and manipulation are the negative side of the Earth personality, along with the tendency to assert authority and ownership. Like Water, Earth can forgive with little effort or hold a grudge for years, constantly exacting revenge.

Spiritual Considerations for Earth

Auriel is the Archangel for the element of Earth. He brings the awareness of the gods as manifested in the beauty of creation. In short, as we behold the wonders of nature, we are driven to consider the even greater splendor of the forces that originated it. This archangel operates at levels beyond physical sight and teaches a sense of cosmic rightness. Auriel bears a glowing lantern in his left hand and a pair of scales in his right.

Earth Correspondences

Colors	Yellow, brown, russet
Symbols	Square, cornucopia, spindle, scythe, salt
Tools	Shield, pentacle, flail, horn
Plants	Alfalfa, cotton, oats, patchouly, vetivert, wheat
Stones	Moss agate, jasper, malachite, peridot, tourmaline
Places	Caves, forests, fields, gardens, canyons
Zodiac	Capricorn, Taurus, Virgo
Archangel	Auriel
Times	Midnight, winter
Direction	North
Process	Responsible, practical, organized, steady, grounded

Earth Meditation

Earth represents the manifestation of desire. When the Earth element is under control, the individual can balance physical desires with mental and spiritual needs. Earth needs nourishment from the other elements in order to survive. However, if it were not for Earth, no place for the other elements would exist. People must organize their life in a responsible and practical way so they have time for their mundane as well as spiritual activities. For those who tend to be irresponsible and indecisive, meditating on Earth will help ground these tendencies. The reserved and stoic will find that working with the Earth element can be an adventure into unknown and enchanted territories. The following meditation will help you to balance your Earth element.

Choose a symbol or object from the list of Earth correspondences and make yourself comfortable and relaxed. Hold the object and focus your attention on it. Use your breath to control your thoughts. Breathe in to a count of five; then exhale to a count of five. Do this breathing several times until your concentration is fixed upon the object.

Hold and look at your Earth symbol. Visualize a cave set deep within the Earth. Enter the cave, allowing your eyes to adjust to the dark. Proceed deeper and deeper into the cave; downward, spiraling downward, ever deeper into the cave. Hear the trickle of the underwater stream that travels through the cave. Look at the cave walls. What do you see? How do you feel as you go deeper and deeper into the cave? What impressions about yourself do you get in connection with being in the cave?

Look up and see a tiny slit far above; see a shaft of light coming through to light the way, revealing the hidden depths of the cave. Look and see the crystals, different-shaped rocks, and the pale green moss that carpets the floor; everything has such beauty and elegance—the kind of beauty only Mother Nature creates.

Breathe deeply; feel the heavy, Earth-scented air enter your body, giving you strength and vitality that you did not have before. Feel the cave floor beneath you. Pick up a handful of the dark moist Earth; look at it, feel it, smell it; absorb its richness. Feel your connection to the Earth and know you are part of it. Allow the Earth's life-giving qualities to penetrate you, giving you strength and reassurance in your own abilities.

Be still; reflect on the cave and the protection it provides. Slowly begin your journey back. Before leaving, say a prayer to the Earth Mother. Thank her for this time of solitude and companionship. Take the security of the Earth energy with you.

Synopsis

No matter who you are or where you live, the elements in some way affect your life. The elements are everywhere; you cannot avoid their influence. However, there are ways to work with them so they balance within the mind and body. Reaching balance and a point of mental and physical equilibrium is necessary if you are going to create an effective spiritual system.

The simplest and most effective way of achieving balance in your life is by recognizing your dominant and passive elemental qualities. Have your astrological natal chart calculated and interpreted. The chart will also provide information on important personality qualities along with areas in which you will excel. The natal chart is a valuable mirror of your true self and can provide you with advice in all areas of your life.

Almost everything, including the elements, has two sides or aspects to its nature: the physical side and the spiritual side. Physically, the elements can balance the human body so it functions properly. From the spiritual standpoint, the elements can develop composure and bring harmony into our lives through acts of ritual worship. By inviting the higher octaves, or symbolic spiritual representations, of these natural forces to join with us in our rites, we are able to share their light and energy.

ENDNOTE

1. This act of gently breathing into the newborn's mouth was eventually replaced with the patriarchal slap on the buttocks to remove evil and sin.

CHAPTER 16

A Place for Prayer and Worship

The groves were God's first temples.
William Bryant, "A Forest Hymn"

People are coming to church not simply to partake of the sacred but to partake of sacred community.
Milton J. Rosenberg, *Pastoral Psychology*

The Domain of Deity

To our ancestors, who considered mythology an explanation of the workings of nature, all the world was a sanctuary. The gods were the creators and their homes on the earth symbolically revealed their power and presence. What were believed to be the gods' special homes on Earth became early sacred sites. Usually, these sites were areas where vortexes of natural energy existed, such as waterfalls, mountain tops, or underground caverns.

Sacred space has always been important when worshipping deity. Before urbanization, the land itself provided a host of natural sites. Springs and wells were favored locations for shrines to a goddess and were considered places for increasing fertility or curing illness. Trees were venerated as passageways for nature spirits that traveled between heaven and earth. Hills, plateaus, and mountains housed the mighty thunder gods who ruled above all.

As circumstance and necessity dictated, housing and fenced-in shelters became a requirement for survival. Constructed enclosures were essential for protection from dangerous animals, bad weather, and unfriendly humans. The family dwelling soon became a refuge as well as a sanctuary, providing a secure environment where physical and spiritual needs were met.

Before long, humans began to build houses for their gods as well as themselves. From the pyramids of Egypt to the monuments of Avebury, permanently constructed places of worship were an essential part of early culture and society. Because religion was an integral part of daily life, the temples were the focus of most activities, as they fulfilled both the social and spiritual needs of the community.

To the ancient people, the temple was the dwelling place of the god or goddess, represented therein by an invisible oracle, natural symbol, or lifelike statue. The size and quality of the monument was in direct proportion to the power and authority of its resident deity. Temples to state gods and goddesses employed hundreds of people to maintain their vast estates. Because of their size, many early temples became the main source of livelihood for the city or town in which they were located.

One of the most interesting qualities of these early religious centers was their physical placement. For the most part, temples and sacred monuments were aligned with the planetary correspondent or natural element of their resident deity. For example, a temple dedicated to a solar god would be arranged to reconcile with the rising sun; a temple to the moon goddess would be oriented toward lunar energy. If the deity enlisted the power of a natural phenomenon such as water, the temple or shrine would be located on or near a spring or well. This incorporation of the associated element or astrological correspondent into the physical structure was believed to attract and enhance the deity's energy.

Sacred space is just as important and necessary today as it was in our ancestor's time. Now, like then, sacred space provides a sanctuary or haven where communication with a deity is possible. Besides affording a place for peaceful reflection, the quality of sacred space makes a statement about the individual's or group's devotion to deity. Conviction, dedication, and commitment are needed to create and maintain the shrines, temples, and cathedrals that grace our land. If nothing else, mainstream religion has more than proved its high regard for deity through its splendid architecture. This is definitely something to be admired rather than rebuked.

Creating a Place for Prayer and Worship

Sacred space is an area or room set aside for the reverence and worship of deity and should be treated with great respect. Once created, the personal shrine will radiate the glory and sovereignty of the god or goddess whose house it has become. In time, just like the great cathedrals, the area of worship will become filled with energy. When this happens, you only need to come within range of the area to feel the power, hope, and intent projected by its resident god or goddess.

The personal shrine or temple should be considered a living organism, a physical model of the universe whose psychic energy it represents. It should set the standard for inner and outer organization and show an understanding of the cosmology of the natural world. Everything contained within the temple or shrine should have meaning and purpose and, above all, be subject to the exaltation of deity. Whether it is a solitary working space or an actual temple, the area must hold the power and potential to evoke the elusive quality of the spirit, which is manifested when contact with a deity is made.

The whole purpose of creating sacred space is to provide a permanent home for the energy of the god and goddess who are being summoned. Imagine inviting your family or friends over for dinner if you had no house or apartment. You would not be able to provide them with an address, let alone fix them anything to eat. Of course, they could meet you on the bench in the park, but how often do you think they would be willing to do this? The point is that an established place of worship is necessary if you plan to invite the god and goddess to your celebrations.

Although people might disagree on the setting of a permanent sacred space, for the purpose of this book and the practice of Co-Creation Spirituality, it is necessary to establish a permanent area for worship. This setting aside of a sacred space is the starting point of any spiritual quest. It is the first act or acknowledgment of your reverence for deity and is the beginning of the spiritual transformation process.

The sacred space you create provides a place for the deity's energy to focus. You can channel this higher source of power into a comprehensible form of the deity's true nature. This connection with deity causes a transfer of divine energy that penetrates individual consciousness, bringing ecstasy and spiritual wisdom. Simply put, when you invoke the essence of deity, your level of consciousness is elevated and allows you to embrace deity—which is the object of all prayer and worship.

Remember that your sacred space or temple is a physical representation of your inner devotion and therefore reflects your spiritual condition and vision. For example, Catholic churches and shrines are magnificent places for worship. Everything— from the church's front door to the back of the altar—glorifies deity. The attention to detail, appropriate symbolism, and cleanliness are above reproach. I have never been in a dirty, disorganized, or unkempt Catholic church. Unfortunately I cannot say the same about some of the Wiccan spaces I have viewed. These spaces resembled the basements of a slum dwellings, not spiritual sanctuaries. Cleanliness is next to godliness, no matter what your background.[1]

Designing a Temple

You can approach the creation of sacred space in two ways. The first is for those who have a spare room; the second is for those who want to adapt a space in a room already designated for another purpose. In either case, there is always room for the god and goddess if the devotee is dedicated and creative.

When converting a spare room into a ritual area, cleaning is the first order of work. Remove all furniture, wall hangings, and personal objects. Paint the room a neutral color, such as ivory, light gray, or beige. If there is carpet, clean or replace it. Hardwood and tile floors need less care and are easier to keep clean than carpet.

Once you have cleaned and painted the area, you can convert it from an ordinary room into a spiritual sanctuary. When creating a sanctuary, consider everything, even the window treatments. Remember that you are creating an emotional atmosphere of comfort, beauty, and harmony so that all who enter will be at ease. The atmosphere in the room itself should be a blessing.

The Sacred Circle

In most sacred spaces, you will find a circle on the floor.[2] When actively consecrated, this physical border becomes a boundary between the human world and the realm of the Mighty Ones.

Symbolically, the circle represents celestial unity, cyclic movement, and completion. The circle is feminine in nature and serves to contain, as does the womb, all life and energy raised within it. The circle is an important feature of various religious traditions because it can be created anywhere and provides a symbolic ring of protection where a deity can be invoked.

To mark out a circle on the floor, you will need a cord or rope (cut to half the length of the total diameter), chalk, masking tape, and paint. Tie the chalk to one end of the cord. Tape the other end to the center of the room or area to be marked. Pull the cord taut and trace the circle on the floor with the chalk. Paint or tape over the chalk mark to provide a permanent circular boundary in the room.

The Altar

The most important part of any sacred space is the altar setting. The altar will be the focus of all your rituals, prayers, and works; it should be attractive in appearance and large enough to hold your sacred tools. The altar shape is not as important as the overall size and condition of the piece you choose.

A simple square, oblong, or round table are altar options. An important criterion should be size. The altar must fit comfortably into the designated space and allow for movement around it; it should be able to accommodate all the items necessary for ritual.

Remember that the altar's purpose is to be a sacred shrine for the god and goddess. After ritual, the altar does not convert back into a television stand, dining room table, or workbench. The idea of the god and goddess' consecrated tabernacle doubling as a mundane piece of furniture is ludicrous. Can you imagine the Catholic priests, after a High Mass or special religious service, stripping down the altar and putting sandwiches and beer on it? Or worse, putting their feet up on it as they kick back to watch the game? Using the altar for any other purpose besides worship is disrespectful.

To the spiritual devotee, the altar is where all obeisance is directed and focused during ritual. The priests of old understood the laws of the universe and knew how to best use the energy of those who came to pray and worship. As a result, they created imposing altars in churches and cathedrals. These priests captivated their audience with the beauty and majesty of lavish, ornate props. Once they had the congregation's attention, they organized and directed the raising of power through the Mass for the glorification of their gods. It is not hard to see how the churches of old were able to become such a prominent force—thousands of people, for hundreds of years, gave them energy.

All altars should be considered sacred, as they reflect the potential and power of the god and goddess. In an esoteric sense, the altar is a repository for divine energy. The altar then becomes an extension of the devotee's mind, allowing for the acquisition of spiritual wisdom during worship. Thus the altar becomes the point of union between human and god, as it represents an objective-physical arrangement that joins the spiritual and material realms.

When setting up your altar, put on it the objects needed for the work at hand. There is nothing more distracting than a table filled with this and that and some of everything. More is not necessarily better. In most cases, more creates confusion. The point of having an altar is to provide a place for deity; it is not a display counter for religious and magical paraphernalia.

Sacred Space Examples

In spiritual decorating, good examples are invaluable. Below, members of Our Lady of Enchantment share their pictures and ideas. As we are a formal spiritual organization and believe in the sacredness of deity, all our members have created personal altars for their favorite gods and goddesses. Also included at the end of this section is a tour of the chapel and various altars of Our Lady of Enchantment.

Our Sacred Space
(Bob and Ellen)

We are lucky because we have a spare room in our house and were able to create a ritual room, set aside for only that purpose. Our main altar is in the north. On it is a statue of Persephone.

Although our circle is not marked off on the floor, we have a braided cord that we lay down as part of our circle casting. In this room, each of us have set up our own workspaces. The room has a large

Bob and Ellen's Sacred Space

closet where we store our herbs, oils, candles, bottles, and other materials. We do our Full Moon celebrations and important works together at our main altar; personal works or meditations are done at our individual altars.

We love having this sacred space available. By setting it aside for one purpose, we keep outside energies to a minimum. However, on the down side, we must keep people who do not know about our religious involvement away from this area. While it may be easy to explain a statue or candle, it is harder to explain an entire room.

Lady Autumn's Personal Meditation Space

Personal Meditation Space
(Lady Autumn)

From the time I was a teenager, I have been fascinated with the deities of the Hindu pantheon, so it seemed natural to build an altar to them. These deities are both exotic and mysterious. Hinduism is one of the few major religions of the world that is still polytheistic.

This altar is located on top of a bookcase in my study (see photo). Left to right on the lower shelf are: Parvati, Goddess of the Mountain; Ganesh, Elephant-headed God of all good enterprise; Krishna, eighth incarnation of Vishnu; Lakshmi, Goddess of good fortunes and fertility; Shiva Nataraja, dancing the creation of the universe; and Nandi, Shiva's faithful bull companion. On the top left shelf is Kali, the destroyer; on the top right shelf is Shiva in his aspect of God of the Yogis.

I do not actively work with the Hindu deities, but this altar serves as a focal point for my worship of them. Mostly I sit before this altar and meditate. On a daily basis, I burn incense and candles to the gods and goddesses. On a weekly basis, I make offerings of flowers, fruit, and the like. Next to each statue I have placed some of the objects associated with the particular deity. For example, in front of Shiva Nataraja is a lingam representing his phallus, one of his most prominent symbols.

The deities of the Hindu pantheon offer a variety of energies to meditate upon. My altar offers me a sanctuary for contemplation and reflection.

In Honor of the Greek Deities
(Aristaeus)

I like to work with the Greek deities, so I have set up an altar for them. I arranged it in a U-shape, with three pairs of deities on each part of the altar (see photo). Hermes and Athena are to my left (for youth and beginnings), Dionysus and Demeter are in front (for fertility and manifestation), and Zeus and Hecate are to my right (for authority and wisdom). I have specific tools for each one, reflecting the aspects they represent for me. For example, for Athena I have a wand, since she is a goddess of wisdom and intellect and is associated with the element of Air. I keep these personal tools next to each deity's statue.

Altar in Honor of the Greek Deities

When I do personal work or meditate on a particular aspect of deity, I focus on the god or goddess that best matches my intentions. I burn appropriate candles and incense and hold and concentrate on their objects. If possible, I work the personal tool into the ritual for a closer link to the deity. Having all six gods and goddesses in my altar area helps me to keep in mind the many aspects of the Lord and the Lady.

The Anubis Altar
(Lord Cassius)

The ancient Egyptian god Anubis is a deity of medicine and is the Opener of the Ways between our world and the spiritual realms. Anubis as a deity is more focused toward direct spiritual contact than ritual. Because of this, his altar requires less open space and working tools than most other spiritual spaces.

The Anubis Altar

Due to limited apartment space, I keep altars set up in my bedroom. My Anubis altar is set in a corner, between two altars to Roman deities. The central focus of this altar is the large statue of Anubis, which has been consecrated and instilled with a great deal of energy. Also on the altar is a smaller figure of Anubis, depicting him in an alternate human aspect. In honor of Anubis, I keep a candle burning nearly all the time. A small incense burner and an ankh (symbolizing life and the power of deity) are on the altar as well.

Working with Anubis is much more like meditation than ritual. To reach his energy, one simply enters into the mental state that is compatible with his particular flow of influence and force. Entering this mental state requires an alert but detached focus; a calm and mentally composed state. I often do a short invocation and focus on contacting the energies over which Anubis presides. When Anubis is contacted, I feel a sense of presence and inner mental communication flows freely after that. With this altar, the deity statue has been of greatest importance, as it provides an excellent point for focus and contact.

The Chapel and Main Altar at Our Lady of Enchantment

The first thing people want to see when they come to Our Lady of Enchantment is our chapel—which seems to be some sort of an enigma in the world of Wicca and

Neo-Paganism. I find this vexation over a chapel very strange, because the point of religion is the reverence for deity. What better way to show love and appreciation for a god and goddess than by dedicating a space to them for prayer and worship?

To enter our chapel, you pass through a flower-garland arched door, reminiscent of the small archways in Victorian churches. Just inside the archway (ready to meet and greet all who enter) is a life-sized statue of Kuan Yin whose raised brick platform holds offerings and signs of the season. A small step to the right puts you in the chapel and inside our fifteen-foot diameter circle, which has been permanently painted onto the hardwood flooring. (The floor has been sealed and coated to protect it from salt, water, and candle drippings.)

As in most sacred spaces, the main altar is the chapel's focal point. The altar is an oblong, waist-high reproduction of a Roman table. It is finished in white with gold leafing and looks as nice without an altar cloth as it does with one. The clean lines and style of the table make it perfect for an altar because there is nothing about it that distracts from its purpose.

Chapel Door

On the altar, which is framed by arched windows, stands a four-foot high statue of the Goddess. Also present on the altar are the sacred tools used for our rituals and ceremonies. On the left are the Chalice and Pyx;[3] in the center are the athame, salt, and water bowls; to the right are the aspergillum, bells, and hanging censer.

The Main Altar

Under the main altar is a smaller table used during our Sabbats as the altar of offering. During ritual, we place seasonal representations, candles, and symbolic objects on this altar. With this extra altar, we can use the main altar only for invocations and Eucharist blessings. This dual altar set-up works well; it keeps the main altar clear and allows the priesthood and attendants to keep out of each other's way.

Located just inside the entrance to the chapel is our

Buddha

Buddha. He is life-sized and over a hundred years old; he comes from a temple in Taiwan.

Although we do not do any specific rituals to him, his presence is calming and lends dignity to the atmosphere. To the right of the Buddha, on a corner shelf, stands a three-and-a-half-foot high statue dedicated to Vesta. An ever-burning cauldron resides under the statue. On June 9 of every year, the light in the cauldron is extinguished. At the end of an elaborate ritual, the Priestess rekindles it.

A Personal Altar

It is wonderful to have a chapel dedicated to the god and goddess where group rituals and worship can be enacted. However, there is still nothing like having your own personal space. Even though I live on the chapel premises, I find it comforting to have my own places of devotion.

I have several altars, each dedicated to a different goddess. The first is my Vesta altar, located in the south of my bedroom. On it stands a reproduction of Vesta, whose image was recreated from an ancient Roman coin. Also on the altar are an amphora jar, container of salt, and container of flour, as these items are sacred to Vesta.

Next to Vesta is an altar dedicated to Hecate. On this altar are Hecate's symbols of the lion, hound, Three Graces, a key, chalice, and onyx scrying ball. I use this altar to call upon Hecate for strength, power, and wisdom.

The third altar is consecrated to Ishtar, represented by three statues, which represent the goddess' three aspects (see photo). On the left is the Maiden; her vessel is open and held in offering. The second larger statue is the Mother; her vessel is held as if she were pouring something, as in pouring the waters of life. The smallest one to the right is older-looking and represents the Crone aspect. If

Personal Altar

Vesta

Altar to Ishtar   *Altar to Hecate*

you look closely, you can see that her vessel is held tight with her hand clasped over the top, as if she were keeping a close watch over the secrets held within.

Also kept on this altar is the Vessel of Creation, the Rod of Authority, and my personal chalice, pentacle, and athame.

Designation of the Quadrants

Chapter 15 explained the function and purpose of the four elements. As individuals, we rely on these dynamic forces to maintain physical existence and keep our spiritual lives in balance. Because of their influence, the elements have become an inextricable part of

Eastern Quadrant in Chapel

many Wiccan/Pagan and New Age religious rites. In keeping with tradition, Co-Creation Spirituality also recognizes and employs the symbolic attributes of these elements within the context of ritual.

As with deity, it is proper and fitting to have predetermined stations for these energies to reside in. The representations you choose to delineate these archetypal forces will depend on their medium of expression and design of your sacred space.

Once you have marked the circle floor, use a compass to locate the directions east, south, west, and north. Place a token at each point to indicate the positions. If your sacred space is in its own room, marking the designation of the elements or quadrants will not be a problem. In our chapel, small shelves hung at eye level mark each quadrant station. Appropriate colored banners depicting the symbolic significance of the force it represents hang over each shelf. A corresponding colored candle, elemental tool, and an image conveying the archetypal nature of the force itself are placed on the shelf.

For those using a space that serves a dual role, there are various inconspicuous ways to designate the element's position. Hang four wall sconces with appropriately colored globes or use four pictures, each depicting one of the four seasons. Brightly colored Mexican or Native American wall hangings, icons of saints or archangels, and even prints of ancient gods and goddesses provide the necessary symbology. As with all your spiritual endeavors, be creative and use your imagination when creating sacred space.

Synopsis

Maintaining sacred space is an honor, a privilege, and the obligation of all sincere religious practitioners. Whether you create a chapel, such as ours, or use a corner of a room, an area set aside for deity is a priority. The sacred space alone categorically declares the devotee's genuineness, intent, determination, and dedication to his or her spiritual path.

For some people, creating such a space will be a hardship; nevertheless, with a little ingenuity, a space can be made. If an individual has room for a television, stereo, and VCR, he or she has room for an altar.

The time has come for those who say they practice the Old Religions of Paganism to put their money where their mouth is and show the world that they value their gods as much as mainstream Christianity does. Hundreds of thousands of dollars pass through the hands of the Wiccan/Pagan movement every year and yet, to date, only a handful of centers or Pagan sanctuaries are available, and most of these are privately funded.

For example, one New England group boasts a membership of well over 3,000 people, all of whom pay dues of $20 annually and support several group-sponsored festivals throughout the year. These festivals attract over 500 people each time, with every attendant paying an average of $135, not including meals. As these events are held in campgrounds, take advantage of off-season rates, and are composed of an all-volunteer staff and free speakers, a profit is definitely being made. And yet, after some fifteen years this organization still does not have a place to call its own.

For the many people dissatisfied with mainstream religion and yearning for meaning and greater significance in their life, where are their alternatives? If a small order such as Our Lady of Enchantment can set up and maintain a center with a chapel, library, gift shop, office, and room for classes, no reason exists why Wiccans and Neo-Pagans cannot obtain and maintain a permanent place of worship. These places of worship do not have to be great cathedrals or hundreds of wooded acres filled with stone monuments; all they need to be is established places for meeting and worship.

The Co-Creation system supports the idea of small, close-knit groups gathering for ritual and worship at regular intervals. By putting aside a corner of your living room or converting your spare room into a spiritual sanctuary, you invite a continual flow of energy. As this energy expands, it attracts and entices similar forces to it, which in turn help it to grow and increase. In time, these personal sacred spaces become vortexes of divine energy and work like giant magnets, attracting those of similar spiritual persuasion.

All major religious movements have become established spiritual communities by slowly growing and gathering members. They designate and dedicate space for their gods in return for the deity's help and support. The more energy is focused toward the religious objective, the larger it becomes. If followers of Wicca want their spiritual path to become recognized and accepted as a viable religion, then they must provide a stable environment for the nourishing of those seeking its wisdom.

ENDNOTES

1. Some readers may be screaming at my so-called Christian thinking. This is not true, however. I am simply reclaiming what is mine to have—that which was borrowed by the new religion of Christianity from the ancients who created it.

2. In Co-Creation Spirituality, we hold all our rituals inside the boundary of a circle; a common practice among most Wiccan/Pagan and New Age groups. A circle lends equality and cohesion to the group activities.

3. The term Pyx is an old Greek word meaning box; the Pyx contains the hosts or common bread used for blessing during rituals and ceremonies.

Part IV

The Cauldron of Transformation

A New Vision of Expression

Chapter 17

The Office and Obligation
of the Priesthood

*No matter what method, the Priesthood arises, for its practitioners, as
a choice beyond choices, a natural inevitability that cannot be denied.*
Nema, "Comment on the Priesthood," *Mezlim #2,* 1993

*The minister's task is to lead men from what they want to what they
need.*
Ralph Sockman, *The Highway of God,* 1941

The Significance of Priesthood

All organizations, large or small, religious or secular, need leaders who are capable,
controlled, and concerned about the welfare of their constituents. Whether in the
church or corporate structure, knowledgeable officials who understand the business
at hand are a necessity. Frequently, the creative genius of one individual is responsible for the organization's origin. His or her charisma maintains and controls the ties
that bind. If the individual was skilled in the profession, he or she is remembered
long after leaving.

Hierarchy and authority are part of our universal structure. They are consistent
with function and become oppressive only when abused. Each individual has the
same essential worth as any other, but not everyone is equal in the capacity to perform. Nurses and doctors, as individuals, have the same personal worth. In the operating room, however, the value of their functions differs dramatically. The same is
true in the church. The laity have as much right to pray to god as the priests; they do
not have, however, the authority to counsel, teach, or lead others in the sacred rites.

Within the scope of most religions is a hierarchy of priests who administer to the needs of the congregation. These ambassadors of theological wisdom are special people. Through dedication, initiation, and training, they can advise, teach, and lead others in spiritual matters. As emissaries of the divine, their lives should be examples of spiritual responsibility and a focus of discipline not usually practiced by the average individual. They, and they alone, have the right and authority to guide others upon the path and offer the sacraments of their religion.

A priest's principal function is that of spiritual counselor, healer of souls, speaker of truth, and warrior against evil. The priest should be interested in his or her parishioners, listen to their needs, and provide them with guidance where necessary. The priest is a caretaker of souls who is duty bound to live according to divine law and share his or her experience and revelation of the higher mysteries with all who seek.

The priest is not a messiah, savior, or redeemer of sins. He or she is a mediator and an intercessor between divine intelligence and human spiritual inspiration. The priest stimulates and promotes within the disciple spiritual health and awareness, but does not criticize or condemn the frailness of human nature.

Every priesthood, be it Christian or Pagan, carries much responsibility. Once initiated, the priest is endowed with the sacred trust of directing his or her congregation toward the wisdom of the Holy Mysteries. This sharing of enlightenment aids in the evolution of the soul and spirit of humanity.

Because the priest is a summoner of the divine, he or she is held accountable for the preservation of the Holy Spirit when manifested through ritual. This transubstantiation of immaculate energy into the corporeal existence for the exaltation of human consciousness is the act of a sacred trust. Through the ecstasy and rapture of individual perception, the spirit is rekindled and elevated for a momentary reunion with its original potential. For this reason, the invoker of higher wisdom needs to have more than just a superficial understanding of petitioning for and investiture of the sacrament.

None should overlook or diminish the importance of the priesthood in relation to the proper functioning of any religious system. Though each of us, privately, has the right and responsibility to call on deity and worship as we see fit, this in no way invalidates or incapacitates the power or position of the priesthood. Everyone has the ability to heal their bodies, but that ability does not make each individual a doctor. Everyone has the ability to refute allegations of injustice, but that does not make the average person an accomplished attorney. Because someone can recite a ritual or pantomime an invocation, this does not necessarily make them a priest or priestess.

Co-Creation Spirituality and Ecclesiastical Obligation

The priest's position within any system is that of guardian and guide, protector and provider, teacher and counselor. When examined from the secular viewpoint, each position is a vocation or craft unto itself. However, to the prelate of divine wisdom, these offices of obligation merge into one comprehensive declaration of faith. The competency with which the priest handles each of these aspects directly confirms the depth of his or her conviction.

If an individual desires to become a priest or priestess of Wicca or one of the many Neo-Pagan traditions, he or she should find out where to receive proper training. Someone with little or no comparative religious education cannot teach theology. The individual without counseling skills cannot guide others safely through a mental or spiritual crisis. The individual who has not been formally instructed and initiated into the mysteries cannot reveal these unspoken truths to others in their ceremonies.

Unfortunately, for the most part, Wicca, Neo-Paganism, and the New Age movement do not have formal theological training. Although most of these non-Christian missionaries have not set standards, these standards do exist. The universe, whether we like it or not, is wrought with regulations. One of these states that for every action there is a reaction. The reaction from trained theologians to the concept of a do-it-yourself priesthood is one of repudiation and rejection. How can we enter the race when we are not recognized as runners?

For the most part, the sincere student will ferret out a reputable teacher or credible group, which is not as difficult as it may seem. Armed with a few simple guidelines, anyone can procure training in the new religions of Paganism. The key to help unlock the door of the spiritual mysteries is a simple common sense evaluator—something everyone should use when approaching any type of a new religious or philosophical group or organization.

Common Sense Teacher/Group Evaluator

The following common sense guide lists six points to look for when evaluating a teacher or group.

1. Ask for a printed copy of the teacher's/group's basic beliefs, practices, and requirements. If no copy is forthcoming, sincerely question the skills and abilities of the teacher and group. Anyone who has valid information will provide you with printed copies of their doctrine. No hard copy—no deal.

2. Ask the teacher where and by whom he or she was trained and evaluate his or her response. In her answer, did she provide names, dates, and places? Or did he provide

some wild tale of how he was the seventh son of a seventh son and his grandmother (who is dead now) took him aside and initiated him in his early teens? No names or dates of training? Look elsewhere.

3. Observe the living conditions of the prospective teacher. Can the teacher support him or herself and their family? Is the teacher clean, drug-free, and responsible? If the person cannot help him or herself, how can the person help you? No exceptions; if the place is a mess, leave.

4. What does the teacher want in exchange for teaching you? Some sort of exchange should take place, whether it is that old demon cash or help around the house. Everything of value has a price; there are no free rides. People who are afraid to ask for compensation for their time and work may have some hidden agenda, which usually manifests as head count or power tripping. If the teacher does not state his or her price up front, be wary of what might be expected in the future. No price—no commitment from you.

5. Ask the teacher for references or interview other members of the group. The best way to judge the efficacy of any organization is by its membership. Are the other members responsible, mature adults? Are they friendly, outgoing, and responsive to new people, or are they arrogant and secretive? Do they speak of spiritual and uplifting things or hang around and gossip? Did they welcome you in friendship? Consider how you feel about the group before you return.

6. Be observant. What is the main focus or interest of the teacher and group? Do they spend more time discussing what should be on the feast list than they do on spiritual matters and proper ritual procedure? Worse yet, do they have the feast first and then hustle through the ritual if there is time? If the teacher or group is more interested in the chips and dip than in the raising of spiritual consciousness, stay home.

The priesthood of any religion occupies a position of authority and responsibility that should be viewed as a sacred trust. True priesthood requires years of training from recognized ecclesiastics, mental and physical discipline, and dedication to the promotion of the Holy Spirit. Even in the Wiccan and Neo-Pagan traditions, preparation for the priesthood should include more than memorizing magical jargon and Pagan platitudes. Dressing up once a month in flowing robes and lighting incense and candles does not make one a member of the priesthood. It definitely should mean more than saving whales, protesting nuclear power, or supporting the polyamorous lifestyle. These may be valid agendas to some but they hardly qualify as spiritual activities, let alone preparation for priesthood.

One does not read a couple of medical books and then hang out a shingle declaring oneself a doctor. One does not attend a legal seminar and then start practicing law. Yet many have done this very thing with the Wiccan/Pagan priesthood. The zealous wanna-be reads a couple of books, dubs himself or herself Grand High Poobah-Druid Priest/ess, and attempts to teach and lead others in spiritual exploration.

This action is ludicrous and abusive. It censures the ability of the true priesthood to function on both the spiritual as well as material planes. It advertises to the world the lack of training and discipline in the Wiccan/Pagan movement. It also discredits true Wiccan doctrine and invalidates Pagan practices by exhibiting the inability to control that which is of our own making.

What it boils down to is quality verses quantity. Standards need to be set, if not by the priesthood and the religion, then by those seeking admittance into it. When those who are sincerely interested in the spiritual value of the Pagan religions challenge the system, demand competent teachers, and refuse to settle for foolish titles, the Pagan priesthood will reclaim its rightful position in the spiritual community.

Questions and Answers

I asked clergy members of Our Lady of Enchantment several questions about their feelings regarding the priesthood. It is always helpful to have the thoughts and impressions of others regarding controversial topics—and the pros and cons of Pagan priesthood is about as controversial as one can get. The questions I put to those who agreed to participate and their answers are presented below.

Aristaeus, what do you feel it means to be a priest or priestess in a religion that emphasizes individual ability?

Priesthood in such a situation requires a great amount of practical knowledge and ability—much more than superficial book learning or simple group leadership. The priest or priestess must be able to show others how to lead themselves. Where there is a great focus on individual spirituality, the priesthood has to open the way for personal discovery and illumination. Building talent always requires more ability than leading sheep.

Cassius, what standards do you feel the Wiccan/Pagan priesthood should live up to?

The Wiccan/Pagan priesthood *must* live up to both the standards of practicality and the basic social standards of modern society. Without practical training, goals, and organization, no religion can survive. If a religion doesn't hold ethical standards similar to the society around it, people will fear, distrust, and hate it. It is impossible to thrive if you are not effective or if you rub the general populace the wrong way.

Balaam, do you think there should be guidelines and qualifications that the Wiccan/Pagan priesthood must meet?

Of course there must be guidelines and qualifications! If just anybody, no matter how incompetent, can stand up and say, "I am a priest," then the overall quality of the religion goes down the toilet. People who don't know can't teach; people without ability can't do or lead. It just doesn't make any sense for such people to hold positions of responsibility—and, on top of it, be public advocates.

Do you feel that everyone who takes an interest in or gets involved in Wicca and Neo-Paganism should become a priest or priestess?

Cassisus: Absolutely not! There are many ways to be active in religion and do meaningful things in the spiritual field. Priesthood is only one of many—and by far the most difficult. Look at how many effective Christians there are. They are all involved and getting things done. Yet, are they all priests? No, of course not! At least they have had the sense to put egos aside and focus more on the religion than on individual position.

Aristaeus: No. Many people don't have the time or inclination to be members of the priesthood. There is nothing wrong with this as they have their own paths to explore.

Lady Autumn: No, because everyone is not cut out for the priesthood. It is a big responsibility, and many people in training for the priesthood don't realize this. As soon as they find out that they have to do some work, or are responsible for the temple setup and, indirectly, how well the ritual goes, they quit or look for an easier place to be. They look for someplace that doesn't require an effort, where they can pretend to be something they aren't.

Balaam: No. Not everyone is able to be a teacher or leader. Many are able to learn but very few are really able to teach. Just because someone can perform a ritual does not mean he or she is able to comprehend and teach the deeper meanings of the mysteries.

Autumn, do you feel those who devote their full time to the priesthood of the Neo-Pagan faiths should be compensated for their efforts and works?

In the sense of a market economy, yes. There is a big difference between a person of ability earning money and somebody getting a salary. The current standards of the Pagan priesthood are so low, the last thing they need is to be put on the dole. If a leader is truly competent, then he or she has something real and physical to offer. That has worth, and there is nothing wrong with people paying for things that have value.

Having been involved with the Pagan movement, what is your opinion of the vast majority of its leaders who claim to be members of the priesthood? What one thing would you say to them if you were given the opportunity? (As Balaam and Cassius have been more involved, and for a longer period of time, with the Pagan movement, their answers are below.)

Balaam: I'd say the vast majority of the leaders whom I feel are less than competent are self-serving rather than enhancing—at the expense of depriving true searchers of the goal they seek. These leaders are concerned with surrounding themselves with others to feed their ego and they exchange nothing in return. "Water seeks its own level," and it is also true that there are a lot of so-called seekers out there who want nothing more than to be commanded rather than taught, because learning involves work.

Given the opportunity, I would say to them, "If you want to claim religion and want the freedom from persecution for doing this, then you really have to practice religion in the true sense of the word. It appears that you want to use Paganism and the Old Religion as an umbrella to do what you want. When this happens, you do more to destroy the gains that are being made by others, and you do this better than those who deliberately set out to do so, who you consider the enemy. I have seen the enemy and it is thee."

Cassius: Having been involved with the Pagan movement for over ten years, I must say that most of its leaders are unqualified from nearly every standpoint. The average Pagan leader just doesn't have the ability, true leadership vision, or even a competent understanding of his or her own religion to be teaching, let alone leading others. The vast majority of Pagan leaders are just useless talk, and that is a real shame. If they were more interested in the religion than they are in the style of their robe, something just might get done.

The one thing I would like to say to them is: "So, you say you're a Pagan Priest? Friend, when you tell me that, prove it. Show me what you have done, what you have built, and how you have advanced the cause of your religion. That, and only that, is the measure of your worth."

Synopsis

Ecclesiastical obligations are not taken lightly at Our Lady of Enchantment. Because we are a legally recognized religious organization, all who wish to be initiated and ordained into our system must meet certain standards. By maintaining a quality leadership program, we preserve the dignity and stability of our tradition. We ensure that only those qualified to do so speak on our behalf. Our structure and adherence to the basic Co-Creation principles has helped us as individuals, as well as a religious order, to grow and progress.

Proper education and training in the priesthood are not that difficult if the individual is truly interested and willing to do some work. For this reason, Our Lady of Enchantment has a two-step program designed to help educate those who wish to become members of the priesthood.

The program is simple and straightforward. First, the student takes our "Earth, Religion, and Power" course and then the "Metaphysics One" course. Attending these courses qualifies the student for ministerial credentials and helps him or her to establish a ministry. By creating his or her own ministry, the student gains some of the social skills necessary to maintain a group.

Second, the student applies for our "Priesthood Training Program," which is a set of lessons, activity cards, and guidance lectures in group work. The lessons provide the necessary theological education while the activity cards and lectures provide instruction in group dynamics and counseling. By making this program available through the mail, as well as at our center in New Hampshire, there is no reason why anyone who wishes to be a priest or priestess should go untrained. For a free information package on all our programs and activities, write to:

Our Lady of Enchantment
P. O. Box 1366
Nashua, NH 03061

ENDNOTE

1. Most groups have a social hour and feast after their Sabbats and special ceremonies. Note that the feast takes place after the Sabbat or ceremony, not before or during.

CHAPTER 18

The Observance of Essential Requirements

Ritual may be manmade in the sense that human hands fashioned it. But what inspired those hands to do their work is the Divine influence.

Ben Zion Boksar, *Perspectives on a Troubled Decade*, 1950

The Reason for Ritual and Worship

Religion and worship reaches its climax during that moment in ritual when the devotee is brought into alignment with deity. This lining up with the power and potential of the God and Goddess transforms, through a transubstantiation of energy, the individual's consciousness. Once this happens, the devotee becomes aware, deep within his or her soul, of the splendor and glory of the Holy Spirit. Only through a consummate act of genuine devotion is this type of revelation or spiritual rapture possible.

However, before any type of prayer, worship, or ritual can be accomplished, there needs to be a strong connection made with deity. The devotee must be thoroughly convinced of the existence of his or her gods and of their inherent power and wisdom. Without this absolute confidence in the omnipotence of deity, worship becomes empty.

Once a commitment to deity has been made, the individual often experiences an overwhelming desire for interaction with his or her god form. This preoccupation with involvement is part of the human need to connect or unite with one's passion. Simply put, it is like being in love—the need to express deep emotions takes precedence over all other feelings and desires. This love affair with God has inspired humanity to create great religions.

The primary purpose behind an intimate relationship with a deity is the elevation of consciousness that takes place when the human and divine quintessence are united in ritual worship. When the adoration of deity is combined with a properly executed and intense act of religious observance, the individual experiences spiritual ecstasy. This momentary shift in awareness consummates the personal identification and fusion of human spirit with divine potential, allowing the devotee to comprehend the exalted magnitude of deity. In other words, during special rites of worship it is possible for the participants to experience apotheosis, or exaltation of consciousness, within their personal nature.

Because of the possible ramifications (both positive and negative) of extreme elevated states of consciousness, proper procedures must be followed for ritual worship. Simply put, if the ritual is worth doing, then it is worth doing right. There is no excuse for shallow, sloppy, second-rate rituals. Every religious tradition has its own conception of deity, and rituals vary from one group to another. However, this individuality should not diminish the leaders or the group from striving for excellence rather than mediocrity.

If coming together for a ritual is only an excuse to party, a serious problem exists with the leadership and the quality of the group. On the other hand, if you meet to earnestly worship the God and Goddess, then the extra time needed to do things properly will be a welcome incentive rather than an irritation or inconvenience.

Most of the problems with poorly conducted rituals stem from a lack of understanding about the procedure itself. If individuals have no conception of a ritual's fundamental structure, then their final product will be inferior. No matter what type of a project you undertake, if you do not know where to begin, how are you going to construct anything of value, let alone achieve success?

Preliminary Rites and Preparation

Ritual worship should be both solemn and imposing in language and intent. It should lead the devotee step by step to a climax where he or she is made one with the deity, resulting in an intense feeling of profound, heartfelt euphoria. This spiritual ecstasy is only possible when every action of a ceremony is properly coordinated and expressed for the glorification of divinity.

For a ritual to be properly constructed, it must have four separate yet related segments that merge together effortlessly. These segments are the preparation and consecration of the area and members, which include the opening benediction; the prayer and supplication, which defines the purpose of the ritual and includes the invocation of deity; the atonement and Eucharist, which emphasizes the Rite of Union and the Rite of Redemption; and the closing and dismissal of the Quadrants and congregation.

The commentary for each part includes both a definition of the process and the corresponding rites where applicable. It is recommended that everything except the principal liturgy be memorized. Memorized words become second nature, so participants can then experience the moment and emphasize its symbology rather than be distracted by shuffling paper and reading from printed copy.

Preparation and Consecration

The first segment of ritual is the preparation and consecration of the area and the participants. This opening portion is important because it sets the mood and tone of the ritual itself.

Preparation

Composing the Ritual Checklist. This is done by sitting down and reading through the ritual to see what is needed and who will be doing the speaking parts. By reading over the ritual in advance and making notes of items needed and important segments, you reaffirm the purpose and intent of the ritual.

Altar and Quadrant Preparation. Two members will act as ATTENDANTS during the ceremony. One ATTENDANT sets up the altar; the other places the Quadrants in their respective positions. After all is in place, one of the ATTENDANTS lights the altar candles and recites:

(Right candle)
Our Lord is the Sun, he brings forth the light.
He has dominion over all, he is power and might.

(Left candle)
Our Lady is the Moon, she brings forth the night.
She controls the soul of man, she is wisdom and insight.

The ATTENDANT who placed the Quadrants lights them (beginning with the east) and recites:

I light the East, the home of moonlight and consciousness, the realm of the spirit.
I light the South, the home of fire and inspiration, the realm of awareness.
I light the West, the home of the waves of completeness, the realm of our watery beginnings.
I light the North, the home of all that is green and fruitful, the realm of abundance.

By lighting the altar and Quadrant candles prior to ritual, a statement of intention is made and the transformation process begins as the atmosphere becomes receptive to higher spiritual vibrations.

Consecration

Entrance. All the participants follow the lead PRIEST and PRIESTESS into the chapel or ritual area; those with assigned parts move to the appropriate positions.

Priest Anoints Each Member with the Oil

The Benediction (Blessing)

This is the actual beginning of the ritual and sets the criterion for the proper state of mind as a preliminary to the actual mass itself. The benediction begins the ceremony with the blessing of the priesthood and congregation as follows (holy oil and aspergillum required).

The PRIEST and PRIESTESS face the altar and genuflect; the PRIEST rings the bells three times.

The PRIESTESS faces the altar, picks up the aspergillum, and holds it high in front of her as she asks the following blessing:

Our Lord and Father, Divine Solar Radiance,
Ever-Dying King, Guardian of the Threshold,
We invoke thee as Sol Invictus, the Unconquered Sun,
Lord of the Land, Glory of the Heavens
And all that brings light and life.
Let all who seek enlightenment find strength
In the fluid of your passion.

The PRIESTESS asperges the congregation in blessing.

The PRIEST faces the altar and holds the vial of oil high in front of him as he asks the following blessing:

O Blessed Virgin, Sacred Mother,
To whom the glory of the sun belongs.
Universal Goddess, we invoke thee as Sophia,
Holy Wisdom, first among the gods.
Bless us through your most Holy Spirit
That we shall ever walk with love, compassion,
And understanding now and forever.

The PRIEST anoints each member with the oil.

The Litany of the God and Goddess
This begins the process of energy transformation and sets the stage for the mass as the participants are prepared to welcome and accept the God and Goddess into their hearts.

The PRIEST and PRIESTESS face the altar and genuflect. An ATTENDANT comes forward and tones the bells at the appropriate time.

(Bells)

PRIEST
May the power of the Lord conquer confusion,
May the power of the Lord protect us from evil,
May the power of the Lord lead us in righteousness,
May the power of the Lord bring us light and life.

ALL
May the power of the Lord bring us light and life.

(Bells)

PRIESTESS
May the love of the Lady lift up our hearts,
May the love of the Lady grant us more virtue,
May the love of the Lady teach us great wisdom,
May the love of the Lady bring us beauty and grace.

ALL
May the love of the Lady bring us beauty and grace.

(Bells)

PRIEST and PRIESTESS
May the Lord and the Lady who reign from above
Always come forth with great passion and love.
Bring us to stand for God and for right
Ever to lead us from darkness to light.

ALL
Ayea, Ayea, Cerridwen
Ayea, Ayea, Cerridwen
Ayea, Ayea, Cerridwen
Ayea, Ayea, Ayea!

Ayea, Ayea, Cernunnos
Ayea, Ayea, Cernunnos
Ayea, Ayea, Cernunnos
Ayea, Ayea, Ayea!

Note: Substitute the names of the deities you are working with in place of Cerridwen and Cernunnos during the ritual.

Consecration of the Elements and Creation of Sacred Space

The PRIEST and PRIESTESS face the altar. The PRIESTESS takes up the Athame and holds it in offering to the Goddess. She dips the Athame into the bowl of water, saying:

Creature of water, cast out from thyself all impurities and uncleanliness of this world.

The PRIESTESS dips the Athame into the dish of salt and scoops out three small portions, placing each into the bowl of water, saying:

Creature of earth, let only good enter to aid us in our prayer and work.
So shall it be.

The PRIESTESS holds the Athame in offering to the Goddess and draws down the fire from heaven into the Athame, which she directs down onto the circle outline, creating a sphere of protective energy, saying:

I conjure and create thee, O circle of power, which shall be a boundary between the world of men and the realm of the Mighty Ones, which shall preserve and protect all energy raised within. Blessed are the Lord and Lady who guard the gateway to everlasting life. So be it!

"Hear me, O Mighty One ..."

The Calling of the Quadrant Guardians

This is the final segment of the Preparation and Consecration. The PRIEST takes up the Athame and proceeds to the East where he begins his acknowledgment. After each summoning, the PRIEST picks up the associated element, holds it in offering, and proceeds to the next Quadrant.

(East)
Hear me, O Mighty One, Ruler of the Whirlwinds,
Guardian of the Eastern Portal.
Let your essence be as one with ours,
As witness and shield at this gateway between the worlds.
So mote it be!

(South)
Hear me, O Mighty One, Ruler of the Solar Orb,
Guardian of the Southern Portal.
Let your light be as one with ours,
As witness and shield at this gateway between the worlds.
So mote it be!

(West)
Hear me, O Mighty One, Ruler of the Mysterious Depths,
Guardian of the Western Portal.
Let your fluid be as one with ours,
As witness and shield at this gateway between the worlds.
So mote it be!

(North)
Hear me, O Mighty One, Ruler of Forest and Field,
Guardian of the Northern Portal.
Let your fruitfulness be as one with ours,
As witness and shield at this gateway between the worlds.
So mote it be!

Prayer and Supplication

This portion of the rite expresses the theme or reason behind the performance of the mass. At this time, the God or Goddess is invoked as a prelude to the apex of the ritual, the Rite of Union and the Rite of Redemption. Here, the main body of the liturgy will change as does the purpose of the rite. Seasonal celebrations will focus on time-honored earth themes such as planning, planting, harvesting, and remembering. Other rituals, such as the Feast of the Blessed Virgin and the Good Friday Eucharist Remembrance, will focus directly on the majesty of the God and Goddess.

Once the theme of the ritual has been expressed, the PRIEST or PRIESTESS approaches the altar in solemn reverence and genuflects. With great passion, he or she invokes the power and presence of deity. The invocations we use have been memorized and worked until they have become second nature. Through this familiarity, the PRIEST or PRIESTESS who invokes is able to separate the physical enactment from the spiritual penetration taking place, allowing for total involvement with the deity. It also intensifies the spiritual experience and energy within the bounds of the circle.

The Invocation of the Goddess
Thou who whispers gentle yet strong
Thou for whom my soul doth long,
By most men you are seldom seen
Yet you ever reign as virgin, mother, queen,
Through the veil you pass with pride

As I beckon thee now to be at my side,
Cerridwen!

Thou who knows, thou who conceals
Thou who gives birth, thou who feels,
For you are the Goddess and mother to all
Pray thee now come as I call,
Now through the mist I hear your voice
And invoke thee most gracious Goddess by choice,
Cerridwen!

Thou who suffers as all men die
Doth with her victim in love lie,
For you are the Goddess and crone of despair
To our ending with you we must share.
I feel thy passion and feel thy presence;
I desire to be one with thy vital essence,
Cerridwen!

I pray thee, dancer of eternal bliss,
Bestow upon me thy wondrous kiss.
Let now thy light, love, and power
Descend, become one with me this hour,
For you are the creatress of heaven and earth
To my soul and spirit you have given birth,
Cerridwen!

All members in unison praise the Goddess by chanting:

Ayea, Ayea, Cerridwen
Ayea, Ayea, Cerridwen
Ayea, Ayea, Cerridwen
Ayea, Ayea, Ayea!

The Invocation to the God
Father of death, Father of night.
Father of birth, Father of light.
Cernunnos, Cernunnos, Cernunnos.
Come by flame, Come by fire.
Come now, whom we desire.
Cernunnos, Cernunnos, Cernunnos.

O Horned One, O ancient one.
God of the sun, bringer of light.

The powers of Darkness put to flight.
O Horned One, O ancient one,
Who comes from beyond the gates of death and birth.
Come who gives life to all on earth.

Come, I invoke thee,
For you are Pan, Apollo, Cernunnos,
Lord of Hades, Lord of Death.
You are them all, yet you are he,
Come, come, my Lord, as I beckon thee.

Come, come, my Lord of wild delights.
Come, join with us in these secret-mystic rites.
Come, come, my Lord of fire and flame,
As I call out your sacred and holy name
Cernunnos, Cernunnos, Cernunnos.

All members in unison praise the God by chanting:

Ayea, Ayea, Cernunnos
Ayea, Ayea, Cernunnos
Ayea, Ayea, Cernunnos
Ayea, Ayea, Ayea!

Atonement and Eucharist Through the Rite of Union and the Rite of Redemption

The atonement is the final proclamation prior to the actual Eucharist Rite of Union and Rite of Redemption. This is done in anticipation of the actual embracing of the God and Goddess through their most sacred rites. During seasonal ceremonies, there will be an extended portion of liturgy that varies according to the focus of the ritual. When this has been completed, the following method of sacred observance begins.

The Proclamation

An ATTENDANT approaches the altar, genuflects, and rings the bells three times. He or she steps to the side of the altar. The PRIEST and PRIESTESS approach the altar and genuflect.

The ATTENDANT recites the following declaration:

Those who walk in darkness
Shall now experience great light;
Those who hunger and thirst
Shall be quenched at the altar of life;

Those who call upon righteousness
Shall take the hand of the Lord and Lady;
Those who approach with anticipation
Shall receive the gifts of the spirit.

ALL
Our Lord and Lady,
We acknowledge your greatness;
Our Lord and Lady,
We affirm your wisdom and love;
Our Lord and Lady,
We pray for your presence;
Our Lord and Lady,
We now ask for your blessing.
Blessed be Cerridwen and Cernunnos!

The PRIEST and PRIESTESS face each other. The PRIEST kneels before the PRIESTESS and they begin the Rite of Union.[1]

The PRIESTESS holds the container of red wine in her right hand and the container of white wine in her left. She raises both to eye level and silently summons the Lord and Lady into the wine. She lowers the containers over the Chalice and pours both at the same time as she says with great emotion:

I pour the red and the white, that they shall mix as life and death, joy and sorrow, peace and humility, and impart their essence and wisdom unto all.

The PRIEST remains kneeling as he holds the Chalice filled with the wine, saying with great emotion:

For I am the father, lover, and brother unto all, the bringer of life, the giver of death, before whom all time is ashamed. Let my spirit breathe upon you and awaken the fires of inspiration within your soul.

The PRIESTESS returns the containers of wine on the altar, picks up the Athame, and slowly lowers it into the Chalice as the PRIEST (who is still kneeling) rises with the Chalice to meet the blade of the Athame so it touches the wine within. They say, each in turn:

"And they are conjoined to become one …"

PRIESTESS
For as this Athame represents the male and the God…

PRIEST
So this Chalice represents the female and the Goddess.

PRIEST and PRIESTESS (in unison)
And they are conjoined, to become one, in truth, power, and wisdom. So mote it be.

The PRIEST and PRIESTESS each take a sip of wine and place the Chalice on the altar. The PRIESTESS picks up the Paten and faces the PRIEST and again with great reverence says:

Behold the sovereignty of our divine king,
Beloved son and lover,
Radiant and everlasting light,
Guardian of the souls of man who rises triumphant from the tomb!

PRIEST
We honor thee, O sacrificed God,
Who, through the mother, grants eternity.
By shedding your blood upon the land,
All are transformed through your passion as they pass through the gates of judgment.

The PRIEST picks up one of the hosts and holds it over the Paten; in unison, the PRIEST and PRIESTESS say with great reverence:

Let now the mystery be revealed of the light of the Lord within, who in the shadow of the Goddess shall ever reign supreme!

The PRIEST snaps the host in half. He offers half to the PRIESTESS, and he partakes of the other. Both the Chalice with the blessed wine and the Paten with the hosts are passed to the congregation. As each member receives the Chalice and the Paten, they say:

Blessed are the faithful, for they shall receive the gifts of the spirit.

Closing and Dismissal

The closing and dismissal end the principle portion of the mass and begin the return process for the priesthood and congregation. As with the previous sections, certain parts of this division vary according to the focus of the ritual. Those parts that remain the same are the dismissing of the Quadrants, closing benediction, and the banishing of the sacred space. Again, these parts of the ritual should be memorized and given the same emotional expression as they were in their original state of creation. The following text provides the exact method used.

The PRIEST and PRIESTESS approach the altar and genuflect. The ATTENDANT rings the bells three times. The PRIEST takes up the Athame and proceeds to the North where he begins the dismissal of the Quadrants. As he dismisses the Guardian, he also extinguishes the corresponding candle unless otherwise directed.

(North)
Hear me, O Mighty One, Ruler of Forest and Field,
Guardian of the Northern Portal.
We thank thee for thy blessings and protection at this gateway
Between the worlds and bid thee hail and farewell.
So mote it be!

(West)
Hear me, O Mighty One, Ruler of the Mysterious Depths,
Guardian of the Western Portal.
We thank thee for thy blessings and protection at this gateway
Between the worlds and bid thee hail and farewell.
So mote it be!

(South)
Hear me, O Mighty One, Ruler of the Solar Orb,
Guardian of the Southern Portal.
We thank thee for thy blessings and protection at this gateway
Between the worlds and bid thee hail and farewell.
So mote it be!

(East)
Hear me, O Mighty One, Ruler of the Whirlwinds,
Guardian of the Eastern Portal.
We thank thee for thy blessings and protection at this gateway
Between the worlds and bid thee hail and farewell.
So mote it be!

The Closing Benediction

This final blessing on the congregation before they leave the sacred space helps ground the energy and protect all those who participated in the ceremony as they re-enter the physical realm.

The PRIESTESS faces the altar and recites the closing benediction:

We ask our Lord and Father, the Divine Solar Radiance,
Ever-Dying King and Guardian of the Threshold,
To give us strength, power, and wisdom.
We ask of our Lady, Blessed Virgin and Sacred Mother,
She who has been known by many names,

To bless us through her Holy Spirit
And grant to each of us compassion, understanding, and love,
Now and forever. So shall it be!

The PRIESTESS takes up the Athame and banishes the energy of the circle in a counterclockwise motion, beginning in the North. Pointing the Athame at the physical boundary, she draws the energy up and back into the Athame as she speaks the following:

I banish thee, O circle of power, that has been a boundary between the world of men
and the realm of the Mighty Ones.
Let all energy and power be returned as we depart in peace and love.
So mote it be!

Synopsis

Trying to accurately describe the exhilaration and ecstasy generated in a properly conducted ritual is much like trying to describe the true essence of intense, penetrating love. If you have experienced it, you know how it feels; if you haven't—you don't know. Nevertheless, you are left speechless by the experience. Some things cannot be put into words; this is why training and initiation into the mysteries was and still is so important. Until you have been led to the wellspring of the God and Goddess, passed through the gates of regeneration, and felt their presence deep within your soul, you have no point of reference. Without this experience, you remain naive.

This is not to say that untrained people cannot contact deity and have visions or unintentional encounters with the God and Goddess. With the right attitude, emotion, and determination, everyone has the ability to touch the hand of the God or Goddess. However, a chance encounter is not a controlled act of ritual worship whereby the Lord and Lady are regularly brought into a created sacred space. For this type of endeavor, the individual needs knowledge, training, and experience—which can only come through spiritual transformation.

This book is designed to whet the appetite of the sincere seeker so there will be further research, study, and investigation of spiritual concepts. Anyone who can read this book can pantomime the invocations, Rite of Union, and Rite of Redemption. However, only those who have been properly trained, initiated, and ordained in the mysteries of the God and Goddess have the authority and qualifications to actualize the transubstantiation of divine potential into corporeal reality. As with all vocations, one needs time, effort, and training to become proficient at religion—ability is not a free commodity.

ENDNOTE

1. The Rite of Union was designed as a spiritual bringing together of the masculine God energy and the feminine Goddess energy in order to express the essential perspicacity of the Great Mystery. It was never intended to be used as a prelude to or form of actual physical sexual intercourse. At this time during the mass, we are extending our consciousness beyond the realm of physical perception to approach divinity—we are not grounding our vitality through corporeal contact.

CHAPTER 19

Sacraments, Sacred Rites, and Prayers

Worship arises as spontaneously in the heart of the religious devotee as love arises in the heart of the youth who has found in the maiden, beauty, inspiration, and understanding.

Charles C. Jasey, *Journal of Religion*, XV, October 1935

Prayer should be understood, not as a mere mechanical recitation of formulas, but as a mystical elevation, an absorption of consciousness in the contemplation of a principle both permeating and transcending our world.

Alexis Carrell, *Man, The Unknown*, 1935

The Art of Prayer and Worship

Prayer and acts of ritual worship express our love and devotion for deity. Prayer is the process we use to communicate directly with deity and ritual allows us to share this devotion with others. By verbally expressing our thoughts through prayer, we substantiate their existence; by physically acting out our emotions in ritual, we declare our allegiance to deity.

All prayers and acts of ritual worship are channels through which the devotee is able to reunite himself or herself with the light or aura of the Holy Spirit. This channeling is created through a transubstantiation of energy in which the participant's consciousness is made aware of the true significance of the god and goddess being worshiped. The realization, or acknowledgment, of that which is greater provides the devotee with the opportunity to embrace his or her gods on a personal level. This reunion with divine potential is the main objective of all religious ceremonies.

The rituals and sacraments that follow form the principal body of the prayer and supplication segment of each ceremony and therefore constitute the formal portion of the liturgical calendar at Our Lady of Enchantment as recorded in our *Temple Book of Prayer and Scripture*.[1] We use the first two rituals at our Friday Night Church Service. These rituals are followed by our monthly Lunar and Solar rituals and finally by those rites that make up our Ten Holy Days of Obligation.

Our Lady of Enchantment is a legally recognized Church with a large congregation and membership; all our rites and ceremonies are designed primarily for group participation. We also try to divide the rituals' speaking equally, so many participants have the chance to express themselves.

The passages are marked PRIEST or PRIESTESS for those leading the ritual and performing the sacraments; and ATTENDANT for the Attendants who assist the priest and priestess during the ritual. All of the parts, except for the Invocations to the God and Goddess, the Rite of Union, and the Rite of Redemption, are interchangeable. These acts of high ritual worship are sacred to the gods and therefore must be consummated by the appropriate and properly initiated members of the priesthood.

For most of our ceremonies, we use two sets of altar candles. Those placed on the altar itself are lighted prior to the ceremony; those that stand beside the altar are table height and are lighted during the ceremony. A bookstand is used to hold the *Temple Book of Prayer and Scripture* for the conducting priesthood's reference. The bookstand leaves the leaders' hands free so they can gesture when appropriate. Finally, we only perform the sacred Rite of Union and Rite of Redemption during our Holy Days of Obligation. During our Friday Night Church Services and Lunar and Solar Rites, we use a modified Common Wine Blessing to express the symbiosis that occurs during the Rite of Union. The full text of the Common Wine Blessing is included where used. I recommend that you read the footnotes, as they provide some important insights into the meanings and workings of the rites themselves.

If you follow a solitary path, you will need to make some modifications if you wish to practice our ceremonies. However, the process of adapting properly constructed rituals to your own needs can be both physically rewarding and spiritually uplifting. As long as you take care and show attention with regard to deity and composition, our ceremonies should serve as proper guidelines.

Friday Night Church

Ritual of the Prayer Chest

This ritual provides the opportunity for each member to personally petition the God and Goddess on their behalf. Members write their desires on small pieces of paper placed in the prayer chest and blessed during the ceremony. After the ritual, the contents of the prayer chest are emptied into the censer and burned, allowing the smoke to take the prayers and wishes to the gods.

Basic Requirements

The altar is covered with a white cloth; on it are placed the candles, Athame, Chalice filled with a mixture of red and white wine, salt and water bowls, censer,[2] bells, aspergillum, oil for anointing, and a small box with a lid to be used as the prayer chest.

Before the ritual begins, participants write out their wish on a piece of paper, which they take into ritual with them.

The Ritual of the Prayer Chest

ATTENDANTS are responsible for the altar and Quadrant preparation (Chapter 18).

All members enter the Chapel or ritual area.

The Benediction

The PRIEST and PRIESTESS perform the Opening Benediction (Chapter 18).

The Litany of the Lord and Lady

The PRIEST and PRIESTESS perform the Litany of the Lord and Lady (Chapter 18).

The Consecration

The PRIESTESS consecrates the elements and casts the circle.

An ATTENDANT approaches the altar, genuflects, and rings the bells. He or she lights the floor altar candles, saying:

(Right)
Blessed be this torch of truth and illumination
For it shall deliver us from ignorance.

(Left)
Blessed be this torch of reason and wisdom
For it shall bring us toward understanding.

The Consecration

The PRIEST and PRIESTESS consecrate the elements and cast the circle[3] (Chapter 18).

Principle Ritual Liturgy

An ATTENDANT approaches the altar and genuflects. He or she picks up the prayer chest and proceeds around the circle, collecting the petitions in the chest. The ATTENDANT returns to the altar and holds the prayer chest in offering to the Goddess, saying:

> *Blessed shall be all who accept the sacred spirit*
> *For they shall be blessed and endureth forever.*

An ATTENDANT approaches the altar, genuflects, and rings the bells. He or she picks up the prayer chest. The ATTENDANT proceeds to offer the chest at each of the Quadrants, saying with great passion:

(East)
Redeemer of Great Mystery
Whose Secrets are in the Air
Let thy weary traveler
In your secrets share!

(South)
Redeemer of Great Mystery
Whose Powers shine through the night
Let our journey now begin
As we come into your Light!

(West)
Redeemer of Great Mystery
Whose Force comes from the sea
Let us rapture in your Glory
That shall one day make us free!

(North)
Redeemer of Great Mystery
Whose Wisdom comes from earth
As now our journey ends
Through death we gain rebirth!

The PRIEST genuflects, picks up the prayer chest, and holds it in offering as he speaks with great emotion:

> *Eternal Father, our prayers now hear*
> *Great Sire of Gods whom all revere.*

Endow us with your powers strong
For that is what we crave and long.
That in your sacred Name we stand
And only ask you lend a hand.
To help us proudly in your way
As we sing your praises every day.
And to our sacred rite benevolent attend
And grant us happy life and blessed end.

ALL
Ayea, Ayea, Cernunnos
Ayea, Ayea, Cernunnos
Ayea, Ayea, Cernunnos
Ayea, Ayea, Ayea!

The PRIESTESS genuflects and faces the congregation, saying:

We gather in celebration and praise
In honor of our Lord and Lady.
For they bring forth understanding
Of the secret nature of all things.
It is before their sacred altar
That all are refreshed and renewed.
In our Lord we find strength and fortitude
In our Lady we find inspiration and wisdom.
When their power and potential meet
They create and bring forth light and life.
We beseech them this night to forgive our errors
To accept our sacrifice of devotion
And bring forth their blessings upon these petitions.

The Invocation

The PRIESTESS rings the bells, picks up the prayer chest, and hands it to the PRIEST. The PRIEST genuflects, faces the altar, and holds the chest high in offering as he invokes the God (Chapter 18).

ALL
Ayea, Ayea, Cernunnos
Ayea, Ayea, Cernunnos
Ayea, Ayea, Cernunnos
Ayea, Ayea, Ayea!

The PRIEST hands the prayer chest to the PRIESTESS, who holds it in offering, saying:

Blessed is the Sacred Virgin
For She brings forth light
Blessed is the Holy Mother
For She brings forth life
Blessed is the Wise One
For She brings forth Love!

ALL
Ayea, Ayea, Cerridwen
Ayea, Ayea, Cerridwen
Ayea, Ayea, Cerridwen
Ayea, Ayea, Ayea!

The congregation holds hands and chants to raise energy, which is directed into the prayer chest. (The hand holding and chanting are optional; if you wish, you may offer a special prayer, meditation, or appropriate reading instead.)

Common Wine Blessing

The PRIEST and PRIESTESS approach the altar, ring the bells, and genuflect. The PRIESTESS picks up the Chalice and holds it in front of her as the PRIEST picks up the Athame, and holds it over the Chalice. Each recites as follows:

PRIESTESS
Behold the Maiden's Cup of Desire
The Vessel of Creation
Behold the Grail of Great Mystery
The Cauldron of Regeneration.

PRIEST
Behold the Sword of Flaming Passion
The Lance of Strength and Power
Behold the Rod of High Authority
The Bringer of Fruit and Flower.

The PRIEST plunges the Athame into the Chalice as both say:

PRIEST and PRIESTESS
Together yet separate
And always as one
Are the Lord and the Lady
So their will may be done!

The PRIEST passes the wine to the other members, saying as they reciprocate:

Blessed are the faithful, for they shall receive the gifts of the spirit.

An ATTENDANT approaches the altar, genuflects, and extinguishes the Quadrants, beginning with the North, saying:

(North)
Let the North, the home of all that is green
And fruitful, bring forth our desires.

(West)
Let the West, the home of our watery beginnings,
Bring comfort and peace.

(South)
Let the South, the home of fire and inspiration,
Lend us power and strength.

(East)
Let the East, the home of moonlight and consciousness,
Always empower our spirits.

An ATTENDANT approaches the altar, genuflects, and extinguishes the altar candles, saying:

(Left)
Blessed be this torch of reason and wisdom
For it shall bring us toward understanding.

(Right)
Blessed be this torch of truth and illumination
For it shall deliver us from ignorance.

Closing Benediction
The PRIEST rings the bells and recites the Closing Benediction (Chapter 18). The PRIESTESS banishes the circle (Chapter 18).

The Ritual of Candle Blessing
The intent of this ritual is to bring the blessings of the God and Goddess into our homes on a regular basis. Each person attending the ceremony should bring a candle that corresponds in color to his or her God or Goddess. During the ritual, the PRIEST-ESS and PRIEST transfer the power of the Goddess, which has been invoked, into these candles. The participants can take the candles home and burn them as desired.

Basic Requirements

The altar is covered with a yellow or white cloth; on it are placed the candles, Athame, Chalice filled with a mixture of red and white wine, salt and water bowls, censer, bells, aspergillum, oil for anointing, and a large yellow or gold pillar candle.

The Ritual of Candle Blessing

ATTENDANTS are responsible for the altar and Quadrant preparation (Chapter 18).
   All members enter the Chapel or ritual area.

The Benediction

The PRIEST and PRIESTESS perform the Benediction (Chapter 18).

The Litany of the Lord and Lady

The PRIEST and PRIESTESS perform the Litany of the Lord and Lady (Chapter 18).

The Consecration

The PRIESTESS consecrates the elements and casts the circle (Chapter 18).
   An ATTENDANT approaches the altar, genuflects, and rings the bells. He or she lights the floor altar candles, saying:

(Right)
I light the night which they have made
May darkness flee this temple.

(Left)
I light the path which they have set
May we continue in their wisdom. So be it!

   An ATTENDANT approaches the altar, genuflects, and picks up the yellow candle. He or she lights it and holds it in offering, saying:

He who seeks shall learn
He who asks shall receive
He who knows shall teach
He who has faith in the spirit
Shall always remain in the light
So shall it be!

   The PRIEST approaches the altar, rings the bells, and genuflects. He takes the candle from the ATTENDANT and proceeds to offer it at each one of the Quadrants, beginning in the east, saying:

(East)
Raphael, Keeper of the East
Lord of the Morning Light,
Inspiration of the elusive Wind,
Bless us with your Sacred Sight.

(South)
Michael, Guardian of the South,
Lord of Burning Fire,
Awareness of the Midday Sun,
Bring forth our Desire.

(West)
Gabriel, Ruler of the West,
Lord of the Twilight Hour,
Bringer of Emotional Control,
Provide us with Psychic Power.

(North)
Uriel, Preserver of the North,
Lord of the Inner Earth,
Granter of Physical Pleasure,
To our dreams give birth.

The Invocation

The PRIEST hands the candle to the PRIESTESS. She rings the bells, genuflects, and invokes the Goddess (Chapter 18).

ALL
Ayea, Ayea, Cerridwen
Ayea, Ayea, Cerridwen
Ayea, Ayea, Cerridwen
Ayea, Ayea, Ayea!

The PRIESTESS hands the candle to the PRIEST. He follows her around the circle as she anoints each member's candle, saying: *May the power of the Lady be with you.*

ALL
May the power of the Lady be with you.

Common Wine Blessing

The PRIEST and PRIESTESS approach the altar, ring the bells, and genuflect. The PRIESTESS picks up the Chalice and holds it in front of her as the PRIEST picks up the Athame, and holds it over the Chalice. Each recites as follows:

PRIESTESS
Behold the Maiden's Cup of Desire
The Vessel of Creation
Behold the Grail of Great Mystery
The Cauldron of Regeneration.

PRIEST
Behold the Sword of Flaming Passion
The Lance of Strength and Power
Behold the Rod of High Authority
The Bringer of Fruit and Flower.

The PRIEST plunges the Athame into the Chalice as both say:

PRIEST and PRIESTESS
Together yet separate
And always as one
Are the Lord and the Lady
So their will may be done!

The PRIEST passes the wine to the other members, saying as they reciprocate:

Blessed are the faithful, for they shall receive the gifts of the spirit.

An ATTENDANT approaches the altar, genuflects, and extinguishes the Quadrants, beginning with the North, saying:

(North)
Let now the North, the home of all that is green
And fruitful, manifest our desires.

(West)
Let now the West, the home of our watery beginnings,
Stabilize our emotions.

(South)
Let now the South, the home of mental awareness,
Grant us strength and power.

(East)
Let now the East, the home of moonlight and consciousness,
Endow us with great wisdom.

An ATTENDANT approaches the altar, genuflects, and extinguishes the altar candles, saying:

(Left)
Let now the wisdom of the Lady be our light.

(Right)
Let now the power of the Lord be our strength.

Closing Benediction
The PRIESTESS ring the bells, recites the Closing Benediction, and banishes the power of the circle (Chapter 18).

Lunar and Solar Services

The Full Moon Ceremony
In almost every Wiccan/Pagan tradition, it is a common practice to meet and celebrate the energy of the Goddess on her most sacred time of the full pregnant moon. At this time, most practitioners of the Pagan Way set aside time to worship the Goddess, work magic, and share among themselves the secrets of their craft. Essentially, the celebration of the full moon is restricted to those members who have been initiated into the priesthood and form the leadership nucleus of each religious group. At Our Lady of Enchantment, we have long subscribed to this arrangement of limiting participation in our lunar rites to only the ordained priesthood. We have found it is much easier to create and maintain a strong spiritual focus when everyone participating in the ritual is thoroughly trained and in tune with each other. This type of group dynamic is not always possible with a congregation of mixed[4] members.

For the most part, our full moon celebrations follow as closely as possible the previously discussed ritual format. The major differences are the elimination of the Rite of Union and the Rite of Redemption, which have been replaced with blessings that stress the Lunar or Goddess aspect being emphasized.

Basic Requirements
For this ceremony, the altar is covered with a white cloth.[5] On it are placed the two main altar candles, the Chalice filled with white wine, the Athame, salt and water bowl, a censer, and the bells. In addition, you will need a bowl filled with spring water into which has been placed a floating candle. Fresh white, pink, or light yellow flowers make a nice touch and add to the femininity of the ceremony.

When the altar and circle preparations have been completed, the appointed members light the Quadrant and altar candles (Chapter 18).

The Liturgy of the Lunar Rite
All members of the priesthood gather in the chapel or ritual area.

The Opening
An ATTENDANT approaches the altar and lights the floor altar candles, saying:

(Right)
Gentle Mother, meek and mild.
Look upon your seeking child,
With this candle I now light
Please bring us joy on this night.

(Left)
I approach you, Lady of gentle grace
To bless and protect this sacred space,
With this torch of truth and praise
Gently guide us through all our days.
So mote it be!

The Benediction
The PRIEST and PRIESTESS perform the Opening Benediction (Chapter 18).

The Litany of the Lord and Lady
The PRIEST and PRIESTESS perform the Litany of the Lord and Lady (Chapter 18).

The Consecration
The PRIESTESS consecrates the elements and casts the circle (Chapter 18). The PRIEST calls in the Guardians of the four Quadrants (Chapter 18).

The Proclamation
With the preparation of sacred space completed, an ATTENDANT approaches the altar, rings the bells, and genuflects. He or she picks up the bowl with the floating candle and offers it to the Goddess at each one of the Quadrants, staring with the East, proclaiming:

(East)
There is but one spirit and it dwells within
For it is the truth from where we begin.

(South)
There is but one spark and it burns us like fire
It comes from a passion brought forth from desire.

(West)
There is but one feeling and it is our emotion
It swells deep within, crashes forth like the ocean.

(North)
There is but one reason and it comes from rebirth
To live, love, and die with wisdom on earth.

The ATTENDANT returns, faces the altar, and genuflects. He or she holds the cup or bowl in offering to the Goddess and leads the group in the following proclamation:

ALL
There is but one spirit and it dwells within
For it is the truth from where we begin.
There is but one spark and it burns us like fire
It comes from a passion brought forth from desire.
There is but one feeling and it is our emotion
It swells deep within and crashes forth like the ocean
There is but one reason and it comes from rebirth
To live, love, and die with wisdom on earth.

Ayea, Ayea, Cerridwen
Ayea, Ayea, Cerridwen
Ayea, Ayea, Cerridwen
Ayea, Ayea, Ayea!

An ATTENDANT approaches the altar, genuflects, and rings the bells. He or she lights the water candle and holds it in offering to the Goddess, saying:

Lady of desire, reflection of light
You are motion, direction, and our second sight.
Mother of creation the original source
You are potential, power, the ultimate force.
Grandmother of time, wise one from above
Do we summon thee here with honor and love.

ALL
Ayea, Ayea, Cerridwen
Ayea, Ayea, Cerridwen
Ayea, Ayea, Cerridwen
Ayea, Ayea, Ayea!

The Salutation

The ATTENDANT hands the bowl and floating candle to the PRIEST who begins the Salutation of the Goddess in anticipation of her arrival.[6]

Gracious Goddess and Mother of All,
Give us the wisdom to discover you,
The intelligence to understand you,
The diligence to seek after you,
The patience to wait for you,
The openness of mind to accept you,
And the dedication to proclaim you,
We welcome you within our hearts
Now and forever, so shall it be!

The Invitation

The PRIEST places the bowl and floating candle in the center of the altar, rings the bells, genuflects, and picks up the Chalice. He kneels in front of the PRIESTESS and holds the Chalice in offering as he speaks with great reverence:

Lady of the Morning Star
Queen of the Heavenly Sea
Power of the mighty wind
You alone were chosen to be.

Lady who guides the mighty Angels
Mother of selfless devotion
Enchantress of the mysteries
And Keeper of time and motion.

Lady we now invite thee here
As the Virgin of pure love
The one who moves the soul of man
With her splendor from above.

Lady we now invite thee here
As the Mother of sacred earth
Whose power is beyond compare
When dreams are given birth.

Lady we now invite thee here
As the Wisdom from the past
That within this holy Grail
Come blessings that will last.

The PRIESTESS places her hands over the Chalice and speaks with great reverence:

Behold the Brilliant Evening Star
The Virgin of Celestial Light
Behold the Goddess's from afar
The Mother of Second Sight.

Behold the Queen of twilight hour
The Wise and Vigilante Protector
Behold the Goddess's silent power
The Mother most regal and Splendor

Behold the Lady who must descend
The Mystery hidden beneath the veil
Behold the Goddess who rises again
The keeper of the golden Grail.

The PRIESTESS picks up the Athame, and before plunging it into the Chalice exclaims:

I offer to thee courage and wisdom
And I bring thee strength and might
I offer to thee warmth and pleasure
And I bring thee love and light
I offer to thee the seed of the sun
And I bring thee honor and power
I offer to thee the staff of life
And I bring thee fruit and the flower.

The Invocation

The PRIEST rises and hands the Chalice to the PRIESTESS who, with great emotion,[7] performs the Invocation of the Goddess (Chapter 18). All members salute the Goddess by saying:

Ayea, Ayea, Cerridwen
Ayea, Ayea, Cerridwen
Ayea, Ayea, Cerridwen!

The PRIEST and PRIESTESS share the wine and pass it to the other members, saying:

Blessed are the faithful, for they shall receive the gifts of the spirit.

At this point, there is a meditation, group work, or spiritual reflection as determined prior to the ritual.

The Conclusion

An ATTENDANT approaches the altar, ring the bells, and genuflects. He or she proceeds to the North, extinguishing the Quadrant candles in order, saying:

(North)
There is but one reason, it came from the earth
So to our dreams the gods would give birth.

(West)
There is but one feeling, it comes from the ocean
To help us learn control over each emotion.

(South)
There is but one spark, it comes from fire
Brings us the passion to create desire.

(East)
There is but one spirit, it came from the air
And with us its knowledge and wisdom did share.

An ATTENDANT approaches the altar, rings the bells, and genuflects. He or she extinguishes the floor altar candles, saying:

(Right)
Let now the potential, Power, and force
Return unto the original source.

(Left)
Let now the motion, Direction, and sight
Return unto the original light.

Closing Benediction

The PRIEST approaches the altar, rings the bells, and genuflects. He recites the Closing Benediction (Chapter 18). The PRIESTESS takes up the Athame and banishes the circle (Chapter 18).

Sunday Morning Solar Rite

The Solar Rite is optional, mainly because many Wiccans and Pagans are offended and dismayed with anything totally God-oriented. However, many of our students and the vast majority of our members are not so prejudiced and enjoy the balance created by having both Solar and Lunar rites available.

This ritual is dedicated to the God of the Sun and is performed at either sunrise or high noon on the first Sunday of the month. As with our Lunar rite, this celebration is open to only the initiated priesthood. It also follows the same ritual format as the lunar rite, except the blessings are replaced with those that stress the solar god concept.

Basic Requirements

For this ceremony the altar is covered with a red or yellow cloth; on it are placed two orange altar candles, the Chalice filled with red wine, the Athame, salt and water bowls, a censer, and the bells. For the representation of the Sun God, we use a large red candle[8] with four wicks, which we place on a pedestal in the center of the circle.

When the altar and circle preparations have been completed, the appointed members light the Quadrant and altar candles (Chapter 18).

The Liturgy of the Solar Rite

All members of the priesthood gather in the chapel or ritual area.

The Opening

An ATTENDANT approaches the altar and lights the floor altar candles, saying:

(Right)
O Great Father of Burning delight
Let all your children see,
As they revel in full sunlight
The glory that belongs to Thee.

(Left)
O Great Father of Heavenly power
Whose splendor does inspire
Be with us at this morning hour
And grace us with your fire.

The Benediction

The PRIEST and PRIESTESS perform the Opening Benediction (Chapter 18).

The Litany of the Lord and Lady

The PRIEST and PRIESTESS perform the Litany of the Lord and Lady (Chapter 18).

The Consecration

The PRIESTESS consecrates the elements and casts the circle (Chapter 18). The PRIEST calls in the Guardians of the four Quadrants (Chapter 18).

The Proclamation

With the preparation of sacred space completed, an ATTENDANT approaches the altar, rings the bells, and genuflects. He or she recites the following proclamation:

O Great Father to whom the Sun belongs
Providence of great mystery
Keeper of the Primal Fire
Guardian of unapproachable light
Host of the heavenly vault.
Be with us now and forever, Amen!

ALL
Be with us now and forever, Amen!

The ATTENDANT rings the bells three times and places some incense in the censer, which he or she hands to the PRIEST.

The PRIEST walks once around the circle, carrying the incense and saying:

Holy art thou, Lord of the Most High
Blessed is the Son of Your creation
As is the Child of His seed and the
Holy Spirit of Light and Life.

The PRIEST returns to the altar and replaces the censer.

The PRIESTESS approaches the altar, genuflects, and rings the bells. She proceeds to the center of the circle where she delivers the following proclamation:

Praise be the Lord,
The King of Kings,
Sovereignty of the Heavens,
First breeze of breath,
Primal flame of fire,
Initial pleasure of passion,
Principal making of matter,
Sire of the sacrifice,
Father of the Beloved Sun,
Creator of the Holy Spirit,
Be with us now and forever, Amen.

The Salutation

The PRIEST approaches the altar, genuflects, and rings the bells. He lights a small taper candle. He takes the candle to the center of the circle and begins the salutation with great emotion:

At this time on the first of days
God the Father's name we praise,
Who, creation's Lord of Spring
Did the world from darkness bring.
For on this day the eternal Son
The rising King, his triumph won
And when the Holy spirit came
He brought the gift of living flame.
We call the blessed Three in One
Let your will and work be done,
We pray the words that set us free
As we start each day our faith in Thee.

The PRIEST lights each wick of the jumbo candle and then says:

Glory to the Father, to the Son and
To the Holy Spirit;
As it was in the beginning, it is
Now and will be forever.
Amen!

ALL
Glory to the Father, to the Son, and
To the Holy Spirit;
As it was in the beginning, it is now
And will be forever.
Amen!

The Invitation

The PRIEST and PRIESTESS approach the altar, genuflect, and ring the bells. The PRIESTESS picks up the Chalice, kneels in front of the PRIEST, and holds the Chalice in offering, saying with great reverence:

O Sacred Son, life of all below
Thou a fount of life and fire
Surpassing all the joys we know
And all we should desire.

My longing heart calls thy name
For thee I do adore
And seeking thee, itself in flame
To seek thee more and more.

This cup I hold shall thee bless
That we may love alone
And ever in our lives express
The rapture we have known.

The PRIEST places his hands over the Chalice and recites with great reverence:

Behold our Lord and Father,
Eternal heavenly light,
To whom the Sun belongs,
Blessed is His sacrament,
Kept as a covenant,
With the sacrificed God,
Who shed his blood,
For the love of the Land,
That life everlasting,
Should be our reward,
As we drink the elixir of life.

The PRIEST picks up the Athame and before plunging it into the Chalice exclaims:

Let thy grace my sole chief treasure
Love's pure flame within thee raise.
King that my words can't measure
The blessing of your splendid praise.

Within my heart is devoted feeling
Vainly should my lips express.
I come before thy altar kneeling
And pray this wine thee shall bless.

The Invocation
The PRIESTESS rises and hands the Chalice to the PRIEST, who holds it in offering, saying with great emotion:

Sol Invictus is the high Sun Lord
As Pan and Apollo are much adored.
The Christ has risen, a twice-born Son
Ascending to the Father and Holy One.
Wearing a crown of glistening gold
His glory and majesty we behold.
O Savior who became a sun-blessed ray
We rejoice in your rebirth this day
And hope for the Spirit and peace divine
To grace and bless this sacred wine.

The PRIEST faces the group, holds the wine in offering, and speaks the following:

Glory to the Father, to the Son, and
To the Holy Spirit;
As it was in the beginning, it is now
And will be forever.
Amen!

ALL
Glory to the Father, to the Son, and
To the Holy Spirit;
As it was in the beginning, it is now
And will be forever.
Amen!

The PRIEST and PRIESTESS share the wine and then pass it to the other members, saying:

Blessed are the faithful, for they shall receive the gifts of the spirit.

At this point, there is a meditation, group work, or spiritual reflection determined prior to the ritual.

The Conclusion

An ATTENDANT approaches the altar, rings the bells, and genuflects. He or she proceeds to the North, extinguishing the Quadrant candles accordingly (Chapter 18).

An ATTENDANT approaches the altar, rings the bells, and genuflects. He or she extinguishes the floor altar candles, saying:

(Left)
O Great Father of Heavenly power
Whose presence reigns from above
Be with us at this morning hour
And grace us with your love.

(Right)
O Great Father of Burning delight
Your mysteries we now know,
As we extinguish now this light
In peace profound we go.

Closing Benediction

The PRIEST approaches the altar, rings the bells, and genuflects. He recites the Closing Benediction (Chapter 18). The PRIESTESS takes up the Athame and banishes the circle (Chapter 18).

The Ten Holy Days of Obligation

People recognize the changing of the seasons: the smell of spiced cider, a chill in the air, and the ripening pumpkin bring forth the image of autumn. Snow-laced trees, a hearth draped with holly, and the sweet scent of bay remind us of winter. Clear blue skies, daffodils, and the chirping of birds tell us spring is on the way. Hazy skies, high heat, humidity, and an occasional thunderstorm make the presence of summer known. And so the wheel turns, bringing hope, promise, growth, and reward; the cycle of birth, life, and death continues.

Like most Pagan traditions, our system of spirituality professes a belief in the beauty, power, and presence of the energies that prevail during the different seasons. For this reason, we find it spiritually uplifting to celebrate these shifts or transitions with a Sabbat ritual that expresses our appreciation for the times of light and life.

There are two ways to celebrate the seasonal changes or Sabbats. The first approach is one of spiritual thanksgiving, which deals strictly with the honor and glorification of deity and is the way the Sabbats are approached here. The second method is one of magical petition and those rituals can be found, in their entirety, in my first book, *Reclaiming the Power* (Llewellyn, 1992). Although the rituals may seem similar in their approach, they are different in their presentation. In addition to the Solstices, Equinoxes, and mid-solar changes, we have added two exceptionally powerful rituals to our calendar. The first is the Rite of Remembrance, celebrated on the Christian Good Friday; the second is the Feast of the Blessed Virgin, celebrated on September 7. These ten designated times complete our ten Holy Days of Obligation.

One note: At Our Lady of Enchantment, we celebrate the Sabbats on the exact date. We do not feel that it is too much to ask of our members to put aside ten days out of the year, be they weekend or weekday, for the God and Goddess. However, this observation is not a hard and fast rule; it is just the way we prefer to handle our spiritual obligations.

The Winter Solstice or Yule

Yule is a pre-Christian holiday or festival celebrated on the Winter Solstice, around December 21. It is the true New Year, both astronomically as well as spiritually. At this time, we see the simultaneous death and rebirth of the Sun-God represented in the shortest day and longest night of the year. From this time forward, the sun grows in power and strength. We use this time to acknowledge the Sun of Righteousness and welcome back the spiritual aspect of the light that brings life.

In addition to the usual altar tools, there should be a large yellow pillar candle, seasonal incense, and decorations. The ritual begins as usual:

ATTENDANTS are responsible for the altar and Quadrant preparation (Chapter 18).

The Benediction
The PRIEST and PRIESTESS perform the Benediction (Chapter 18).

The Litany of the Lord and Lady
The PRIEST and PRIESTESS perform the Litany of the Lord and Lady (Chapter 18).

The Consecration
The PRIESTESS consecrates the elements and casts the circle (Chapter 18).

The Calling of the Quadrant Guardians
The PRIEST calls in the Guardians of the four Quadrants (Chapter 18).

The Declaration
An ATTENDANT lights the floor altar candles, saying:

(Right)
Blessed be the fire of faith which brings
Forth the light.

(Left)
Blessed be the light of the world which brings
Forth life.

An ATTENDANT approaches the altar, genuflects, and rings the bells. He or she recites the following:

Blessed be the White Goddess
Blessed be the Sacrificed King
Blessed be their Spiritual Seed
Blessed be their Children of Light.

The PRIEST approaches the altar, genuflects, and rings the bells. He picks up the yellow candle and holds it in offering, saying:

Desolate and dormant is the earth above
Fertile and vital is its soul below.
Our mind knows what our eyes cannot see
For all is resting and waiting.
The canopy of death hangs heavy about us
Life ends and life begins all in a moment.
We attain spiritual strength and happiness
When we seek from within rather than from
Without.

An ATTENDANT approaches the altar; the PRIEST hands the ATTENDANT the candle, which he or she offers at each Quadrant, saying:

(East)
Blessed be the light coming from the East
Which inspires us.

(South)
Blessed be the fire coming from the South
Which warms us.

(West)
Blessed be the moisture coming from the West
Which refreshes us.

(North)
Blessed be the fertile earth of the North
Which nourishes us.

The ATTENDANT returns, genuflects, and places the candle on the altar.

The Salutation

The PRIESTESS approaches the altar, genuflects, and rings the bells. She lights the yellow candle[9] and places it in the center of the circle, saying:

Lord and Lady of the Night
Of mist and of moonlight,
Though you are seldom seen
We meet you in the heart of dream,
Bless now our thoughts and deeds
And help us to fulfill our needs,
On this night we honor thee
To make your presence a reality,
Love and honor we give to thee
For all our blessings, so mote it be!

ALL take hands and chant:

God of Glory
God of Light
Return to us
This Solstice night!

The Invitation

The PRIEST approaches the altar, genuflects, and rings the bells. He addresses the congregation:

On this night we petition the presence of the
Lord of Light and the Lady of Life,
We revel in their wonderment and bathe
In their illumination,
We are guided and guarded by their love,
Wisdom, and understanding,
And only seek their blessings.
Let us sing their praises as they
lift up our hearts in joy and exaltation.

ALL
Ayea, Ayea, Cerridwen
Ayea, Ayea, Cerridwen
Ayea, Ayea, Cerridwen
Ayea, Ayea, Ayea!

Ayea, Ayea, Cernunnos
Ayea, Ayea, Cernunnos
Ayea, Ayea, Cernunnos
Ayea, Ayea, Ayea!

The Invocations

The PRIEST and PRIESTESS approach the altar and genuflect. An ATTENDANT
rings the bells three times. The PRIESTESS does the Invocation of the Goddess
(Chapter 18). The PRIEST performs the Invocation of the God (Chapter 18).

The Proclamation

The ATTENDANT approaches the altar, genuflects, and rings the bells three times,
saying:

Those who walk in darkness
Shall now experience great light;
Those who hunger and thirst
Shall be quenched at the altar of life;
Those who call upon righteousness
Shall take the hand of the Lord and Lady;
Those who approach with anticipation
Shall receive the gifts of the spirit.

ALL
Our Lord and Lady
We acknowledge your greatness;
Our Lord and Lady
We affirm your wisdom and love;

Our Lord and Lady
We pray for your presence;
Our Lord and Lady
We now ask for your blessing.
Blessed be Cerridwen and Cernunnos!

The Rite of Union and the Rite of Redemption

The PRIEST and PRIESTESS approach the altar, genuflect, and face each other. The ATTENDANT rings the bells and the PRIEST and PRIESTESS perform the Rite of Union and the Rite of Redemption (Chapter 18).

ALL respond to the passing of the wine and host:

Blessed are the faithful,
for they shall receive the gifts of the spirit.

The Conclusion

The PRIEST approaches the altar, genuflects, and rings the bells. He proceeds to dismiss the Guardians (Chapter 18).

An ATTENDANT approaches the altar, genuflects, and extinguishes the floor altar candles, saying:

(Left)
Blessed be the fire of faith for bringing
Forth the light.

(Right)
Blessed be the light of the world for bringing
Forth new life.

Closing Benediction

The PRIEST recites the Closing Benediction (Chapter 18). The PRIESTESS banishes the circle (Chapter 18).

Imbolc or Oimele

Imbolc, also known as Oimele or Brigantia, is celebrated on February 1. This is the feast of the waxing light or feast of lights and is related to the Goddess Bridget or Bride. This great day is associated with the return of life and light. Imbolc marks the awakening of the earth and the promise of spring, a time of new beginnings.

The Eleusinian Mysteries included a torchlight procession on February 1 in honor of Demeter when she searched for her lost daughter, Persephone; when Persephone was found, light was brought back to the world. This is also the time of the virgin-maiden aspect of the Goddess, being courted by the young Lord God. Their passion for each other is felt in the seasonal energy at this time. Close in relationship to Imbolc is the Christian festival of Candlemas, celebrated on February 2, and is a time of purification.

In addition to the usual altar tools, there should be a white or pink Goddess (pillar) candle, seasonal incense, and fresh new flowers.

ATTENDANTS are responsible for the altar and Quadrant preparation.

The Benediction
The PRIEST and PRIESTESS perform the Benediction (Chapter 18).

The Litany of the Lord and Lady
The PRIEST and PRIESTESS perform the Litany of the Lord and Lady (Chapter 18).

The Consecration
The PRIESTESS consecrates the elements and casts the circle (Chapter 18).

The Calling of the Quadrant Guardian
The PRIEST calls in the Guardians of the four Quadrants (Chapter 18).

The Declaration
An ATTENDANT lights the floor altar candles, saying:

(Right)
Fearless Lord, Protector and Father of All
Bring forth Light, Life, and Wisdom.

(Left)
White Maiden, Gentle Mother, Silent One
Deliver us from Ignorance and Darkness.

The ATTENDANT approaches the altar, genuflects, and rings the bells. He or she picks up the Goddess candle, saying:

Our Lady has been with us from the beginning
She is our Light and Life.
Our Lord comes from the glory of the Lady
And he is our Strength and Power.

Together they bring forth the wonderment
Of all things past and present.

The ATTENDANT hands the candle to another ATTENDANT who offers it at each of the Quadrants, saying:

(East)
Let now the Dawn and Spring of Life come forth.

(South)
Let now the Fire and Spirit of Life come forth.

(West)
Let now the Passion and Love of Life come forth.

(North)
Let now the Balance and Wisdom of Life come forth.

The ATTENDANT returns to the altar and, still holding the candle, recites the following and ALL join in:

Out of Death comes Life,
Out of Darkness comes Light,
Out of Winter comes Spring.

The Salutation

The PRIESTESS approaches the altar and genuflects. She faces the group, saying:

The Sun has been reborn and
Our Lord has risen,
The Moon reflects his glory and
Our Lady is transformed.
Together they bring forth Light and Life
Delivering us from Darkness, Death, and Sorrow.
Out of Death comes Life,
Out of Darkness comes Light,
Out of Winter comes Spring.

ALL
Out of Death comes Life,
Out of Darkness comes Light,
Out of Winter comes Spring.

The Invitation
The PRIEST approaches the altar, genuflects, and rings the bells. He faces the group, saying:

Let us banish the Winter and welcome the Spring,
As Light brings Life to every living thing.
The Glory of the Gods we now behold,
For all that is given returns threefold.
As we revel in the warmth of their presence and light,
We pray they will bless and protect each of us this night.

The PRIEST lights the Goddess candle,[10] saying:

For out of Death comes Life,
Out of Darkness comes Light,
Out of Winter comes Spring.

ALL
Out of Death comes Life,
Out of Darkness comes Light,
Out of Winter comes Spring.

Ayea, Ayea, Brighid[11]
Ayea, Ayea, Brighid
Ayea, Ayea, Brighid
Ayea, Ayea, Ayea!

Ayea, Ayea, Cernunnos
Ayea, Ayea, Cernunnos
Ayea, Ayea, Cernunnos
Ayea, Ayea, Ayea!

The Invocations
The PRIEST and PRIESTESS approach the altar and genuflect. An ATTENDANT rings the bells three times. The PRIESTESS does the Invocation of the Goddess (Chapter 18). The PRIEST performs the Invocation of the God (Chapter 18).

The Proclamation
The ATTENDANT approaches the altar, genuflects, rings the bells three times, and recites:

Those who walk in darkness
Shall now experience great light;
Those who hunger and thirst
Shall be quenched at the altar of life;

Those who call upon righteousness
Shall take the hand of the Lord and Lady;
Those who approach with anticipation
Shall receive the gifts of the spirit.

ALL
Our Lord and Lady
We acknowledge your greatness;
Our Lord and Lady
We affirm your wisdom and love;
Our Lord and Lady
We pray for your presence;
Our Lord and Lady
We now ask for your blessing.
Blessed be Brighid and Cernunnos!

The Rite of Union and the Rite of Redemption

The PRIEST and PRIESTESS approach the altar, genuflect, and face each other. An ATTENDANT rings the bells. The PRIEST and PRIESTESS perform the Rite of Union and the Rite of Redemption (Chapter 18).

The Conclusion

The PRIEST approaches the altar, genuflects, and rings the bells. He proceeds to dismiss the Guardians (Chapter 18).

The ATTENDANT approaches the altar, genuflects, and extinguishes the floor altar candles, saying:

(Left)
Lady of Light, Wise One, thou art pure in Spirit
And Love Eternal.

(Right)
Lord of Fire, Passionate One, thou art true Force
And Endless Power.

Closing Benediction

The PRIEST recites the Closing Benediction (Chapter 18). The PRIESTESS banishes the circle (Chapter 18).

The Spring (Vernal) Equinox

The Vernal Equinox is celebrated around March 21. This is the time when the sun crosses the plane of the equator, making the day and night of equal length. The Vernal Equinox is the beginning of Spring and the agricultural season. Many Christian

Easter customs come from this festive occasion. The most popular of these practices is that of decorating eggs. In ancient Egypt, Rome, Greece, and Persia, brightly colored eggs were eaten at this time as symbols of immortality, fertility, and resurrection.

The Equinox is a time of balance, when we seek equality and harmony between the masculine and feminine forces in nature. It is also a time of resurrection when all life returns—one reason why Christianity decided upon this time for the resurrection of their divine king. The dates for Good Friday and Easter Sunday are calculated from the time of the Equinox.

In addition to the usual altar tools, there should be a basket filled with decorated eggs and bouquets of fresh flowers tied with ribbon and packages of seeds. Have enough so that each member can have an egg, seed packet, and bouquet of flowers to take home for their own altars.

ATTENDANTS are responsible for the altar and Quadrant preparation. All enter the chapel or ritual area.

The Benediction
The PRIEST and PRIESTESS perform the Benediction (Chapter 18).

The Litany of the Lord and Lady
The PRIEST and PRIESTESS perform the Litany of the Lord and Lady (Chapter 18).

The Consecration
The PRIESTESS consecrates the elements and casts the circle (Chapter 18).

The Calling of the Quadrant Guardian
The PRIEST calls in the Guardians of the four Quadrants (Chapter 18).

The Declaration
An ATTENDANT approaches the altar, genuflects, and rings the bells. He or she lights the floor altar candles, saying:

(Right)
Lord of the Dark realm descend,
And move the spirit of our soul.
Renew within the vital force,
Blend thy energies, make us whole.

(Left)
Lady from the Dark realm come,
Lead us into the new dawning day,

Protect us from the passions of man,
Guide us along thy secret way.

The ATTENDANT approaches the altar, genuflects, and picks up the basket of flowers and eggs. He or she offers them at each one of the Quadrants, beginning in the East, saying:

(East)
May the blessings of the Spirit of Air
Bring forth new beginnings and insight.

(South)
May the blessings of the Spirit of Fire
Bring forth personal power and wisdom.

(West)
May the blessings of the Spirit of Water
Bring forth rest and regeneration.

(North)
May the blessing of the Spirit of Earth
Bring forth endurance and stability.

The ATTENDANT returns and places the basket on the altar.

The Salutation

The PRIESTESS approaches the altar, genuflects, and rings the bells. She faces the group, saying:

Our Lord and Lady are known by many names;
They are our light and life.
We stand within their sacred temple and
Feel their presence, passion, and power.
This is their house, their home, their season
All hail to thee, Cerridwen and Cernunnos.

ALL
Ayea, Ayea, Cerridwen
Ayea, Ayea, Cerridwen
Ayea, Ayea, Cerridwen
Ayea, Ayea, Ayea!

Ayea, Ayea, Cernunnos
Ayea, Ayea, Cernunnos
Ayea, Ayea, Cernunnos
Ayea, Ayea, Ayea!

The Invitation

The PRIEST approaches the altar, genuflects, and rings the bells. He picks up the basket of eggs and flowers, offers it to the Goddess, and turns and faces the group. Still holding the basket, he says:

We invite Thee, O Ancient One
White Maiden, Blossoming Mother,
Seed of Spring.
Thou who are the bounty of desire,
Pregnant with promise and the
Living Earth.
Come, be with us now.

We invite Thee, O Horned One,
Antlered Stag, Green Lord
Quickening will of Light.
Thou who dies and returns
With the first bud of Spring
Come be with us now.
We invite Thee, Lord and Lady
Forces of regeneration
Powers of blessed earth and
Sacred sky to be with us
From dawn to dusk
In work and prayer
Now and forever, so be it!

The PRIEST places the basket in the center of the circle and leads everyone in the chant:

Blessed be the flower and seed
Grant to all what they need.

The Invocations

The PRIEST and PRIESTESS approach the altar and genuflect. An ATTENDANT rings the bells three times. The PRIESTESS does the Invocation of the Goddess (Chapter 18). The PRIEST performs the Invocation of the God (Chapter 18).

The Proclamation

The ATTENDANT approaches the altar, genuflects, rings the bells three times, and recites:

Those who walk in darkness
Shall now experience great light;

Those who hunger and thirst
Shall be quenched at the altar of life;
Those who call upon righteousness
Shall take the hand of the Lord and Lady;
Those who approach with anticipation
Shall receive the gifts of the spirit.

ALL
Our Lord and Lady
We acknowledge your greatness;
Our Lord and Lady
We affirm your wisdom and love;
Our Lord and Lady
We pray for your presence;
Our Lord and Lady
We now ask for your blessing.
Blessed be Cerridwen and Cernunnos!

The Rite of Union and the Rite of Redemption

The PRIEST and PRIESTESS approach the altar, genuflect, and face each other. An ATTENDANT rings the bells. The PRIEST and PRIESTESS perform the Rite of Union and the Rite of Redemption (Chapter 18).

The Conclusion

The PRIEST approaches the altar, genuflects, and rings the bells. He proceeds to dismiss the Guardians (Chapter 18).

The ATTENDANT approaches the altar, genuflects, and extinguishes the floor altar candles, saying:

(Left)
Blessed be the Seeds of Earth
That bring promise and hope.

(Right)
Blessed be the Light of the Spirit
That brings us new beginnings.

The ATTENDANT approaches the altar, genuflects, and retrieves the basket in the center of the circle. He or she offers it in closing to the four Quadrants, saying:

(North)
Let us always remember the Earth,
For it provides hope and promise.

(West)
Let us always remember the Waters of Regeneration,
For they render rest and renewal.

(South)
Let us always remember the Fires of Passion
For they give us protection and power.

(East)
Let us always remember the Eternal Spirit
For it brings forth the first light of Spring.

Closing Benediction

The PRIEST recites the Closing Benediction (Chapter 18). The PRIESTESS banishes the circle (Chapter 18).

The ATTENDANT stands at the edge of the circle and allows each member to take his or her seed package, egg, and flower bouquet as they leave.

Good Friday, Eucharist, Rite of Remembrance

The word *Eucharist* comes from the Greek *Eucharistein,* meaning to give thanks. During the Last Supper, Jesus broke bread with his Apostles in an upper room of a house in Jerusalem, and the celebration of the Eucharist[12] came into being. By blessing the bread and the wine, which Jesus then shared with his disciples, the rite of the Eucharist was instituted and in time became the focal point of the Christian mass.

On Good Friday, at sunset, Christians all around the world gather in solemn reverence to remember their Son of God, Jesus the Christ. They gather to celebrate his symbolic passion and love for humanity and pray for his resurrection in the days to follow. With such an outpouring of love and emotion at this time, the energy levels are extremely high. It seems only reasonable to experience some of the spiritual ecstasy so abundant at this time.

I realize that many Wiccans and Pagans tremble with terror at the prospect of expressing any emotion whatsoever for the Christian Savior God, Jesus Christ. However, keep in mind that Jesus is just another version of the Pagan dying and resurrected god who gave his life for the good of the land and the people who lived on it. From a religious standpoint, everyone should be able to appreciate what Jesus said and did during his time. He was indeed a divine victim or sacrificial king in every sense of the word—one reason why every year at Our Lady of Enchantment, we repeat the Rite of Remembrance and celebrate the Eucharist of Christ.

At least four people are needed to perform the speaking parts for this ritual. Because the main focus of the ritual is on the blessing of the sacred Wine and Bread through the Rite of Union and Rite of Redemption, the entire ritual is memorized.

The main altar is in the North and a smaller altar is placed in the center of the circle. Both are covered with white altar cloths and draped with purple vestments. Candles on the main altar as well as those used for the Quadrants are purple. The floor altar candles are white and are placed next to the altar of offering. Easter lilies are placed on both altars and one at each of the Quadrants. In addition to the regular altar tools, the PRIEST uses his Staff, which should be decorated with a wreath of white flowers tied with purple ribbon.

ATTENDANTS are responsible for the altar and Quadrant preparation (Chapter 18).

The Eucharist Rite of Remembrance
ALL follow the PRIEST, carrying the staff, into the chapel or ritual area.

The Benediction
The PRIEST and PRIESTESS perform the Benediction (Chapter 18).

The Litany of the Lord and Lady
The PRIEST and PRIESTESS perform the Litany of the Lord and Lady (Chapter 18).

The Declaration
The two ATTENDANTS approach the main altar, genuflect, and light their candles. They go to the altar of offering and light the floor altar candles, saying:

(Right)
Lord of Blood
Red Glory, Pulsing Bright
Cast away shadows
Bring in the light!

(Left)
Lady of Gleaming Beauty
Jewel of power
Enter our souls
For this hour!

The PRIESTESS and PRIEST approach the altar and genuflect. The PRIESTESS picks up the water bowl and the PRIEST picks up the salt bowl. They each offer them, saying:

PRIESTESS (water)
Blessed shall be this sacred fluid
Born of the raging sea

Transformed into passion
Bringing us love and harmony!

PRIEST (salt)
Blessed shall be this sacred remembrance
Brought from the dark forest floor
Transformed into power
Bringing us life ever more!

The Consecration
The PRIESTESS consecrates the elements and casts the circle (Chapter 18).

The Calling of the Quadrant Guardians
The PRIEST calls in the Guardians of the four Quadrants (Chapter 18), using his staff rather than the Athame.

When the PRIEST returns to the altar, he genuflects, rings the bells three times, and faces the altar. Holding up his staff, he recites:

The Salutation
Praise the Divine Victim and His glory,
Of His love we now sing;
Of the blood, the price exceeding,
Shed by our immortal King,
Destined for the world's redemption,
From the noble womb did spring.

From the Goddess as Virgin pure,
Born to us on earth below,
He was the man to teach the Word,
Spread the seeds of truth to sow;
Then he closed the solemn order
Miraculous his life of woe.

On the night of his Last Supper,
Seated with his chosen band,
He, the Paschal Victim eating,
Fulfills the Law's first command,
Then the food passed to his brethren,
Gives of himself back to the Land.

Praise be to the Father, and to the Mother,
And to the Lord of the Land. Amen.

ALL
Praise be to the Father, and to the Mother,
And to the Lord of the Land. Amen.

The Invitation

An ATTENDANT takes his or her place in front of the altar of offering, ringing the bell three times and saying:

(ring the bell and say)
In thee we are reconciled.

(ring the bell and say)
In thee we feel harmony.

(ring the bell and say)
In thee we find love.

(ring the bell and say)
In thee we are made new again.

(ring the bell and say)
Blessed are the Lord and Lady, for they
Bring unification of the mind and soul.

Praise be to the Father, and to the Mother,
And to the Lord of the Land. Amen.

ALL
Praise be to the Father, and to the Mother,
And to the Lord of the Land. Amen.

An ATTENDANT rings the bell three times and the PRIEST and PRIESTESS genuflect, as do the attendants who are standing in front of the altar of offering.

The PRIEST picks up the Host container in offering and says the following:

(Hosts)
Lord of the Sacred and most Holy
Source of all Life,
Be thou ever constant and within us
So that we may remain in thy abundant joy!

The PRIESTESS picks up the vessels of red and white wine in offering and says the following:

(Red and white wine)
Lady of the night, Queen of all Mysteries
Source of invisible power,

Be thou ever constant and within us
So that we may remain in thy abundant joy!

The Proclamation
An ATTENDANT standing in front of the altar of offering genuflects and rings the bells three times, saying:

Those who walk in darkness
Shall now experience great light;
Those who hunger and thirst
Shall be quenched at the altar of life;
Those who call upon righteousness
Shall take the hand of the Lord and Lady;
Those who approach with anticipation
Shall receive the gifts of the spirit.

ALL
Our Lord and Lady
We acknowledge your greatness;
Our Lord and Lady
We affirm your wisdom and love;
Our Lord and Lady
We pray for your presence;
Our Lord and Lady
We now ask for your blessing.
Blessed be the Lord and Lady!

The Rite of Union and the Rite of Redemption
The PRIEST and PRIESTESS approach the altar, genuflect, and face each other. An ATTENDANT rings the bells. The PRIEST and PRIESTESS perform the Rite of Union and the Rite of Redemption (Chapter 18).

One ATTENDANT reads the Twenty-Third Psalm, "The Lord is My Shepherd,"[13] as the other ATTENDANT passes out the Remembrance tokens. (See the end of this ritual for token suggestions.)

The Conclusion
An ATTENDANT takes his or her place in front of the altar of offering, ringing the bell and saying:

(Ring the bell)
In thee we are reconciled.

(Ring the bell)
In thee we feel harmony.

(Ring the bell)
In thee we find love.

(Ring the bell)
In thee we are made new again.

(Ring the bell)
Blessed are the Lord and Lady for they
Bring unification of the mind and soul.

Praise be to the Father, and to the Mother,
And to the Lord of the Land. Amen.

ALL
Praise be to the Father, and to the Mother,
And to the Lord of the Land. Amen.

Closing Benediction

The PRIEST recites the Closing Benediction (Chapter 18). The PRIESTESS banishes the circle (Chapter 18).

The ritual area is left with candles lit so that all may return for personal prayers and blessings if they wish.

At Our Lady of Enchantment, we make up little cards with an explanation of what the cross symbolizes (see below) on one side and a copy of the selected reading done during the rite on the other and attach a small cross to it. These are wrapped in purple paper, tied with white ribbons, and given as ritual remembrances to all who participate.

Key Symbol—The Cross

The cross is a universal symbol of communication between heaven and earth. The cross also represents the Tree of Life and the Tree of Nourishment. The vertical line represents the masculine, positive, and active polarity; the horizontal line represents the feminine, negative, and passive side of nature. The cross is dualism in nature and the union of opposites as the material and spiritual planes cross and unite with each other.

Beltane or May Eve

Beltane is celebrated on April 30 (May Eve) and is primarily a fire and fertility festival. Beltane, meaning "Bel-Fire," is named after the Celtic God Bel, also known as Beli or Balor, which means Lord. Some seem to think that Bel was comparable to the Celtic Gaul god, Cernunnos. This is possible as most male gods relate to the sun and fire aspects.

Beltane is also the time of the May Queen, in which a young woman was chosen from the village to represent the Earth Goddess and reflected the transformation of maiden to mother. This was also the time of the kindling of the "Need Fire," when all fires in the village were extinguished and ritually relit the following day.

Fertility played an important role in the Beltane celebrations. The most significant symbol of this was the May Pole, also known as the *axis mundi*, around which the universe revolved. The pole personified the thrusting masculine force; the disk at the top depicted the receptive female. Tied to the pole were seven colored ribbons, which represented the seven colors of the rainbow. Fire and fertility, for the most part, dominated the rituals at this time.

Beltane is one of the two highest of the Holy Days of Obligation (the other being Samhain on October 31). As the aspect of fertility and growth is personified at this time, the Rite of Union and Rite of Redemption take on a greater significance, as these are the two rites that allow us to unite spiritually with the God and Goddess.

In addition to the usual altar and tools, there should be a cauldron placed in the center of the circle, surrounded by flowers and with a candle inside. There should also be a crown of fresh flowers that the PRIEST places on the head of the PRIESTESS in remembrance of the May Queen and Goddess reigning as the Queen of heaven.

ATTENDANTS are responsible for the altar and Quadrant preparation (Chapter 18).

The Benediction
The PRIEST and PRIESTESS perform the Benediction (Chapter 18).

The Litany of the Lord and Lady
The PRIEST and PRIESTESS perform the Litany of the Lord and Lady (Chapter 18).

The Consecration
The PRIESTESS consecrates the elements and casts the circle (Chapter 18).

The Calling of the Quadrant Guardian
The PRIEST calls in the Guardians of the four Quadrants (Chapter 18).

The Declaration
An ATTENDANT approaches the altar, genuflects, and rings the bells. He or she lights the floor altar candles, saying:

(Right)
Blessed be our Lord of Light and Power,
For He transforms our souls for this hour.

(Left)
Blessed be our Lady of Love and Passion
For our Hearts and Future She shall fashion.

An ATTENDANT approaches the altar, genuflects, rings the bells, and recites the following:

Let now the Light and Life of the Creative Spirit
Deliver us from Darkness, bring us
Wisdom and Clear Vision, as we progress
Toward our Lord and Lady. So be it!

The Salutation

The PRIEST approaches the altar, genuflects, and rings the bells. He lights a taper candle and proceeds to the center of the circle where he recites the following and lights the candle in the cauldron:[14]

By the Oak and by the Stone,
Stands the Cauldron of the Crone,
Mistress of our Birth and Death
From who comes life's first breath,
We approach your altar on this Night
To summon forth thy sacred Light,
And all of those who dare to seek
Of your Mysteries we shall speak,
With torch and flame this fire we fashion
To arouse your tempting passion,
For you are the Maiden, Mother, and Wife
Whose Triple Will brings forth all Life!

ALL
Ayea, Ayea, Cerridwen
Ayea, Ayea, Cerridwen
Ayea, Ayea, Cerridwen
Ayea, Ayea, Ayea!

The Invitation

The PRIESTESS approaches the altar, genuflects, and speaks the following:

Cerridwen, Glorious Lady of the Moon,
Holiest of Holy, we honor thee this night.
Thou art the Maiden, the Mother and the
Crone, Transcendent and Ageless Splendor,

To whom we pay homage. Now do we celebrate
The cycle of return, the promise. For all
That shall be touched by Thy Light, shall
Be Transformed.

ALL
Ayea, Ayea, Cerridwen
Ayea, Ayea, Cerridwen
Ayea, Ayea, Cerridwen
Ayea, Ayea, Ayea!

The PRIEST approaches the altar, genuflects, and picks up the crown of flowers. He escorts the PRIESTESS to the center of the circle where they stand beside the cauldron. The PRIESTESS kneels and the PRIEST holds the crown in offering, saying:

Thou who rises from the Raging Sea,
Shall now accept thy destiny.
Let now the Lady of Inner Earth,
To the Land of promise give birth.
So that all the seed, fruit, and grain
Shall in abundance come forth again!

The PRIEST places the crown on the head of the PRIESTESS and she rises.

ALL
Ayea, Ayea, Cerridwen
Ayea, Ayea, Cerridwen
Ayea, Ayea, Cerridwen
Ayea, Ayea, Ayea!

The Invocations
The PRIEST and PRIESTESS approach the altar and genuflect. An ATTENDANT rings the bells three times. The PRIESTESS does the Invocation of the Goddess (Chapter 18). The PRIEST performs the Invocation of the God (Chapter 18).

The Proclamation
An ATTENDANT standing in front of the altar of offering genuflects and rings the bells three times, saying:

Those who walk in darkness
Shall now experience great light;
Those who hunger and thirst
Shall be quenched at the altar of life;
Those who call upon righteousness

Shall take the hand of the Lord and Lady;
Those who approach with anticipation
Shall receive the gifts of the spirit.

ALL
Our Lord and Lady
We acknowledge your greatness;
Our Lord and Lady
We affirm your wisdom and love;
Our Lord and Lady
We pray for your presence;
Our Lord and Lady
We now ask for your blessing.
Blessed be the Lord and Lady!

The Rite of Union and the Rite of Redemption

The PRIEST and PRIESTESS approach the altar, genuflect, and face each other. An ATTENDANT rings the bells. The PRIEST and PRIESTESS perform the Rite of Union and the Rite of Redemption (Chapter 18).

The Conclusion

The PRIEST approaches the altar, genuflects, and rings the bells. He dismisses the Guardians (Chapter 18).

An ATTENDANT approaches the altar, genuflects, and extinguishes the floor altar candles, saying:

(Left)
Blessed be the Lady who came from the night
For she has brought to all love and light.

(Right)
Blessed be the Lord who shines forth as the sun
For his will and work shall now be done.

Closing Benediction

The PRIESTESS recites the Closing Benediction and then banishes the circle (Chapter 18).

The Summer (or Midsummer) Solstice

Summer or Midsummer Solstice is celebrated around June 21, and is the longest day and shortest night of the year. The festival of the Summer Solstice is concerned with both fire and water. From this point on, the sun declines in its power; the symbology of fire was used in keeping the sun alive. The water element was used for the ritual blessing of individuals, sacred wells, and springs.

One of our ancestors' customs was to leap over or pass through fires. It was believed that the higher one jumped, the higher the crops would grow. As with Beltane, cattle were driven through the fires for purification and fumigation. It was also believed that the fire repelled the powers of evil and protected the cattle as well as all who passed through it.

Another symbol used at this time is that of the wheel. The wheel's turning suggests the season's turning or progression. Wheels were decorated with flowers and lighted candles. The decorated wheels were taken to a body of water and set afloat.

In addition to the usual altar tools, there should be a yellow floating candle placed in a bowl of water. The altar of offering should be set in the center of the circle with the floor altar candles next to it. Fresh flowers should be used to decorate the area. For this ritual, we make wheels out of fresh flowers for each of the Quadrants.

ATTENDANTS are responsible for the altar and Quadrant preparation (Chapter 18).

All enter the chapel or ritual area.

The Benediction
The PRIEST and PRIESTESS perform the Benediction (Chapter 18).

The Litany of the Lord and Lady
The PRIEST and PRIESTESS perform the Litany of the Lord and Lady (Chapter 18).

The Consecration
The PRIESTESS consecrates the elements and casts the circle (Chapter 18).

The Calling of the Quadrant Guardian
The PRIEST calls in the Guardians of the four Quadrants (Chapter 18).

The Declaration
An ATTENDANT approaches the altar, genuflects, and rings the bells. He or she lights the floor altar candles, saying:

(Right)
Cernunnos be with us in truth and might
As in your honor this candle we light.

(Left)
Cerridwen now send your divine guiding power
Through candle flame bless each this hour.

An ATTENDANT approaches the altar, genuflects, and picks up the bowl with the floating candle in it. He or she offers this at each of the Quadrants, saying:

(East)
Let the winds of consciousness bring
Forth insight and wisdom
As the East gives rise to the light.

(South)
Let the fires of awareness bring
Forth motivation and inspiration
As the South gives host to the Sun.
(West)
Let the waves of completeness bring
Forth love and passion
As the West accepts the twilight.

(North)
Let the blossoming fertile Earth bring
Forth manifestation of desire
As the North returns from darkness.

The ATTENDANT places the floating candle in the bowl on the altar of offering.

The Salutation

The PRIESTESS approaches the altar, genuflects, and picks up a taper candle. She lights it and proceeds to the altar of offering where she lights the floating candle, saying:

Our Lord is the fire of the Golden Sphere,
Our Lady's time now draws near,
For through the candle flame they speak,
Bringing insight and wisdom to all who seek.
The mystery of life within their power lies,
That will in time allow mankind to rise,
Above the limitations of this confined earth,
To all we know and see they have given birth.

ALL
Ayea, Ayea, Cerridwen
Ayea, Ayea, Cerridwen
Ayea, Ayea, Cerridwen
Ayea, Ayea, Ayea!

Ayea, Ayea, Cernunnos
Ayea, Ayea, Cernunnos
Ayea, Ayea, Cernunnos
Ayea, Ayea, Ayea!

The Invitation

The PRIEST faces the group and delivers the following message:

At this time of Light and Life
Do we celebrate the Summer Solstice,
For all life has blossomed forth
And Nature flourishes around us.
Great indeed is our joy this night
As our Lord and Lady bless us with
Their abundance.
Our Lord provides strength and passion
And our Lady love and understanding.
They allow us to progress and grow
As they free us from past restrictions.
Great indeed are their blessings.

The PRIESTESS goes to the altar of offering and picks up the floating candle. She holds it in offering to the Goddess as she recites the following:

To the Lord and Lady
Our gratitude we show
As in life and spirit
We progress and grow.
Let us all thank them
By our work and deed
That we may all receive
What we wish and need.

The Invocations

The PRIEST and PRIESTESS approach the altar and genuflect. An ATTENDANT rings the bells three times. The PRIESTESS does the Invocation of the Goddess (Chapter 18). The PRIEST performs the Invocation of the God (Chapter 18).

The PRIEST asks everyone to take hands and form a circle around the altar of offering as they chant the following:

Candle and flame
Bring joy and gain!

The Proclamation

An ATTENDANT standing in front of the altar of offering genuflects and rings the bells three times, saying:

Those who walk in darkness
Shall now experience great light;
Those who hunger and thirst
Shall be quenched at the altar of life;
Those who call upon righteousness
Shall take the hand of the Lord and Lady;
Those who approach with anticipation
Shall receive the gifts of the spirit.

ALL
Our Lord and Lady
we acknowledge your greatness;
Our Lord and Lady
we affirm your wisdom and love;
Our Lord and Lady
we pray for your presence;
Our Lord and Lady
we now ask for your blessing.
Blessed be the Lord and Lady!

The Rite of Union and the Rite of Redemption

The PRIEST and PRIESTESS approach the altar, genuflect, and face each other. An ATTENDANT rings the bells. The PRIEST and PRIESTESS perform the Rite of Union and the Rite of Redemption (Chapter 18).

The Conclusion

The PRIEST approaches the altar, genuflects, and rings the bells. He dismisses the Guardians (Chapter 18).

An ATTENDANT approaches the altar, genuflects, and extinguishes the floor altar candles, saying:

(Left)
Blessed be the Lady, for she is life and light.
(Right)
Blessed be the Lord and all who gathered here this night.

Closing Benediction

The PRIESTESS recites the Closing Benediction and then banishes the circle (Chapter 18).

Lughnasadh or Lammas

Lughnasadh (Celtic) or Lammas (Christian) is held on August 1. *Lughnasadh* means loaf feast and refers to the first loaves baked from the first grain harvested. The priesthood blessed these loaves and distributed them among the members of the congregation. Observing this festival ensured an abundance of fruit and grain in the months to come. The first fruit picked or sheaf cut was considered sacred to the Gods and therefore treated in a special manner.

Corn and grain are the primary features of rituals at this time because they symbolize the fertility of the earth, awakening of life, and life coming from death. The golden ears of corn are seen as the offspring of the marriage of the sun and virgin earth. Corn and wine, like bread and wine, represent human's labor and ability to sustain life.

Wine and candle making were also done at this time of year, along with food preserving and other preparations for winter. Some customs include rush-bearing, decorating water wells with vines, and blessing food.

In addition to the usual altar tools, there should be a large John Barleycorn, which is a man shaped out of cookie dough that contains seven grains, including cornmeal and barley flour. There should be a basket large enough to hold the corn that each member brings. Every participant should bring at least one ear of corn.

ATTENDANTS are responsible for the altar and Quadrant preparation (Chapter 18).

All enter the chapel or ritual area.

The Benediction
The PRIEST and PRIESTESS perform the Benediction (Chapter 18).

The Litany of the Lord and Lady
The PRIEST and PRIESTESS perform the Litany of the Lord and Lady (Chapter 18).

The Consecration
The PRIESTESS consecrates the elements and casts the circle (Chapter 18).

The Calling of the Quadrant Guardian
The PRIEST calls in the Guardians of the four Quadrants (Chapter 18).

The Declaration
An ATTENDANT approaches the altar, genuflects, and rings the bells. He or she lights the floor altar candles, saying:

(Right)
Our Lord is the passion
He brings forth the light
The harvest is of his seed.

(Left)
Our Lady is the power
She brings forth the life
The harvest is her reward.

An ATTENDANT approaches the altar, genuflects, rings the bells, and recites the following:

Our Lady teaches that naught receives naught.
That as we have sowed, so shall we reap.
On this night all shall receive accordingly,
Nothing shall be withheld for those deserving.
For blessed are the fruits of our labors.

The ATTENDANT goes around the circle, gathering the corn and leading all in the chant:

As the corn—we are reborn!

The PRIEST takes the basket of corn from the ATTENDANT and offers it at each one of the Quadrants, saying:

(East)
I call upon soft and whispering winds
The realm of intellect and perception
Bring forth the spirit of wisdom.

(South)
I call upon the warm and quickening light
For thou art fire and inspiration
Which warms the hearth and heart.

(West)
I call upon the cool waters of sea and stream
The realm of our watery beginnings
Temper our emotions with love and compassion.

(North)
I call upon flowering field and forest
For thou our land of beauty and pleasure
Bring forth abundance and great bounty.

The PRIEST places the corn in the center of the circle.

The Salutation
The PRIESTESS approaches the altar, genuflects, and recites the following:

Once again has the Goddess provided,
For our seeds, once planted, became flowers
And those flowers became the fruit of our Desires.
Bountiful is our Harvest and great shall be our reward
We rejoice, as we once again come full cycle.

The Invitation
The PRIEST picks up the John Barleycorn, holds it in offering, and asks the blessing upon it as follows:

Corn and barley are of this earth
With love and work we gave them birth,
Though they were just once small seeds
Through them we achieved our wishes and needs.
Behold John Barleycorn who was our plight
Brings us joy and abundance this night,
Because of him we know and see
The truth of our own reality.

The PRIEST hands the John Barleycorn to an ATTENDANT who offers him at each Quadrant while another ATTENDANT reads the legend of John Barlycorn:[15]

(East)
There were three kings into the east,
Three kings both great and high,
And they hath swore a solemn oath
John Barleycorn should die.

They took a plough and plough'd him down
Put clods upon his head,
And they hath sworn a solemn oath
John Barleycorn was dead.

But the cheerful spring came kindly on,
And show'rs began to fall;
John Barleycorn got up again,
And sore surpris'd them all.

(South)
The sultry suns of summer came,
And he grew thick and strong,

His head weel arm'd wi' pointed spears,
That no one should him wrong.

The sober autumn enter'd mild,
When he grew wan and pale;
His bending joints and drooping head
Show'd he began to fail.

His color sicken'd more and more,
He faded into age;
And then his enemies began
To show their deadly rage.

They've ta'en a weapon long and sharp,
And cut him by the knee;
They ty'd him fast upon a cart,
Like a rogue of forgerie.

(West)
They laid him down upon his back,
And cudgell'd him full score;
They hung him up before the storm,
And turn'd him o'er and o'er.

They filled up a darksome pit
With water to the brim,
They heaved in John Barleycorn—
There let him sink or swim.

They laid him out upon the floor,
To work him farther woe;
And still as signs of life appear'd,
They tossed him to and fro.

(North)
They wasted o'er a scorching flame,
The marrow of his bones;
But the miller used him worst of all,
For he crush'd him between two stones.

And they have ta'en his very heart's blood,
And drank it round and round;

And still the more and more they drank,
Their joy did more abound.

John Barleycorn was a hero bold
Of noble enterprise;
For if you do but taste his blood,
T' make your courage rise.

The ATTENDANT returns to the altar and hands the John Barleycorn to the PRIESTESS. She holds it in offering and says:

Our Lord and Lady shall provide
Long after all has withered and died,
Though they have given us life through the land
What we now hold, is the work of our hand,
And always remember, just as the corn
We, like they, are ever dying and reborn.

The PRIESTESS places the John Barleycorn in the center of the circle with the corn. All take hands and chant the following to bless the corn and grain:

Corn and grain
Bring joy and gain!

The Invocations
The PRIEST and PRIESTESS approach the altar and genuflect. An ATTENDANT rings the bells three times. The PRIESTESS does the Invocation of the Goddess (Chapter 18). The PRIEST performs the Invocation of the God (Chapter 18).

The Proclamation
An ATTENDANT standing in front of the altar of offering genuflects and rings the bells three times, saying:

Those who walk in darkness
Shall now experience great light;
Those who hunger and thirst
Shall be quenched at the altar of life;
Those who call upon righteousness
Shall take the hand of the Lord and Lady;
Those who approach with anticipation
Shall receive the gifts of the spirit.

ALL
Our Lord and Lady
We acknowledge your greatness;
Our Lord and Lady
We affirm your wisdom and love;
Our Lord and Lady
We pray for your presence;
Our Lord and Lady
We now ask for your blessing.
Blessed be the Lord and Lady!

The Rite of Union and the Rite of Redemption

The PRIEST and PRIESTESS approach the altar, genuflect, and face each other. An ATTENDANT rings the bells. The PRIEST and PRIESTESS perform the Rite of Union and the Rite of Redemption (Chapter 18).

The Conclusion

The PRIEST approaches the altar, genuflects, and rings the bells. He dismisses the Guardians (Chapter 18).

An ATTENDANT approaches the altar, genuflects, and extinguishes the floor altar candles, saying:

(Left)
Blessed be the Maiden, Mother, Crone
As we now approach the Harvest Home.

(Right)
Blessed be the King of corn and grain
As now the season of abundance does wain.

Closing Benediction

The PRIESTESS recites the Closing Benediction and then banishes the circle (Chapter 18).

The John Barleycorn is usually placed on the feast table for everyone to partake of. Members take their ear of corn home, dry it, and use it to make their corn babas for Autumn Equinox (See Endnote 16).

The Feast of the Blessed Virgin

The Feast of the Blessed Virgin occurs on September 7 and/or 8. It is a celebration of the Nativity of the Blessed Virgin Mary who, like many Christian deities, was a compilation of many early Pagan goddesses. Much of the symbolism that surrounds Mary is identical to that of Ishtar and Isis.

For this ritual, we emphasize the principle of everlastingness and realize the nature of constant motion from birth through life to death. All matter moves, progresses, and evolves whether it wants to or not. As we are moving from a season of life to one of death, the concept of birth and honoring the Goddess for her life-giving properties is important.

The purpose of the ceremony is to bring down the blessings of the Goddess as we ask her to help us improve our lives.

In addition to the usual altar tools, there should be an empty cornucopia placed on the altar of offering in the center of the circle. All members bring a fruit or vegetable.

ATTENDANTS are responsible for the altar and Quadrant preparation (Chapter 18).

All enter the chapel or ritual area.

The Benediction
The PRIEST and PRIESTESS perform the Benediction (Chapter 18).

The Litany of the Lord and Lady
The PRIEST and PRIESTESS perform the Litany of the Lord and Lady (Chapter 18).

The Consecration
The PRIESTESS consecrates the elements and casts the circle (Chapter 18).

The Calling of the Quadrant Guardian
The PRIEST calls in the Guardians of the four Quadrants (Chapter 18).

The Declaration
An ATTENDANT approaches the altar, genuflects, and rings the bells. He lights the floor altar candles, saying:

(Right)
Hail, Great Mother shining light,
Bring us birth and all that's bright.

(Left)
Hail, Great Mother from Heaven above,
Bring us life and all that is love.

The PRIESTESS approaches the altar, genuflects, and recites the following:

Lady of all life, below and above
We gather here with warmth and love.
So that all who come before thy throne
Shall learn of mysteries yet unknown.
Let each now behold your beauty and grace
As this now becomes your sacred space.

The PRIEST approaches the altar, genuflects, and reads the following prayer:

Holy sweet Virgin Mary, Mother of God,
daughter of the Highest King and Mistress
Of the Angels. Mother of our Creator,
Queen of Heaven, receive us under your protection.
Queen of Mercy, we implore you and your
Holy Son for health, comfort, and strength
To serve your righteous cause. We ask for
Your blessings now and forever, Amen.

The Salutation

The PRIESTESS stands in front of the altar of offering. She genuflects, picks up the cornucopia, and recites the following:

Our Lady's love is deep and wide
To some her secrets are denied.
But we shall fearless still proceed
To follow where she may lead.
She fills our life with hope and laughter
So we have no fear of what comes after.

Praise be to the Virgin, to the Mother and
To the Queen of Heaven, now and forever, Amen.

ALL
Praise be to the Virgin, to the Mother, and
To the Queen of Heaven, now and forever, Amen.

Each member approaches the altar of offering, genuflects, asks the Goddess' blessing, and puts a fruit or vegetable into the cornucopia. Before returning to his or her place, each says:

Praise be to the Virgin, to the Mother, and
To the Queen of Heaven, now and forever, Amen!

The Invitation

The PRIEST approaches the altar, genuflects, and rings the bells. He recites the following with great emotion:

Blessed be the Lady, Mother of All
For you are our wisdom and hope.
Thou, who was before mankind,
Who was at our birth and shall
Claim us at our death.
We now ask your blessings this night.
Be with us now and forever,
In this life and all those to come

ALL
Praise be to the Virgin, to the Mother, and
To the Queen of Heaven, now and forever, Amen!

An ATTENDANT approaches the altar, genuflects, and speaks the following with great reverence:

For each morning with its light
My Lady, we thank thee.
For rest and shelter in the night
My Lady, we thank thee.
For health and wealth, love of friends
For everything thy goodness sends,
My Lady, we thank thee.

ALL
Praise be to the Virgin, to the Mother, and
To the Queen of Heaven, now and forever, Amen!

The Invocation

The PRIESTESS approaches the altar, genuflects, and does the Invocation of the Goddess (Chapter 18).

The Proclamation

An ATTENDANT standing in front of the altar of offering genuflects and rings the bells three times, saying:

Those who walk in darkness
Shall now experience great light;
Those who hunger and thirst
Shall be quenched at the altar of life;

Those who call upon righteousness
Shall take the hand of the Lord and Lady;
Those who approach with anticipation
Shall receive the gifts of the spirit.

ALL
Our Lord and Lady
We acknowledge your greatness;
Our Lord and Lady
We affirm your wisdom and love;
Our Lord and Lady
We pray for your presence;
Our Lord and Lady
We now ask for your blessing.
Blessed be the Lord and Lady!

The Rite of Union and the Rite of Redemption
The PRIEST and PRIESTESS approach the altar, genuflect, and face each other. An ATTENDANT rings the bells. The PRIEST and PRIESTESS perform the Rite of Union and the Rite of Redemption (Chapter 18).

The Conclusion
The PRIEST approaches the altar, genuflects, and rings the bells. He dismisses the Guardians (Chapter 18).

An ATTENDANT approaches the altar, genuflects, and extinguishes the floor altar candles. He or she then says:

Beloved Lady of Light and Life,
Who art blessed amongst women,
Mother of all upon the earth,
Be with us now in our hour of need,
For we are your children conceived in love
And brought forth to honor your name.
Guide us and guard us in all we do,
That we shall bring only honor to your name.

ALL
Praise be to the Virgin, to the Mother, and
To the Queen of Heaven, now and forever, Amen!

Closing Benediction
The PRIESTESS recites the Closing Benediction and then banishes the circle (Chapter 18).

Autumn Equinox (or Mabon)

The Autumn Equinox, also known as Mabon, is celebrated sometime around September 21. As with the Spring Equinox, this is a time of equal day and equal night. However, after this night, the days grow shorter and the sun begins to wane in power.

This festival is also known as the Harvest Home and is the end of the agricultural year. All the crops have been gathered. Canning and storage for the winter is a priority and wine making is in full progress. Leaves turning color, bird migrations, corn harvesting, and bonfires remind us of the time of year.

The purpose of the Autumn Equinox is thanksgiving. We want to thank the God and Goddess for all of our gifts and pledge ourselves to maintain what we have gained throughout the year. This is a wonderful time to decorate the house and the ritual area with signs of the season. Pumpkins, corn stalks, basket of Indian corn, and gourds add to the autumn atmosphere and bring the symbolic meaning of the harvest into the home and sanctuary of the God and Goddess.

In addition to the usual altar and tools, the altar of offering should be placed in the center of the circle. On it are placed a basket, the corn baba,[16] and a red candle. Each participant brings his or her own corn baba for blessing during the ceremony.

ATTENDANTS are responsible for the altar and Quadrant preparation (Chapter 18).

All enter the chapel or ritual area.

The Benediction
The PRIEST and PRIESTESS perform the Benediction (Chapter 18).

The Litany of the Lord and Lady
The PRIEST and PRIESTESS perform the Litany of the Lord and Lady (Chapter 18).

The Consecration
The PRIESTESS consecrates the elements and casts the circle (Chapter 18).

The Calling of the Quadrant Guardian
The PRIEST calls in the Guardians of the four Quadrants (Chapter 18).

The Declaration
An ATTENDANT approaches the altar, genuflects, and rings the bells. He or she lights the floor altar candles, saying:

(Right)
Lord of the Dark Realm descend
Your strength and power now lend.

(Left)
Lady of the Moons bright light
In your name we gather on this night.

An ATTENDANT approaches the altar of offering and genuflects. He or she picks up the corn baba and offers it at each Quadrant, saying:

(East)
Equal day and equal night
Golden leaves, icy wind and the Dying Sun,
Shadows cast from the fading light
And the spirit of the Harvest is upon us.

(South)
Flaming Autumn Fires
The memory of a Summer past,
Fills our hearts with warmth and passion
As we revel in the bounty of the Harvest.

(West)
Water cooled by a setting Sun
Reflecting the last glimmer of day,
Thou art the twilight, the time of passing
Do we realize the wisdom of the harvest.

(North)
Barren land reveals the pitted soil
Gathered crops provide food and joy,
Death awaits rebirth
And the promise of the Harvest sustains.

The ATTENDANT replaces the corn baba on the altar of offering and hands the red candle to the PRIESTESS.

The Salutation
The PRIESTESS holds the candle in offering to the God and Goddess and recites the following:

Golden-haired Corn Mother
Red Dying King,
Leaves turn, sickles gleam
Summer's end is at hand.
Our Harvest has been hearty
And our dreams fulfilled.
Blessed is the Autumn Fire

Which brings hope and promise,
Blessed be our Lord and Lady
Who brought us Life and Light.

ALL
Blessed be our Lord and Lady.

The PRIESTESS lights the candle and places it on the altar of offering in front of the corn baba.

The Invitation

PRIEST approaches the altar, genuflects, and rings the bells. He delivers the following invitation:

This is the time of equal day and equal night
The time of gathering and celebration,
A time when the abundance of life flows freely
And yet the chill of Death lingers near.
For now the Corn Maiden, our Silver Moon Goddess
Offers up her bounty and withdraws,
The Corn King, Red Lion of the South, Giver of Life,
Bringer of Death remains ever steadfast.
Is the time for petitions
Is the time for reward,
Is the time for Thanksgiving,

Blessed be the Lady
Blessed be the Corn
Blessed be the Lord
Blessed be the Harvest.

ALL
Blessed be the Lady
Blessed be the Corn
Blessed be the Lord
Blessed be the Harvest.

An ATTENDANT approaches the altar of offering and the PRIEST rings the bells. The ATTENDANT picks up the basket and collects the corn babas from each member. The ATTENDANT returns to the altar of offering.

The Invocations

The ATTENDANT places the basket on the altar of offering and steps aside. The PRIESTESS comes forward and blesses the corn babas by doing the Invocation to the

Goddess (Chapter 18). Then the PRIEST comes forward and empowers them by doing the Invocation of the God (Chapter 18).

The PRIEST asks everyone to take hands and chant the following over the corn babas:

Blessed be the harvest.

The Proclamation

An ATTENDANT standing in front of the altar of offering genuflects and rings the bells three times, saying:

Those who walk in darkness
Shall now experience great light;
Those who hunger and thirst
Shall be quenched at the altar of life;
Those who call upon righteousness
Shall take the hand of the Lord and Lady;
Those who approach with anticipation
Shall receive the gifts of the spirit.

ALL
Our Lord and Lady
We acknowledge your greatness;
Our Lord and Lady
We affirm your wisdom and love;
Our Lord and Lady
We pray for your presence;
Our Lord and Lady
We now ask for your blessing.
Blessed be the Lord and Lady!

The Rite of Union and the Rite of Redemption

The PRIEST and PRIESTESS approach the altar, genuflect, and face each other. An ATTENDANT rings the bells. The PRIEST and PRIESTESS perform the Rite of Union and the Rite of Redemption (Chapter 18).

The Conclusion

The PRIEST approaches the altar, genuflects, and rings the bells. He dismisses the Guardians (Chapter 18).

An ATTENDANT approaches the altar, genuflects, and extinguishes the floor altar candles, saying:

(Left)
Death is upon us but rebirth will follow and
The Lady will guide us through the night.

(Right)
Our hearts are filled with warmth and passion and
The Lord will provide for us through the Winter.

Closing Benediction

The PRIEST recites the Closing Benediction (Chapter 18). The PRIESTESS banishes the circle (Chapter 18).

Samhain or All Hallows Eve

Samhain, which means Summer's End, is celebrated on October 31. It is the end of the agricultural season and the beginning of the Celtic New Year. Samhain is the festival of the dead and was Christianized as All Souls or All Saints Day. This is a time of chaos and the reversal of normal order due to the simultaneous aspects of ending and beginning something.

For our ancestors, Samhain was when the majority of the herd was butchered, providing food for the winter months. Slaughter, barren earth, and decreasing daylight made the concept of death an ever-present reality. Because of this, Samhain has always been considered a time when the veil between the worlds was thin, a night of magic charms and divination—when the dead could be easily contacted.

On this night, we see the goddess of vegetation and growth return to the underworld, for it is the time of the Horned God of the hunt, the god of death and regeneration. He rules the winter months, the time of transition when we switch from life to death. As Beltane was a time of life and growth, Samhain is its opposite: a time of death and decay.

In addition to the usual altar tools on the main altar, there should be a skull and a pair of horns. Place the cauldron in the circle with a red candle in it. For this ritual, the altar cloth is black. The candles on the main altar are red and the floor candles next to the altar are black. Fill a basket with bundles of dried herbs tied with black ribbon, which will be given to the participants during the ritual. These bundles are taken home and placed above the doorway for protection during the winter months.

ATTENDANTS are responsible for the altar and Quadrant preparation (Chapter 18).

All enter the chapel or ritual area.

The Benediction
The PRIEST and PRIESTESS perform the Benediction (Chapter 18).

The Litany of the Lord and Lady
The PRIEST and PRIESTESS perform the Litany of the Lord and Lady (Chapter 18).

The Consecration
The PRIESTESS consecrates the elements and casts the circle (Chapter 18).

The Calling of the Quadrant Guardian
The PRIEST calls in the Guardians of the four Quadrants (Chapter 18).

The Declaration
An ATTENDANT lights the floor altar candles next to the altar of offering, saying:

> (Right)
> *Blessed be our Lord of Death*
> *For he brings rest and regeneration.*

> (Left)
> *Blessed be the Death Crone*
> *For she transforms the soul of man.*

The PRIESTESS approaches the altar, genuflects, and addresses the group, saying:

> *We gather together this night*
> *In a place that is not a place*
> *And a time which is not a time.*
> *All that was green has died*
> *And memories are our retribution and reward.*
> *For now the season of life draws to a close*
> *So begin the dark times of rest and reevaluation.*
> *Death brings life, life brings death.*

> ALL
> *Death brings life, Life brings death.*

The Salutation
Two ATTENDANTS approach the altar and genuflect. One picks up the skull and the other picks up the horns; they say in turn:

> (Holding the skull)
> *Blessed is the Death Crone*
> *As her silent tides of death and birth,*

For she alone brought love,
Life, and wisdom to our Earth.

(Holding the horns)
Blessed is the Dying King
And the sacrifice of blood he shed,
For he alone will guide us
Through the Dark times of Dread.

ALL praise the God and Goddess:

Ayea, Ayea, Cerridwen
Ayea, Ayea, Cerridwen
Ayea, Ayea, Cerridwen
Ayea, Ayea, Ayea!

Ayea, Ayea, Cernunnos
Ayea, Ayea, Cernunnos
Ayea, Ayea, Cernunnos
Ayea, Ayea, Ayea!

The Invitation

The PRIEST approaches the altar and genuflects. He lights a taper candle and hands it to an ATTENDANT who offers it at each of the Quadrants, saying:

(East)
Death brings awareness of the Eternal Spirit.

(South)
Death brings awareness of the Divine Spark.

(West)
Death brings awareness of the Mother's Grace.

(North)
Death brings awareness of the Final Atonement.

The ATTENDANT returns to the main altar and hands the lighted taper to the PRIEST.

The PRIEST proceeds to the middle of the circle and lights the candle in the cauldron, saying:

As with life, so with death
We have come full circle,
Let us now bid farewell to all
Which has not been productive,

The past does not bring sadness
But produces guidance for the future,
All which passes away shall make room
For what we wish to bring about.

The PRIESTESS joins the PRIEST at the cauldron. An ATTENDANT comes forward and picks up the basket with the herbal bundles in it. He or she holds the bundles so the PRIESTESS can bless them, saying:

The land has died, the earth is cold
The Horned One comes from times of old.
He brings the word, he is the death
He whispers to all with icy breath.
The spirits of the dead are abroad this night
Take heed, find comfort in the cauldron light.
For all across the land, Death does roam
But the Lord guides, and guards his own.

ALL
Ayea, Ayea, Cernunnos
Ayea, Ayea, Cernunnos
Ayea, Ayea, Cernunnos
Ayea, Ayea, Ayea!

The ATTENDANT proceeds around the circle with the basket and each member takes a bundle of herbs. All chant while the ATTENDANT is coming around:

Death brings life, life brings death!

The Invocations
The PRIEST and PRIESTESS approach the altar and genuflect. An ATTENDANT rings the bells three times. The PRIESTESS does the Invocation of the Goddess (Chapter 18). The PRIEST performs the Invocation of the God (Chapter 18).

The Proclamation
An ATTENDANT standing in front of the altar of offering genuflects, rings the bells three times, and then recites:

Those who walk in darkness
Shall now experience great light;
Those who hunger and thirst
Shall be quenched at the altar of life;
Those who call upon righteousness
Shall take the hand of the Lord and Lady;

Those who approach with anticipation
Shall receive the gifts of the spirit.

ALL
Our Lord and Lady
We acknowledge your greatness;
Our Lord and Lady
We affirm your wisdom and love;
Our Lord and Lady
We pray for your presence;
Our Lord and Lady
We now ask for your blessing.
Blessed be the Lord and Lady!

The Rite of Union and the Rite of Redemption

The PRIEST and PRIESTESS approach the altar, genuflect, and face each other. An ATTENDANT rings the bells. The PRIEST and PRIESTESS perform the Rite of Union and the Rite of Redemption (Chapter 18).

The Conclusion

The PRIEST approaches the altar, genuflects, and rings the bells. He dismisses the Guardians (Chapter 18).

An ATTENDANT approaches the altar, genuflects, and extinguishes the floor altar candles, saying:

(Left)
Blessed be the Death Crone
For she transforms the soul of man.

(Right)
Blessed be the Lord of Death
For he brings rest and regeneration.

Closing Benediction

The PRIEST recites the Closing Benediction (Chapter 18). The PRIESTESS banishes the circle (Chapter 18).

Allow the candle in the cauldron to burn out completely.

Synopsis

For those who have been practicing the old Pagan ways and Wiccan religion, the rituals that make up the yearly calendar of Sabbats take on a special significance. Besides being times of worship and fellowship, these celebrations allow us to connect with the potent, intoxicating presence of deity. This is why so much attention should be given to the Sabbat rituals and their presentation. It is important that everything be as perfect as it can be to show proper respect and devotion for the Gods, as well as our dedication to the religion itself.

Many things can make a ritual work, besides the mouthing of memorized script. The rituals must correspond geographically to the hemisphere in which they are being enacted. Mythically, they should progress—as do the seasons themselves—revealing the mystery of their intention to the participants. The leaders of the ceremonies should be well trained, competent, and poised in both their spiritual awareness as well as in their delivery of liturgy.

Attention to proper symbolism, atmosphere, and ritual attire should be taken into consideration long before the event is to take place. Preparation of the Chapel or ritual area should be done with respect and reverence for the god and goddess who will be called forth. And everyone should be made to feel as if their participation, no matter how minor, in some way contributed to the overall effect of the ceremony itself.

In conclusion, everyone has the right to worship as they see fit. What people do not have the right to do is make a mockery of deity, religion, and spirituality in general. When it comes to religion, no one true, right, and only way exists; but there is definitely a right and a wrong way of performing religion's rituals and ceremonies.

ENDNOTES

1. *The Temple Book of Prayer and Scripture* is the equivalent of the Wiccan/Pagan Book of Shadows or Witches' Grimoire. We changed the name so it was both recognizable and distinguishable from the works of other traditions and acceptable to non-Wiccan/Pagan seekers.

2. Use of the censer and incense is solely up to the discretion of those doing the ritual. Some people like a lot of incense and some cannot stand it. Use common sense here, please.

3. For Friday Night Church services we do not call in the Guardians of the Quadrants. These rituals are less formal than Full Moons and Sabbats because they are open to the public and people who have never experienced ritual before.

4. *Mixed* refers to initiated and non-initiated members. As most of our rituals are open to students, members, and sincere seekers, most of the people are not formally trained or ordained priests.

5. White is universal but not mandatory; you may use seasonal colors for the altar cloth and flowers. Keep the altar candles white for this ceremony.

6. This is the part that everything else has been leading up to: the actual calling in of the Goddess to manifest through the priestess. In some Pagan traditions, the segment that follows the salutation is called Drawing Down the Moon.

7. This segment of the mass is difficult if not impossible to do if you have not been properly trained and initiated. At the moment of the blessing, the priestess must be able to open herself as a channel for divine energy to flow through into the Chalice, permeating the wine with the sovereignty of the Goddess.

8. Three-, four-, and five-wick candles are twelve inches high and from four to six inches in diameter. These candles frequently come in the primary colors; you can purchase them at most candle shops.

9. This candle is left to burn out.

10. The Goddess candle is left to burn out completely. When the ritual is over, the candle can be placed in a coffee can or metal pan with some water and then set in the tub for safety.

11. For Imbolc, we use the Goddess Brighid in our rites, for this festival is also Oimele or Brigantia.

12. The early Roman Church developed the Eucharist as a formal rite. However, the blessing of bread and wine or bread and water was a common practice in almost all of the early, Pre-Christian mystery religions.

13. For those who do not wish to use the twenty-third Psalm from the Bible, you may substitute "Of the Office of the Anthem" section VII, from the Gnostic Mass, *Gems of the Equinox,* Israel Regardie, Falcon Press (see Bibliography).

14. If the rite is performed outdoors and it is permissible to have a fire, the fire would take precedence over the candle in the cauldron.

15. "John Barleycorn" is from the book *Egyptian Myth and Legend,* by Donald A. Mackenzie (see Bibliography).

16. To make a corn baba, strip dried husks from a corn cob and soak the husks in water until pliable. Use the cob as the body. Use paper or a small Styrofoam ball for the head. Cover the ball with strips of husks and attach them to the cob. Cut a narrow strip of husk and roll it into a seven-inch length; tie off at the ends with string for arms. Attach it to the cob and then fashion a dress from strips of corn husks.

CHAPTER 20

The Creative Spirit

I must create a new system or be enslaved by another man's; I will not reason and compare: my business is to create.

William Blake

New Beginnings

One of the main objectives of this book is to introduce you to our system of Wicca, Co-Creation Spirituality, and make you aware of some of the options available to you regarding the practice of Pagan ways. Another purpose is to encourage you to refresh your present religious tradition—or inspire you to create a new and better method of religious worship.

Religion and spirituality are a part of life. In order for them to be effective, they need to be progressive and timely. The priests and leaders of today's religions need to be aware of changing attitudes and ideals. They also need to regularly improve and renew their theology and rituals to keep pace with contemporary thought. We can learn from the past. However, it is the moment we experience, and the future to which we look forward, that shapes and gives life to our endeavors.

Getting started is usually the hardest part of any project, whether it is upgrading something old or creating something new. This is especially true when it comes to spirituality. It is easier to start with the fun stuff first, like rites and symbolism, and leave the history and theology for last. Unfortunately, this approach does not work, because without a realistic and functional belief system, there is nothing upon which devotion can be based. There must be reason and logic behind the new concept of worship before it can become a legitimate and workable spiritual path. All lasting religions began by building strong theologies, then adding the appropriate symbolism, rites, and ceremonies to enhance their existing beliefs.

With something as vague and autonomous as Paganism and Wicca, it is difficult to get a hold on anything substantial. In general, most of the followers of the Pagan way gloss over theology because they do not want to appear dogmatic. The more vocal members of the Wiccan movement will not take a stand on anything relating to established doctrine because they fear they might jeopardize their popularity—and goddess forbid they lose some of their adherents. These attitudes leave the Wiccan/Pagan seeker stumbling around in the dark, looking for the light and a place to begin.

However, there are options available when the individual's motivations are sincere and reasonable. For the most part, there are three reasons for addressing personal spirituality. The first comes from the individual who is not happy with what he or she has been exposed to and wants to create something new and different. The second comes from the individual who likes his or her basic belief system but wants to update it. The third response comes from the person who is happy with his or her religious tradition, but wants to stimulate and strengthen his or her spiritual skills and knowledge.

It does not matter which type of person you are because the following syllabus will help you organize your thoughts and ideas. Once arranged in a logical order, these personal observations and viewpoints will substantiate your present beliefs or help you design a new system. Basically, this is how all religious and spiritual traditions start. Someone puts his or her theories about god, the universe, and life into a coherent format and then promotes the conclusions. If the new theory has been properly arranged, it will attract others who are of like mind.

Of course, this does not mean you have to share your thoughts with others. If you do decide to share, however, you will have something of value to present. With all your thoughts and ideas organized and recorded, you have a readily available program that will provide the doctrine and guidelines for your group activities.

The Spiritual Seeker's Plan of Action

The categories and associated statements that follow should be dealt with in the order in which they appear. So often when we begin to deal with deeply spiritual thoughts and emotions, all sorts of wonderful ideas begin to emerge. By keeping things in order and not jumping around, you allow for a greater expansion on each topic presented. This makes it easier to deal competently and completely with the proposed subject matter.

1. Beliefs and Faith

a. List the positive and negative aspects of the religion in which you were raised. Even if you hated the religion, try to find at least one positive thing to say about it.

b. From the above answer, which concepts of your early religious training would you keep and which are of no value to you now?

c. Make a list of the things you feel religion should, in general, help you accomplish on a spiritual level.

d. Explain your feelings about deity as in the Creator, God the Father, Goddess the Mother, and secondary gods and goddesses who provide spiritual stimulation to their disciples.

e. Choose a god and a goddess to work with and make clear your reasons for picking them.

f. Write down the major myths associated with each deity you have chosen.[1] If available, collect illustrations and photographs that express the major concept of the associated myths.

2. Practices and Ceremonies

a. Make a list of the dates and festivals held sacred to your God and Goddess. These should be clearly noted on your calendar of spiritual events.

b. List and then describe in detail any additional times or celebrations that you wish to include in your spiritual system.[2]

c. If you are not using the invocations and rituals in this book, design your own. These should be written down exactly as they will be performed.[3]

d. Design a special prayer or invocation for the goddess you have chosen.

e. Design a special prayer or invocation for the god you have chosen.

f. Make a list of the offerings that would be appropriate to present to your god and goddess on their special days or occasions.[4]

g. If you are going to perform your rites within the bounds of a circle, write out how the circle will be cast.

h. If you are going to call on Guardians, as we do, create a process for doing so and write it down as well. Describe how you see the Guardians and what it feels like when they are called into your sacred space.

3. Religious Objects and Places

a. Make an inventory of all the symbols and objects that are held sacred to your god and goddess and those special items that represent your religious beliefs.

b. If you are going to use additional symbols, such as the traditional Wiccan tools,[5] list these and their purpose along with their meaning and how they are to be used.

c. You will need an altar and an established place for your worship—consider these carefully. Once set up, the altar and surrounding area will become sacred and should not be used for any other purpose. If you do not already have an altar and place of worship, consider setting one up at this time.

4. Values and Morals

a. Compose a set of spiritual values that you feel should be followed by yourself and those people you may work with in the future.

b. List what is acceptable behavior within the bounds of ritual and what is not.

c. If you plan to include others in your circle, set some basic standards of practice and ethics that the group must follow. These standards should be written out and copies made for every member.[6]

5. Leaders and Priesthood

a. If you will be working with others, pick a group leader. He or she should be someone everyone respects and can get along with. List the possibilities.

b. Conductors of ritual will need to be decided upon in advance. This can be done by group vote or rotation.[7] Again, a list should be made of who will be doing what ritual and when. Prepare a calendar for three months in advance that designates who will be in charge of each ritual.

c. A list of duties for the leaders of the ritual should be prepared and given to each leader, along with their personal responsibilities and obligations toward the group.[8]

d. Proper initiation and ordination are necessary for those who wish to call themselves priest or priestess. If this is something you desire, whether you are working alone or with a group, make the arrangement to get the proper training. For more information on priesthood training, contact *Our Lady of Enchantment, P. O. Box 1366, Nashua, NH 03061.*

Synopsis

Imagination and creativity are the keys to formulating a religious system that will be both functional and spiritually beneficial. Reach out and learn about other traditions and their religious viewpoints. Always compare what you are doing with what others are doing. Keep a journal about the different methods others use to achieve the same thing you are doing. Make notes about their ideas on theology, ritual, and symbolism.

If you have been taught one way to do something, try a new approach. You can always go back to the way you were doing things before if the new way does not work. After all, if our ancestors had not tried new things, we would still be living in caves.

I remember being uncomfortable with the way I had been taught to do the symbolic Great Rite; however, I continued to do it the same way for years. Then I happened upon someone doing it a bit differently and I liked what I saw, so I tried it their way. The new way seemed more fitting than the old, and eventually I was able to develop the Rite of Union we use today. I did not lose anything by trying something different, but gained from the experience. Trying new things helps us grow and progress.

If you are a solitary and do not have access to any other groups or a teacher, read. You can find hundreds of books about Wicca, Paganism, Mystery religions, and ritual. Compare what the different traditions have to say about deity, theology, and ritual practice. Select what you like from each one and put these ideas together. Begin with the traditions in this book. This is what I did to come up with the system we now have today.

I chose European deities and incorporated their traditional seasonal celebrations into a basic theological doctrine. I added the esoteric symbolism from the early Greek and Roman Mystery traditions. This was structured around a common sense approach to the basic prevailing religious ideals of our time.[9]

Creating a system of your own is not complicated. The basic framework for a working religion already exists within this book and others which pertain to the art of religious crafting. All you need to do is choose the god and goddess you want to work with. Include their personal, as well as traditional, symbolism and combine this with active ritual worship. If you are going to be working with others, you will also need to incorporate a code of ethics for all to follow. It is that simple.

In closing, I want to say that starting your own religious tradition shows your creativity, sincere dedication to the gods, and willingness to incorporate spirituality into your life. It does not make you a priest or priestess—these are stations that must be conferred by the proper authorities. If priesthood is something you wish to acquire, go through the proper channels, get the training, and submit to the initiation process. Those who are willing to work and are respectful of their teachers achieve and develop spiritual maturity. Those who are looking for overnight enlightenment and superficial titles for ego gratification never endure.[10]

ENDNOTES

1. For this project, you will need some good mythology books. Compile as many myths as possible about the gods you are working with, as this makes them that much more real.

2. If you are going to use the Ten Holy Days of Obligation offered in this book (Chapter 19), then these dates should go onto your calendar of events as well.

3. The power in ritual is in repetition. If you do not write everything down exactly as it will be done, you will not be able to repeat it.

4. Special offerings can include flowers, foods, special objects, candles, and beverages.

5. Traditional Wiccan tools include: Athame, Chalice, Wand, Pentacle, Censer, Salt and Water Bowls, God and Goddess Candles, and Cauldron.

6. Standards include proper dress, being on time for ritual, necessary items others need to bring, and any monetary obligations.

7. At Our Lady of Enchantment, we use a rotation so all the initiates get a chance to lead ritual. Only initiated and ordained priests lead ritual. The congregation and members training for the priesthood assist with speaking parts and other ritual duties.

8. This list should mention that participants should notify the group if they are unable to attend, and should also arrange for coverage of their functions in advance.

9. Religious ideals of our time include the patriarchal neurosis of Fundamental Christian thought and practice.

10. This is obvious in the number of Wiccan and Pagan groups, covens, groves, newsletters, etc., that have come and gone just in the last five years. On the other hand, those who were properly trained are still around, serving their community.

Bibliography

Angus, S. *The Mystery Religions.* New York: Dover Publications, 1975.

Armstrong, Karen. *A History of God.* New York: Ballantine Books, 1993.

Baring and Cashford. *The Myth of the Goddess.* New York: Viking/Arkana, 1991.

Barrett, Clive. *The Egyptian Gods and Goddesses.* New York: Aquarian/Thomas, 1992.

Benko, Stephen. *Pagan Rome and the Early Christians.* Bloomington, IN: Indiana University Press, 1984.

Blofeld, John. *Bodhisattva of Compassion: The Mystical Tradition of Kuan Yin.* Boston: Shambhala, 1988.

Bonwick, James. *Irish Druids and Old Irish Religions.* New York: Dorset, 1986.

Brandon, George. *Santeria from Africa to the New World.* Bloomington, IN: Indiana University Press, 1984.

Budge, E. A. Wallis. *Egyptian Heaven and Hell.* Peru, IL: Open Court Publishing, 1974.

Budge, E. A. Wallis. *Egyptian Religion.* New York: Dover, 1987.

Carr-Gomm, Philip. *The Druid Tradition.* New York: Element Books, 1991.

Cotterell, Arthur. *The Macmillan Illustrated Encyclopedia of Myths and Legends.* New York: Macmillan Publishing, 1989.

Davidson, H. R. Ellis. *Myths and Symbols in Pagan Europe*. Syracuse, NY: Syracuse University Press, 1988.

Dolfyn. *Shamanic Wisdom*. Earth Spirit, 1990.

Drury, Nevill. *The Elements of Shamanism*. New York: Element Books, 1989.

Drury, Nevill. *The Shaman and The Magician*. New York: Arkana, 1982.

Earhart, Byron H. *Religious Traditions of the World*. New York: Harper, 1993.

Eliade, Mircea. *Religions of Antiquity*. New York: Macmillian Publishing, 1987.

Eliade, Mircea. *Shamanism, Archaic Techniques of Ecstasy*. Princeton, NJ: Princeton University Press, 1964.

Fatunmbi, Awo Falokun. *Iwa-Pele, Ifa Quest: The Search of Santeria and Lucumi*. Bronx, NY: Original Publications, 1991.

Finegan, Jack. *Myth and Mystery: An Introduction to the Pagan Religions of the Biblical World*. Grand Rapids, MI: Baker Book House, 1989.

Fowler, William Warde. *Roman Ideas of Deity*. Indianapolis, IN: Books for Library Press, 1969.

Fox, Robin Lane. *Pagans and Christians*. New York: Harper & Row, 1986.

Goodwin, Joscelyn. *Mystery Religions in the Ancient World*. New York: Harper & Row, 1981.

Graves, Robert. *Larousse Encyclopedia of Mythology*. Hanlyn, 1968.

Hooke, S. H. *Babylonian and Assyrian Religion*. Norman, OK: University of Oklahoma Press, 1963.

Jacobsen, Thorkild. *The Treasures of Darkness: The History of Mesopotamian Religion*. New Haven, CT: Yale University Press, 1976.

James E. O. *The Ancient Gods*. New York: G.P. Putnams Sons, 1960.

James, E.O. *Myth and Ritual in the Ancient Near East*. New York: Thames & Hudson, 1958.

Karade, Baba Ifa. *The Handbook of Yourba Religious Concepts*. York Beach, ME: Weiser, 1994.

Leeming, David Adams. *The World of Myth.* New York: Oxford University Press, 1990.

Lurker, Manfred. *The Gods and Symbols of Ancient Egypt.* New York: Thames & Hudson, 1974.

Macmullen and Lane. *Paganism and Christianity.* Minneapolis, MN: Fortress Press, 1992.

Matthews, Caitlin. *The Celtic Tradition.* London: Element Books, 1989.

Meyer, Marvin W. *The Ancient Mysteries: A Source Book.* New York: Harper & Row, 1987.

Neimark, Philip John. *The Way of the Orisha.* New York: Harper, 1993.

Newsome, James D. *Greeks, Romans, Jews.* Philadelphia: Trinity Press, 1992.

Nichols, Ross. *The Book of Druidry.* London: Aquarian Press, 1990.

Pelikan, Jaroslav. *Jesus Through the Centuries.* New York: Harper & Row, 1985.

Reitzenstein, Robers. *Hellenistic Mystery Religions: Their Basic Ideas and Significance.* San Francisco: Pickwick Press, 1978.

Robertson, Lawrence Durdin. *The Year of the Goddess.* London: Aquarian Press, 1990.

Robinson, John S. *Born in Blood: The Lost Secrets of Free Masonry.* New York: M. Evans & Company, 1989.

Ross, Nancy Wilson. *Buddhism: A Way of Life and Thought.* New York: University Books, 1981.

Rutherford, Ward. *The Druids: Magicians of the West.* New York: Sterling Publishing, 1879.

Sabrina, Lady. *Reclaiming the Power: The How and Why of Practical Ritual Magic.* St. Paul, MN: Llewellyn Publications, 1992.

West, John Anthony. *The Traveler's Key to Ancient Egypt.* New York: Alfred A. Knopf, 1985.

Wilken, Robert L. *The Christians as the Romans Saw Them.* New Haven, CT: Yale University Press, 1984.

Willis, Roy. *World Mythology.* New York: Henry Holt & Co., 1993.

Index

Abred, 17

Abred, Spiral of, 17

absorption, 195

active force, 130

Adonis, 58

Africa, 63-65, 67, 69, 71, 73, 75

Air, 17-18, 20, 49, 68, 72, 90, 93-94, 104,
109, 114, 116, 127, 139-140, 144, 147-
151, 153, 157, 164, 226

altar, 20, 29, 50, 65, 94, 124, 130, 132-
133, 161-169, 183-187, 189-192, 196-
202, 204-208, 210-228, 230-233,
235-245, 247-262, 268

Annwn, 17

Apollo, 90, 103-104, 115-116, 137, 189,
214

Archangel, 150, 152, 154, 156

Asia, 41, 47, 75-77, 79, 81

aspergillum, 10, 131, 166, 184, 197, 202

athame, 124-125, 133, 166, 168, 186,
190-193, 197, 200, 202, 204-205, 209-
211, 214-215, 231, 270

authority, 10-11, 16, 26, 29-30, 33, 58,
61, 122, 128-129, 131, 133, 140, 144,
156, 160, 164, 168, 173-174, 176, 193,
200, 204

Autumnal Equinox, 9, 19, 248, 253

Babaluaiye, 35, 37

baptism, 27-28, 153

bell, 29, 81, 97, 112, 150, 232-234

Beltane, 9, 19-20, 106, 234-235, 239, 257

benediction, 80, 131, 137, 182, 184, 191-
192, 197, 201-202, 205-206, 210-211,
215, 217, 220-221, 224-225, 229-230,
234-235, 238-239, 242-243, 248-249,
252-253, 257-258, 261

birth, 6-7, 17, 28, 45, 58, 77-78, 88, 92,
97, 99-100, 102-103, 108, 115, 125, 130,
141, 144, 149, 153, 188-189, 203, 208,
210, 216, 236-237, 240, 245, 249, 251,
258

Blessed Virgin, 9, 184, 187, 192, 216, 248

blessing, 28, 123-124, 131, 133, 137, 152,
162, 170, 184, 190, 192, 196, 200-202,
204, 214, 220, 224, 226, 228-229, 233,
238-239, 242-243, 245, 248, 250, 252-
253, 256, 261, 263

blood, 24-25, 30, 37, 58, 70, 78, 91, 115,
152, 191, 214, 230-231, 246-247, 259

bread, 20, 24, 45, 67, 70, 87-90, 93, 98,
114, 116, 124, 170, 229, 243, 263

Buddha, 41-42, 44-45, 80, 82, 167

Buddhism, 13, 41-45

candles, 28, 32, 81, 97, 132-133, 163-166, 176, 183, 196-197, 201-202, 205-206, 210-211, 215, 217, 220-221, 224-225, 228, 230, 234-235, 238-239, 242-243, 248-249, 252-253, 256-258, 261-263, 270

catholic, 5, 25-34, 72, 97, 110-111, 161-162

cauldron, 1, 10, 18, 20, 36, 53, 70-71, 98, 100-101, 106, 119, 130, 154, 167, 200, 204, 235-237, 257, 259-261, 263, 270

Celts, 15-18, 21, 96, 98, 106

censer, 10, 29, 131-132, 166, 197, 202, 205, 211-212, 262, 270

ceremony, 28, 36, 49-50, 85, 93, 115, 132, 136, 180, 182-184, 192, 196-197, 201, 205, 211, 249, 253, 262

Cernunnos, 9, 101, 185-186, 188-190, 199, 219-220, 223-224, 226, 228, 234, 239, 241, 259-260

Cerridwen, 9, 100, 130, 185-186, 188, 190, 200, 203, 207, 209, 219-220, 226, 228, 236-237, 239-240, 259

chalice, 10, 20, 27, 29, 116, 123-124, 154, 166-168, 190-191, 197, 200, 202, 204-205, 208-209, 211, 213-214, 263, 270

chapel, 10, 82, 130, 163, 165-169, 183, 197, 202, 206, 211, 225, 230, 239, 243, 249, 253, 257, 262

Christian, 4-6, 10-11, 16, 23-26, 28-29, 33, 37, 48, 72, 75, 83, 113-116, 122-123, 131, 144, 170, 174, 216, 221, 224, 229, 243, 248, 270

Christianity, 5, 12-13, 16, 23-27, 29-30, 32-33, 84, 94, 96-97, 108, 113, 115, 134, 169-170, 225

church, 3, 5-6, 8-9, 25-33, 62, 97, 113, 116, 123-124, 131, 145, 159, 161, 173, 196-197, 262-263

circle, 17, 29, 51-52, 127, 137, 143, 150, 162-163, 166, 168, 170, 186-187, 197-198, 201-203, 205-206, 210-212, 215, 217-218, 220-221, 224-225, 227-231, 234-239, 241-244, 247-249, 252-253, 257-261, 267-268

cleansing, 49-50, 85, 94, 137

Co-Creation, 8-13, 19, 21, 28, 30, 38-39, 52, 57-58, 83, 94, 122, 124, 136, 148, 161, 168, 170, 175, 179, 265

communication, 5, 35, 45, 51, 93-94, 103, 110, 121-123, 125-126, 128, 136, 145, 149, 160, 165, 234

compassion, 80-81, 114, 184, 193, 244

confession, 27

confirmation, 27-28

consecration, 36, 129, 132, 137, 182-183, 186, 197-198, 202, 206, 211, 217, 221, 225, 231, 235, 239, 243, 249, 253, 258

Consecration, Rite of, 132

craft, 32, 99, 175, 205

creator, 6, 16, 27, 49, 66-67, 84, 92, 94, 97, 110, 212, 250, 267

custom, 13, 49, 64, 96-97

death, 4-7, 17, 19, 21, 24-27, 30, 34, 44-45, 77-78, 80, 86-91, 102-103, 106, 129-130, 149, 153, 188-190, 198, 216-217, 243, 249, 254-255, 257-261

dedication, 28, 38, 95, 160, 169, 174, 176, 208, 262, 269

Diloggun, 35

divination, 8, 16, 33, 35, 45, 69, 96, 102-103, 134-136, 138, 144, 257

Divine Victim, 9, 58, 229, 231

divinity, 7, 16-17, 24, 53, 55, 57, 59, 62, 84, 94, 111, 117, 123, 133-134, 182, 194

druid, 16-17, 20, 95, 97

drumming, 50, 63

dynamic energy, 56, 133, 147

Earth, 17-20, 47-52, 56, 58, 67-68, 70, 77-78, 86-88, 93, 98, 101-106, 109-113, 127, 130, 139, 142-143, 147-148, 155-157, 186-189, 198, 203, 207-208, 210, 217-218, 220, 226-228, 231, 234-235, 237, 240, 243, 245, 252, 257, 259-260

Earth Mother, 50-51, 58, 105, 157

east, 44-45, 75, 150, 168, 183, 186, 192, 198, 201-204, 206, 210, 218, 222, 226, 229, 240, 244-245, 254, 259

Eleggua, 35-36, 38, 67-68, 71-72

elements, 3, 8, 17-18, 25, 29, 48, 50, 57, 63, 68, 77-79, 86, 88-90, 93, 101, 103, 109-112, 116, 125, 127, 133, 136, 139-140, 144, 147-149, 151-155, 157-158, 168, 186, 197-198, 202, 211, 217, 221, 225, 231, 235, 239, 243, 249, 253, 258

enchantment, 9-11, 13, 15, 19, 30, 35, 50, 82, 130, 163, 165, 169, 177, 179-180, 196, 205, 216, 229, 234, 268, 270

enlightenment, 6, 42-43, 45, 59, 75, 82, 123, 174, 184, 269

Eucharist, 9, 27-28, 30, 123-124, 166, 182, 187, 189, 229-230, 263

Europe, 15, 95-97, 99, 101, 103, 105-106

feast, 9, 28, 37-38, 57, 65-67, 69-72, 77, 81, 85, 87, 92, 98, 100, 102-103, 112, 114, 176, 180, 187, 216, 220, 243, 248

Fire, 17-20, 33-34, 37, 49, 56, 68-69, 71, 78-79, 89-91, 96-97, 100, 116, 127, 129, 139-141, 144, 147-148, 151-153, 183, 186, 188-189, 201, 203, 206-207, 210-213, 217-218, 220, 222, 224, 226, 234-236, 238-240, 244, 254, 263

Full Moon, 28, 59, 116, 163, 205

function, 10, 38, 56-57, 61, 85, 107, 122, 125, 136, 148, 168, 173-174, 177

fundamental, 11-12, 16, 41, 47, 59, 76, 106, 121, 128, 147, 182, 270

god, 5-6, 9-10, 17-21, 25-30, 33-38, 47-48, 50, 55-59, 65-66, 69-71, 75-79, 81, 87-88, 90-92, 96, 101, 103-104, 106-110, 113-117, 126, 128-135, 147-148, 152-153, 159-167, 181-182, 187-189, 191, 193-197, 199, 201, 213-214, 218-219, 221, 227, 234-235, 237, 241, 250, 253-254, 256-257, 259-260, 269-270

goddess, 9-10, 34-38, 50, 58-59, 61-62, 77-78, 80-81, 83, 85-86, 88-89, 91, 94, 96-97, 100, 102-111, 113-114, 117, 122-127, 130, 132-134, 143-144, 153, 159-167, 181-182, 184-189, , 193-198, 201, 203, 205-209, 217, 219-221, 227, 231, 235, 237, 241, 245, 249-251, 253-257, 259-260, 262-263, 266-267, 269-270

Good Friday, 9, 28, 30, 116, 187, 216, 225, 229

grail, 95, 98, 114, 123, 125, 130, 154, 200, 204, 208-209

Great Spirit, 50-51

Greek, 24-25, 27, 29-30, 86-89, 91-92, 95, 103, 106, 115, 117, 145, 164-165, 170, 229, 269

growth, 8-9, 11, 29, 32, 38, 87-88, 114, 155, 216, 235, 257

guardian, 34-36, 49, 51, 64, 68, 76, 101-103, 152, 175, 184, 186-187, 191-192, 203, 212, 221, 225, 235, 239, 243, 249, 253, 258

Gwynyd, 17

harvest, 7, 19, 48, 88, 100-101, 105, 108-109, 148, 244-245, 248, 253-256

Heaven, 27-28, 30, 52, 77, 108, 113, 159, 186, 188, 234-235, 249-252

Hecate, 59, 102-103, 126, 137, 164, 167-168

Hermes, 77, 102-104, 115, 131, 164

Hindu, 45, 75, 77, 164

Holy Communion, 27

Holy Days of Obligation, 19, 28, 196, 216, 235, 269

Holy Orders, 27-28

home, 3-5, 10, 15, 19, 32, 63, 65, 67, 69, 71, 73, 81-82, 97, 108, 134, 155-156, 161, 176, 183, 201, 204, 225-226, 248, 253, 257

Horned One, 101, 188-189, 227, 260

host, 27, 124, 159, 191, 220, 232, 240

Ifa, 33, 35-37, 64, 73, 136

Ifa, Table of, 35

illumination, 45, 69, 132, 177, 197, 201, 219

Imbolc, 9, 19, 97-98, 106, 220-221, 263

initiation, 5, 9, 11, 24, 28, 33-38, 58, 70, 73, 105, 115, 174, 193, 268-269

inspiration, 45, 55, 59, 78, 96-97, 100-101, 119, 123, 130, 137, 149, 174, 183, 190, 195, 199, 201, 203, 240, 244

invitation, 208, 213, 218, 223, 227, 232, 236, 241, 245, 251, 255, 259

invocation, 132, 165, 174, 182, 187-188, 199, 203, 209, 214, 219, 223, 227, 237, 241, 247, 251, 255-256, 260, 267

Ishtar, 86, 108-109, 111, 114, 126-127, 137, 143, 167-168, 249

Isis, 78, 86-90, 109, 114, 117, 137, 249

Jesus, 23-30, 32, 88, 94, 97, 113, 115, 117, 124, 229

John the Baptist, 25

judgment, 27, 30, 66-67, 75, 77, 87, 116, 138, 140, 142, 191

justice, 8, 23, 34, 58, 68, 79, 109-110, 149

Key Stones, 126-127, 137, 143, 145

knowledge, 9, 11-12, 35, 43, 49-50, 75-77, 98, 100, 102, 131, 138-142, 148-149, 151, 153, 155, 177, 193, 210, 266

Kristos, 117

Lady, 9-11, 13, 19, 30, 35, 50, 65, 67, 82, 91, 108, 111, 124, 130, 133, 163-165, 169, 177-180, 183, 185-186, 190, 192-193, 196-197, 199-200, 202-209, 211, 216-222, 224-230, 232-244, 247-258, 260-261, 268, 270

lance, 29, 95, 200, 204

leadership, 4, 11, 21, 177, 179, 182, 205

life, 6-7, 9-10, 16-18, 24-25, 30-33, 41-43, 56, 59, 61, 63-68, 70, 76-77, 80-82, 91, 98-102, 106-112, 115, 121-123, 125, 127-130, 132-133, 136, 138-139, 144, 147-149, 162, 167, 169, 184-186, 189-190, 199-200, 209, 212-214, 216-217, 219-223, 225-226, 228-229, 231-234, 240-244, 246-247, 249-252, 255-260, 265-266, 269 light, 19, 55, 59, 79, 89-90, 99-100, 108, 115-116, 122, 133, 143, 150-152, 157-158, 162, 167, 187-189, 191, 195, 198-200, 202-203, 205-207, 209-212, 214-224, 226-230, 233, 235-242, 244, 247, 251-252, 254-256, 260, 266

Lord, 4, 9, 27, 76, 78-79, 87, 89, 101, 109, 133, 165, 183-186, 189-193, 197, 199-200, 202-206, 211-214, 217-222, 224-228, 230-236, 238-244, 247-249, 252-253, 255-258, 260-261

Lughnasadh, 9, 19, 99-100, 106, 243

lunar, 88-89, 109, 129, 160, 196, 205-206, 210-211

magic, 7, 32, 58-59, 61, 63, 65-66, 76, 79-80, 82, 84, 86, 95, 99-100, 102, 110, 131, 205, 257

Mary, Virgin, 23, 25-26, 32, 81, 86, 94, 109, 111, 113-115, 248-250

Mass, 4, 9, 28, 78, 124, 144, 162-163, 184-185, 187, 191, 194, 229, 263

matriarchal, 149

medicine power, 49, 52

medicine wheel, 50-51

meditation, 50-52, 92, 123, 145, 150, 152, 154, 157, 164-165, 200, 209, 215

messiah, 23-25, 30, 115-117, 174

Michael, 47, 152, 203

Mithraic Mysteries, 24, 115

Mithras, 24, 115

moderation, 10, 45, 67

monotheism, 57

moon, 20, 28, 44, 51, 59, 78-79, 89-90, 100, 102-103, 109, 114, 116, 127, 160, 163, 183, 205, 222, 236, 255, 263

omnitheism, 12, 57-59

oracle, 35, 125-127, 135-139, 141, 143-145, 160

ordination, 9, 11, 27-28, 268

Orisha, 33-37, 63-69, 71-73

Orpheus, 24, 30

Orphism, 24, 30

Orunmila, 35

Oshun, 34, 36-37, 65-66, 111

Osiris, 58, 78, 86-90, 131

Our Lady of Enchantment, 9-11, 13, 19, 30, 35, 50, 82, 130, 163, 165, 169, 177, 179-180, 196, 205, 216, 229, 234, 268, 270

Oya, 34

Pagan, 4-5, 10-11, 24-25, 28, 30, 33, 37, 84, 97, 113, 115-116, 122, 124, 147, 168-170, 174, 176-179, 205, 216, 229, 249, 262-263, 265-266, 270

Paganism, 5-6, 15, 17, 19, 21, 25, 169, 175, 179, 266, 269

palm branches, 28, 30

pantheism, 57

pantheon, 33, 38, 58, 61, 64, 70, 84-85, 93, 106-107, 111, 164

passion, 26, 28, 34, 37, 56, 76, 122, 148, 151-153, 184-185, 187-188, 191, 198, 200, 204, 206-207, 210, 221-222, 226, 229, 231, 236, 240-241, 244, 254, 257

paten, 10, 29, 123-124, 191

patriarchal, 158, 270

Persian, 25

Pisces, 12, 153-154

politics, 4, 13, 30

polytheism, 57, 84

power, 4, 16, 18, 20, 24, 29, 34-35, 37-39, 43, 49-50, 52, 56, 58, 63-64, 66, 68-69, 71-73, 76, 78, 81, 83-85, 87, 89, 91, 96-99, 108-109, 112-113, 116-117, 124-125, 127, 138, 140-141, 143-144, 147-149, 156, 159-161, 163, 167, 174, 176, 179, 181, 185-188, 191-193, 199-201, 203-205, 215-216, 221, 224, 226, 229-232, 235, 238-240, 253,

prayer, 8, 10, 50, 52, 62, 131, 157, 159-161, 163, 165-167, 169, 181-182, 186-187, 195-200, 227, 250, 262, 267

priest, 7-9, 27, 32, 36, 38, 85, 88, 113, 124, 174-175, 177-180, 183-187, 189-192, 196-204, 206, 208-215, 217-221, 223-225, 227-239, 241-245, 247-253, 255-261, 268-269

priestess, 9, 36, 38, 85, 88, 124, 137, 167, 174-175, 177-178, 180, 183-187, 189-193, 196-206, 208-215, 217-243, 245, 247-258, 260-261, 263, 268-269

priesthood, 8-9, 11-12, 15-16, 20, 26, 48, 83-85, 166, 173-179, 184, 191, 196, 205-206, 211, 243, 268-270

proclamation, 189, 206-207, 212, 219, 223, 227, 233, 237, 242, 247, 251, 256, 260

prophecy, 16, 97, 115, 135-136

quadrant, 168-169, 183, 186, 197, 202, 205, 210-211, 215-218, 221, 225, 230-231, 235, 239, 243, 245, 249, 253-254, 257-258

quest, 4-5, 49, 125, 161

Raphael, 150, 203

reading cloth, 126-127, 137-139, 144-145

Redemption, Rite of, 124, 182, 187, 189, 193, 196, 205, 220, 224, 228-229, 233, 235, 238, 242, 248, 252, 256, 261

regeneration, 87, 90, 101-103, 106, 112, 130, 193, 200, 204, 226-227, 229, 257-258, 261

religion, 3-9, 11-16, 24-25, 29-39, 41-42, 44-45, 47-48, 50, 52, 73, 83-84, 94-96, 110, 116, 122-123, 135-136, 160, 166, 169-170, 174, 176-179, 181, 193, 195, 262, 265-267, 269

requirement, 3, 12, 125, 134, 159

respect, 8, 11, 18, 21, 30, 37, 48, 51, 61, 72, 92, 96, 108, 132, 141, 160, 262

resurrection, 24-26, 28, 87-90, 225, 229

rites, 6-7, 18, 33, 48, 85, 96, 102, 110, 130, 137, 144, 148, 158, 168, 173, 182, 189, 195-197, 199, 201, 203, 205, 207, 209-211, 213, 215, 217, 219, 221, 223, 225, 227, 229, 231, 233, 235, 237, 239, 241, 243, 245, 247, 249, 251, 253, 255, 257, 259, 261, 263, 265-267

ritual, 6-8, 10-11, 16, 18, 20, 27, 33, 43, 47-48, 50, 59, 64, 82, 85, 89, 100, 106, 108, 110-111, 122, 124-125, 131-133, 136-137, 144-145, 148, 158, 161-163, 165-168, 170, 174, 176, 178, 181-184, 186-187, 189, 191, 193, 195-198, 201-202, 205-206, 209-211, 215-216, 225, 229-230, 233-234, 239, 243, 249, 253, 257, 262-263, 268-270

Rod of Authority, 10, 122, 128-129, 133, 168

Roman Catholic, 5, 25-34, 72, 97, 110-111, 161-162

Rome, 25, 225

Sabbat, 9, 19, 123, 180, 216, 262

sacrament, 27, 174, 214

sacred fluid, 127, 129, 230

sacred pipe, 50-51

sacred symbol, 19

sacrifice, 33, 35, 37-39, 64, 70, 72, 131, 199, 212, 259

saint, 32, 34-35, 37, 68-69, 71-72

salt, 29, 67, 130, 132-133, 156, 166-167, 186, 197, 202, 205, 211, 230-231, 270

salutation, 208, 212, 218, 222, 226, 231, 236, 240, 245, 250, 254, 258, 263

salvation, 24, 30, 75, 80

Samhain, 9, 19-20, 98-99, 101, 106, 235, 257

Santería, 13, 31, 33-39, 64, 66, 69, 73, 110-111

season, 19, 166, 224, 226, 239, 248-249, 253, 257-258

shamanism, 13, 21, 47-49, 51-52

smudge, 50

Sol Invictus, 24, 30, 116, 184, 214

solar, 24, 86, 91, 106, 115, 129, 160, 184, 187, 192, 196, 205, 210-211

soul, 5, 7, 20-21, 45, 55, 66, 117, 149, 174, 181, 183, 187-188, 190, 193, 208, 217, 225, 232, 234, 258, 261

south, 79, 104, 152, 167-168, 183, 187, 192, 198, 201, 203-204, 206, 210, 218, 222, 226, 229, 240, 244-245, 254-255, 259

Speaking Stones, 35, 126-127, 136-139, 143-144

spirit, 17, 19-21, 28, 31, 49-51, 56, 65, 113, 119, 139, 141, 148-150, 153, 161, 174, 176, 181-184, 188, 190-191, 193, 195, 198, 201-202, 206-207, 209-210, 212-215, 219-220, 222, 224-226, 228-

229, 233, 236, 238, 241-242, 244, 247, 252, 254, 256, 259, 261, 265, 267, 269

spirituality, 4-13, 19, 25, 28, 30, 38, 45, 47, 49, 51, 57-58, 83, 94, 122-124, 128, 136, 139, 148, 161, 168, 170, 175, 177, 216, 262, 265-266, 269

staff, 52, 71-72, 92, 98, 104, 109-110, 112, 114, 116, 130-131, 150, 169, 209, 230-231

statue, 81-82, 85, 94, 114, 132, 160, 163-167

Stone People, 50

structure, 8, 10-11, 15, 21, 48, 59, 95, 147, 160, 173, 179, 182

Summer Solstice, 9, 19, 238, 241

sun, 19-20, 24, 28, 44, 51, 56, 58, 67, 79, 84-85, 88-91, 94, 96, 99, 112, 116, 150-151, 155, 160, 183-184, 188, 203, 209-212, 214, 216, 222, 224, 234, 238-240, 243, 253-254

Sun God, 88, 90-91, 94, 99, 211

Sweat Lodge, 49-50

sword, 18, 20, 69, 77-78, 81, 99-100, 103, 114, 124-125, 152, 200, 204

symbol, 12, 19-20, 27, 30, 51, 58, 64, 68, 71, 86-87, 90-91, 101, 106, 119, 121, 130-131, 150, 152, 155, 157, 160, 234-235, 239

system, 4-5, 7-9, 13-14, 16-17, 19, 26, 30-31, 35, 38-39, 42, 47, 50, 52, 57, 62, 84, 94, 105, 122, 125, 136, 148, 154, 157, 170, 174-175, 177, 179, 216, 265-269

Tammuz, 58, 88, 129

temple, 24, 26, 29, 38, 43, 76, 80, 82-83, 85, 87-94, 105, 108, 114-115, 160-161, 167, 178, 196, 202, 226, 262 tools, 7, 10, 34-35, 50, 70, 72, 87-88, 98, 110, 121-125, 127, 129, 131-133, 144, 150, 152, 154, 156, 162, 164-166, 216, 221, 225, 230, 235, 239, 243, 249, 253, 257, 268, 270

totem, 49-51, 67, 100, 127, 143-144

tradition, 1, 8, 12-16, 24, 30, 34, 39, 42, 84, 94, 107, 114, 124, 131, 136, 168, 179, 182, 205, 265-266, 269

transcend, 44, 116

transformation, 5, 9, 32, 43, 70, 90-91, 101, 108, 125, 130-131, 151, 161, 181, 183, 185, 191, 193, 222, 235, 237, 261

transubstantiation, 174, 181, 193, 195

truth, 3, 8, 14, 19, 25, 29-30, 41-42, 52, 58, 79, 103-104, 121, 135, 137, 139, 141, 143, 145, 149, 174, 191, 197, 201, 206-207, 231, 239, 245

Union, Rite of, 28, 123-124, 182, 187, 189-190, 193-194, 196, 205, 220, 224, 228-229, 233, 235, 238, 242, 248, 252, 256, 261, 269

universal, 6, 26, 29, 42, 59, 75, 112, 148, 153, 173, 184, 234, 262

unmanifested, 8-9, 17

values, 8, 10, 122, 141, 268

Vernal Equinox, 9, 28, 116, 224

vessel, 10, 35-36, 39, 109, 122, 125-128, 131-133, 136-137, 143, 154, 167-168, 200, 204

Vessel of Creation, 10, 35, 122, 125-128, 132-133, 136-137, 168, 200, 204

virgin, 9, 32, 34, 65, 77, 81, 86, 93, 97, 109, 111, 113-114, 184, 187, 192, 200, 208-209, 216, 231, 243, 248, 250-252

vision quest, 49

wand, 29, 69, 71, 104, 110, 112, 150, 164, 270

Water, 17-18, 20, 29, 36, 45, 49, 64-66, 68, 76-79, 81, 86, 88-89, 97, 101, 103, 105, 109-112, 131-133, 137, 139, 141-142, 144, 147-148, 153-156, 160, 166, 178, 186, 197, 202, 205, 207, 211, 226, 230, 238-239, 243, 246, 254, 263, 270

west, 15, 44-45, 88-89, 154, 168, 183, 187, 192, 198, 201, 203-204, 207, 210, 218, 222, 226, 229, 240, 244, 246, 254, 259

Wicca(n), 10-11, 21, 83-84, 122, 124, 147, 161, 165, 168-170, 175-178, 205, 210, 229, 262, 265-266, 268-270

wine, 20, 24, 66, 68, 70-71, 87-88, 91, 93, 111, 116, 123, 190-191, 196-197, 200-202, 204-205, 209, 211, 214-215, 220, 229, 232, 243, 253, 263

wisdom, 8, 11, 17-18, 29-30, 41, 43, 48-49, 61-62, 66-67, 69, 76-77, 79-80, 97-98, 101, 121, 123, 133, 148, 161, 163-164, 167, 174-175, 181, 183-185, 190-192, 197-199, 201-202, 204-205, 207-210, 219, 221-222, 226, 228, 233, 236, 238, 240, 242, 244, 251-252, 254, 256, 259, 261

worship, 4, 7, 9-10, 16, 20, 27, 31-33, 36-37, 52, 56-57, 59, 62, 73, 75, 77, 83-84, 87, 115-116, 123, 132, 147, 153, 158-167, 169-170, 174, 181-182, 193, 195-196, 205, 262, 265, 268-269

Yemoja, 34, 36-37, 64-65

Yeshua ben Joseph, 25

Yule, 9, 28, 216

Stay in Touch

On the following pages you will find listed, with their current prices, some of the books now available on related subjects. Your book dealer stocks most of these and will stock new titles in the Llewellyn series as they become available. We urge your patronage.

To Get a Free Catalog

To obtain our full catalog, you are invited to write (se address below) for our bi-monthly news magazine/catalog *Llewellyn's New Worlds of Mind and Spirit*. A sample copy is free, and it will continue coming to you at no cost as long as you are an active mail customer. Or you may subscribe for just $10 in the United States and Canada ($20 overseas, first class mail). Many bookstores also have *New Worlds* available to their customers. Ask for it.

To Order Books and Tapes

If your bookstore does not carry the titles described on the following pages, you may order them directly from Llewellyn by sending the full price in U.S. funds, plus postage and handling (see below).

Credit card orders: VISA, MasterCard, American Express are accepted. Call us toll-free within the United States and Canada at 1-800-THE-MOON.

Special Group Discount: Because there is a great deal of interest in group discussion and study of the subject matter of this book, we offer a 20% quantity discount to group leaders or agents. Our special quantity price for a minimum order of five copies of *Cauldron of Transformation* is $67.80 cash-with-order. Include postage and handling charges noted below.

Postage and Handling: Include $4 postage and handling for orders $15 and under; $5 for orders over $15. There are no postage and handling charges for orders over $100. Postage and handling rates are subject to change. We ship UPS whenever possible within the continental United States; delivery is guaranteed. Please provide your street address as UPS does not deliver to P.O. boxes. Orders shipped to Alaska, Hawaii, Canada, Mexico, and Puerto Rico will be sent via first class mail. Allow 4–6 weeks for delivery. International orders: Airmail—add retail price of each book and $5 for each non-book item (audiotapes, etc.); Surface mail—add $1 per item.

Minnesota residents add 7% sales tax.

Mail orders to:
Llewellyn Worldwide, P.O. Box 64383, Dept. K600-9
St. Paul, MN 55164-0383, U.S.A.

For customer service, call (612) 291-1970.
All prices subject to change without notice.

Reclaiming the Power
The How & Why of Practical Ritual Magic
Lady Sabrina

By far one of the most usable and workable approaches to magic written in a long time, *Reclaiming the Power* is for anyone who has ever wondered about magic, ever wanted to try it, or ever had a goal to achieve. This is the first book to explain just what ritual magic is without the trappings of a specific tradition. It is a simple, straightforward approach to magic, stressing the use of natural and seasonal energies to accomplish what needs to be done.

Getting results is what *Reclaiming the Power* is all about. The average person, untrained and uninitiated, will learn magic that can be performed anywhere and for any purpose. Everything, from what magic is to spell-casting, is explained in simple, easy-to-understand language. All of the rituals presented are complete and can be easily adapted to solitary working.

0-87542-166-0, 256 pp., 5¹/₄ x 8, illus., softcover   **$9.95**

The Ancient & Shining Ones
World Myth, Magic & Religion
D.J. Conway

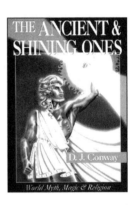

The Ancient & Shining Ones is a handy, comprehensive reference guide to the myths and deities from ancient religions around the world. Now you can easily find the information you need to develop your own rituals and worship using the Gods/Goddesses with which you resonate most strongly. More than just a mythological dictionary, *The Ancient & Shining Ones* explains the magickal aspects of each deity and explores such practices as Witchcraft, Ceremonial Magick, Shamanism and the Qabala. It also discusses the importance of ritual and magick, and what makes magick work.

Most people are too vague in appealing for help from the Cosmic Beings—they either end up contacting the wrong energy source, or they are unable to make any contact at all, and their petitions go unanswered. In order to touch the power of the universe, we must re-educate ourselves about the Ancient Ones. The ancient pools of energy created and fed by centuries of belief and worship in the deities still exist. Today these energies can bring peace of mind, spiritual illumination and contentment. On a very earthy level, they can produce love, good health, money, protection, and success.

0-87542-170-9, 448 pp., 7 x 10, 300 illus., softcover   **$17.95**

To order, call 1-800-THE-MOON
All prices subject to change without notice

Global Ritualism
Myth & Magic Around the World
Denny Sargent

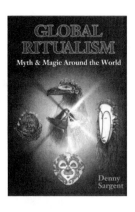

The concept of ritual and spirituality is common to all peoples, as the same archetypal powers dwell in the psyches of people everywhere. From Haiti to Egypt, *Global Ritualism* analyzes the common themes and archetypal symbols of higher ritual so that you can define how these archetypes play out in your own life. As you build a "global vocabulary" of such spiritual and magical symbols, you will be able to construct your own vibrant, living rituals—actively following a mythos that you create rather than one that has been given to you.

Let the subconscious language of human archetypes become your path to spiritual evolution and meaning. Become an "eclectic ritualist" and dare to live a more fulfilling life! Includes 300 photos of actual rituals as they are enacted around the world, including 16 pages of color photos.

0-87542-700-6, 256 pp., 7 x 10, 271 photos, 16 color pgs., softcover   **$19.95**

Dancing Shadows
The Roots of Western Religious Beliefs
Aoumiel

At last, a contemporary Pagan perspective on Western religious history! Discover the historical roots of Neo-Paganism and its relationship to modern religions. Learn the story of how the Pagan deities have been absorbed into the hierarchy of mainstream religions, and why Pagan beliefs have been borrowed and refuted by Aryan religions over the centuries. *Dancing Shadows* traces Western religions back 3,000 years to the Dravidian god/goddess beliefs of the ancient Indus Valley (which evolved into the Western Pagan tradition) and the patriarchal sky-god religion of the Aryans from Central Asia (on which modern Christianity, Judaism, and Islam are based). This book will show you how the cross-fertilization of these two belief systems—both traceable to a common religious ancestor—is the source of conflicts that continue today.

Aoumiel draws together current research in the fields of history, religion, archeology, and anthropology to formulate a cohesive theory for the origins of modern Neo-Paganism … and presents a refreshing affirmation of the interconnection between all Western peoples and beliefs.

1-56718-691-2, 224 pp., 6 x 9, softcover   **$12.95**

To order, call 1-800-THE-MOON
All prices subject to change without notice

Buckland's Complete Book of Witchcraft
Raymond Buckland

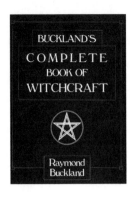

Here is the most complete resource for the study and practice of modern, non-denominational Wicca. This is a lavishly illustrated, self-study course for the solitary or group. Included are rituals; exercises for developing psychic talents; information on all major "sects" of the Craft; sections on tools, beliefs, dreams, meditations, divination, herbal lore, healing, ritual clothing and much, much more. This book unites theory and practice into a comprehensive course designed to help you develop into a practicing Witch, one of the "Wise Ones."

Never before has so much information on the Craft of the Wise been collected in one place. Traditionally, there are three degrees of advancement in most Wiccan traditions. When you have completed studying this book, you will be the equivalent of a Third-Degree Witch. Even those who have practiced Wicca for years find useful information in this book, and many covens are using this for their textbook. If you want to become a Witch, or if you merely want to find out what Witchcraft is really about, you will find no better book than this.

0-87542-050-8, 272 pp., 8½ x 11, illus., softcover   **$14.95**

Santeria: The Religion
Faith, Rites, Magic
Migene González-Wippler

When the Yoruba of West Africa were brought to Cuba as slaves, they preserved their religious heritage by disguising their gods as Catholic saints and worshiping them in secret. The resulting religion is Santeria, a blend of primitive magic and Catholicism now practiced by an estimated five million Hispanic Americans.

Blending study with her experience, González-Wippler describes Santeria's pantheon (orishas); the priests (santeros); the divining shells used to consult the gods (the Diloggún) and the herbal potions prepared as medicinal cures and for magic (Ewe) as well as controversial ceremonies—including animal sacrifice. She has obtained remarkable photographs and interviews with Santeria leaders that highlight aspects of the religion rarely revealed to nonbelievers. This book satisfies the need for knowledge of this religious force that links its devotees in America to a wisdom seemingly lost in modern society.

1-56718-329-8, 400 pp., 6 x 9, 64 photos, softcover   **$12.95**

Celtic Myth & Magic
Harness the Power of the Gods & Goddesses
Edain McCoy

Tap into the mythic power of the Celtic goddesses, gods, heroes and heroines to aid your spiritual quests and magickal goals. *Celtic Myth & Magic* explains how to use creative ritual and pathworking to align yourself with the energy of these archetypes, whose potent images live deep within your psyche.

    Celtic Myth & Magic begins with an overview of 49 types of Celtic Paganism followed today, then gives instructions for evoking and invoking the energy of the Celtic pantheon. Three detailed pathworking texts will take you on an inner journey where you will join forces with the images of Cuchulain, Queen Maeve and Merlin to bring their energies into your life. The last half of the book clearly details the energies of over 300 Celtic deities and mythic figures so you can evoke or invoke the appropriate deity to attain a goal. This inspiring, well-researched book will help solitary Pagans who seek to expand the boundaries of their practice to form partnerships with the divine.

1-56718-661-0, 464 pp., 7 x 10, illus., softcover   **$19.95**

The Crafted Cup
Ritual Mysteries of the Goddess and the Grail
Shadwynn

The Holy Grail—fabled depository of wonder, enchantment and ultimate spiritual fulfillment—is the key by which the wellsprings of a Deeper Life can be tapped for the enhancement of our inner growth. *The Crafted Cup* is a compendium of the teachings and rituals of a Pagan religious Order—the Ordo Arcanorum Gradalis—which incorporates into its worship ritual imagery based upon the Arthurian Grail legends, a reverence toward the mythic Christ, and an appreciation of the truths and techniques found scattered throughout the New Age movement.

    The Crafted Cup is divided into two parts. The first deals with the teachings and concepts which hold a central place within the philosophy of the Ordo Arcanorum Gradalis. The second and larger of the two parts is a compilation of the sacramental rites and seasonal rituals which make up the liturgical calendar of the Order. It contains one of the largest collections of Pagan, Grail-oriented rituals yet published.

0-87542-739-1, 420 pp., 7 x 10, illus., softcover   **$19.95**

To order, call 1-800-THE-MOON

All prices subject to change without notice

The Sabbats
A New Approach to Living the Old Ways
Edain McCoy

The Sabbats offers many fresh, exciting ways to deepen your connection to the turning of the Wheel of the Year. This tremendously practical guide to Pagan solar festivals does more than teach you about the "old ways"—you will learn workable ideas for combining old customs with new expressions of those beliefs that will be congruent with your lifestyle and tradition.

The Sabbats begins with background on Paganism (tenets, teachings, and tools) and origins of the eight Sabbats, followed by comprehensive chapters on each Sabbat. The last section provides 16 complete texts of Sabbat rituals—for both covens and solitaries—with detailed guidelines for adapting rituals to specific traditions or individual tastes. Includes an extensive reference section with a resources guide, bibliography, musical scores for rituals, and more.

This book may contain the most practical advice ever for incorporating the old ways into your Pagan lifestyle!

1-56718-663-7, 320 pp., 7 x 10, illus., photos, softcover $14.95

Ancient Ways
Reclaiming the Pagan Tradition
Pauline Campanelli, illustrated by Dan Campanelli

Ancient Ways is filled with magick and ritual that you can perform every day to capture the spirit of the seasons. It focuses on the celebration of the Sabbats of the Old Religion by giving you practical things to do while anticipating the sabbat rites, and helping you harness the magical energy for weeks afterward. The wealth of seasonal rituals and charms are drawn from ancient sources but are easily performed with materials readily available.

Learn how to look into your previous lives at Yule . . . at Beltane, discover the places where you are most likely to see faeries . . . make special jewelry to wear for your Lammas Celebrations . . . for the special animals in your life, paint a charm of protection at Midsummer.

Most Pagans and Wiccans feel that the Sabbat rituals are all too brief and wish for the magick to linger on. *Ancient Ways* can help you reclaim your own traditions and heighten the feeling of magick.

0-87542-090-7, 256 pp., 7 x 10, illus., softcover $14.95